A "Splendid Idiosyncrasy":
Prehistory at Cambridge 1915-50

Pamela Jane Smith

3Brooklyn Court
Cambridge CB1 7HF
07976 919083

BAR British Series 485
2009

This title published by

Archaeopress
Publishers of British Archaeological Reports
Gordon House
276 Banbury Road
Oxford OX2 7ED
England
bar@archaeopress.com
www.archaeopress.com

BAR 485

A " Splendid Idiosyncrasy": Prehistory at Cambridge 1915-50

ISBN 978 1 4073 0430 4

Printed in England by CMP (UK) Ltd

All BAR titles are available from:

Hadrian Books Ltd
122 Banbury Road
Oxford
OX2 7BP
England
bar@hadrianbooks.co.uk

The current BAR catalogue with details of all titles in print, prices and means of payment is available
free from Hadrian Books or may be downloaded from www.archaeopress.com

Professor John Hutton's retirement party with members of the Cambridge Faculty of Archaeology and Anthropology dressed in museum artefacts, 1950. (Courtesy of the late Mina Lethbridge.)
"We all knew each other. We were all friends — or enemies", said the late Professor Stuart Piggott, in conversation with Julia Roberts, 1994.

Contents

Acronyms

CAS   Cambridge Antiquarian Society
CUA   Cambridge University Archives. These archives are held at the Cambridge University Library
CUL   Cambridge University Library
DNB   *Dictionary of National Biography*
FRC   Fenland Research Committee
ILN   *Illustrated London News*
MAA   Museum of Archaeology and Anthropology, Cambridge University
MAN   Musée des Antiquités Nationales

Illustrations

Preface

In this study, I ask and answer questions as to how and why a set of ideas and practices becomes articulate, systematic and professionalised within a university setting. The oldest school of prehistoric archaeology in a British university which granted degrees is at Cambridge. Because of its central importance, prominence and location, the history of Cambridge prehistory offers a clear example of the successful establishment of a new academic subject.

Three different theoretical approaches were used in the course of the inquiry. Investigations into the success and failure of research schools, geography-of-knowledge analyses and results of gender and science studies were all shown to have both salience and limitations when applied to this case study.

The work focused on three central personalities, one key figure for each decade described. The research school approach was least relevant when applied to Miles Burkitt and to the early establishment of academic prehistory during the 1920s. Before there were formalised controls over recruitment and institutionalised avenues of entry, religious beliefs, motivations, philosophies, gendered relationships and informal settings such as tea-rooms were clearly significant.

In contrast, J.B. Morrell's (1972) research school material worked well for Grahame Clark as an example of a male, university-based, intellectual entrepreneur during the 1930s. Morrell's (1972) and G.L. Geison's (1981) list of ingredients for academic achievement — a strong coherent set of research questions and methods, exploitable techniques, an avenue for publication, a pool of recruits and an ability to establish administrative support — was found to be important. Personal reminiscences and unpublished correspondence revealed that the Museum tea-room became a central knowledge-making place and that interpersonal relationships of trust fostered innovative thought.

Gender and science studies illuminated Dorothy Garrod's difficult experiences in the 1940s as the first woman and first prehistorian elected to a professorship at Cambridge University. Changing gender definitions, student creativeness, the collegial nature of knowledge production and the informality and flexibility of social and academic relationships were considered as possible additions to Geison's and Morrell's list. Based on this study of prehistory, it would appear that small, informal and intimate groups may create splendid university subjects.

Pamela Jane Smith
Lucy Cavendish College
30 June 2004

Dedication and Acknowledgements

It was an honour and joy to meet and to work with the many individuals who made this research possible; their varied help is mentioned within the text. I hope that my book is worthy of all who contributed their time and light-hearted energy.

"Cambridge's Splendid Idiosyncrasy" is dedicated to Mina and Tadzio.

I thank Supervisor Paul Mellars, Advisor Jane Renfrew, History and Philosophy of Science Department Advisor Jim Secord, Jane Woods and the members of the Faculty of Archaeology and Anthropology and the staff of the Haddon Library; Elisabeth Leedham-Green and the Superintendents of the Cambridge University Library Manuscripts Reading Room, The President and Fellows of Lucy Cavendish College, T.C. Champion and the Librarians of the Society of Antiquaries, John Barnes, Robert and Linda Braidwood, the Miles Burkitt family, Mrs Geoffrey Bushnell, Christopher Chippindale, Desmond Clark, Grahame Clark, Lady Clark, Mary Kitson Clark, Judy Cowell, Mrs Glyn Daniel, Alison Duke, Jeremy Elston and the Garrod family, John and Evelyn Evans, Clare Fell, Peter Gathercole, Jack Golson, David Hall, Lady Hamilton, Sonia Hawkes, Phyllis Hetzel, Bruce Howe, John Hurst, Ray Inskeep, Tadzio Jamiolkowski, Lady Jeffreys, Robin Place Kenward, Anne McBurney, Alan Macfarlane, Jessica Martin, Donald Mitchell, John Mulvaney, Joan Oates, John Osborn, Kate Perry, John Phillips and Charles Phillips's family, John Pickles, Stuart Piggott, John Plumb, Steven Plunkett, Merrick Posnansky, Joyce Reynolds, Julia Roberts, Mrs Kenneth St Joseph, George Salt, Freydis Sharland and the C.S. Leaf family, Gale and Ann Sieveking, Tessa Stone, Chris Stray, William E. Taylor Jr, Mary Thatcher, Anne Thomson, Bruce G. Trigger, Jane McFie Waley, Richard West, John Wymer and Patrick Zutshi.

Contributions from Lucy Cavendish College, Cambridge, the Social Sciences and Humanities Research Council of Canada, the Overseas Research Students Award, the Cambridge Commonwealth Trust, the Garrod Fund of the Cambridge Department of Archaeology, the James Bay Housing Co-operative, the Wenner-Gren Foundation for Anthropological Research, the American School of Prehistoric Research, the LEE Foundation, Anne and Christopher Chippindale, Jane Callander, Francis McManus, Thurstan Shaw and Loren Reed Smith, Jr funded this research.

Foreword

Prehistory as a field of systematic research emerged during the nineteenth century, with such significant contributions as the Three Age System, the establishment of the antiquity of humankind, and the formation of the evolutionary framework in which the "Descent of Man" came to take an important place. Several distinguished historians of archaeology, from Glyn Daniel to Alain Schnapp and Bruce Trigger, have examined this theme. But the development of prehistory as an academic discipline, and the establishment of prehistoric archaeology as a significant university subject, is a different story. Here Pamela Jane Smith is a pioneer, and *A Splendid Idiosyncrasy* is the first full treatment, certainly in the English-speaking world, of this process. As she so clearly shows, many of the significant developments which established the study of prehistory as a professional undertaking, up to the middle of the twentieth century, including the inception of a full Honours Course in prehistory and archaeology, first took place in Cambridge. That this is so was largely the result of the endeavours of three remarkable people whose contributions she examines here.

One of the strengths of this highly readable study is that the author has made such effective use of unpublished sources. With the support of the family of the first of her protagonists, Miles Burkitt, she has used his letters and other material to bring out his crucial influence in the early stages and his significant role up to the time of Dorothy Garrod's election as Disney Professor of Archaeology in 1939. Moreover she was the first to locate and to realise the importance of the Garrod archive, lying unremarked in the Musée Nationale des Antiquités at St Germain-en-Laye. This has allowed her very effectively to reconstruct, with Jane Callander, the background to Dorothy Garrod's pioneering excavations in Gibraltar, Palestine and Bulgaria. She has also used great persistence in uncovering the story of Garrod's election in 1939 to the Disney Chair, making her the first woman professor at Cambridge. "Gentlemen, you have presented us with a problem" the Vice Chancellor is alleged to have said to the Electors, for women, although able to take courses at Cambridge at that time, were not then entitled to take degrees, and indeed were not able to do so until 1948. Perhaps most significantly of all, she has discerned and defined the importance of the young Grahame Clark, appointed lecturer at Cambridge in 1935, in influencing the nature of the new discipline. Clark was elected to the Disney Chair upon Garrod's retirement in 1952, so his tenure as Disney Professor falls outside the scope of this study. But his development in the 1930s of an approach (which the author here rather challengingly terms "the New Archaeology"), with its interdisciplinary emphasis and the inception of the ecological approach, was greatly influential on the development of the discipline. So too was his role in The Prehistoric Society, newly re-constituted with an international dimension, and his work for many years as the editor of its *Proceedings*.

Why and how did these things happen at Cambridge? Pamela Jane Smith has interviewed systematically most of the surviving protagonists of these early years at Cambridge, as well as other involved figures, such as the late Stuart Piggott, and compares the early development of prehistoric archaeology with those of other new university disciplines such as chemistry or physiology. Here her focus upon the importance of the departmental tea-room is at first surprising and then persuasive. It reminds us that the story is one of human personalities as much as it is about scholarship. That the author keeps this thoroughly in view is one of the aspects which makes this such a sympathetic and intriguing study as well as an exceptionally well-researched one.

The text presented here is essentially the one which she submitted for the degree of Doctor of Philosophy at Cambridge in 2004. It will, I predict, find many followers, as a case study which discerns the important general trends among the carefully researched detail. For there are other strands to the story. Archaeology at Liverpool, for instance, had a notable start with the foundation of the Liverpool Institute of Archaeology, through the energy of John Garstang, in 1904. But the initial momentum was not maintained. The story of the Department in Edinburgh, initiated with the appointment of the great prehistorian V. Gordon Childe as the first Abercrombie Professor in 1927, has yet to be written. So too does that of the Institute of Archaeology in London, founded by Mortimer Wheeler shortly before the Second World War. In the United States prehistoric archaeology lies rather uncomfortably in the university world between classical archaeology on the one hand and anthropology on the other, and there are very few university departments where the undergraduate teaching of archaeology escapes the shadow of its two neighbours. This did not happen in Britain, where the interactions between anthropology and archaeology, conceived in a different way as separate although related disciplines, have taken another direction. Here is another theme ripe for review. The French and German traditions have also their particularities and the author here notes that it was the Abbé Breuil who was mentor not only to Burkitt but also to Garrod in her early days.

If it was once possible to view archaeology and anthropology as Cambridge's "splendid idiosyncrasy" — the term is from the Oxford philosopher Lord Quinton — Pamela Jane Smith analyses with great clarity why that is no longer the case. As Quinton remarked: "Archaeology was a comparatively marginal subject in Cambridge … and many of its exponents were amateurish or odd or both". Over the period of her study, from 1915 to 1950, prehistory became established in Britain as a professional discipline, splendid perhaps but no longer idiosyncratic. This pioneering study describes with great clarity how that came to be so.

Colin Renfrew

1 Introduction

1.1 Prehistory — Cambridge's splendid idiosyncrasy

It is often assumed that, in Britain, archaeology has always been a university-inspired course. However, the identification of qualified scientific archaeology with a formal education is a twentieth-century phenomenon. Archaeology as a waged, educated, vocational pursuit is a recent development. At the beginning of the twentieth century, there were no degree courses in archaeology, no profession or professionals, no formal controls over recruitment, nor institutionalised avenues of entry, nor established examination-based qualifying standards, certainly no faculties, textbooks, lectures, practicals, Tripos[1] nor archaeological libraries.

British universities have produced great lineages of descendants who practise archaeological specialisations the world over. Yet, it is not known why or how archaeology became a university option. There are no specific histories of how archaeology was institutionalised as a university degree subject in Great Britain and Eire.

The entire history of all twentieth-century archaeologies, not just prehistoric, but classical, Romano-British, Anglo-Saxon, mediaeval and historic, can be viewed through the lens of amateur *versus* university professional and how these terms became defined and used. A university-based group emerged during the twentieth century, whose members gainfully asserted that anyone who was not university-centred, or at least university-trained, was an amateur. It is widely accepted today that if you do not have a degree you are not a professional archaeologist. How did this happen? Who considered themselves professionals? Who preferred to be defined as amateur and how did the self-identity of archaeologists change?

This twentieth-century professionalisation of archaeology did not happen in isolation. Historian Harold Perkin, in *The Rise of Professional Society*, observes that the twentieth was the century "of the uncommon and increasingly professional expert"; modern Britain "is made up of career hierarchies of specialised occupations, selected by merit and based on trained expertise . . . professional society is based on human capital created by education and enhanced by closure, that is, the exclusion of the unqualified." He claims that an intellectual class came "into existence, along with the word 'intellectual' as a noun, from the 1880s" onward and that the "invasion of the ancient universities" by the sciences was "an aspect of the professionalisation of university teaching" (Perkin 1989: 2, 86, 87). This broad historical shift is documented for numerous disciplines: Soffer (1994) studies

the development of history at Cambridge and Oxford from 1870 to 1930; Tillyard (1958) describes the founding of the Cambridge English Tripos in 1917; Porter (1982) investigates the success of the Natural Sciences Tripos and the Cambridge school of geology. However, these developments are not at all documented or analysed for archaeology.

My work, a start, focuses on one small crucial beginning. It is the first history of its kind and is intended to be a block for the building of a broader informed history of British academic archaeology. It will hopefully set an example for other historians of archaeological institutions to follow. "A Splendid Idiosyncrasy: Prehistory at Cambridge, 1915–50" is a micro-environmental "thick description" (Geertz 1973) of prehistoric archaeology at one of the most important academic centres in the world. It is a detailed and locally specific study of "The oldest school of prehistoric archaeology at a University which provided an Honours Course as well as a Diploma"(Daniel 1950: 137). According to historian of science, James Secord, this study is a good example of cultural history.

During much of the twentieth century, "the Cambridge faculty was the only one in Britain producing a flow of honours graduates" (Clark 1989a: 53). The title of this study emphasises this point and is derived from Anthony Quinton's review of Disney Professor Glyn Daniel's (1986) *Some Small Harvest: the Memoirs of Glyn Daniel*. Quinton (1987: 139) observed that Daniel "started as a geographer at Cambridge, but moved in his second year to that university's splendid idiosyncrasy, archaeology and anthropology. Archaeology was a comparatively marginal subject in Cambridge when he [Daniel] embarked on it and many of its exponents were amateurish or odd or both."

In 1915, at the invitation of the Reader in Ethnology, A.C. Haddon, shy, young Miles Burkitt, "essentially unconventional, he flaunted incongruously an Old Etonian tie"(Fox 2000: 44), became the first in Great Britain to offer lectures on prehistoric archaeology as part of a degree course to undergraduates. "The antiquity of man as determined by the earliest remains of his handiwork" (Read 1906: 57) or "Prehistoric Anthropology"[2] had been mentioned as a possible part of the post-graduate curriculum of the Board of Anthropological Studies at Cambridge since its inception in 1904. Ethnologist A.C. Haddon, Woodwardian Professor of Geology T. McKenny Hughes, the University Lecturer in Physical Anthropology, W.L.H. Duckworth, Disney Professor of Archaeology William Ridgeway, Curator of the Museum of General and Local Archaeology and of Ethnology Baron Anatole von Hügel and Mrs A. Hingston

---

[1] "From the custom of printing the list of successful candidates on the reverse side of the sheets of verses which had long been circulated on the occasion of the Bachelor's Commencement (or formal graduation) came the Cambridge term 'tripos' for an examination for an honours degree since the author of the verses, an annually selected BA, had originally declaimed them sitting, as a licensed jester like the Praevaricator, on a three-legged stool. Hence he acquired the name of 'Mr Tripos' and his verses were designated 'tripos verses'" (Leedham-Green 1996: 126).

[2] *Reporter*, 1904: 806.

Quiggin were all involved with the establishment of the Board. They were all fascinated by archaeology as well as anthropology.

By 1912, Quiggin had been offering courses of lectures in prehistory for some years at Homerton Training College and had published her textbook *Primeval Man: the Stone Age in Western Europe*. Duckworth had also published his short primer, *Prehistoric Man*. However, no one had offered a course of lectures in prehistory to undergraduates; Quiggin was specifically barred from doing so because she was a woman; Homerton was not yet a constituent College of the University. Teaching within Cambridge was, therefore, to be Burkitt's contribution. In 1915, when Haddon and Duckworth agreed to Burkitt's first course of lectures on "Prehistoric Archaeology and Primitive Art", a one-part Tripos course had just been approved; the Board of Anthropological Studies had begun to accept undergraduates as well as Diploma and research BA candidates.

It should be mentioned that the history of the anthropological side of the joint Honours Tripos course is not within the scope of this study. I do not document the life of Cambridge anthropology. This has been thoroughly studied by many others. Sandra Rouse's unpublished Ph.D dissertation "Ethnology, Ethnobiography, and Institution: A.C. Haddon and Anthropology at Cambridge, 1880–1926" is especially useful, as are innumerable additional accounts. A few of these are: Haddon's manuscript (1923), Clarke (1925), Fortes (1953), Gathercole (1977), Langham (1981), Leach (1984), Stocking (1984, 1996), Urry (1985) and Rouse (1999). Although anthropology is not the focus of my research, it will be often heard as a *basso continuo* in the following study.

During the 1920s and 1930s, the archaeological side of the Cambridge Tripos course attracted increasing numbers of competent students who eventually defined the scope and purposes of what they began to refer to as their new profession. Many Tripos and Diploma graduates from these decades went on successfully to pursue archaeology as a paid full-time career. These included A.J.H. Goodwin who was Professor at the University of Cape Town, known as the first professional South African prehistorian. Others were: Maud Gwladys White, who worked at the Royal Commission on Ancient Monuments for Wales and Monmouthshire (White 1934a, 1934b, 1935, 1936) and later collaborated with her husband, Grahame Clark, on excavations and reports; Mary Kitson Clark, who was a member of Dorothy Garrod's 1929 famed all-female team at el Wad, Mount Carmel, Palestine; Elisabeth Kitson, who excavated with Leakey in Africa; Jacquetta Hawkes, later known widely as an author; Clare Fell, who became Assistant Curator of the University Museum of Archaeology and Anthropology; Glyn Daniel, later Disney Professor of Archaeology and Editor of *Antiquity*; Thurstan Shaw, the father of British West African archaeology and Professor of Archaeology at the University of Ibadan, Nigeria; J. Desmond Clark, Professor of Anthropology at Berkeley, USA and world-leading

Africanist; Bernard Fagg, head of the Nigerian Antiquities Service and Curator of the Pitt-Rivers Museum at Oxford; John Brailsford, Keeper of British and Medieval Antiquities at the British Museum; John Hamilton, Inspectorate of Ancient Monuments; H.G. Wakefield of the Victoria and Albert Museum; Charles McBurney, who became Cambridge Professor of Quaternary Prehistory; R.R. Clarke, Curator, Norwich Castle Museum; and T.G.E. Powell, foundation Rankin Lecturer in Prehistoric Archaeology at University of Liverpool. Aileen Henderson (Fox 2000: 108), later Lady Fox, founding mother of archaeology at Exeter, suggests that it was Miles and his wife, Peggy Burkitt, who introduced her to field archaeology while she was at Cambridge in 1928. The prehistorian, Gertrude Caton-Thompson, known for her work in Zimbabwe and the Fayum, although not a Tripos graduate, was a student of Haddon's in 1923 (Caton-Thompson 1983).

In addition to the above, by 1932, Cyril Fox's work on the Cambridge region, L.S.B. Leakey's work on the Stone Age cultures of Kenya, H. O'Neil Hencken's work on the archaeology of Cornwall and Scilly, and Grahame Clark's work on the Mesolithic had all begun as research dissertations of the newly instituted Ph.D degree, "a German invention",[3] in the newly established Board of Archaeological and Anthropological Studies. By the 1950s, prehistoric archaeology had become one of the most successful and widely exported subjects produced by Cambridge; the Tripos became the gatekeeper for post-graduate research and archaeological careers in Britain and beyond. Cambridge-educated archaeologists continue to dominate certain areas of investigation. For example, in a recent conversation, Regents' Professor G.A. Clark of Arizona State University stated, "probably ninety percent of English-speaking people involved in Palaeolithic archaeology have come through Cambridge."

Archaeology is today defined as the study of past material culture (Renfrew and Bahn 2000: 12). "Archaeology is a broad church, encompassing a number of different 'archaeologies'," Renfrew and Bahn (2000: 13) explain. All archaeologies are united by established, acknowledged theories, methods and practices. British prehistoric archaeology, as currently defined, studies the periods before written records. These periods, known in Britain as the Palaeolithic, Mesolithic, Neolithic, Bronze and Iron Ages, span 3 million years. Romano-British, Anglo-Saxon, mediaeval, and historical are additional archaeologies which study periods after the introduction of writing. These distinctions are debated by some but are still widely used (Renfrew and Bahn 2000).

When the period of my research begins in 1915, such definitions and distinctions were not yet established. For example, "Mesolithic" was a term rarely used in Britain before the appearance of Macalister's 1921 *A Textbook of European Archaeology*, Burkitt's (1926b) article "The Transition

---

[3] Joan Oates, in conversation, 2000.

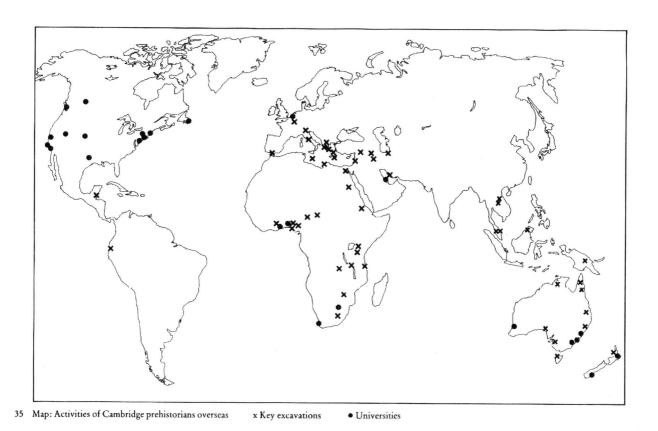

35   Map: Activities of Cambridge prehistorians overseas   x Key excavations   ● Universities

FIGURE I   This ever-increasing map of accomplishments hung for decades in the Disney Professor's Downing site office. "The Cambridge intellectual imperium endures across prehistoric landscapes . . . every continent is liberally sprinkled with the Cambridge mark," wrote John Mulvaney (1990: 115) in his review of Clark's (1989a) Prehistory at Cambridge and Beyond. Clark's "academic career virtually spans the currency of the discipline which is termed Prehistory. Prehistory has changed from a subject rarely taught in universities to an important inter-disciplinary undergraduate experience. In all these vital developments, Cambridge archaeologists have been prominent" (Mulvaney 1990: 119). Mulvaney, considered to be the founding father of Australian archaeology, graduated from the Tripos course in 1953. (Disney Professor Sir Grahame Clark's map courtesy of Cambridge University Press and Clark's Estate.)

between Palaeolithic and Neolithic Times: the Mesolithic Period" and Grahame Clark's seminal Cambridge Ph.D thesis *The Mesolithic Age in Britain* (1932a). The definitions, methods and practices which many archaeologists take for granted today did not exist in 1915. Historian of archaeology, Bruce Trigger (1989: 270), states that entire areas of archaeological study in Britain, such as the current specialisations of zooarchaeology, bioarchaeology and palaeoethnobotany, grew from work championed by Clark at Cambridge. As my work shows, this research, heavily influenced by previous developments in British and Scandinavian archaeology, was introduced by Clark and the botanist, Sir Harry Godwin, during the 1930s. This period at Cambridge was characterised by innovations in methods and rapid conceptual change.

This research traces and analyses these changes; it details the establishment of prehistoric archaeology as an academic endeavour for which the Cambridge Faculty of Archaeology and Anthropology is justly celebrated. The activities of Cambridge prehistorians will be the focus of my analysis. However, the early Special Board of Archaeological and Anthropological Studies offered courses of lectures

or supervisions in all archaeologies including Classical. Since 1879, classical archaeology had also been taught in Section D in the Faculty of Classics. In addition, during the early twentieth century, courses of lectures in classical archaeology were offered under the Special Board of History and Archaeology. At this time, the Disney Professor of Archaeology, Ridgeway, (1853–1926), who simultaneously held the Brereton Readership in Classics, gave courses of lectures in what would today be called classical archaeology under all three Boards.

As the twentieth century unfolded, the term archaeology began to refer only to those courses of lectures and papers offered by the Faculty of Archaeology and Anthropology. By 1928, the Board of History and Archaeology had become the Faculty of History and had dropped the archaeological section. Also, by the late 1920s, classical archaeology was no longer referred to as archaeology but more precisely as classical archaeology and had fallen decisively within the domain of the Faculty of Classics. This research does not study the development of classical archaeology. Excellent histories of the Classical Tripos at Cambridge written by Christopher Stray (1998, 1999) and Mary Beard (1999)

1930

Definition of archaeology
"the study of past distributions of culture-traits in time and space, and of the factors governing their distribution" (Clark 1933b: 232)

Goal
creations of typologies for surface finds in order to determine spatial and chronological connections

Theme
interaction of cultures as represented by lithic assemblages

Method
"We archaeologists did a good deal of walking" (Phillips 1987: 38)

Subject matter studied
lithic surface finds

Questions
How does one lithic artefact relate morphologically to another?

Focus
the use, manufacture and distribution of implements

1939

Definition of archaeology
"the study of how men lived in the past" (Clark 1939a: 1)

Goal
economic and social reconstruction of prehistoric life

Theme
nteraction of society and environment as expressed in material culture

Method
"The crux of archaeology is excavation" (Clark 1989a: 66)

Subject matter studied
settlement sites

Questions
How does material culture relate to the environment and to society?

Focus
the activities that the use, manufacture and distribution of implements imply

FIGURE II Dramatic intellectual shifts occurred in Grahame Clark's thinking during the 1930s, a decade in which prehistoric archaeology emerged as a hybrid interdisciplinary university-based subject in Britain.[4] G.R. Willey (1991: 222), doyen of American archaeology, observes, "The successful bringing together of prehistorians and people from the natural sciences has been the Cambridge achievement . . . this is the reason why Cambridge, in the scope of the 20th century, has led the way in making the world conscious of the importance of prehistory".

already exist and will be used as background information.

Because of its central importance, success, prominence and location, Cambridge prehistory offers the possibility for an excellent case study through which we may investigate history-of-science questions of why and how knowledge becomes academic. The history of the Faculty of Archaeology and Anthropology offers a clear example of the establishment of a new subject and provides a fascinating site for excavation.

1.2 Research Questions and Literature Review

Research Schools
How, then, "could spirit be made flesh" (Ophir and Shapin 1991: 3)? How do ideas become practice? How are definitions, goals and methods centralised and institutionalised

in one place? How is academic knowledge generated? Following R.N. Soffer (1982): why and how does one set of ideas and practices become articulate, systematic and professionalised within a university setting? In "Why do Disciplines Fail? The Strange Case of British Sociology," Soffer (1982) states that the processes by which academic subjects are established remain elusive and unexplained. However, she suspects that "the success of a discipline is not determined by its powers of protection or patronage". Successful professions must maintain "a monopoly over a special body of knowledge and skills . . . which is of a real benefit to the public". British sociology at first failed because of a fatal weakness in its intellectual content. "Charismatic personalities, the energetic activity of a group of believers, and the receptivity of institutions were necessary factors" but, most importantly, successful university professions must maintain "a monopoly over a special body of knowledge and skills" (Soffer 1982: 801).

Historians of science W. Coleman (1985: 49) and C. Rosenberg (1979) also argue that "cognitive content" cannot be ignored in the analysis of what they call "discipline

---

[4] For discussion of the emergence of interdisciplinary archaeology at Cambridge, see P.J. Smith 1997; 1997–8, 2000b.

formation". Rosenberg (1979: 447) suggests it is necessary to see "knowledge itself as a central element in shaping the structure of disciplinary cultures" within universities; Coleman, in his superb account of the establishment of nineteenth-century physiology, assigns an "indispensable role to cognitive content in the analysis of the disciplinary phenomenon". In "The Cognitive Basis of the Discipline: Claude Bernard on Physiology", Coleman (1985) demonstrates how Bernard's innovative conception of life and science provided an intellectual foundation for the new discipline of French physiology; this foundation was then used to assure intellectual, institutional and pedagogical independence. "The cognitive elements of experimental physiology were to Bernard a decisive instrument in translating bold explanatory ideas and proposed methods of a science in the making into the worldly needs of laboratory space, financial support and provision for training students" (Coleman 1985: 50, 69).

This work shows that it is vital to understand the concepts that provided an identity to early-twentieth-century Cambridge archaeologists. However, J.W. Servos (1993: 9) notes that T.S. Kuhn's *The Structure of Scientific Revolutions* "offered historians of science a powerful justification for studying the institutions in which science is done." For several decades since that publication, historians have gravitated "toward study of social institutions of science". S. Shapin (1992: 349), in his review of the externalist/ internalist debate in historical analysis, asserts "fundamentally the division of the e/i [externalist/internalist] explanatory world into the cognitive (science) and the non-cognitive (society) has never been systematically defended. There is as much 'society' within the scientific community, and scientific work-places, as there is outside them." In their analyses, Coleman, Rosenberg and Soffer pay ample attention to social parameters. "The concept of a discipline," Coleman (1985: 68) writes, "demands at least a minimal level of social organisation"; a community of scientists, the means to disseminate views to a wider public through publication and instruction, and sustained relations with authorities who may provide funding and other types of support. Organised institutions, such as great universities, Soffer adds (1982: 774), play an obvious role: while they do not "create disciplines, they can produce a resonant intellectual environment that transmutes a fragmented subject into a tradition through continuing discussion, influential publications and a significant number of students."

These suggestions parallel the conclusions made by other authors. A considerable literature on research schools (essays in *Osiris* 1993, Secord 1986) documents the importance of vibrant research agenda for the successful establishment of a new subject. Certainly the seminal article written on this subject is J.B. Morrell's (1972) study "The Chemist Breeders: the Research Schools of Liebig and Thomas Thomson". "It is commonplace," Morrell states, that "during the nineteenth century the activity known as science" began to be professionalised; Liebig's opening of his chemistry laboratory at the University of Giessen "was a crucial event" in this process. To help us understand this event it is possible "to postulate the propitious conditions under which a laboratory [and university][5] based research school could flourish." Morrell suggests that we take account of "intellectual, institutional, technical, psychological or financial" elements in our analysis. For example, a research school may require a charismatic director whose leadership qualities are "most effectively exerted in informal pre-bureaucratic contexts" (Morrell 1972: 1–6). Morrell's elements are succinctly charted by G.L. Geison in his 1981 article "Scientific Change, Emerging Specialties and Research Schools". Here Geison (1981: 23) defines research schools as "small groups of mature scientists pursuing a reasonably coherent programme of research side-by-side with advanced students in the same institutional context and engaging in direct, continuous social and intellectual interaction".

There are difficulties in applying the term "research school" to the emergence of prehistoric archaeology at Cambridge. During the time covered by my study, the Archaeology and Anthropology Tripos course consisted of one Part only. Until 1948, a student could focus on archaeology and anthropology for either Part One or Part Two of their degree. Usually a student read history or classics before a final year of archaeology and anthropology as Part Two of a three-year degree. This one part included two sections. A student could take papers in either Section A, which covered physical and social anthropology and prehistoric archaeology, or Section B, Norse, Celtic and Anglo-Saxon history and language, taught under the Elrington and Bosworth Professor of Anglo-Saxon, H.M. Chadwick.

Geison's (1981: 23) definition of a research school was derived from the study of laboratory-based activities and may not always be completely applicable to the development of prehistoric archaeology at Cambridge, where undergraduates and quasi-hierarchical pedagogical techniques were crucial to the establishment of the subject. Interestingly, by the 1960s, Brian Fagan and Ray Inskeep[6] were writing home from Africa to their former teacher, Miles Burkitt, enquiring how the "Cambridge school" of prehistory was progressing. However, here Fagan and Inskeep were using the term "school" to mean a somewhat looser group of teachers and students "united by the possession of common doctrine, method, or style" (Servos 1993: 4) rather than a tight group of researchers working side-by-side. Discipline, on the other hand, as loosely defined by Servos as "a community of scientists, publications, instruction, funding", may appear a more fitting concept than Morrell's research school. Still, I suggest that this concept may be too broad and does not fully apply to archaeology as it existed at the beginning of my research, when it was a small, growing part of a fragmented curriculum within an emerging Tripos course. This study begins as the "discipline" was barely forming.

[5] Geison (1981: 35) notes how "research schools are so closely associated with the institutionalisation of science in the universities."
[6] Burkitt, M.C. Papers CUL Add. 7959 Letters found in Box III.

Despite these problems of definition, Morrell and Geison's list is useful in that it provides a structure within which to present a vast amount of collected historical material about the development of prehistoric archaeology at Cambridge. Geison's chart, commonly referred to in history-of-science literature as "Morrell's model" (Geison 1993: 227), points us in the right direction. It offers a framework and a container for the description of events. It suggests ideas as to appropriate variables which may have facilitated the growth of prehistoric archaeology in an academic setting. Factors delineated by Morrell and Geison serve analytical and research purposes.

A focused research programme, a pool of recruits, new exploitable techniques, new fields of research and a publication outlet are all evident in the evolving Cambridge experience. Geison (1993: 228) notes that Morrell's schema for an ideal research school, although referred to as a "model", should not be taken as prescriptive but instead is intended to be a useful "systematic catalogue of the factors to be considered when examining a research school." This "model", then, is simply intended to familiarise us with comparative work and illuminate possible areas of investigation. On the one side it encourages biography; on the other, histories of disciplines and universities (Servos 1993). "More important than the label," Secord (1986: 264) suggests, "is the idea underlying the historical study of research schools, for it focuses attention on small groups within the scientific community, and the social and intellectual ties that bind them together."

This is the first time that such models, developed in the discipline of history of science, have been used to explicate a study of the history of archaeology. The strength of the application of this literature to a data base drawn from archaeology will be examined.

Geography of knowledge

My study of a small group dedicated to archaeology within the larger scientific community of Cambridge would also seem to fit within a tradition of research which investigates the "place of knowledge". Such approaches may prove well suited to a study of Cambridge prehistory and may help to augment research school approaches. In his 1998 article on "Historical and Sociological Problems in the Location of Science", Shapin argues that local and spatial situations should be "attended to in order to understand how scientific knowledge was made, how it secured credibility, how it travelled". He notes that there has been a "rise in a geographical perspective on science in recent years" (Shapin 1998: 5, 6) which has been eclectically influenced by the social theorists Bruno Latour, Anthony Giddens, Pierre Bourdieu and Michel Foucault. This literature offers insights into knowledge creation and dissemination. In particular, the work of Latour and his followers draws attention to the ways in which patterns of

colonialism "have established channels" which facilitate the standardisation and spread of knowledge (Shapin 1998: 7). These insights are especially applicable to prehistory at Cambridge and its many graduates who followed the setting sun of the Empire. "My father was very proud of the Empire; a civilising force for good," explains Thurstan Shaw, who took a First in the 1936 Tripos; "The Empire provided us with jobs" (in conversation, 2003).

The geography of knowledge analyses scientific achievements and their spread as the outcome of local training and traditions. An increasing number of localised case studies answer broader questions about academic practices. Soraya de Chadarevian (2002: 3), in her history of molecular biology at Cambridge, states, "My choice of a local study is based . . . on the thesis that widely distributed experimental practices and scientific institutions embody local expertise and negotiations. It is only by studying in detail these local solutions, the resistances they met, and the eventual 'export' of local practices to other laboratories, that one may understand the construction of a new scientific field." It is legitimate and necessary to study the "place" of scientific activity, whether it be a classroom, laboratory, tea-room or excavation. Ophir and Shapin (1991: 9) describe the "situated" character of knowledge; the "embeddedness" of science in "knowledge-making sites". Although using terms unfamiliar to archaeologists, Shapin is suggesting that attention be paid to what happens, for example, at excavations or in tea-rooms in order to understand how archaeology became an academic subject. Certainly this approach suits a profession in which "Real Archaeologists" must get mud on their boots (Stoddart and Malone 2002: 917) in practical activities. Clark is remembered by students as occasionally expressing disapproval for colleagues who "didn't get their boots dirty".[7] See also Clark's criticism of Glyn Daniel as quoted in Stoddart and Malone (2002: 918), or Kent Flannery's (1982: 275) caricature of a well-known colleague as the man who "couldn't dig his way out of a kitty litter box".[8]

In a similar vein to Shapin's work, historian of science, Paula Gould, during a discussion at the 1998 Cambridge Conference for Women and Higher Education, suggested that we "go back to the 'small' to get to the 'large'". When attempting to understand how science works, Gould (1998: 23) suggests that we look at "science clubs, the coffee room discussions, meeting groups. How are they set up; who has access to them?" We should be aware of the roles different men and women occupied within those groups. It is these interactions "we need to get into, we need to get closer to" (Gould 1998: 23). Shapin (1994) and J. Hardwig (1991) look at the role of trust in such interactions; an issue which becomes a lyric vocal line throughout my research, heard especially in the Faculty tea-room. Ophir and Shapin (1991: 12) state "our understanding of face-to-face interaction in modern science is still rudimentary".

---

[7] Gillian Tennant, 1952 Tripos, personal correspondence, 1998.

[8] This ultimate archaeological put-down was taken by many as referring to celebrated New Archaeologist, Lewis Binford.

CHART II. Factors in the success or failure of research schools.

Degree of success	Sustained success			Temporary success		Partial or relative failure			
	Liebig's School	Foster's School	Noyes' School	Arcueil School	Fermi's Group	Thomson's School	Burdon-Sanderson's School	Remsen's School	Bancroft's School
1. 'Charismatic' leader(s)	+	+	+	+	+	−	−	−	+
2. Leader with research reputation	+	+	+	+	+	+	+	+	+
3. 'Informal' setting and leadership style	+	+	?	−	+	−	−	−	−
4. Leader with institutional power	+	+	+	+	+	−	+	+	+
5. Social cohesion, loyalty, esprit de corps, 'discipleship'	+	+	+	+	+	−	−	?	+
6. Focused research program	+	+	+	+	+	+	+	+	+
7. Simple and rapidly exploitable experimental techniques	+	−	+	?	+	+	+	+	−
8. Invasion of new field of research	+	−	+	−	+	−	−	−	+
9. Pool of potential recruits (graduate students)	+	+	+	+	?	+	+	+	+
10. Access to or control of publication outlets	+	+	+	+	+	?	+	+	+
11. Students publish early under own names	+	+	+	+	?	−	−	?	+
12. Produced and 'placed' significant number of students	+	+	+	+	?	−	−	+	+
13. Institutionalization in university setting	+	+	+	−	?	+	+	+	+
14. Adequate financial support	+	+	+	+	+	−	−	+	+
Total of " + 's"	14	12	13	10	10	5	7	9	12

+ means that this feature appears to be present

− means that this feature appears to be absent

? means that presence or absence of feature is unclear

FIGURE III Geison's Chart. Geison (1981: 27) states, "any such chart does all sorts of violence to the particularities and nuances of the circumstances surrounding the success or failure of a research school [but] the chart does have some value as a rough guide to the sorts of factors to be considered by students." Geison's list of ingredients for success illustrates the results of comparative studies in the emergence of science and adds perspective to the case study of Cambridge prehistoric archaeology. It heuristically suggests fruitful areas of investigation and provides a structure for this investigation.

Gender and Science

This study will hopefully illuminate face-to-face inter-action in modern science by using the above perspectives. However, much of the work conducted on research schools was begun during the 1970s before gendered analyses became commonplace. It would, therefore, be productive to look at relevant recent gender and science studies. This would be especially interesting because current research school analyses, such as the articles which appear in *Osiris* (1993), tend to ignore the study of gendered relationships in science production.

Gender may have many attributes, but ease of definition is not one of them. "Gender is emphatically not another way of talking about women, nor is it a topic or a subject area; it is an analytical category. It has this in common with terms that express forms of social difference — age, caste, clan, tribe — that it is simultaneously a way of ordering experience, a system of representation and a metaphor for particular kinds of relationships," writes L. Jordanova. Gender is a concept "that expresses a widespread and highly complex phenomenon: the representation of the multiple relationships between masculine and feminine," she continues. Gender analysis, a product of scholarly interests that have emerged since the 1960s, can be a powerful tool for interpreting the past (Jordanova (1993: 474, 483). It draws attention to nu-anced relations long held to be natural and unquestionable. Gendered analysis invites us to look at our self-concepts and behaviours and at how they are structured and used. A gendered perspective suggests new questions for inves-tigation and offers insightful understandings of personal relationships integral to science.

Such an approach is especially applicable to Cambridge from 1915 to 1950 when definitions of masculinity and femininity were shifting (Phillips 1979, Gould 1997, Howarth 1998). "Gendered characteristics have pervaded all aspects of social life," Jordanova (1993: 475) states. The masculine and the feminine are linked with occupa-tions, skills, talents, virtues, vices, places, objects, col-ours, shapes, scientific activities and university subjects. Interviewees often reminded me that the Archaeological and Anthropological Tripos was considered a "soft op-tion" in which "undergraduettes"[9] might excel.[10] Entire "scientific fields became professionalized along gender lines that functioned to exclude women, while others such as nutrition, home economics and teaching became feminized," states the historian C. Merchant (1982: 406).

Archaeology presents an intriguing combination of both; it was academically professionalised along masculine Cambridge lines during the early twentieth century. However, my study will document how some women, with the active support of male colleagues, creatively and successfully fashioned archaeological spaces both in the field and within the Faculty.

By 1915, women had been admitted to Tripos examina-tions[11] since 1882 but membership of the University was still an exclusively male privilege. By the end of World War I, it appeared that changes wrought in attitudes and behaviour by courageous female war work "might bring major institutional and structural change," writes historian Gill Sutherland (1998: 6). The Franchise Act granted women over 30 the right to vote. "The 1919 Sex Disqualification Removal Act launched a more general removal of barriers," she continues. Yet in 1921 a proposal before the Senate for full female membership was "catastrophically defeated by 904 votes to 712" (Leedham-Green 1996: 192). What eventually did secure a majority "was a half-a-loaf proposal: that women should be granted the titles of degrees but none of the privileges that went with them" (Sutherland 1998: 8). The women I interviewed irreverently referred to their title degrees as the "Tits". The *Historical Register: Supplement* (1921–30: 9), states that, despite the lack of membership, the position of women was improved by the New Statutes of 1923 "which made women eligible for all University teaching offices and these offices give membership of Faculties".

However, my analysis of Garrod's experience as the first woman elected to a Professorship at Cambridge reveals that being a female academic within a "Men's University" (Sutherland 1998: 7) presented problems. Studies taken from the literature on women and science enlighten Garrod's diffi-culties and place her academic experiences in perspective.[12] Literature on gendered roles in scientific careers shows that although academic achievements are dependent on an innovative cognitive base, they are also rooted in skilled attitudes and necessary learned behaviours. A successful academic must know how to work the system.

These three approaches, research school analyses, ideas derived from the geography of knowledge literature, and the insights from research into gender and science, will be used in this study to understand the flourishing success of Cambridge prehistory.

---

[9] "Undergraduette" was a term that became popular during the 1960s in Cambridge but has since fallen out of use.

[10] Betty Saumarez Smith, Tripos 1936; Former Secretary for the Faculty and Tripos graduate in 1945, Mary Thatcher; classicist Alison Duke, in correspondence and in conversation, 1996–9.

[11] The history of women and higher education at Cambridge is told in numerous publications, some of which are: McWilliams-Tullberg (1975); Sutherland (1994); Stephen (1927); Phillips (1979) and Richmond (1997). Gould's (1998) unpublished Ph.D thesis, *Femininity and Physical Science in Britain 1870–1914,* is also recommended.

[12] The following studies will provide relevant information: G. Sonnert and

G.J. Holton (1995) *Gender Differences in Science;* P.A. Graham (1978) "History of Women in American Higher Education"; T. Stone (1999) unpublished Ph.D "The Integration of Women into a Military Service"; C.F. Epstein (1991) "Constraints on Excellence"; D.R. Kaufman (1978) "Associational Ties in Academe: some Male and Female Differences"; S.E. Widnall (1988) "Voices from the Pipeline"; D. Wright (2000) "Gender and Professionalization"; A. Oram (1989) "Embittered, Sexless or Homo-sexual"; L. Sciama (1984) "Ambivalence and Dedication: Academic Wives in Cambridge University 1870–1970"; and J. Howarth's (1998) research on "Gender at Cambridge and Oxford, 1900–1950".

1.3 Sources

All knowledge is community based. This is especially true when secondary published material did not exist and unpublished sources had not yet been located. This research is substantially based on information from material I collected with the support and generous help of many contributors. Extensive detective work and conversations with former Archaeology and Anthropology students, their families, supervisors and colleagues resulted in the creation of new archives. Many of these papers are now placed in the Cambridge University Library. The discovered sources are listed in the footnotes and under References or Manuscripts. The transcripts of some of the interviews conducted are attached in the Appendix. Correspondence is listed alphabetically by surname under Manuscript Sources. Notes from interviews which have not been transcribed are also listed by the interviewees' surnames under Manuscript Sources.

1.4 Qualitative Methodology

Ethical Procedures and Evidential Constraints

Standard ethical procedures suggested by the widely-published qualitative methodologists, Egon Guba and Yvonna Lincoln (1981),[13] were followed when using evidence from living subjects and from oral historical interviews. In this section, the procedures used are reviewed. Evidential constraints and how they were established are also discussed. Firstly, it should be stated that oral historians give interviewees the right to comment on and approve anything used. This has been done as carefully as possible.

I first wrote to Grahame Clark in 1987 to seek permission to study his career. He was consistently receptive. I requested that he read my articles prior to publication, which he did. Both he and his wife, Lady Clark, were astute editors yet never interfered with interpretations. They allowed complete academic freedom. Fortunately, my study of Clark was mostly completed before his death in 1995. When I returned to Cambridge in 1997, after an intermission, I concentrated on Garrod and, after further delays away from Cambridge, Burkitt became the focus. A final piece of research which discussed Clark's contributions to the transformation of the Prehistoric Society of East Anglia (Smith 2000b) was shown to Lady Clark for comment by research adviser, Jane Renfrew. My chapter on Dorothy Annie Elizabeth Garrod has been sent to all who wrote letters or were interviewed during that research for their comment and approval. Interviewees had the right to change quotations and only approved quotations are used. Very seldom has anyone requested changes. The Garrod family was strongly supportive. The Burkitt family has also been kind and generously helpful and has reviewed the Burkitt

chapter. The family has made available an extensive collection of Miles Burkitt's published papers and unpublished notes. In the following text, I refer to this collection as the "Burkitt Family Archive". This archive is listed amongst the sources in Manuscripts.

In 2000, I recorded 30 life histories in an oral history project funded by the Wenner-Gren Foundation for Anthropological Research. These tapes have been placed at the Society of Antiquaries of London and are publicly available. Two hundred bound pages of transcriptions are also stored at Cambridge University's Haddon Library and some transcripts are included here as an Appendix. After painstakingly reviewing the transcripts, a process which took months, most interviewees gave me written permission to have these interviews and the transcriptions used in my work. I found, however, that interviewees were much less willing to talk openly and were less candid on publicly available recordings. The approved Wenner-Gren interviews are the only interviews which have been made public.

Oral historical evidence is used here as a small piece of a large project which is subject to evidential constraints. Oral responses are only quoted in conjunction with supporting and corroborating evidence from other types of sources. I searched for independent lines of information, looking for what the philosopher Alison Wylie (1992: 25) terms a "network of resistances". Wylie argues that interpretations are strengthened when based on converging lines of evidence. She suggests that we work towards a "concatenation of inferences" (Wylie 1989: 15). Conclusions are improved by using collateral lines of documentation. Following Wylie's suggestions, results were enhanced through a system of checks and balances. This may be best explained by using an example. In 1950, a divisive controversy burst open within the Faculty. Ethel John Lindgren had been appointed to a Lectureship just before the William Wyse Professor of Social Anthropology, John Hutton, retired. When Meyer Fortes succeeded Hutton to the Chair, he felt that Lindgren should be replaced by someone more appropriate to the newer, pressing research and teaching demands of the Faculty.[14] This split the Faculty between the older, moneyed "amateurs" and the younger professionals and ushered in a new era. If there were to be a need to reconstruct this controversy, there would be seven sources of information. There are three differing oral historical accounts from the then Secretary for the Faculty, Mary Thatcher,[15] and from two former post-graduate students, Lindgren's Ph.D student, Ian Whitaker, and the physical anthropologist, Marie Lawrence. Glyn Daniel's (1986) version of events is printed candidly in *Some Small Harvest*. The Faculty and Appointments Committee Minutes[16] and the Faculty of Archaeology and Anthropology Board Minutes[17] have records of discussions

---

[13] Egon G. Guba and Yvonna S. Lincoln are the American 'gurus' of qualitative methodology, widely cited by educators. Dr Matt Jaren of Edinburgh University suggested this reference.

[14] Fortes Papers. CUL Add. 8405/1/41.

[15] I thank Mrs Charles McBurney for suggesting that I meet and interview Miss Mary Thatcher and Mrs Geoffrey Bushnell.

[16] Faculty and Appointments Committee Minutes CUA Min.V.93.

[17] Faculty of Archaeology and Anthropology Board Minutes CUA Min. V.95.

and decisions. Finally, there are Fortes's and Lindgren's revealing correspondence.[18] The oral historical accounts can be placed alongside equally solid written evidence from archival sources. An unfortunate situation may be more accurately and fairly analysed using several lines of complementary and competing evidence.[19]

In this manner, oral historical evidence as well as evidence from other types of sources may be successfully used to reconstruct crucial events. Occasionally, one especially reliable witness, respected within the small Cambridge community, may augment thin written evidence with a few key memories. For example, Garrod's momentous election as the first female professor is barely mentioned officially. Regardless of her accomplishments, Garrod has remained a "shadowy figure" in Cambridge.[20] There is no official record of who was considered or what was discussed on the evening of 6 May 1939. The scant Minutes from Elections to Professorships[21] reproduced later in this study is the *only* existing document. The eight Electors, pillars of respectability and academic power, appear to have met in the usual way, discussed an apparently small field of candidates, reconvened the following morning and quickly voted for Garrod. There is no hint of controversy surrounding this important election. There was no attempt to suspend the proceedings, to suggest alternatives or to request time to advertise for or to interview additional applicants as had happened during some previous Cambridge professorial elections.

The late Lady Jeffreys's testimony greatly enhances this scarce evidence. By good fortune, I met a former undergraduate named Barbara Wallis while having tea in the Cambridge University Library. I discovered, as we talked, that she had come up to Cambridge to read Archaeology and Anthropology during the Second World War. Months later, she approached me to suggest that I speak to her elderly friend, Lady Jeffreys, a mathematical physicist, then in her nineties. At that time, I was living as a guest at Elisabeth Leedham-Green's home. Leedham-Green, the Deputy Keeper of University Archives at the University of Cambridge, assured me that Lady Jeffreys was a highly respected member of the Cambridge community, known for her clarity, good memory and intelligence. She would be a reliable witness.

In fine, vivid detail, Lady Jeffreys remembered, how she had met "outside Elector", Manchester Professor of Geography, H.J. Fleure, on a train from Cambridge to Manchester the morning following Garrod's election. She recounted Fleure's humour and good spirits, the sepia light drifting through the train window; Fleure's memory of the Vice-Chancellor's response when the Electors gave their decision was, "Gentlemen, you have presented us with a problem."[22] When I cross-checked this phrase with Alison Duke, who had known Vice-Chancellor Dean well, she

immediately confirmed that the wording was exactly his. Jeffreys' memories are historically invaluable and helped in the reconstruction of Garrod's academic career.

Oral Historical Interviews

The established ethnographic fieldwork method of interviewing was used when confronted with no known sources to study the development of archaeology. "Of all the means of gathering data perhaps the oldest and most respected is the conversation," write widely published social scientist qualitative methodologists, Egon Guba and Yvonna Lincoln. "Interviewing — 'the conversation with a purpose' — is perhaps one of the best tools the inquirer can use" (Guba and Lincoln 1981: 153, 154). It is a preferred tactic of data collection in the social sciences. The authors explain that an interview may be either highly structured, essentially an oral questionnaire focusing on a narrow enquiry for a specific purpose, or so broad and unstructured that the unexpected may emerge. Guba and Lincoln suggest that broad, unstructured interviews are best used for the purpose of collecting oral histories.

Structured Interviews

Guba's "structured interviews" are used for a specific purpose only. This type of interview often functions well as a first research step toward documentation. My early work on reconstructing the history of the Fenland Research Committee is an example of how this method may be applied. The Committee, which occupies a mythical presence in archaeological minds, exists just beyond living memory. Little was known as to how it was founded, its day-to-day goals and activities, who was involved, what excavations were conducted and what publications resulted. Few realised that the Committee was the predecessor of the Cambridge Sub-department for Quaternary Research and that it developed the stratigraphic-geological approach for archaeology in Britain. In search of sources, I interviewed a sample of 34 people including the then only surviving Committee members, Grahame Clark and Stuart Piggott. My sample also included Cambridge college archivists and librarians such as Clare College's Suzanne Johnston, the archivist, Bill Holliwell, from the Fenland office of the British Sugar Company and Cambridge researchers such as Harry Godwin's student, Richard West. I then talked to archaeologists involved in recent Fenland research, John Coles, David Hall, Charly French and Sylvia Hallam, as well as curators of local museums, e.g. Steven Plunkett, the then Keeper of Archaeology at Ipswich Museum, and finally Faculty elders such as Peter Gathercole. Events snowballed as each person put me in touch with others. In this case, the structured interview led to considerable relevant information which is presented in Chapter 3.

The search to find Fenland Committee members provides other examples of how the structured focused interview

---

[18] CUL Add. 8405 /1/41.

[19] This controversy will be discussed in full in an upcoming book and is mentioned here so that interested readers may know the pertinent sources.

[20] Paul Mellars, in conversation, 1996.

[21] Elections to Professorships CUA O.XIV.54.

[22] This quotation is fully explained in Chapter 4.

method may work. Charles Phillips was a Fellow of Selwyn and a founder of the Committee. Although the University Library, the Cambridge Museum of Archaeology and Anthropology and Selwyn College had no information, a passage in Phillips's (1987) published autobiography stated that his son took a position at the Greater London Council's map collection in 1965. Fortunately, when I rang the City map division, John Phillips answered the telephone, invited me to tea and offered his father's previously unknown and unpublished memoirs. Tom Lethbridge, another founder of the Committee, was deceased but rumour was that his younger wife was alive in Girton. However, there was no Lethbridge in the directory. After a day of knocking on doors in Girton, I was told that if I followed a black cat named Sam, I would find Mina Lethbridge, whose lilting accent would make BBC English sound vulgar. Once again, Mina Lethbridge offered me tea, a trunk of letters and her husband's unpublished autobiography.

A mass of information therefore emerged from these interviews. The research on Garrod is another example of the effectiveness of structured interviews when used to uncover sources. Garrod's correspondence and manuscripts were believed to have been destroyed. Persistent rumours suggested that she had burnt her literary remains. In consequence, Garrod's life and brilliant career had not been thoroughly documented. After much intensive questioning of many people, Jane Renfrew suggested that I approach Phyllis Hetzel of the Newnham College Roll Office. Through Phyllis Hetzel, L. Pulvertaft-Green (Tripos 1948–49) was found. Pulvertaft-Green was the first to mention a counter-rumour; Clark had once told her that Garrod had saved correspondence and field notes and that this unpublished material was stored in France. Jane Renfrew then suggested that I contact Paul Bahn, a good friend of Suzanne Cassou de Saint-Mathurin. Saint-Mathurin, who had died in 1991, had excavated with Garrod in France and Lebanon and stayed with her in the Charente. Bahn's first response in March 1996 was not hopeful. "Suzanne de St Mathurin left me Dorothy Garrod's desk in her will but it was empty — no papers, no secret drawers!" But a later letter, written on 2 April 1996 states "I have just returned from Paris where I spoke with Geneviève Pinçon, another friend who was involved with the de St Mathurin legacy . . . There is indeed considerable Garrod material . . . now gone to the Musée des Antiquités Nationales."[23] When Saint-Mathurin died, boxes of Garrod's diaries, letters, field notes, photographs and manuscripts were bequeathed to the MAN along with Saint-Mathurin's papers. This material, not yet accessioned, is kept under Saint-Mathurin's name.

The depth and literary wealth of the preserved material is astonishing. Only a few photographs of Garrod had been

well known; now hundreds are available. Her field notes and diaries from excavations and expeditions to Kurdistan, Anatolia, Bulgaria, France and Lebanon detail exciting personal experiences. Crucial archaeological discoveries can now be better reconstructed. Photographs and diaries document the 1932 discovery at Mount Carmel, Palestine, of the Neanderthal female skeleton, Tabun I. According to Christopher Stringer, who is the custodian of Tabun I at the Natural History Museum, this skeleton is "the most complete Neanderthal female yet discovered and remains one of the most important human fossils ever found" (Callander[24] and Smith 1998). Diaries discuss excavation activities and illuminate important archaeological work. Harvard archaeologist, Ofer Bar-Yosef, who is an expert in Levantine archaeology, states that Garrod's work "remains decisive in interpreting the course of human evolution" (Callander and Smith 1998). Garrod's papers, photographs, letters, field notes and diaries found at the Musée des Antiquités Nationales have now been disseminated and used in several publications.[25]

Unstructured Interviews[26]

In comparison to the narrow, goal-oriented structured approach to interviewing, oral historical interviews can also be unstructured and may be used to record general, broad-ranging life stories. Unstructured oral historical interviewing, a new and growing field, is defined as "the evocation and recording of individual memories of the past" (Johnson and Dawson for the Popular Memory Group of University of Birmingham: 1998: 81). "No more elegant tool exists to describe the human condition than the personal narrative" asserts anthropologist Marjorie Shostak (1998: 402). A primary merit of oral recollections is that they recreate the complexity and uniqueness of past experiences. Oral recordings capture the tone, volume, silence, emotion and personal meaning of events. Attitudes can be rediscovered more accurately and descriptions made colourful. History becomes enriched and more complete. "The collector of the spoken word," a founder of the History Workshop movement and journal in Britain, Raphael Samuel (1998: 391) states, "is in a privileged position."

I was privileged to work with the people I have met and experienced few of the difficulties in communication described by other oral historians who, for example, recorded the painful memories of an oppressed or traumatised group (William Westerman, 1998, on Central American refugee testimony; Irina Sherbakova, 1998, on Gulag memories). Interviewees were no less powerful but certainly had more enjoyable memories; people were thoroughly willing, communicative, articulate and co-operative.[27] They immediately saw the value of this history. In fact, the first response was often, "Why has this not been done before?"

[23] Bahn, in correspondence, April 1996.
[24] Since 1997, at Bahn's suggestion, I have collaborated with Jane Callander on exhibitions. Jane is an historian of Near Eastern archaeology with an MA from the Institute of Archaeology, University College London. She had been working simultaneously on Garrod since 1994. We are now

planning a pictorial biography of Dorothy Garrod based on the hundreds of unpublished photographs held at the MAN.
[25] Davies and Charles 1999; Bar-Yosef and Callander 1999; Bar-Yosef and Callander in press; Smith *et al.* 1997; Smith 1998, 2000a; Callander and Smith in press.

Most interviewed were Cambridge graduates; the undergraduate and female student of the 1920s, '30s and '40s were an already highly selected group upon arrival at Cambridge. They were usually from the middle classes although some such as Sylvia Hallam and Jack Golson, who identified themselves as working-class, appeared after the Second World War. All exhibited a profound self-awareness. "Yes, we knew we were pioneering something," Golson, (First, 1951 Tripos), wrote in 1999 about the beginnings of the Deserted Mediaeval Village Research Group. The interviewees' recall was detailed and vivid; memories were accurate when cross-checked against other evidence. Perks and Thomson (1998: 183) observe that, as one ages, a "life review" memory phase emerges. Recent memory fails with age but ability to recall distant memories improves. In discussing the fallibility of memory, Stone (1998: 8) writes "research has in fact demonstrated that interviewing elderly people presents fewer problems in this regard than interviewing the young or the middle aged".

Tea was often offered and was an absolutely delight. It may have helped that the interviewees and myself came from similar backgrounds and, as a Canadian, I spoke a variation of the English language. My "outsider within" status also must have been a "plus"; as a beginning Ph.D researcher, there was no position to protect in the Cambridge Faculty and no privileged standpoint to defend. I was genuinely fascinated by the interviewees' remarkable lives and their candid responses.[28]

Nor were there difficulties, as some historians report (Stone's manuscript, 1998), with sample construction. In addition to the other interviews mentioned, as many students as possible were contacted. This sample was "self selecting" (Stone 1998: 2) in that I could only write to the survivors. I attempted to interview all female Faculty graduates from 1915 to 1950 whether or not they had specialised in archaeology. Phyllis Hetzel and Kate Perry, the Archivist of Girton College, matched addresses with the names identified from the *Historical Register* Class Lists. All but three of the 75 female survivors responded with written comments and about one third agreed to follow-up interviews. Several, such as the late Mrs Robin Place Kenward, who took a First in 1947, wrote to male Faculty graduates and sent me their responses and their class notes. The general questions in my letters to all were as follows: Why did you read archaeology? What are your memories of Burkitt, Clark, Garrod or other Faculty members? What careers have you chosen? The face-to-face interviews were wide-ranging, loosely structured and varied with each person. The surviving men who had specialised in archaeology were well known and easily reached. I did not attempt to contact men who were not archaeologists.

Historian Paul Thompson (1998) mentions that oral history results can be unpredictable and may force a shift of research focus. One of the first interviews I conducted was with a now

deceased personality. My question about the "rural" nature of Cambridge versus Oxford was misheard as "moral" at which time he happily launched into a personal discussion of past loves. Much to my embarrassment, this happened again three months later. The interviewee heard "moral" rather than "rural". Armed with Morrell and Geison's model for success, I thought that perhaps this new oral information could fit under the category of effectiveness "in informal pre-bureaucratic contexts" (Morrell 1972: 6). On a later occasion, I brought up the topic of "rurality" again with Thurstan Shaw. "Oh," he responded, "we all knew who the womanisers were."[29] I realised then that I was asking the wrong question. Human relations were more important than rurality. Perhaps one of the strengths of the Faculty was its smallness and its endogamy. There was a history of long-committed couples who worked together for the advancement of the subject, as well as a commitment to the tea-room as a sanctuary. This point will be returned to in the conclusion of this study.

1.5 Preview, 1915–50

The first course of lectures in prehistory was listed in the Michaelmas Term of 1915. By 1950, the full Tripos course for Archaeology and Anthropology had been effectively instituted. Spanning this time, my study will end with the 1950 post-war burst of students, the admission of women to full University membership and the diaspora of graduates to foreign and British posts. Biographies of personalities provide an entry into the development of prehistory's social, intellectual and institutional aspects. Each chapter focuses on a central player and covers a decade: Miles Burkitt and his contributions occur primarily in the twenties (Chapter 2); Grahame Clark's New Archaeology emerges throughout the thirties (Chapter 3); and Dorothy Garrod's experiences as the first woman and as the first prehistoric archaeologist elected to a professorship occupies the forties (Chapter 4). Because this was, when written during the 1990s, the first study to investigate these figures and because their lives had not been documented elsewhere, I included detailed accounts of their careers.

Each chapter revolves around a central biographical and historical crescendo. Miles Burkitt (1890–1971), a self-proclaimed amateur and antiquarian, son of the greatly respected Cambridge Norrisian Professor of Theology F.C. Burkitt (1864–1935), was never considered to be an intellectual, but was the first to offer lectures. His contributions require resurrection and analysis. Some forgotten actors will hopefully be resuscitated. William Ridgeway, the Anglo-Saxon archaeologist Tom Lethbridge, young Cyril Fox, the elegant Curator Louis Clarke remembered because "you could always smell the violet scent upon his handkerchief", energetic Librarian Miss Fegan, Boy Denston and the Museum Demonstrator Maureen O'Reilly,[30] will be a few of the personalities described.

---

[28] This was one of the most enjoyable things I have ever done with my life.
[29] Shaw, in conversation, 1996.

[30] Quotations from Mary Thatcher, Mrs Chitty, *née* Mary Kitson Clark, and Thurstan Shaw, in conversation 1996, 1997, 2003.

Clark, a successful, professionalising, intellectual entrepreneur, rapidly changed archaeological theory and method during the 1930s and consequently dramatically altered the Faculty's archaeological curriculum. He is remembered for his "scientific cutting-edge" teaching as a young Assistant Lecturer.[31] Garrod, a female outsider, a woman professor in a university that still barred her from full membership, was well-known for her non-university based archaeological research in England, Gibraltar, Palestine, Kurdistan and Bulgaria. She suffered personally when elected to the oldest and most prestigious university chair of archaeology in Great Britain. Her experiences reveal the gendered operation of academic careers.

Each biographical sketch leads to rediscovered contributions and reconstructed lives. Based on these individual stories, I paint a broader analysis of how new subjects work within academia. Themes of tea, trust and masculine and feminine identities thread through the chapters, hopefully tying the narrative into a coherent piece about the processes of academic professionalisation. A final section in Chapter 4 will discuss the diaspora of a few of the young students following the establishment of the full Tripos course. A conclusion which re-evaluates the research school chart/model and combines it with the geography of knowledge and gendered approaches will act as a book-end to the study. This research is illustrated throughout with photographs I have located, many of which have not been previously presented.

There is a widespread perception among archaeologists that history must entail sweeping accounts of grand accomplishments. Lists of dates and events demonstrate the ever-increasing maturation of our discipline. Archaeology progresses, more or less lineally, through stages of scientific development leading to the pinnacle of our present state of knowledge. Antiquarianism inevitably leads to cultural-historical archaeology which then leads to the 1960s successes of scientific enquiry. But the usefulness of the lineal, stage-oriented archaeological history of the world in 300 pages is no longer obvious. Room is needed for the detailed historical analysis of motives, intentions, personalities, intellectual assumptions, cognitive content, ideational changes, attitudes and social, political and gender relationships. The following history of archaeology seeks to recover intentions, reconstruct conventions and restore context[32] in a fine-grained analysis. The theoretical orientations outlined above at times fit this case study; at other times they do not apply to the establishment of prehistoric archaeology at Cambridge. In this lack of fit, in filling that crack and by paying attention to the discrepancy between my work and the work of others, I hope to contribute to our understanding of academic life.

---

[31] Desmond Clark, who took a First in the 1937 Tripos, in conversation, 1996.

[32] After Skinner (1969).

2 God, Empire and Prehistory

"We may look forward to our School and Museum being the real centre of your branch of research in the Empire"
A.C. Haddon to Miles Burkitt, 18 December 1920.[1]

Morrell (1972) begins his investigation of research schools by suggesting that an ideal school requires a charismatic director with a solid research reputation. However, preliminary investigation into the establishment of prehistory as an academic subject at Cambridge revealed immediately that the institutionalisation of prehistory did not depend on one charismatic leader of great standing. Miles Burkitt, who was the first lecturer in prehistory, was neither charismatic nor brilliant. He had no research reputation. How and why, then, did Burkitt become so important to the beginning of Cambridge prehistory? The answers to these questions are given in this chapter when Burkitt's strong religious beliefs and his unselfish devotion to prehistoric archaeology are investigated.

The collegial nature of prehistory as a subject will be stressed. The personalities and philosophies of powerful scholars at Cambridge, who greatly influenced the successful institutionalisation of this new subject, are described. In addition to Burkitt, key players, such as William Ridgeway, Museum Curator Louis Clarke and Cyril Fox, are depicted. Miles Burkitt and his father, F.C. Burkitt's contributions are examined first. Louis Clarke and his relation to the establishment of the Museum tea-room will also be explored.

Because there were no historical studies of Miles Burkitt and of the development of Cambridge prehistoric archaeology, Burkitt's life and contributions are here reconstructed in detail. His experiences at Cambridge and abroad indicate that the research school chart may not sufficiently describe prehistory at Cambridge. In order to give a fuller account, an analysis of the gendered definitions of undergraduate and female students in the twenties is needed and is therefore included in this chapter. A wide range of background information is also presented to give the reader the general knowledge necessary to understand Grahame Clark's subsequent success in the 1930s and Dorothy Garrod's difficulties as a woman professor during the 1940s.

Since the history of prehistory at Cambridge is interwoven with the history of the Cambridge Museum of Archaeology and Anthropology, and because no detailed account of the Museum exists, the history of the Board of Anthropological Studies and of the Museum will also be told.

The chapter begins with a study of the Burkitts' beliefs, followed by an investigation into the relationship between the Board of Anthropological Studies and the Museum. A thorough biographical study of Miles Burkitt is then presented along with an analysis of relationships within the

Archaeology and Anthropology course. The foundation of the tea-room is taken into account. Finally, a preliminary re-evaluation of Morrell's model will increase our perspective and understanding of how 1920s Cambridge prehistory was institutionalised.

2.1 The Burkitts, God and the Museum

Miles Crawford Burkitt (1890–1971) was the only child of F.C. Burkitt (1864–1935), Norrisian Professor of Divinity and Fellow of Trinity. F.C. Burkitt was "one of the most distinguished Divinity Professors she [Cambridge] ever had."[2] Celebrated as the first layman elected to a Cambridge theological Chair, F.C. Burkitt was a vivid personality and vigorous, prolific scholar, accomplished in the textual criticism of the New Testament, Syriac Gospel studies, Hebrew and Old Testament studies, Rabbinic studies, Franciscan history and Latin as well as East and West Syrian liturgiology (Souter *et al.* 1935). Archaeology was also a fascination and, as a member of the Cambridge Antiquarian Society, F.C. Burkitt published archaeological studies on Palestine in their *Proceedings* (1929: 67–71, 1931: 72–3).

The Burkitt family had been "strong upholders of the Protector Cromwell, with whom they were connected by marriage". John Bunyan is also said to have been a friend and to have held meetings in the family home. Over the centuries, a succession of Burkitts had been "scholars and parsons of the Puritan type" (Bethune-Baker 1936: 445), and had been known for their generosity, "unworldliness and reforming spirit". In keeping with this reformist tradition, F.C. Burkitt and young Miles attended Matins and read lessons at a "liberal evangelical" church near their home. According to A.M.G. Stephenson, author of *The Rise and Decline of English Modernism*, F.C. Burkitt was one of the Cambridge Modernists[3] who fostered a forward-looking intellectual critique of Anglican practice and thought within the Church of England, much in advance of their contemporaries. The Modernist movement, which flourished between 1920 and 1940 in Cambridge, advocated ordination of women, the use of contraception and marriage of the divorced in church. Modernists were favourably inclined to reunion with Nonconformists, had little use for ritual and considered the Church a "necessary evil" (Stephenson 1984: 8). F.C. Burkitt was a Vice-President of the Modern Churchmen's Union and regularly spoke at Churchmen conferences.

Professor Burkitt belonged to the London Society for the Study of Religion which had been founded in 1904 by

[1] Burkitt Papers. CUL Add. 7959 Box III.
[2] Obituary: *The Times* 13 May 1935.

[3] Other Modernists were the well-known pacifist Canon Charles Raven, who was the Master of Christ's during the 1930s, and Kathleen Wood-Legh, a founding member of Lucy Cavendish College.

Friedrich von Hügel, Baron of the Holy Roman Empire. The London Society drew members from all religious communities and met several times yearly for tea and lively informal theological discussions at the home of Jewish biblical scholar and philanthropist, Claude Montefiore. Von Hügel, described as "the most profound writer on religious subjects" in the twentieth century (Stephenson 1984: 86), was a leading member of the Modernist movement within the Roman Catholic Church.

Friedrich von Hügel's younger brother, Anatole,[4] was the first Curator of the Cambridge Museum of General and Local Archaeology and of Ethnology.[5] According to Curator Louis Clarke[6] (1925: 415), writing in *The Antiquaries Journal*, "The Museum chiefly owes its existence to the Cambridge Antiquarian Society which was founded in 1839; part of whose activities consisted of collecting local antiquities." In 1875, the Antiquarian Society wrote a letter to the Council of the Senate (*Reporter* June 1875: 486) suggesting that it would "make over to the University the antiquities it had gathered" on condition that the University would provide suitable accommodation. This offer was supported by Disney Professor of Archaeology Churchill Babington and Geology Professor McKenny Hughes, prominent members of both the Antiquarian Society and the University. In a subsequent report to the University in 1883, the Society stated that its collections and its library were the "nucleus of a good Museum"; "valuable and instructive" (*Reporter:* November 1883: 155). Drawing attention to the "importance of the connexion between Archaeology and Ethnology" as well as "the promise of a 'lacustrine series from Switzerland' and of Ethnographical collections from the South Sea Islands", the Society suggested that they had heard of a suitable candidate for Curator for their proposed Museum, Anatole von Hügel (Clarke 1925: 417). The resulting University Museum of General and Local Archaeology, with Baron von Hügel as Curator, was opened in 1884, housed at first in the "most cramped and unhealthy conditions" (Haddon 1928: 169).[7]

Members of the London Society for the Study of Religion, Baron Friedrich von Hügel, F.C. Burkitt, Claude Montefiore and their colleague the archaeologist and Hellenist, Edwyn Bevan, were keen supporters of Anatole von Hügel's efforts to build a large new museum on the Downing College Grounds,[8] specifically to house ever-increasing archaeological and anthropological collections. Edwyn Bevan was the brother of Cambridge Professor of Arabic, Anthony Ashley Bevan. The Bevan Gallery in the Cambridge Museum of Archaeology and Anthropology is named after A.A. Bevan,

FIGURE IV   Block I, The New Museum, 1911. (Courtesy of MAA.) "Please let me contribute this as a nest-egg toward Block II in honour of this auspicious day of materialization!" F.C. Burkitt congratulating Curator Baron Anatole von Hügel, 21 December 1909, on the beginnings of the Downing Site Museum.[9]

a munificent donor to von Hügel's cause; his name appeared prominently and repeatedly in Museum reports early in the century: "Professor Bevan's subscription has again enabled the Curator to make some notable additions" *(Reporter* 1906;150). "The Melanesian series has been enriched by Professor Bevan" (*Reporter* 1909: 209). In addition to A.A. Bevan, Rev. J.W.E. Conybeare, mentioned by Stephenson (1984: 25–6) as an inspiration for Modernism within the Church of England, was also a strong supporter of the Museum. "The Museum has been and continues to be enriched by the generosity of . . . Rev. J.W.E. Conybeare."[10]

Tea gatherings for the study of religion and the resulting friendships and alliances of religiously like-minded colleagues certainly paid off handsomely for the Museum. "My Dear von Hügel," F.C. Burkitt writes in 1905, "It so happens that I got a half year's stipend out of the University

---

[4] Anatole von Hügel was "to labour patiently for the opening of Cambridge to his fellow catholics" (Leedham-Green 1996: 175).

[5] The name of the Museum was changed to the University Museum of Archaeology and of Ethnology when it moved, in 1913, to its present Downing Street site.

[6] In addition to Clarke's concise work, the history of the Cambridge Antiquarian Society and the Museum of Archaeology and Anthropology is well told in several publications: Thompson (1990) *The Cambridge Antiquarian Society 1840–1990*; V. Ebin and D.A. Swallow (1984) *"The Proper Study of Mankind . . ." — Great Anthropological Collections in Cambridge*; J.D. Pickles *Library History* 1988: 8(1); J.G. Pollard (1978) "The Cambridge

Antiquarian" in the *Proceedings of the CAS*; as well as the histories in the *Historical Register*. Unpublished histories, including Joan Cunning's research, are available in CUMAA Box 259 mm1/1/14.

[7] "The old cluttered museum was simply a small leasehold in Little St. Mary's Lane." (John Pickles, in conversation, 2003.)

[8] By the end of the nineteenth century, the University had bought and begun to develop Miles Burkitt's beloved Downing College gardens as a place dedicated to Science.

[9] CUMAA 1909 Letter Box.

[10] No date, no author. Manuscript in CUMAA Box 23 mm1/1/1.

. . . it won't occur again, so I must get rid of some of it at once and therefore enclose a cheque for £15 for the New Museum." Again in 1908, "My Dear von Hügel, It is about now that my ship, *i.e.* the Norrisian title comes in, so I am very glad to be able to add a little more to your Building Fund . . . do you begin to build at £1000?"[11]

Judging from Committee Minutes, before formalised controls over recruitment, institutionalised avenues of entry and established qualifying standards, affairs of the Museum were informally run. Baron von Hügel, described as "good looking", "a dear, charming, sensitive man",[12] seemed to have controlled the Museum in a personal and dignified manner. Concerns were easily discussed privately with the Vice-Chancellor or members of university syndicates. Other Board members were always readily available. When Burkitt's first lectures in the Museum were attended by students and dogs, von Hügel wrote an agitated note to Haddon[13] suggesting that dogs were perhaps inappropriate in lecture halls close to unique collections. The presence of dogs with students continued to be periodically noted in correspondence well into the 1930s. Von Hügel also requested that students refrain from smoking in the Museum's gothic stone stair-well. When this practice continued, von Hügel suggested that if Board members would refrain from smoking under the "No Smoking" notice on the staircase, students may be more easily dissuaded.[14] At this point, as students were increasingly in the Museum, von Hügel complained to Burkitt, "with tears in his eyes" that artefacts should not be used in games of marbles.[15] Upon von Hügel's resignation in 1922, owing to ill-health, the Board noted his "zeal, ability and *self-sacrifice*"; his "generous and opportune" gifts of money and his great work in amassing "valuable and instructive archaeological, antiquarian and ethnological collections"(*Reporter* 22: 742). The beautiful Museum building is a lasting monument to his memory.

2.2 The Museum and the Board

From the inception of anthropological and prehistoric archaeological instruction at Cambridge, the Museum provided a home and inspiration. The history of the future Faculty and that of the new Museum are impossible to separate. Abundant evidence exists of intertwining purpose. Destined to become a fruitful marriage of interests, the relationship between Anthropology and Curator von Hügel began to take formal shape in the early 1900s. In May 1903, the then University Lecturer in Ethnology, A.C. Haddon, William Ridgeway, and the Cambridge Antiquarian Committee, which governed the affairs of the Museum, defended Curator von Hügel's demand for additional facilities and more appropriate space. "The inadequacy of the present Museum building has already obliged [us] repeatedly to call attention to the overcrowded galleries" claimed Haddon and Ridgeway (*Reporter* May 1903).

Ridgeway, a powerfully built man and most persuasive orator, Disney Professor since 1892, served on innumerable Syndicates and important Boards during his long and demanding career. He was overwhelmingly important to the establishment of Anthropology and to the health of the Museum. When von Hügel's request for more adequate facilities was challenged in the Senate, Ridgeway silenced the opposition with "into our hands [have come] valuable collections which, if lost to the University, would take more than 500 years to replace" (*Reporter* 2 June 1903: 893).

The following October, von Hügel, F.C. Burkitt and A.A. Bevan defended and signed Haddon and Ridgeway's Memorial on the Study of Anthropology at Cambridge. "We the undersigned members of the Senate wish respectfully to lay before you . . . The study of all branches of Anthropology — Archaeology, Ethnology, Physical and Mental Anthropology — has within the last decade made extraordinary advances . . . The materials for the teaching of Pre-historic Archaeology and Ethnology have been rapidly accumulating in the Museum . . . We therefore ask you to take steps . . . to establish a Board of Anthropological Studies" (*Reporter* October 1903: 80). During two years previously, A.C. Haddon had delivered several courses of lectures in the Museum's lecture theatre. It had also been formally announced that "Explorers" and "Military Officers, Civil Servants, Missionaries and others who may desire to undertake scientific work when stationed abroad" (*Reporter* January 1903: 337) could call on Haddon at the Museum to arrange instruction.

The Board of Anthropological Studies was established in May 1904, composed of Ridgeway, Haddon, Duckworth, the University Lecturer in Physiological and Experimental Psychology, W.H.R. Rivers, and philologist and Anglo-Saxon specialist, H.M. Chadwick. Von Hügel was invited to serve on this Board and was consistently present until illness interrupted his Curatorship in 1921. In letters to von Hügel throughout the 1910s, Ridgeway clearly stated that the advancement of the interests of the Museum would benefit Anthropology, which included the study of Pre-historic Archaeology. When the Museum profited in 1910 from benevolent donations, he wrote to von Hügel "My heartiest congratulations on the latest thousand. Fortune indeed is smiling on us . . . the patient work is now beginning to convince the public that Anthropology has a great importance not only for Science but for practical life."[16]

Certainly Ridgeway's behaviour and effectiveness bring to mind Morrell's (1972: 6) claim, "For a potentially valid intellectual programme to be implemented, power was necessary. Quite simply the director had to possess or be rapidly gaining sufficient power within his institution to realize his

---

[11] Museum correspondence from this era is kept in boxes sorted by year in the CUMAA.
[12] Burkitt, memoirs [1961], in Burkitt Papers. CUL Add. 7959 Box III.
[13] CUMAA 1920 Letter Box.

[14] Smoking was mentioned various times in Board Minutes. CUA Min. V.92.
[15] Burkitt, memoirs [1961], in Burkitt Papers. CUL Add. 7959 Box III.
[16] 7 January 1910, CUMAA 1910 Letter Box.

ambitions." By 1910, Ridgeway was a Fellow of Gonville and Caius College (1880–87; 1893–1926), Disney Professor of Archaeology (1892) and Brereton Reader in Classics; thus solidly established within the University community. In fact, Ridgeway was simultaneously on the Board of History and Archaeology, the Board of Classical Studies, the Board of Anthropological Studies and the General Board of Studies and thus held considerable administrative power. "He was a great puller of strings, but never for his own hand" wrote Burkitt.[17] Considered conservative in some areas, he is described as having limited "enthusiasm for reform" (Johnson 1994: 71; Conway *DNB* 1922–30: 720). "Even the normally bland language of the obituarist stretched to the word 'pulverize' in describing his handling of academic opponents."[18]

With his curmudgeonly reputation, Ridgeway was a strong and faithful champion of new subjects.[19] Throughout the early 20th century, Ridgeway exerted decisive influence on University, Museum and Board affairs. For example, in a 1908 letter, he urged von Hügel, Haddon and Duckworth to attend the luncheon at Caius he had organised for the Royal Anthropological Institute specifically to get "more representatives of Cambridge anthropology" in appropriate positions of influence. In 1908, Ridgeway was President of the Anthropological Institute and had just opened negotiations with the Prime Minister to establish an Imperial Bureau of Anthropology which would make available information on races within the Empire. In another letter, he expressed his wide interest in University and British politics. Ridgeway suggested that von Hügel back "Larmor [the Lucasian Professorship of Mathematics, Sir Joseph Larmor] against Cox," arguing that Larmor was preferable because he was "a strong Imperialist and Unionist".[20] Larmor would have appealed to Ridgeway who was a Unionist from Ulster. His family had migrated under James I and intermarried with Cromwellian settlers (*DNB* 1922–30: 720).[21] Again, in January 1913, Ridgeway wrote to von Hügel "It is most desirable to get Walker off the Antiquarian Board." Rev. F.G. Walker is described as an energetic and effective Secretary of the Society in M.W. Thompson's (1990) history of the CAS. It is not clear why Ridgeway found it necessary "to deal strongly with his [Walker's] conduct" but Thompson notes that Walker left the Society, at the height of his success, in late 1913.

Judging from these and other letters deposited in the CUMAA, Ridgeway was probably the person who inspired the Antiquarian Committee's "Report to the Senate" in 1910: "Inasmuch as the teaching of Archaeology and Anthropology has become an important part of the practical work of the University, two official teachers . . . the Disney Professor [Ridgeway] and Reader in Ethnology [Haddon], should be *ex officio* members"(*Reporter* 1910: 1034) of the governing Antiquarian Committee of the Museum. As a result of Ridgeway's persuasive abilities, by 1910, the Board of Anthropological Studies was permanently and officially situated to control Museum affairs.

2.3. Anthropology and Empire

Although not a central theme in research school literature or in the other approaches discussed, philosophical and religious beliefs clearly supplied a justification for the institutionalisation of archaeology and anthropology. During the late nineteenth and the early twentieth centuries, the ancient universities of Oxford and Cambridge stressed a core of liberal training of character; ideal precepts of conduct and thought were learned through the rigorous study of classics, mathematics and later history. University education was intended to enhance gentlemanly moral and spiritual qualities. University teaching was directed towards establishing a sense of personal responsibility and producing well-bred intelligent leaders. Soffer (1994) suggests that the ancient universities were conceived as schools for statesmanship. The classicist, Christopher Stray, would agree. "Each year they [Cambridge and Oxford] sent out cohorts of men who went on to positions in the Church, the law, and politics, and later in the expanding civil service at home and abroad" (Stray 1999: 2). Cambridge was a seminary preparing young men to govern colonies and homeland. This was true of many subjects other than history, classics and maths. Roy Porter (1982: 201), in his study of the Cambridge School of Geology, states "Sedgwick likewise used his geological lectures, warm, personal, and rich in anecdotes, to turn his audience into manly, liberal, Christian gentlemen, with an enthusiasm for God's Creation." Basil Willey (1968: 16) in his history of the English Tripos writes, "It [the Tripos] could turn out men who were sane, wise, balanced, free from specialisation and all kinds of lopsidedness." Such courses, Stray (1999) argues, played a central role in the transmission of culture and the production of elites. With the growing professionalism in the late nineteenth and early twentieth centuries, two-part Triposes were introduced at Cambridge. Part I represented "traditional amateur learning, Part II the specialised knowledge of the professional scholar" (Stray 1999: 1).

The liberal education ethos and the growing need for specialisation were united within anthropological studies at Cambridge. In 1913, the Board of Anthropological Studies recommended to the Senate that an Honours examination

---

[17] Burkitt's notes from a lecture given to the CAS, 1961. CUL Add. 7959 Box III.

[18] Mary Beard; draft of upcoming biography of Ridgeway.

[19] Ridgeway supported C.S. Myers's effort to introduce Psychological Studies (*Reporter* March 1920: 690); he also fought for the establishment of the Board of Architectural Studies

[20] This undated letter may refer to Larmor's election as the University's representative in Parliament. Cox may be Harold Cox (1859–1936) of

Jesus College. From 1911 to 1922, Larmor represented Cambridge as a Unionist. CUMAA Letter Box, 1913.

[21] Ridgeway was said to have kept the skull of a priest, "cut off by some ancestor of his for leading a rebellion in Ireland" (Tom Lethbridge's unpublished autobiography, "The Ivory Tower", no date, page 13). Mina Lethbridge supplied a copy of this source.

[22] Previously the Board had granted diplomas only.

for an undergraduate BA Honours degree in Anthropology be established. This degree would be a specialised course, would rank as a second part of existing Triposes[22] and would be well suited for students who "may be engaged subsequently in administrative and missionary work in the Colonies".[23] As early as 1904, Sir Richard Temple, who had 20 years of military experience in India, Afghanistan and Burma, had stressed the importance of anthropology "for those whose work lies in distant lands" (Fortes 1953: 427). Temple hoped that the necessary accumulation of scientific knowledge needed to educate colonial officers appropriately would be encouraged by the University. Fortes (1953) claims that Temple, Haddon and other early-twentieth-century anthropologists believed that knowledge of customs and institutions of the peoples in India, Africa and Oceania could be used for the benefit of native peoples. In his masterful tome, *After Tylor: British Social Anthropology 1888-1951,* George W. Stocking (1996: 413–15) describes how, in addition to Haddon, Bronislaw Malinowski considered "'practical anthropology' to be the means by which the interests of natives, colonizers, administrators, and anthropologists could be advanced". "Unenlightened exploitation, without regard to the welfare of native populations," was considered inadvisable because it might produce resentment and resistance.

In her analysis of Haddon's contributions, Sandra Rouse (1999) agrees with Stocking's historical interpretations. Haddon was a keen promoter of the merits of anthropological training for missionaries and colonial officers. "The advantages to the colonial administration of an appreciation of local practices would be a smoother, more efficient, less confrontational atmosphere." Anthropological data could be used for the benefit of the colonial administration. It could, in addition, be used "in such a way as to lead to a more enlightened rule" (Rouse 1999: 22) to benefit the local people; the native population would then be treated more humanely.

Following the establishment of a Board for Indian Civil Service Studies at Cambridge in 1899, Haddon made various attempts to sell the value of anthropological knowledge to the colonial service and to missionaries. He argued that anthropologically trained Europeans "would form less fraught relationships with native people" (Rouse 1999: 23). In his history of Cambridge anthropology, Haddon (1923: 3) mentioned that his son, E.B. Haddon, was an Acting Provincial Commissioner in Uganda and that "other students had gone into the Colonial Civil Service. Several Missionaries have studied Anthropology and they admit

that this has been of great service." In a 1918 statement, the Board of Anthropological Studies claimed "The importance of a knowledge of the conditions of life, customs and beliefs of the natives of the British Dominions and Protectorates cannot be overestimated."[24] As late as 1934, the then Curator of the Museum, Louis Clarke, was still writing, "The Museum houses the Faculty of Archaeology and Anthropology. The Faculty gives instruction not only to those who will be professed students . . . but to others whose work may be among various peoples as administrators, missionaries, and planters."[25]

Stocking (1996: 378) suggests that the "clubby" colonial bureaucracy preferred men who would benefit from some anthropological training but "whose main qualifications were the moral attributes associated with a gentlemanly background". In *The Rise of Professional Society,* Perkin (1989) argues that a new concept of gentleman had emerged during the late nineteenth century; the new gentleman was an educated, courteous, well-spoken man, defined by a myriad of subtle, skilled social behaviours. Gentlemen did not engage in any occupation for personal gain; they spoke proper English, had appropriate manners and, in particular, knew how to treat women. They were not "cads".[26]

2.4   Prehistory, God and Miles Burkitt

Certainly, Miles Burkitt would have agreed with the definition of a gentleman presented in the previous paragraph. He thought that the colonial service would be best administered by educated, considerate men with some anthropological and archaeological training. Burkitt was precisely the person needed by the Board to introduce future colonial gentlemen to prehistory. There is some evidence from correspondence that Haddon had been looking for a person who could lecture gratis on prehistoric topics and by 1913 Haddon had found his man. In correspondence to French archaeologist, Henri-Martin, Haddon now referred to Burkitt as his "assistant".[27]

Burkitt had been admitted to Trinity[28] in 1909 with the rank of pensioner[29] and by 1912 had taken a one part BA degree in Natural Sciences and was working in the Sedgwick Museum on the Downing site. "I was bored, perhaps rotten" he wrote.[30] When Burkitt was young, teaching was "still done within the Colleges"; the University was an intimate community of scholars and he was friends with many academics including Woodwardian Professor of Geology, T. McKenny Hughes, who was an accomplished

[23] No author. CUMAA Box 19 mm1/3/2.
[24] Board Minutes. CUA Min. V. 92.
[25] Clarke, CUMAA Box 120 mm2/2/3.
[26] Shaw remembered from a conversation with his mother when he was four years old, "A gentleman is not a cad!" (in conversation 1998).
[27] Sandra Rouse pointed this out; the correspondence is amongst the Haddon Papers (Envelope 3; CUL).
[28] Jacqueline Cox of the Cambridge University Archives traced Burkitt's degree. Burkitt graduated after completing one part of the Natural Science

Tripos in 1911 because it was possible before World War I to graduate with Part I of "traditional amateur learning" in a Tripos course.
[29] At this time, pensioners were students who paid fees to their colleges for teaching, board and lodging; scholars were those who held scholarships; sizars had originally financed their studies by undertaking menial tasks within their colleges (Leedham-Green 1996) but by the late nineteenth century, sizarships were in effect minor scholarships (Stray, personal communication, 2003).
[30] Burkitt Papers, Memories. CUL Add. 7959 Box III.

FIGURE V Burkitt as a Young Man, no date. (Reproduced by kind permission of the Syndics of the Cambridge University Library.)[31] "When you are sitting under a Juju Tree, in some foreign land, administering Justice, — never let the sun set on an unmarked artefact", Miles Burkitt, speaking to his students, as quoted by Desmond Clark and Ray Inskeep.

archaeologist.[32] In 1913, McKenny Hughes[33] asked Burkitt for help sorting an extensive collection of Palaeolithic and Neolithic implements which were then on display at the

Sedgwick Museum. When Burkitt enquired as to the nature of his collection and the meaning of the word "Pre-history", McKenny Hughes offered to arrange a meeting with l'Abbé Henri Breuil (1877–1961), considered at that time to be the "greatest living authority on early Man's implements . . . and on prehistory in general" (Brodrick 1963: 12). Within days, Burkitt was invited to lunch with Breuil at Haddon's home; "*C'est notre première rencontre, sous le toit hospitalier du Professeur Haddon, après mes conférences sur l'art préhistorique à L'Université de Londres (1913), quand vous m'exprimiez votre souhait de suivre mes recherches*" (Breuil 1921: x).[34]

The irrepressible Breuil clearly made an immediate and indelible impression on young Burkitt. Within weeks they were roaming Spain together in search of prehistoric adventures. With excitement and enthusiasm, they joined Père Teilhard de Chardin, "Alsatian" Paul Wernert and the Bavarian priest, Hugo Obermaier, at the excavation of the great cave of Castillo near Puente Viesgo in northern Spain. Obermaier, the Director of the excavation, was, at that point, before World War I, Professor at the Institut de Paléontologie Humaine in Paris; Teilhard de Chardin, also associated with the Institute, would later call the period 1912 to 1923 his "phase of palaeontological research in Europe" (Cuénot 1965: 18).[35]

"*Et bientôt,*" Breuil (1921: x) wrote, in his lively preface to Burkitt's (1921a) *Prehistory: A study of early cultures in Europe and the Mediterranean Basin*, "*vous descendiez dans les profondes mais pacifiques tranchées de la grotto de Castillo . . . tout l'intérêt que suscitaient pour vous ces questions encore neuves et peu connues de l'évolution intellectuelle de l'humanité primitive.*"[36] Letters home reveal Burkitt's delight and wonder at Castillo's prehistoric art, long succession of Palaeolithic and Upper Palaeolithic industries and its sequence of Pleistocene fauna.[37] He was deeply impressed by his eminent companions who, with generosity and good will, adopted the slightly eccentric, gangling, shy, young Englishman. "It was a pleasure to be of assistance as [you] were anxious and willing to learn and also most appreciative of the beauties of Spain," Wernert wrote in May 1914.[38] After a season of excavation at

---

[31] Burkitt Papers. CUL Add 7959 Box I. This photo was found in the section labelled "Postcards from Spain".

[32] Burkitt recalled the opening ceremonies, in 1904, for the first building to be erected on the Downing College grounds, the Sedgwick Museum of Geology. He remembered how Professor Hughes had insisted that "I be fetched away from St Faith's School for that historical occasion". He also remembered that the small group of University children lived for the most part in a sheltered enclave round the newly-built Roman Catholic Church on Lensfield Road and "were not encouraged to speak to any child of the Town or County." Despite the "slums" of East Road, Burkitt described a quietly secluded Edwardian "misty English Valhalla". He retained elegant and romantic images of his Cambridge childhood. King's College and the Senate House were "the most beautiful sight"; acres of Downing College gardens stretched to Downing Street, ancestral trees, flowers and fields bordered Cambridge's avenues and a horse-drawn tram stopped at Hyde Park Corner near the Burkitt home. Letters from Eton implied that he dearly missed Town, Gown and family. ([1961]; Burkitt Papers. CUL Add. 7959 Box III).

[33] Hughes had excavated at Cissbury with General Pitt-Rivers and was an

expert in Anglo-Saxon pottery (John Hurst, in conversation, 2000). His wife, Mrs McKenny Hughes was an accomplished flint collector. McKenny Hughes was also an active excavator with the Cambridge Antiquarian Society and had an extensive lithic collection which was "all collected when travelling with either Sir Charles Lyell, Sir John Evans or Professor Prestwich while many other experts of our own country as well as foreigners joined them and gave me the benefit of their advice and guidance" (McKenny Hughes 1914 , notes found in the Burkitt Family Archive).

[34] "It was at our first meeting, under the hospitable roof of Professor Haddon, after my lectures on prehistoric art at the University of London (1913), that you expressed your desire to follow my research."

[35] The Teilhard de Chardin expert, Professor Ursula King of the University of Bristol, supplied the Cuénot reference.

[36] "Soon you descended into the deep but peaceful trenches of the Castillo cave . . . which aroused for you new and little known questions about the intellectual evolution of primitive humanity."

[37] Burkitt Papers. CUL Add. 7959 Box I and III.

[38] Burkitt Papers. CUL Add. 7959 Box III.

FIGURE VI   Spring at Castillo, 1913. The excavators, left to right: Père Teilhard de Chardin; Miles Burkitt, "Breuil's pupil"(wearing the white linen hat); Director, Dr Hugo Obermaier; Assistant Director of the excavation, Paul Wernert; and finally Nels C. Nelson of the American Museum of Natural History in New York. (Courtesy of the CUL.)[39]
"Please bring me a white linen hat," Miles wrote to his parents, who were about to visit Spain. In his letters home, Burkitt clearly found his adventures wonderful.[40] *The many chambers of the large Castillo cave contained paintings, engravings, monochrome signs, and red and black bison, hinds and horses. The deposits were well stratified, representing all stages from the Mousterian to Neolithic.*[41]

Castillo, Burkitt, Teilhard de Chardin, Wernert and Breuil toured *"les Grottes ornées"* of north-west Spain and then hiked to the Hautes-Pyrénées' cave of Gargas, where Breuil had recently discovered a new gallery; Burkitt was here enthralled by the mutilated hands stencilled on cave walls which he interpreted as an early form of magic amongst the Aurignacian people (Burkitt 1921a).

Burkitt was proud to be "Breuil's pupil"; he often referred to Breuil and Obermaier as his honoured "teachers"; without classes or formalised courses "much archaeological and geological information was gleaned" (Burkitt 1921a: vi) at informal evening camp conversations. He learned excavation methods by observation and imitation on site amidst rough living. In 1914, Burkitt again joined Breuil for new explorations. *"Enfin vint l'expédition d'hiver en Andalousie, les longues chevauchées à travers les âpres collines griseuses à demi-couvertes de chênes lièges . . . Et d'Espagne, nos esprits s'élevaient et s'envolaient bien loin, vers d'autres faits humains, qu'il serait bon de comparer à ceux que nous avions sur les yeux; la Scandinavie, la Sibérie, l'Afrique"*(Breuil 1921: xi).[42] Years after, Burkitt reminisced about his "happy trails" with Breuil. "We set out

for months at a time; mules loaded with foodstuffs; sleeping in any chance peasants' hut up in the mountains or even in rock shelters . . . or a loft over a stable. It was all great fun as well as intensely interesting for the study of cave paintings . . . the temples of prehistoric man."[43]

During their wanderings through the mountains of Spain, Breuil had explained to Burkitt the phases of evolution which cave paintings and engravings were thought to follow. Breuil (1906) had established a chronology for cave paintings in northern Spain and southern France by comparing pictures in regard to technique, mastery of colour, refinement and perfection of form. Engravings from mobiliary art, which had a stratigraphic age already determined, were used as comparisons. Breuil observed the sequence of superpositions when paintings and engravings occurred as in a palimpsest. He also used archaeological occupation when it had buried paintings and engravings as evidence for relative dating. Breuil then deduced an order of succession for cave paintings which suggested that, for example, linear outlines painted in red or black were Early Aurignacian, whereas monochrome and linear paintings with attempts at modelling with shaded colour were Late

[39] Burkitt Papers. CUL Add 7959 Box I, found amongst Postcards from Spain.
[40] Letters, in Burkitt Papers. CUL Add. 7959 Box I.
[41] As described by Macalister (1921: 489).
[42] "At last came the expedition to Andalusia in the winter, the long rides over the harsh grey hills, half covered with cork-oaks . . . And, from Spain, our spirits rose and flew very far toward other human facts which it would

be good to compare with those we had before our eyes; Scandinavia, Siberia, Africa."
[43] Notes "for a public lecture"; 1930; Burkitt Family Archives. This collection of Burkitt's published and unpublished papers is in possession of Miles Burkitt's son, Miles Burkitt Jr and Mrs Caroline Burkitt. Mrs Burkitt is Eleanor Dyott's daughter. Eleanor Dyott, who dug with Garrod, appears in Chapter 4.

Aurignacian; the polychromes of Altamira and Castillo were Late Magdalenian. Burkitt was to use exactly this reasoning years later to suggest chronologies for rock art in his 1928 book, *South Africa's Past in Stone and Paint*.

Breuil and Obermaier introduced Burkitt to other colourful, accomplished continental archaeologists and their ideas. He met the fatherly Émile Cartailhac, who had occupied the chair of prehistoric archaeology at Toulouse, and Count Napoléon Henri Bégouën, whose sons had just discovered, in 1912, the now famous modelled clay bison at Tuc d'Audoubert. These scholars agreed that mural cave paintings and mobiliary art were expressions of totemism and magical beliefs. Cave men had been driven by mystical religious beliefs to penetrate the dark and inhospitable recesses of caves, many of which were thought not to have been inhabited. The paintings were often not contemporary with any industrial deposits which might be found and only a selected number of caves had been chosen for art work. Animals pictured were beasts of the chase, not beasts of prey. This evidence pointed to the interpretation that the animal pictures were manifestations of hunting magic. The caves were interpreted as sanctuaries; the anthropomorphic figures must have been primitive priests (Bégouën 1929; Obermaier 1924; Reinach 1903). Burkitt was deeply impressed by these arguments which he then repeated, unchanged, throughout decades of ensuing publications and to generations of students.

Breuil and Burkitt continued their exploration of southern Spanish prehistory at the cave of La Pileta, Malaga, just discovered in 1911. Here they studied the transition of rock art paintings from Palaeolithic realistic paintings to stiff conventional forms and finally to post-Palaeolithic geometrical, conventionalised designs. Burkitt used this evidence in later publications on the transition from the Palaeolithic to the Neolithic (1921a, 1926a, 1926b). During this trip, Burkitt suggested that Breuil write an introductory text for tourists and novices. This little book, Burkitt (1921a: xi) explained, must be full of the interest *"que l'on peut encore trouver au coeur de l'Espagne"*.[44] When Breuil declined, Burkitt volunteered to write the book fully using Breuil's research. Breuil applauded this attempt to introduce

his view of prehistory to *"l'immense empire Britannique"*. As discussed below, Breuil, Obermaier and Cartailhac contributed extensively to Burkitt's *Prehistory: A Study of Early Cultures in Europe and the Mediterranean Basin* (1921a). This book and Burkitt's *The Old Stone Age* (1933) became the standard texts for generations of students in Cambridge and in the Empire beyond. Many carried these books with them to Africa and New Zealand.[45]

In October 1913, Haddon announced that Burkitt would give a course of public lectures on "The Upper Palaeolithic Culture" and "The Art of the Cave Man". This was the first public lecture series given at Cambridge on prehistory. By 1912, Physical Anthropologist, W.H.L. Duckworth, had published his primer on *Prehistoric Man* and Mrs A. Hingston Quiggin had been offering courses of lectures in prehistory at Homerton Training College, but neither Duckworth nor Quiggin had given public lectures or lectures to Cambridge undergraduates on prehistoric topics.[46] Also, although the Disney Professorship of Archaeology was endowed in 1851, the holder was only required to "deliver lectures on . . . things connected with Antiquarian research and the Fine Arts" rather than prehistory.[47]

By 1915,[48] Burkitt felt sufficiently prepared by his archaeological apprenticeship to suggest to the Board of Anthropological Studies that he offer a course of lectures on "Prehistoric Archaeology and Primitive Art" to Cambridge undergraduates.[49] After consideration of Burkitt's "training and attainments", it was "unanimously agreed that Mr. Burkitt be a Recognised Lecturer under the Board."[50]

Burkitt's[51] non-stipendiary course for Michaelmas was never presented because the war intervened. After a time with Breuil in the French Red Cross, Burkitt joined his mother and father at a YMCA recreation hut in a camp hospital of 5000 beds near Rouen. While working there, Burkitt took every opportunity to meet with Breuil to assist in arranging the vast lithic collection from the rock shelter of Laussel, Dordogne. This material had been unearthed by Breuil's friend, Gaston Lalanne, during excavations conducted from 1909 to 1911.[52] The rock-shelter had been inhabited and then abandoned six different times and was therefore considered

---

[44] "that one can still find in the heart of Spain."

[45] Shaw, in conversation, 2000; Golson, in conversation, 1996.

[46] Elsewhere in Great Britain, Robert Munro had given Edinburgh University a gift in 1910 to fund the now well-known Munro Lectures on Anthropology and Prehistoric Archaeology; Munro gave his first five public lectures on "Palaeolithic Man in Europe" under this scheme in 1912. "The course was a great success and attracted exceptionally large crowds" (Munro 1921: 74). This was a public not a degree oriented course of lectures.

[47] CUA Foundation Deed O.XIV.4.

[48] In June 1914, Colonel Willoughby Cole Verner, the discoverer of La Pileta, again demonstrated the consistent intellectual openness and generosity shown to Burkitt by his continental mentors. Verner loaned expensive lantern slides and made succinct suggestions for the exhibition on prehistoric drawings "painted as a form of magic" that Burkitt successfully mounted for the Royal Society in London. According to John Pickles, Verner was a polymath, professional soldier and prolific author who produced a monograph with Breuil on the Upper Palaeolithic cave

of La Pileta in 1915 (in conversation, 2003).

[49] In this, Burkitt was supported by his friend, Mansfield D. Forbes, known as Manny Forbes, the young, brilliant, Clare College English don who was to be so important to the establishment of the English Tripos in 1917. Manny Forbes was an active excavator with the Cambridge Digging Club of the Cambridge Antiquarian Society. He was a close friend of and co-excavator with V. Gordon Childe (letters; Burkitt Papers; CUL Add. 7959; Minutes of the CAS Council; volume 5; 1919; Haddon Library). I thank J.D. Pickles for arranging access to the Minutes of the CAS Council Meetings and Ordinary Meetings.

[50] Board of Anthropological Studies Minutes. 12 May 1915: Minute Book CUMAA Box 19 mm1/3/2.

[51] Burkitt offered this course gratuitously.

[52] Although Burkitt does not refer to it in his memoirs, Laussel was well known for its remarkable reliefs cut into limestone of corpulent nude female forms known as Venus figures. These were interpreted by the discoverer, psychopathologist Lalanne, as religious idols.

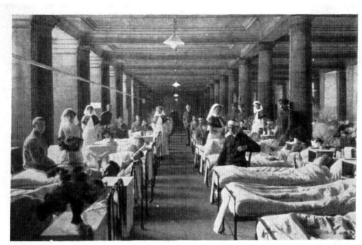

R.A.M.C. 1st EASTERN GENERAL HOSPITAL, 1914. TRINITY COLLEGE, CAMBRIDGE

FIGURE VII   August in Cambridge, 1914. (Courtesy of the CUL.)[53]
In August 1914, the 1st Eastern General Hospital was opened at Nevile's Court in Trinity, where the cloisters served as wards for the wounded. The whole area of Kings' and Clare's ground, eleven acres, was eventually covered by the Hospital.[54] *"When will it all be over and, even then, will we ever be able to go back to our old lives," Burkitt wrote to Haddon.*[55]

to be an important example of clear industrial stratigraphy (Obermaier 1924). The Laussel section illustrated the early Palaeolithic Late Acheulean layer of occupation underneath Mousterian and rich Aurignacian levels. These layers were then superseded by the more recent Solutrean.

It was during this volunteer sorting work that Burkitt learned Breuil's methods of lithic typological analysis. Here Burkitt was taught to identify Acheulean as opposed to Mousterian as opposed to Solutrean stone implements. Burkitt later claimed that this training in the skills of typological analysis "became the basis for the archaeological side of the Cambridge school".[56] Students, such as Desmond Clark, remembered Burkitt as a "remarkably good typologist."[57]

Burkitt's Beliefs
Some time during World War I, Burkitt began to believe that humans "moved Godward in spite of or maybe partly owing to struggles against overwhelming odds;" evil itself could help a nation and a person grow. As a result of difficult struggles, Burkitt suggested that our "soul", which he seemed to equate with "conscious intelligence" (Burkitt 1923; 212) developed in humans during the transition to the Upper Palaeolithic. He argued that this was obvious from reading the Old Testament and from archaeological studies.[58]

There is no doubt that Burkitt was a deeply religious prehistorian. This was testified to by Burkitt's many students. Desmond Clark[59] remembered him saying grace before the scrumptious formal teas served by Peggy, his "very pretty, very grand"[60] wife, daughter of Sir John Pease Fry. Tea was

always served prior to the weekly seminars which were held at Burkitt's gracious home in the village of Grantchester near Cambridge. If a student, during the 1920s and 1930s, occasionally stayed the night to study Burkitt's extensive private library, a brief prayer, attended by the servants, preceded breakfast.

Burkitt clearly articulated his religious beliefs and their relationship to prehistory in sermons and addresses published in *The Modern Churchman,* the journal of the Modernist Church movement to which his father had introduced him. In a Lenten address at Cambridge's All Saints Church in 1929, Burkitt argued "A knowledge of the ancient past and the part played in it by our forerunners . . . becomes important in the great study of Man, next to the study of God, the chief object of all intellectual effort . . . The study of humanity's past is a study of God and His purpose as it is being worked out through each succeeding age" (Burkitt 1930a: 265–6). In a follow-up paper for *The Modern Churchman,* he suggested that the Great War was the current test but something new had been born in our ancestors through similar ancient suffering; in the story of early man and his reactions to and conflict with the world around him, "we see, as a culmination, the result of struggle and failure, the generation of the soul". The study of natural sciences revealed the teachings of Jesus Christ by revealing the emergence of human character (Burkitt 1932b: 267). The study of prehistoric man, a vast new subject, was especially important because it illustrated precisely such questions as the development of our spirituality; the knowledge gained from this fascinating study offered a new, broader outlook on mankind and

[53] Burkitt Papers. CUL Add. 7959 Box I.
[54] As reported in the *Historical Register Supplement;* 1911 to 1920.
[55] No date; Haddon Papers; CUL Envelope II. I thank Sandra Rouse for recommending this letter.
[56] Burkitt, memoirs, in Burkitt Papers. CUL Add. 7959.
[57] Desmond Clark, personal correspondence, 2000.

[58] Quotation from "Sermon preached in Barrington Church"; Burkitt Family Archives.
[59] Desmond Clark, personal correspondence, 2000.
[60] Quotation from an interview with former Secretary for the Faculty, Mary Thatcher, 1999.

his place in nature; such "cultural education" trained "the minds of the young" (Burkitt 1934).[61]

It is not clear who influenced Burkitt to intertwine the study of prehistory with God's design. Desmond Clark[62] suggested the influence originated with Father Ewing who was the excavator of Ksar Akil, an Upper Palaeolithic site in Lebanon. Clark distinctly remembered Ewing stating that the soul entered the body in the Upper Palaeolithic; he also remembered that Burkitt openly discussed this idea with students. However, there is no evidence that Burkitt and Ewing knew each other in the 1910s. Ursula King,[63] theological expert on Teilhard's thought, is certain that Teilhard wrote nothing at that time about the arrival of the soul. The French archaeologist, Alain Schnapp, assures me that the influence was not from Breuil.[64] Amongst the many letters from continental prehistorians held at the CUL, there is only one mention of the "soul". Émile Cartailhac wrote his thoughts about religion, during a discussion of the Trois Frères sorcerer, in an undated letter to Burkitt "*L'âme humaine a pensé cela durant des millenaires*."[65] There is no further discussion of the "soul" in any private correspondence or published source.

Whatever its exact origins, the belief that prehistory illuminated God's purpose is understandable when considered in light of the evidence presented above concerning the London Society for the Study of Religion and its connection with the founding of the Museum of Archaeology and Anthropology. Certainly Miles Burkitt could have been influenced by any of the many deeply religious figures who were contributors to the health and growth of the young Board and new Museum and to archaeology and anthropology as academic pursuits. His beliefs reflect well the religious aspects of the Museum's foundation.

The interconnections between religious belief and the teaching of prehistory are clear. Burkitt's belief provided a justification to teach undergraduates and Colonial Probationers at Cambridge. Interrupted by the War, Burkitt returned armed with a powerful new philosophical/religious motivation. He argued that through the study of the past, we gain knowledge of ourselves. In a similar vein to Haddon and other anthropologists, Burkitt hoped that Cambridge men, educated in prehistory, would be public-spirited, just, intelligent leaders and fair, peaceful colonial administrators. As Burkitt stated in the *Parish Magazine*, the goal of education

was to develop personal character and the qualities of self-reliance necessary to be leaders.[66]

The study of the past would make men wiser. In 1929, speaking to the Cambridge Rotarians, Burkitt suggested that prehistory provided a sobering perspective; we are a small part of a large whole; we are "not the centre of the world".[67] Archaeology was the perfect subject dealing with "the beginnings of ourselves; our thoughts; our religion" (Burkitt 1949a, 1949b: 414). Understanding how past civilisations have grown and disappeared put our present lives in proper proportion. A knowledge of the past would enable the societies of the Empire to live "happily together and form one united Royal community".[68] Equipped with a prehistoric perspective on the struggles of humanity, gentler undergraduates would be "cultivated men";[69] they would administer justice to an Empire with understanding and humility. They might even avoid another war. In various unpublished notes and papers collected and ordered chronologically by Burkitt and kept by his family, a desire that Cambridge men would promote peace in the Empire was expressed.[70]

Burkitt's Teaching

In 1923, Burkitt was making ten guineas yearly from fee-paying students who attended his lectures. This was his total income since he was not a Fellow of Trinity and did not teach within that college. Money, however, was never discussed. Throughout his life, Burkitt believed that "If you are fortunate enough to be born paid, you must give something back to the public."[71] From the beginning, he defined himself as a knowledgeable "amateur" or "Antiquarian". When he delivered his description of a trip abroad to the Cambridge Antiquarian Society in November 1922, he described himself as "An Antiquarian in Crete". Burkitt clearly saw himself as a lover of prehistoric art, a Dilettante[72] with moral purpose.

As late as 1955, in a speech on "Archaeology and Education" to the Pan-African Congress, Burkitt reiterated that archaeology "reigns supreme as an intellectual hobby subject . . . an admirable and fascinating study to train the minds of the young" but usually not appropriate for "vocational teaching".[73] When Thurstan Shaw, while revising for his 1936 Tripos exams, asked Burkitt's advice on archaeology as a profession, Burkitt emphatically responded "Not unless you have a private income of £1000 a year!"[74]

[61] Notes, Burkitt Papers. CUL Add 7959 Box II.

[62] Desmond Clark, personal correspondence, 2000.

[63] King, personal correspondence 2003.

[64] Others in England were thinking along somewhat the same lines as Burkitt around 1915. Ambrose Fleming, Professor of Engineering at University College London and President of the Evolution Protest Movement, was arguing that Cro-Magnons were Adamites whereas the Neanderthals were pre-adamites (personal correspondence, David Livingstone, 2003). However, Burkitt was not a member of the Protest Movement.

[65] "The human soul has thought that for thousands of years" (Burkitt Papers. CUL Add. 7959 Box III).

[66] No date; no parish mentioned. CUL Add. 7959 Box II.

[67] 1929, notes; Burkitt Family Archive.

[68] Burkitt; quoted from draft paper "Archaeology and Education", 1955. CUL Add. 7959 Box II.

[69] In 1998, Mary Thatcher stated in an interview, "cultivated men went into Service".

[70] Stated in several unpublished essays in the Burkitt Family Archives.

[71] Statement to local newspaper, 1965, Burkitt Family Archives.

[72] from the Italian word, *dilettare*, to delight. Burkitt delighted in the avocation of prehistory.

[73] Burkitt Papers. CUL Add. 7959 Box II. This is quite a remarkable statement considering that many Cambridge-trained professional archaeologists, such as Desmond Clark and Haddon's student, Louis Leakey who was the founder of the Pan-African Congress, were in his audience.

[74] Shaw, in conversation, 1996.

FIGURE VIII   The Burkitts in Brno, Moravia, 1926. (Photograph courtesy of the MAA.)
Burkitt did not excavate after Castillo, partly because of frail health, but travelled extensively visiting sites and
museums, collecting material for teaching and for the archaeological travelogue reports written for numerous journals
and newspapers. His wife, Peggy Burkitt, a talented draftswoman, illustrated many archaeological publications gratis.
The Burkitts believed that archaeology was a non-professional and gracious avocation. Commenting on a visit to the
Museum in Brno and to Dr Adolf Mahr's Neolithic dig in Burgenland, where they helped with the excavation, Peggy
Burkitt commented, "We arrange a carriage for 10.00 and are much laughed at as bed lovers, but reply that it is our
holiday."[75]

Men did what they did for religious and moral motivations, not for money or plaudits. If you had income "and your driving force was curiosity, rather than *restless ambition*, archaeology at the Museum was a great life in the Golden Age," wrote Tom Lethbridge, a man of independent means who was the Museum's Honorary Keeper of Anglo-Saxon Artefacts during the 1920s.[76]

Burkitt had no intent of being original; his mission was to disseminate faithfully his mentors' interpretations in a self-professed amateur manner. In 1915, the Ph.D degree and other post-graduate research degrees had not yet been instituted at Cambridge. Burkitt's conception of himself as a pupil and, later, as a university lecturer did not require that he produce an original contribution to knowledge. Intellectual and personal faithfulness were manifest in his first book, *Prehistory: A study of early cultures in Europe and the Mediterranean Basin*, and in his course of lectures. He repeated his mentors' material *verbatim*.

Unabridged and uncritical use of Obermaier and Stehlin's research and teachings is found in Burkitt's Chapter 3 of

Prehistory. Breuil, Obermaier, Cartailhac and H.G. Stehlin had willingly sent Burkitt detailed notes explaining their geological and archaeological views.[77] Obermaier wrote a series of letters giving evidence for "synchronizations" between the geological stages of the "Glacial Epoch" and the stages of Palaeolithic industries. Such correlations established relative chronologies for Palaeolithic industries in Germany, France and Spain. According to Burkitt's correspondence, Albrecht Penck had discovered Magdalenian deposits within the Alpine terminal moraines of what he claimed was the fourth and final (Würm) glaciation. Therefore, the Magdalenian was assigned to the post-glacial Bühl advance. Acheulean handaxes had been found embedded in clay at Conliège; this clay was more recent than the third (Riss) glacial stage. Therefore, the Early and Late Acheulean belonged to the "Third Interglacial Stage". In 1905, Obermaier had demonstrated the existence of four series of fluvio-glacial deposits of gravels which were thought to be clear evidence of four glaciations, in the basin of the Garonne. There, in the third terrace, were found Acheulean industries, once again "dating" the Acheulean industries to the "Third Interglacial Stage" for France/Spain. In the cave

[75] Peggy Burkitt, letter to family; Burkitt Papers. CUL Add. 7959 Box III.
[76] Lethbridge unpublished autobiography; [1965]. Again, I thank Mina

Lethbridge for this source.
[77] The letters and notes mentioned in this paragraph are in Burkitt Papers. CUL Add. 7959 Box III.

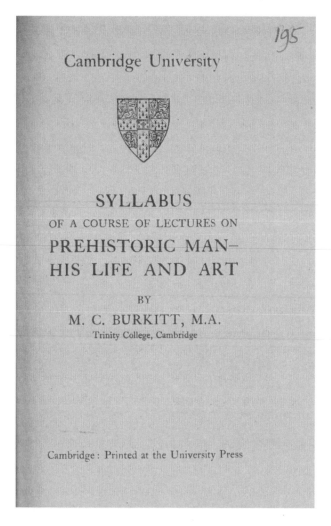

Cambridge University

195

SYLLABUS

OF A COURSE OF LECTURES ON

PREHISTORIC MAN–
HIS LIFE AND ART

BY

M. C. BURKITT, M.A.

Trinity College, Cambridge

Cambridge : Printed at the University Press

FIGURE IX Syllabus for "Prehistoric Man: His Life and Art", the first and for decades the only course taught on Palaeolithic archaeology in Great Britain. (Courtesy Burkitt Family Archives.)

of Bouichéta (Ariège), Mousterian implements were found on deposits left by the Rissian glacier, demonstrating the post-Rissian character of the Mousterian for France. H.G. Stehlin wrote to Burkitt, in 1920, stating that he had discovered Mousterian deposits within the terminal moraine of the Würm in the caves near Neuchâtel; this discovery assigned the Mousterian of central Europe to a date anterior to the maximum of the Würm glaciation. Therefore, an early Mousterian followed the Late Acheulean during the "Third Interglacial Stage" and a Late Mousterian was assigned to the Würm glaciation.

Without the slightest alteration, Burkitt repeated this information in articles published during the decade (1920a, 1922b,1924a). Obermaier and Stehlin's evidence for correlations between Penck and Brückner's four-stage

glaciations and archaeological finds was often used, with little or no acknowledgement or change, in 1930 as well as in his textbook *The Old Stone Age* in 1933. In his 1930 *Nature* article (Burkitt 1930b), Burkitt did not cite Obermaier but nevertheless explained glacial and archaeological correlations exactly as Obermaier had in *El Hombre Fósil,* translated and published as *Fossil Man in Spain* in 1924. Burkitt used Breuil's material in a similar apparently uncritical manner. In 1919, Breuil had sent an illustrated description of the anthropomorphic figure, the "Sorcerer", found partly engraved, partly painted in the huge cave of Les Trois Frères.[78] Burkitt repeated Breuil's exact description of this figure, not only in *Prehistory* and in an article in *Man* (1921b), but also in *Our Forerunners*, published in 1923, a Home University Library book intended for the general public.

Throughout the twenties, Burkitt used his colleagues' opinions and evidence faithfully, apparently with full permission but without full acknowledgement. Examples of others' material are legion in Burkitt's work.[79] He did not use footnotes or references as would currently be required. The personal relationships of knowledge were apparently different from today. Ownership of ideas, research results and interpretations seemed less important. Before the era of scholarly professionalisation, knowledge seemed to have been openly shared with little concern for individual intellectual property rights. This was perhaps because the community of European prehistorians was still very small and Obermaier or Breuil's views were widely informally recognised and acknowledged. The need for specific acknowledgement for specific work may not have been necessary. However, Burkitt not only used information but also shared information generously without the expectation of returns. This implies that he was operating under a different set of values in relation to ownership of knowledge from those we assume today.

In his devotion to a few representatives of continental thought, Burkitt ignored competing theories and local knowledge. He seriously underplayed the breadth of geological and archaeological debates which were raging at the time in England and abroad. There is no mention in his early books and articles of the monoglacial theory for England supported by the biologist A.S. Kennard. "Don't believe any of the fantastic continental theories," Kennard wrote to Burkitt in 1920.[80] The theory that only one glacial had occurred in Britain was well argued by Burkitt's contemporary, the Irish prehistorian R.A.S. Macalister (1921), but Burkitt never referred to this important work. Nor did he discuss Marcellin Boule's well-known criticism of Penck and Brückner's Günz glaciation or S. Hazzledine Warren's (1922: 182) respected interpretations in his "Man and the

[78] Letter, in Burkitt Papers. CUL Add. 7959 Box III.
[79] Examples from the early 1920s would be Cartailhac's (no date; Burkitt Papers. CUL Add. 7959 Box III) letter referring to dolmens and menhirs, which is associated with Burkitt's 1923 lecture on dolmens (CAS Ordinary Minutes; volume III), and Burkitt's (1920b) report on Minoan sites in Crete, which is a summary of Alan Wace's chronology, J.L. Myres' geological and

archaeological investigations and Childe's research on Minoan ware. Since Burkitt gave no references or indication as to whom he was indebted to, I thank the classical archaeologist, David Gill, for pointing out the origin of Burkitt's Minoan arguments.
[80] Kennard to Burkitt. Letter in Burkitt Papers. CUL Add. 7959 Box III.

Ice Age". Warren, remembered as "that splendid amateur" by Stuart Piggott,[81] argued that temperate plant beds were more reliable than migrating animals in giving insight into climatic conditions; all evidence pointed to greater, not lesser, cold during the Magdalenian. This suggested that the British Mousterian and Aurignacian were interglacial rather than glacial or post-glacial industries.

Under Burkitt's instruction, generations of students were introduced to the four-stage glacial sequence named after Alpine rivers, the "Günz, Mindel, Riss, Würm" mantra, with little appreciation for how controversial that sequence really was. Burkitt (1920a) taught that this succession was applicable to Britain, but in fact there were recurrent long-running discussions concerning this. Geologists such as the new Woodwardian Professor of Geology, "Johnny" Marr, the young geologist, J.D. Solomon, who later dug with Leakey in Africa, and the Geology Professor, P.G.H. Boswell of Imperial College, debated if and how the Günz, Mindel, Riss, Würm catagorisations were applicable to Britain. Reid Moir is most remembered for his adamant support of the theory that man-made, pre-Palaeolithic implements had been recovered from Tertiary deposits at Foxhall in East Anglia.[82] But, at the time, Reid Moir was also known for his proposed correlations between British archaeological industries and geological stages which disagreed with Burkitt's French-inspired assertions.

Interpretations of the number and chronology of glaciations and their relationship to archaeological remains were hotly debated in the early 1920s. None of this complexity was ever discussed by Burkitt in his textbooks. Reviewers of *Prehistory* noted this simplified approach. "It is perhaps this extreme concentration on the Abbé Breuil's work" which was at fault, wrote C.H. Read (1922: 189). "A volume on Prehistory should at least give a summary account of [all] arguments." "One would imagine from reading his account that the French theory was the only one . . . that the German view of the Mindel-Riss age of the Chellean flints had been abandoned . . . to write of the neolithic age and omit the Baltic evidence is like producing Hamlet without the Prince of Denmark." (Peake 1921: 189). Burkitt was unfamiliar with crucial Scandinavian material. Discussing the art of the Neolithic "without dealing with racial and trade movements is to make the subject unintelligible" (Peake 1921: 190). Both reviewers noted "evidence of haste," poor writing style, frequent repetitions, apparent contradictions and possible errors.

Johnny Marr's copy of *Prehistory,* which is available at the Earth Sciences Library, Cambridge, is filled with his marginalia; exclamation points of frustration exist alongside scribbled criticisms and corrections. However, the students I interviewed were primarily impressed with Burkitt's warmth for the subject, his excellent memory and vast general knowledge, rather than his exact intellectual abilities. They were not concerned with the accuracy or specific content of his lectures; they were attracted instead by his engaging presentation.

Surviving students from the 1920s and 1930s much appreciated Burkitt's personal approach to prehistory in the "small and intimate" Archaeology and Anthropology Faculty.[83] "Miles' great ability was to make prehistory exciting with his memories of sites and prehistorians; " his lectures were "enlivened and enriched by his great store of amusing anecdotes . . . I was much attached to Miles," stated one of Burkitt's most famous students, the Africanist Desmond Clark.[84] Even in the early 1950s, when Burkitt's knowledge was clearly dated, students held endearing memories. "I loved Miles Burkitt, not because I learned anything more than his out-of-date books could have told me, but because of his delivery; he captured one for prehistory," remembered Merrick Posnansky.[85] "His lectures were enormously enjoyable," stated Warwick Bray,[86] Professor emeritus of Latin American Archaeology at University College London and first Lecturer in European Prehistory at Sheffield in the Department of Ancient History. "It was almost as if your favourite Uncle was up there, reminiscing about olden days. You didn't go there to get the new but what fascinated me was that he was so obviously a bridge to the past. He had been there and had worked with the Abbé Breuil in the old days and nobody else had," Bray continued.[87]

If Geison's (1981) model is taken as a guide, a growing number of students would be expected as a subject becomes progressively recognised within an institutional structure and there is evidence that Burkitt's approach of "Burins and Tea"[88] increasingly recruited students to the new academic subject of prehistory. Tea at the Burkitts' was well remembered as an important occasion. "During my time at Cambridge, Burkitt befriended me and encouraged me to come out to their house in Grantchester for tea anytime. I did this several times and always ran into a stimulating group; students, visitors. The teas were often full of shop talk and provocative prehistory. Peggy Burkitt was a delightful conversationalist," testified archaeologist Bruce Howe.[89]

---

[81] Piggott, in conversation, 1994.

[82] An excellent discussion of the Eoliths controversy is presented by S.J. Plunkett in his unpublished manuscript, *Prehistory at Ipswich* (1996).

[83] Joan Lillico, First Class Honours, 1935 Tripos, personal correspondence, 1998.

[84] Desmond Clark, in conversation, 2000.

[85] Archaeologist, Professor Merrick Posnansky, Diploma,1953, personal correspondence, 2000.

[86] Bray is Professor emeritus of Latin American Archaeology at University College London and was the first Lecturer in European Prehistory at Sheffield in the Department of Ancient History. Bray's efforts laid the foundation for the Sheffield Department of Archaeology.

[87] However, there were others, especially students reading social anthropology and post-graduates, who, by 1948, found Burkitt simple-minded and uninspiring (Anthropology Professor R.T. Smith, in correspondence 4 April 1999); Burkitt's "now we are a tree" pose to illustrate human evolution was wearing to some and widely imitated by former students during interviews. One of these, Joan Oates, Fulbright Scholar at Cambridge in 1950–52, does the fairest demonstration.

[88] "Burins and Tea" was a phrase referred to by several former students and was apparently used by Burkitt himself to describe his approach to education.

[89] Howe, personal correspondence, 1997. I thank Robert and Linda Braidwood for putting me in touch with Bruce Howe.

By February 1926, members of the Board could state in their Minutes, "The growth of the study of prehistory now forms a substantial part of the courses" for the Board. By then, Burkitt was teaching 60 to 70 students who were attending a two-term subsidiary course for the Ordinary Degree; 13 who were reading for the Tripos, four or five for the Diploma and three who were from the Colonial Service reading for the Diploma.[90] At this point, there were various categories of students which do not exist today. "Honours Tripos" undergraduates paid 25 guineas for a one-year course and an additional 20 guineas for a second year to the Board. "Non-Tripos Ordinary Degree" students paid by the course of lectures; two guineas was the fee for a week of three lectures. It appears, from the Board Minutes, that anyone interested could become a student, since an additional category of "Non-matriculated" students also paid two guineas for a week of lectures.[91] Burkitt's simple teaching methods seemed to appeal to all.

Burkitt thought of himself as an intellectual emissary who served the Empire by introducing new knowledge to a wide range of students of prehistory which was not readily available elsewhere. In 1924, for example, Burkitt reported in the *Proceedings of the Prehistoric Society of East Anglia* that Professor Kozlowski of Lwow who had finished a large work on "Neolithic pottery cultures of Eastern Europe . . . alas, in Polish! . . . had kindly communicated to me the following chart" (1924b: 180). In response, Childe, who was fond of Burkitt, wrote a courteous note in a follow-up issue of the *Proceedings* stating that Burkitt had made certain mistakes in this chart.[92] Again in 1924, Burkitt reported, in *Man* (1924a) and in *the Proceedings of the Prehistoric Society of East Anglia (*1924c), the results of Count de la Vega del Sella's research in the caves of Asturias. The Burkitts had visited the Count during their honeymoon in 1923. Such reports and notes abound in the *Proceedings of the Prehistoric Society of East Anglia* and in *Man*. "All that I was trying to do was incite their [the audiences'] curiosity" Burkitt wrote retrospectively.[93]

Burkitt did not conceive of himself as an original researcher, intellectual or excavator but he was an engagingly effective communicator and mentor for introductory students. "One should never underestimate the importance of a good teacher" stated Desmond Clark during an interview.[94] Clare Fell, who earned a First Class degree in 1933, remembered Burkitt playfully joking with pupils.[95] Mary Kitson Clark, who took a post-graduate year in 1927, found him attentive, kind-hearted and helpful.[96] Burkitt's great desire was to teach. In the 1920s, he was definitely not a careerist. Unlike the archaeologists who were to succeed him, Burkitt would never have considered himself to be a professional.

2.5 Sir William Ridgeway and the Board

The Board, Women and Men

In May 1919, Burkitt returned to teach his "very successful course"[97] on "Man of the Old Stone Age" under a Board of Anthropological Studies which was particularly receptive to women.[98] Newnham students, Alice Selby and Camilla Wedgwood, described as notably fashionable in her "woven lavender blue" (Halliday 1979: 139) dress, were earning First Class degrees under Haddon's encouragement. When Haddon "could not find a suitable man to instruct Economics and Material Culture" in 1923, he suggested Mrs Quiggin.[99] Since women were not allowed to lecture to undergraduates, the Board labelled Quiggin as "Haddon's Deputy" in the *Reporter*.[100] Ridgeway vociferously supported this decision. In 1925, Ridgeway himself proposed Miss Wedgwood as a lecturer.[101] The Board took considerable care and time to seek special permission for her to have the right to lecture openly to Tripos men.[102] Ethel Sophia Fegan was yet another woman welcomed and valued by the small, new Board. Known to generations as simply "Miss Fegan", she started working in the Museum in 1918. In recommending Miss Fegan for a yearly honorarium as Librarian in 1919, C.E. Sayle stated, "I repeat that there is no one in England who can do the work better."[103]

[90] Board Minutes, February 1926. CUA Min.V.92.
[91] Board Minutes. CUA Min.V.92 30 May 1923.
[92] There was some question as to how accurate Burkitt was in these reports.
[93] Notes 1965: Burkitt Family Archive.
[94] Desmond Clark, in conversation, 2000.
[95] Fell, in conversation, 1996.
[96] Kitson Clark, in conversation, 1996.
[97] 1919, Board Minutes. Min.V.92.
[98] Interviews with various Newnham graduates published by Ann Phillips (1979) give fascinating insight into women who attended Cambridge classes during this period. "All England had gone dancing mad," wrote Frances Partridge (1981: 62), when referring to the 1920s at Cambridge in her celebrated *Memories*. According to Newnhamite D.L. Halliday (1979: 136), matriculated 1920, the early Twenties were "years of renaissance . . . Cambridge was on a wave of exhilaration." Euphoria, enthusiasm and high spirits were victorious. Town and Gown had gone chaotically joyful as the Armistice was announced and a gay atmosphere conquered all. The afternoon diversion for female students was light tea and dancing, "thé-dansants", with your boyfriends at the elegant Dorothy Café on Sidney Street. All seemed ready "for the new world". Chaperon regulations at Newnham were relaxed, rules on smoking were revised; women may

not have won full University membership but they were certainly having great fun; "six May Balls on six nights running," wrote Newnhamite, D.C. Booth (1979: 126), *m.* 1916. The twentieth century released women from "an intolerable thraldom in dress"; bare backs at the Balls were now buoyantly acceptable. "The war freed us." stated E.M. Lang (1929: 192, 194). However, all wore hats and white, not blue, stockings, to lectures. Silver Street was the demarcation point after which Newnhamites covered themselves "decently" before proceeding (S. Keith-Walters, matriculated in 1925, 1979: 164).
[99] In addition to offering courses of lectures at Homerton Training College, Mrs Quiggin had worked as Haddon's secretary and later wrote his biography, *Haddon the Head-hunter* (1942).
[100] Quotations from Board Minutes. CUA Min.V.92.
[101] Wedgwood was deeply admired in the Faculty for her excellent academic work. She was the daughter of 1st Baron Wedgwood, MP, and later became a successful anthropologist in Australia.
[102] 25 November 1925. Board Minutes. CUA Min.V.92.
[103] Sayle was under-librarian for the University Library and was just retiring as Honorary Librarian for the Cambridge Antiquarian Society's Library when he wrote this letter to the CAS, who still nominally controlled the book collection. CUMAA 1919 Letter Box.

Ridgeway's support of Wedgwood is remarkable because he had belligerently and rather crudely opposed the admission of women to full membership in 1921. In a serious attack, he had questioned women's commitment to academic work: "the best researchers all get married, and those who do not get married seem to do nothing."[104] It is clear from Lethbridge's [1965] unpublished autobiography that Ridgeway privately did not approve at all of having women in positions on the Board. However, Ridgeway did treat Wedgwood well; one suspects that his behaviour was determined by the specific situation rather than by his entrenched attitudes towards women's right to study at Cambridge. He was a politically astute strategist who recognised talent; Wedgwood had not only talent but also came from a family which was a respected member of Annan's (1955) "Intellectual Aristocracy" and which was intermarried with Cambridge's academic elite.

In their reaction to women, Board members embody the historical contradictions of the time. Cambridge was still a "men's university, though of a mixed type" (Sutherland 1998: 89). The Board provided training for gentleman probationers and Burkitt's philosophy defined what "good men" should be. But there were no gentlewomen in the Colonial Service and women could not serve as District Commissioners. Women did not fit the definition of what a good student might be and had little place within Burkitt's educational percept. As discussed in the section on anthropology and empire, the definition of a gentleman and the role that undergraduates would take in governmental positions were clearly demarcated. Women students, on the other hand, at this point, did not have a well-defined status or clear future. Female students were fully aware of this. When discussing her colourful memories of the anthropologist, Jack Driberg, Eleanor Robertson, who took the Tripos in 1938, wrote, "Anthropologists of his generation had been Colonial Administrators with a classical background. There was of course no future for females in the Colonial Administration — so it was a bit unreal."[105]

Nevertheless, there is no evidence in letters or interviews that women felt dismissed by Burkitt or other Board members. There is no reference to discriminatory behaviour. Burkitt was consistently described by both men and women as an enthusiastic man of "avuncular kindness" who "made European archaeology really exciting".[106] All interviewed considered Burkitt's kindness and hospitality to be one of the most valued aspects of his teaching: "One of my happiest archaeological memories . . . was the delicious home-made cake," wrote Joyce Perry (Tripos 1937).[107]

The seemingly contradictory situation of women students and lecturers illustrates what Janet Howarth refers to as an "uncertain post-war mood" concerning women at universities. In the early twentieth century, there was a deep ambivalence and much confusion expressed about women's presence in Cambridge. The definition of a gentleman as "not a cad" was based partly on how men should behave towards women. How, then, was a gentleman supposed to behave toward female students in a male institution? Which was more representative of post-war Cambridge, Howarth (1998: 101) asks., "the mob that destroyed Newnham's gates in 1921 after the Senate once again voted against the opening of degrees, or the horde that rushed out to Girton" excitedly wanting to dance? Howarth suggests that the same men may have been involved in both instances.

This prevalent ambivalence was evident by the varying actions and attitudes of Board members. Haddon was known as a champion of women's right to education.[108] Ellis H. Minns, who succeeded Ridgeway as Disney Professor of Archaeology in 1927, appears to have been equally helpful to women and men. Joyce Perry[109] stated that Minns first offered her the position as Curator of the newly founded David Livingstone Memorial Museum at the Rhodes-Livingstone Institute in Northern Rhodesia. This post was apparently taken by the soon-to-be-renowned Desmond Clark only after Perry declined in order to marry. In contrast to these positive experiences, Joan Townsend distinctly remembered being "incensed" by the attitudes of Haddon's replacement, T.C. Hodson, "an anthropological mediocrity whose years in the Indian Civil Service made him a likely mentor for colonial probationers" (Stocking 1996: 293). Hodson held the "instinctive and unashamed view of women as 'lesser breeds'".[110]

Unfortunately, the research school literature reviewed has not yet discussed such issues as gender definitions of men and women. Investigations into the establishment and functioning of research schools has not yet considered how these definitions may have benefited or harmed the development of research institutions such as scientific laboratories. Gender is not referred to in Morrell's model. It would appear, however, that, if archaeology is to be used as a case study, it would be relevant to consider these issues. As this study unfolds, the importance of gender categorisations will become more obvious. First, however, it is important to reveal something about the great transition which made the Board of Anthropological Studies into the Faculty of Archaeology and Anthropology.

The Board and Faculty

During the 1920s, Board members made concerted and persistent efforts to establish resources to service the growing student numbers. Although Burkitt generously allowed students to use his extensive private collection, there began to be a new awareness that a library should be organised in the Museum. Since 1883, the library of the Cambridge

---

[104] Ridgeway as quoted by Beard, unpublished draft in Beard's possession.
[105] Robertson, personal correspondence, 1998.
[106] Joan Townsend, student in 1928, personal correspondence, 1998.
[107] Perry, personal correspondence, 1998.
[108] Rouse, in conversation, 1996.
[109] Perry, personal correspondence, 1998.
[110] Townsend, personal correspondence, 1998.

*FIGURE X   Disney Professor of Archaeology, Sir William Ridgeway,[111] 1920. (Photograph courtesy of the Master and Fellows of Gonville and Caius College.) Ridgeway is said to have resembled a "west country Elizabethan". He would "fight anybody with the greatest avidity" stated Tom Lethbridge's wife, Mina.[112]
In his lecture entitled "The Relationship of Archaeology to Classical Studies", Ridgeway argued that the meaning of archaeology was best expressed "by the term anthropology, which embraces not only the material productions of man, but also all that pertains to his sociology and to his religion."[113] Armed with this definition of archaeology in 1920, Ridgeway transformed the Board of Anthropological Studies into the Board, later Faculty, of Archaeology and Anthropology.*

Antiquarian Society had been regarded as part of the general collections of the Museum. In the late 1910s, there was growing concern at its uncatalogued, disorganised state. There was no inventory, librarian or fixed hours of access nor designated secure room. The point was made that members of the University would benefit if these books

were available. In a report to the CAS in 1919, the Honorary Librarian, C.E. Sayle, complained that the Society had paid little regard. The Antiquarian Committee, which governed the Museum, was unsure of its own authority on the matter. No one quite knew who was in control. The Museum housed Von Hügel's and Haddon's[114] private collections as well; von Hügel's library was uncatalogued.

After some thought, the Committee recommended that all book collections stored in the Museum be consolidated into one catalogued official library, placed in one room, labelled "Library". This task was accomplished by Miss Fegan with aplomb. Together with Haddon in 1921, Fegan set up the library in the Keyser Gallery on the Museum's ground floor. Grand book cases were used as improvised walls; a wire mattress became the door.[115] In the midst of this hard effort to establish a formal, accessible working library, Ridgeway reasserted his power and his driving ambition for archaeology as anthropology. Soffer's (1982) claim that a subject's success depends ultimately on the potency and vitality of those ideas on which a subject is based is supported by Ridgeway's effective use of his definition of archaeology to transform the Board of Anthropological Studies.

At Ridgeway's request, in late 1919, Haddon suggested that the Antiquarian Committee with its members from the Cambridge Antiquarian Society[116] be reconstituted and placed under the control of the Board of Anthropological Studies.[117] The new teaching of archaeology and anthropology was based on Museum collections; Haddon argued that the body most directly interested in the Museum should have full control of its affairs. This suggestion certainly "ruffled the dovecotes".[118] Replying on behalf of the CAS, Committee member, Dr D.H.S. Cranage, Litt.D, FSA, objected to the proposed change. He reminded Haddon of the Society's position as founder of the Museum. Other members of the Antiquarian Committee such as Arthur Gray, who was the Master of Jesus, and F.J.H. Jenkinson, the University Librarian, raised similar objections. When the Board of Anthropological Studies, represented by Rivers, Haddon, von Hügel, Ridgeway and Duckworth, submitted their report on the management of the Museum to the Senate in January 1920, Dr Cranage argued that the Museum's archaeology and the Board's anthropology were not related subjects.

The proper definition of archaeology was Ridgeway's cue. Elaborate distinctions between anthropology and archaeology simply didn't hold, he argued. Ridgeway pointed out that a Royal Commission on state aid for Oxford and Cambridge

[111] Sir William was knighted in 1919.

[112] Mina Lethbridge, in conversation, 1995.

[113] Ridgeway Paper in the Cambridge Classical Library OL, Box C.9. I thank Grahame Clark for pointing out this reference.

[114] Much of the equipment as well as the ethnological teaching material was Haddon's personal property (Board Minutes. 1917 Min.V.92).

[115] This description of the Library is a reconstruction from several sources, including Sayle's 1919 report presented in CAS Council Minutes, Volume 5, stored at the Haddon Library, Cambridge, and Fegan as quoted in J.D.

Pickles (1988).

[116] By Graces of the Senate in 16 June 1904 and 16 June 1910, the management of the Museum had been vested in the Antiquarian Committee. The Vice-Chancellor, as well as members of the Council of the Cambridge Antiquarian Society, the Fitzwilliam Syndicate, Ridgeway, Haddon and von Hügel served on this Committee.

[117] Antiquarian Committee Minutes, CUMAA Box 19 mm/2/5.

[118] Quoted from archaeologist, Bruce Howe, who dug with Garrod at Bacho Kiro.

Universities had recently been established.[119] For the first time in its history, the University had made application for public funds. Ridgeway suggested that there was now a unique opportunity to secure financing for the Museum and Board united as one vigorous university teaching institution dedicated to the future of archaeology and anthropology combined (*Reporter* 1920: 692-5). Ridgeway's compelling financial argument and his convincing definition of archaeology as anthropology won the day. By a Grace of the Senate in June 1920, the Antiquarian Committee that had hitherto controlled the Museum was abolished and "its functions transferred to a new Board of Archaeological and Anthropological Studies" (*Reporter* 1921: 606).

The official taking-over of the Museum by the Board is remembered today as a power struggle between the local, county Cambridge Antiquarian Society and a powerful University. "The Society had no choice . . . the University had the money and owned the Museum." M.W. Thompson[120] argues that the new power arrangement was beneficial to the Board but seriously detrimental to the position of the Society. Certainly the CAS has little say in running the Museum or the Faculty today. However, at the time, the Antiquarian Committee and the Council of the CAS clearly voted for this change with good majorities.[121] The CAS retained four key representatives on the new Board, including Gray and Rev. Canon H.P. Stokes, Fellow of Corpus Christi. Both were respected members of their Colleges and of the CAS. These members continued to contribute in much the same way as before.

It is worth noting that the vocal opponents to this change were powerful members of Colleges. This implies a College/University power struggle rather than a local Society *versus* University conflict. Gray, the Master of Jesus, may have had additional motives; he may not have wanted Ridgeway to gain control of a university-museum Board with access to public money.

The Royal Commission, and subsequent Statutory Commissioners (1922 to 1926), were often referred to in the Board Minutes. Consultation and discussion with University officers and College Fellows were ongoing and the Commission's final recommendations affected the financial distribution of power between the Colleges and the University. After 1926, a large part of the fees paid by students went to the University rather than to college tutors as formerly. The Royal Commission had recommended a transference of formal teaching from the college to University officers and the Statutory Commissioners ac-

cordingly enjoined the appointment of many new University Lecturers and Demonstrators from among College lecturers. As College teachers became University officers, the new system of Faculty Boards shifted considerable educational power to the University and its Boards.

Ridgeway steered Archaeology and Anthropology firmly through this period of bureaucratic restructuring, seizing every opportunity to increase the Board's hegemonic control of archaeology. This was evident in his dealings with Cyril Fox who was first mentioned in the Board Minutes in 1920 when Burkitt motored him to Toft to assess antiquities donated to the Museum.[122] Fox eventually became one of Archaeology's most celebrated graduates.

In 1920, arrangements for entry to a College were still personally oriented. Before the Previous Examination was prescribed by the Commission, a student could enter a college by personal invitation. This individualistic arrangement for entry into Cambridge worked well both for Fox, who was a mature man with a family, and for the Board who benefited from his astute volunteer work sorting mediaeval collections. Fox had entered Magdalene on the invitation of Quick Professor of Biology, G.H.F. Nuttall,[123] where his brilliance was soon recognised. However, Fox did not have a first degree and was not attached to any Board.[124] At this point, Chadwick, then affiliated to the new English Tripos, "agreed to take him on" (Scott-Fox 2002: 25). One invaluable advisor was O.G.S. Crawford,[125] who came to Cambridge to "meet Mr Fox and to arrange with him the mapping of the archaeological finds of the Cambridge district."[126] Crawford, a known advocate of space-time presentation, was not affiliated to any university and he contributed to Fox's work freely as a colleague. When Fox wished to submit his thesis in 1922, he was directed to the Board of History and Archaeology.[127] As mentioned earlier, various archaeologies were still taught under different Boards and the Board of History and Archaeology[128] offered lectures in Greek and Roman numismatics and sculpture.

Ridgeway, however, clearly realised that a brilliant Ph.D thesis would be a feather in Archaeology and Anthropology's cap; he vehemently argued that Fox's subject was archaeology as defined by the Board of Archaeology and Anthropology. As a powerful, forthcoming member of both Boards, Ridgeway proposed to the History and Archaeology Board that "the subject of archaeology be removed from that Board and should in the future be dealt with solely by the Board [of Archaeology and Anthropology] which was now in a strong enough position to take full charge of the subject."[129]

[119] For a readable history of the Royal Commission and the follow-on Statutory Commissioners for Cambridge, which resulted in the establishment of the Faculty system and annual state aid for Cambridge, see Leedham-Green's (1996) *A Concise History of the University of Cambridge.*
[120] M.W. Thompson, in conversation and correspondence, 1996, 2003. Also see Thompson (1990), *The Cambridge Antiquarian Society 1840–1990.*
[121] Antiquarian Committee Minutes. CUMAA Box 19 mm/2/5.
[122] Board Minutes. 1920 CUL Min.V.92.
[123] Nuttall was Chairman of the Agricultural Board. The circumstances of Fox's entry into Cambridge are detailed in the biography, Scott-Fox's

(2002) *Cyril Fox: Archaeologist Extraordinary.*
[124] Unthinkable today.
[125] Crawford was, at that point, Secretary to the Congress of Archaeological Societies and had just begun to work as Archaeological Officer at the Ordnance Survey.
[126] CAS Council Minutes November, 1920. Volume 5, Haddon Library, Cambridge.
[127] Fox was one of the University's first Ph.D candidates.
[128] This Board was reorganised as the Faculty of History in 1927.
[129] Board Minutes. Min.V.92, May 1922.

Divisions between Boards were still fluid; this led to confusion but also possibilities. The Assistant Registrary for Research Studies wrote a conciliatory letter to Haddon and Ridgeway stating that there had been no intent to insult them and that the University administration would be flexible and approachable. It was agreed that Fox's Ph.D thesis could be attached to the Board of Archaeology and Anthropology. It was then decided that archaeology would forever fall within the clear domain of the future Faculty of Archaeology and Anthropology in 1927.[130]

Cyril Fox is celebrated today and well remembered for his fine intellectual work. His thesis "was to prove one of the most accomplished ever presented for the degree" (Clark 1989b: 7). Fox's thesis became crucially important to the definition of archaeology under the new Board. By setting a high in *The Archaeology of the Cambridge Region; A Topographical Study* for future candidates, Fox's research and theoretical contributions constructively defined what "original" research was. This set a good example for Grahame Clark's Ph.D in the early 1930s.[131]

One of the Board's main requests, in light of the Royal Commission's work on restructuring, was full pay for and ownership of the Disney Professorship of Archaeology.[132] In 1926, the Board reiterated, "in view of the fact that the Statutory Commissioners are engaged in revising the Statutes of the University," the Board begged leave to suggest alterations in the regulations governing the Disney Professorship of Archaeology: the Professorship should be raised to the status of a full Professorship with a full stipend of £1200 yearly; the title should be altered to the Professor of Archaeology and Anthropology; and, most importantly, the Professorship, currently not assigned to any Board, should be attached to the new Faculty of Archaeology and Anthropology. Ridgeway would resign his post of Brereton Reader in Classics and devote himself solely to the work of the new Faculty. A report to the Council and debate ensued. Burkitt stated that he and his father did much behind-the-scenes visiting of important people.[133] When the issue came before the Senate in May 1927, some suggested that the Professorship be assigned to the Classics Faculty.

In a characteristically inspired response with religious overtones, Miles Burkitt spoke for anthropology and archaeology. Nobody wanted less to underrate the importance of Classical Archaeology, he argued, but his own subject of prehistory was the basis of archaeology. Classics "in the words of John Bunyan, came into the narrow way by the winding lane at the side. After all, the narrow and strait gate is through Geology and Natural Science." In his experience, archaeology was akin to geology and to all natural sciences[134] as well as anthropology (*Reporter* 3 May 1927). As if by God's way, the immense, basic field of general archaeology should be the special work of the Disney Professor. The future of the Faculty, set up by the Commission, should be in the hands of the Disney Professor as strong Head of Archaeology and Anthropology. From the Board Minutes for Classics, there seems to have been little resistance from the Classics Board which already had a Reader in Classical Archaeology. That Board seemed more concerned with successfully converting the Brereton Reader to the Brereton-Lawrence Readership dedicated to the study of ancient philosophy.[135] On 17 May 1927, just months after Ridgeway's unexpected and deeply mourned death, the Disney Professorship with full stipend was successfully assigned to the Faculty of Archaeology and Anthropology.

Ridgeway's loss may have devastated the young Faculty since the omniscient Haddon was about to retire. But, most fortunately, the quietly respected Elrington and Bosworth Professor of Anglo-Saxon, H.M. Chadwick, decided to remove his students from the Faculty of English to Archaeology and Anthropology. Chadwick had been involved with Anthropological Studies since 1904, was on the Board for years and had offered courses of lectures in archaeology of La Tène to Viking periods. He is often mentioned in Board notes and Museum letters. Chadwick felt that Anglo-Saxon language could not be divorced from its cultural settings. He sought the opportunity to broaden his studies by including Norse, Celtic and Romano-British research and hoped to find a haven in the newly organised Faculty to combine the "study of Language, Literature, History and Civilisation — by which we mean both Institutions and Archaeology." Chadwick wished to promote the study "of the Teutonic and Celtic peoples — the civilisation, intellectual, social, and material, of these people"(*Reporter* October 1926). Chadwick brought with him two excellent University Lecturers, Toty de Navarro,[136] who for years taught Bronze and Early Iron Age archaeology, and Dame Bertha Phillpotts.

The Faculty benefited enormously from the addition of a full-time, full-paid Disney Professor as well as from the learned Chadwick's contributions. The added breadth of expertise along with Chadwick's bright, paid, congenial Lecturers gave new confidence. The ongoing administrative structural change from Board to Faculty spurred an increase

---

[130] Letter in the Haddon Papers. CUL Envelope III.
[131] Fox mapped artefacts against ecological backgrounds in order to test an assumption that had been "frequently advanced over the last dozen years that early settlements were always on open land" (Peake 1924: 111). His thesis produced major new generalisations about the relationship between landscapes and culture-history. Early agricultural settlement had been on light, permeable soil, whereas in the Iron Age and Anglo-Saxon period, the settlement shifted to heavier, harder-to-work but more productive soil. In later work, Fox showed that south-eastern English lowlands had been exposed to migration and diffusion yet the highlands were more protected.

His 1920s conclusions held well into the late 1940s.
[132] Board Minutes. CUA Min.V.92 June 1920.
[133] Burkitt, memoirs [1961]. CUL Add. 7959 Box III.
[134] The Board had repeatedly requested that Anthropology and Archaeology be defined on the scientific side of literary and scientific groupings under the new Faculty system (Board Minutes from 1922 and 1924. CUA Min.V.92).
[135] Board of Classics Minutes. CUA Min.V.89.
[136] "Toty" was a successful Lecturer whose contributions were appreciated by many that I interviewed until he retired in the early 1950s.

in students; the largest Tripos class of the 1920s graduated in 1926. This class included Louis Leakey and Gregory Bateson who took First Class degrees before proceeding to lives of fame.

2.6 Louis Clarke, Gentlemen and Tea

The above description of institutional changes documents one of Geison's (1981: 24) factors listed as most important in his analysis of the success of research schools, the "Institutionalization in university setting". This was clearly accomplished by the Board during the 1920s.

United, the Board and Museum entered a period of excitement and efflorescence, supported by devoted volunteer effort. Honorary Keepers abounded; when Haddon, as Acting Curator, "toppled over" one of many distinguished elderly gentleman working on strange objects, his "gruff but kindly" comment was "are you one of those damned fools who work for nothing!?"[137] The elderly Honorary Treasurer, consistently referred to as "Daddy Bird", was a trusted, highly competent volunteer in charge of all Museum and Board accounts. For years, he and other Keepers were valuable, respected members of the Board.

Before the Faculty system was introduced in 1926–7, the Board relied heavily on non-stipendiary lecturers. As Reader in Ethnology, Haddon held the only stipendiary position. The acclaimed W.H.R. Rivers, who "contributed more than anyone else to the methodology of ethnology" (Haddon 1923: 1), held no official position.[138] This situation was difficult but also could be opportune. Anyone who had knowledge, wanted to share it and was willing to work for small sums of student fees, could apply to be a "Recognised Lecturer". The only qualification required was a Cambridge degree.

Describing this same era in the new English Tripos, Tillyard (1958: 13) states "with the weakest professional qualifications, I became one of the first teachers for the new Tripos." This "haphazard" process would have been "out of the question eight years later when things had become organised." Since there was no set curriculum, lectures were widely varied and innovative. This openness and lack of formal entry arrangement welcomed young talent and new ideas. T.F. McIlwraith, who was to become the founder of anthropology in Canada, spent unpaid months sorting the Museum's African material as an undergraduate. Shortly after taking a First class degree in the Tripos in 1921, he offered a course to eight students on African Ethnology. Other

post-graduate students also generously contributed. L.W.G. Malcolm, who later become Curator at the Bristol Museum, spent his years as a M.Sc student cataloguing the Tremearne collections. Even undergraduates could become involved. "Mr Gordon Ruck of Caius has compensated for the absence of Mr Benson and Mr Bushnell who have gone down," stated a Museum report to the University. These undergraduates had been working on the preservation and arrangement of monumental brass rubbings (*Reporter* 1926: 812).

During this decade, work in the Museum was an integral part of undergraduate education. It was noted in the Faculty Minutes that Miles Burkitt, his father Professor Burkitt and Miles Burkitt's twelve students had been "indefatigable" in sorting stone artefacts and pottery. H.M. Chadwick was ever-present with his students, cleaning and identifying Bronze Age artefacts.[139] Cambridge men, now members of the public, who had speciality knowledge, were also involved. The Minutes noted that "Rev. W.A. Crabtree of Ipswich lectured to post-graduates" on ethnological topics. Col. T.C. Hodson, who replaced Haddon as Reader, took the opportunity to introduce himself by offering a course of unpaid lectures on "Social Anthropology of India" in 1923.[140]

This community effort of undergraduates, young researchers, ex-colonial officers and elderly gentlemen was at first a tentative success. By all accounts, the Museum operated pleasantly, if chaotically. Everyone appears to have been learning. "It was a fascinating period," wrote Burkitt. Some items were still privately owned and many had never been sorted or displayed. "We all began to realise how rich the Museum's collections were."[141] Improvisation was encouraged; volunteer work was greatly appreciated and well recognised. "I don't think some of you can realise how amateur it all was . . . and how excellent," remarked Burkitt in a speech to the CAS in 1962.[142] Miss Fegan and Mrs Quiggin donated chairs for the undergraduates to sit on and desks; curtains for the windows were made by Girton College volunteers. On occasion, students scrubbed the entire Museum.[143] Former Tripos men began to collect artefacts abroad and send them home. Burkitt returned after World War I with a teaching collection of French Palaeolithic implements donated by the well-known French prehistorian, Salomon Reinach.

In 1920, the President of the Society of Antiquaries of London, C. Hercules Read, introduced Louis Clarke to Curator Baron von Hügel, describing him as "a great traveller and an old Trinity Hall man,"[144] who had studied with Henry Balfour at the Pitt Rivers Museum in Oxford.[145] When von Hügel retired in

[137] Burkitt, memoirs [1961]. CUL Add. 7959 Box III.
[138] It was only after Rivers' sudden death, in June 1922, when the subject "was left totally unprovided for" (Board Minutes 1923. CUA Min.V.92), that the Board petitioned the General Board for a stipend of £200 for a replacement. W.E. Armstrong, one of Rivers' students, was chosen over the soon to be famous B. Malinowski, who also applied. As will be clear in my discussion of Garrod's appointment, the Cambridge Faculty consistently preferred its own.
[139] Board Minutes. 1920–21, CUA Min.V.92.

[140] Board Minutes. 1920–21, CUA Min.V.92.
[141] Burkitt, memoirs [1961]. CUL Add. 7959 Box III.
[142] Burkitt, memoirs [1961]. CUL Add. 7959 Box III.
[143] Board Minutes. CUA Min.V.92 1921.
[144] Read to von Hügel, CUMAA 1920 Letter Boxes
[145] In *Prehistory at Cambridge and Beyond,* Clark (1989a: 40) states that Clarke had taken the Diploma of Anthropology at Oxford before coming to Cambridge.

FIGURE XI L.C.G. Clarke[146] MA, FSA; The Gentleman Curator by Augustus John 1915. (By courtesy of the Fitzwilliam Museum.)
"His splendid hospitality did much for our subject", bringing together varieties of gifted people in gracious Museum surroundings "littered with beautiful things" (G.H.S. Bushnell 1961: 192). Clarke was apparently the person who introduced the tea-room to the Museum and its Board. His Museum teas were well attended by students and Faculty members. The place of the tea-room and the friendly, relaxed and enjoyable times encouraged by the occasion of tea provided an opportunity to develop trusting relationships which worked well for the expansion of the Tripos course.

1922, Clarke was appointed over numerous other applicants to the Curatorship of the Museum. Named Louis "because he was the fourteenth child"(Scott-Fox 2002: 49), he came from a wealthy Lancashire family who had made its fortune in coal. Along with his considerable wealth, he brought artistic presence and cultivated grace to the Museum. Clarke's Museum parties and receptions are legend, well-remem-

bered by Museum employee, Charles Bernard Denston and others interviewed. Champagne and exquisite catered hors d'oeuvres,[147] elegantly served by maids in peaked white caps and black dresses, were evening affairs for patrons, prehistorians and anthropologists. "And who can forget the *soigné* figure, the handmade pastel silk shirts or invariable black tie, the velvet smoking suit in the evening," wrote Assistant Curator Maureen Hutton, *née* O"Reilly (Hutton and Bushnell 1962: 3), in her fine tribute to Clarke after his death in 1960.[148] Students from the 1930s vividly remember his aristocratic demeanour, his dressed presence[149] and his efficiency in gaining financial support and benefactions.[150]

One of Clarke's first actions as Curator was to formalise the custom of mid- morning and afternoon tea. "In those days the typewriter and the telephone were hardly regarded as the mode of communication between gentlemen" (Hutton and Bushnell 1962: 2). Some informal pleasant space was required for appropriate discourse. A meeting place was necessary for the smooth running of business and personal affairs. Professor Christopher Hawkes, who knew Clarke during the 1930s, remembered him in "*pince-nez* and flowing white dustcoat . . . rushing around the Museum, checking on everyone . . . At eleven o'clock precisely he would stand in the middle of the ground floor displays shouting *'Tea'"* (Hawkes as quoted by Scott-Fox 2002: 47). All present, whether students, staff, visitors, or academics from adjacent Faculties, would abruptly stop and casually assemble "so that '*everyone will get to know each other, otherwise they will hate each other,*'" stated Clarke to Hawkes as quoted by Scott-Fox (2002: 47). According to Hutton and Bushnell (1962: 3) both of whom worked for decades in the Museum, Clarke was "at his wittiest and most delightful at tea in the Museum on a dark, wet afternoon" even with a modest audience. Mary Kitson Clark, who is one of the few students surviving from the 1920s, well remembered sneaking into the enjoyable, delectable Museum teas which were "always full of good talk" and good cakes.[151]

Although not well documented or researched, according to historian Gregory Blue, there is some evidence that tea was important as a "place of significant scientific socialising"[152] in Cambridge University institutions at this time. Blue, who is doing biographical work on Joseph Needham, suggested that I look at practices at the Sir William Dunn Institute of Biochemistry under its first Director, Frederick Gowland Hopkins. He noted that Needham gave an interview to *The Caian* in 1976 when he retired as Master of Gonville and Caius College, in which he stated "My life revolved very much more around the lab [Hopkins's Biochemical

---

[146] Louis Clarke's name was universally pronounced "Lew-ey" Clarke (Mina Lethbridge, in conversation, 1996).

[147] As remembered by Denston, in conversation, 2000. Denston was first employed in the Museum in 1937. His unpublished autobiography, which I will refer to later, is in his possession.

[148] Known for his humour, Clarke was an entertainingly unconventional host. Among the many Clarke stories I heard from Mina is the following retold by Tom Lethbridge [1965]: "One day a Nonconformist Missionary of very serious demeanour arrived. Louis swept him off to look at Maori

artefacts . . . There is one 'feather box' in the Museum which is noted for the indecency of the carving. 'There' said Louis proudly 'I could never get into that position myself!'"

[149] Shaw, in conversation, 2000.

[150] "Clarke was responsible for attracting large benefactions," Pickles, in conversation, 2003.

[151] Kitson Clark, personal correspondence, 1999.

[152] Blue, personal correspondence, 2000.

Laboratory], and in the lab, than it did in College . . . after all we were having lunch and tea everyday, and that was the main centre of interest"(Needham 1976: 40). In a further article about Hopkins, Needham (1962: 34–5) wrote, "Throughout the half-century of Hopkins' life and work at Cambridge there were tea-club meetings each week or fortnight, when one or other of the research workers would give an account of experiments in progress. The atmosphere at these meetings was unforgettable." They were characterised by constructive, astute, helpful criticism; it was agreed that "no one could speak or act with passion or prejudice . . . Nor were the young excluded," Needham continued, Part II students of the Natural Sciences Tripos were always welcomed "to the tea-club meetings".

Blue[153] has indicated that Hopkins may have modelled his tea-club on the practice of scholarly tea-meetings at the Cavendish Laboratory. Donald Opitz, describes tea at the Cavendish in his unpublished dissertation "The Country House as Laboratory: Science and the Aristocracy in Late-Victorian and Edwardian Britain." Opitz states, "researchers gathered daily in the Professor's room for tea, a tradition that according to [Cavendish Professor Lord] Rayleigh's contemporaries began during his term." Opitz[154] states that this tradition was instigated by Lady Rayleigh. In *John William Strutt, Baron Rayleigh 1842–1919,* Arthur Schuster (1921: xxiii) suggests that Rayleigh's afternoon tea "was an innovation which may appear to be trivial, but the custom, which affords opportunities for informal discussion of scientific matters and encourages friendly personal intercourse, has been copied in many laboratories." Opitz noted that the tradition continued for years after Rayleigh's departure.

It would seem from the above that tea was an established social and intellectual occasion among scientists in the University. By the early 1930s, afternoon tea was also an established tradition among undergraduates in their rooms. At Cambridge, no lectures or supervisions were held between lunch and Hall or dinner. This time was reserved for various undergraduate athletic activities, usually on the river, which were followed by tea. Male boat club friends enjoyed their afternoon tea which interviewees remembered as an opportunity "to joke and exchange rude stories".[155]

However, evidence as to the social and intellectual importance of tea at the Museum is difficult to find. Tea was so embedded in everyday Faculty practice and was such a taken-for-granted occurrence, that it was seldom discussed in minutes, correspondence, diaries, published literature or interviews. References to tea persistently appeared in interviews only as background noise. I listened to endless people discussing their archaeological lives before noticing how important tea was.

From some correspondence saved at the Museum, it appears that Clarke often invited potential patrons and valued guests to attend morning coffee and afternoon tea. It is also clear from his statement quoted above, "*everyone will get to know each other otherwise they will hate each other,*" and from Kitson Clark's letters, that tea in the twenties was a relaxed social, learn-to-work-together opportunity rather than a place for significant scientific socialising. The smooth running of the expanding Board and Museum was the key concern. One suspects that business and policy decisions were made and gentlemen's agreements kept.

There is evidence that this was true until recently. Mary Cra'ster, former Assistant Curator of the Museum, remembers that administrative decisions were still agreed upon at Museum coffee and tea during the 1960s. "Everything was arranged over a cup of coffee in the tea-room," she stated. A gentleman's agreement atmosphere prevailed. "If you said you would do something, you did it." This trust was possible, Cra'ster thought, because "everyone knows everybody". Archaeologists were part of a small, known community.[156] Cra'ster remembered the "fascinating informal academic discussions" which occurred during tea and coffee when participants would "knock ideas around".[157]

In correspondence from the 1920s, there is, as yet, no mention of the tea-room as a place for scientific debate or discussion of ideas. However, this changed with the arrival of Grahame Clark and the fledgling scientific professionals of the thirties discussed in the following chapter. The atmosphere of trust based on familiarity established in the tea-room during the twenties would then support the creation of new approaches to archaeology. As explained by the philosopher, John Hardwig (1991), who has researched the role of trust in scientific knowledge, a climate of trust is required to support much of our academic knowledge. Research as a collegial activity is based on trusting the expertise of others. No one can know enough and "In most disciplines, those who do not trust cannot know. . . the trustworthiness of epistemic communities is the ultimate foundation" for knowledge (Hardwig 1991: 694). Certainly, evidence of how the Museum tea-room was used would support Hardwig's conclusions.

Louis Clarke, with his socially astute, learned and cultivated approach and with the tea-room as a civilising and socially binding influence, turned the Museum into a 1920s roaring success. Energies coalesced and everyone pitched in, soliciting collections. The Museum entered a period of gracious, productive expansion. "Our mutual friend O.G.S. Crawford tells me that you are trying to get together a collection of sherds for teaching," Haddon wrote to Clarke in February 1921.[158] Fox and Burkitt, as Honorary Keeper of

[153] Blue, in conversation, 2000.
[154] Opitz, in conversation, 1999.
[155] "We were the good ship Venus, You really should have seen" etc., etc. Sidney Sussex College Boat Club song. Shaw, in conversation, 1996.
[156] So much so that nicknames were common; Grahame Clark was Sweetie, Gordon Childe, Foetus Face, O.G.S. Crawford, Uncle OGPU, after the

initials for the Soviet secret police, referring to Crawford's avowed Communist leanings. Caton-Thompson was Gravel Pit Kate, a well-known female was Powder Pigeon, *etc.*
[157] All quotations, Mary Cra'ster, in conversation, 1999.
[158] CUMAA 1921 Letter Box.

the Stone Implements, worked keenly together. "He supplied the knowledge and myself the organisation," wrote Burkitt.[159] Tom Lethbridge and Louis Clarke successfully scoured the Fenland for artefacts. With "his zeal for collecting and his flair in the sale-room, it is no wonder" the Museum was "so notably enriched," wrote Grahame Clark (1989a: 40–41). The varied members of the Museum thoroughly enjoyed themselves. "I don't think there could have been a happier or better place to work than Louis Clarke's Museum," concluded Hutton, *née* O'Reilly (Hutton and Bushnell 1962: 3).

2.7 Chapter Conclusion

God, Empire and Prehistory proved a powerful trinity. By the end of the 1920s, Cambridge was indeed becoming the real centre of prehistoric research in the Empire. Based on a strong philosophical/spiritual justification that such knowledge would contribute to a better world, Archaeology and Anthropology had a functioning meeting place, the tearoom, which fostered peaceful co-operation. It also had an established library, a Ph.D qualification, ongoing courses of lectures and the first graduated students specialising in prehistory. With a base of continuing institutional support, a resonant intellectual environment was beginning to transmute a subject into a tradition through continuing discussion and a significant number of students (Soffer 1982).

A.J.H. Goodwin was the first archaeologist trained by the Board and the first of Burkitt's archaeology students to gain a position in the Empire. Graduating in 1923, Haddon went to great trouble to find him a post under Professor A.R. Radcliffe-Brown at the University of Cape Town,[160] where he became known as the first professional archaeologist in the Union of South Africa. Goodwin, who according to Desmond Clark (1994: 7) was "the founder of systematic archaeological research in South Africa," and "Peter" Van Riet Lowe, in Johannesburg, published, in 1929, their great synthesis, *The Stone Age Cultures of South Africa.* In this classic, the authors proposed an independent African nomenclature and terminology to replace Eurocentric Stone Age categories; the chronological sequence they introduced is still used generally in Africa south of the Sahara. By 1936, Louis Leakey (Tripos 1926), another famous graduate, had already published a series of influential books, *Adam's Ancestors, The Stone Age Cultures of Kenya Colony* and *Stone Age Africa,* which synthesised and popularised Eastern, Central and Southern African archaeology. In Northern Rhodesia, major discoveries were also made. By 1922, the famous Broken Hill mine had yielded an extensive fauna thought to be associated with an ancient skull from the same site and in 1924, F.B. Macrae (Tripos 1924), a District Commissioner and former Cambridge Archaeology and Anthropology student, had conducted Northern Rhodesia's first excavation; this was in a cave at Mumbwa which Desmond Clark (Tripos 1937) would re-excavate in 1939.

Although the importance of such students is emphasised by Morrell's model, a detailed description of the history of the Board, Museum and Faculty of Archaeology and Anthropology suggests that the model/chart should heuristically include several other appropriate areas of investigation suggested by the gender and geographical approaches. Although helpful in suggesting that students are necessary for institutional success, staying within the limitations of Morrell's findings would not have permitted a complete account of the development of prehistoric archaeology at Cambridge. The importance of personal beliefs, motivation, philosophies, gendered relationships and informal settings such as tea-rooms to the establishment of this academic subject should also be indicated. Burkitt's religious beliefs turned out to be important to the institutionalisation of prehistory. Motivated by a strong religious and emotional commitment to prehistory, Burkitt successfully inspired students. Social spaces such as the tea-room provided a suitable supportive environment.

In a time of professed amateurs, how, then, did ideas become practice? In Burkitt's case, he was proud to communicate the knowledge learned as the sole young pupil of the Abbé Breuil. Burkitt prepared to teach prehistory while lying in the mud at Gargas and digging by the light of an acetylene lamp with honoured intellectual guardians. Burkitt's mentors were gentlemen. Cartailhac was consistently charming and cultured. According to Burkitt, Teilhard de Chardin was described as courteous and "well-bred . . . a Christian mystic and gentleman combined" (Burkitt as quoted by Cuénot 1965: 20). "One's first emotion was affection" (Burkitt 1922a: 43) for the prehistorians he met in Spain and France. In an uncritical way, when Burkitt began to teach, one of his firm desires was to communicate his feeling of excitement and to demonstrate his devotion to Obermaier and Breuil's ideas. He never aspired to be the charismatic researcher described by Morrell and Geison.

Before formalised controls over recruitment, institutionalised avenues of entry and established qualifying standards, Ophir and Shapin's (1991: 3) "spirit" was made "flesh" through personal attachment and companionship. Ophir and Shapin's place of knowledge was the nightly camp fires, at which Burkitt "had much conversation" or on the back of a horse while travelling through acres of waterlilied lagoons in Spain. Before the establishment of the social structures necessary for Geison's research schools, I may conclude that archaeological knowledge was packaged within an individual, trade-like apprenticeship based on loyalty.

If Burkitt were applying for his post today, with the current stress on original research, he would likely not be shortlisted. He may not have even qualified for Cambridge if the Previous were mandatory before coming up from Eton. In an era before a standardised qualifying entry examination, before self-conscious attempts at "meritocracy" and before paid positions, Burkitt's comparative wealth and place as a

---

[159] Burkitt memoirs, [1961] in Burkitt Papers. CUL Add. 7959 Box III.

[160] Haddon Papers. CUL Envelope III.

male child of the University allowed him to contribute freely on his own terms. As recorded in the Faculty Minutes, the Board felt fortunate to have him.[161] He was precisely the right man, a fine historical fit.[162] Without Burkitt, prehistoric archaeology may never have been taught to undergraduates. The subject may not have been introduced in Cambridge. Burkitt is criticised by some (Daniel 1986) for his apparent lack of professional ambition and for his rumoured refusal to accept the new Abercromby Professorship of Prehistoric Archaeology at Edinburgh before V.G. Childe in the late 1920s. Yet he is remembered with great affection. Thurstan Shaw clearly described a "generous man of good

will".[163] Desmond Clark stated that Burkitt was "a dedicated lecturer" obviously happiest while teaching Cambridge introductory courses on the Palaeolithic. Burkitt remained as a non-professional lecturer in the Faculty until 1958 when he retired in order to commit himself more fully to local government. Over the years, he was particularly well thought of as the Chairman of the Education Committee of the County Council for Cambridgeshire where he fought for the inclusion of archaeology in secondary school curricula.[164] However, his dream of a united world governed by judicious, historically-informed men, resulting in peace among nations, has eluded us.

---

[161] Board Minutes 1919. CUA Min.V.92.

[162] In contrast, the qualified but poorer Fox could not afford to stay at Cambridge. After working for Louis Clarke for two years as his privately paid Assistant Curator at £300 yearly, during which he offered lectures on the archaeology of the Cambridge region, Fox accepted the post of Keeper of Archaeology at the National Museum of Wales and Lecturer in

Archaeology at the University College, Cardiff. Several years later, in 1930, a stipendiary Assistant Curatorship was finally established at Cambridge (Various dates. Board Minutes Min.V.92).

[163] Shaw, in conversation, 2003.

[164] Clark, in conversation, 2000.

3 Grahame Clark's New Archaeology

"Young and irreverent persons in Cambridge . . . were making the first conscious and concerted effort to professionalise prehistory." (Abercromby Professor of Prehistory, Stuart Piggott, addressing the Prehistoric Society in 1963).[1]

I have now described the beginnings of the institutionalisation of prehistory as a taught subject, introduced by a well-read, self-defined gentleman of congenial nature. Miles Burkitt was an independently wealthy man who shared his private library, lithics collections and wide knowledge with students in an atmosphere of generosity and good will. He was motivated by the belief that archaeology, as part of a liberal education, would produce Godly men of value and sound judgement who would justly administer an Empire. Archaeology was not to be seen as a career. It was a humane study to better mankind not individual desires. Men of "ambition" were suspect; they could easily be corrupted by the seduction of power, money and fame. Those who put their own academic ambitions before the common good were "rude".[2] Research was not the prime goal of Burkitt's academic life; the Ph.D was still, in the 1920s, a questionable, even at times disreputable, degree.[3] Such a degree was too narrow and could be viewed as self-serving. "No one took a Ph.D because that was considered vulgar," observed Mary Cra'ster.[4] Research for its own sake was still an "ungentlemanly, boorish, and even foolish German idea" (Morrell 1993: 122).

In contrast, in this chapter, Burkitt's most famous Ph.D student, Grahame Clark, a self-proclaimed man of Science, is introduced. Matriculating in 1926, he achieved First Class Honours in the Archaeology and Anthropology Section A[5] Tripos, concentrating on north-western European prehistory, a specialisation specifically set up at his request.[6] Motivated by his love of science, Clark became one of the first research students in archaeology in the new Faculty of Archaeology and Anthropology. Upon hearing of his decision to pursue a Ph.D in prehistoric archaeology, Clark's guardian approached his supervisor, Miles Burkitt, and Disney Professor Ellis Minns to enquire about employment possibilities. He was promptly told that Clark had no employment future.[7] Although Clark came from a very respectable middle class background,[8] he did not have a private income. He was, nevertheless, very determined to become a "professional archaeologist".[9]

Certainly Harold Perkin's (1989: 2) observation that the twentieth was the century "of the uncommon and increasingly professional expert" is manifest in archaeology at this time. Clark's wish to be a "professional" would have been an impossible dream when Burkitt dug with Obermaier in 1913. However, during Clark's undergraduate years, Cyril Fox had already become a successful professional role model. As mentioned above, with Louis Clarke's support, Fox had secured the post of Keeper of Archaeology at the National Museum of Wales in 1924. In an interview in 1994, Abercromby Professor emeritus, Stuart Piggott observed that, in the late 1920s, although "archaeology didn't exist as a subject at all . . . and I had no means of getting training . . . I did take a chance . . . going as general assistant to the Museum of Reading"[10] at the age of 17 for ten shillings a week in 1927. By 1930, then, a few rather poorly paid positions were in place at Museums including Piggott's, Reginald Smith's at the British Museum and Wheeler and Fox in Wales. V. Gordon Childe,[11] the Abercromby Professor of Prehistoric Archaeology was at Edinburgh and Burkitt had obtained a position as Cambridge University Lecturer in 1926.

On completion of his Ph.D, Clark began to achieve his desired archaeological profession, beginning his long and distinguished career with the tenure of a Bye-Fellowship at Peterhouse. Following this, he was Faculty Assistant Lecturer from 1935–46, University Lecturer 1946–52, Disney Professor of Archaeology 1952–74, Head of Department of Archaeology and Anthropology in 1956–61 and 1968–71, and Master of Peterhouse 1973–80. Clark was a pre-eminent twentieth-century archaeologist. Trigger (1989: 269) states that, by the 1940s and 1950s, Clark had begun to pioneer an ecologically oriented, functionalist approach to prehistory, the first scholar to apply A.G. Tansley's (1935) concept of an ecosystem to archaeological evidence. Willey (1990: 371) agrees that Clark developed the ecosystem concept, introducing to English archaeology a view of culture which attempted "to say something about the interrelationship of environment, technology, social forms,

[1] Piggott 1963: 5.

[2] Mina Lethbridge, in conversation, 1999.

[3] Although original research was always respected by Haddon and others who promoted the post-graduate Diploma, the debate about whether or not the more intensive Ph.D was a worthy degree recurred in the Faculty Minutes right into the 1930s.

[4] Mary Cra'ster, in conversation, 1999.

[5] As alluded to earlier, the Archaeology and Anthropology course was a one-part degree usually taken over two years. After 1926, it was divided into two Sections, A and B. Section A covered physical and social anthropology and prehistoric archaeology. This study only deals with Section A. Section B was dedicated to Norse, Celtic and Anglo-Saxon history and languages taught under the eminent Elrington and Bosworth Professor of

Anglo-Saxon, H.M. Chadwick.

[6] Faculty Board Minutes, 7 October 1928. CUA Min.V.92a.

[7] Clark, in an interview on 20 April 1994, stated that his guardian had spoken to Professor Minns. Miles Burkitt claimed to his students that Clark's guardian had also questioned him (Shaw, in conversation, 2000).

[8] His father was a stockbroker and Lieutenant Colonel in World War I who died in the 1919 influenza pandemic.

[9] Clark, in conversation, 12 July 1994.

[10] Quoted, with permission, from the interview Julia Roberts conducted with Stuart Piggott in 1994. Roberts is a Ph.D student at the University of Wales; the interview transcript is in Roberts's possession.

[11] "Childe . . . was the sort of remote and strange scholar that everyone respected and no one understood." (Piggott, in conversation with Roberts,

and idea systems". It is generally thought that Clark's stress upon an interdisciplinary approach led to the development in England of the subdisciplines of bio- and zooarchaeology as well as palaeoeconomy and palaeoethnobotany.

During the 1930s, Clark was a successful intellectual entrepreneur who, more than any other individual in Cambridge archaeology, personified the new generation of prehistorians who believed that archaeology was a profession. Whereas Burkitt felt that archaeology was an amateur avocation which must serve the Empire and promote world peace, Clark felt that archaeology was a professional endeavour which must become academically institutionalised. In the following discussion, Burkitt's "narrative" archaeological approach is compared to Clark's self-conscious scientific approach. I demonstrate how the social organisation of archaeology in Cambridge was changed with the establishment of the Fenland Research Committee in 1932 and how Clark used a new knowledge base developed during the interdisciplinary excavations of the Committee to gain institutional support for a new definition of archaeology. During this decade, Clark coldly waged a successful war with personal and intellectual weapons to institutionalise prehistory. Without doubt, he was responsible for gaining increased status for prehistory as a specialisation at Cambridge. Questions to be answered are: how was science defined by Clark; what exactly was a scientist in Clark's conception; and how did a "Scientist" differ from Miles Burkitt's conception of an academic gentleman? Also, what difference did this make to the practice of archaeology?

Heuristic "models" of research schools taken from the history of science literature reviewed earlier apply well to a study of Clark and his influence. As mentioned previously, Coleman (1985), Geison (1993), Morrell (1972) and Secord (1986) suggest that certain factors, such as a charismatic leader, a strong coherent set of research questions and methods, an avenue for publication and an ability to establish administrative support, must be present for an academic research school to develop successfully. Informed by this literature, I answer questions such as: how did Clark redefine archaeology; did his work begin to draw students to Cambridge; was the training he offered a lasting contribution to his students' careers; did he provide editorial support and publication opportunities as the literature on research schools suggests as necessary for success? As alluded to earlier, a pool of recruits, exploitable techniques, and new fields of research may be evident in the evolving Cambridge experience. Clark's contributions, and whether or not he can be said to have started his own school, will be evaluated in the light of these questions and the reviewed literature.

The geography-of-knowledge literature, which analyses scientific achievements and their spread, suggests that Clark's intellectual influence may be fruitfully traced through his students as they travelled to work in Africa in 1936 and 1937. The export of environmental archaeology will therefore be reviewed through two case studies,

Thurstan Shaw, First Class Honours 1936, who went to Ghana, and Desmond Clark, First Class Honours 1937, who travelled to Northern Rhodesia. In this way, knowledge travel will be documented. The place of the tea-room as a knowledge-making site is also examined. Finally, a gendered point of view will enlighten my search for understanding the multiple relationships between masculine and feminine which developed within the maturing social structures of Cambridge prehistory.

3.1 Grahame Clark (1907–1995)

"A Young Man in a Hurry"

In their investigation of emerging specialties and schools, Morrell (1972, 1993) and Secord (1986) stress the importance of charismatic leadership in the development of successful research institutions. Morrell suggests that Liebig's persuasive personal magnetism was one of the major reasons that he attracted recruits and funds to his chemistry laboratory at the University of Giessen during the 1820s. He was able to inspire and hold students' loyalty simply by how he behaved. "Liebig was the spirit as well as the leader of his battalions; and if he was followed so heartily it was because, much as he was admired, he was loved even more. Each word of his carried instruction, every intonation of his voice bespoke regard; his approval was a mark of honour" (Morrell 1972: 36). In contrast to Liebig, Thomas Thomson, who was head of the less prestigious chemistry laboratory at the University of Glasgow, could "hardly be called a charismatic figure or leader." His less attractive features were his "chilling sarcasm" and "uncontrollable propensity to sneer"(Morrell 1972: 38, 39). It should be noted that three of the four research schools which are listed in FIGURE III as having failed, lacked congenial, revered leaders.

How, then, is Clark described by students and contemporaries and in personal correspondence and literature in the 1930s? According to many I interviewed, Clark was the embodiment of the "*Young Man in a Hurry*" from F.M. Cornford's well-known 1908 satire of Cambridge University politics, *Microcosmographia Academica: Being a Guide for the Young Academic Politician*. "*A Young Man in a Hurry* is a narrow-minded and ridiculously youthful prig, who is inexperienced enough to imagine that something might be done before very long, and even to suggest definite things." Clark also appears to have been one of Cornford's *Adullamites* who inhabited "a series of caves near Downing Street". *Adullamites* were dangerous because they knew what they wanted; "and that is, all the money there is going."

By 1914, Downing Street had become the building site for the new science Tripos courses, laboratories and museums. Among these were the famous Cavendish Laboratory as well as Chemistry, Engineering, Zoology, Mineralogy, Geology, Botany and the new University Museum of Archaeology and Ethnology. In keeping with the location, the Faculty of Archaeology and Anthropology had consistently fought to be classified on the Science rather than the Arts side of the

FIGURE XII   Grahame Clark.[12]
This photograph dates from December 1950, two years after the final Fenland Research Committee meeting, when Clark was excavating the famous Mesolithic site of Star Carr. It was taken by the renowned Cambridge studio of Lettice Ramsay and Helen Muspratt. (By courtesy of the Cambridgeshire Collection.)

General Board of the Faculties.[13] *Adullamites* were indeed men of Science who "It will be seen . . . are not refined, like Classical men" (all quotations, Cornford 1908: 3).

Clark was a self-focused, very ambitious, determined young man. Apparently aloof, cold and driven, stories describing his inscrutable, difficult-to-know nature abound. For example, as an undergraduate Warwick Bray[14] remembered

Clark rushing by in the hall exclaiming, "The difference between your generation and mine is that you're going to be cremated." "I never had any luck with Grahame," Bray continued, "I shaved my beard off in mid-term and for a long time he thought I was two people." Post-graduate students were referred to as "the crows on the wall."[15] Requesting references was sometimes awkward and daunting; "*Another* application, Miss Place?!"[16] An anonymous applicant for a post-graduate grant was told "You know, there's some good jobs in industry." Students invited to tea at Grahame Clark's house were greeted with "So, you think you did well in the exams?"[17] Such occasions "tended to be the opposite of relaxed."[18] Tea was often a sobering experience to which Jack Golson was "summoned on my own"; this only happened when Clark "had something serious to convey — advice about your future, particularly when he felt you were going in the wrong direction." This was "the way Grahame expressed his concern for his students when he felt you were worth supporting."[19] Golson distinctly remembers being pelted with gravel by Clark's children as he and his colleagues approached the entrance to the Clark home.[20]

There is, in fact, a persistent rumour that Clark, who had a reputation for being politically right-wing later in life, was a Nazi during the 1930s.[21] This is such a commonly held belief that any one who has done historical work on Clark has been repeatedly confronted by this statement. Both Peter Rowley-Conwy, who wrote the biographical section on Clark for Murray's encyclopedia[22] and Brian Fagan have discussed this rumour with me.[23]

There is no evidence to support this accusation. The term should not be interpreted as an accurate, literal description of Clark's politics but, instead, it should be seen as a metaphorical crack regarding Clark's behaviour. Mina Lethbridge,[24] who knew Clark in the late 1930s and would have had no reason to protect him, categorically denied that he was ever a Nazi sympathiser or Mosleyite. She stated that he was, in fact, "liberal" or "slightly left-wing". It was apparently a practice to call someone whom you disliked a "Nazi" during the decade before World War II, as when Reid Moir labelled Clark and the archaeologist, Charles Phillips, "those little Nazis".[25] I suggest that the Nazi rumour resulted from and

---

[12] According to archaeologist and Clark biographer, Brian Fagan (in conversation, 2000), Professor Sir John Grahame Douglas Clark preferred to be known simply as Grahame Clark.

[13] Board Minutes. CUA Min.V.92 various dates, 1926.

[14] Warwick Bray, Professor emeritus of Latin American Archaeology at the Institute of Archaeology at University College, London, in conversation, 2000.

[15] L. Pulvertaft-Green, Tripos 1948–49, in conversation, 1998.

[16] Robin Place Kenward took a First in the Tripos in 1947, personal correspondence, 2000.

[17] Professor emeritus of Archaeology at the University of New England at Armidale, Graham Connah, in conversation, 2000.

[18] Foundation Professor of Prehistory in the School of Pacific Studies at ANU, Jack Golson, in conversation, 1996.

[19] Jack Golson, personal correspondence, 17 March 1997.

[20] "This was the occasion of Dorothy Garrod's retirement, when Grahame

and Molly put on a garden party, to which archaeology students were invited. It was a lovely summer day . . . a group of us students were [arriving] . . . when we received a cascade of gravel from the three Clark children in the bushes," Jack Golson, in correspondence, 2003.

[21] This rumour was first reported to me by John Carman (in conversation, 1996) and Julia Roberts (in conversation, 1994).

[22] Murray 1999.

[23] Rowley-Conwy, personal correspondence, 1995 and Fagan, in conversation, 1996.

[24] Mina Lethbridge, in conversations, 1994, '95, '96. Mina Lethbridge considered Clark to be "rude".

[25] Steven J. Plunkett, author of the 1996 manuscript entitled "Prehistory at Ipswich: an Idea and its Consequences," in conversation, 1996. This is a quotation from Moir correspondence which Plunkett found in the Ipswich Museum. I thank Plunkett for this source.

was based on Clark's 1930s' personal severity and remoteness rather than his politics.

Clark apparently mellowed with age as he accumulated power. Glyn Daniel (1986: 212) did claim that Clark's years as Disney Professor of Archaeology were not entirely happy ones in the Department because of Clark's "alarming and chilling self-centredness." Discussions always focused on Clark and his work rather than on Departmental or even visitors' concerns.[26] However, Mrs Anne McBurney[27] stated that Clark was "very helpful" and congratulatory to Charles McBurney, her husband, as a post-graduate. By the 1950s, after Clark had been elected to the Disney Chair, Ray Inskeep found him considerate and attentive. When Inskeep came to Cambridge to apply for an adult bursary through the Cambridge Extramural Department, Clark "talked to me in his office, took me around the Museum, pointed out the major things of interest to me and encouraged me to publish. That was not the action of the kind of man who deserved the reputation of an unapproachable person. I was always grateful to him."[28] Robin Place recalled Clark taking a "lot of trouble to get a job for a badly shell-shocked chap who had been wounded at Anzio."[29] Merrick Posnansky wrote "I personally owe him a great deal for setting me up as an archaeologist. In the 1950s, jobs were hard to get and many students dropped out, abandoning their ambitions. Clark told me that if one wanted something really hard, one would get it."[30] Another famous post-graduate of the 1950s, John Evans, stated "I began very seriously to question if the Ph.D was worth carrying on and I nearly gave up. Clark persuaded me not to. After dinner at Peterhouse, he marched me up and down, talking to me about his own experiences when he had very nearly gone into the Coal Authority when he was my age. He really was remarkable."[31]

This evidence suggests that Clark began to exhibit benevolent qualities of leadership as he matured. He could be fatherly and caring toward a select few in whom he inspired loyalty.[32] However, his behaviour during much of his academic life does not compare favourably to Morrell's description of Liebig or to the fatherly personality of Henry De la Beche, the first Director of the Geological Survey of Great Britain. In his study of the Survey, Secord (1986:

251) details how De la Beche took young geologists under his wing. "Continue to think me a kind of daddy," De la Beche wrote to one protégé. "As Director De la Beche fostered this sense of familiar closeness." Survey *esprit de corps* was supported by dinner celebrations of communal solidarity, thoroughly enjoyed by all, facilitated by De la Beche's memorable sense of humour (Secord 1986: 240, 241). Clark, on the other hand, was known for his lack of humour or buoyancy.[33] He was described by one student as having "a permanent slice of lemon in his mouth."[34]

Clark's personal behaviour does not seem to conform to the expectations suggested by the literature on successful research schools. I would suggest that Clark's personality was not important in attracting students or in the process of institutionalisation of prehistory. It is clear that Clark's ideas, clarity and brilliance of presentation and definition of science was what attracted students and supported institutional gains. As stated by former undergraduate Bray, "Thinking about my days, I have come to the conclusion that Clark *as a person* was irrelevant. What he had to say was up-to-date, exciting, clearly and well argued. The books were fabulous; I used to read them for pure pleasure. It didn't matter that the man himself was cold as a crocodile."[35] Personal magnetism, or lack thereof, was not an issue. Instead of personality, Clark's innovative intellectual approach and how it evolved are crucial to understanding Cambridge prehistory in the 1930s. During this period, Clark changed his definitions, goals, methods, research questions and subjects studied. In order to examine the cause and effect of Clark's changing intellectual agenda, it is best to start with his conception and approach to archaeology prior to the establishment of the Fenland Research Committee.

"A Passionate Connoisseur of Flints"[36]

"As an undergraduate I had already been a passionate connoisseur [of flints] for more than a decade, a result, perhaps, of having attended boarding schools from the age of seven, each of them situated on chalk downs . . . rich in flint industries," Clark (1974: 35) has remarked. He published several lithic reports as a member of Marlborough School's Natural History Society while still a teenager.[37] Clark's interest in archaeology was also engendered by astute schoolmasters and by his

[26] Returning from Ghana in the late 1940s, former student, Shaw, found that after a precursory five minutes on Africa, the remaining hour centred on Clark. Shaw, in conversation, 2000.

[27] Mrs Charles McBurney, in conversation, 1996 and from personal correspondence 21 May 1996. Clark was very fond of Charles McBurney (Cambridge Professor of Quaternary Prehistory); "they got on very well."

[28] Ray Inskeep, Professor emeritus of Archaeology at Cape Town University, in conversation, 2000.

[29] Personal correspondence, 29 August 2000.

[30] Professor emeritus Merrick Posnansky, Department of History, University of California at Los Angeles, personal correspondence, 8/3/99.

[31] John Evans, Professor emeritus of European Prehistoric Archaeology at the Institute of Archaeology in London, in conversation, 2000.

[32] Mrs Anne McBurney, evidenced by letters to Charles McBurney from the 1940s and early 1950s, personal correspondence to author, 21 May 1996. Clark was supportive of McBurney, favouring his application, over Desmond Clark's, for the Faculty Lectureship in 1952.

[33] At a dinner party in the 1960s, Any Mellars remembers Clark using the term "frivolous". Mrs Mellars was surprised by this uncharacteristic, for Clark, expression. "I had no idea he knew the word" (in conversation, 1996).

[34] Dr Marie Lawrence, *née* Nutter, post-graduate student in Physical Anthropology in the early 1950s, in conversation, 1998.

[35] Bray, in correspondence, 10 November 2003.

[36] I published some of the following material in 1997 as "'A Passionate Connoisseur of Flints': an Intellectual Biography of the Young Grahame Clark based on his Pre-War Publications," *Archaeologia Polona* 35–6: 385–408 and "Grahame Clark's New Archaeology: the Fenland Research Committee and Cambridge Prehistory in the 1930s," *Antiquity* 71: 11–30.

[37] For information on Clark's young interest in archaeology and how it was encouraged while at St Wilfrid's see the Clark Archive CUL Add. 9409/30. Detailed notes on his life and interest in archaeology while at Marlborough are also in this archive, which has been carefully preserved by his Executors.

Map I

*N.B.   The area enclosed by a dotted line is covered on a larger scale by **Map II***

FIGURE XIII   Surface Finds, Typologies, Distributions and Relative Dates.
This map, from Clark's The Mesolithic Age in Britain,[38] shows the distribution of British Mesolithic sites as known in 1932. Prior to his association with the Fenland Committee, Clark relied on distributional mapping and typological analyses to ascertain relative dates for the surface lithics found at these sites. (By courtesy of Cambridge University Press and the estate of Professor Sir Grahame Clark.)

[38] For his Ph.D, Clark submitted a compilation of published and unpublished
research, including *The Mesolithic Age in Britain.*

association with the Sussex Archaeological Society. By the 1930s, he was a recognised lithics expert, often called upon to classify flint remains (Kingsford 1934: 53; Percival 1934: 251; Curwen 1931: 137–41, 1934: 121–3; Leaf 1938: 61).

The Mesolithic Age in Britain and several associated articles are characteristic of Clark's early work. At this point in his career, he defined the "science of archaeology . . . as the study of past distribution of culture-traits in time and space, and of the factors governing their distribution"(Clark 1933b: 323). One of his first published articles was a short study of the use, morphology, distribution and evolution of "horned hollow scrapers" (Clark 1927; 274) in which he traced the morphological changes in lithic forms collected as surface remains. "The phrase which marks the evolution of the [horned] type from the common hollow scraper is the reduction of superfluous flint from the sides of the protrusions," Clark (1927: 276) reasoned. In "Discoidal Polished Flint Knives: their Typology and Distribution", Clark (1928) again arranged the differing lithic forms into an evolutionary sequence based on subtle morphological changes. He then studied the distribution of the various forms. When mapped within Britain, the different categories of artefact forms fell into marked geographical areas and their distributions remarkably coincided with that of beakers produced by the early Bronze Age Beaker civilisation. "There does seem to be some ground for attributing the diffusion [of this type of knife] to the Beaker folk themselves," Clark (1928: 53) concluded.

Clark's typological analyses were based on two assumptions, both standard conventions of prehistoric archaeology at the time.[39] He assumed that artefacts could be arranged in evolutionary sequences by studying changes in attributes such as shape. For example, of two harpoons found in Yorkshire, Clark (1932: 17) wrote "technically the harpoons are more evolved than those from the Maglemose station of Svaerdborg, comparing more closely with those from Kunda of rather later date." Here, he was emphasising evidence of links between British Mesolithic assemblages and the western Baltic by comparing artefact forms. Clark also took an assemblage as equivalent to a culture and equated a culture with a people. Two types of microlithic industry, one "broad blade" with non-geometric types, the other "narrow blade" with frequent geometric forms, had been discovered in the Marsden area of the Pennines. Clark (1932) concluded that there were two peoples in the region. "Thus, whereas the non-geometric folk almost invariably utilized rather poor whitish to pale grey flint, the geometric folk employed . . . a smooth semi-translucent" (Clark 1932: 26).

As was common practice in the early 1930s, Clark used mapping of categorised artefact forms to suggest relative dates for assemblages. The non-geometric and geometric assemblages were dramatically different typologically, exploited different types of flint supply but, when locations of these two types were mapped, they occupied the same

region. Clark concluded that the industries could be arranged chronologically, with the less evolved broad blade preceding the more sophisticated narrow blades. The use of concurrent mapping of artefacts had been pioneered by Fox in his Ph.D thesis (1923), *The Archaeology of the Cambridge Region* and discussed by Childe (1935: 6) in his Presidential address to the Prehistoric Society: "The technique of archaeological mapping which has been so splendidly developed in this country thanks to Crawford, Curwen, Chitty, Clark, Fox, Phillips and others is very helpful both in deciding to what culture a type belongs and in determining the chronological relation between several cultures."

The question of the origin of these widely accepted assumptions and methods is not discussed in histories of archaeology. I suggest that Clark and others might have been influenced by Oswald Menghin and the ethnographic method and theory of the diffusionist Vienna School of *Kulturkreislehre*. Both Childe (1931b) and Clark (1931) had enthusiastically reviewed Menghin's massive 1931 tome on the prehistory of Europe, *Weltgeschichte der Steinzeit*, and Childe (1933: 182), in his review of *The Mesolithic Age in Britain,* had pointed out the influence of Menghin and the school of "culture cycles" on Clark's analyses. As described by the American anthropologist, Clyde Kluckhohn (1936), the method and theory of *Kulturkreislehre* were as follows. The prehistorian or ethnographer must first know one area intimately, taking into account "not merely typological resemblances of a single trait but also the whole number of such similarities between traits or groups of traits" (Kluckhohn 1936: 163). Neighbouring regions must also be studied intensively. The student should make distribution maps, proceed to analyse the distribution of culture traits, and must be concerned with whether or not the culture is relatively homogeneous. If a culture seems to exhibit the same combination of characteristics as another, a genetic connection between the two should be assumed. The main goal is "the establishment of spatial and temporal distribution [which reveals] that certain culture elements appear in association in a fashion too consistent to be fortuitous" (Kluckhohn 1936: 162). Such geographical culture complexes were called *Kulturkreise* and might sometimes exist contemporaneously in one region. At that point, it might be possible to suggest a relative chronology. This approach, as described by Kluckhohn, paralleled the practice of Clark and others in England in the early 1930s.

Clark first departed from common practice in *The Mesolithic Age in Britain* and, to some degree again, in two articles on the classification of lithics published in 1933 and 1934. Here, he first consciously used what he defined as a scientific approach.

3.2   Clark and "Men in White Coats"[40]

At some point in *The Mesolithic Age in Britain*, Clark's style of presentation and reasoning seemed to diverge notice-

---

[39] For example, Gordon Childe (1925) used similar typological methods in *The Dawn of European Civilization.*

[40] "What archaeology needs is men in white coats [*i.e.* scientists]," Clark to West at Star Carr in 1951 (West, in conversation, 2003).

ably from his colleagues. In an era before the excavation of stratified Mesolithic sites, accomplished famously at Star Carr from 1949–51, and long before the radiocarbon-based chronologies of the 1950s and 1960s, Clark became aware that he must use every possible line of evidence because the Mesolithic industries studied were mainly surface finds "collected on an unscientific and selective principle" with little or no evidence of stratigraphic succession (Clark 1932: 92).

Clark began to argue explicitly for the inclusion of a wide range of evidence when attempting to classify and date Mesolithic industries. It was important to consider the "character of the industry" rather than "selected types" (Clark 1932: 111). The lithic industry should be considered as a whole and all lithic categories must be studied. The presence or absence of tool types may be recorded but conclusions should not be based on the presence of one characteristic tool alone. Several lines of evidence must be used to support conclusions. State of preservation of artefacts, percentage of different artefact types present, material and technique used in the manufacture of the tools, associated finds, and archaeological remains from the vicinity must all be considered before stating results. Lithic analysis was then supported with other evidence such as the distribution and patination of artefacts. Several lines of inference were always to be used to enhance conclusions.

Clark defined this analytical approach as scientific reasoning. He hoped to use independent information from varied sources of data in order to support hypotheses. The science of archaeology required an argument supported by evidence explicitly used for stated goals. When separate lines of inference converged, Clark felt that his argument was greatly strengthened. In comparison, when Williamson (1930) and E.C. Curwen[41] (1931, 1934) included sections on lithics, pottery, charcoals, iron slag or animal bones in their excavation reports, there was no effort to reason multilaterally. Reasoning from different lines of evidence was not explicitly championed. The summary and conclusion sections of the report were short and not emphasised. Information was not manipulated to make a specific argument. The word "science" was never used.

Again, the influential pair, H.J.E. Peake and O.G.S. Crawford[42] (1922: 509–10) attempted to use several specialist sources of data to date the flint assemblage of *tranchet*-edged axes and non-geometric points found under peat at Thatcham in south-

eastern England. In a section entitled "general remarks", A.S. Kennard reported that the shells found in the peat were pre-Roman, "Dr Andrews of the British Museum" studied the animal bones and Crawford compared the Thatcham types of implements with similar ones from a Yorkshire site found under peat where the predominant tree was *Pinus sylvestris.* This implied that both the Yorkshire site and Thatcham might be contemporary with the Late Shell-mound Period in Scandinavia. This was considered interesting work at the time but Crawford's report was not consciously organised around the idea of an argued thesis. As with the Curwens, Crawford's "general remarks" were a broad, discursive presentation without an effort to establish certainty or to win the reader over to a single point of view.

Clark seems to have taken what was an implicit, incipient way of thinking and of presenting research, articulated it strongly and clearly, and then called this science.[43] He explicitly, rather than implicitly, argued a thesis and supported it with several sources of evidence. In order to support his claim, for example, that Grimes Graves and Cissbury flint mines were Neolithic in origin, Clark (1932: 111); Clark and Piggott (1933) compared typological lithic analyses with the results of pottery, mollusca and fauna studies, finding that all "lines of evidence" were in favour of a Neolithic date. Here, Clark sought to confirm his hypothesis by presenting different results which supported each other.[44] By using several types of data, he hoped to set up constraints and check his results.

This type of reasoning and argumentation may have been modelled on the 1923 published version of Cyril Fox's acclaimed thesis, *The Archaeology of the Cambridge Region; A Topographical Study.*[45] Fox (1923: xxi; xxiv; 314) had organised his book into clear sections beginning with the "Object of the Research," followed by "Method". He cogently presented findings and analyses, ending with a separate section marked "Conclusions" in which he concisely and clearly argued his thesis that the Cambridge region should be divided into primary and secondary settlements areas.

In the 1920s, the general euphoria following World War I had some relevance to Cambridge academic life and its plethora of new degrees. By the 1930s, however, as the Archaeological and Anthropological Tripos course became established, the social and intellectual influences on Clark were localised. It

---

[41] Dr Eliot Curwen, a former medical missionary in China and his son, physician E. Cecil Curwen, who was at Cambridge with Clark, were skilful archaeologists. Clark (1989a: 50) claimed to have learned to excavate from 1928–30 while at the Curwens' excavations of the Iron Age fort known as the Trundle. Future members of the Fenland Research Committee, Charles Phillips and Stuart Piggott were also present. Clark dug at the Whitehawk Neolithic causewayed camp excavation as well.

[42] Crawford preceded Clark at Marlborough and was well remembered there by Clark's tutors (Clark Archive. CUL Add 9409/30). Charles Phillips (1951), Stuart Piggott (1989), Christopher Hawkes (1989) and Grahame Clark (in conversation, 20 April 1994) all claimed that Crawford had a deciding intellectual influence on their archaeological lives. Crawford was remembered by Clark as "one of my first heroes" (Clark Archive. CUL Add. 9409/30).

[43] Alan Macfarlane, after reading this chapter of my original thesis, com-

mented as follows. "It all seems to be kind of a status game and perhaps to do with funding. Colin Renfrew in the 1980s managed to get archaeology re-classified as a 'light science' so its student and other grants (needing labs) would be higher. I am called 'Professor of Anthropological Science', at the suggestion of Professor Ernest Gellner, in the belief that this might add to the status (and maybe funding) of our Department" (Macfarlane, in correspondence, 30 September 2003). Macfarlane went on to mention that "The idea that 'multilateral thinking' makes something scientific is extremely naive. It is what all good historians have done for centuries, without pretending to be scientific." Macfarlane gave invaluable advice on this and the previous chapter.

[44] A Neolithic date is today considered correct.

[45] This was the first Ph.D thesis in archaeology approved by the Board of Archaeology and Anthropology, and likely the first Ph.D in prehistoric archaeology in Britain.

would seem that it was the milieu of Cambridge which supported Clark's quest for scientific clarity. His Ph.D degree demanded an argumentative, narrowed, very specialised, reasoned presentation of evidence. Although still a new degree an example of how to do a thesis was set by Fox. In a time of expanding scientific activity and creativity, so well documented by Leedham-Green's (1996) history,[46] the University setting offered the intellectual models and motivation Clark needed. I would suggest that the Downing site presented Clark with both the intellectual and the social structures necessary to support his definition and use of scientific reasoning.

Following a thesis format, Clark, in the first pages of *The Mesolithic Age in Britain,* set out the ideas he wished to argue: a Mesolithic Age, distinct from the preceding Palaeolithic and following Neolithic, did in fact exist and could be distinguished by characteristic lithic assemblages. He suggested that the most striking feature of the Mesolithic was the remarkable spread of microlithic industries (small points, triangles and crescents) across Europe. In addition to distinctive industries, "The Mesolithic Age as a whole is demarcated from the Upper Palaeolithic by a great geological and climatic divide" (Clark 1932: 6). Broad shifts from Upper Palaeolithic to Mesolithic were caused by climatic and environmental factors. "The drastic [post-glacial] environmental changes playing upon human cultures of relatively simple character, were conducive to developments of far-reaching importance," Clark (1932: 6) wrote. The Mesolithic could be recognised not only chronologically and industrially but also by distinctive environmental changes. This definition and the published version of his Ph.D were well received; "for an exhaustive exposition and sound interpretation of the mesolithic industries of Britain . . . the book is indispensable and admirably fills a real gap," wrote Childe (1933a: 18).

Clark implied that his definition of the Mesolithic was controversial. He cleverly used the hiatus theory as a foil to enhance his argument.[47] Actually, Clark's thesis was not as controversial as suggested. The Mesolithic was already recognised as a time and/or cultural stage by many. R.A.S. Macalister had a generous section on the Mesolithic Period in *A Text-book of European Archaeology* in 1921. Burkitt (1926a: 8–49) devoted an entire chapter to "Mesolithic Times" in *Our Early Ancestors* and had also written a solidly descriptive summary of the Azilian, Tardenoisian, Maglemosean, Shell Mound, Asturian and Campignian "cultures" as comprising the Mesolithic Period in an article published in the *Proceedings of the Prehistoric Society of East Anglia* (Burkitt 1926b). He had suggested that it would be convenient to create a Mesolithic stage to include "all those industries and

cultures . . . that start at the end of the Magdalenian times on the change of climate" (Burkitt 1926a: 4). Childe (1931a: 347) had published an intensive study reviewing the extensive Scandinavian literature on the Forest Cultures of "the Mesolithic phase". Leading archaeologists, such as the Scot, Robert Munro, Hugo Obermaier of Spain, the famous Polish prehistorian, Leon Kozlowski ,and numerous local workers in Britain, such as Francis Buckley,[48] had used the term and studied the Mesolithic as an age and/or culture.

Nevertheless, Clark felt that he was "in at the beginning".[49] He was indeed the first to systematise, synthesise and organise the vast and varied material collected by many others and to propose such a clearly articulated definition. *The Mesolithic Age in Britain* is now viewed as forming a seminal boundary, marking the beginning of British Mesolithic studies. The current Disney Professor of Archaeology, Colin Renfrew (1986: 238) has stated, "Grahame Clark is widely esteemed as the leading prehistorian of our time . . . for his pioneering work on the Mesolithic period." Specialist, T.D. Price (1983: 761), considers Clark the "doyen of Mesolithic studies".

In addition to multilateral reasoning, Clark also used extensive categorisations as the basis for his approach to science. Clark proposed that evidence in archaeology must, above all, be systematised. Good science was ordered clearly. This point is explicitly made in his many books and typological studies and can be demonstrated by an examination of examples of his work. In "The Classification of a Microlithic Culture; the Tardenoisian of Horsham", Clark (1933c: 55) categorised microlithic finds from eight sites in Sussex in order to provide an "objective basis for comparison" to other collections. Microliths were sorted into eight classes on the bases of morphological and technological differences: Class A contained microliths blunted obliquely down part of one edge; Class B were blunted straight down one edge; and C, blunted down one edge and across their base, etc. The simplest forms belonged to A, B, and C; the more evolved to Class D. Once the microliths were sorted, the eight sites could be compared by studying the proportions of different classes which occurred at each location. The substantial uniformity between inventories implied one culture, which Clark referred to as the Horsham Culture. Again, Clark (1934) described derivative forms of a type of British arrowhead, the *Petit Tranchet*. Various classes were identified and a basic general parent form, Class A, was recognised. All subsequent forms, Classes B-I, were apparently derived from Class A. Since Classes B and C were always associated with Neolithic finds, they could be used for dating purposes. Classifying arrowheads in this way could therefore have "chronological value for excavators" (Clark 1934: 33).

---

[46] Leedham-Green (1996: 195) argues that the Ph.D was in fact established as a result of pressure from Cambridge's scientists: "It was among the pure scientists, probably, conscious as they were of their international standing, that the need was most felt for some more telling inducement for overseas researchers to come to Cambridge than the right to take a tripos after two years, or the award of a BA for a dissertation."

[47] The hiatus theory suggested that there was a break in occupation between the Upper Palaeolithic and the Neolithic periods and denied the existence

of possible transitional industries.

[48] A well-respected "amateur", Buckley had been the first to distinguish narrow from broad blade industries in the Pennines Hills and had shown the exact similarity between the earliest Pennines Mesolithic assemblages and those of the Tardenoisean in Belgium (Buckley 1921, 1924).

[49] Clark, in conversation, 20 April 1994; "At my time of life, it naturally happens that, in a subject as young as prehistory, one is willy-nilly bound to become an historical monument" (Clark, personal correspondence, 15 June 1988).

In *The Mesolithic Settlement of Northern Europe*, Clark (1936) systematised the antler and bone artefacts from the Maglemosean assemblages by dividing them into ten classes based on probable function. The tenth class, for example, was comprised of bone points. Such bone points appeared in many forms. Clark divided the points into 25 classes according to differences in shape and then studied the distribution of each classified shape, finding that certain forms occurred generally over all of northern Europe. This implied to Clark (1936a: 115) that the Maglemose was a uniform culture over a wide area. These lithic typologies developed by Clark were used until recently. Forty-three years after their publication, S. Palmer (1977: 15) could write in her survey of British Mesolithic cultures, "Professor Clark's definition and classification of British microlithic types . . . still form a basis for the assessment of lithic industries."[50]

Clark's mode of presentation, style of writing and stress upon systemisation of evidence and use of "science" differed dramatically from Burkitt's approach. Burkitt presented ideas on the basis of authority, not argument. As explained above, he was proud to be "Breuil's pupil" and, with sincere loyalty and faithfulness, disseminated Breuil's, Obermaier's and Cartailhac's educated opinions and research. He summarised others' material either for the sake of discussion or for the edification of the audience. Burkitt may have felt it rude or self-centred to present a personal opinion too forcefully. Defending a thesis would not have been appropriate. One did not need a platform to further one's career. In fact, Burkitt never explicitly argued his own views; in addition, he was consistently courteous in dealing with the views of others. For example, when reporting the infamous Glozel, apparently forged, artefacts, Burkitt (1926c: 221) graciously wrote, "Dr Morlet has done me the honour of forwarding me" information about his finds which were allegedly of "a very early date". "I am bound to say that I am a bit skeptical," Burkitt (1926c: 221) wrote, but even if it should prove that the Glozel finds "are really much later in date, it will not detract one whit from their importance as the objects themselves seem to be of very considerable interest." We know, however, from private correspondence[51] that Burkitt thought Dr Morlet to be completely mad.[52]

Clark was well-known for his "easy and lucid style" (Curwen 1941: 203) of writing. Burkitt, in comparison, wrote informally by today's academic standards; he often digressed or proceeded peripatetically through a subject. He made a concerted effort gently to educate and to discuss engagingly rather than to argue a point. In his descriptions, for example, of beautiful Magdalenian cave paintings and

dancing sorcerers,[53] Burkitt appealed to the emotion and imagination of his readers rather than their ability to reason. Multiple lines of evidence to support a conclusion were never a concern and never explicitly detailed. He wrote discursively for a wide audience and made no attempt to publish systematisations and classifications. Burkitt seemed uninterested in ordering the world around him. He never used the word "science".

Since so little research on the history of archaeology exists, and since no one else has investigated the development of British academic scientific archaeology in the early twentieth century, it is difficult to know for certain how representative Burkitt's and Clark's approaches were for their respective decades. However, as one example, we may observe the immensely popular 1920s books of Gordon Childe. If reviews of Childe's *The Dawn of European Civilisation* (1925) are considered, it appears that the reviewers considered Childe's subtle, gentlemanly presentation to be one of the most valued attributes of his work. "He presents us with the facts on both sides, and sometimes even goes out of his way to warn us of the objections to the particular hypothesis he adopts" wrote Crawford (1926: 90). In his 1929 review of Childe's *The Danube in Prehistory*, W.A. Heurtley (1931: 124) observed "Above all, one must respect the disarming modesty with which the author expresses his own opinions as well as the courteous deference with which he treats the opinions of others." Preserving an open mind was complimented and admired. Inclusion of detail and thorough treatment of others' views was valued. Focused scientific argumentation was less important.

Clark, on the other hand, was a 1930s Cambridge Ph.D man, living amongst the "caves" of Downing Street, surrounded by scientists from the Sedgwick Museum of Geology and the School of Botany. The Downing site presented Clark with both the intellectual and social models necessary to support scientific thinking and the sharing of ideas and dreams.

3.3 Tea and Scientists

Tea

The tea-room had been set up by elegant Curator Louis Clarke for students, staff, visitors and academics from adjacent faculties to assemble casually. By the early 1930s, with an increasing number of post-graduate researchers present, tea seems to have become more than a place for sophisticated banter and more than simply a space in which peaceful friendships could be formed and administrative decisions settled in a civilised manner. As in other depart-

---

[50] However, some of Clark's efforts at classification were criticised in the 1930s. In his report on the excavation of the Arminghall henge monument, Clark (1936d) placed the site in a category he created comprising henge monuments with a similar layout, all of which he argued had been used as "sanctuaries". Clark drew a distinction between henge sacred monuments and disc, bell and palisade barrows from the Netherlands which he claimed had been used as burial sites only. The archaeologist, A.E. van Giffen (1938), strongly disagreed, suggesting that Clark's criteria for classification were arbitrary and baseless.

[51] Burkitt Family Archive.

[52] Most observers today would agree with Burkitt's private assessment. For an up-to-date examination of the Glozel controversy see Bahn and Renfrew (1999).

[53] "As we wander to-day through the weird and silent caves which Palaeolithic Man decorated with the wonderful paintings and engravings of animals, we seem to see the sorcerer himself leading the hunter who is about to perform or witness the magic ritual . . ." (Burkitt 1921b: 183).

T.P. FILE

Vol. x + 1, No. 1   27 Nov., 1939

THE
TEA PHYTOLOGIST

FOUNDED IN 1912

EDITED BY
E. F. CALAMENTHA, P.M.

CONTENTS

CAMBRIDGE
JOHN ARLISS
ST. TIBBS ROW

AGENTS IN TRINIDAD, TORONTO, TRUMPINGTON

All plants preserved
All funds conserved

Price One Shilling & Sixpence
Subscription Price, Two Shillings ; Composition Fee :—Fifteen Guineas, C.O.D.

PRINTED IN GREAT BRITAIN

" VERT, A ST. ANTHONY'S CROSS ARGENT, ON A CHIEF OF THE
SECOND. PER FESSE, THREE CROSSES BOTONNY OF THE FIRST."

SUPPORTERS : TWO RAMPANT HELIANTHS, ORE HUMANO, PROPER.
MOTTO : " HINC LUCEM ET POCULA THEÆ."

EDITORIAL

LONG years again have passed away
   Since last we sang our merry lay ;
   But now the sunbeams once more see
The pages of a new *T.P.*

Behold, the slight Botanic Muse
Has not grown feeble with disuse.
Enough ! We hope that you'll agree
No sugar's needed with the tea.

New faces shine on every hand
And strangers walk about the land.
We welcome all ; to prove it, we
Invite them all to **COME TO TEA.**

FIGURE XIV *The Tea Phytologist. (Title page, Courtesy of Richard West and the Clare Archivist Mrs S. Johnson, the Clare College Archives and the Master and Fellows of Clare College.)*
"We welcome all; to prove it, we
Invite you all to COME TO TEA"
(E.F. Calamentha, Editor, The Tea Phytologist, founded 1908.)[54]
Produced by members of the Downing Street Botany School, The Tea Phytologist was a light-hearted version of the innovative and respected scientific journal, The New Phytologist. Clark's "men in white coats", experts in pollen analysis, were members of Harry Godwin's school of research. The Godwins were visitors to the Museum tea-room and founders of the interdisciplinary Fenland Research Committee.

ments, tea became an important social arena for scientific talk. A gentlemanly time for home-made cake began to provide a safe space to share expertise. Research friendships and working alliances were formed; intellectual plans and thoughts appear to have been discussed with ease and friendliness. Attendance at tea and later membership in the new Fenland Research Committee were at least partially based on what a person could contribute intellectually to discussion. Louis Clarke had successfully founded a place were the emerging experts could get to know each other and share new ideas.

Research school investigations would lead us to suspect this. Although not referring to tea, historian Joel Hagen (1993: 194) argues, in his study of the internal dynamics

of the Frederic Clements' school of ecology, that the social context created by small informal groups may "greatly speed the conceptual development of a science". Ideas may be modified and transmitted much more quickly than they can through formal channels. Settings such as tea-rooms may offer the opportunity for groups to respond to changing methods and ideas.[55] Such co-operation could play a crucial role in establishing a research tradition (Hagen 1993: 194).

Studies of the geography of knowledge are also relevant. Shapin (1998: 8) states that his work on seventeenth-century English science points to gentlemanly identity as a "powerful answer to the question of whom to trust" but "twentieth-century scientists are not gentlemen . . . solu-

---

[54] The 1908 issue states that the *Tea Phytologist* was a "private botanical journal edited by members of the Cambridge University Botany School Tea Club."

[55] Macfarlane points out that "in many disciplines the same function

was performed by the pub, certainly with the famous Eagle and DNA and the various pubs which Oxford and Cambridge anthropologists have frequented, ending up with the King's College Bar in our Department" (in correspondence, 2003).

tions to the questions of trust appear to be different; they seem to point towards *expertise* and the institutions that produce and vouch for expertise. But modern science is no less trust-dependent than in the past." Certainly the trust-dependent side of archaeological practice was serviced by a functioning tea-room.

The Fenland Research Committee was set up so that diverse experts could investigate the English Fenland, a region of low-lying wetlands north of Cambridge which promised special opportunities for geological, botanical and archaeological field research. Grahame Clark's first entry in the Committee's Minutes stated,[56] "The desire to form a committee for Fenland research was first voiced by archaeological workers who sadly felt the lack of essential geological, botanical and zoological knowledge." This committee was "to be known as 'The Fenland Research Committee' with the investigation of the history of the fen deposits as its aim and object." The Committee's first meeting occurred on 7 June 1932, in the Upper Parlour of Peterhouse. Those present were: Miles Burkitt; transport manager at the Ely Beet-sugar Factory Major G.E. Fowler; Tom Lethbridge; J. Reid Moir; Grahame Clark; Dr and Mrs Godwin; Foraminifera specialist from the Sedgwick Museum, W.A. Macfadyen; Trinity Classicist, E.J.A. Kenny; and Charles Phillips. C.S. Leaf[57] and A.G. (Bertie) Brighton, the young, recently appointed Curator of the Sedgwick Museum, were elected *in absentia*.

There is evidence that the idea of establishing such a Committee was birthed in the Museum tea-room. Importantly, according to C.W. Phillips's unpublished memoirs,[58] all the "archaeological workers, who sadly felt" the need for an organisation of specialists, met together for daily tea in the Museum for several years preceding the formation of the Committee. When, in 1929, Phillips[59] became acquainted with Clark, he felt fortunate since Clark "had a proper status in the official world of archaeology at Cambridge and was already a well known figure in the Museum . . . through him I was admitted to a group of teachers, pupils, and others who met mid-morning in the Museum for tea and conversation." Phillips states that the people who attended tea together were Miles Burkitt, Tom Lethbridge,[60] C.S. Leaf, E.J.A. Kenny, Grahame Clark and, sometimes, the Godwins. All were future founding mem-

bers of the Committee. Although Phillips did not mention Gordon Fowler and Louis Clarke being present, we know from correspondence to Louis Clarke,[61] that Fowler was consistently around the Museum reporting Fen finds and discussing Fenland archaeology with staff; he would certainly have been at tea.[62] Also, we know that Louis Clarke joined the Committee at its second meeting[63] and was active financially behind the scenes from the beginning.[64] He and Assistant Curator, Maureen O'Reilly, were very supportive to new initiatives at the Museum.

In commenting on these early years, Phillips[65] wrote, "It was being increasingly realized that major archaeological problems could only be solved with speed and efficiency by co-operative effort." "It was a small beginning but we needed a broad front," Clark stated.[66] "A remarkable revitalisation was becoming manifest in British archaeology where professionals and amateurs were becoming acutely aware of the great advantages that could follow integration with the natural sciences," (Godwin 1978: 7). In announcing the formation of the Committee, Burkitt (1932a: 453) wrote, "for some time past several people at Cambridge have felt that a research committee of experts in the various branches of science required should be formed to undertake a comprehensive study . . . for a proper study of the fens, many lines of investigation are required."

Scientists

Certainly Shapin's suggestion that modern scientific co-operation involves sharing expertise is upheld by the tea-room clientele and by the make-up of the emerging Fenland Committee. Brief biographical sketches of Committee members Phillips, Fowler, Leaf, Lethbridge and the Godwins are here used to illustrate the diversity of the experts involved.

Phillips was one emerging specialist who played an important role in the Committee as its Treasurer and expert on Romano-British archaeological investigation. According to his memoirs,[67] he had been attracted to archaeology as a child but when he came up to Cambridge in 1919, the Archaeology and Anthropology specialisation was "a new thing and largely directed to preparing for entry into the Colonial Service" (Phillips 1989: 35). He, therefore, accepted a History Exhibition, and upon graduation found work as

---

[56] Fenland Research Committee Minute Book: 7 June 1932. CUL Add. 9426.

[57] According to Clark, Leaf was a First World War veteran who had suffered "shell shock". Clark, in conversation, 1994.

[58] I quote these memoirs with the permission of the Phillips family.

[59] Phillips became acquainted with Clark following a meeting called to establish an alternative to the Cambridge Antiquarian Society. This meeting had been organized by N. Teulon Porter, a member of the Society. Neither Clark nor Phillips were impressed and neither joined. There is some correspondence from Porter to Fowler, concerning extinct waterways, among the papers in Mina and Tom Lethbridge's trunk. Quotation from Phillips' memoirs [1975–80]: 182.

[60] In his unpublished Memoirs, Tom Lethbridge also mentioned the tea-room several times as a centre for discussion.

[61] Fowler to Clarke, CUMAA letter boxes for 1929, '30, '31.

[62] Leslie J. Oakley, who has done biographical research on Fowler, confirmed Fowler's close involvement with the Museum and Louis Clarke (in conversation, 1996).

[63] Fenland Research Committee Minute Book: October 1932. CUL Add. 9426.

[64] The CUMAA letter boxes have Phillips's correspondence, including a letter to Clarke, requesting financial support for the Welney excavation that was sponsored by the Committee to investigate Romano-British settlement of the Fen. Clarke, who joined the Committee in October 1932, gave £10, which corroborates Piggott's (in conversation, 1994) observation that Louis Clarke was "always good for a fiver".

[65] Phillips memoirs [1975–80]: 234.

[66] In conversation, 1994.

[67] Phillips memoirs [1975–80]: 141.

Wyman Abbott	Peterborough	Peterborough archaeology
D.F.W. Baden-Powell MA FGS	Hinksey Hill, Oxford	geology
H.L. Bradfer-Lawrence FSA	North Wootton, Lynn	Kings Lynn archaeology
A.G. Brighton MA	Sedgwick Museum, University of Cambridge	geology
M.C. Burkitt FSA	Grantchester	archaeology
J.G.D. Clark BA *(Secretary)*	Peterhouse [college], University of Cambridge	archaeology
L.C.G. Clarke MA FSA	Museum of Archaeology & Ethnology, University of Cambridge	archaeology
Lt-Col. J.E.E. Craster	Cambridge	surveying
O.G.S. Crawford BA FSA	Ordnance Survey, Southampton	archaeology, maps, air-photographs
Wing-Commander F.P. Don	Cambridge	air-photographs
Curtis Edwards	Curator, Wisbech Museum, Cambridgeshire	Wisbech area archaeology
Major G. Fowler *(Vice-President)*	Ely, Cambridgeshire	extinct waterways
Dr Cyril Fox FSA	Director, National Museum of Wales	archaeology
Dr & Mrs H. Godwin	Cambridge	peat
F. Hanley MA	Department of Agriculture, Cambridge	soils
C.F.C. Hawkes FSA MA	Department of British & Medieval Antiquities, British Museum	archaeology (Early Iron Age, Romano-British)
Dr Wilfrid Jackson	University Museum, Manchester	domestic animal bones
Professor O.T. Jones FRS	Sedgwick Museum, University of Cambridge	geology
A.S. Kennard FGS	Beckenham, Kent	mollusca
A. Kenny BA	Trinity College, University of Cambridge	hydraulics
C. Leaf MA	Cambridge	archaeology, topography
T.C. Lethbridge MA FSA	Shelford, Cambridgeshire	archaeology (Anglo-Saxon)
Dr W.A. Macfadyen	Sedgwick Museum, University of Cambridge	foraminifera
Reid Moir FRAI	Ipswich, Suffolk	archaeology
C.W. Phillips MA *(Treasurer)*	Selwyn College, University of Cambridge	archaeology, Lincolnshire
Dr A.C. Seward FRS *(President)*	Downing College, University of Cambridge	paleo-botany
Professor Swinnerton FRS	Nottingham University	geology, S. Lincolnshire
F.M. Walker	Manea, Cambridgeshire	Manea archaeology

TABLE 1. *Membership of the Fenland Committee, from a list made after its second meeting on 15 October 1932. Found in the Sedgwick Museum's 'Macfadyen Dead File', this list accompanied a note from Clark soliciting the 70/- daily necessary to begin test-boring at Plantation Farm, the Committee's first excavation.*

By courtesy of Dr David Norman and Mr Roderic Long of the Cambridge Sedgwick Museum of Geology.

FIGURE XV Membership of the Fenland Committee, from the list made after its second meeting on 15 October 1932, shows the significant variety of scientific talent involved. At peak membership, the Committee benefited from the participation of 42 specialists, combining the resources of many disciplines. Meeting biannually throughout the 1930s, the Committee remained free of institutional control until it dissolved and was recreated after the Second World War, in 1948, as the Sub-department of Quaternary Research with Dr Godwin as Director. The above list, found in the Sedgwick Museum's "Macfadyen Dead File", accompanied a note from Clark soliciting the 70 shillings daily necessary to begin test-boring at Plantation Farm, the Committee's first excavation. By courtesy of Dr David Norman and Mr Roderic Long of the Cambridge Sedgwick Museum of Geology.

a history lecturer and coach for Ordinary Degree students. In 1927, Crawford enlisted Phillips as one of his volunteer "archaeological ferrets"[68], suggesting that he revise the state of Lincolnshire's field archaeology and maps. Because of this work, before the Committee was formed, Phillips had already "received a large amount of air photographic cover of the central Fenland from Crawford for use. I could not fail to see the evidence of farmsteads, fields, connecting droveways, and extinct waterways . . . over many areas from which the peat had been removed by modern cultivation." The progressive disappearance of peat "had begun to reveal the Roman pattern of settlement once more."[69] As founding member, Phillips stressed the importance of air photography, the possibility of co-operation with the RAF, and the need to obtain a set of 6″ and 2″ Ordnance maps. He and O.G.S. Crawford, when Crawford first attended in June 1933, set up a sub-committee to investigate the Roman occupation of the Fens. In addition, Phillips had already, while excavating for the Bristol Spelaeological Society during the late 1920s, co-operated with several specialists, including J.W. Jackson, a faunal expert and geologist from the Manchester Museum, A.C. Kennard, the mollusca analyst, and J.C. Maby who studied charcoal; all were future members of the Fenland Committee.

[68] O.G.S. Crawford, as Archaeology Officer to the Ordnance Survey, "set up a personal network of young people whom he used to call his archaeological ferrets and when he wanted, he was in the course of map revision, and when he wanted some entries checked and he knew someone reliable, he'd send you the maps and say 'Do go and have a look at so and so'" (Stuart Piggott to Julia Roberts, in interview, 1994).
[69] Phillips memoirs [1975–80]: 237.

FIGURE XVI   A recent aerial view of the Fenland, showing the meandering banks of silt locally known as roddons that represent the extinct drainage of the Fens. (By courtesy of the Cambridge University Collection of Air Photographs, Unit for Landscape Modelling.)

FIGURE XVII   Aerial photo of the Fenland north of Cambridge with the locations of Plantation Farm, "the first considerable enterprise undertaken by the Committee in the Autumn of 1932" (Phillips 1951: 263) marked in ink by Clark. (By courtesy of the MAA.)

Gordon Fowler was another budding expert and indispensable to the formation of the Committee; he soon become its Vice-President and is still pleasantly remembered. "Oh! Fowler! Fowler was great fun!"[70] He was an enormously energetic man who was interested in archaeology, geology, and botany, "the most enthusiastic collector of objects and information you could possibly have wanted".[71] As Transport Manager for the Ely Beet-sugar Factory, Fowler was required to collect beetroot promptly from local farmers by using the waterways. He therefore had an intimate knowledge of the Fens and the people who lived there.[72] "He was very widely known" (Godwin 1978: 46), on good terms with the local drainage authorities, gave lectures at village gatherings on Fenland archaeology and geology, and could always be counted on to recruit labour or gain permission for Fenland research projects.[73] "Few new [archaeological or geological] discoveries failed to come to his notice. When a site he had visited seemed to merit closer attention telephone calls would inform the members . . . and next day with gum-boots, spades and peat-indifferent clothing a small party would *rendezvous* at some agreed point," remembered Godwin (1978: 46).

Many suggest that it was through Fowler that the Committee began. He "was to act as catalyst and bring a number of workers from different disciplines to work on Fenland problems," wrote Phillips.[74] "He succeeded in linking up and co-ordinating workers in different branches of science, and they have now formed themselves into a Fenland Research Committee," commented Geologist James Wordie (1934: 38) during discussion following a 1934 presentation

by Fowler to the Geographical Society. In this discussion, Fowler had described four types of extinct waterways he had identified during years of Fenland residency. During the course of his work, he had "noticed meandering banks of silt locally known as roddons, which formed a connected system . . . [and] rose a number of feet above the surrounding levels." When viewed from the air and plotted on maps, they appeared to be artificial or natural drainage courses running from higher ground. In 1932, Fowler (1932: 212) published the first of several articles in which he stated that the "roddons evidently represent the natural drainage of the Fens" and that their raised position was due to differential shrinkage.[75] The discovery of an extinct water system "is much the most important geological discovery round Cambridge within the last generation," commented Wordie (1934: 38). It should be realized that his work (Fowler 1933, 1934) of "mapping and transfer to the six-inch Ordnance Survey map was done under fearfully daunting field conditions." The recovery and documentation of the Fenland's waterways was Fowler's "very special contribution to Fenland research," observed Godwin (1978: 81).

As evidenced by correspondence,[76] by 1929, Fowler was well acquainted with Tom Lethbridge and C.S. Leaf. In addition to knowing these archaeological workers, the

---

[70] Mina Lethbridge, in conversation, 1994. Fowler was later awarded an Honorary MA by the University of Cambridge.
[71] Lethbridge, unpublished autobiography: 72.
[72] Clark, in conversation, 1994.
[73] Clark, in conversation, 1994.
[74] Phillips memoirs: 238.

[75] This explanation was later disputed by Godwin (1938a) who found that roddons had not suffered shrinkage and that the surrounding peat was wasting away rather than merely compacting. Fowler helped Godwin during this investigation and agreed with the new conclusion.
[76] Letters donated to me by Mina Lethbridge.

Sedgwick Museum Dead Files and the Sedgwick Fenland Research Committee File contain letters from Fowler to Geologists, Professor O.T. Jones, A.G. Brighton, and W.A. Macfadyen prior to the formation of the Committee. These letters suggest that Fowler had good working relationships with these men before they joined the Committee. For example, on 30 May 1931, he wrote to Jones to thank him for the "valuable diagrams and notes."[77] They appear to have been discussing roddon sedimentation. In May 1932, Fowler wrote a letter to Brighton, asking him to thank Macfadyen for the Foraminifera slides.[78] It was from Macfadyen's work that Fowler concluded that the roddons were produced by flooding of tidal rivers.

Founding members C.S. Leaf, described by Piggott as an "eccentric but clever amateur,"[79] and Lethbridge were both astute, expert excavators. Leaf is credited with discovering the Committee's Plantation Farm site around 1930. Lethbridge, who helped Leaf at Plantation Farm previous to the formation of the Committee, was Honorary Director of Excavations for the Cambridge Antiquarian Society for over 30 years and a specialist in Anglo-Saxon remains found in the Fens. In 1931, he had reported a skeleton found in Southery Fen, dated to the Bronze Age by her biconical jet bead bracelet. This short article (Lethbridge 1931) included a separate section by Fowler detailing the geological setting and a report by R.U. Sayce[80] identifying the skeleton as female. Lethbridge was already accustomed to interdisciplinary approach and would have appreciated the value of the Committee when it began in 1932. Godwin (1978) recalled that there was quite a lot of discussion about the Southery skeleton during Committee meetings and that it was eventually named 'Nancy'. In 1933, he did pollen analysis of the Upper Peat at the Southery site and established a stratigraphic correlation with Plantation Farm.

The "men in white coats" included Harry Godwin and Mrs M.E. Godwin who were intellectually and bureaucratically vitally important to the Committee. Both were young and well respected scholars. M.E. Godwin had a London BSc. degree in botany with subsidiary geology at Nottingham University College and later taught biology. H. Godwin had achieved a double First Class Honours in the Cambridge Natural Science Tripos and, in 1925, obtained one of the first Ph.Ds awarded by the University Board of Research Studies. In 1927 he was appointed Senior University Demonstrator in the Botany School. By 1932 he was already deeply involved in ecological research in Wicken Fen, studying succession and deflected succession of Fenland vegetation. In 1931, Sir A.G. Tansley had suggested to M.E. Godwin that she begin research in pollen analysis. "The method had been worked out by the great leader of Swedish geology, Lennart

von Post, although all accounts in English were due to his pupil, Erdtman" (Godwin 1985: 155).

The Godwins developed experimentally an ability to prepare, identify, and count samples. They also began to solve the problems of using a pollen spectrum to indicate forest composition, taking into account differential preservation and production, time of flowering, and transport factors. In addition, they studied local influences, concluding that successional conditions may obscure the effects of climatic changes and noted that archaeological data could prove chronologically useful when reconstructing forest sequences (H. Godwin 1934a, 1934b). "It seems, therefore, particularly desirable that the post-Boreal story of development of the British forests should be directly linked to as many independent time indices as possible, whether geological, climatic or archaeological," wrote Harry Godwin (1934b: 352).

As founding members, the Godwins attended all meetings, participated in all excavations, worked on the Essex Coast sub-committee, organised the Committee's 1934 analysis of a spearhead found in Methwold Fen, and conducted extensive independent research for the Committee on roddon formation, peat stratigraphy, vegetational history, and land- and sea-level changes. Several references in the Minute Book point out the contributions made by the Godwins to the establishment and successful functioning of the Committee. They were especially adept at recruiting valuable members. During the first meeting, "It was decided that Dr. Godwin approach Dr. Seward with a view to securing his services as President."[81] A.C. Seward, Professor of Botany at Cambridge from 1906 to 1936, was a renowned palaeobotanist, and H. Godwin's friend. Fortunately for the Committee, Seward was a Trustee of the Sladen Fund of The Linnean Society of London. Correspondence in the Minutes suggests that he was helpful in obtaining grants from this organisation to support the Committee's excavations. H. Godwin also attracted one of his Ph.D students, M.H. Clifford, to the Committee in 1934. Clifford was a palaeobotanist who specialised in the analysis of macrofossils such as roots, twigs, and rhizomes, and who worked with the Godwins on their excavations at Peacock's Farm and Mildenhall Fen, and with H. Godwin at the Wood Fen and Woodwalton investigations of peat stratigraphy. Clifford's Ph.D fieldwork on Fenland postglacial vegetational stages is mentioned in the 14 November 1936 Minutes, when the Committee voted him £5 toward his expenses.

Apparently it was the Godwins who attracted two other close associates, H.H. Swinnerton,[82] Professor of Geology at Nottingham, and the Sedgwick Professor of Geology, O.T.

---

[76] Letters donated to me by Mina Lethbridge.
[77] Fowler May 30, 1931 Jones Letter: Fenland Research Committee File. Dead Curator's Cabinet. Sedgwick Museum of Geology.
[78] Fowler, May 31, 1932 Brighton Letter: Fenland Research Committee File. Dead Curator's Cabinet. Sedgwick Museum of Geology.
[79] Piggott, in conversation, 1994.
[80] Sayce lectured on material culture for the Faculty in the late 1920s and

early 1930s; his textbook *Primitive Arts and Crafts* (1933) was read by many.
[81] Fenland Research Committee Minute Book 7 June 1932. CUL Add. MS 9426.
[82] Phillips also knew Swinnerton; he had used Swinnerton's (1931) geomorphological knowledge of the Lincolnshire coast to substantiate the argument that the Romans had operated a ferry across the Wash (Phillips 1932).

Jones. "As he [Jones] was a member of my own college, night after night we sat together at dinner and a Fenland problem habitually lasted through coffee, and the trip home" (Godwin 1978: 46). Godwin suggests that Jones exercised a "watchful and benevolent geological supervision" over the Committee's research.

In 1938, when Harry Godwin presented his first proposal for the development of an institute of Quaternary Research at Cambridge University, he stated that Quaternary research "aims to establish a valid scheme of world events through and since the ice-age, in which the results of botany, zoology, geology, archaeology, climatology, geography and related sciences have been correlated . . . It is always the <u>combination</u> of these activities which really advances knowledge. . . The work of the Fenland Research Committee since 1932 illustrates the nature and value of such co-operative work."[83]

3.4 The Fenland Research Committee[84]

Although the Committee was not a "research school" in terms of being a long-term established institution, it is clear from the above sketch of participants that some factors delineated by Geison's (1981) list of ingredients for academic success, such as a focused research programme, the development of new exploitable techniques and the exploration of new fields of research were characteristic of the Committee's activities. In addition, the various experts and their areas of specialisation illustrate well the suggestion that successful academic endeavours must maintain "a monopoly over a special body of knowledge and skills" (Soffer 1982: 801). A special body of knowledge emerged during the first decade of the Committee's excavations and, as we see below, this new knowledge had lasting consequences for archaeology at Cambridge. As Coleman (1985: 49) and Rosenberg (1979) argue, the importance of "cognitive content" in social analysis of scientific life cannot be ignored.

Most importantly, Morrell (1972) argued that the success of Liebig's chemistry lab at the University of Giessen was primarily the result of Liebig's development of a reliable experimental technique of analysing organic compounds. In a similar way, the introduction of pollen "statistics" was pivotal to the success of the Committee's work. The Godwins demonstrated how pollen analysis could be a viable and applicable technique for interdisciplinary explorations in Britain. Their pollen analytical work successfully provided British archaeologists with a relative climatological time scale for their finds. This indispensable technique allowed the Committee's members to use a stratigraphic-geological approach to archaeology. It made an enormously important contribution to archaeological knowledge.

In addition, it was clear that the Committee was organising, promoting and cementing in academic history a new way of producing knowledge. This type of organisation of knowledge is not sufficiently discussed in the research school material but is central to understanding the Committee's productiveness and contributions. From the first meeting, participants appear to have been acutely aware that multiple authorship would benefit everyone. There was a conscious effort and commitment to exploit and incorporate specialists' contribution by the Committee members. Although "separate publications by individuals of their own particular researches"[85] were not precluded, the members immediately agreed upon and upheld the principle that communally produced results had more power and would benefit science in a potent new way. In the Minutes from the foundation meeting, there appears the statement: "The question of publication was discussed and it was agreed that in principle, scattered publication was . . . undesirable."[86] This point was reiterated strongly in the second meeting, when a major policy was agreed upon. Co-authored publications should result "from the correlation of results from different sciences. This should be the ultimate aim."[87] The Committee would have the most impact as a unified team; knowledge should be communally created, owned and exported. Science would hence benefit.

In his unpublished manuscript on the history of Quaternary research in Britain and in conversations, Richard West[88] argues that, by 1932, the knowledge base necessary for the operation of such a committee had already been produced in Scandinavian countries and that precedents for this type of organisation of knowledge production existed in Britain.

In Scandinavia, "The mapping of the sediments, the construction of methods of correlation via varved clay studies, marine limits and peat stratigraphy, and palaeontological studies of organic and marine sediments combined to lead to a chronology of late-and post-glacial history," writes West [2003: Chapter 2, p. 1].[89] "This chronology became the basis for the expansion of the subject in Europe, especially after the meeting and publications of the International Geological Congress in Stockholm in 1910." By the early twentieth century, it was known that the withdrawal of ice sheets at the end of the Pleistocene was indirectly important to dating archaeological sites. As the ice receded, sediments were left in distinctive successive layers, or varves, and sections of varves from separate locations had been correlated, establishing a geochronology. This geochronology outlined the retreat of ice over 12,000 years. Also as ice melted, sea levels changed and as the weight of the ice lessened on the earth's crust, land mass rose. The changing relations of land and sea were complicated but had been documented for the Baltic area. Raised beaches and extinct coastlines had been identified and the maximum age of any site could

[83] On the Development of Quaternary Research in the University. Clare College Archives. Godwin Papers. Clare College Archives. ACC 1992.
[84] For a full analysis of the FRC, please refer to Smith 1994, 1997, 1997–8.
[85] FRC Minute Book. CUL Add. MS 9426, 15 October 1932.
[86] FRC Minute Book. CUL Add. MS 9426, 7 June 1932.
[87] FRC Minute Book. CUL Add. MS 9426, 15 October 1932.
[88] West, in conversation, 2003
[89] West's unpublished work is quoted with his permission.

be judged by observing its relation to ancient and modern sea levels. Postglacial alterations in climate had been established through vegetation, faunal and marine studies; it was known that northern Europe had undergone a cycle of warm/dry and warm/damp climatic phrases: Pre-boreal, Boreal, Atlantic and Sub-boreal. As a result of extensive pollen analysis on samples taken from water-logged and unaerated deposits, Scandinavian scientists had developed a general forest succession, had established outlines of forest history from the Pre-boreal through Atlantic phrases over wide areas of continental Europe and had roughly correlated the Boreal with Mesolithic sites, the Atlantic with the late Mesolithic and early Neolithic and the Sub-boreal with the Early Bronze Age.

These findings were available to British archaeologists before the establishment of the Fenland Committee; there is evidence that this research was well known to the Committee's archaeologists. According to West, the Geologist, T.W. Woodhead (1863–1940), appears to have invited Pollen expert, O.G.E. Erdtman, to Britain to study the pollen content of peat profiles in the early 1920s. West reports that, in 1922, Erdtman visited many sites, collecting samples with the co-operation of the Geological Survey and that Woodhead became a pioneer in the application of Scandinavian methods to British vegetation history. By the time Clark (1932) wrote *The Mesolithic Age in Britain,* he was well aware of Woodhead's efforts to date microlithic finds by relating them to peat stratigraphy in the southern Pennines. Clark also knew of and reported on Erdtman and J.P.T. Burchell's work to assign a relative date to the Lower Halstow site in 1928; this work resulted in the wide dissemination of pollen analysis techniques (West [2003]: 7). In addition, a thorough, popular summary of the Scandinavian climatological time scale evidence on the correlations of geological, climatic, and archaeological epochs in northern Europe had already been published by Childe (1931a) for the British archaeological audience.

West has discovered that a now forgotten interdisciplinary "Central Committee for the Survey and Study of British Vegetation" was held in Leeds with an ecologist, a botanist and a geologist as members in 1904. West suggests that, although short-lived, this committee may have set a standard for the Fenland Committee. Again, in 1923, the British Association for the Advancement of Science in Liverpool appointed a Committee to investigate Quaternary peats in the British Isles. This was an attempt to increase interest in the interdisciplinary study of peat stratigraphy and its relation to archaeology. Interdisciplinary Scandinavian and German research such as K. Bertsch's (1931) extensive wetland excavation of the Federseeried in Württemberg may also have provided a model.[90] "Pollen diagrams and analysis of macroscopic plant remains were used to reconstruct the history of the lake . . . Archaeological investigations were

linked to the vegetation and environmental history in a very detailed way. The organic sediments were associated with occupation evidence" (West [2003]: Chapter 3, p. 1).

In addition, West points out that the 5th International Botanical Congress was held in Cambridge in August 1930. The President of this conference was the future President of the Committee, A.C. Seward. The Phytogeography and Ecology Section Sub-committee was chaired by A.G. Tansley with H. Godwin as a member. Papers considered the results of pollen-analytical work on British peats and the vegetation history of Britain as well as some evidence of correlation with archaeological finds.

It is against this background of academic activity on the Downing site that we must view the founding of the Committee. The Downing site specialists were university-educated, well aware of research in other countries and of the need to apply it to British circumstances. Importantly, they were also within walking distance of each other. There were many accessible meeting opportunities offered not only by Museum tea but also by the Cambridge traditions of Formal Halls and close College life that conveniently supported interdisciplinary sharing of knowledge. As Ophir and Shapin (1991: 16) state, "Perhaps the days in which ideas floated free in the air are truly nearing an end. Indeed, what we believed to be a heavenly place for knowledge, we will come to see as the result of lateral movements between mundane places." One of the reasons for the Committee's longevity was this local availability of expertise and what historian of science, David Livingstone (1996: 23), terms the "social-cognitive arrangements" which local settings such as the Museum tea-room could offer.

The interdisciplinary Fenland Research Committee embodied and made manifest Clark's scientific reasoning approach. The Committee's social structuring of research demanded that several lines of evidence be considered. Once again, West suggests that Clark must have already been influenced by exposure to multilineal ecological thinking before the founding of the Committee and that the change in his reasoning evident in his dissertation in 1932 and the ensuing development of what Clark called a "scientific approach" may have been the result of exposure to the knowledge described above.[91] Clark apparently first met the Godwins when he was writing his Ph.D thesis and, as reported above, shared tea. Certainly Grahame Clark would have known about the 1930 Botanical Conference convened within a few steps of the Museum of Archaeology and Ethnology.[92] He had also clearly recognised the importance of Scandinavian contributions even as an undergraduate. "My first view of the glories of Scandinavian archaeology was obtained when I visited Denmark and Sweden as a guest of the late Dr John af Klercker in 1929" wrote Clark (1936a: ix) in the Preface to his *The Mesolithic Settlement of Northern Europe.* According to that book, Clark

---

[90] Bertsch was described by Clark (1936a: xi) as a natural historian. I thank Richard West for this reference.

[91] West, in conversation, 2003.

[92] Brooks and Chipp (1931) published the presentations as well as a list of participants.

was introduced to ecologically oriented and interdisciplinary Scandinavian achievements during his 1929 visit. Agreeing with West, Godwin (1978: 45) has stated, "The stimulus to fresh advance came . . . in the expansion of ecological ideas, particularly of dynamic succession, in adoption of the techniques of pollen analysis, and finally in the whole concept of Quaternary research."

Clark and The Fenland Research Committee
"The whole affair was the individual result of Grahame Clark's fanatical pertinacity," stated Piggott,[93] referring to the archaeological side of Committee activities. Clark frenetically thought in terms of getting things done. As keen organiser and hard worker, Clark, the Committee's Secretary, arranged and set agenda for meetings, took minutes, kept members informed, corresponded on behalf of the Committee, sought new members and made appeals for funds. It appears that his aloofness enhanced his ability as Committee administrator.[94] He was able to treat each point of view without emotion and coldly keep control of agenda. Astutely, Clark and Gordon Fowler felt that the Committee should always dine together to encourage informal accord. These dinners, arranged before the business section of the meetings, were not for enjoyment alone but to assure the smooth running of Committee activities.[95] Certainly he and C.W. Phillips were the key archaeologists who directed the archaeological portion of the Committee's excavations and quickly published the joint results. Godwin[96] remarked, in a speech to the British Association, Clark "was really responsible for organising and pushing through most of the [archaeological] field work."

From 1933 to 1940, Clark co-authored eight site reports and articles in co-operation with the Fenland Research Committee and worked with members on other reports from outside the Fenland area. This published work documents the intellectual links between the Committee and Clark's redefinition of prehistory as taught at Cambridge during the 1930s. Two of these publications, the Plantation Farm and the Peacock's Farm reports, especially and clearly illustrate the new structure of the social organisation of knowledge as well as the restructuring of Clark's scientific approach.

At the first meeting, the "problem of financing"[97] the Committee's first excavation was discussed. The purpose of this excavation at Plantation Farm in the Fens was to establish the stratigraphical context for the early Bronze Age and to "study post-glacial changes in environment in relation to man"(Clark 1933a: 266). According to correspondence,[98]

Clark had begun working on the Plantation Farm site prior to June 1932. As the Committee began, there are several letters requesting equipment and advice. Clark then produced sectional diagrams, illustrating the site's stratigraphy and the positions of the finds.

From study of the stratigraphy, Clark saw that occupation of the sand-hill had begun after a few inches of the upper peat had formed. The Godwins' analysis of aquatic plant pollen implied that the hillock had been surrounded by a shallow swamp. Clark concluded that the sand-hill, a dry island in a swamp, must have been a very desirable location for occupation.

The Godwins concluded from their pollen analysis that the lower layer of peat began to form in the Late Boreal, when the floor of the southern part of the North Sea was covered by fens. The authors also found evidence that following the formation of this lower peat, a subsidence of land levels occurred during the Atlantic climatic phase when the area was covered with tidal estuarine silts. Re-elevation of the land followed, permitting the formation of the upper peat during the Sub-boreal. This sequence, upper peat over tidal silt over lower peat, became central to understanding the Fenland stratigraphy as it was found at other sites. Godwin attempted to demonstrate a correspondence between lithology, stratigraphy and time in order to date archaeological finds relatively. This correspondence was questioned at the time by Committee members[99] and has since been re-evaluated by Fenland scholars (Hall and Coles 1994) as new study shows that the sequences of peat and clay are not simple divisions that apply broadly across the southern Fenland.

The Plantation Farm site report consisted of several distinct sections. Jackson, the Manchester Museum faunal expert mentioned above, analysed the animal bones recovered from the excavation. Macfadyen added an account on Foraminifera found in the clay. A.S. Kennard reported on the non-marine mollusca found in the channel cut into the semi-marine silts. Kennard and Macfadyen's results corroborated the Godwins' conclusion that a subsidence and re-elevation of land had occurred. The Godwins' suggestion that the upper peat layer had been formed during the Sub-boreal climatic phase meshed with Clark's typological analysis dating the artefacts to the early Bronze Age. Combining these reports, the authors used the convergence of several lines of investigation to reconstruct a history of the human occupation of the site in relation to the geological, geographical, climatic and botanical changes of the Fenland.

[93] Piggott was 23 when Clark invited him to join the Committee. Piggott identified the pottery found at Runcton Holme, Peacock's Farm (1935) and the Essex Coast (1936). I interviewed Professor Piggott at his home on 5 April 1994.
[94] Mina Lethbridge, in many conversations, August and September, 2000. Years later, archaeologist Paul Ashbee remembered Clark as an excellent committee chair and moderator precisely because he was "above it all" (Ashbee, in conversation, 1 March 2003).
[95] Grahame Clark remembered these dinners and their purpose in conversations on 20 April and 12 July 1994.
[96] Godwin, H. History of the Fenland. Paper Given at the British Association Evening Meeting, Cambridge, 19 August 1938. Clare College Archives ACC 1992/2.
[97] FRC Minute Book, 7 June 1932. CUL Add. MS 9426.
[98] FRC File. Dead Curator's Cabinet. Sedgwick Museum of Geology.
[99] "The last meeting of the Committee was interesting; it seems to be dawning on people that a bed of buttery clay may be diachronic when traced over wide areas." (Jones 27 May 1936 letter to Macfadyen: Fenland Foraminifera: Fenland Research Committee File; Sedgwick Museum.)

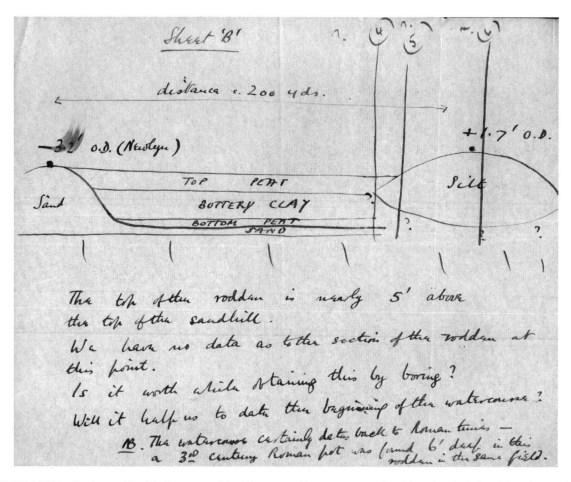

FIGURE XVIII Grahame Clark's diagram of the Plantation Farm stratigraphy. This sketch defined the classic three-phrase sequence of the Fenland: upper peat over buttery clay over lower peat. Clark's drawing, found in the Macfadyen Dead File, accompanies a letter from Clark to Professor of Geology, O.T. Jones, seeking advice on where to place borings to verify and complete "the section of the sandhill and the fen deposits through which it protrudes". (By courtesy of Dr David Norman and Mr Roderic Long of the University of Cambridge Sedgwick Museum of Geology.)

"Before dinner a preliminary report on the excavations at Peacock's Farm was presented to the Committee by the Secretary and by Dr. Godwin."[100] From their excavation trenches, Clark and the Godwins obtained flints that corresponded to the early Bronze Age level at Plantation Farm. Neolithic "A" pottery was found in the lower peat below that Bronze Age surface. For the Mesolithic, a typical Tardenoisian core was discovered with other worked and calcined flints in a well-defined black band below the Neolithic "A" pottery. The stratigraphy was clear. "The recovery of Early Bronze Age, Neolithic 'A' and Late Tardenoisian remains in vertical stratigraphical succession in one section is unique," Clark *et al.* (1935: 318). This was "the first time that a vertical succession of these cultures has been obtained in one section in England" (Clark 1935: xxix).

In the site report, Clark discussed the typological affinities of the microlithic industries excavated from the lower peat. He used information about microburins from *The Mesolithic Age in Britain* to help establish these affinities. As in earlier typological work, Clark assumed lithic forms evolved,

that they could be arranged in an evolutionary sequence by comparing morphological changes and that specialised forms were later than unspecialised forms.

A full picture of the environmental setting of the site became clearer when M.H. Clifford's work on plants remains, ash stem wood, dogwood, reeds and buckthorn, as an index of the vegetation growing *in situ*, the Godwins' report on pollen and A.S. Kennard's and C. Oldham's results of mollusc shell studies were combined with Clark's typological analysis. During the Mesolithic, a period of relative geological stability, a cross-over of falling pine and rising alder was evident in the woodlands and the site was surrounded by open water or swamp. During the Neolithic "A" horizon, the climate may have been becoming warmer and the area drier. By the early Bronze Age, after a period of submergence, willows and reeds grew near the settlement.

The team had reconstructed a history of the human occupation and of the general and varied changes of the Fenland in which people lived. At the end of the report, Godwin presented a synthesis that hypothesised botanical, geological and archaeological correlations and attempted to set the archaeological remains in an environmental context.

---

[100] FRC Minute Book: 27 October 1934. CUL Add. MS 9426.

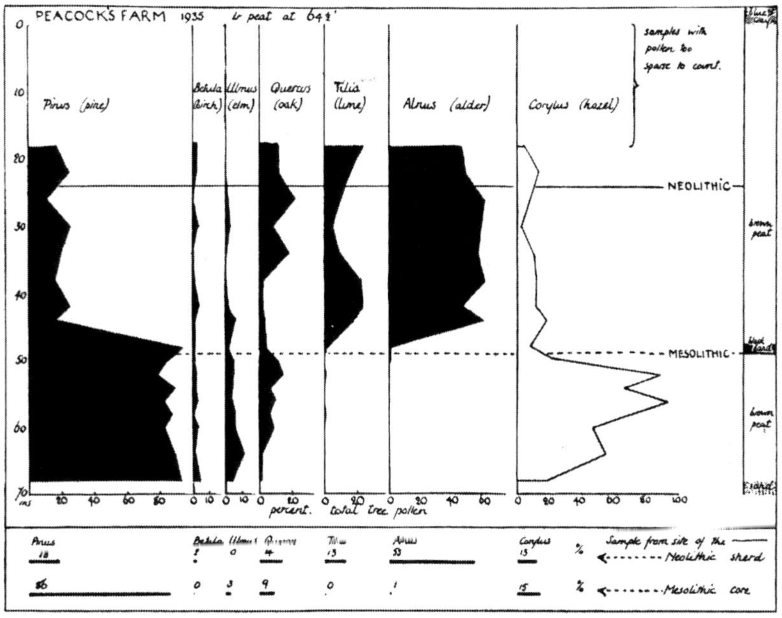

FIG. 16. Pollen analyses taken in series through the lower peat at Peacock's Farm, at 64½ ft. on the base line. Below are shown the analyses of two separate samples from the site of prehistoric objects

FIGURE XIX   The celebrated Peacock's Fen excavation during the summer of 1934. Grahame Clark and C.W. Phillips are at the base, while the palaeobotanist Sir Albert Seward and Harry Godwin stand on the step marking the lower peat. (By courtesy of the MAA.)

FIGURE XX   Sir Harry and Mrs M.E. Godwin's pollen analyses taken in series through the lower peat at Peacock's Farm. The sequence is typical of the end of the Boreal climatic period. This knowledge of forest history "forms a background scale against which other events can be seen, and by which they can sometimes be dated," wrote Godwin (Clark and Godwin 1940: 69). (Illustration from the Antiquaries Journal 15: 309.)

3.5 Archaeology Redefined

In some ways, Clark (1933b: 232) continued to consider archaeology as "the study of past distributions of culture-traits in time and space" during his association with the Fenland Research Committee. Clark used typological analyses similar to those used in his earliest studies, classifying artefacts according to morphological differences, mapping the differing classes to establish their distribution as with the Committee's Mildenhall report (Clark 1936b: 29), and assuming that complimentary distributions implied contemporary cultures (Clark and Godwin 1940: 60). As in earlier work, Clark equated an assemblage with a culture and a folk and continued to arrange forms in an evolutionary sequence by comparing morphological changes, assuming that lithics and pottery must have evolved from simple general ancestors to more complex descendants.

In practice, alongside these conventional methods, Clark was re-defining his archaeology, emphasizing excavation along with the study of surface finds. In contrast to his earlier research, his major Fenland investigations involved intensive digging. "The crux of archaeology is excavation"

Clark (1989a: 66) was later to write. Clark's archaeology, no longer typological analyses alone, had become based on a stratigraphic-geological approach. When Clark wrote *The Mesolithic Age in Britain,* mapping of surface finds was one of the few methods he could use to establish relative dates. In all the Fenland reports, Clark could correlate his typological and mapping results with quantities of relevant botanical and climatic evidence.

Clark's choice of subject also dramatically changed. He became well acquainted with natural events and their relevance to dating archaeological sites.[101] In *The Mesolithic Age in Britain*, Clark had used environmental factors to explain shifts from the Upper Palaeolithic to Mesolithic. By 1936, when he published *The Mesolithic Settlement of Northern Europe,* environmental change explained variations between assemblages as well as between prehistoric periods. Instead of invasion or migration, environment was the independent variable.

As the decade proceeded, the team continued to take advantage of new pollen and natural science analyses to produce a broad, contextual picture of the climatic, geological,

---

[101] In the Plantation and Peacock's Farm reports, the Godwins had explained the Blytt and Sernander climatic periods which had "been closely correlated, especially in Sweden, with post-glacial forest history, with the Baltic lake periods, with de Geer's geo-chronology, and with chief phases of archaeological development." As Godwin (1978: 24) later wrote, "In a period before absolute physical means of dating were available, the importance of such a background means of correlation and reference was immense."

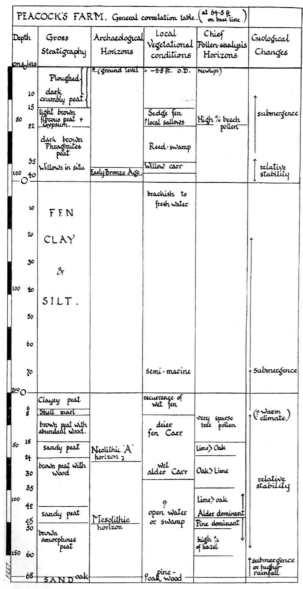

FIG. 19. Table to show general correlations of botanical, geological, and archaeological events throughout formation of the fen beds at Peacock's Farm

FIGURE XXI   Peacock's Farm General Correlation Table from the 1935 Peacock's Farm report. The Plantation and Peacock's excavations, Godwin (1978: 55) later wrote, "have properly been regarded as something of a landmark in British archaeological method, convincingly demonstrating, as they did, the enormous potentialities of a stratigraphic approach in sites . . . : it heralded a widespread change in manner of approach to the problems of British prehistoric archaeology." In addition to introducing new approaches, the Committee's concerted use of interdisciplinary teamwork was particularly prescient. Such teamwork has become an inescapable feature of modern science. (Illustration from the Antiquaries Journal 15: 317.)

---

[102] I am indebted to Childe (1952) for this insight into Clark's intellectual growth.

[103] For a thorough analysis of the transformation of the PSEA, see "'The Coup': How did the Prehistoric Society of East Anglia Become the Prehistoric Society?" (Smith 2000b).

floral, faunal and geographic circumstances that formed the ecological settings for the Fenland's prehistoric occupation. During this time, the Committee began to provide information on life-ways; what food was preferred, what wood was relied upon for fuel and what weather and changing climates had affected people's lives. The researchers learned that the Peacock's Farm residents ate pig, bred oxen and burned alder and oak in their fires (Clark *et al.* 1935). At Methwold Fen, where the Bronze Age spear-head had been found, the inhabitants would have endured "a great increase in wetness of the fens" (Godwin *et al.* 1934: 398). By the later Bronze Age, because of increased dampness, the Peacock's Farm site had been abandoned and people had chosen to settle on higher ground (Clark 1936b).

This increased knowledge was one of the influences that led Clark (1939a: 1) in *Archaeology and Society* to re-define archaeology as "the study of how men lived in the past". It is clear that Clark not only learned to apply multilineal thinking during his association with the Fenland Committee; he also had become an expansive thinker. One scientific question led to answers but then further questions. Interest in dating a site relatively had led to the reconstruction of life-ways. He began the decade with dating as his prime typological goal but found that "science" could lead from one small question to many amplified arenas of discovery. As a 20-year-old in 1927, Clark wondered how one artefact related morphologically to another yet ended the next decade by investigating how material culture related to environment. His fascination with the interaction of cultures had changed to a fascination with the reconstruction of prehistoric subsistence and social patterns. Clark began as an archaeologist interested in the use, manufacture and distribution of implements but became an archaeologist interested in the activities that the use, manufacture and distribution of implements imply.[102] As Childe (1952: 209) wrote in his review of Clark's seminal *Prehistoric Europe: the Economic Basis*, culture was now "conceived as action, not as the fossilized results of action."

3.6   The New Archaeology Institutionalised

Coleman (1985) suggests that a specialty or discipline emerges when a community of scientists gains access to the means to disseminate a new knowledge base through publications and instruction and is successful at soliciting material and institutional support and at establishing relations with authorities who influence funding. In the 1930s, there was a community of archaeologists within the Faculty of Archaeology and Anthropology who worked closely together, valued new environmental knowledge, had similar goals, were united by their stated desire to benefit from interdisciplinary explorations and who were also establishing the means to disseminate their views.

The Proceedings

The legend of the take-over of the Prehistoric Society of East Anglia[103] and its journal, the *Proceedings of the Prehistoric Society*, is one of the great tales of British archaeology. It was vividly remembered by Stuart Piggott:

"With the Fenland Research Committee, I was constantly going over to Cambridge and talking to Grahame Clark . . . we frankly decided to take over the PSEA and make it into the Prehistoric Society."[104] To this day, the transition of the regional PSEA to the national Prehistoric Society in 1935 is remembered as a well-planned coup by Young Turks headed by Clark. However, a different version of events can be recreated from the PSEA's Minute Books, the Memoirs of C.W. Phillips, interviews conducted by myself and by Peter Rowley-Conwy and prehistorian Steven Plunkett's comprehensive analysis of the unpublished letters to and from the many involved.[105] These sources suggest that there was no need for a take-over. They reveal that for years the membership of the PSEA had discussed the possibility of changing its name; years before 1935, the Society had been recognised as a national organisation, critically important to the development of prehistoric studies in Britain.

Although initially dedicated, in 1908, to the study of "all matters connected with prehistoric man in East Anglia,"[106] the PSEA had become the premier society for the study of prehistory in Britain; by the 1920s, A.C. Haddon, Miles Burkitt, Professor Ridgeway, Louis Clarke, Sir Arthur Keith, Nina Layard, J. Reid Moir, Professor V. Gordon Childe, O.G.S. Crawford and Johnny Marr were all active members. There is no space here to detail the intricate inner politics of this Society; suffice it to report that by the time Grahame Clark was first elected to the Society's Council in 1932, grave concerns about the competency of the Editor of the Society's journal had been repeatedly raised. As a result of the controversy, the Editor, Guy Maynard, suggested at the 24 May 1933 Council meeting that "he was not willing to carry on the responsibility of all branches" of his office.[107] Following Miles Burkitt's suggestion, "it was unanimously resolved . . . that J.G.D. Clark be invited at once to relieve" Maynard of the function of Editor of the *Proceedings*.[108] As Acting Editor, Clark immediately took control, efficiently producing on-time publications for 1933 and '34. The Young Turk had thus been invited to take over. Shortly before the Annual General Meeting in February 1935 in Norwich, Grahame Clark suggested to the Council "That the title of the Society shall be The Prehistoric Society"[109] in order to facilitate soliciting nationally and internationally acclaimed contributions for the *Proceedings*. This proposal was carried by a large majority in the postal ballot.

In 1935, Clark became Honorary Editor of the new *Proceedings,* a position he retained for 35 years. In his assessment of Clark's work, G. Sieveking (1976: xvii) commented "it was as a result of the transformation of the Prehistoric Society of East Anglia into the Prehistoric Society . . . that a platform was made available in Britain"

for the publication of evidence from the natural sciences. The content of the new *Proceedings* stressed national, interdisciplinary concerns. Writing in the *Archaeological Journal*, Ward Perkins (1936: 295–7) noted the predominance in the new *Proceedings* of articles which discussed "aspects of archaeology in which physiographical changes have played a determining part." Clark often solicited articles from specialists other than archaeologists. In 1936, the zoogeographer, P. Ullyott, explained how a study of the distribution of flatworms could be used to date relatively the separation of England from the Continent. Geologist, P.G.H. Boswell, in his Presidential address in 1936, argued the case for continued co-operation between disciplines.

During the late 1930s, in his editorial notes and in the section "Current Prehistory", Clark (1936c, 1937b, 1937c) often discussed the usefulness of geological, botanical and zoological evidence. He used the *Proceedings* to describe and publicise new advances which had emerged from the Fenland Committee's work. By 1936, he was publishing research conducted by the Committee, such as Warren *et al.*'s Essex coast report in the *Proceedings*.

The headquarters of the *Proceedings* were moved from Ipswich to the Cambridge Museum of Archaeology and Ethnology in 1935. In 1936, Phillips became Honorary Secretary of the Prehistoric Society, retaining that position until 1946. With Clark as Honorary Editor, the journal quickly became a major vehicle of communication amongst British archaeologists. During its first years, the *Proceedings* published several landmark papers that set the frame of study for the next generation and became some of the most cited articles in modern British archaeology. Clark (1985: 12) states, "the fact that [the] *Proceedings* were edited for some four and a half decades in Cambridge . . . put us in the position to publish some of the most original work of generations of young prehistorians."

Instruction
At the Faculty Board meeting of 16 October 1934, Burkitt noted, "After some discussion it was agreed to ask Dr Grahame Clark to give a short course of lectures on Mesolithic Europe in Lent Term for a fee of ten guineas."[110] Lecturing gave Clark the opportunity to present his views on cultural sequences within their environmental context. In the preface to *The Mesolithic Settlement of Northern Europe,* Clark (1936a: ix) wrote, "The subject-matter for the book was covered in a course of lectures . . . during Lent Term of 1934." In his review of this book, Armstrong (1937: 68–9) observed that Clark's conclusions were "immensely strengthened by the synchronisation of independent researches by geologists, biologists, archaeologists and botanists. The

---

[104] Quoted from Piggott's 1994 interview with Julia Roberts, with permission.
[105] The letters are in the Ipswich Museum's archives; Plunkett's unpublished research, entitled "Prehistory at Ipswich; an Idea and its Consequences" is in his possession.
[106] *Proceedings of the PSEA* (1910: 4).
[107] Prehistoric Society of East Anglia Minute Book, 24 May 1933. The

Minute Books for the Prehistoric Society of East Anglia are stored at the Library of the Society of Antiquaries of London. John Coles and David Hall suggested this source.
[108] Prehistoric Society of East Anglia Minute Book, 24 May 1933.
[109] Prehistoric Society of East Anglia Minute Book, 23 February 1935.
[110] 16 October 1934, Faculty Minutes CUA Min.V.92a.

book is a striking example of what can be achieved by co-operation of this nature." At the beginning of *The Mesolithic Settlement* Clark (1936a: xi) stated, "From my association with the Fenland Research Committee I have experienced directly the extreme value of co-operative approach."

The following year, "The Board approved an arrangement by which Dr Grahame Clark should give a course on geo-chronology and climatic history."[111] By then, Clark was giving 44 hours of "lecturing and teaching" on material closely related to his research with the Committee.[112] In 1936, he was appointed Faculty Assistant Lecturer, his first paid, full-time, official position. In the Faculty Minutes, Clark was described as having "given valuable lectures . . . and also provided instruction on the practical side in fieldwork and excavation."[113] From 1937–39 "Archaeology with the selected area Europe" was listed as one of three selected area options available for Tripos papers, along with Anthropology of Africa and India.[114] It would appear that Clark was the lecturer for this option. By 1939, Burkitt noted, "Dr Clark's subject is central to the work of the Archaeological side" of the Tripos course.[115]

Teaching became one of Clark's major concerns and he immediately attracted students. "The development of post-graduate research in prehistoric archaeology at Cambridge had to wait on the provision of undergraduate teaching," Clark (1989b: 6) observed. "The Cambridge faculty was the only one in Britain producing a flow of honours graduates in prehistoric archaeology," he wrote (1989a: 53). He noted that the number graduating from Section A sharply increased after his appointment (1989a: 52). As Clark stated, the Faculty and Appointments Committee Minutes record increases in student enrolment throughout the 1930s; Archaeology and Anthropology was apparently becoming an exciting academic alternative. Since Section A was a combined Archaeology and Anthropology one-part Tripos course, it is difficult to ascertain if the students enrolled were specifically attracted to Clark's teaching and his new environmental archaeology. The most popular selected area option listed in the *Historical Register* for the Tripos course from 1937–39 was African Anthropology, perhaps because of the presence of Evans-Pritchard on the Faculty. However, the Faculty Board Minutes described Clark as "a capable and enthusiastic teacher whose value has been well appreciated by his students."[116] In 1928, there were 17 students enrolled in Section A, in 1934 there were 41, and by 1939, 60.[117] In 1935, when Clark was first present as a Faculty Board member, Disney Professor Ellis Minns noted that the quality and quantity of students was very satisfactory.

Charles McBurney (1976: xii), who joined the Tripos course in 1935, wrote, "The intellectual climate, as I recall it, was

one of new ideas characterised everywhere by an atmosphere of excitement and optimism. Discussion and criticism indeed abounded . . . rendered fruitful by important new discoveries and often spectacular developments in method and technique." In his "A Tribute to Grahame Clark", McBurney (1976: xii) stated, "From you, we began to hear . . . of new and exciting developments quite outside the scope of classic text-books of the day. Outstanding among these topics were the growing fields of Post-Glacial and environmental studies based on the then new and rapidly growing techniques of pollen analysis, varve dating, Post-Glacial sea-level changes . . . exemplified as near at hand as Peacock's Farm and in the activities of the Fenland Research Committee."

The results of the Fenland Research Committee's work provided a new cognitive base for teaching prehistoric archaeology. It also provided a training ground for future professionals. In 1935, Clark proposed that the Cambridge University Field Archaeological Society, founded by undergraduates Thurstan Shaw and Rainbird Clarke, become associated with the Committee "for the purpose of assisting with excavations."[118] An agreement was then drawn up, signed by students, J.C. Mossop, J.K. St Joseph, Rainbird Clarke and T.G.E. Powell. Most of the work of the Committee's Mildenhall (Clark 1936b) excavation was done by volunteers of the Archaeological Society and members are recorded as attending the lecture segment of Committee meetings. All of the above students found employment and professional success: Thurstan Shaw as Professor of Archaeology at the University of Ibadan, Nigeria; St Joseph as Director of Aerial Photography in Cambridge; Clarke as Curator at Norwich Castle Museum; and Powell as Rankin Lecturer in Prehistoric Archaeology at Liverpool. Six other students, Desmond Clark, Bernard Fagg, John Brailsford, John Hamilton, H.G. Wakefield and Charles McBurney, who graduated between 1935 and 1939, "went on to pursue archaeology as a profession" (Clark 1989a: 52).

Facilities

There is considerable evidence in the Faculty Minutes that the Board was expanding its facilities to deal with the level of enrolment. This stress upon obtaining teaching and library space contrasts with the emphasis in the Faculty Board Minutes of 1928 upon adding rooms for Museum collections. After 1935, the need for additional facilities for students was regularly discussed. In the 1935 Faculty Appointment meeting, Minns announced that rooms in the old Law School had been solicited for teaching purposes.[119]

In 1936, Clark raised the question of the new Library and was assured that it would soon be staffed. By 1937, there was a note in the Minutes stating that the Library was now "working

[111] 19 July 1935, Faculty Minutes CUA Min.V.92a.
[112] 19 July 1935, Faculty Minutes CUA Min.V.92a.
[113] 8 June 1936, Faculty Minutes CUA Min.V.92a.
[114] *Historical Register Supplement* 1931–40: 399–401.
[115] 8 June 1939, Faculty Minutes CUA Min.V. 92a.
[116] 8 June 1936, Faculty Minutes CUA Min.V.92a.

[117] 10 November 1939, Faculty and Appointments Committee Minutes CUA Min.V.93.
[118] 24 January 1935, Faculty Minutes. CUA Min.V.92a.
[119] 7 November 1935, Faculty and Appointments Minutes. CUA Min. V.93.

well under the charge of [Librarian] Rishbeth."[120] It was also suggested in the Minutes that Section A was understaffed; in 1938, Glyn Daniel, who had achieved a First in Section A in 1934 and finished his Ph.D in June 1938, was asked to give a course on Megalithic tombs of Europe. By 1938, "the problem of space" was becoming acute and permission had at last been obtained "from the University to issue an appeal for funds to extend the buildings up to the Botany School."[121] However, as we discover in Chapter 4, this period of growth was abruptly arrested by the Second World War.

3.7   Knowledge Travel

By the late 1930s, the "young and irreverent persons in Cambridge" (Piggott 1963: 5) had successfully begun to institutionalise themselves. In the above section, it was demonstrated that the cognitive aspects of Clark's agenda were established by active dissemination of ideas and methods through a designated journal, by creative instruction and through the gaining of necessary institutional support. Presenting innovative views that placed cultural sequences within environmental contexts in his lectures, Clark promoted an interdisciplinary approach to the problems of post-glacial history as a core subject for Cambridge archaeology. In my interviews with his 1930s students, Clark is consistently remembered as a cutting-edge intellectual, employing new, rapidly developing techniques to solve archaeological problems. He was not loved[122] but he was certainly respected and made a lasting impression on his students.

In order to access properly the strength of Clark's influence and the research agenda that emerged from the Committee's work, it would seem appropriate to apply the concept of knowledge travel as developed by Shapin (1998). Did this teaching translate successfully to new settings? Two case studies which would illuminate this question are those of Thurstan Shaw and Desmond Clark. Both Shaw and Clark[123] went out to Africa after taking their degrees at Cambridge. "Unquestionably Grahame was a major influence in my life," stated Desmond Clark.[124] J.G.D. Clark's lectures were "so solid, so sound, so scientific" remarked Thurstan Shaw.[125] In the following section, a history of the early careers of these two men will be reconstructed in order to trace Cambridge archaeological training as it applied to new territory.

FIGURE XXII   Shaw at Hembury Fort, 1932.
Miss Liddell's staff consisted of Thurstan Shaw, Aileen Henderson, who later married Sir Cyril Fox and became a Lecturer in archaeology at Exeter University, and Mary Nicol, who married Louis Leakey[126] and became world-famous for her Pleistocene discoveries at Olduvai Gorge in Tanganyika. Both Liddell and foreman, W.E.V. Young, took great care to introduce them to excavation techniques. "In subsequent years, Mary Leakey used to reflect on what a good training it was."[127] (By courtesy of Thurstan Shaw.)

Thurstan Shaw (1914–)[128]
As with so many I interviewed, Thurstan Shaw was introduced to archaeology as a schoolboy;[129] his parents also had "a good historical sense"[130] and summer vacations were spent exploring ancient sites. An article on one of these sites, the underground passages of Exeter, in the *Proceedings of*

[120] 10 November 1937, Faculty and Appointments Minutes. CUA Min.V.93.

[121] 10 November 1938, Faculty and Appointments Minutes. CUA Min.V.93.

[122] "People always speak of Burkitt as if they really did love Burkitt, and that Burkitt was the person who helped them become interested," I said to Desmond Clark in an interview on 18 April 1996. "That's right!" he answered. "But Professor Clark was the one. They don't speak of Clark as if they loved him, but they do speak with respect," I added. "Yes, I think you got it exactly," Clark responded.

[123] There were others who also became Africanists. For example, Bernard Fagg (1915–1987), after taking the Tripos in 1938, was accepted as a cadet for the Colonial Administrative Service and posted to the Provincial Administration of Plateau Province in Nigeria. In his spare time, he conducted field research into prehistoric remains and immediately recognised the importance of the remarkable terracotta Nok figurines when they came to his notice in 1943. In 1947, he was appointed Assistant Surveyor of Antiquities and, when Kenneth Murray retired in 1957, Fagg became

Director of the new Nigerian Department of Antiquities.

[124] Desmond Clark, in conversation, 1996.

[125] Shaw, in conversation, 1996.

[126] When Shaw came up to Cambridge, Leakey was a Research Fellow in St John's and a Faculty Board member. He was forcefully advocating that geology be a required Tripos subject and that the Tripos course be expanded. Tripos administrative changes will be explored in Chapter 4

[127] "Skeleton in my Luggage; Memoirs of an Africanist Archaeologist" (Shaw [1975–95]: 123). This unpublished autobiography is in Shaw's possession and is quoted with his permission.

[128] Shaw is known as the father of British Western African Archaeology. Shaw's ceremonial African name, Onunu Ekkwulu-Ora, is translated as "the mouth which speaks on behalf of Igbo-Ukwu".

[129] A teacher at Blundell's recommended Breasted's *Ancient Times*, which enthralled him.

[130] Shaw, autobiography: 84.

the Devon Archaeological Exploration Society led him first to C.F. Moysey's work on surface flint hunting of artefacts and then to the newly founded Devon Archaeological Exploration Society. It was through this Society that Shaw had the opportunity to dig the Iron Age and Neolithic site, Hembury Fort, under the direction of Dorothy Liddell.[131]

Upon arriving in Cambridge in 1933 to read Classics, Shaw attended a public Museum lecture on Fenland archaeology by Charles Leaf; he later accompanied Leaf to Fenland excavations and joined Phillips and Clark at Phillips' excavation of the long barrow on Therfield Heath. Beginning Part II in Archaeology and Anthropology in 1935, Shaw noted that the total lack of practical courses was the reason he and Rainbird Clarke founded the University Field Archaeological Society. In 1936, Shaw joined the Fenland Research Committee's excavation at Mildenhall and remembered Clark plotting "the removal of Miles Burkitt from his post [because] he had never done any real archaeological research, never directed an excavation."[132]

Shaw was well aware of Clark's brilliance and thankful for the introduction to scientific reasoning[133] and to Fenland soil and artefact analyses, but it was Burkitt who gave Shaw access to an excellent private library, who personally encouraged him to strive for a First in the Tripos exams and who worked to secure him a position at the British Museum after graduation. However, having been introduced to African missionaries and pastors as a boy, Shaw had long desired to work in Africa and accepted a teaching post at Achimota College in the Gold Coast. Achimota was "the nearest thing to a university in Black Africa" (Shaw 1990: 207) with a racially integrated staff. Established to train Africans to assume self-governing rule, it was a forward-looking, "subversive"[134] institution, generally resented by the Colonial Government.

Archaeology was not abandoned when Shaw was invited not only to teach, but to assume the post of Curator at the Achimota Museum. Here was his opportunity to apply British learning. Achimota's "concept of a museum was simply a place where you put things and left them for people to look at." Shaw preferred the Cambridge model of a Museum as a teaching and research institution.[135] The museum "needed a lot of active organisation to become a centre of education and research as well as of conserva-

tion."[136] Following examples set by Louis Clarke and Miles Burkitt, Shaw transformed the Achimota Anthropology Museum. As Burkitt had done in Cambridge, "By means of purchase, collection and donation" artefact "series from the Gold Coast" were made "as complete and representative as possible," for use by students and teachers (Shaw 1946: 189). Education was a key concern; as Leaf did before him, Shaw gave public lectures for the "dissemination of archaeological awareness" (Shaw 1990: 211). And, as Louis Clarke had done for the Fenland Committee, "People were encouraged to report sites and finds to the museum, and to donate specimens" (Shaw 1990: 209).

In carrying out research, Shaw quickly found that much of what he had learned in Britain was not applicable to tropical Africa. He was, firstly, in a completely unexplored area. Gold Coast archaeology did not exist. Leakey (1936) in his *Stone Age Africa: An Outline of Prehistory in Africa,* dedicated only one page to archaeology in West Africa. This "constitutes a fair indication of our ignorance," Shaw (1943: 140) commented. As he began to explore, he immediately discovered that aerial photography, to which he had been introduced by Crawford and Keiller's (1928) book *Wessex from the Air,*[137] had no realistic application because of the thick tropical ground cover. He also found that many of the British lithic categorisations he had learned did not apply to African finds. The morphological forms simply did not correspond. African microlithic artefact material was white quartz rather than the European flint that Shaw had been accustomed to. This material was "hard to read"[138] or analyse and because of this he was forced to develop new typological methods which suited a new material.

When Shaw conducted his first major excavation, at Bosumpra Cave, Abetifi, Kwahu, with the aim of proving that a Stone Age had existed in West Africa and that prehistoric peoples had inhabited the forests, he unexpectedly discovered an extensive microlithic industry associated with pottery. Such an association was completely unknown from his British experience and Shaw found that the European terms of Neolithic and Mesolithic were inapplicable in Africa. Clark had suggested that microliths were characteristic of the Mesolithic but the British Mesolithic was not associated with pottery. The term Neolithic was equally inappropriate to describe what was discovered.

---

[131] Although space does not allow a description of the archaeological field activities in southern England in the early 1930s, I will mention that, at this time, there were two competing groups. Liddell was the sister-in-law of the marmalade millionaire and archaeologist, Alexander Keiller, and was therefore in his "camp". Keiller is remembered for his excavations at Windmill Hill and Avebury. The opposing team was led by Mortimer Wheeler who excavated Maiden Castle. Wheeler's and Keiller's excavations attracted much publicity; each team felt superior archaeologically to the other. People I interviewed worked either with one team or the other but never both. Wheeler and Keiller were flamboyant womanizers; I routinely heard stories of their competing exploits. I would hear that women, or in the case of Keiller, women and men, would be involved with either Keiller or Wheeler, but never both. I concluded that the social boundaries of the two groups were taken seriously. This would make an interesting study. A biography of Keiller, *A Zest for Life; the Story of Alexander Keiller* was

recently written by Lynda J. Murray (1999).

[132] Shaw, autobiography: 168.

[133] Shaw, in conversation, 2003.

[134] Shaw, autobiography: 232. "There was very little social intercourse between Achimota and official and government circles in Accra; the latter regarded Achimota as subversive — which we were."

[135] "Out of the teaching in the Museum . . . grew the Department of Archaeology and Anthropology. It is first and foremost a laboratory meant for, and arranged for, study and research in Anthropology." (T.T. Paterson, 1938. CUA Min.V.92a.)

[136] Shaw, autobiography: 228.

[137] This book had "provoked an awakening interest in aerial photography as a method of determining archaeological sites" (Murray 1999: 29),

[138] Shaw, in conversation, 2000.

The European Neolithic was a food-producing stage but at Abetifi there was no evidence of food production. European terminologies were therefore not applicable. The association of microliths, ground stone axes and pottery has since been found repeatedly in Western Africa and Shaw's Abetifi work is now considered to be the first "attempt at scientific excavation in the Gold Coast"(Nunoo 1993: 29).

Shaw also found that his African colleagues, whom he was duty bound to educate and train, were reluctant to dig and resisted the idea of excavation. Manual labour was not done by educated men. Digging for anything was beneath their dignity.[139] The past was known from oral tradition and legend and many felt that archaeology and excavation were unnecessary. Local people were also reluctant to permit him to excavate anything involving burials. As a European he had taken for granted that examining skeletons was appropriate, but in West Africa this was not understood or valued. Despite this resistance, Shaw's assistant at the Abetifi excavation, Richard Nunoo, eventually became interested in archaeology and later served as the Curator of the Ghana National Museum. In fact, many of Shaw's students at Achimota did succeed either in archaeology or as future administrators of an independent Ghana. Kofi Busia, for example, became Ghana's Prime Minister.

According to Shaw, the "scientific" thinking he had learned at Cambridge translated well to Africa.[140] Although there was a scarcity of evidence in the Gold Coast, using many lines of inference, when possible, resulted in a better argument (Shaw 1944). This was clearly a result of Clark's influence.[141] At Abetifi, for example, he found stratified evidence of a Stone Age occupation; this later led to questions about subsistence and economy (Shaw 1943). Also, as Burkitt and Clark had argued before him, Shaw felt that archaeology had practical value. "Archaeology," Shaw (1943: 145) wrote, "gives us knowledge of the past by which alone we can properly understand the present, and without this understanding we cannot hope to control or plan the future." This parallels Grahame Clark's (1959: 12) statement, "for me prehistory is only worth pursuing because it sets not merely history but contemporary life in the kind of perspective allowed . . . by modern science."

Clark's way of reasoning and the Committee's manner of doing interdisciplinary science as well as a Cambridge philosophy concerning archaeology's purpose had successfully jumped continents even if exact British archaeological methods and definitions failed to apply.

Desmond Clark (1916–2002)[142]

In contrast to the intense humid heat, dense vegetation, numerous diseases and intellectual isolation which Shaw

suffered in the Gold Coast, the climate and terrain in Northern Rhodesia were conducive to archaeological exploration. Also, unlike the Gold Coast, Northern and Southern Rhodesia had a conspicuous white settler population and an accompanying European administration which understood the concept of an archaeological past and tended to value amateur artefact collecting.[143] By 1938, when Desmond Clark accepted the posts of Curator of the newly founded David Livingstone Memorial Museum and Secretary of the Rhodes-Livingstone Institute for Social Anthropology, East, Central and Southern Africa had a growing, transplanted, European-based tradition of Quaternary and archaeological investigation.

This tradition of research was led by scholars from the Geological Surveys such as E.J. Wayland, the Director of the Geological Survey of Uganda Protectorate. As a result of his research, Wayland had proposed a widely accepted relative climatological time scale of alternating wet/dry or pluvial/interpluvial periods which were thought roughly to correspond with the European glaciation sequence. Wayland had also suggested a sequence for Stone Age cultures in East Africa. As mentioned previously, A.J.H. Goodwin and Van Riet Lowe had already published their great synthesis, *The Stone Age Cultures of South Africa* in 1929 and by 1936, Leakey was synthesising and popularising Eastern, Central and Southern African archaeology. In Northern Rhodesia, major discoveries had been made with the find of an ancient skull at Broken Hill mine. Cambridge-trained District Commissioner, F.B. Macrae, had conducted Northern Rhodesia's first excavation at the Mumbwa Caves.

By 1938, the Rhodes-Livingstone was an established research Institute, located only a few miles from the archaeologically rich Zambezi and Victoria Falls. The Institute staff included Godfrey and Monica Wilson, *née* Hunter,[144] who had completed several years' work among the Nyakusa in southern Tanganyika and, later, Max Gluckman who worked with the Barotse. "The Wilsons' friendship and intellectual stimulus were invaluable" wrote Desmond Clark (1994: 6). Through the Wilsons, Clark was introduced to the importance of ethnographic studies and what would be termed today ethnobotany. During an interview, Clark remembered the joy of walking through the country with African carriers and guides and, later, African colleagues; "I learnt about plants and animals and their relationship to them, and of course, most important of all, water."[145] This experience reinforced his knowledge of ecological archaeology learned from Grahame Clark and Harry Godwin in Cambridge.

According to his autobiographical sketches, Desmond Clark had no particular fascination with Africa but had been

---

[139] Shaw, autobiography: 306–8.
[140] Shaw, in conversation, 2001.
[141] Shaw, in conversation, 2003.
[142] Desmond Clark was Professor emeritus of Anthropology at Berkeley and an eminent Africanist.

[143] Shaw, in conversation, 2000.
[144] Hunter is often mentioned as a valued Cambridge Ph.D candidate in the Faculty's Minutes in the early 1930s.
[145] Desmond Clark, in conversation, 2000.

TENTATIVE CORRELATION OF CLIMATES AND CULTURES I[N]
ZAMBEZI VALLEY, SOUTH AFRICA, THE BELGIAN CONGO AN[D]

North of Southern Rhodesia

ZAMBEZI VALLEY GEOLOGICAL EVENTS	Congo Basin Events	Congo Basin Cultures	East Africa Events	
Erosion to present contours	Downcutting to		Present phase	
Low-level denudation terrace	Present Contours	Tsitolian	Nakuran Wet Phase	
Wind-blown sand			Dry	
Calcareous Aluvium erosion	Sands	Lupemban	Makalian Wet Phase	
Kalahari Sands II	?	—	Dry	
Calcification and Pink Alluvium III in some tributaries			Gamblian	Late Kenya Aurignacian
Minor erosion Younger Gravels and Sands Erosion	Gravels and sands of lower terrace of the Kasai Erosion	Upper Sangoan (Djokocian)	Pluvial	Proto-Stillbay Upper Sangoan
Redeposited Kalahari Sand	Red sands		with	
	Sandy clays	Middle Sangoan (Kalinian)	three	Upper Kenya Aurig. Middle Sangoan
Younger Gravels Erosion Ferruginization	Gravels Erosion and formation of high-level terrace of the Kasai Ferruginization	Middle Sangoan (Kalinian)	sub- Maxima	Lower Kenya Aurig. Lower Sangoan Levalloisian
Land rubble Kalahari Sands I	Kalahari Sand?		Volcanicity	
Older Gravels II Ferruginisation? Older Gravels I Erosion Ferruginization	Sands and fine clays (Ruashi) High-level Kamoa gravels	Congo Chelles-Acheul	Kamasian Pluvial	East African Chelles-Acheul Pre-Chelles-Acheul (Oldowan)
Silicification	Kalahari Sand? Earth movement		Volcanicity	
Freshwater limestones and sands High-level pebble-beds Formation of end-Tertiary Peneplain	Plateau gravels	Pre-Chelles-Acheul	Kageran Pluvial	Pre-Chelles-Acheul (Kafuan)

FIGURE XXIII Desmond Clark and son, with his Tentative Correlation of Climates and Cultures in the Upper Zambezi Valley, South Africa, the Belgian Congo and East Africa and Table of Geological Events, Climates and Stone Age Cultures. These tables, taken from the published result of Clark's Ph.D research, The Stone Age Cultures of Northern Rhodesia (Clark 1950), illustrate the extent of Desmond Clark's commitment to interdisciplinary research. This work rivals reports produced by the Fenland Research Committee. (By courtesy of The South African Archaeological Society.) (Photograph by courtesy of John Clark.)

introduced to archaeology as a child by schoolmasters at Monkton Combe.[146] His first experience with excavation was not with the Fenland Research Committee, but with Wheeler, when Grahame Clark suggested that he dig for two seasons at Maiden Castle. In all interviews, Desmond Clark repeatedly stated that Grahame Clark was the important intellectual influence.

Northern Rhodesia was fertile ground for the application of Grahame Clark's and Godwin's multidisciplinary scientific approach; from the start, Desmond Clark's work was interdisciplinary. His earliest publications, before the Second World War, are collaborative efforts with natural scientists. In 1939, Desmond Clark co-authored a report with Quaternary scientist, Dr H.B.S. Cooke. This was a preliminary note on the geology and archaeology of a site at Victoria Falls. In reference to this era, Desmond Clark (1989: 141) wrote, "The Zambezi valley gave me my first opportunity to apply what I had learned at Cambridge . . . I was able to work out the geomorphological sequence of terraces and their contained artifact assemblages and, more rarely, faunas." His second publication was seemingly even more directly affected by Grahame Clark's influence. His "Further Excavations (1939) at the Mumbwa Caves, Northern Rhodesia" contained a section on "ecological notes" (D. Clark 1942: 133) which described "the ecotone between the grasslands of the Kafue Flats and the savanna woodlands"(D. Clark 1994: 80). In this study, Desmond Clark argued that the evidence suggested seasonal movements of prehistoric people.

Desmond Clark claimed, during interviews, that his 1939 use of the concept of ecology and his "scientific" approach of using multiple lines of evidence was directly the result of Grahame Clark's teaching. Grahame had provided the lasting example of how scientific investigation should proceed from hypothesis, to evidence, to conclusion.[147] In an autobiographical sketch, Desmond Clark (1989: 139) wrote, "For me, Grahame's emphasis on palaeo-ecology has been all important since, without an understanding of the habitat of any prehistoric group, it is impossible to begin to understand their behaviour — how changes in climate and environment brought about the particular adaptations that resulted."

Certainly, there could be no clearer example of knowledge travelling with hardly any alteration to its principles. This successful transfer of a way of thinking might be partially explained by the fact that "social-cognitive arrangements," such as a supportive Colonial administrative system, facilitated Desmond Clark's desire to follow Grahame Clark's scientific agenda. It should be noted that African people were excluded professionally from archaeology longer in Northern Rhodesia than in the Gold Coast. Native ar-

chaeologists were not produced in Zambia until the 1970s when Desmond Clark was able to train archaeologists at the University of California at Berkeley. Nevertheless, Desmond Clark's accomplishments in Northern Rhodesia imply that Grahame Clark and Harry Godwin's teaching was very successful and travelled well.

3.8 Chapter Conclusion

We may conclude that Geison's (1981) research school "model" constructively illuminates Grahame Clark's contributions to the progressive institutionalisation of prehistory at Cambridge during the 1930s. As Geison's work suggests, prehistory became steadily stronger as the result of the introduction of an innovative cognitive base. Geography-of-knowledge concepts also seem to have intellectual value in that they point to important variables. The spread of what Grahame Clark defined as scientific thinking resulted in increased status for Cambridge archaeology.

During the 1930s, the Faculty was the "centre of prehistoric research in the Empire"[148] as indicated by the two case studies presented. The Cambridge diaspora had begun. Although this may make a good solid conclusion, it should be noted that research school approaches tend to avoid important aspects of the story I wish to tell. Lesser souls, with supporting duties, are forgotten if we only study the importance and success of innovative research agenda, how these agenda were institutionalised and how well they apply abroad. Two final short biographical sketches will now be used to present historically important actors. Their contributions are relevant but do not fit easily within the research schools or even geography-of-knowledge perspectives.

Both O'Reilly and Denston were from working-class backgrounds. O'Reilly was from a poor Northern Irish family and arrived at Girton in 1920 as a Clothworkers' Scholar to read English and Anglo-Saxon archaeology. Upon graduation, she was appointed a Girton Research Scholar and by 1925 had several good archaeological publications. In 1925, she replaced Cyril Fox as Louis Clarke's personal Museum assistant. From 1925, informally and unrecognised by the University, O'Reilly managed the Museum whenever Clarke suffered from poor health. At such times, Museum correspondence for the 1920s and 1930s was often addressed to Dear Sir (Mr O'Reilly) or to Mr O'Reilly Esq.

In addition, Maureen taught prehistoric and Anglo-Saxon archaeology as a demonstrator within the Faculty. There are several letters in the Museum from her ex-students describing her as "down to earth" and a reliable, good demonstrator for both Section A and for Norse, Celtic and

---

[146] This is a common theme in all interviews; students came up to Cambridge already attracted to archaeology as a possible profession.
[147] Desmond Clark, in conversation, 1996, 2000.
[148] As quoted previously: "We may look forward to our School and Mu-

seum being the real centre of your branch of research in the Empire," A.C. Haddon to Miles Burkitt, 18 December 1920. (Burkitt Papers. CUA Add. 7959 Box III).

FIGURE XXIV   Maureen O'Reilly, described as "built for comfort not for speed,"[149] was the first woman to be formally elected to a paid position at a Cambridge Museum when she became the Assistant Curator to Louis Clarke in the Museum of Archaeology and Anthropology in 1930. (By courtesy of Mina Lethbridge.)

FIGURE XXV   Charles Bernard Denston, First Technician of the Duckworth Laboratory 1945–86. Known as "Boy Denston" when he was hired in 1937 as a young, able teenager, C.B. Denston was initially employed to make tea, clean and guard the Museum. "Two brews were made for the academics. One China, the other Indian." [150] Denston would then ring a bell . . . "the peals of the bell echoing up the stairs of the Museum" and "go around to all the Faculty offices, 'The tea's made, Sir or Ma'am'." [151] (By courtesy of C.B. Denston.)

C.B. Denston

First Technician of the Duckworth Laboratory

1945-1986

Self Portrait

Anglo-Saxon history and languages of Section B.[152] Mary Kitson Clark, who dug with Dorothy Garrod at Mount Carmel in 1929, and who was one of the first female students to take the Diploma in Archaeology as a post-graduate in 1927, considered O'Reilly a strong influence, "The star at the Museum was Miles Burkitt for the Palaeolithic but Maureen took me for everything else."[153] Desmond Clark credited O'Reilly with helping him to secure work after his graduation in 1937.[154]

Importantly, O'Reilly contributed to the Faculty tea-room by making the biscuits and cakes, described by Denston as "all sorts of cakes for consumption, plain and iced, jam and cream rolls, all kinds of biscuits,"[155] which the staff enjoyed every weekday from 1925 to 1946 until she retired. In this way, O'Reilly successfully supplied and supported the creation of a knowledge-making place.

---

[149] Mary Thatcher, in conversation, 1996.

[150] Quoted with permission from Denston's unpublished autobiography [no date]. The autobiography is in the possession of Charles Bernard Denston.

[151] Denston, autobiography: 407.

[152] Letters from CUMAA Letter Boxes.

[153] Chitty, *née* Kitson Clark, in conversation with Julia Roberts, 1994.

[154] Letter, CUMAA Letter Box 1937.

[155] Quoted, with permission, from Denston's autobiography [no date].

From Faculty Minutes it is clear that O'Reilly was behind every Faculty scene. She seems to have known the charlady of each important person. At momentous decisions, Maureen O'Reilly would suggest a strategy, in effect: "we mustn't make this demand this week of the General Board because the vote will be against us, but, if we wait, I am told confidentially, by the bedder, that certain persons will be away . . . the Board may then be on our side." When, for example, in 1944, Grahame Clark's future stipend was discussed, O'Reilly suggested that "from an informal conversation with the Secretary-General's clerk, she had gathered that it might be advisable to make a recommendation now regarding the rate of the stipend."[156]

Maureen knew how to manoeuvre. She was politically wise in a practical way; she knew the University's weaknesses and strengths and how the University operated. She quietly and competently worked for the Faculty's success.

How then do we include and evaluate this type of contribution in a history? Certainly O'Reilly's contributions were recognised at the time. In 1939, "The Faculty has agreed to forward a vote of thanks to Miss O'Reilly for the magnificent way she has grappled with the difficult situation arising in the Museum owing to the outbreak of war . . . a great responsibility has fallen on her which she has ably discharged."[157] She and Tom Lethbridge had packed and stored the Museum's materials for safety. In the following year, the University's Council appointed O'Reilly Deputy Curator. "She got to the top," Mary Thatcher said; "for her status and her time, for her class, the society in which she lived, she couldn't have done better."[158] In 1945, Maureen O'Reilly married Professor Hutton and peacefully retired.

Denston also contributed in major ways to the smooth running of the Faculty. Arriving in 1937 at the Museum from a "poor, money-wise family,"[159] son of a Cambridge tailor who made clothing for the undergraduates, Denston described Faculty members as "toffs" whom he addressed as "Sir". "I never felt I was one of them." One of his many tasks, in addition to cleaning and tea, was to operate visual aids such as epidiascopes at lectures. "There were no automatic projectors in the early days." "The lecturers had no idea! In they tramped with a pile of books under the arm, paper markers, sometimes with numbers, a box of slides," wrote Denston in his autobiography. "A slide was put into a holder . . . while this was being shown another slide was put into another holder and one leaned over [so as to not] disturb the first slide . . . the pointer banged on the floor for the next slide . . . [then retrieving the first holder so as to not disturb the second slide]. In between the slides, the lecturer would want a picture from a book projected." If the picture was on the thin side of the book, "it meant stretching one's arm right round the epidiascope to hold the heavy side of the book while fiddling to get the picture central on the platform" which had to be raised and held, "trying not to let any of the paper markers fall out" while switching quickly between slides and books.

This mundane yet essential assistantship work is not mentioned in studies of academic life and certainly not in any histories of archaeology. Denston, however, cleverly used his pedestrian position to learn. During many hours of attendance at undergraduate lectures, he absorbed the equivalent of an undergraduate degree, educating himself, choosing to concentrate on Physical Anthropology. After returning from a difficult war, during which he was a prisoner under the Japanese, Denston became assistant to Jack Trevor, the Director of the newly established Duckworth Laboratory of Physical Anthropology located in the "Gods" of the Museum. As Trevor's assistant, Denston helped sort the recently acquired Pearson Collection of skeletal remains "which numbered at least 10,000 skulls, thousands of post-cranial bones and primate material other than human."[160] Staff assistants in the Anatomy Department suggested that Denston read anatomy text books and soon Trevor was using him to identify skeletal remains. "Tables [in the Laboratory] were piled high with hundreds of broken femora and tibiae, radii and ulnae, and my job was to sort the broken segments and reconstruct the complete bones."[161]

By 1950, the Duckworth Laboratory had the largest collection of human skeletal material in Britain and the Faculty was able to afford the lab's first Demonstrator, Peter Longton. According to Denston, Longton and subsequent Demonstrators helped in "attaining knowledge of Osteology, Paleopathology" and in teaching him how to present data in written reports. In 1954, Denston co-authored his first report on the identification of skeletal remains from an archaeological site; by 1958, he had become sole author of these publications. By retirement in 1986, Denston had produced 255 reports and 45 published physical anthropological studies. As the Director, Trevor's, health failed, it is rumoured that Denston took over his position and produced many publications, some of which are wrongly attributed to Trevor.

During his career, Denston studied and reconstructed many important finds, including Thurstan Shaw's skeleton from Akure in Nigeria, known as the "oldest African man,"[162] and Wheeler's "skulls of the defenders of Maiden Castle, still bearing the marks of Roman butchery." In 1986, Denston was awarded an Honorary MA by the University of Cambridge. "We honour today a man who joined the ranks of the assistant staff half a century ago, as a boy of fourteen, and, almost unprompted, certainly untutored, created for himself a name in scholarship, the expert practitioner in an art which he made his own, guide and helpmate of generations of students, counsellor and peer of scholars at home and abroad."[163]

---

[156] Faculty Minutes. CUA Min.V.94.

[157] Faculty Minutes. CUA Min.V.92a.

[158] Mary Thatcher, in conversation, 1996.

[159] All quotations in this paragraph are from Denston's autobiography.

[160] Denston's autobiography: 415.

[161] Denston's autobiography: 417.

[162] *Cambridge News* 21 February 1967.

[163] Quoted from the text of Denston's Cambridge Honorary MA, 1986, in Denston's possession.

Both Denston and O'Reilly were eventually recognised by their contemporaries for their accomplishments and both were suitably congratulated for their importance to academic life and to the establishment of prehistory as a subject. Nevertheless, the heuristic perspectives encouraged by research school investigations do not readily accommodate the type of contributions that Denston and O'Reilly made. Denston's work as tea boy and cleaner in the 1930s might not be included in a research school study, yet this work was crucial to the development of the Faculty. O'Reilly's presence on the Faculty Board and as a baker of cakes affected positively the growth of university archaeology but would not be included in investigations.

As will be discussed further in the conclusions to this study, the research school "model" could be augmented in order to deal appropriately with a greater variety of evidence. When a gendered perspective is added to research school and to geography-of-knowledge approaches, attention is more effectively focused on additional accomplishments. The Morrell/Geison model could be broadened to include lesser figures. The above case studies imply that it is important to incorporate many faceted approaches to the history of science when reconstructing the history of an academic subject.

In the following Chapter, Dorothy Garrod will be centre stage; she was the first woman and first prehistorian to be elected to a professorship at Cambridge. Once again, the question of the appropriateness of research school literature will be considered.

4   Dorothy Garrod in the Field and Faculty

At the end of her life, an acquaintance suggested to Garrod that she had been lucky. *"Pas la chance,"* Garrod replied, *"c'est courage et persévérance."*[1]

The last chapter revealed how the institutionalisation of prehistory as a taught subject at Cambridge during the 1930s was furthered by the intellectual accomplishments of a "young man in a hurry" and his association with scientists. Heuristic models taken from the history of science literature were used to study Grahame Clark and his influence. The suggestions made by Coleman (1985), Geison (1993), Morrell (1972) and Secord (1986) that certain factors are present in a successful academic research school proved applicable to Clark and his experiences at Cambridge. The most relevant argument from the literature was Morrell's idea that the success of Liebig's chemistry lab at the University of Giessen was primarily the result of his development of new experimental techniques. In a clearly similar way, the introduction of pollen analysis, known as pollen statistics during the 1930s, was shown to be pivotal to the success of Clark's new archaeology. Using the results of Scandinavian-inspired, innovative scientific techniques, Clark developed new research agenda which attracted and inspired his students. These young men and women were then among the first professionals who travelled abroad and successfully spread their scientific archaeological knowledge. It was concluded that Geison's research school chart should be expanded to accommodate additional evidence.

By the end of the 1930s, the archaeological side of the fledgling Faculty of Archaeology and Anthropology was offering a growing number of students a solid interdisciplinary core of new knowledge and the promise of careers. There was, by then, an expanded library to service the new undergraduates,[2] university-educated, specialised staff, classrooms for teaching, museum space and material for instruction and demonstration, an innovative journal, *The Proceedings of the Prehistoric Society*, for publication of new archaeological research as well as a thriving intellectual/social place to meet, the tea-room. By December 1938, the new Museum Curator, T.T. Paterson, who was a Faculty Ph.D candidate in Palaeolithic archaeology and earth sciences, could confidently write, "Ten years ago there were seventeen students reading for the Tripos; there are now sixty in addition to an average of thirty Colonial Probationers, and there is every reason to believe this

expansion will continue even more rapidly as the necessity for education in the social sciences becomes widely recognised."[3] "It can be said immediately that this is the foremost school of Archaeology and Anthropology in Europe."[4]

In 1939, Dorothy Annie Elizabeth Garrod entered the Faculty as the first woman and the first prehistorian ever elected to a professorship at either Cambridge or Oxford. Before her election, she had had an illustrious excavation and expedition career as a superbly accomplished "dirt" archaeologist in the field.[5] In this chapter, I discuss her experiences as one of the finest British Palaeolithic archaeologists of the twentieth century. Her field career and accomplishments will be considered before proceeding to an analysis of her academic experiences and an account of her contributions toward the establishment of a full Archaeological and Anthropological Tripos during the 1940s.

Unpublished papers and personal recollections of colleagues and former students reveal a contrast between Garrod's personality as professor and her behaviour in every other context.[6] In the field she was at ease and gently humorous; reserved but fun. In the Faculty, however, she is described as "cripplingly shy" — dry, distant, difficult to know. A comparison between Garrod's extraordinary effectiveness in the field and her more muted success as an academic will be made using excerpts from her correspondence and field diaries to document the contrast. Garrod's earliest letters, before her Professorship, show a spontaneous attitude toward life and work. However, evidence will be presented which suggests that Garrod had a peculiarly trying time as a prehistorian and professor at the University of Cambridge.

The questions addressed in this chapter were not inspired by the research school literature which applied so effectively to Clark's experiences. Morrell's model, which worked brilliantly to illuminate Clark's career, is less helpful when Garrod's academic life and contributions are considered. It appears that research school approaches do not sufficiently address the corporate and the gendered nature of academic archaeology and do not clearly suggest appropriate ques-

---

[1] As told to Jane Callander by Garrod's colleague, Lorraine Copeland.
[2] In 1935, part of the old Law School was transferred to the use of the Faculty to provide for the rapidly expanding Library. The Library was moved from the Museum to a space in the adjacent building which is now called the McBurney Room. "The Library is the biggest anthropological library in Britain, other than that of the Royal Anthropological Institute" (*ca.* 1939/40, T.T. Paterson; draft memorandum for the Committee of the General Board on the Department of Archaeology and Anthropology; Faculty Minutes. CUA Min.V.92a).

[3] T.T. Paterson, December 1938 draft report, appeal for funds: CUMAA Box 111 mm2/2/9.
[4] Faculty Minutes. CUL Min.V.92a. Draft memorandum for the Committee of the General Board on the Department of Archaeology and Anthropology; *ca.* 1939/40 by T.T. Paterson.
[5] Garrod described herself as doing "dirt archaeology, as Crawford called it" in a 1964 letter to her former student, Mrs Robin Kenward. Letter in possession of the Kenward family.
[6] Smith *et al.* 1997, Smith 2000a.

FIGURE XXVI   Dorothy Garrod as a child; photograph by Photographer to Her Majesty The Queen, ca. 1898. Garrod was a solid member of Annan's (1955) British intellectual aristocracy. Her father, Sir Archibald Garrod, KCMG, FRS, MD, FRCP, had been St Bartholomew's first director of the new Medical Unit in 1919 and subsequently Regius Professor of Medicine at Oxford. He is regarded as the founder of biochemical genetics. Her grandfather was Sir Alfred Garrod, FRS, MD, FRCP, of King's College Hospital, Physician Extraordinary to Queen Victoria and a leading authority on rheumatic diseases;[7] her uncle, Alfred Garrod, FRS, was a noted physiologist and zoologist and Professor of Physiology of the Royal Institute and Professor of Comparative Anatomy at King's College. Her mother, Laura Elisabeth Smith, was also from a distinguished medical family; the maternal grandfather, Sir Thomas Smith, first baronet, was "one of the great surgeons of his time",[8] Consultant Surgeon to St Bartholomew's, Surgeon Extraordinary to Queen Victoria and Sergeant Surgeon to Edward VII. (Photograph in possession of the author.)[9]

and what were her contributions as an academic, not only to the successful institutionalisation of prehistory but to the successful integration of women into Cambridge life? Finally, what was Garrod's difficulty in being professor?

A biographical introduction follows, after which I analyse Garrod's accomplishments in the field and detail her lasting contributions to archaeology. Garrod's attitudes and experiences in the field will then be compared with her experiences as an academic.

tions when people who are not primarily academics become the focus of investigation. In order adequately to describe the growing success of Cambridge prehistoric archaeology in the 1940s once Dorothy Garrod is professor, we must first consider Garrod's early career.

Garrod was not academically the leader of a research school. She was experienced in the field and as professor participated in and contributed to a broader, co-ordinated effort by the entire Faculty to expand archaeology to a full degree course. Questions which must be answered to understand Garrod's experience and which are addressed in this chapter are, how did Garrod become involved in archaeology at a time when few women would have had the inclination or opportunity? What were her experiences and contributions in the field and did gender definitions hinder her performance as an excavator? How did she become elected as the first woman professor ever at Cambridge

4.1   Dorothy Annie Elizabeth Garrod (1892–1968)

Born in 1892 in London and educated at home, Garrod was exposed to archaeology as a child by her beloved tutor, Miss Isabel Fry, with whom she visited Roman archaeological sites.[10] Her father, who served for a time on the Ipswich Museum Committee,[11] may have been another childhood influence.

Coming up to Cambridge in 1913, before archaeology was available as a subject, Garrod read ancient and classical history at Newnham College[12] where she became respected

---

[7] Garrods have held 13 professorial Chairs in the last three generations (Garrod relative, Professor Jeremy Elston, in conversation, 1998). Information on members of this very successful academic family may be found in the *DNB*. For an in-depth study of Sir Alfred Garrod, see R. Porter and G.S. Rousseau's (1998) *Gout: the Patrician Malady.* For additional information on Garrod's immediate family, read Gertrude Caton-Thompson's (1969) entry on Dorothy Garrod in the *Proceedings of the British Academy* 55: 338–61.

[8] Suzanne Cassou de Saint-Mathurin writing to Gertrude Caton-Thompson, letter from Fonds Suzanne Cassou de Saint-Mathurin. Box 71, 33432, MAN.

[9] Copy also in Garrod Papers. Box 71, MAN.

[10] Suzanne Cassou de Saint-Mathurin writing to Gertrude Caton-Thompson, no date, letter from Fonds Suzanne Cassou de Saint-Mathurin. Box 71, 33432, MAN.

[11] Plunkett, S.J. 1996. "Prehistory at Ipswich — an Idea and its Consequences." Garrod's father served on this Committee before Garrod was elected the President of the PSEA in 1928.

[12] Women were not allowed to take degrees at Cambridge in 1913 but could attend lectures and some supervisions, depending on the subject. They were allowed to sit the same exams as undergraduates. Newnham and Girton were the two colleges associated with Cambridge University established specifically for women students. Women students were not members of the University and were not referred to as "undergraduates".

for her quick wit and gentle humour.[13] She regularly participated in the Newnham College debates, successfully defending the motion, "Heredity is of more importance than environment." Her contributions to the student monthly publication, *Thersites,* reveal a quiet literary talent. At Newnham, "a golden autumn term transformed Cambridge into a magical city,"[14] before the start of World War I. By the time of her graduation in 1916, Garrod had tragically lost two brothers; Lt Alfred Noël Garrod, killed while serving with the R.A.M.C, and Lt Thomas Martin Garrod who died of wounds in 1915, aged 21. Her third brother, Lt Basil Rahere died, aged 22, in February 1919 from influenza before demobilisation. It is rumoured that Garrod also lost a fiancé.[15] Perhaps trauma-induced, she suffered poor health as a student and, after serving in the Catholic Women's League in France and the Rhineland,[16] she joined her father in Malta in 1919. There as Head of War Hospitals, Sir Archibald "in his wisdom distracted her mind towards interest in the antiquities" (Caton-Thompson 1969: 342).

Garrod's closeness to her father and his influence is often mentioned in unpublished letters.[17] Caton-Thompson writes that the "closeness of family ties . . . particularly with her father was a frequent element in her conversation."[18] Also, apparently Garrod's first comment upon election to the Disney Professorship of Archaeology was "I wish my father had been alive and the others"[19] (Caton-Thompson 1969: 340). Although there is no indication in models of research schools that father/daughter relationships are important to academic success, there is some literature which does address this influence. In commenting on the early careers of female researchers at the Cavendish Laboratory, Gould (1997: 134) writes, "Since there was no prescribed route for aspiring female physicists to follow, influence and support from family members effectively shaped their lives. Patterns of behaviour between fathers and daughters, uncles and nieces, brothers and sisters, became a model for gendered working relationships." Gould (1997: 134) notes that P.G. Abir-Am and D. Outram (1987) "have claimed that the nature of the home environment was of the utmost importance in determining the career patterns of women." In addition, R. MacLeod and R. Moseley (1979) have documented the possibility that daughters might take inspiration from the example of their fathers' successful scientific careers.

Certainly Garrod openly admired her father's inventive-

ness and scientific adventurous nature as when she mused about his experiments in the family home. "I remember one conversation with Dorothy, in which she contrasted the conditions under which her father did his research work, with that of the 1940's and 50's; specialised team work, with elaborate facilities, whereas her father had developed his genetic ideas in the solitude of a make-shift study room in their Chandos Street house with a bootlace equipment."[20] Her parents' home would have obviously "remained a source of intellectual stimulation and perhaps inspiration" (Gould 1997: 135).

Garrod's intellectually aristocratic family would have provided her with a set of values which served her well in the exploration of new areas of knowledge and the pursuit of excellence in research. Caton-Thompson (1969: 341, 340) reports that Garrod "once told me that she resolved" at the time of her brothers' deaths "to try to compensate her parents . . . by achieving a life they could feel worthy of the family tradition." Here Caton-Thompson noted the "remarkable Garrod tradition of eminence in the advancement of scientific learning." As shown below, her father's pioneering spirit was also characteristic of Garrod's archaeological work. Garrod demonstrated considerable adventurousness while digging abroad. "She was eager, fastidious, apparently not robust, but with a clear sense of values . . . and courage . . . hence the very strenuous field work [in] — France, Spain, Palestine, Kurdistan . . . caves and underground rivers, " observed Miss Jean Smith, a Newnham College friend.[21]

After Sir Archibald was appointed Regius Professor of Medicine at Oxford in 1920, Garrod enrolled in Oxford's post-graduate Diploma in Anthropology in 1921. It is clear from her lecture notes, which survive at the MAN, that the Diploma course was an intensive introduction to both archaeology and anthropology. R.R. Marett, who was Reader in Social Anthropology as well as the experienced excavator of the Palaeolithic site, La Cotte de St Brelade (Marett 1912, 1916), and physical anthropologist, Professor Arthur Thomson, were her instructors.[22] Garrod's notes reveal detailed lectures on "Method in Physical Anthropology", including instruction on how to excavate graves, how to record orientation, position, grave goods and how to photograph, measure, preserve, label and pack skeletons. "Great care should be exercised in removing bones; undermine them and support them," she carefully notes. "Cave burial: each layer should be removed separately," she continues.

[13] Favourable comments on Garrod's debating talents appear in the Newnham College, Cambridge, student publication, *Thersites* from 1913–15.

[14] Quoted from *Thersites*, 11 November 1913, volume 33.

[15] Jane Callander and I persistently heard this rumour but it was confirmed by only one witness, Miss Lovedy Smith, in an interview with Callander in 1997.

[16] Although there is some disagreement over the exact date, Garrod apparently converted to Catholicism prior to coming up to Cambridge. While at Cambridge, she enjoyed Museum Curator Baron von Hügel's hospitality, finding it supportive to the Catholic community (Letters to Caton-Thompson from Jean Smith, Fonds Suzanne Cassou de Saint-Mathurin. Box 71, MAN).

[17] Caton-Thompson to Saint-Mathurin, Saint-Mathurin to Caton-Thompson, Saint-Mathurin Papers. Box 71, MAN.

[18] 6 February 1976 correspondence, found in Saint-Mathurin Papers. Box 71, MAN.

[19] Garrod was here referring to her brothers.

[20] 6 February 1976 correspondence, found in Fonds Suzanne Cassou de Saint-Mathurin. Box 71, MAN.

[21] Smith 1968 letter to Barbara White of Newnham College on the occasion of Garrod's death, Fonds Suzanne Cassou de Saint-Mathurin. Box 72, MAN.

[22] See George W. Stocking's (1996) *After Tylor: British Social Anthropology 1888–1951* for an understanding of Oxford Anthropology at this time.

Such knowledge was to prove extremely useful to Garrod while removing skeletons during subsequent excavations. Garrod was also provided with a thorough introduction to prehistory, to de Mortillet's system of unilinear, evolutionary classification of Stone Age assemblages and to an understanding of the importance of geology and climate change. "The Mousterian begins in warm, ends in cold conditions, Magdalenian climate becoming warm and moist," Garrod noted under the heading, "Wanderings of peoples."[23] She was also introduced to Oxford's Professor of Geology, W.J. Sollas, who was at that time writing his influential and important text, *Ancient Hunters.* "*Je crois me souvenir que le livre qui a déterminé sa vocation est Ancient Hunters,*" observed Garrod's close colleague, Suzanne Cassou de Saint-Mathurin.[24] Garrod used this text throughout her field and teaching career.[25]

It may have been R.R. Marett who finally inspired Garrod to devote her life to prehistory. Years later, while presenting the first Marett Lecture established in his honour, Garrod referred to the "many enchanted hours" she had spent listening to Marett in his Acland House room. "The lectures and tutorials of that Trinity Term of 1921 opened a new world of the mind." "Marett the genial colleague, the brilliant talker, the beloved friend," Garrod stated.[26] Mrs. Chitty, *née* Mary Kitson Clark, one of Garrod's companions during the now famous Mount Carmel excavation of 1929, stated, in an interview, that Garrod experienced her conversion to prehistory with a religious depth of feeling. "The determination to be a prehistorian and particularly in the Stone Age, came over her in one second, like a conversion. She was, after the War, in turmoil, what was she to do with her life? And, it came over her in a flash, that was what she was to do."[27]

The possibility that Marett, Oxford and family were behind Garrod's conversion to prehistory is supported by her recollections during her acceptance speech for an Honorary Doctorate from the University of Toulouse in 1952. "*C'est au cours des grandes vacances de 1921 que je suis venue à Toulouse pour la première fois, ayant en poche une lettre d'introduction auprès de Cartailhac, de mon maitre le Dr Marett, ami de toute la vieille génération des préhistoriens français . . . il y avait tout juste un an que j'avais découvert la préhistoire, révélation qui devait déterminer l'orientation de toute une vie.*"[28]

Describing this trip, Garrod wrote to Jean Smith in September 1921, "My dear Jean, The last week in France was great fun. It was really almost too moving to be true. You crawl on your stomach for hours . . . climbing up yawning abysses (lighted only by an acetylene lamp which you had to carry with you somehow) and get knocked on the head by stalactites and on the legs by [stalag]mites, and in the end arrive at all sorts of wonders; bison modelled in clay, and portraits of sorcerers, and footprints of Magdalenian man which have been sealed since Palaeolithic times." The humour and *joie de vivre* evident in this letter were typical of Garrod's later approach to life.[29]

Garrod was about to meet Breuil, by then Professeur at the Collège de France and at the Insitut de Paléontologie Humaine, who became her life-long intellectual father. "Comte Bégouën, our host who discovered the caves is a dear, and we also met the Abbé Breuil who knows more than anyone else about these things and explores impossible caves in a Roman collar and bathing dress. He got an Hon. degree at Cambridge last year, but more fully clothed." After earning her Oxford Diploma with distinction, Garrod joined Breuil, on Marett's recommendation, at the Institut de Paléontologie Humaine in Paris in 1922. Her preserved notes,[30] as well as comments in an obituary she later wrote at Breuil's death,[31] attest to a rigorous introduction to Commont's research on the Quaternary gravels of the Somme. Breuil also introduced Garrod to the French typological system of classification of lithic collections[32] and to the opportunity to work at the famous excavations of the Palaeolithic sites of La Quina with Henri-Martin ("*qui fouille alors dans la grande tranchée où la femme de la Quina a été trouvée*")[33] Les Eyzies with Denis Peyrony, Isturitz with the Saint-Périers and with Jean Bouyssonie in Corrèze. At La Quina, Garrod had the opportunity to learn to identify Neanderthal remains and also to meet her future friend and collaborator, Germaine Henri-Martin. "La Quina was to produce remains of 27 Neanderthal individuals: particularly important for Dorothy Garrod's future work were fragments of a juvenile cranium," observed Jane Callander.[34]

Grahame Clark, in his biographical study of Garrod written for Tim Murray's (1999) *Encyclopedia of Archaeology,* claims that the future research agenda of Garrod's life

[23] Quotations in this paragraph are taken from Garrod's notes found among many other notes in Box 61, 33431, MAN. Garrod's lecture notes for her own lectures at Cambridge University are intermixed with her early student notes from Oxford.

[24] Saint-Mathurin to Miss Sheldon, n.d. Fonds Suzanne Cassou de Saint-Mathurin. Box 71, 33432, MAN.

[25] Teaching notes; Garrod Papers. Box 67, MAN.

[26] Manuscript of Garrod's Marett Lecture, Garrod Papers. Box 67, MAN.

[27] Mrs Chitty (*née* Mary Kitson Clark) in conversation with Callander and myself, 26 October 1996.

[28] "It was during the Long Vacation of 1921 that I came to Toulouse for the first time, having in my pocket a letter of introduction for Cartailhac from my teacher Dr Marett, friend of all the old generation of French

prehistorians . . . just a year after I had discovered prehistory, a revelation which would guide the course of a whole life." Manuscript of draft speech, Garrod Papers. Box 64, MAN.

[29] This and the following quotation describing Breuil are from a letter found in Box 72, MAN. It should be noted that, at times, Saint-Mathurin's papers are intermixed with Garrod's at the MAN.

[30] Garrod Papers. Box 64, 33431, MAN.

[31] A draft copy of this obituary is in Box 72, MAN.

[32] Breuil was able to classify a lithic artefact typologically, blind, by feel alone (Desmond Clark, in conversation, 2000).

[33] "who was excavating the large trench where the woman of La Quina was found." Notes on Garrod's student life at the IPH by her friend, Germaine Henri-Martin, found in Box 72, MAN.

[34] Callander, in conversation, 1999.

FIGURE XXVII   M. l'Abbé H. Breuil, the great French prehistorian who had introduced Miles Burkitt to prehistory in 1913, was an intellectual father also to Dorothy Garrod. He is here pictured with Garrod in 1926 when she was awarded a B.Sc. from Oxford University. (Photograph by courtesy of the Pitt Rivers Museum, University of Oxford.)

were determined by her association with Breuil in the early 1920s. Clark might presumably trace all of Garrod's various research themes to Breuil's influence. Her interest in the origin, distribution and classification of Middle and Upper Palaeolithic assemblages; her fascination with the questions of the origin of modern humans and the demise of the Neanderthals; the concern with relative dating by geochronology; and her declaration that "Europe was after all only a peninsula of Africa and Asia" (Clark 1999: 402) could all be interpreted as Garrod being the intellectual child of the Abbé Breuil.[35]

As Breuil had encouraged Burkitt to write *Prehistory*, he also suggested to Garrod the wish "*de voir réunis en une publication d'ensemble convenablement raisonnée les résultats acquis depuis plusieurs générations par vos compatriotes*" (Breuil 1926: 7).[36] In 1926, Garrod published her first synthesis, *The Upper Palaeolithic Age in Britain* (1926),[37] for which she was awarded a B.Sc from Oxford University. This was Garrod's first experience working with industries to which the classic French sequences did not apply.

In this detailed compilation and analysis of British assemblages, Garrod described a local variation of French Upper Palaeolithic industries which she labelled Creswellian. This term, named after the famous cave-sites of Creswell Crags where it was most in evidence, is still used today. "I would suggest that this industry is sufficiently well characterized to deserve a name of its own which will serve to differentiate it, on the one hand from the classical Magdalenian of France, on the other from the true Upper Aurignacian." "We can no longer expect"Garrod (1926: 194) continued "the classification of Gabriel de Mortillet to hold good all over the Palaeolithic world."

At this point in her career,[38] Garrod wrote a postcard to Burkitt cryptically stating that Palaeolithic research in England and the Fayoum was "crowded."[39] By 1924, she was clearly looking for exploration opportunities. According to Alison Roberts (1999), Garrod had planned to excavate Kent's Cavern but access was denied by the Cavern proprietors in August 1925. Shortly afterwards she accepted Breuil's invitation to explore Mousterian sites in Gibraltar.

[35] Clark, in conversation, 1994.

[36] "I expressed to you the desire to see the results, acquired over several generations by your compatriots, collected in one suitably argued published synthesis."

[37] Used by Clark as a model for *The Mesolithic Age in Britain.*

[38] There are some aspects of Garrod's career which I do not address, e.g. the Glozel affair, because they are not relevant to this publication. Refer to Bahn and Renfrew (1999) and Garrod (1968).

[39] Letter from Garrod to Burkitt, 1926. CUL Add. 7959 Box III.

FIGURE XXVIII Dorothy Garrod, "a valued member of a valued class,"[40] at the Devil's Tower, Gibraltar, June 1926. "FOUND MOUSTERIAN SKULL" Garrod wired her parents on 12 June.[41] Here she holds the skull remains of a young Neanderthal child, whom she named Abel, uncovered during her excavation at Devil's Tower. This achievement soon became known to a wide public. "The Gibraltar skull, an important new link in the record of prehistoric man, was found last June by Miss D.A.E. Garrod . . . Miss Garrod recently read a paper on her discovery before the Anthropology Section of the British Association at Oxford," reported the Illustrated London News. [42] "The success of the excavation," Garrod stated modestly, "was largely due to the very sound advice" from Breuil.[43] (Photograph by courtesy of the Pitt Rivers Museum, University of Oxford.)

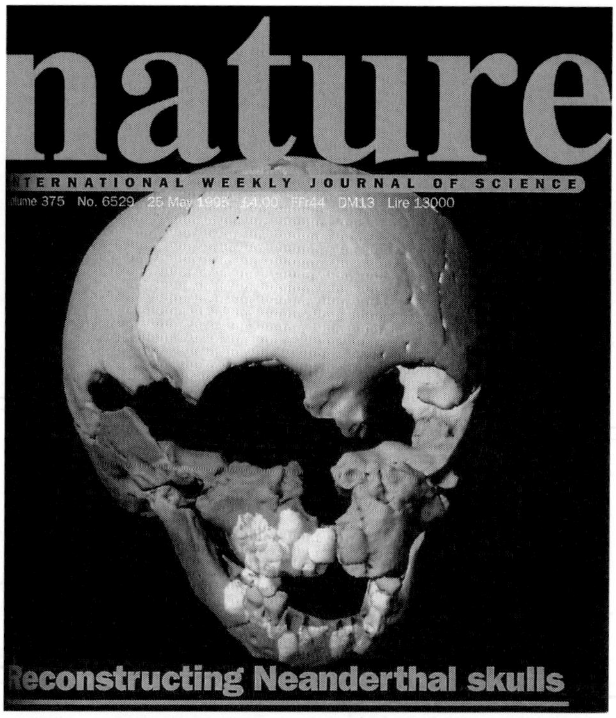

FIGURE XXIX Reconstruction of the Devil's Tower skull, Nature (Zollikofer et al. 1995).
The Gibraltar crania are not yet securely dated but evidence suggests late Neanderthal survival in the Iberian peninsula. This may have been their final refuge. The Gibraltar dig provided important information for our present understanding of the dispersal throughout Europe of Middle Palaeolithic people. Garrod's date of 20,000 B.C. retains its resonance today. Dates of 26,000 B.P. for the age of the remains and four years old for Abel's age at death are considered approximately correct.[44] "Professor Garrod's discoveries on Gibraltar remain as significant today as they did 70 years ago. Indeed they are still a source of scientific interest and an active focal point for Neanderthal studies. The Devil's Tower excavation was a major scientific landmark. It helped broaden the focus of the Mousterian beyond the narrow confines of northern Europe and into the Mediterranean zone," states Dr Nick Barton, Co-director, with Professor Chris Stringer, of the Gibraltar Caves Project.[45]

4.2 Garrod as Explorer and Excavator: "Small, Dark and Alive"

Gibraltar

According to Caton-Thompson (1969), Breuil had noticed fossil bone in the talus at the foot of Devil's Tower while on war missions to Gibraltar in 1917. A sounding in 1919 had produced Mousterian implements. At his invitation, Garrod excavated the site over a total of seven months between 1925 and 1927. This was her first internationally recognised dig and she soon struck skeletal gold.

Skilfully, Garrod found the scattered fragments of one tiny skull over a period of two separate excavation seasons. Garrod's photograph album, stored at the MAN, testifies to the personal importance of these spectacular finds. Surrounded by red stars, she sits holding the pieces. The

photograph is entitled "Abel", "b. B.C. 20,000. d. *aet*. 5, Disinterred, June 11, 1926."

In her 1928 interdisciplinary excavation report, Garrod produced the physiographic and typological analysis while Oxford anatomist, L.H. Dudley Buxton, and the well-known human anatomist/diffusionist from University College, London, G. Elliot Smith, commented on the hominid remains. Because Garrod was to find many anomalous skeletons during her ensuing career, it is worth mentioning here

---

[40] Mrs Chitty (Mary Kitson Clark), in conversation, 1996.
[41] Telegram in possession of Jane Callander.
[42] *ILN* 28 August 1926.
[43] Quotation from Garrod's draft obituary of Breuil. Box 72, MAN.

[44] Callander, in conversation, 1998.
[45] Quoted from Callander, J. and P.J. Smith. 1998. *Handbook for Exhibition in Honour of D.A.E. Garrod.*

that Dudley Buxton (1928: 61, 64, 65, 83) at first thought that the skull did not fit within the definition of Neanderthal. The massive size of the cranium was "remarkable" in comparison to the Neanderthal child from La Quina; there was a "very large proportional breadth" and an unusual cephalic index; in addition, the frontal bone was "extremely slenderly built," "entirely unlike those which are usually associated with Neanderthal man." The abnormalities suggested a brain-case built "more after the fashion of modern than of Neanderthal." However, the child's permanent dentition was of the normal massive Neanderthal type. Primarily because of this certainty, despite serious concerns as to how to categorise the remains, Dudley Buxton decided "to ascribe it to Neanderthal man".

Garrod's friend, an expert from the Natural History Museum, London, Dorothea M.A. Bate, dealt with the faunal remains. Garrod concluded that Neanderthals, with an Upper Mousterian industry, lived at Devil's Tower in a period of regression. "The sands and travertines with their terrestrial fauna and remains of human occupation can only have been deposited in a period of emergence when the Rock was once more joined to the mainland." The Director of the Institut de Paléontologie Humaine, Marcellin Boule, considered the travertine "to have followed on the deposition of the Monastirian beaches" which were assigned to the Last Interglaciation (Garrod *et al.* 1928: 44, 46). With this reasoning, Garrod provided her finds with a relative chronology and was therefore not solely dependent on typological analysis for establishing relative sequences.

As Grahame Clark suggested, Garrod's intellectual directions were firmly set by the 1920s. Her research goals remained basically unchanged throughout her life. Garrod's use of geochronology during the Gibraltar excavations and her search for hominids, "skulls — the best fund-raiser,"[46] were to be hallmarks of all her future work. Such goals were evident in Garrod's first statement of purpose, delivered to the Prehistoric Society of East Anglia as its incoming President in 1928. Here she declared that Palaeolithic archaeology was at a critical stage, that the heroic age of French archaeology was past, that de Mortillet's original unilinear framework of assemblage classification was conceptually inadequate and that prehistorians should think of cultural evolution in phylogenetic terms rather than narrow stratigraphic units.[47]

With her PSEA address, Garrod inaugurated a "new era in palaeolithic studies which will ever be her enduring monument." Clark (1939b: 280). "The centre of interest is rapidly shifting away from Europe and new discoveries make it clear that the classic sequence from Chellean to Magdalenian cannot be universally applied,"Garrod argued. "'Western Europe is only an advanced cape of Eurasia, a kind of cul-de-sac where successive waves of many human tides come to break and die out'" (Garrod 1928a: 260; Garrod quoting Boule 1928a: 261). Garrod would, from then on, look to Eurasia for the origins of the Palaeolithic invasions of Europe.

Kurdistan

Shortly before Garrod articulated this vision of Palaeolithic archaeology, she conducted a preliminary survey of Southern Kurdistan in search of Stone Age sites and the skeletal remains of Mousterian, i.e. Neanderthal, man. The area was archaeologically unexplored, "a blank on the distribution map of the Old Stone Age;"[48] hers was the first expedition to enter the district and was, according to Ralph Solecki (1972: 16), who excavated the Neanderthal site of Shanidar Cave, "to stand as the only prehistoric research in that country [north-eastern Iraq] for over two decades." Dudley Buxton and the American prehistorian, Henry Field,[49] had found, in 1927, extensive Palaeolithic surface lithics over the North Arabic desert. This implied to Garrod that Palaeolithic people migrated between Upper Mesopotamia and Syria and she hoped to discover evidence to support this hypothesis in Iraq's limestone caves. During her first brief survey, Garrod (1930: 13) discovered "Mousterian implements in gravels near Kirkuk". On a follow-up expedition in late 1928, she uncovered lithic evidence of an Epipalaeolithic, known then as Upper Aurignacian, occupation in the cave of Zarsi and an Upper Palaeolithic lithic assemblage overlying a Middle Palaeolithic level at Dark Cave, Hazar Merd. This was the first discovery of the Mousterian *in situ* in that region, proving that the Mousterian, previously thought to be primarily European, had existed as far afield as north-east Iraq.

At that point, Iraq was under British Mandate but there had been several rebellions, attempts at secession by the Kurds. Garrod's expedition took place between the second and third uprising and she therefore travelled and excavated under constant, heavy, armed guard. In fact, during one cave exploration, Garrod noticed that the police guard's "loaded gun, slung over his back, was aimed at the nape of my neck."[50] However, according to her vivid draft story, which survives at the MAN, she and her team were treated cordially by the local population. Garrod's numerous and thoughtful photographic studies of the local Kurd population imply good relations and a fascination with the people and with the country, which she thought particularly beautiful.[51] Her comments suggest that the team enjoyed themselves, despite dangers and oncoming bitter winter cold.[52]

[46] Bar-Yosef, in conversation, 1999.
[47] As did Clark, Garrod equated an assemblage with a culture and a culture with a people.
[48] Quotation from Garrod's Kurdistan Manuscript. Box 72, MAN. Garrod's vivid story of the Kurdistan/Persian border expedition and excavations is accompanied by dozens of photographic studies of the local Kurdish people who apparently visited Garrod's camp sites. These photographs were clearly intended as ethnographic records of how people lived, reflecting Garrod's training in anthropology at Oxford. These photographs are stored with Garrod's papers at the MAN.
[49] In *The Track of Man*, Field (1955) describes meeting Garrod and later Breuil when Field was a student at Oxford in the early 1920s.
[50] Kurdistan manuscript. Box 72; MAN.
[51] Garrod's notes record these reactions. Garrod Papers. Box 72, MAN.
[52] Saint-Mathurin to Caton-Thompson, describing the cold, no date. Box 71, 33432, MAN.

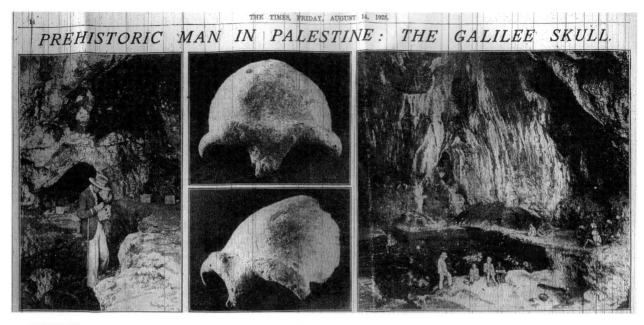

THE TIMES, FRIDAY, AUGUST 14, 1925.

PREHISTORIC MAN IN PALESTINE: THE GALILEE SKULL.

FIGURE XXX "GALILEE SKULL" New Light on Early Man, The Times, 14 August 1925. "We publish today the first photographs of the human skull of an extremely primitive type." "The skull is now in this country and has been examined by Sir Arthur Keith who explains the significance of the discovery." As with the Gibraltar cranium, the Galilee skull differed from the Neanderthal varieties found in Europe. Keith suggested that the specimen approached a modern type, that skeletal remains seemed to become more Neanthropic, i.e. modern, the further east one went; the skull must represent a particular "race or breed of Neanderthal". What then was the relationship of "Neanthropic man" and "Neanderthal man"? Who was our common ancestor (Keith 1925)?[53]

Did the fact that Garrod was a woman affect her field archaeology in Gibraltar and Kurdistan? I have found no evidence that Garrod's gender either helped or hurt her archaeological explorations. Once again, as Mary Thatcher observed, Garrod was indeed a valued member of a valued class. She was an established upper-middle-class educated English woman whose family's scientific and personal reputation was beyond dispute. Gibraltar was a long-occupied British Crown colony, military garrison and an important naval base. As is clear from the extensive acknowledgements in her Gibraltar publication, Garrod experienced cordial and privileged alliances with government and military officials. Kurdistan was under British Mandate and Garrod had the full co-operation of the military; relationships with government officials were solid. If there had been difficulties, her position in British society, and as a British citizen in an occupied territory, would have easily surmounted concerns about her being a woman.

The Levant, the Galilee Skull and Shukbah

In 1928, Oxford Professor J.L. Myres[54] invited Garrod to excavate Shukbah Cave in Palestine for the British School of Archaeology in Jerusalem. This was the first of a series of monumental excavations she was to conduct in the

Levant, but before this excavation is discussed, it should be explained that prehistoric research in that area was still in its infancy, just beginning to excite much European interest. The methodological and theoretical foundations of Western Asian archaeology were established during the 1920s and '30s. The ground work for the expertise and theoretical background we now know to be necessary to understand the Levant's complex sites was just beginning.

The period between the World Wars was the formative era in Levantine archaeology.[55] "The foundation for all fields of archaeology from the Stone Age to the Islamic were laid in the years of the British Mandate," writes Jane Callander (in press). "The necessary academic atmosphere [was] created by the establishment of the Department of Antiquities, the British School of Archaeology, the American School of Prehistoric Research, the Hebrew University, and the presence in Jerusalem of the French Ecole Biblique." It was during this time that René Neuville was posted to the French Consulate in Jerusalem, that Moshe Stekelis fled Russia and that the German archaeologist, Alfred Rust, arrived in Palestine by bicycle. Neuville excavated Natufian sites in the Judean Desert on behalf of the Institut de

---

[53] The Zuttiyeh (Galilee) skull is today considered by many to be evidence of hominid travel through the Levantine corridor from Africa rather than from the East. Researchers such as Jean-Jacques Hublin (2000: 162) perfectly echo Keith: "The Zuttiyeh skull . . . does not display clear Neanderthal affinities at a time when Neanderthal derived features are already well developed in European hominids." The date and classification of the Zuttiyeh skull are still questioned; Bar-Yosef (1992, 1998a) suggests a date >300,000 BP; a possible relative date would be within OIS 9. According to Callander (2002), most current archaeologists would agree with Keith

that the Zuttiyeh specimen exhibits traits of anatomically modern humans (AMH). The specimen may be part of a population which was ancestral to the Levantine AMH populations from Skhul, Qafzeh and which is represented by the jaw from the lower part of layer C at Tabun. Some archaeologists claim that there is evidence of successive waves from the south associated later with Afro-Arabian fauna (Tchernov 1998); the fate of these early AMH populations is unknown.

[54] Callander, in conversation, 2004.

[55] Bar-Yosef, in conversation, 1999.

Paléontologie Humaine of Paris, and would later explore Qafzeh Cave. Stekelis, now considered the "father of Israeli prehistory,"[56] discovered the important Palaeolithic and pre-Natufian site of Kebara. Rust excavated the Jabrud Rockshelter in Syria; his Palaeolithic sequences would eventually challenge Garrod's typological classifications from Mount Carmel.

However, the most remarkable prehistoric archaeological event of the 1920s in Western Asia was considered at the time to be Francis Turville-Petre's discovery of an ancient cranium at Mugharet ez-Zuttiyeh, near the Sea of Galilee.[57] This was the first time that "human remains of Mousterian date have been found outside the limits of Europe" (Keith 1927: 53).[58] George Grant MacCurdy, founder of the American School of Prehistoric Research, suggested that this discovery, together with the International Congress of Archaeology at Jerusalem and Beirut in 1926, "inaugurated a new era of prehistoric research in Palestine" (MacCurdy 1937: Foreword). Reviewers referred to the fragments as the "well-known Galilee skull" (Close 1928: 373) and Sir Arthur Keith (1927) devoted more than 50 pages to describing and analysing the remains.

The excitement that this discovery generated is completely unexplained in the history of archaeology literature. The political and social reasons for the explosion of European interest in the Palaeolithic of Western Asia during the 1920s have never been critically examined; such an examination is well beyond the scope of my analysis.[59] Nevertheless, the ample, sensational coverage in *The Times,* including large photographs, implies that English readers were fascinated by Neanderthals and that the questions posed by Keith in his newspaper article were of interest. Since the replacement of Mousterian (associated with Neanderthal) assemblages by the Aurignacian (associated with a "Modern European type") was rapid in Europe, where did modern man come from?

Where did modern man come from was exactly Garrod's guiding research question. It may be concluded that Garrod's questions were very much being considered in the public realm and were not dependent on new technical developments in a research school setting. Research school models were not designed to describe this way of doing science in the field outside of a university structure. Garrod's questions were developed during exploration abroad while working within a wider public arena. Such research was openly advertised in newspaper articles. As during Garrod's Gibraltar excavation, skeletal discoveries appear to have been applauded by the English middle classes. Ideas were presented before a non-academic readership and Garrod, along with an educated public, was looking further to the East for the ancestor of modern man.[60]

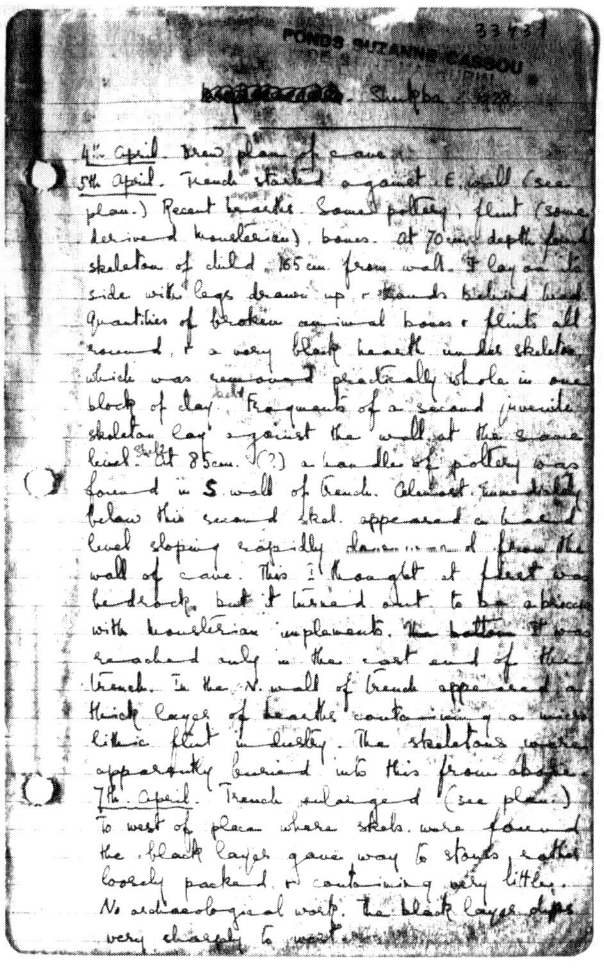

FIGURE XXXI Garrod's unpublished Shukbah field diary, first day of excavation, 5 April 1928.[61] "Trench started against E. wall . . . Some pottery, flint (some derived Mousterian), bones. At 70 cm depth found skeleton of child. It lay on its side with legs drawn up . . . Fragments of a second juvenile skeleton lay against the wall at the same level." On 5 April 1928, as well as finding evidence of a Mousterian unknown in Europe, Garrod also immediately unearthed the first remains of the Natufians who were "perhaps the earliest farmers" (Bar-Yosef 1998b: 162). "Larger blunted-back knives are common," Garrod (1932a: 258) observed, "and a number of these have on their edges the peculiar polish produced by cutting corn or grass." These discoveries at Shukbah set the agenda for future research by raising new and persistent questions concerning the origin of agriculture and the proper definition of the Neolithic. (By courtesy of the MAN.)

Certainly Garrod's discoveries, although not associated at the time with a university research setting, helped to congeal agenda taught today in university classes. Current research

---

[56] Callander, in conversation, 1999.

[57] For an evaluation of Turville-Petre's archaeological contributions, see Bar-Yosef and Callander (1997).

[58] The skull remains the oldest human fossil found in the Levant.

[59] As with Desmond Clark's and Thurstan Shaw's experiences in Africa,

archaeological exploration was supported by the expanding British Empire.

[60] It should be remembered that "Java Man" had already been reported and was in the public consciousness (Shaw, in conversation, 2002).

[61] Found in Garrod Papers. Box 63, MAN.

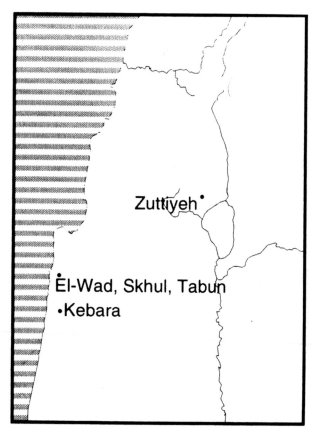

FIGURE XXXII Map of Sites.
On this map, after Goldberg and Bar-Yosef's 1998
study of Levantine prehistoric caves, we see the close
geographic location of Zuttiyeh, el-Wad, et-Tabun, Skhul
and Kebara caves. Over hundreds of thousands of years,
this small area, surrounding the modern city of Haifa,
appears to have been an environmental refuge and
crossroads for many prehistoric peoples. (By courtesy of
Goldberg and Bar-Yosef.)

questions are reminiscent of those which directed Keith and Garrod's explorations during the 1920s. The agenda for Levantine Palaeolithic research appear to have been set by 1926. The questions of origins, dates, migrations, climatic change and ancestors still dominate the literature.[62]

At Shukbah,[63] as in Gibraltar, Garrod (1928a, 1928b, 1942) again found anomalous industries and made radically new skeletal discoveries. During the first extraordinary day of excavation, she uncovered three stratigraphic layers: A, Early

Bronze Age to recent; B, an unknown microlithic flint and bone industry, later named the Natufian, which included microlithic "lunates" (Garrod 1957: 214) and sickle-blades; and D, an Upper Mousterian which "differs markedly from the industries of the same stage in Western Europe in the greater variety of its forms and in its more delicate technique, which approaches that of the Upper Palaeolithic." These Upper Palaeolithic forms occurred in clearly Mousterian, Middle Palaeolithic, layers and were not a result of mixture. Breuil at first suggested the name Aurignacio-Mousterian. The evidence of Upper Palaeolithic forms in a stratigraphically Middle Palaeolithic industry implied to Garrod that here there had been an "earlier and much more intimate contact between the two industries" and that in Palestine "we are much nearer to the centre of dispersion of the Upper Palaeolithic"(Garrod 1928b: 183, 185).[64] Garrod explained that she was slightly in favour of an Asiatic origin but that this could remain an open question (Garrod 1928a).

According to Bar-Yosef (1998b: 159), the most documented sequence from foraging to farming is in the Near East and the Natufian, with its evidence of cereal harvesting, is the "threshold for this major evolutionary change." "The Natufian," wrote Caton-Thompson (1969: 346) "is the turning point between the desert and the sown, between food gatherers and food producers, between wild animal and the domestic." Garrod did not seem to recognise the importance of the Natufian finds at first; she was surprised that there was no pottery nor domesticated animals as would be expected in Europe (Garrod 1932a). Although Dorothea Bate later found that the then Middle Natufian, or Shukbah Natufian, had domesticated dogs, Garrod's 1928 report concentrated on the Mousterian with its implications for the origins of the Upper Palaeolithic in Europe rather than the origins of agriculture or the Neolithic revolution in the Near East. "Little at that time could she have realised that she had found the nucleus of future discoveries," observed Caton-Thompson (1969: 346). Only later did Garrod (1957: 226) clearly note that her discovery of evidence of harvesting and of the domestication of dogs, without evidence of pottery, questioned the European definition of the Neolithic; "the old terms Mesolithic and Neolithic are no longer strictly applicable," she concluded.

el-Wad, Mount Carmel

With great fortune, I was able to track and to interview Mrs Chitty, *née* Mary Kitson Clark, who knew Garrod in 1929

---

[62] The literature is vast; see the well-equipped Haddon Library for Levantine prehistory. Aitken *et al,* (1992), Akazawa *et al.* (1998) and Bar-Yosef & Pilbeam (2000) offer an introduction to current debate.

[63] The definitive study of Garrod's Shukbah excavation and of her Middle Palaeolithic lithic finds is Jane Callander's (2002) "A Very Beautiful Mousterian Industry" Dorothy Garrod's Discoveries in Layer D of Shukbah Cave in Palestine Reconsidered. Unpublished MA Thesis; University College London; Institute of Archaeology; Forthcoming as an article in the *Proceedings of the Prehistoric Society.*

[64] Because the Levallois knapping technique was extensively used in the production of flakes in this industry, Garrod re-named it the Levalloiso-Mousterian; today it is known as the Late Levantine Mousterian. Bar-Yosef (1998a) and Callander and Bar-Yosef (forthcoming) suggest that at this

time in Europe, the Levalloisian and the Mousterian were considered to be separate industries. In fact, during the 1920s and '30s, there was considerable confusion about the relationship between the Levallois technique and the Mousterian but it was recognised that the two could at times be part of one industry. According to Burkitt, reporting in his draft of a "Handbook for the 1932 Congress of Prehistory and Protohistory Archaeology" (CUL Add 7959 Box I), Levalloisian flakes had been found intermixed with early Mousterian industries in England. Also, on the Continent, "The true Mousterian industries are characterized by flake tools such as Levallois flakes" (Burkitt and Childe 1932: 190). The re-definition, then, of the Aurignacio-Mousterian as Levalloiso-Mousterian could have been an effort by Garrod to make this unusual industry more accessible intellectually to Europeans.

FIGURE XXXIII   Garrod's 1929 photograph of the Mount Carmel Caves prior to excavation. El-Wad is to the left; et-Tabun, which appeared at first "to be quite small" (Garrod 1934: 85) and insignificant, is to the right. Referring later in life to her early Levantine adventures, Garrod (1962: 233) stated, "In those ten years the whole regional succession, from the close of the Lower Palaeolithic through to the mesolithic was revealed, and a new type of fossil man brought to light. 'Bliss it was in that dawn to be alive'." (Photograph by courtesy of the Pitt Rivers Museum, University of Oxford.)

and who was at the excavation of el-Wad. For the first time, eyewitness accounts of archaeological procedures and of Garrod's behaviour with Arab excavators and toward her own team members were available.[65] As an historian, rather than archaeologist, I was most interested in reconstructing human relationships between all the team players. Relevant to this reconstruction were the rich unpublished literary finds at the MAN. Sources saved include Kitson Clark's field notebook from el-Wad, April-June 1929,[66] Garrod's unpublished handwritten notes from el-Wad, entitled "Athlit, Wady Mughara 1929–30", 3 April–18 June,[67] Garrod's working notes for the discovery of the skeleton, Tabun I,[68] handwritten notes from Kebara[69] as well as camp diaries, personal diaries, card indexes and extensive notes from the other excavation seasons. These records were accompanied by hundreds of photographs, taken by Garrod, some of which are reproduced in this chapter. With these data, new perspectives were opened and Garrod's personal experiences could be re-created.

The extensive joint excavation funded by the British School of Archaeology and the American School of Prehistoric Research in the Valley of the Caves, Mount Carmel, lasted seven seasons and involved the excavation of three sites, Mugharet el-Wad (Cave of the Valley), et-Tabun (the Oven) and Mugharet es-Skhul (Cave of the Kids). A fourth cave, Kebara, initially noticed by Garrod while travelling on the Haifa–Jerusalem train, was also explored. The joint endeavour resulted in the discovery of the longest stratigraphic record for this crucial region of Western Asia. This sequence is believed to span over 600,000 years, from a crude, early "chunks of flint" pre-handaxe industry, referred to by Garrod as Tayacian (Layer G) (Garrod and Bate 1937: 89), to the modern era. The long Palaeolithic succession uncovered still serves "as a techno-cultural yardstick for the entire Levantine Mousterian" (Bar-Yosef 1992: 134).

The archaeological richness of the Mount Carmel Caves was astonishing. "The group of caves . . . has proved to be richer than any other Mediterranean coastal group" wrote MacCurdy (1937) in his introduction to *The Stone Age of Mount Carmel*. The first archaeological layer discovered at et-Tabun, Layer B of the Upper Levalloiso-Mousterian,

[65] Team members came from women's colleges in Cambridge, Oxford and the USA. I thank Julia Roberts for putting me in touch with Mrs Chitty.
[66] Garrod Papers. Box 63, MAN.
[67] Garrod Papers. Box 58, MAN.
[68] Garrod Papers. Box 57, MAN.
[69] Garrod Papers. Box 58, MAN.

FIGURE XXXIV "Palestine People."
Notebooks and diaries from the very strenuous excavations document bonhomie and courage under stress. Dorothy Garrod with the members of her first excavation crew at the el-Wad, Mount Carmel, 1929. Standing in their camp are, left to right: Elinor Ewbank (Lady Margaret Hall, Oxford), Dorothy Garrod, Mrs Chitty, née Mary Kitson Clark (Girton College, Cambridge), Dean Harriet M. Allyn (Mount Holyoke College, USA) and Dr Martha Hackett. When I asked "how would you describe Garrod?," Mrs Chitty instantly and emphatically responded "Small, dark and alive!"[70] (Photograph courtesy of the Fonds Suzanne Cassou de Saint-Mathurin, MAN.) Jacquetta Hawkes (left), who also dug at Mount Carmel Caves, 1932. (Photograph courtesy of Mrs Caroline Burkitt, Mrs Kennedy Shaw's daughter.)

had an average depth of 3.50 metres (Garrod 1934). Archaeological deposits for the inner chamber reached 8.30 m in depth. The trench dug in the outer chamber had a maximum depth of 15.50 m filled with archaeological layers. The maximum thickness of all the deposits was over 24 m (Garrod and Bate 1937). The stratigraphic layer E of et-Tabun alone "yielded in addition to innumerable flakes, blades and cores, no less than 7,113 hand-axes, 26,758 racloirs [scrapers] and 3,009 other implements" (Clark 1937a: 487). More than 87,000 stone implements were eventually excavated, classified and catalogued.[71]

The skeletal remains were equally challenging and remain controversial. Extensive burials were uncovered at el-Wad, et-Tabun and Skhul. The remains from Tabun and Skhul, which will be discussed below, continue to be contentious. Most archaeologists today argue that two species of prehistoric humans, Neanderthal and Anatomically

Modern Humans (AMH), using similar tools, occupied the caves either concurrently or alternately during the Middle Palaeolithic. Others might agree with Keith's final judgement that Tabun I and II, Skhul and even Zuttiyeh all represent only one highly variable people in the throes of evolutionary change, having affinities to both *Homo neanderthalensis* and *Homo sapiens*. Still others suggest that the morphological evidence for Neanderthal presence at Tabun is poor and that the remains can be seen, instead, as evidence for a regional evolution of *Homo sapiens*. Despite all debate, it is generally agreed that the Levant provided an "inevitable land corridor" for the "long voyage to the West" (Arensburg & Belfer-Cohen 1998: 319).

According to Callander,[72] activities prior to Dorothy Garrod's digs at Mount Carmel were high-level stuff; government reports and telegrams about the site of paramount importance. "Yet the whole thing seems to fall to Garrod with merely good will. What a burden!" She was in charge

---

[70] Chitty (Kitson Clark), in conversation with Callander and Smith, 1996.
[71] "The study of the archaeological material which I undertook myself," wrote Garrod in her 1939 application for the Disney Chair (copy found in Garrod Papers; Box 72; MAN), "involved the classification . . . of more

[72] Callander, in conversation, 1998.
[73] "Kebara was re-excavated by Stekelis, from 1951–65, and a team led by Bar-Yosef, from 1982–90, revealing in 1983 an almost complete Neanderthal burial" (Callander & Smith 1998).

than 87,000 stone implements."

FIGURE XXXV   The el-Wad Terrace; levelled area and rock cut basins at base of layer B. Close to 100 burials[74] were found in a cemetery on the terrace of el-Wad cave during the 1930 and '31 excavation seasons; these were associated with rich material cultural remains, lithics, bone tools, decorative objects, a ground stone assemblage and architectural features. "It was clear that basins, wall, and pavement formed a single scheme" wrote Garrod (1932b: 48), connected, she thought, with a cult of the dead. (Photograph by courtesy of the Pitt Rivers Museum, University of Oxford.)

of all four excavations, including Theodore D. McCown's work at Skhul and Francis Turville-Petre's investigation of Kebara.[73] At el-Wad and et-Tabun, Garrod was specifically responsible for designing the excavation strategies for four, sometimes simultaneous, excavation sites during seven seasons, soliciting and budgeting finances, setting up camps, choosing, hiring, training and supervising her co-workers, arranging for equipment and supplies, dealing with British Mandate officials and maintaining cordial relationships with the local Arab employees and their community. She was notified of all finds and made the decisions on how to preserve and to catalogue the abundant archaeological remains. The analysis of artefacts required an extraordinary effort; Garrod was responsible for analysis of all material, writing field reports and publication of results. She handled these formidable tasks expertly. "It was an enormous project and she did it quite single-handedly," remembered 1929 crew member, Kitson Clark.[75]

Inspired by the "sensational results" (Garrod 1929: 220) that Charles Lambert, from the British Mandate Department of Antiquities, had uncovered in 1928,[76] Garrod began to excavate el-Wad in early April 1929. Her first notebook entry, 3 April 1929, records that six women and four men, from neighbouring Palestinian villages, had begun preparing the site. Shortly after, in the outer chamber, she uncovered a collective burial of ten individuals associated with a Shukbah-like microlithic and bone industry. By her last entry on 18 June, Garrod could record eight archaeological levels from Bronze Age to Mousterian, the most complete prehistoric sequence in Palestine to date. A sounding was made at Tabun, finding Mousterian implements identical to that of Shukbah and el-Wad; according to Kitson Clark's notes, she made the first sounding at Skhul, discovering a Levalloiso-Mousterian industry, thought today to correspond to Tabun's Layer C.[77]

---

[74] Estimate from Belfer-Cohen *et al.* (1991).

[75] Chitty (Kitson Clark), in conversation with Callander and Smith, 1996.

[76] In early 1929, Keith had reported in the *ILN* (NPR.c.313 West Room, CUL) a find in Palestine of great interest and importance; prehistoric objects "not so far found outside of Europe". In 1928, Charles Lambert had

uncovered, during a preliminary investigation at el-Wad, the first prehistoric art object discovered in the Near East, a finely carved bone animal head. He had also discovered human, later identified as Natufian, burials.

[77] The sounding was also mentioned during interviews. Kitson Clark, in conversation with Callander and Smith 1996.

FIGURE XXXVI HOMO 25.
Garrod's photograph of a decorated Natufian skeleton. "It rested on its side . . . on the head was a circlet, perfectly in place, made up of seven rows of dentalia" (Garrod 1932b: 48). El-Wad is today considered to have been a major base camp; no "research of Natufian culture [dated ca. 12,900 to 10,200 BP] is complete without taking the site into full consideration," states Weinstein-Evron (1998: 9), who is re-excavating the cave. (Photograph courtesy of the Pitt Rivers Museum, University of Oxford.)

Kitson Clark's journal for this first season radiates excitement but the excavation was particularly difficult. Both Shukbah and et-Tabun are karstic caves with sinkholes and vaulted ceilings; the stratigraphy in all caves was convoluted. Many layers were disturbed and occasional gaps occurred, as at Shukbah between Layer B and Layer C. No complete sequence was ever found in any one section at el-Wad; the archaeological layers were unevenly distributed. Only Natufian remains, for example, were found on the cave's terrace.

Living and health conditions at the el-Wad excavation were as difficult as the stratigraphy. "Unfortunately, the Arabs

kept their goats in this cave, so we picked up lice . . . they did run freely around our legs and one of the Americans [Allyn] and I got Relapsing Fever. She got it rather badly with weevils . . . very unpleasant."[78] In Garrod's reports as Field Director to the American School of Prehistoric Research, she frequently mentioned the weather. "On 4 October [1932] the camp was flooded out by an excessively severe thunderstorm. Work was impossible the next day." Later in October, Garrod wrote, "the damp heat is very trying. An epidemic of influenza has spread to the members of the expedition." During the first week of November as the excavation of el-Wad was concluding, "Work was stopped for four days owing to very heavy rain, quite unusually violent;" and, at the end of November, "Weather has been vile . . . a tent is a bad place to live in during a succession of gales and thunderstorms."[79]

Nevertheless, Kitson Clark remembered Garrod as an excellent archaeologist "who knew her stuff"[80] and who remained composed, calm, and generous. Although reserved and shy, Garrod was "a very warm and feeling person." Kitson Clark noticed that relationships between the Mandate Government and the Arab population were definitely strained in 1929. During a procession on Good Friday, the way was cleared but "in front of every alleyway was part of Colonel Glubb's police with a whip. The crowds gave us the feeling of being hostile." Despite this, Garrod developed friendships with the Arab personnel who worked on the dig. Dr Martha Hackett set up a small medical clinic for the local people which was apparently much appreciated. Garrod, herself, was well respected and seemingly loved.[81]

et-Tabun, Mount Carmel

Work at et-Tabun was started in 1931; in the same season, Ted McCown, a 21-year-old palaeontologist from the University of California, began his excavation of Skhul cave. Both excavations revealed invaluable hominid remains, still pivotal to the archaeological debate on human evolution. In his first season, McCown found a single archaeological deposit resting on bed-rock yielding a Levalloiso-Mousterian industry identical to that of Tabun C as well as the first burials embedded in breccia. In the following season, he uncovered an ancient prehistoric necropolis with individuals who appeared to combine Neanderthaloid and Neanthropic features.[82]

At Tabun, with characteristic skill, Garrod quickly discovered that the deepest layer (G) in el-Wad corresponded to the first undisturbed layer (B) of Tabun which was a Levalloiso-Mousterian industry with abundant triangular flakes; the evidence of prehistoric occupation at Tabun started where the evidence of occupation at el-Wad had

[78] Kitson Clark, in conversation with Julia Roberts, 1994.
[79] "Reports of Miss Dorothy Garrod, Field Director, Wady al-Mughara, Autumn Season 1932, to the Directors and Trustees of the American School of Prehistoric Research," copies in Box 72, MAN, others in possession of Jane Callander.
[80] According to Kitson Clark, Garrod judged changes in stratigraphy by

the changing feel of stone artefacts.
[81] All quotations from Kitson Clark, in conversation, 1996.
[82] As mentioned above, the Skhul people are now considered to be AMH and are dated to *ca.* 100,000 BP by ESR (Bar-Yosef 1998a). They are today thought to ante-date the Neanderthal of Tabun and Kebara.

FIGURE XXXVII Palestinian villagers visiting Garrod's camp. Relationships with Arab neighbours and employees were warm; Garrod was often invited to weddings or other celebratory occasions. "She was called Sitt Miriam, Lady Mary." "When we had a fantasia at the end, a party, the girls made a ring all around us and danced round us singing," Kitson Clark remembered. This photograph was taken by Eleanor Dyott, later Mrs W.B. Kennedy Shaw, who was a crew member for three seasons at et-Tabun. (Photographs courtesy of Mrs Caroline Burkitt, Mrs Kennedy Shaw's daughter.)[83]

stopped. Tabun, therefore, complemented the prehistoric record preserved at el-Wad. Although it revealed

no Natufian, Upper Palaeolithic or transitional material, Tabun harboured an endless surprise of Mousterian and

[83] Miles Burkitt was responsible for recruiting several members of Garrod's Mount Carmel team. Among these were Mary Kitson Clark and Eleanor Dyott. Miles Burkitt's son, Miles Burkitt Jr, later married Eleanor Dyott's daughter, Caroline. Dyott's extensive photograph album from the Mount Carmel dig is in Mrs Caroline Burkitt's possession. Also, Miss Hilda Wills was the Burkitts' long-term friend and most likely learned of the dig through them.

FIGURE XXXVIII   Garrod's photograph of Tabun in 1934 which appeared in The Stone Age of Mount Carmel *(1937) with her stratigraphy superimposed. This photograph, taken from Layer B, shows the grandeur of the dig. Layer D contained Lower Levalloiso-Mousterian (Middle Palaeolithic) deposits characterised by long and narrow Levallois points; Layer E and F were Lower Palaeolithic. According to Professor Avraham Ronen, leading Levantine expert who has re-evaluated the Mount Carmel Caves, "Garrod's stratigraphical subdivision of Tabun Cave is the clearest ever made."[84] (Photograph courtesy of the Pitt Rivers Museum, University of Oxford.)*

Acheulean finds associated with abundant fauna, a discovery "so far unknown in this region"(Garrod 1932b: 50)[85] In her correspondence to G.G. MacCurdy, of the American School of Prehistoric Research, Garrod claimed to be embarrassed by Tabun's unexpectedly great depth of the deposits and the need for additional time and funds.

The skeleton of what is today considered to be a Neanderthal female, Tabun I, was discovered in December 1932 in Terrace West near the surface of Layer C. Because of the continued controversy surrounding this skeleton, its proper stratigraphic provenance and its relationship to the remains from Skhul, it is worth putting on record Garrod's unpublished opinions.

[84] Quotation from Callander & Smith (1998).
[85] The faunal evidence at Tabun was unrivalled in richness and allowed Dorothea Bate, who had worked with Garrod at Gibraltar and Shukbah, to reconstruct Tabun's prehistoric climate. In her now famous chart, Bate suggested that *Dama Mesopotamica,* a species of deer, abundant in Layer

B, implied forest conditions and considerable rainfall. Layer B also gave evidence of "a great faunal break having taken place," "an abrupt change to fauna of modern type" (Garrod and Bate 1937: 155). A rapid increase in *Gazella,* on the other hand, in Layer C implied drier conditions.

In a letter I recovered from the MAN,[86] written to Caton-Thompson, dated 22 January 1933, Garrod stated, "The probability of its being a woman is strengthened by the fact that we found vestiges of a very young infant close to the left humerus."[87] Although the skeleton was, therefore, immediately recognised as female, Garrod had grave concerns as to its classification. Garrod observed that the skeleton had "the most receding lower jaw I know on any human." "It has Neandertaloid brow-ridges but the bone is thin." "The skeleton is small, and the bones are delicate in contrast with Neanderthal man and with Ted's [Skhul's] people."

Some weeks earlier, a massive, powerful lower jaw with a well-developed chin had been recovered from the base of Layer C in Terrace East considerably below the level of Tabun I in Terrace W. "It [the woman]," Garrod noted "contrasts most strikingly with the isolated jaw from the base of the same level which has a well marked chin and seems to compare with Ted McCown's people." McCown's people had, by then, been classified by Keith as a Palestinian race of Neanderthal, *Palaeoanthropus palestinensis*, which was characterised by strong chins and considered to be closer to modern humans than their chinless, European Neanderthal relatives.

Since it was generally assumed that Neanderthals evolved from a common ancestor before modern humans, Garrod was surprised to find such strong evidence of two types of "humans", with the more modern type living so clearly stratigraphically *beneath* the chinless (even *more* chinless than European Neanderthals) primitive woman.

Bar-Yosef and Callander (1999) have argued that Garrod's MAN letter and corroborating evidence from a report Garrod wrote for the Jerusalem Department of Antiquities in 1932, which repeats the same statements, explains why Garrod wrote her well-known conclusion concerning Tabun I. In *The Stone Age of Mount Carmel*, Garrod (1937: 64), "The skeleton lay so near the surface of C that the question must arise whether it does not represent a burial from Layer B. There was no obvious sign of disturbance, but . . . I feel that this must remain an open question." As this statement shows, Garrod had doubts not only about Tabun I's classification but also about its provenance. Bar-Yosef and Callander believe that Tabun I is a burial from Layer B and therefore not associated with Layer C and its industries as are the skeletons from Skhul.[88]

The information in the MAN letter does not lead to an explanation of Garrod's doubt as to the Tabun skeleton's proper stratigraphic provenance. Garrod did not discuss the stratigraphical position in relation to Layer B or Layer C in the MAN letter; she discussed only her concerns as to how the skeleton should be morphologically classified. She also made it clear that she thought the skeleton was a

FIGURE XXXIX   Dorothy Garrod with Yusra, the woman who found Tabun I, the adult female Neanderthal skeleton. According to Jacquetta Hawkes,[89] Yusra acted as foreman in charge of picking out items before the excavated soil was sieved; over the years, she became expert in recognising bone, fauna, hominid and lithic remains and had spotted a tooth which led to the crushed skull. Hawkes remembered talking to Yusra about coming up to Cambridge. "She had a dream. She was very able indeed. Yusra would obviously have been a Newnham Fellow."[90] The villages of Jeba and Ljsim were destroyed in 1948 and I was unable to trace any members of the Palestinian team. (Photograph courtesy of the Pitt Rivers Museum, University of Oxford.)

"true" earlier Neanderthal type. MacCurdy had suggested to her that it was perhaps akin to Krapina.[91] Krapina was, at that time, assigned to the Riss-Würm interglaciation. Neanderthals and the Mousterian generally were considered to be correlated with the European Würm glaciation. Bar-Yosef (Bar-Yosef and Callander 1999: 82) argues that because of evidence of Bate's great faunal break, Tabun B was thought to be correlated with the Würm glaciation and that Garrod would have preferred that Tabun I correspond to the Würm of Europe. However, there is no clear evidence that Garrod was thinking in this way. In fact, she seemed to believe that Tabun I pre-dated Neanderthals in Europe.

The letter does, however, clearly show that Garrod did not agree with Keith and that she felt that two different human types lived at Tabun, within the same stratigraphic unit; the modern one represented by the jaw, preceding the more primitive Tabun I, the woman. This was a

---

[86] Garrod Papers. Box 71, MAN.

[87] It would appear that Tabun I died in childbirth or shortly there after.

[88] Callander, in conversation, 2003.

[89] Jacquetta Hopkins, later Hawkes, from Newnham College, was a member of Garrod's 1932 Autumn team.

[90] Jacquetta Hawkes, in conversation with Jane Callander, 1990. I found some evidence in the Faculty Minutes that Garrod attempted to bring Yusra to Cambridge in 1936.

[91] Unpublished MacCurdy letter to Garrod, 3 February 1933. Garrod Papers, Box 71, MAN.

FIGURE XL   The removal of the skeleton, Tabun I, from her grave. (Photographs courtesy of the Pitt Rivers Museum, University of Oxford.)

revolutionary thought indeed and is today considered by many to be correct. However, Garrod apparently deferred to Keith and McCown on this issue; she never publicly countered their eventual conclusion that Tabun I belonged to *Palaeoanthropus palestinensis*.[92]

Conditions at et-Tabun were harsh. The crew endured uncomfortable, primitive living conditions, terrible heat (119 degrees in Autumn 1932), 'sticky' humidity, limited and contaminated water, faulty equipment, dust, hot 'Khamseen'

winds, violent electrical storms, torrential rains and again exposure to serious disease. Team members were again repeatedly very ill. During the final 1934 excavation season at Tabun, one crew member, Ruth Waddington, was rushed to the German Hospital in Haifa with malaria.

Garrod's 1934 diary is permeated with light-hearted stories that belie these difficult circumstances. "There was considerable consternation as there had been predictions of a cloudburst, an earthquake and the end of the world."[93]

[92] Since it has not been noted in current literature, it should be recorded here that Tabun I's feet were burnt and that the body lay in a hearth (Garrod

1932 letter to MacCurdy, Garrod Papers. Box 57, MAN.)
[93] Garrod 1934: 25 May 1934, Garrod's Diary, found near Box 62, MAN.

"Mud, muck, ooze upon the floor, torn tents and thunder – all were forgotten as the sherry bottle was opened. Though it might be mentioned all knives were carefully cleared off the table . . . as the dark showed blue lightning."[94] The women named their tents and tiny mud brick huts the "Tibn Towers", arranged daily tea, "Sabbath" sherry at 6.00 p.m. and an occasional Sunday seaside holiday. Although Garrod was affectionately called "The Boss", all daily living and working routines were group decisions, informally decided at breakfast or tea.

Numerous and frequent official European visitors were handled with patient humour. "The Towers must above all things keep up appearances," Fuller writes in Garrod's April Diary. "The afternoon was awaited with some anxiety, as Miss Hilda Wills had announced her intention of visiting the Towers," reports Garrod on 14 April 1934. "At 2.0 precisely Miss W.'s car was sighted turning into the 'drive'. DG hastened down to receive her, putting the finishing touches to her toilet as the car approached the causeway . . . though ignorant of prehistory [Miss Wills] displayed just the right amount of interest — in short behaved like the best type of Cultured English Hat . . . drank tea in the parlour of the Towers, and drove away, leaving a cheque . . . Sabbath Sherry was drunk at 6.45, the toast being . . .

> a 'hat' of the best, named Miss Wills,
> a presenter of gifts and not bills,
> drove up to the Towers
> and stayed several hours,
> leaving twenty-five pounds and no mils."

The "Tibnites" decided at tea to spend part of this gift on improving an "essential piece of furniture" — their crude outdoor loo.[95]

On 27 August 1934, according to Garrod's Diary, Levels F and G were completed. On 29 August, "The lorry for the flints arrived; 5 tonnes of flint." "At 12.45pm DG and ED [Eleanor Dyott] sailed away in a taxi. Au revoir au Mughâret et-Tabun." The diary is then marked, "Finis". Garrod's description and analysis was published in 1937 to critical acclaim. Grahame Clark, who was to succeed Garrod to the Disney Chair in 1952, described her massive tome, *The Stone Age of Mount Carmel* (1937), as "pure gold" (Clark 1937a: 488). Following the publication of this volume, Garrod was awarded Honorary Doctorates from the University of Pennsylvania and Boston College and a DSc. from Oxford University.

Anatolia and Bacho Kiro

The 1938 expedition to Anatolia and the subsequent trip to and excavation of the key Palaeolithic cave site in Bulgaria, Bacho Kiro, on behalf of the American School of Prehistoric Research, were Garrod's last field adventures before her election to the Disney Professorship. Once again, eyewitness accounts suggest that Garrod was poised and archaeologically successful as Director.

FIGURE XLI   *Dorothy Garrod with bear cub, Anatolia, 1938. "She was calm and self-assured, conversed easily and put me completely at ease, and I took to her at once," reported Dr Bruce Howe on his first meeting with Garrod in 1938. Howe was a "green-horn graduate student" at Harvard University when he joined Garrod's five-month expedition to Anatolia and Bulgaria to document Palaeolithic sites. Although Director, Garrod "very much treated us . . . as equals . . . she seemed perfectly confident . . . authoritative and forth putting in all her fieldwork and planning interactions. Dorothy was unique, rather like a glass of pale fine stony French white wine."[96] (Photograph courtesy of the Pitt Rivers Museum, University of Oxford.)*

During her 1938 reconnaissance expedition in Anatolia, Garrod was once again "largely self-propelled". As in early field situations, her "demeanor and dealings with the various Institutes and with the Turkish authorities were . . . civil, effective and sure-footed with mutual respect and cordiality evident at all times". Although ultimately in charge of key decisions, she always encouraged contributions from the young Harvard researchers who accompanied her, James Gaul as well as Bruce Howe. Meeting at meals for "good talk and work", Garrod suggested that Howe spend his next year (1938–1939) in Cambridge to benefit from the Museum's extensive collections of Stone Age material and

---

[94] Garrod 1934; Anne Fuller's April 1934 entry in Garrod's Diary, MAN.

[95] Garrod 1934, Garrod's Diary, 14 April 1934, MAN.

[96] Bruce Howe, personal correspondence, 1997.

to attend Grahame Clark's and Glyn Daniel's lectures on prehistoric archaeology.[97]

Archaeologically, the expedition and excavation were a success. At Bacho Kiro, Garrod uncovered evidence of a number of Aurignacian levels superimposed on Mousterian material. This was the first Palaeolithic sequence to be found in Bulgaria; Garrod's conclusions about the Bulgarian Aurignacian remained the foundation of Upper Palaeolithic studies in that country for decades (Kozlowski 1999).

This detailed reconstruction and analysis of Garrod's excavation experiences and remarkable discoveries has documented how and what Garrod contributed to the foundation of twentieth-century Palaeolithic research during the period prior to her professorial election. By 1939, her very successful archaeological explorations had became known throughout Europe and Western Asia. Garrod's field research led the way in the 1930s. She is, today, considered to be one of the founders of modern prehistory for the Levant. The Mount Carmel sequence, possibly spanning over 600,000 years, still serves as a yardstick for the entire Levantine Mousterian. Many of Garrod's concerns, such as the emergence of anatomically modern people, remain issues of great anthropological concern. The skeletal evidence she uncovered is still studied and continues to be the centre of controversy and debate. Garrod's research was not only seriously important in the 1920s and 1930s but has remained relevant to current archaeological investigation. Her discoveries and analyses are part of university curricula in prehistory the world over. Garrod's life and accomplishments are worthy of great interest.

Garrod's academic career is now discussed; literature which analyses women's academic experiences will be used to understand Garrod's professorial years. Dozens of former students and colleagues shared their memories; these recollections helped to reconstruct Garrod's life as professor at Cambridge.

4.3 Garrod as Professor: Reserved and Shy

In May 1939, the mathematical physicist, Dr Bertha Swirles, later Lady Jeffreys, was taking a train from Cambridge to Manchester when she met Manchester Professor of Geography H.J. Fleure. Fleure had just participated in the Cambridge meeting that had elected Dorothy Garrod to the Disney Professorship of Archaeology. According to Fleure, when the Electors gave their decision to Vice-Chancellor Dean, the Vice-Chancellor replied "Gentlemen, you have presented us with a problem."[98]

The Vice-Chancellor was correct. Being female, Garrod was not a full member of Cambridge University. Yet, as

FIGURE XLII "Dear Mr Vice-Chancellor, I beg to submit myself as a candidate for the vacant Disney Professorship of Archaeology," Dorothy Garrod wrote in her professorial application, 16 March 1939.[99] Although women became eligible for all University teaching offices and for membership to Faculties and Faculty Boards under Cambridge University's New Statutes of 1926, they were still not admissible to degrees and could not thus become members of the Senate and the Regent House. Garrod's election highlighted the contradiction inherent in this situation. (Reproduced by kind permission of the Syndics of the Cambridge University Library.)

Professor she became eligible to serve on the Council of the Senate, and all members of the Council were by definition members of the University. Had she been chosen to serve on the Council, an awkward situation would have occurred. This amused Fleure,[100] who was favourably disposed to electing Garrod (Daniel 1986: 98).[101] He was from Manchester, where women were admitted to degrees, and

[97] Bruce Howe, personal correspondence, 1998.

[98] Lady Jeffreys, in conversation, 1998. I am grateful to Lady Jeffreys for sharing her memories before she died.

[99] Garrod Papers. Box 72, MAN.

[100] Lady Jeffreys, in conversation, 1998.

[101] Daniel, Disney Professor of Archaeology from 1974–81, met Fleure shortly before the 5 May 1939 Election. Daniel recalled Fleure favourably discussing Garrod's candidacy. Several family members and colleagues of the Electors, whom I interviewed, felt that this particular group of Electors might have been pro-women.

was accustomed to the idea of women in higher academic ranks. The Electors seem to have chosen the best candidate without concern for administrative repercussions.

As mentioned earlier, there is no hint of controversy surrounding this important election. There is not the least sign of strong disagreement among the Electors. Dorothy Garrod was apparently chosen because of her qualifications. She was the best candidate for the position in several ways. By 1939, Garrod was one of Britain's finest archaeologists. In addition she had shown some administrative skill and some ability as a supervisor. Garrod was Newnham's Director of Studies for Archaeology and Anthropology from 1934 and had served on Newnham College committees. Although she had never held a position as a University officer, Garrod had offered a short course on the Palaeolithic in Eastern Europe and the Near East for the Faculty in 1938.[102] She was remembered by her Newnham students, at individual supervisions, as an "excellent supervisor, gentle and organised."[103] "Dorothy was my supervisor and she was very nice . . . she was a wonderful relief."[104]

Garrod's application was helped by political considerations and by who her competitors were. There is no official record of who was considered, but a list can be reconstructed from unpublished and published memoirs and interviews with relatives and former students. One possibility is problematical. There are conflicting reports on whether Gertrude Caton-Thompson, respected internationally for her intensive, innovative archaeological investigation of the Later Stone Age in Egypt, wanted the Professorship. A close relative of Garrod clearly remembers Caton-Thompson expressing regret that she was not chosen for the position.[105] But former Disney Professor Glyn Daniel (1986: 98) wrote in his Memoirs that "the Electors first offered the Chair to Caton-Thompson, who had not applied, and . . . when she declined, appointed Dorothy Garrod". Since there is no corroborating evidence either way, I can say no more than that Caton-Thompson was considered.

Christopher Hawkes, in 1946 appointed foundation Professor of European Archaeology at Oxford, did certainly apply (Webster 1991: 234).[106] But, in 1939, he was a man of merely 34 years whose career, in comparison to the other candidates, was not yet established.

The first of the major contenders was Miles Burkitt. "It was thought by many inevitable that the Disney Chair ought to

and would go to Miles Burkitt," wrote Daniel (1986: 97). Burkitt was, by then, a long-term devoted member of the Faculty Board of Archaeology and Anthropology, an able administrator, the generous and hard-working Secretary to the Board since its inception. Burkitt's publications, *Prehistory* (1921a) and *The Old Stone Age* (1933) were standard introductory texts for Faculty courses. As documented earlier, he was remembered by all as an inspiring lecturer. Yet he had no experience directing excavations and he was not reputed to be an original researcher. The Faculty Board had declined to nominate him for a Senior Doctorate.[107] In addition, internationally known, influential prehistorians, such as Breuil, considered Garrod to be a superior candidate.[108]

Daniel (1986: 97) also claims that the Anglo-Saxon archaeologist, Tom Lethbridge, "put in" for the Professorship. This claim is supported by a passage from Lethbridge's unpublished autobiography. He had taught archaeology from the mid 1920s to the early 1950s at Cambridge and entered the arena at the request of those opposed to an outsider. "There was an obvious candidate [Burkitt] for the Professorship but there was also a candidate from outside. Louis [Clarke, the Museum Curator] said it would be a real disaster for Cambridge if this one were elected and . . . persuaded me to stand to keep this man out" (Lethbridge [1965]: 100).

Possibly the "candidate from outside" was Mortimer Wheeler, who Daniel (1986: 97) states wanted the position. Wheeler at that time was involved as Honorary Director of London University's Institute of Archaeology that he and his wife, Tessa, founded in the mid-1930s, and had not formally applied, but the British archaeological community was small and an informal inquiry would have been sufficient. He was "a brilliant organizer, a born excavator, a dynamic and forceful character" but was also considered a "bounder" by some members of the Cambridge Faculty (Daniel 1986: 407–8). He could easily have been one of those discussed among the "other persons mentioned by the electors".[109] By implication one of the Electors who might have voted for Wheeler was diverted by Lethbridge's candidacy.

On the other hand, the "outsider" may have been Louis Leakey[110] who, although with a brilliant Ph.D from St John's College, had scandalised Cambridge by leaving his pregnant first wife for Mary Nicol in 1934. Eyewitness accounts claim that the uproar was considerable and that Leakey was harshly judged for what was considered a rash and irresponsible act.[111]

[102] Faculty Minutes, 3 November 1938. CUA Min.V.92a.
[103] Joan Lillico, First Class Honours 1935, personal correspondence, 1998.
[104] Clare Fell, who was awarded a First in 1933, in conversation with Julia Roberts, 1994.
[105] Callander, referring to Madeleine Lovedy Smith's memory of the incident, personal communication, 1998.
[106] During an interview with me in 1996, Sonia Chadwick Hawkes confirmed that Hawkes applied.
[107] Faculty Minute Book: 5 March 1929. Min.V.92a.
[108] Testimonial on Garrod's qualifications for the Disney Professorship by

Breuil. Box 72, MAN.
[109] Elections to Professorships. CUA O.XIV.54, 5 May 1939.
[110] Mary Kitson Clark was the first to claim that the "outsider" was Leakey, personal correspondence, 1998.
[111] Shaw was a good friend of Mary Nicol and knew Leakey and Nicol when they were first together. He remembers the reaction well (in conversation, 1996). Shaw's 60 years of correspondence with Mary Leakey is now in the CUL. It is clear, from letters Leakey wrote to Garrod, that he did wish to apply for the Disney Professorship in 1952 but may have decided against it for financial reasons. Leakey's correspondence with Garrod is stored in the CUMAA letter box for 1951.

A highly qualified, scandal-free, established British-born woman was apparently a more pleasing alternative than any outsider. Thus the fact that Garrod was a "Cambridge man" may be added to her list of qualifications.[112] "All went well," Lethbridge ([1965]: 100) concludes: "the proper man got in."

Reaction to Election

Garrod's appointment "was rather a bombshell as far as I could gather," reports Howe.[113] Her election was greeted with excitement and high expectations, especially by the women's colleges. The Newnham College *Roll Letter* announced with pride, "Miss Garrod's election as Disney Professor has been the outstanding event of the year and has filled us with joy."[114] Fellow female scholars felt uplifted by her achievement[115] and Rosalind Franklin, then a first-year undergraduate, later known for her part in the elucidation of the DNA structure, wrote to her parents, "The chief news in Newnham is the first female professor ever to be elected in Oxford or Cambridge has been elected from Newnham. It is not yet known whether she is to be a member of the University!"[116]

For contemporary women students, "the excitement of her appointment was great", reports Eleanor Robertson, Newnham Archaeological and Anthropology student, class of 1938.[117] Many enthusiastically recall the summer of 1939 "college feast" given at Newnham in Garrod's honour, where each dish was named after an archaeological item. For Jane Waley, *née* McFie (Double First, 1945 [Section A] and 1946 [Section B]), Garrod and Newnham dons, such as E.M. Butler, elected Schröder Professor of German in 1944, and Jocelyn Toynbee, elected Lawrence Professor of Classical Archaeology in 1951, were inspiring: "They seemed to me to tower over the male versions in other subjects! I suppose there were some males among my fellow students, but my self confidence was undaunted!"[118]

The wider University community also took note. "The election of a woman to the Disney Professorship of Archaeology is an immense step forward towards complete equality between men and women in the University. The disabilities that remain here, being purely formal, are certain to be swept aside next time any changes in the University affairs are introduced" (R. English, May 1939). Many observers assumed that full membership for women in the University would soon follow.

However, Shaw[119] recalled that he and other undergraduates were particularly proud that Cambridge had held off a womanly invasion during the 1930s; they were pleased that it had remained a male domain. Oxford, on the other hand, had surrendered and there was a rumour that Oxford's performance in the Boat Race had slumped precisely as a result of the feminisation of that University. In fact, many of the male undergraduates interviewed had no memory of Garrod's election. It simply didn't register. As one undergraduate from the late 1930s, who read Archaeology and Anthropology in order to enter the Civil Service in India, stated, Cambridge was a "delightful, secluded club" where undergraduates "never took notice of girls in classes." "There weren't many of them" and "women were there on sufferance."[120] This was quite a consistent response from undergraduates interviewed.

There is a persistent rumour that Garrod's election was the precipitating event that resulted in the formation of a temporary syndicate on the Status of Women in the University during the early 1940s. There is no evidence at all in the Council or any Minutes that this is true.[121] War was declared before Garrod took office in October 1939. Most University activities were concentrated on emergency measures and accommodating 2000 evacuated members of colleges and institutions of the University of London; there was neither time nor staff to consider the extensive, detailed change to Statutes which was required later when women were admitted to degrees in 1948.

Two surviving signatories of the 30 September 1946 Memorial to the Council that initiated the long-awaited changes granting women full status clearly stated to me that Garrod's election was not a determining influence in their decision to back the petition. Professor Sir John Plumb and Dr George Salt suggested that the basic absurdity was introduced years previously when women were admitted to all University teaching offices and Faculty Boards, yet denied full membership. According to Plumb, Garrod's election was part of an ongoing process rather than a separate event. He felt that it would have happened much earlier if war had not intervened; Plumb remembered much discussion before 1939. Support for his claim emerged when I consulted the student newspapers of the era. *The Granta,* for example, had a number of questioning articles on females and their status. Plumb also stated that the University administration was behind the change, that it was not difficult to gather support for the Memorial and that Garrod's election as the first woman was noted receptively by all.[122]

Nevertheless, there is some specific evidence that Garrod's election forced an interesting administrative change for all

---

[112] It should be noted that, when members of the Faculty organised a sweepstake on who would win, Lethbridge was the only member of the staff to put his money on Garrod. "No one for a moment thought that she would win . . . I held on and won twenty-five shillings" (Lethbridge ([1965]: 100).

[113] Howe, personal correspondence, 1998.

[114] *Letter* of January, 1940: 11.

[115] Classicist, Alison Duke, in conversation, 1998.

[116] May 7, 1939, letter in possession of Franklin's sister, Mrs Jenifer Glynn.

[117] Robertson, personal correspondence, 1998.

[118] Waley, personal correspondence, 1998.

[119] Shaw, in conversation, 1996.

[120] Mr R.E. Lawry, in conversation, 1998.

[121] Council of the Senate Minutes 1938–1942. I thank Leedham-Green for searching these sources.

[122] Plumb, in conversation, 1998. It was an honour to interview both signatories. I thank Leedham-Green for suggesting that I contact Plumb and Salt.

involved. In the Minutes for the Council of the Senate for 17 March 1941, it is noted that a committee had been set up to advise the Registry on the Seniority of titular graduates and women Professors "in relation to the Order of Seniority of Graduates."[123] According to Leedham-Green,[124] the concern here was the proper rank order, for example, for processing at official Cambridge functions. Since Garrod was the only woman Professor, it can be assumed that the Council was discussing her and was concerned as to how to include her in official occasions or how and where to list her in official lists. Garrod was Professor and must process but had no proper Cambridge degree and therefore could not process.

The dilemma was solved on 5 May 1941 when it was agreed that "the Registry should be authorised to give to a woman's name the place which it would have if the Order of Seniority of Graduates applied as well to titles of degrees as to degrees." This was the model for and wording used when women were eventually granted degrees in 1948. It was agreed at that time that all University Statutes and Ordinances should apply to holders of titles of degrees as to degrees,[125] or as stated in the *Reporter*: "Women who hold titles of degrees shall be deemed to hold the corresponding degrees."[126]

Garrod's election clearly not only foreshadowed but also precipitated major change not just to one "research school" but to an entire research university.

The public reaction to Garrod's election seems to have been as extraordinary as the administrative response. There were very few women in teaching posts in Cambridge University in 1939. Garrod was a modest, shy person and appears to have been uncomfortable with the attention her election elicited. Her reticence is revealed in a story recounted by Howe. At the moment of her appointment, Garrod invited him to accompany her to a performance of "Fidelio" at a University theatre to celebrate. "She said that I could provide a sort of shield between her and the surrounding colleagues sure to show up . . . on all sides . . . she didn't want to be swamped with congratulations and chatter," wrote Howe.[127]

The reaction of the Faculty was as demanding as that of the public and University. When Garrod assumed the Disney Chair, the Archaeological and Anthropological Tripos course consisted still of one part only. As mentioned above, a student usually read history or classics before taking a final year of archaeology and anthropology as Part Two of a three year degree. This one part still included two sections: Section A which covered Physical and Social Anthropology and Prehistoric Archaeology; and Section B which covered Norse, Celtic Britain, and Anglo-Saxon history and language. By the end of the 1930s, the increasing demand

FIGURE XLIII   Professor Garrod in her Cambridge garden, 1939. As Professor, "she struck me as a lonely, self-contained figure and not particularly convivial in large groups . . . her total non-participation in Museum/ Department background or behind-the-scenes life struck me then as a major circumstance and fact of her University life," observed Bruce Howe during his year as a student in the Faculty.[128] "She was apprehensive at every junction . . . very shy to be the Head [of the Department]," stated Garrod's secretary, Miss Mary Thatcher.[129] (Photograph by courtesy of Madeleine Lovedy Smith and Antonia Benedek, Professor Garrod's cousin and god-daughter.)

for social anthropology and prehistoric archaeology, which was documented in the previous chapter, suggested that the Tripos course should be expanded.

Faculty Responsibilities

Garrod was expected by the Faculty to meet this increased demand for prehistoric archaeological expertise and to play a key administrative role in the development of a full Tripos.

[123] Council of the Senate Minutes 1938–1942.
[124] Leedham-Green, in conversation, 1999.
[125] For information on the Syndicate appointed to consider the status of women in the University, see file CUA R2930. I thank Leedham-Green for finding this file.
[126] *Reporter*, 3 June 1947.
[127] Howe, personal correspondence, 1998.
[128] Howe, personal correspondence, 1998.
[129] Thatcher, in conversation, 1998.

Leakey[130] had introduced the idea of an expanded Part I as early as 1934 when he presented a four-page document strongly suggesting that archaeologists in Section A be better prepared for the field with courses in geology. He suggested a generalised first year for both social anthropological and archaeological students followed by a specialised second year with a new curriculum and more practical, field preparation for the prehistorians. Although the Faculty did not respond and Leakey left soon after with Mary Nicol for Africa, there was a general feeling recorded in the Minutes that social anthropology, in particular, must modernise in order to compete with Malinowski and the London School of Economics.[131]

At the end of the decade, a new Faculty member, young Glyn Daniel, went further and recommended a Part I and II for archaeologists.[132] Daniel, who succeeded Grahame Clark to the Disney Chair in 1974, earned a Double First in Sections B and A and was so well-liked by Professor Chadwick and well-known to his Examiners that the Faculty waived his *viva voce* examination and recommended him immediately for the Ph.D in June 1938.[133] In March 1939, Daniel[134] wrote to J.H. Hutton, William Wyse Professor of Anthropology, just as Hutton was formulating a Part II for social anthropologists. "One day we will have an advanced archaeological Part II — of that I have no doubt. Why not start it now; we have men coming up who want to do specialised archaeological work," argued Daniel. Signed "The Prophet", Daniel suggested a Part II that would allow men to specialise in all branches of archaeology from the "earliest times to the dawn of history". Daniel's planned Part II was delayed by the declaration of war but revived by Garrod on 23 January 1946 after she and Daniel had returned from war service; Daniel, Clark, Burkitt and Garrod served on the revision committee and it was their combined endless committee labour which eventually produced the desired result of a Part II in archaeology. The full Tripos course was established by early 1948.[135]

With her election in 1939, Garrod was catapulted into a challenging situation within a changing Faculty that was on the verge of expansion and needed a famous archaeologist to engineer a new curriculum. Although she did not have experience as a university lecturer, Garrod immediately assumed responsibility for teaching prehistory to advanced students. It should be remembered that Garrod was the first prehistorian rather than classicist to assume the Disney Chair; she became a professor of a subject that had been comparatively recently introduced to the University curriculum which was not yet fully institutionalised. Her predecessor, Ellis Minns, a respected classicist, palaeographer and former lecturer in Slavonic studies, did most of his teaching in the respected Classics Tripos rather than in Archaeology and Anthropology.[136] "Archaeological studies other than Classics [classical archaeology] were still considered to be in an [institutionally] embryonic state," wrote archaeologist Charles Phillips in his memoirs, who served with Garrod on the Faculty Board during the 1930s.[137]

Cambridge continued to be the only university in Great Britain offering an undergraduate degree specialising in prehistoric archaeology; archaeology was still considered by some, including Burkitt, to be a "hobby pursuit". By others it was considered a "last resort" or "soft" option.[138] Although institutional circumstances had greatly improved during the 1930s, both prehistory and anthropology were still fighting for academic recognition, funding and accommodation (Rouse 1997, Smith 1997).

Lethbridge ([1965]: 99) observed in his autobiography that Garrod's position on the Board of the Faculty of Archaeology and Anthropology was "one of considerable frustration and difficulty". The University was in a period of rationalisation and progressive bureaucratisation. Relationships between the Faculties and the General Board of the Faculties, a powerful University body that controlled finances and final decisions on innumerable Faculty matters, had become noticeably more formal and distant.[139] Previously, during the 1920s and '30s, a sense of informality pervaded the Faculty Minutes; individual discussions with university administration personnel were permitted; decisions to meet a particular Faculty demand or student situation could be negotiated; interactions were more relaxed; there seemed to be more time for personal attention to Faculty exceptions. Mutually beneficial decisions seemed more possible.

During the late 1930s, matters were beginning to be rigorously conducted according to form. Flexibility was no longer encouraged by the General Board. It appeared that the Faculty did not react well to this new regime. The

---

[130] Faculty Minutes 18 February 1934. CUA Min.V.92a.

[131] Professor Hodson's concern, 18 February 1934. Minutes.

[132] It is Daniel who must be given credit for the idea of a full Tripos course for archaeologists.

[133] In the same month, June 1938, Charles McBurney, the future Cambridge Professor of Quaternary Prehistory, was accepted as a research student with a proposed thesis of "A Critical Study of Mousterian Industries in Europe"; he was assigned Burkitt as Supervisor. (10 June 1938, Minutes. CUA Min.V.92a.)

[134] Letter in the CUMAA Box 111 W07/1/1.

[135] Daniel graduated too late to be considered in depth in this study. However, because of his importance academically and his national popularity on the television show "Animal, Vegetable, Mineral" during the 1950s, it is worth mentioning that students from 1939 and 1940 (John Barnes and Bruce Howe to name just two, in conversation, 1998, 1999), genuinely

enjoyed his good will and were impressed with his desire to bring archaeology to a wider audience. As early as 1938, Daniel introduced free lectures for the Cambridge public which were successful.

[136] Ellis Hovell Minns was a specialist in the archaeology of the Scythians. Clark remembered him as being especially supportive to the study of prehistory (Clark, in conversation, 1994). Decades of Minns's correspondence, a fascinating read, are kept in the CUL Add. 7722.

[137] Phillips, Memoirs [1975–80]: 141. Memoirs in possession of the Phillips family. Phillips was absolutely correct; the great expansion of archaeological departments did not happen until the 1960s.

[138] Mrs Betty Saumarez Smith (Tripos 1936), Alison Duke, Mary Thatcher and others, personal correspondence and in conversation, 1998.

[139] Documented by numerous correspondences reported in the Faculty Minutes.

anthropologists and archaeologists valued their autonomy and rejected attempts by the General Board to formalise procedures and establish regulations. Illustrations of the expectations of the General Board and the Faculty's responses abound; a few examples follow. In 1936, the General Board noted that the Faculty Board's Report "appears without the customary opening sentence begging leave to report,"[140] that the Faculty apparently had done this before and that their current manner of addressing the General Board was unacceptable. In the same letter, Secretary General to the General Board of the Faculties, John T. Saunders, inquired "whether you [the Faculty] have any machinery for regulating the acceptance of gifts offered to the Museum." Minns responded promptly that in the future the Faculty would beg to report and that indeed there was no machinery. "The problem of the selection of objects to be accepted by the Museum does not appear to me to be one that can be solved by any kind of machinery," wrote Minns. The Faculty relied, instead, on the "extraordinary knowledge and judgement of the Curator."[141]

When, at the beginning of 1939, the General Board recommended that a "less haphazard method of appointing supervisors"[142] be established and again later in the year when the General Board requested that the Faculty regulate "how much Supervisors of candidates working for research degrees should help in preparation of theses," the Faculty responded that "it was impossible to formalize these personal relationships."[143] In 1938, when T.T. Paterson, the university-trained geologist, assumed control of the Museum from its gracious patron, Louis Clarke, rumblings in the Faculty Minutes suggest that University officials wished to put the informal system of volunteer Keepers, which persisted in the Museum, under regulatory control.[144] Paterson finally suggested "that, in the future, such Keepers would only be appointed when the Curator really asked for them." Again in 1944, when the General Board wished to set the number of hours of lecturing required from a University Lecturer and to establish an inclusive stipend covering all the officer's services, in response, "All members of the [Faculty] Board agreed on emphasising the importance of College supervisions in University teaching and the difficulty of attempting to control hours and methods of each teaching officer."[145]

Before and during Garrod's tenure in the Disney Chair, the Faculty Board wrangled continually with the General Board and repeatedly disagreed over definitions of jobs, funds and accommodation. The Faculty had less need to regulate and ran well in its "haphazard" manner. Certainly the phrase "The Faculty Board did not agree with the view of the General Board" became the Faculty's refrain.

The change in style and tone of administration could have been necessitated by the growth in size of the University, or perhaps caused by broader contextual demands from society or government, but this change may also have been a result of the personal influence of John T. Saunders, a zoologist, who served as Secretary General to the General Board of the Faculties from 1935–53. Saunders had an excellent reputation for strictness, effectiveness and efficiency.[146] He was known as a "hard man".[147] After retiring from Cambridge, he was brought as Vice-Chancellor to University College, Ibadan, Nigeria from 1953–6, where he solved a serious financial crisis of over-spending in three short years.[148] Saunders's written messages to the Faculty radiate control.

It would appear that Garrod was often caught between the General Board's desires and the Faculty's resistance. Shortly after assuming office, Garrod was requested to represent and explain the Faculty's needs to the General Board. Prior to the outbreak of war, the General Board had begun a lengthy investigation into the expenditures of the Faculty of Archaeology and Anthropology on teaching, personnel, accommodation, and equipment. The organisation and regulation of courses, the size and grading of teaching and assistant staff, the status of the Curator of the Museum and the relationship of Section A to Section B within the Tripos course were being scrutinised. The relationship of Section A, which was exclusively prehistoric archaeology, to Section B, which covered the culture and language of early historic Britain, was the most sensitive and contentious of these issues. As mentioned previously, section B had been brought into the Archaeological and Anthropological Faculty from Modern and Medieval Languages in 1927 by Professor of Anglo-Saxon, H.M. Chadwick. The Archaeology and Anthropology Faculty unanimously wished to keep Section B within its ranks.

Yet some members of the University wanted Section B to be transferred to the control of the Faculty of English; there was vocal agitation and occasional letters to the General Board advocating this change. Professor J.H. Clapham of King's, an occasional member of the General Board, had circulated a fly sheet in November 1937, forcefully posing the question, "Is there any reason for maintaining the 1927 divorce from English?"[149]

Having met with Garrod and also Hutton, the Committee for the General Board sent a draft report to the Faculty Board. A major paragraph of this report referred to Garrod. According to the General Board Committee, Garrod "expressed the opinion" that Section A and B "appeal to different kinds of persons," that "Section A and B together did not make a

[140] Letter from Saunders, to Burkitt, 30 April 1936; letter kept in 1936 Letter Box, CUMAA.
[141] Letter to Saunders, 1 May 1936; Letter Box, CUMAA.
[142] 23 January 1939, Faculty Minutes. CUA Min.V.92a.
[143] 25 April 1939, Faculty Minutes. CUA Min.V.92a.
[144] 18 October 1938, Faculty Minutes. CUA Min.V.92a.
[145] 22 November 1944, Faculty Minutes. CUA Min.V.94. I thank Dr T.J.

Mead for arranging access to restricted Faculty Minutes.
[146] According to Harry Godwin (1985: 184), who served with Saunders on the General Board, he was a "supremely competent Secretary General of the Faculties."
[147] Leedham-Green, in conversation, 1999.
[148] Shaw, in conversation, 1999.
[149] Found in Faculty Minutes for 1937. CUA Min.V.92a.

coherent whole and that it was neither necessary nor desirable that they be linked. The Committee agreed to place these opinions on record so that they may be considered when the General Board undertake their inquiry into" the future of Section B.[150] In response, Garrod asserts that she "has no recollection of making statements that Section A and B together did not make a coherent whole" and that she "considers any separation between prehistory and the later archaeology represented by Section B . . . undesirable." The Faculty Board then suggests "that the whole of this paragraph be deleted" because Garrod and the Faculty do "not want this paragraph to prejudice the promised inquiry" into Section B's future.[151]

In November 1940, the General Board sent another draft of their report to the Faculty for approval. The paragraph attributing quotations to Garrod had not been changed or deleted. The Board unanimously once again expressed their concern that these statements were misquoted and that these misquotations could prejudice the future of their Tripos course. The final General Board Report nevertheless retained the objectionable paragraph intact. In addition, on 20 November 1940, Saunders wrote to the Board, "the statement attributed to Professor Garrod appears to the Committee to be the view which should be taken into account when the future of Section B is considered." In final response, the Faculty Board "renews their protest against the placing on record of statements which are in their opinion inaccurate."[152]

This was Garrod's first experience with University administration and politics. It is not clear how the General Board could have so completely misinterpreted her testimony or why it persisted in using quotations that could surely damage Garrod's reputation and might completely discredit her within her Faculty, so soon after her election and before her reputation was established. However, it does explain her fearful concerns.

It was precisely her administrative encounters with the General Board that appeared to have caused Garrod the most consternation. As a professor in the Faculty and as Head of her Department, Garrod dealt continually with Saunders and the General Board. According to Garrod's Secretary, Miss Mary Thatcher, it was during the period when Garrod was Department Head from 1950 to her retirement in 1952, that the Faculty "grossly overspent" on their allowance for electricity.[153] The Board received a letter from Saunders suggesting that Garrod please go and explain. "She might

have been a schoolgirl," states Thatcher, who accompanied Garrod, "she shook with fear." During the meeting, Garrod asked Saunders what the Faculty might do to improve the situation. He answered, "Well, Professor Garrod, when you see a light on, turn it off."[154]

Garrod would have found this type of treatment confusing if not humiliating or at least demeaning. She was an older, cultured, reserved, upper-middle-class woman from an established and highly accomplished family. Garrod would have been accustomed to being treated with an understated respect.

According to Professor George Salt, who was a long-term member of several University Syndicates and had many opportunities to observe Faculty activities, Garrod had a reputation as a dutiful administrator.[155] Throughout her years of tenure, although never "enamoured of University administration" (Daniel 1986: 99), Garrod was nevertheless conscientiously reliable and hard-working within the Faculty. She served for years on every Faculty committee of import. In 1947 alone, Garrod participated on the Faculty Degree Committee, the Faculty Appointments Committee and a committee to consider a possible move from Downing Street to the newly proposed Sidgwick Avenue lecture-rooms. She was also on a committee dealing with the late Professor Chadwick's benefaction, the committee to reformulate regulations for the post-graduate Diploma, the committee to revise courses and regulations for the Tripos and on a committee to organise an archaeological expedition to Bolivia. In addition, Garrod regularly attended Faculty Board meetings and acted as an Examiner.

This is quite in contrast to Elsie M. Butler,[156] Garrod's good friend, who became the second female Cambridge Professor in 1944 when she was elected Schröder Professor of German. In her autobiography, Butler (1959: 153) wrote, "Oh those committees! *I hadn't bargained for them* . . . Yet, strangely enough, many of the dwellers in the groves of academe actually seem to enjoy it. Perhaps this has something to do with the lust for power."[157]

Garrod's Responses

When Garrod's responses to the General Board are studied, she presents herself as relating to University officials as she had related to officials while on excavations and expeditions. As quoted earlier, while on expeditions, Garrod's "demeanor and dealings . . . were civil . . . with mutual respect and cordiality evident at all times."[158] Garrod as-

[150] Faculty Minutes, 22 May 1940. CUA Min.V.92a.
[151] Faculty Minutes, 22 May 1940. CUA Min.V.92a.
[152] Faculty Minutes, 22 January 1941. CUA Min.V.92a.
[153] Thatcher, in conversation, 1998.
[154] Thatcher, in conversation, 1997.
[155] Salt, in conversation, 1998.
[156] According to Salt, Butler had a weaker reputation as a committee person.
[157] The full quotation is: "This was my first experience of University administration; and it was the reason in my heart of hearts I regretted the

day when women were made full members of Cambridge University. They too, I knew from my own bitter experience, would begin to slide down the slippery slope to the bottomless pit of paper precedents. They too would be strangled by the coils of red tape winding and twining round these modern Laocoons. They too would expend the best energies of their minds in wrangling over statutes and ordinances. Yet, strangely enough, many of the dwellers in the groves of academe actually seem to enjoy it. Perhaps this has something to do with the lust for power" (Butler 1959: 153).
[158] Howe, personal correspondence, 1997.

FIGURE XLIV   Cartoon, drawn by a Disney cartoonist during war service in England, of Garrod with members of her Photographic Reconnaissance Section at Medmenham. Garrod was best in small groups where status was not a strong issue. She was "delighted" when Dr Hamshaw Thomas, Cambridge University Reader in Palaeobotany, recruited her in 1942 for the Medmenham Air Intelligence Unit, and was "jolly well not reserved" while there, remembers Hamshaw Thomas's daughter, Mrs Ursula Whitaker.[159] "Rank was of no importance . . . there was an atmosphere of tremendous conviviality" within the Unit and within Garrod's Section of three or four people who worked closely together.[160] Garrod served as Section Officer at Medmenham for three years along with other Cambridge archaeologists, Charles Phillips, Grahame Clark, Glyn Daniel, T.G.E. Powell (class of 1937) and Charles McBurney. (Cartoon reproduced by courtesy of the family of Dr Hugh Hamshaw Thomas, who served as Wing Commander at the RAF Medmenham Unit for Photographic Interpretation.)

sumed that the other side was eminently reasonable and that a fair debate could solve all. She was forthcoming with Faculty needs and seemed to expect the General Board to give a clear answer. Her actions are reminiscent of her writing style, described by Clark (1937a: 488) as "dispassionate . . . scientific . . . modest." She seemed to believe in an idealised scientific model of discourse whereby if her hypothesis was wrong, open discussion would lead to a better solution.

Garrod often argued on a moral basis. After World War II, as a professor returning from National Service, Garrod received her stipend for several months while lesser Faculty members, such as Assistant Faculty Lecturer Grahame Clark, did not. She argued with the General Board that this was crass discrimination. The General Board ignored her argument, stating that all Faculty were not allowed stipends until they started to lecture. When she pointed out that she herself had not started lecturing, the General Board responded that it could consider only hardship cases within

her Faculty. Garrod responded that since it was an issue of discrimination between officers of the same Faculty and as all the junior teaching officers were not receiving stipends, all were hardship cases. The General Board responded that all Faculty were not allowed stipends until they started to lecture. At this point, Garrod stopped responding.

An instructive comparison is made when Garrod's behaviour during war service from 1942–5 is investigated; she is once again described as light-hearted. Garrod seemed thoroughly to enjoy her time away from Cambridge. Eyewitness accounts suggest that she was at ease in small, informal working settings where there was little or no concern with rank and nuanced power relationships. Fred Mason,[161] who was a young language graduate when he temporarily joined Garrod's section, reported that she was a modest, helpful and congenial officer.[162]

In contrast, Garrod seemed ill at ease in all hierarchical or formal situations when back at Cambridge, especially

[159] Whitaker, in conversation, 1998.
[160] Whitaker, in conversation, 1998 and Fred Mason, personal correspondence, 1998.

[161] I thank Ursula Whitaker for introducing me to Fred Mason.
[162] Mason, personal correspondence, 1998, 1999.

where she represented the Faculty. Although she had been an excellent supervisor in informal, small groups of female students while at Newnham College — "her mother joined us for a cup of tea before proceedings began. It was all very friendly and easy"[163] — Garrod was known as a "dead loss" as a lecturer, or even as a supervisor, within the more structured Faculty setting. The unremitting boredom and uniform dullness of her presentations are remembered by many. There was "never a light or bright moment" recalls former 1950s student, John Mulvaney, who later became foundation Professor of Prehistory at the Australian National University in 1970.[164] "She gave one of the poorest public lectures I ever attended," writes archaeologist Merrick Posnansky.[165] Her presentations were "dull, routine, dutiful, lifeless things," observed Howe.[166] Kitson Clark found Garrod to be a "dry-as-dust lecturer" and suggested that this was part of Garrod's misunderstanding of how a Cambridge lecturer should act.[167]

Lecturing was "not her chosen form of communication," stated Ann Sieveking, *née* Paull, who listened to Garrod discuss the Upper Palaeolithic, the Palaeolithic in Asia, and Palaeolithic art and religion as her student from 1951–52.[168] Sieveking's observation is supported by Garrod's own statement to her friend, Mlle Germaine Henri-Martin: "*J'aime mieux écrire que discuter de vive voix*" [I much prefer to write than discuss aloud].[169] Even in small and informal Tripos classes, Garrod seemed uncomfortable with her role and the format of University teaching.

In sharp contrast to the testimonial letters and statements of gratitude I have found from Garrod's "students in the field",[170] many former undergraduates remembered meeting Garrod face-to-face only once, when admitted to the Department, and did not appear to be influenced by her work or personality. She did not seem to be a strong presence in the Faculty and attracted few students. "She was a rather remote figure to us," stated Felicity Beauchamp, who read

Archaeology from 1945-46.[171] "Professor Garrod was busy and distant,"wrote Millicent Munro-Harrap,[172] who graduated in 1951. A "very private person," observed John Evans.[173] "A humble scholar,"concluded Mary Thatcher.[174]

In November 1950, Garrod wrote to her close friend, Mlle Germaine Henri-Martin, "*Je n'ai* rien *pu faire pour Angles* [Garrod and Saint Mathurin's Upper Palaeolithic rock shelter excavation in France] *depuis ma rentrée et je n'arrive pas à préparer mon cours pour le trimestre prochain — je serais obligée de le faire à Paris, ce qui remettra encore le travail d'Angles. Au fond, je mène une vie impossible! La décision de prendre la retraite est absolument nécessaire.*" [I haven't been able to do *anything* for Angles since my return and I haven't managed to prepare my course for next term. I'll have to do it in Paris, which will again delay Angles' work. Basically, I lead an impossible life! The decision to retire is absolutely necessary."[175]

4.4 Theoretical Literature

In order to recount Garrod's story and the story of the Archaeology and Anthropology Faculty during this period, other points of view are needed than those provided in the research school literature. Research school analyses were first developed during the 1970s slightly before gender and science investigations became popular. Current literature which discusses women as academics must be reviewed in order to put Garrod's experiences in proper perspective and to understand fully her academic life. Fortunately, there is substantial theoretical material that applies to these issues.[176]

One of the most referenced analyses of women in academe is Sonnert and Holton's (1995) *Gender Differences in Scientific Careers*.[177] This study was based on two separate models of behaviour. The first focuses on how women are treated as strangers; the second concentrates on how women act as strangers in academic settings. Post-doctoral women

[163] Lillico, personal correspondence, 1998.
[164] Mulvaney, in conversation, 1998.
[165] Posnansky, personal correspondence, 1998.
[166] Howe, personal correspondence, 1997.
[167] Kitson Clark, personal correspondence, 1999.
[168] Sieveking, in conversation, 1998. Ann Sieveking, who dug with Garrod at the Upper Palaeolithic site of Roc aux Sorciers, Angles-sur-l'Anglin, remembered that Garrod, in her role as a Professor from the Faculty, treated students in a formal manner even while on digs. Garrod ate lunch separately and did not converse easily.
[169] Garrod to Henri-Martin, 19 February 1961. Box 38, MAN.
[170] Lorraine Copeland, who dug with Garrod at Bezez Cave and Ras-el-Kelb, remembered "I presented myself and said I'm very interested . . . I know absolutely nothing but would I be able to help? And she [Garrod] was indeed extremely kind and let me come in and . . . they were wonderful to me . . . and of course I learned on the job; learned by doing" (in conversation with Callander, 1993). James Skinner, who also dug at Bezez Cave, claimed that Garrod was an excellent mentor (Letter to Garrod, Garrod Papers. Box 58, MAN). Bruce Howe felt that she was one of the most personally influential archaeologists he met during his long career as a Near Eastern prehistorian (Letter from Howe to Garrod, 9 September 1952, Box 59, MAN). In fact, the students that Garrod did attract to the Faculty were usually people she had had experience with during excavations or expeditions. Garrod recruited Anne Fuller to the Cambridge post-graduate

Diploma in 1934 after they had dug together at Mount Carmel. Again, in November 1945, Garrod suggested to the Faculty that John D'A. Waechter, just released from the RAF, should be admitted as a research student. She argued that, although Waechter had no first degree, he had had extensive experience excavating. Waechter took his Ph.D in 1949 with a thesis entitled "The Mesolithic Age in the Middle East" and went on to teach at University College, London.
[171] Beauchamp, personal correspondence, 1999.
[172] Munro-Harrap, personal correspondence, 1998.
[173] Evans, in conversation, 1998.
[174] Thatcher, in conversation, 1998.
[175] Garrod to Henri-Martin, 21 November 1950. Box 34, MAN.
[176] Gerhard Sonnert and Gerald James Holton's (1995) *Gender Differences in Science;* P.A. Graham's (1978) 'History of Women in American Higher Education'; C.F. Epstein's (1991) "Constraints on Excellence"; D.R. Kaufman's (1978) "Associational Ties in Academe: some Male and Female Differences"; S.E. Widnall's (1988) "Voices from the Pipeline"; D. Wright's (2000) "Gender and Professionalization"; T. Stone's (1999) unpublished Ph.D "The Integration of Women into the Military Service"; A. Oram (1989) "Embittered, Sexless or Homosexual" and the papers as well as the transcripts of the proceedings of the Conference on Women in Higher Education, privately printed in *"The Transformation of an Elite? Women and Higher Education since 1900"* (1998) are especially relevant.
[177] Maureen Linker suggested the Sonnert and Holton book.

and men from top American universities were the subjects of this investigation and were extensively interviewed. The study found first that women in science usually had, as did Garrod, highly educated parents. Repeatedly the study also found that women are more likely to interrupt their academic careers, especially to care for families, and normally take longer to gain degrees. Certainly this was true of Garrod, who was in her thirties before she received her B.Sc from Oxford.

The straight academic road into science is clearly more likely travelled by men. This statement is also true of Garrod's entrance into the academic world, which differed greatly from Clark's, who advanced from undergraduate to Bye-Fellow, Faculty Assistant Lecturer, University Lecturer and finally to Professor, all within the same university system. Women post-graduates in Sonnert and Holton's study had more difficulty establishing collegiate networks of important contacts once within the university; earlier lack of appropriate institutional education could have adversely affected them. Most women interviewed found that the university environment was not supportive and was sometimes frightening. They tended to feel excluded from informal social events such as going for drinks and feel out-of-place in predominantly male groups.

These findings may suggest the reason why Garrod never participated in Faculty gatherings. According to Bruce Howe, she did not frequent the tea-room. "The Museum coffee and teas were very stimulating shop-talk occasions. Daniel, Bushnell, Phillips, Lethbridge, Clark were the regulars; Garrod not at all . . . O'Reilly saw the pot was brewing, contributed cakes, cookies without fail."[178] Garrod might have felt reluctant as a professor to behave as a woman must, contributing tea and cake; there may have been a sense of informal exclusion. In addition, since so many Faculty and research plans were informally concocted over tea, Garrod might have had difficulty remaining up-to-date on the definition of Faculty issues and the formulation of subsequent decisions.

Sonnert and Holton's (1995) study also found evidence that styles of doing science differed between men and women. Women preferred a less aggressive approach; men demonstrated more entrepreneurial spunk, were more combative, self-promoting and preferred higher visibility. These statements well describe Clark who was indeed an intellectual entrepreneur who believed firmly that his own self-promotion would benefit the archaeological enterprise as a whole. In contrast, Mrs Phyllis Hetzel reported at the 1998 Cambridge Women and Higher Education conference, that in her experience while interviewing for the Civil Service and as Register of the Role at Newnham, "women simply do not blow their own trumpets."[179] This is true of Garrod,

who seemed not to know how to or did not care to promote herself or her research within an academic setting.

Finally, Sonnert and Holton also found that women tended to be more "pure" scientists and were less concerned with the political aspects of science, such as influence and power. The women interviewed stressed the intellectually stimulating process of science rather than results, were more cautious, perfectionistic, comprehensive, published less and took fewer risks with data.

Widnall's (1988) paper reviewed graduate Stanford and Harvard student surveys which revealed that women were uncertain about how to combine a family and career and many women who chose academic life remained single as did Garrod. Women students also often reported discomfort with the combative style of communication within their research groups. Men studied tended to be comfortable with a style "that seeks to reduce one of the protagonists to rubble" (Widnall 1988: 1744). Women interviewed generally found this unacceptable. Kaufman (1978: 11) asked if collegiate ties differ for men and women and found that women felt often excluded by the "exclusive club-like context of male professional society".

Discussions during the conference held in Cambridge on "The Transformation of an Elite? Women and Higher Education since 1900"(1998) focused on gendered self-definitions and informal and formal obstacles which women experience in academe. The results from these discussions, as well as the findings presented in A. Oram's (1989) "Embittered, Sexless or Homosexual" and in T. Stone's (1999) "The Integration of Women into the Military Service", illuminate Garrod's experiences and the problems she faced. As these studies suggest, Garrod appears to have had difficulty in defining her role. When considering Garrod's self-presentation, immediately the manner of her dress is brought to mind. As Professor she chose to dress in an understated, sensible, serious, almost manly manner which led to rumours that she might be lesbian. Elsie M. Butler, Schröder Professor of German, on the other hand, dressed in flowing gowns, wore ribbons in her white hair and smoked a cigarette using a long, elegant holder. This may have been the reason she was considered frivolous by some.

As pointed out by Louise Braddock during the Conference on Women in Higher Education since 1900, women, when they entered Cambridge in greater numbers, found that they were "de-skilled". Oxford and Cambridge have peculiar structures in that they have enormously elaborate committees and women did not know how to behave on University Syndicates, "That's a separate skill," remarked Gill Sutherland. University roles, argued Felicity Hunt, demand "the sorts of skills" for which women were not trained.[180]

---

[178] Howe, personal correspondence, 1999.
[179] Hetzel, speaking during discussion at the University of Cambridge conference entitled "The Transformation of an Elite? Women and Higher Education since 1900". These discussions are recorded in *"Transcript of*

the Day's Proceedings" (1998).
[180] Braddock, Sutherland and Hunt speaking during discussion at the University of Cambridge conference entitled "The Transformation of an Elite?" recorded in *"Transcript of the Day's Proceedings"* (1998).

This material suggests that academic achievements are not only dependent on an innovative cognitive base but are also dependent on skilled attitudes and necessary learned behaviours.

4.5 Chapter Conclusion

Taking into account this literature, exactly what was Dorothy Garrod's difficulty in being Professor? It would seem that she found distasteful exactly the type of behaviour that had resulted in her election. Garrod would not have been capable of running a candidate to divert a vote.

Garrod had obviously never read F.M. Cornford's famous satire of 1908 on Cambridge University politics, *Microcosmographia Academica. Being a guide for the young academic politician*, and was untrained in the types of political manoeuvres this book so accurately describes. The "political activity" of casually negotiating deals while strolling King's Parade was alien to her. "Remember this:" Cornford (1908: 42) warns, *"the men who get things done are the men who walk up and down the King's Parade, from 2 to 4, every day of their lives."*

In addition, Garrod's lack of full membership in the University before 1948 and also the fact that she was a woman barred her from some behind-the-scenes interactions and also from social settings where deals might have been struck. Women were not allowed, for example, to dine at the men's colleges where issues were broached and resolved during conversations at High Table. She would not have been present at important informal discussions where bureaucratic manoeuvrings might have been agreed upon.

Negotiating scrimmages with powerful bureaucratic officers or committees was difficult partly because some members of the General Board of the Faculties were particularly hard to deal with. She was unaccustomed to the often sharp style of Cambridge institutional interactions and was uncomfortable with the verbal sparring and sarcastic retorts which were an acceptable part of the negotiating process. In the electricity budget incident previously mentioned, Garrod would have felt it rude to respond to Saunders. However, when she did not retort, he would have judged her as weak. Saunders might have reacted thus to whomever he dealt with. However, as a result of Garrod's background, personality and gender, she was poorly suited to such interactions.

Garrod had no experience in hierarchical, institutional settings, where she would have been under a General Board, yet over undergraduates. She had never gone to a public school such as Marlborough, as had her brothers, or entered Cambridge and stayed there to build her career, as had Grahame Clark. She was accustomed to leading small, egalitarian research teams where she had control of funding and final decisions, or to supervising one or two students over tea; Garrod was ill-prepared for the University's ranked system.

Throughout, Garrod seems to have been operating on the more co-operative, reasoned, and even dignified mode of behaviour she had enjoyed in the practice of research. This behaviour was maladaptive within Cambridge's arcane institutional, hierarchical arena where control and manipulation of scarce resources were critical and where bureaucratic effectiveness required a tacit knowledge of how to act.

Garrod adequately fulfilled the formal requirements of her office. Her diligent service on the Faculty was well-appreciated. She conscientiously worked on Faculty committees and with Burkitt, Clark and Daniel to formulate regulations and to establish a curriculum for the new Tripos course. According to Daniel (1986), Garrod insisted, while serving on the committee to revise and expand the course, that students be required to gain experience excavating abroad and that the new curriculum stress world prehistory. Daniel considered this to be Garrod's most valuable contribution, commemorated today by the Department's Garrod Fund established specifically to pay students' travel expenses. Garrod thus wished to encourage non-Eurocentric perspectives, hoping that with experience abroad and knowledge of the prehistory of other nations, students could consider the place of prehistoric England within a broader context.

However, Garrod never seemed to have tried to institutionalise her own research agenda. In comparison to Clark, who immediately taught his own material, pushed an ecological approach to archaeological analysis and who also fought to institutionalise what was to become known world-wide as environmental and palaeoeconomic archaeology, Garrod did not suggest that her many outstanding discoveries or her views on the evolution of *Homo sapiens* should become part of the required curriculum. Papers on the prehistory of the Near East and on the Levantine corridor were conspicuously absent from the newly established Part II. Although she made it clear that she wanted world prehistory to be taught at Cambridge, Garrod seemed completely incapable of "blowing her own trumpet" or championing her own material. In addition, she simply did not appear to understand the importance of attracting students in order to further her own research agenda.

Garrod never became acculturated to the type of informal behaviour needed to be a "Cambridge man". All indications are that she was uncomfortable in her Professorial role and left as soon as her sense of duty allowed. She did a competent job but longed to return to her field research.[181] Clare Fell, who was Assistant Curator of the Museum of Archaeology and Ethnology from 1948–53, remembered "how shocked and saddened everyone was when she resigned. Dorothy was one of the few women professors and the female academics thought it terrible she should resign. But she was right, as she wanted to finish her research and not get bogged down in administration."[182]

---

[181] Thatcher, in conversation, 1998.

[182] Fell, personal correspondence, 1998 and 1999.

FIGURE XLV   Garrod processing with Butler at Cambridge in academic dress as full members of the University, 1948. (Photograph courtesy of the Pitt Rivers Museum, University of Oxford.)

FIGURE XLVI   Dorothy Garrod and Queen Elizabeth at Newnham College. In 1948, Queen Elizabeth was awarded an honorary degree to celebrate the right of all women to take degrees from Cambridge University. (Photograph courtesy of the Pitt Rivers Museum, University of Oxford.)

Although she did not function happily within the University hierarchy and certainly was not an intellectual careerist or entrepreneur as was Clark, Garrod was very well-liked by her Archaeology and Anthropology staff colleagues. "Oh, we loved her. She was quite awe-inspiring" remembered Thatcher.[183] According to Daniel (1986: 211), in personal situations, "Dorothy Garrod had been easy to get on with; she was a generous, lovable, outgoing person." Upon retirement, thirty-four members of the Faculty Board presented her with an ornate scroll, inscribed in Latin, which reveals their sadness and respect, which can be translated as:

> *To Dorothy Annie Elizabeth Garrod*
> *most illustrious teacher and indefatigable explorer of antiquity, who for thirteen years professed the science of archaeology in Cambridge with such great learning, such great splendour, such great friendliness and humanity, her colleagues, acquaintances, friends, whose names are written beneath, joyfully giving thanks for so many things well done, earnestly mourning her sad and premature departure, following her in all excellent things, moved not only by love but also by regret, to one who has deserved it, who tomorrow will emigrate to Gaul, yet will quite often return to Britain, give with pleasure this clock as a gift.*

> *"caelum non animum mutant, qui trans [mare] currunt"*
> *[Horace. Epistles, Book I, 11, line 27]*
> *"those who hasten across [the sea] change their horizon, not their soul"[184]*

In the same year that women became full members of Cambridge University, Burkitt, Clark and Garrod succeeded in establishing a full two-part Tripos course for archaeology coupled with anthropology. With the story of the graduation of women and the institutionalisation of a full degree course, my work is almost complete. In the late 1940s, Garrod began exploring the beautiful Magdalenian friezes of bison, horses and women in the rock shelter, Roc aux Sorciers, at Angles-sur-l'Anglin. Clark (1949: 64) was about to excavate Star Carr, "one of the richest and most informative sites of Maglemosian culture anywhere;" the results, fully published in 1954, demonstrated the profound intellectual power of combining archaeology with Quaternary research. Burkitt, ever the "avuncular Edwardian gentleman"[185], had retired as Secretary to the Faculty Board in 1939 and was increasingly involved in local government, where he championed archaeology as a

secondary school subject; this involvement culminated in Burkitt's appointment as High Sheriff of Cambridgeshire and Huntingdonshire.

As the 1940s drew to a close, the Faculty of Archaeology and Anthropology experienced one of its most creative periods with an explosion of students who scattered to posts in Britain and beyond. Post-war undergraduates tended to be bright and independent colleagues who were trusted by the Faculty to have projects of their own. Students entering Cambridge after World War II were often veterans on exhibitions offered by some colleges, such as Peterhouse, to ex-servicemen. Others who read archaeology came up on the new state scholarships introduced by the wartime Coalition government. A socially diverse group arrived.[186] Some interviewed were the first in their families to have this opportunity. "Meritocracy was coming to Cambridge," observed Whitaker.[187] "The prevailing attitude among both dons and students was that one worked hard to make up for lost time," writes Gathercole (1993: 1). Students whose courses had been interrupted thronged back to Cambridge. Undergraduates, older and feeling wiser after their war-time experiences, were self-starters who were to contribute fully to Cambridge's intellectual imperium.

By 1950, Glyn Daniel (1950) could note that Terence Powell (Tripos 1937) was pioneering prehistoric archaeology as an undergraduate subject at Liverpool. K.D.M. Dauncey (Tripos 1940), who Ray Inskeep (Tripos 1957) remembered as "a brilliant field archaeologist and brilliant lecturer and teacher", was the only appointment in prehistoric archaeology at Birmingham University. Cyril Fox (Ph.D 1922) had retired from Cardiff but Lady Fox, influenced by the Burkitts, was beginning her campaign to institutionalise archaeology at University College, Exeter. In fact, the only university offering undergraduate courses in Britain which did not have a Cambridge connection was Edinburgh; this was soon to change when Grahame Clark secured a research position for Ian Whitaker (Tripos 1951) under Stuart Piggott at the School of Scottish Studies in 1952.

The Cambridge influence increased in breadth and strength as more dots were added to Clark's world map.[188] John Mulvaney[189] (Tripos 1953) became the foundation Professor of Prehistory in the Faculty of Arts at ANU and is today considered to be the father of Australian prehistory. Jack Golson[190] (Tripos 1951) was instructed by Clark to apply to an academic position in New Zealand. "So, Jack . . . went out to New Zealand and founded New Zealand archaeol-

[183] Thatcher, in conversation, 1998.
[184] Quoted from *Exhibition in Honour of D.A.E. Garrod*, Callander and Smith (1998) with permission from Madeleine Lovedy Smith and Antonia Benedek, Professor Garrod's cousin and god-daughter. Translated from the Latin by Susan Bourne.
[185] The full quotation is "He looked and spoke like an avuncular Edwardian gentleman and his data seemed to belong to that era." John Mulvaney (Tripos 1954), personal correspondence, 1999.
[186] This change in the undergraduate population was noted by several interviewees (e.g. Antonia Rose, *née* Sewell, Peter Gathercole.)

[187] Whitaker, in conversation, 2002.
[188] Unfortunately, space does not allow me to mention many other fascinating interviewees. I plan to expand this section in a future book in which I will concentrate on Cambridge graduates and how they became gate-keepers for positions world-wide. For a detailed description of the Cambridge diaspora, see Clark (1989a).
[189] The full transcript of Mulvaney's interview is appended to this study.
[10] The interview I recorded with Jack Golson is deposited at the Society of Antiquaries of London.

FIGURE XLVII.   Professor Dorothy Garrod in retirement, "tying up one of her beloved nut trees". (Photograph by courtesy of Madeleine Lovedy Smith, Professor Garrod's cousin; caption by Madeleine Lovedy Smith.)

ogy."[191] In 1961, Golson took up his appointment at the ANU Research School of Pacific Studies where he "set the Department of Prehistory so firmly on its feet . . . as the first fully trained and academically qualified prehistorian in the Australian National University" (Clark 1993: ii). John Hurst[192] (Tripos 1951) became one of the founders of the Deserted Mediaeval Village Research Group which championed the "study of Mediaeval settlement as a multi-disciplinary research project" (Hurst 1986: 1).[193] Hurst and the DMVRG effectively introduced open-area excavation methods to Britain.[194] Peter Gathercole[195] (Tripos 1952) began his academic career in 1958 when Golson attracted

him to a joint appointment as Lecturer in Anthropology at the University of Otago and as Keeper of Anthropology at the Otago Museum, New Zealand, where he developed the Otago Department and established undergraduate and post-graduate degrees in archaeology and anthropology. Sylvia Hallam[196] *née* Maycock (Tripos 1948, 1949) became the University of Western Australia's first permanent appointment in prehistoric archaeology. Her students now form a body of professional Australian archaeologists. John Evans (Starred First, Tripos 1949), who worked in the field with his wife, Mrs Evelyn Evans, *née* Sladdin (Tripos 1957),[197] succeeded Gordon Childe in the Chair of European Prehistoric

---

[191] Mulvaney, in conversation, 2000.

[192] The full transcript of Hurst's interview is appended to this study.

[193] This quotation is from a manuscript entitled "The Work of the Medieval Village Research Group 1952–1986", sent to me by John Hurst.

[194] According to Jack Golson (in correspondence 2004), "open-area excavation was widely practiced on prehistoric sites in central Europe and Steensberg's mentor, the geographer Gudmund Hatt, had employed it on

Iron-Age settlement sites in Jutland. The German refugee G. Bersu had brought it to England before WWII and used it at Little Woodbury. But it was not widely practised in Britain."

[195] Tapes of Gathercole's interviews are deposited at the CUMAA.

[196] Hallam's interview is in my possession.

[197] The transcript of the Evans' interview is appended to this study.

Archaeology at the Institute of Archaeology in London. One of his many accomplishments, as the Institute's Director, was the establishment in 1969 of an undergraduate course leading to a first degree in archaeology.

When commenting on the successful institutionalisation of academic archaeology in 21 British universities and on the presence of Cambridge graduates in Asia, Africa, North America, Australasia, continental Europe and Britain, geographer and the then future Director of the Institute of Archaeology, David R. Harris (1977: 113), wrote, "It is a remarkable story, for there can be few scholarly subjects that owe their academic rise so exclusively to one university, Cambridge."

5 Conclusion

How do we explain the sustained success of prehistory at Cambridge? To return to questions posed at the beginning, how are definitions, goals and methods centralised and institutionalised in one place? Why and how do a set of ideas and practices become articulate, systematic and professionalised within a university setting? With Cambridge's splendid idiosyncrasy, prehistory, as an exemplary subject, a solid attempt has been made to answer these questions.

This is one of the few times that work in the history of science has been applied to the history of archaeology. By using three different approaches in the course of this inquiry, the relevance of history-of-science research when investigating the history of archaeology has been demonstrated. It was revealed that each approach had salience and applicability. It is hoped, therefore, that future studies of archaeology will be informed by and benefit from approaches developed within the discipline of the history of science.

This study examined the utility of Morrell's model in a different context from the laboratory schools upon which it was originally based. It was acknowledged that the definition of a research school did not entirely fit the Faculty of Archaeology and Anthropology, and that Geison's comparative research on scientific schools, conducted in the 1980s and early 1990s, was outdated by the mid 1990s. Nevertheless, Geison's (1981: 26) "systematic catalogue of factors to be considered when examining a research school" raised appropriate issues. It was found that Geison's (1981: 24) chart did suggest fruitful areas of investigation. In fact, Morrell's (1972) and Geison's (1981, 1993) work proved remarkably relevant and meaningful, especially when applied to Grahame Clark, *"a young man in a hurry"*(Cornford 1908: 3). The results of research on the development of chemistry (Morrell 1972) and physiology (Coleman 1985) constructively illuminated Clark's contributions to the institutionalisation of prehistory at Cambridge during the 1930s.

Morrell's model (1972) worked well for Clark as an example of a male, university-based, intellectual entrepreneur. Geison's (1981) list of ingredients for academic success, a strong coherent set of research questions and methods, exploitable techniques, an avenue for publication, a pool of recruits and an ability to establish administrative support were shown to be present at Cambridge. A focused research programme and the exploration of new fields of research were characteristic of Clark and the Fenland Research Committee's accomplishments. Certainly a monopoly over a special body of knowledge and skills, following Soffer (1982), was established.

Following Coleman's (1985: 49) and Rosenberg's (1979) suggestion, the importance of "cognitive content" in social

analysis of scientific life has been stressed. As Morrell (1972) indicated, the introduction of an exploitable experimental technique turned out to be crucial for the success of the Committee's work and for the institutionalisation of prehistoric archaeology at Cambridge. It was shown that pollen analysis enabled Clark, Godwin and the Committee to use a stratigraphic-geological approach to archaeology, thus making an enormously important contribution to archaeological knowledge.

Clark used a new knowledge base developed during the interdisciplinary excavations of the Fenland Research Committee to gain institutional support for an innovative definition of archaeology. His efforts to professionalise prehistory by establishing a university degree were successful. As Coleman (1985) suggested, the specialisation of prehistory was supported when the means to disseminate new material through publications and instruction was obtained. This was illustrated by reconstructing the events which led to the rationalisation and nationalisation of the Prehistoric Society of East Anglia in the early 1930s. As Sieveking (1976: xvii) acutely commented, with the establishment of the *Proceedings of the Prehistoric Society*, "a platform was made available in Britain" for the publication of interdisciplinary evidence from the natural sciences. As mentioned previously, the content of the new *Proceedings* stressed broad, national concerns. During its first years, the *Proceedings'* papers set a frame of study for the next generation. Piggott's "The Early Bronze Age in Wessex" appeared in 1938 along with Bersu's "Excavations at Woodbury". Shortly after, Daniel's "The Dual Nature of the Megalithic Colonization of Prehistoric Europe", Crawford's "Air Photography Past and Present", and Garrod's "The Upper Palaeolithic in the Light of Recent Discovery" appeared.

The number graduating with a specialisation in archaeology from Archaeology and Anthropology, Section A, increased during the 1930s. Clark, as "a capable and enthusiastic teacher whose value [was] well appreciated,"[1] attracted students exactly as Morrell's model would indicate. Testimony from former students was gathered to show that Clark was presenting "new and exciting developments quite outside the scope of classic text-books of the day" (McBurney (1976: xii) which inspired undergraduates. Coleman's (1985) and Morrell's (1972) suggestion that funding and facilities were required for a research school to be successful proved to be relevant to Clark and Cambridge prehistory. Evidence was presented that the Faculty expanded its facilities during the 1930s. Teaching and library space was acquired when Minns announced that rooms in the old Law School had been solicited for teaching purposes.[2]

In addition to the research school literature which proved so helpful, the concept of knowledge travel, as developed

---

[1] Faculty Minutes; 8 June 1936. CUA Min.V.92a.

[2] Faculty and Appointments Minutes 7 November 1935. CUA Min.V.93.

by Shapin (1998), was also fruitfully employed. The travel of ideas and the ways of doing science were investigated to access the strength of Clark's and Godwin's research agenda. When compared to other archaeologists from the 1920s and 1930s, it was shown that Clark was explicitly using several lines of inference to enhance conclusions; he defined this as "scientific reasoning". Clark looked for the convergence of separate lines of inference because he believed that this greatly strengthened his arguments. Through two case studies, Cambridge's archaeological training as it applied to new territory was traced and documented. It was concluded that Clark's use of evidence and of scientific reasoning had indeed impressed his students and that the Committee's manner of conducting interdisciplinary science, as well as a Cambridge philosophy concerning archaeology's purpose, had successfully jumped continents. When Shaw's and Desmond Clark's mode of presentation is examined, their style of writing and their stress upon the systemisation of evidence deeply resembled Clark's cool, lucid scientific presentations rather than Burkitt's discursive articles written in a genial, peripatetic style.

Morrell (1972) suggested that we take account of intellectual, institutional, technical, psychological and financial factors in our historical analyses of research schools and this I have done for Clark and the Committee with good results.

However, when applied to Burkitt's and Garrod's contributions, Morrell's model loses some of its force and salience. Certainly, some factors taken from Geison's (1981) chart did apply to Miles Burkitt's long academic career. Morrell (1972) was correct when suggesting that a growing number of students was to be expected and that a pool of recruits contributed to the success of a school. Evidence was given that Burkitt's approach of "Burins and Tea" increasingly attracted students to the new academic subject of prehistory. It was argued that Burkitt did have what Geison might term an effective leadership style. As the archaeologist Bruce Howe and others testified, Burkitt successfully inspired students to pursue archaeology. As Howe remembered, the Burkitt teas "were often full of shop talk and provocative prehistory."[3]

Nevertheless, many themes and issues of interest emerged from the examination of Burkitt's and Garrod's careers that were not mentioned as relevant in either the research school material and the geography-of-knowledge literature. If I were to have directed my inquiry using only Morrell's or Shapin's results and arguments as guides, historically important factors might have been missed. Burkitt, for example, was neither charismatic nor brilliant. Counter to expectations, he had no research reputation yet turned out to be seriously important.

Rather than academic brilliance, Burkitt's religious beliefs were shown to be relevant to the institutionalisation of pre-

history. "The great study of Man, next to the study of God, the chief object of all intellectual effort . . . The study of humanity's past is a study of God" (Burkitt 1930a: 265–6). Prehistory reveals "a culmination, the result of struggle and failure, the generation of the soul"(Burkitt 1932e: 267). The study of prehistoric man illustrated precisely the development of humanity's spirituality. By knowing our pasts, we know ourselves. A knowledge of prehistory will make us wiser, better people and peaceful and responsible rulers of the world.

I have attempted to recover intentions, reconstruct conventions and restore context. Following those goals, Burkitt's religious motivations were dutifully recovered. The importance of philosophical and religious beliefs to the establishment of prehistory was clarified. It was also made clear that before formalised controls and qualifying standards were established, ideas became practice through personal attachment and companionship. Ophir and Shapin's (1991: 3) "place of knowledge" occurred not within a laboratory or university setting but instead during conversations at nightly camp fires. Archaeological expertise was imparted in the field while travelling on horse-back or exploring painted caves. Before the establishment of the structure necessary for Geison's research schools, archaeological knowledge was packaged in individual, trade-like apprenticeships based on loyalty.

Some difficulty with Morrell's approach was also found when the contributions of lesser players were analysed. Denston's and O'Reilly's careers were historically important but did not fit smoothly within either the research school or geography-of-knowledge perspectives. These archaeologists did not attract students or propose great theories but were productive both intellectually and socially. It was shown that Denston and O'Reilly were important participants in the success of Cambridge prehistory. Historical models of research schools may benefit from the inclusion of these quieter players and from an examination of the contributions of good support staff.

When considering the case study of Dorothy Garrod, the history of science literature reviewed was helpful in some ways. Morrell's, Geison's, Soffer's and Coleman's research did lead to the conclusion that Garrod's unwillingness to "blow [her] own trumpet,"[4] to champion her own innovative views or to attract students would and clearly did hurt her as an academic. However, Morrell's analysis as well as approaches from the geography of knowledge did not completely illuminate Garrod's experiences as the only woman professor in a "'men's university" (Sutherland 1998: 89). As noted above, the investigation into the factors which may contribute to the success of research institutions was begun before the results of gender and science research was fashionably available. Many appropriate questions were therefore not suggested by Geison's work. Instead, questions were raised and answered by considering the substantial

---

[3] Howe, personal correspondence, 1997.
[4] Hetzel in the privately printed *Transcripts of the Day's Proceedings.*

The Transformation of an Elite? Women and Higher Education since 1900 (1998).

recent theoretical material which analyses women's experiences as academics. This literature, part of a vast literature on the analysis of gendered behaviours and relationships, was used to provide a wider context and to cast perspective on Garrod's reactions to academic life. The importance of skilled attitudes and learned behaviours was documented. It was argued that Garrod never became acculturated to the type of informal behaviour needed to be a "Cambridge man". It was concluded that Garrod's manner of behaving seemed maladaptive within Cambridge's arcane institutional, hierarchical arena where control and manipulation of scarce resources were critical and where bureaucratic effectiveness required a tacit knowledge of how to act.

Although Garrod did not succeed according to research school standards, her presence heralded the admission of women to an ancient university. Garrod's election clearly precipitated major change, not just to a research school, but to an entire university system. Garrod's successful field career also resulted in valuable and enduring contributions to academic research agendas. It was concluded that this success should somehow be relevant to research school analyses.

It would seem that a contribution may be made to historical analysis if Morrell's work were to be augmented by including other perspectives along with the results presented here in this publication. It may prove profitable to use my findings to extend the analysis in order to construct a fuller description and explanation of academic life. Morrell and Geison's chart would then embrace an example from the history of archaeology as well as from other subjects.

5.1 Enhancements

Motivations

The results of Burkitt's case study suggest that strong emotions, motivations and/or belief systems should be examined during investigations of research schools. As Geison (1981: 32) suggests, "personal, social, conceptual and technical factors interact to shape scientific research" in complex ways. However, personal religious beliefs were not discussed in any of the literature. For example, of the eleven studies published in the 1993 volume of *Osiris*, "Research Schools: Historical Reappraisals", none describes spiritual beliefs or broader philosophical motivations; none discusses personal feelings. Yet the importance of these issues must be stressed when considering the establishment of prehistory at Cambridge.

In any interview I conducted, in the end, people wanted to be remembered for whom and what they loved, not for what they had accomplished. Their uniform passion unites

prehistory at Cambridge. From Burkitt, who believed that the soul was illuminated by a knowledge of the past, to Clark, who believed that prehistory could be the great leveller[5] and therefore must be professionalised, to Garrod, who named the Neanderthal child, Abel, and came to prehistoric archaeology as if converted to a religion, the common thread is a certain belief that this subject will enlighten our lives and strengthen the world. Devotion to archaeology is the one embracing emotion always evident and expressed by all interviewed. Burkitt, Clark and Garrod were strikingly different, individualistic personalities. Yet they were all committed to prehistory as if to a faith. It is clear that this deep emotional and philosophical commitment was one of the major reasons for the success of prehistoric archaeology.

Gender

The analysis of Garrod's academic experiences demonstrated the value of exploring gender differences in science. Garrod's case study illustrated the importance of applying the results of investigations into gender and science issues. The examination of Garrod's academic difficulties suggests that research school studies might benefit from taking gender factors into consideration. A fuller understanding of how a set of ideas and practices become articulate within a university setting might result if the social organisation of sexual differences and the definitions of masculine and feminine roles were explored. Gender issues should, therefore, be included as an appropriate factor in Geison's chart.

Considering how certain gender definitions and their changes either benefited or delayed the development of research schools might prove productive. For example, according to Howarth's (1998) "Gender at Cambridge and Oxford", definitions of masculinity and femininity were shifting during the 1920s and 1930s at the ancient universities. This appears to have been true for members of the Faculty of Archaeology and Anthropology. In the 1920s, women students were not defined as undergraduates. Full female membership had been defeated in 1921 and women were still not allowed to offer lectures. Although the Faculty was particularly receptive to women, deep ambivalence and much confusion was being expressed about women's presence by the wider Cambridge community. At this point, Burkitt taught prehistory as part of a liberal education for future judicious gentlemen probationers who were well-defined as fair-minded District Commissioners or civil servants. A liberal education would train gentlemen in the right habits of thought, steadfastness and consistency. Since there were no gentlewomen in the Colonial Service, female students had little place within Burkitt's educational percept; the role of educated women was much less clearly defined than that of educated men. As one former undergraduate interviewed stated, women were in Cambridge on sufferance.

---

[5] Clark (1956: 615) often repeats his belief that Prehistory "promotes human solidarity by comprehending the whole history of all mankind". See also *Archaeology and Society* (Clark 1939a, 1947: viii) "Those who study the prehistoric past common to the great mass of mankind may help to foster that awareness of human solidarity without which it is difficult to conceive how any world order can be organised on a democratic basis." Refer also to articles such as Clark (1959: 12), "For me prehistory is only worth pursuing because it sets not merely history but contemporary life in the kind of perspective."

As the decades proceeded, however, the definition of male archaeology students seemed to change. When Clark and the Committee dominated the archaeological side of the Tripos course during the 1930s, educating future professionals and scientists became a priority. Until his retirement in 1958, Burkitt did not encourage students to go into archaeology unless they had a private income.[6] Clark, in contrast, was interested in educating archaeologists as scientists who had entrepreneurial drive and who would secure jobs and further the future of prehistoric studies world-wide rather than promote gentlemanly values and behaviour.

As the archaeological side of the Tripos course gained financial and institutional increased status, women, such as O'Reilly, were able to make new options for themselves by creatively and successfully fashioning archaeological spaces within the Faculty. Female students began to be able to contribute in more varied and fuller ways as the definition of an undergraduate was expanded to include them. In addition, working-class men, such as Denston, found ways to participate and to change their self-definition by securing positions.

This would imply that periods of change in the social organisation of gender difference and in the definitions of masculine and feminine may also be periods in which space opens for the creation of new academic knowledge. Times of changing gender roles may be times of academic expansion. This would seem to be true from the experience of prehistory at Cambridge. I would conclude that organisations which are in the midst of change in definitions of gender roles may provide privileged sites for conceptual innovation.

Corporate Knowledge

In his 1993 article, Geison (1993: 235) wrote, "Nothing is more important to the success or failure in a research school than the intellectual and personal qualities of its leader." This top-down nature of Geison's model has been criticised by some (Hagen 1993) who claim that the role of a school's leader is "exalted at the expense of other factors" (Geison 1993: 234). Certainly Ridgeway, for example, had great power and could be considered to fit Morrell and Geison's expectations. Nevertheless, Ridgeway was also a skilled team player and worked well with other strong participants, such as Haddon, on the emerging Board. When Clark and Burkitt are considered, it is clear that Clark's personality and Burkitt's lack of brilliance do not conform to expectations suggested for leaders by the literature on successful scientific laboratories. In addition, Garrod's contributions to the establishment of the full Tripos course and her contributions to social change within the Faculty and University would have been ignored if we were to have looked only for charismatic leadership.

There is no evidence, presented by interviewees or to be found in correspondence or minutes, to suggest that any one person was considered to be the only charismatic leader of this Faculty. Clark was clearly the most intellectually influential, as was pointed out repeatedly by former archaeology students. For example, when asked "Who do you think was the most influential lecturer in terms of ideas," both Professor and Mrs Evans replied quickly and simultaneously, "Undoubtably Grahame Clark. Some of his ideas sounded very strange at that time but he, certainly, with the environmental and economic approaches, this was really something that was the cutting edge."[7] Again, Jack Golson was "much taken by Grahame's course on European economic prehistory . . . this was new and innovative stuff and it was very exciting to be a part of it."[8] But interviewees also stated that Clark was not seen as, and did not act as, a charismatic leader. Golson found him to be "low key, focused and humourless . . . you didn't get the impression that he was a leader . . there was no pedagogical technique". He was "not a crusading figure."[9]

In addition, although some commentators suggest that the Cambridge archaeological diaspora, during the late 1940s or early 1950s, was a direct product of Grahame Clark's design and influence, students interviewed clearly stated that they felt indebted to a variety of Faculty participants. They often argued that the success of the Tripos course was a result of collegial contributions by many and also a clear result of their own ability to create opportunities. After all, as previously mentioned, it was Golson, not Clark, who attracted Gathercole to a joint appointment at the University of Otago and the Otago Museum, New Zealand. Rather than Clark, it was the Curator of the MAA, Geoffrey Bushnell, who worked with Hurst on mediaeval pottery and Gerald Dunning who found Hurst his job at the Inspectorate of Ancient Monuments, Ministry of Works. Daniel was the person who suggested to Evans that he apply for Gordon Childe's position in the Chair of European Prehistoric Archaeology at the Institute of Archaeology in London. Mulvaney followed his own plan to return home to Australia.[10] And Shaw went to Africa fulfilling a boyhood desire, and Desmond Clark found his position in Northern Rhodesia partly through help from O'Reilly.

The Department was composed of "very different personalities" and "You got a bit from each," remembered Mrs Evans.[11] Garrod was "withdrawn"; Daniel, just the opposite, conducted supervisions in the nearest pub. "Glyn of course was a very informal character," enjoyed by many. Burkitt was "kind indeed, very helpful, he threw his library open to any of us . . the moneyed man with leisure pursuing his interests and sharing his interests with you but regarding the whole thing as something that was not a profession."[12]

---

[6] Professor emeritus John Evans and Mrs Evans, in conversation, 2000.

[7] Professor emeritus John Evans and Mrs Evans, in conversation, 2000.

[8] Golson, in conversation, 1996.

[9] Golson, in conversation, 1996.

[10] Taking what had been accomplished at Cambridge as a model, "I

decided,"Mulvaney stated, "that if there were archaeology in Britain, there should be archaeology in Australia" (in conversation, 2000).

[11] Mrs Evans, in conversation, 1998.

[12] Quotations from John Evans, in conversation, 2000.

An unsung hero, also thoroughly respected, was Toty de Navarro, a man with wide, exacting knowledge of the Iron Age, who published little but was an excellent teacher with an encyclopaedic mind, well-liked during the 1920s, '30s and '40s.

From interviews, Faculty records and from correspondence, it is clear that the effectiveness of Cambridge prehistory was the result of a collective enterprise. This was always the nature of the subject ever since Haddon and Ridgeway co-operated to make room for Burkitt's first course of lectures proposed in 1915. However, as the Tripos became established, co-operative, co-ordinated teaching became more organised. Students relied on many specialists, not just one teacher. Evidence from Faculty Minutes and correspondence suggests that, in most cases, the health and future of archaeology and anthropology overrode any one person's goals. There was a strong, common desire to produce a working curriculum and qualifying degree course for future research school leaders.

This approach to the organisation of knowledge production is not sufficiently stressed by the research school literature and it is therefore difficult to make comparisons. However, it is apparent that the Faculty's approach is reminiscent of the Fenland Research Committee's openly declared policy that the results it produced should be communally owned. It was understood that the Committee would have more impact as a unified team; knowledge would be communally created and exported. Science would hence benefit. Perhaps taking support from the Committee's example, the Faculty assumed what may be termed a corporate identity. As Shapin (1994: 127) argues, "identity at once belongs to an individual *and* to the collectivities of which that individual is a part." Academic archaeology at Cambridge was a collective, staff product. Just as scientific knowledge could be better produced collegially, so could students. The education of students was understood to be a corporate and co-operative affair.

When the experience of Cambridge is used as an example, it would seem that a successful research endeavour resulted from a corporate effort. From the beginnings, archaeology and anthropology attracted strongly ambitious and powerful personalities, von Hügel, Haddon, Ridgeway, Louis Clarke, Fox and Leakey to name only a few. Less powerful characters were also shown to be productively involved. During the 1920s, a community of undergraduates, young researchers, ex-colonial officers and elderly gentlemen ran the Museum effectively. Rather than having *a* leader, it was certainly more important to have a group, that, despite sometimes deep differences and possible rivalries, could work together. "Big science" had not yet developed, but the Faculty had quietly discovered the principle of consensual team work. There was no need for only one persuasively magnetic or creative personality. Research schools led by one charismatic leader may prove less successful than faculties and schools comprised of diversely talented people who function well together.

Student Pioneers
The effectiveness of the Tripos course was partly a result of the students' own personal initiative and inventiveness. Cambridge archaeology students tended to be self-starters. Although Morrell stresses the importance of a pool of recruits, the independent, self-motivated nature of the Faculty's student body is worth noting. The number of "fathers", "mothers", foundation lecturers and founders of departments of prehistoric academic archaeology world-wide is remarkable. Tripos graduates were clearly self-directed and should be given full credit for their innovation of productive research and degree programmes and for their fruitful move to and success in foreign places or in British posts.

John Hurst may be mentioned as one example. Hurst helped to initiate, without supervision or Faculty support, the study of mediaeval rural settlement as a multidisciplinary research project. Coming up to Cambridge already fascinated by archaeology, he "had no intention of doing Palaeolithic but Grahame Clark took me aside and said I must take Garrod's option or else she would not be paid." Hurst was Garrod's only pupil and she lectured "as if there were 100 people in the hall."[13] By Part II, Hurst had redirected himself to developing research in mediaeval archaeology.

Many undergraduates in 1949 and 1950, according to Hurst (1986),[14] were appalled at the lack of practical instruction within the Faculty. With no teaching of excavation techniques, they began their own excavations to train themselves. He and Harry Norris (First Class Honours, Tripos 1949) chose the mediaeval moated manor at Northolt and started a 20-year project. The next year, 1951, Hurst, with Golson assisting, directed one of the first urban rescue excavations in Britain. In 1952, Golson went to Denmark to excavate at Steensberg's deserted village site of Store Valby, learning to marry historical documents with archaeological fieldwork. During this time, Hurst started working with the economic historian, M.W. Beresford, who had begun preliminary investigations at Wharram Percy.

When Golson returned from Steensberg's excavation, "we managed to get as many experts on mediaeval settlement together as possible and formed the interdisciplinary Deserted Mediaeval Village Research Group in October 1952," remembered Hurst.[15] The DMVRG co-ordinated work on rural mediaeval settlement, then a new subject. In effect, Hurst and Golson were founding a specialisation. They and the DMVRG applied the Scandinavian concept of open-area excavation by uncovering the total area while charting layers of clay, charcoal, fireplaces, pavements, postholes, etc. Clearing the whole site layer by layer was a

[13] Hurst, in conversation, 2000.
[14] Manuscript, entitled "The Work of the Medieval Village Research Group

1952–1986" by Hurst, in the possession of the Hurst family.
[15] Hurst, in conversation, 2001.

revolutionary method. Over most of England, in the 1920s, 1930s and 1940s, excavations were still carried out either by trenches or by the grid method with baulks as championed by Wheeler at Maiden Castle. The grid method was proving fine for some sites, especially Roman buildings, but inappropriate for subtler mediaeval remains.

According to Hurst, open-area excavation was an important development. "There was certainly no way that the mediaeval peasant house, with its flimsy foundations, could be understood by digging grids," commented Hurst in an interview. "Really the whole process of archaeology has been changed by this method of open-area excavation which has enabled excavators in the second half of the twentieth century to produce very much more remarkable results than was possible in the earlier time," he concluded.[16]

Desmond Clark's and Shaw's pioneer work in Africa as earlier described and John Hurst's work as one of the first graduates of the full Tripos course suggests that students' perseverance was as important as the factors stressed by Geison (1981), Morrell (1972), Soffer (1982) and Coleman (1985), such as publications, charismatic leaders, lively cognitive research agendas, new research techniques, journals and structural and financial support.

Cambridge student self-sufficiency implies that research schools, which desire to be effective, should encourage student independence and set up structures and means to support it.

Tea-rooms
Shapin (1994) and Hardwig (1991) argue that a climate of trust is required to support much of our academic knowledge. No one can know enough and "In most disciplines, those who do not trust cannot know. . . the trustworthiness of epistemic communities is the ultimate foundation" for knowledge (Hardwig 1991: 694). In his well-known study, *A Social History of Truth*, Shapin (1994: 409–17) suggests that familiarity may support scientific consensus. Trust in known people could form a basis for scientific communities. "When people assessed the credibility of what they were told, they were able to draw upon the resources of familiarity" (Shapin 1994: 410). The Museum tea-room appears to have been the Faculty space where the Ophir and Shapin's (1991) practical solution to the problem of trust could be worked out.

According to Christopher Hawkes, Louis Clark founded the custom of Museum tea so that *everyone will get to know each other, otherwise they will hate each other"* (Scott-Fox 2002: 47). Curator Louis Clarke appears to have understood Hartwig's and Shapin's pronouncements on trust. While meeting for morning coffee or afternoon tea, staff, students, visitors, or academics from adjacent faculties could become familiar with each other's limits, faults, strengths and intel-

lectual specialisations. As Stuart Piggott said, "We all knew each other. We were all friends — or enemies".[17] Based on this familiarity, reasoned actions could be taken and sound decisions made. Regular face-to-face interactions could be academically productive. As quoted earlier, "In those days the typewriter and the telephone were hardly regarded as the mode of communication between gentlemen" (Hutton and Bushnell 1962: 2). An informal pleasant space required for intellectual discourse and a meeting place necessary for the managing of personal and scientific affairs was important. A functioning tea-room, where people could relax and engage in easy conversations would promote informal community friendships, the smooth running of a small, young faculty and eventually the creation of new knowledge. Here researchers who knew each other could "knock ideas around" and engage in "fascinating informal academic discussions".[18]

This early mode of functioning informally, the "haphazardness" that the Faculty fought to maintain, characterised by informal relationships established in the tea-room, served the Faculty well. The relaxed nature of graded divisions made the tea-room open to students as well as staff. This fostered a sense of social coherency which exudes from the Faculty Minutes during the 1920s, 1930s and into the early 1940s. This sense of belonging to a meaningful group was noted during interviews with students who were then affiliated with the Faculty. Social loyalty was also evident in reactions to Saunders' efforts to formalise procedures and to standardise individual teaching and staff behaviour. Certainly, when Garrod was faced with a threatening University administration, she was unanimously supported.

This informality and lack of strict rules and structures allowed for innovative teaching and promoted creative contributions by numerous participants. During the 1920s, anyone who had knowledge, wanted to share it and was willing to work for small sums of student fees, could apply to be a "Recognised Lecturer". There was no set curriculum; lectures were widely varied and inventive. Openness and lack of formal entry arrangements welcomed young talent and new ideas. During the 1930s, Clark could easily insert what he, the Godwins and thc Fenland Research Committee had learned the day before in the Fens. Clark was able immediately to offer lectures on his strongest and most exciting material.

The novelty of the ideas presented and the Faculty's relaxed atmosphere attracted students. "Small really was beautiful," stated Joan Lillico.[19] "My third year was by far and away the best when I switched from Modern Languages to the Archaeological and Anthropological Tripos; the Modern Language school was huge and impersonal and A and A was small and intimate." "It was a happy and relaxed time, only 5 or 6 of us in a class . . . entertained by Mrs Burkitt with tea and delicious cakes,"remembered Joyce Perry.[20]

---

[16] Hurst, in conversation, 2000.
[17] Stuart Piggott, in conversation with Julia Roberts, 1994.

[18] All quotations, Mary Cra'ster, in conversation, 1999.
[19] Joan Lillico, Tripos 1935, personal correspondence, 1998.

This relaxed time included fancy dress parties, such as the one pictured on the cover, which commemorated Professor Hutton's retirement. Such festive occasions, when members of the Faculty wore Museum artefacts, were happily remembered. Punting parties led by Faculty members in plus-fours, with painted students dressed as "Indians" beating Museum drums, were an important part of a student's education. As one undergraduate said, "The Anthropology and Archaeology Department was far more interesting than any primitive tribe."[21]

For many years, dogs continued to be allowed in class, smoking persisted under the "No Smoking" sign in the Museum staircase, and students were allowed keys to the Library.[22] Periodically, members of the Faculty Board would resolve never to wear their gowns again. Predictably the General Board would sternly comment that it had come to its attention that the Faculty members were not wearing gowns. Appropriately, on 19 February 1951, the new professional Faculty, following the amateurs who came before, in an honoured tradition of rebellion against University strictures

and in continued dedication to their haphazard ways, passed a firm resolution unanimously resolving that the wearing of gowns would be forever discontinued.[23]

The history of prehistory at Cambridge provided a fascinating site. My investigation suggests that historians must discuss and describe student creativeness, the collegial nature of academic knowledge production, the informality and flexibility of social and academic relationships as well as emotions, personal motivations, religious beliefs and changing gender definitions in order fully to understand our disciplinary past. Research school studies seem to assume that the only "knowledgemaking site" (Shapin 1991: 9) is the laboratory. The literature tends to ignore the importance of other social spaces and how such spaces may support innovation. Tea-rooms are supremely important and the investigation as to the benefits of informal meeting places in research institutions would be an appropriate future project. Based on this study of prehistory, it would appear that small, informal and flexible groups, drinking tea together, create splendid subjects.

---

[20] Joyce Perry, Tripos 1937, personal correspondence, 1998.
[21] I.M.R. Summers (*m.*1949), in conversation, 1998.
[22] There were reports that students actually slept in the Library.
[23] Faculty Minutes. CUA Min.v.95.

CHART II. Factors in the success or failure of research schools.

Degree of success	Sustained success				Temporary success		Partial or relative failure			
	Liebig's School	Foster's School	Noyes' School	Prehistory at Cambridge	Arcueil School	Fermi's Group	Thomson's School	Burdon-Sanderson's School	Remsen's School	Bancroft's School
1. 'Charismatic' leader(s)	+	+	+	?	+	+	−	−	−	+
2. Leader with research reputation	+	+	+	+	+	+	+	+	+	+
3. 'Informal' setting and leadership style	+	+	?	+	−	+	−	−	−	−
4. Leader with institutional power	+	+	+	+	+	+	−	+	+	+
5. Social cohesion, loyalty, esprit de corps, 'discipleship'	+	+	+	+	+	+	−	−	?	+
6. Focused research program	+	+	+	+	+	+	+	+	+	+
7. Simple and rapidly exploitable experimental techniques	+	−	+	+	?	+	+	+	+	−
8. Invasion of new field of research	+	−	+	+	−	+	−			+
9. Pool of potential recruits (graduate students)	+	+	+	+	+	?	+	+	+	+
10. Access to or control of publication outlets	+	+	+	+	+	+	?	+	+	+
11. Students publish early under own names	+	+	+	+	+	?	−	−	?	+
12. Produced and 'placed' significant number of students	+	+	+	+	+	?	−	−	+	+
13. Institutionalization in university setting	+	+	+	+	−	?	+	+	+	+
14. Adequate financial support	+	+	+	?	+	+	−	−	+	+
15. Strong beliefs and philosophical motivations				+						
16. Change in gender roles				+						
17. Co-operative knowledge production				+						
18. Inventive, self-starting, creative students				+						
19. A tea-room and a climate of trust				+						

FIGURE XLVIII. Reformulated "Model". A vehicle for a fuller understanding of how one set of ideas and practices became articulate, systematic and professionalised within a university setting is here provided.

Appendix: Interviews with Archaeologists

"Memories," as one of those interviewed said, "are like gathering roses in winter."

Transcripts

Professor emeritus Warwick Bray
Professor emeritus J. Desmond Clark
Professor Graham Connah
Professor Ekpo Eyo
Professor emeritus John Evans and Mrs Evans
Professor Norman Hammond
Mr John G. Hurst
Professor emeritus R.R. Inskeep
Professor Pierre de Maret
Professor emeritus John D. Mulvaney
Dr Innocent Pikirayi
Professor emeritus Merrick Posnansky
Professor emeritus Thurstan Shaw
Professor emeritus Peter Shinnie
Professor Paul J.J. Sinclair
Professor emeritus Frank Willett

For ease of reading the transcripts, notes concerning the tape-recordings are in sans-serif Roman type.

The interviewer's questions and comments are in sans-serif italic type.

The correspondent/interviewee's answers/narratives are in serif Roman type.

Professor emeritus Warwick Bray

11 September 2000, recorded at the McDonald Institute, Cambridge University, by Pamela Jane Smith pjs1011@cam.ac.uk
This transcript is incomplete. Portions of the interview, especially my comments, are inaudible.

We are talking to Warwick Bray, Professor emeritus of Latin American Archaeology at the Institute of Archaeology at University College London. Professor Warwick Bray was just telling me his memories of Stuart Piggott, whom he admired.

It goes back to the days when I was still a Mediterranean archaeologist and, of course, Stuart Piggott was one of the people you had to read and talk to. I was doing my Ph.D in Sardinia at the time when *Animal, Vegetable, Mineral* was on the Television and Glyn Daniel, Piggott and Mortimer Wheeler were household names. One of the stories that comes to me [Inaudible bit]. In Italian terms, it was just when Luigi Bernabo Brea was making important discoveries on Sicily and the Lipari Islands, and somehow or other, I don't know the story except when I got to be involved, the Government there invited a set of scholars from Britain, mainly from Cambridge, to go and see all these new discoveries. They chartered a fishing boat and filled it with academics. Glyn was there, Stuart was there, a number of others, and a group of students. I was in Sardinia at the time and I came over, and we went from island to island looking at excavations, and at every island, there was a reception with wine. We all had a good time. Where Stuart comes into this — we were talking about his breadth of interest, he was not a narrow-minded archaeologist — we were sitting around at one of these receptions, and Stuart came up with a poetic quotation and offered a bottle of wine to anyone who could recognise it. I was the only person in the room who also had a career in English Literature. I got the quotation, and he paid up like a gentleman. Piggott could happily sit down and talk about anything.

[I say something about him being an historian.]

I think that's how he saw himself as well. He was certainly first and foremost a serious archaeologist but if you look at the breadth of what he wrote about, he wasn't one of those narrow specialists who only had one interest. He was capable of getting into any historical, archaeological or literary subject, and he was interested in people as well. He was very good with students.

Was he responsible for building up the Department at Edinburgh, as opposed to Gordon Childe?

I am not quite sure, because I only once went up there in Piggott's days. I really don't know, but it was very much his Department when he was there. The students thought that he was marvellous. Gordon Childe was a very different personality. Whether he had the capacity to build up something or not, I simply don't know.

Who were some of Piggott's students?

One of the theses I had to read was Beatrice Blance's, who wrote about Mediterranean topics. I had to go up there to read her thesis once. [Inaudible bit.] Here was I, nobody very much from Cambridge, a fairly junior person. I arrived with no appointment. Stuart wasn't there. I came to his house and there I found him in a great woolly pullover. "Let's make lunch!" he said. We then had a very good lunch. "And how about Beatrice Blance? I have a problem with Beatrice," he said. "You can read the thesis but she came to my office not long ago and said 'Stuart, I think that I am going to drop out of Archaeology.'" Stuart said "Who is the lucky man?" And she said "No, I have been called by God. I am going to be a Missionary." And she never wrote anything else for him.

When was this?

It must have been around 1960.

When did you come up to Cambridge?

Early fifties. 1953, I think. I have to check; but I didn't come up to be an archaeologist. To understand how I fit in, you have to go a little bit back to the school days because one of the things that made me believe in Stuart Piggott was that I wasn't a specialist archaeologist either. Up to the age of 16, I was going to be a biologist, which means I had read all the evolutionary biologists at that stage, and when the New Archaeology broke upon the world, I didn't get it through Leslie White. I actually got it through biology. Then I did a switch and was going to be a writer and poet [small inaudible bit]. I did that for two years and realised that the course wasn't really about literature at all. It was about becoming a literary critic, and that was not what I wanted to be at all. After two years of this, I looked around for a change. When it came to it, there were only two things that I could change to. One was Economics and the other was Archaeology and Anthropology, because they had one-year Part Ones. My family background, my father was a field geologist who had worked in Africa. So I had always been interested in other cultures and antiquities and landscapes and that sort of thing. Archaeology was the choice. That first year, the old Part One, was a real mind-blower. It was the most interesting single year of education I have ever had in my entire career, and I found I was good at it. I stayed and did Part Two in one year instead of two, just to get a proper Archaeology degree, and at that point, came on the job market, the thesis market. At that stage, I had already decided I wanted to get a long way from Cambridge. I had had enough of Cambridge, and I thought the biggest possible contrast there could be would be to go to a Catholic country far away. So I sent off letters for scholarships to Turkey, Portugal and Italy. Two said "No" and one said "Yes". I ended up doing my Ph.D in Sardinia. That is the early stage of the career.

Who did you have in Part One?

All sorts of people were teaching in those days. It just overlaps with the end of the period you are most interested in.

[I asked something inaudible about G.I Jones.]

Jones, yes, and Geoffrey Bushnell was there.

Did he teach American Archaeology?

Not very much. He sometimes gave a token course on American Archaeology. It was never something that Cambridge did, but he was a good academic. They more or less gave him a token course. Jack Trevor did Physical Anthropology. It was the end of the Burkitt era in Palaeolithic. There was Clark, McBurney, Audrey Furness, John Coles and, of course, Glyn Daniel.

John Coles?!

Yes, just beginning. I was here a long time, changing subjects and doing a Ph.D. All of those at one time or another taught me, very exciting people to listen to.

Charles McBurney was there?

Yes, I didn't do a great deal of Palaeolithic because I knew that was not where my interest was going to be. But he was certainly one of my teachers and I dug with him as an undergraduate and graduate student as well.

Lethbridge?

No, he was a presence of someone who had been there before. Extraordinary people came along. Glyn Isaac, Paul Mellars, Nic David. There were lots — strange things used to happen. McBurney could not organise flash photographs and was never quite sure how much to compensate. So he used to go out in the dead of the night to photograph his excavation sections, so there would be no interference from sunlight and the flash. All sorts of strange and wonderful things were happening. It was a very good and very varied Department.

Could you say something about Burkitt?

When I first came into contact with him, he was virtually at the end of his career, a long career, and everybody knew and he himself knew that he was no longer on the cutting edge of things. Remember, McBurney and Grahame Clark were teaching in the same building. The comparison was very cruel to Burkitt. He did most of his teaching to first-year beginners. It is probably a good idea to begin small and then become more complicated. His lectures were enormously enjoyable, partly because the man himself was so obviously enjoying them. It was almost as if your favourite uncle was up there, reminiscing about olden days. You didn't get a great deal of very new archaeology. He didn't say much beyond what was in his book, The Old Stone Age. You didn't go there to get the new, but what fascinated me was that he was so obviously a bridge to the past. He had been there and had worked with the Abbé Breuil in the old days, and nobody else had. Clark and McBurney were the rising stars. They hadn't worked in sub-Saharan Africa. They weren't particularly interested in art. The world that Burkitt would talk about was a different world, not enormously relevant and certainly not the way things were to go, but I have always liked the history. I used to find it fascinating just to listen to the asides and anecdotes.

[Inaudible question by me.]

The person who most often came up was the Abbé Breuil. He didn't actually teach about the excavations he did with Obermaier in any formal sense, but he was full of references to that world. If you ever got him over a cup of tea, there would be more of that. He looked a happy man in those days, and it was infectious. We all felt, I felt happy too, just to be there for an hour relaxing, after all this hard-core stuff in the other courses.

What about The Old Stone Age?

Yes, it was used for the want of anything better. There were not a lot of general textbooks on the Palaeolithic in those days. As soon as I got to Part Two level, I sold it. It was clearly not the textbook for the future.

What about Archaeology and Society? *Was that used?*

Yes. We didn't have formal textbooks in the American sense where you have a course book but this was one of the books that most of us bought. The lectures went beyond that. He didn't lecture from the book as I remember. That was certainly a book I bought. But we weren't advised to. It wasn't a formal part of the course training.

When did you have Grahame Clark?

Mainly in Part Two. Having done Part One, the question was, where to specialise? I knew I wanted to travel. I first tried to get into Meso-potamia archaeology, but Munn-Rankin sat me down and gave me a cup of tea and told me why I was unsuitable for this. Quite rightly, no hard feelings, but I was turned down there. I had a go at Egyptology. I eventually found a home in what was then the Neolithic, Bronze and the Early Iron Age Option. Remember, Grahame wasn't just a Mesolithic man, but was teaching the whole prehistoric economy of Europe. He taught us more about that than the Mesolithic. I found it absolutely fascinating, because it was personally where I was at. I had always had an interest in landscapes and what people have done with them. It combined ethnographic analogies and things that you could relate to that were being done by real people. Clark, as an archaeologist, is still my great hero. I still kept his book on *Prehistoric Europe; the Economic Basis* long after I'd sold others.

So many people say that to me.

Interesting. I did go to tea once to his house. I got on my bike and set off to pedal to his house and the chain came off. I arrived there all covered with oil, half an hour late and very apologetic, and he looked at me and said "Well, it was tomorrow, anyhow." I tried again the next day. I never had any luck with Grahame Clark. I shaved a beard off in the middle of the term and he thought I was two people for a very long time. He did write beautiful books. He wrote like a dream and his drawings and maps were good.

Why did he ask you to tea?

He asked all the students.

[I say something about Jack Golson.]

The second time he asked me to tea, he had just done one of his tours around central Europe. He put a huge book on my lap and said "Ah, are you interested in Czech folk art?" He wasn't good with undergraduates.

[I say something about Clark helping Posnansky.]

The person who was my manager, because of the College connection, was Glyn Daniel. He was one of the world's great fixers, because of all his editorial and general work, he knew everybody. So, he could get in touch with anybody. And, since he was teaching the Mediterranean part of the course, he was closest to what I was doing. Geoffrey Bushnell also looked after me, once I went to Colombia. Glyn was my minder for getting grants and getting introductions. Whether he got me the job I eventually got at Sheffield, I don't know. I can't even remember how I heard about it. Having finished my Ph.D, my father kept on entering me for jobs I had no chance of getting, and didn't want anyhow. So quite how the one at Sheffield came about, I don't remember. I remember what happened on the first day, but not how I got there.

[I say something about Sheffield.]

It is a long story. Since I was the only one who was there in those days, let's tell it properly. It was a combination of myself as the archaeologist and Professor Robert Hopper as the university politician. Hopper was Professor of Ancient History and there were also Professors of Latin and Greek. So, they had the Classics and Hopper was a very astute man. He realised that the market in straight Classics, people weren't doing Latin at the time, was obviously going downhill and doomed to go further. He also realised that this was just at the time that archaeology was becoming popular. So, the way his mind worked was that if he took on archaeology, it would build up his power base within the University. But also he was thinking in the long term; his ambition was that when he retired this joint Department would split and that Archaeology would become an honours degree, giving the Department independence, and that is exactly what happened. He had a ten-year plan. He was a very good university politician. He was a Welshman with a loud voice and a belligerent manner. He must have been a devil to be with in a committee, and that may have been how he got away with it. He would announce his plans. The division of labour we had was that I would feed him archaeological ideas; what I thought the Department ought to be doing archaeologically. He would 'politic' in committees. Basically, although I was the first-job junior Lecturer, I was having major policy decisions on what a future Department was going to do. He was a front man and we were a very happy combination. We got on well as people. He was a very reasonable man to work for, once you had his confidence. I know people who didn't. Once he felt that you were up to the job, he would allow you to contribute. I remember the day I got the job, I was so excited I fell down the front stairs of the university and got up again and said, "What would you want me to teach?" "Well, we paid you to tell us that," he said. I set the syllabus. I asked for the Library to get at least two periodicals from every country in Europe, and they did it. It was to be a European Department.

Was that your idea?

No, I applied for a job in European Prehistory, so the premise was set up before I put in. In those days I still was a European Prehistorian. Again, it was Hopper's politics. I would like to acknowledge what this man did. Very few people there today know, and it is not talked about. He did everything he could to build archaeology up. This was in the days of easier State money. There was more money and a slightly more relaxed attitude. Every year we would deliberately overspend and the next year we would overspend again. We were robbing them blind. *[All this was said in humour by Warwick Bray.]* At the same time we bumped our members up by rather shamelessly taking people, malcontents from other Departments, and turning them into quite reasonable archaeologists. Our numbers went up. Consequently, every few years we would get another

Lecturer. The second one was Colin Renfrew. The money was there, and having committed all these bureaucratic manoeuvrings, Hopper would then turn around and say "Look, we have so many students now, we need another Lecturer." And we got one.

I ask about Colin Renfrew.

He had just finished his excavations in Bulgaria. He was obviously the man to watch. So much so that people occasionally come up to me and ask, what was it like working for Colin Renfrew? Then Paul Mellars turned up on a Fellowship.

What year was that then?

1962 or '64 when I went up, and I was there for four years, and at the end of it we had two Lecturers, one Fellow and we were just about to get our third Lecturer. In a matter of four to five years, we built up a small university archaeological Department, and that was very much Robert Hopper's brainchild. He had the vision before I ever got there. He was the strategist. I was the tactician.

Did you ever write this down?

No, it was not something I ever wrote it down. It just shows what one can do with team work. It was a very happy place; there were a lot of bright people around, not just in archaeology. A lot of bright people started off there. It is still a good Department. All of this is so long ago. In the early days, you didn't do an Honours Degree. It was just part of a more general course. I didn't see the founding of a definite school of archaeology known by your products, ex-students, Ph.Ds. I missed that.

Often people say that Cambridge was a 'School'.

Not in the intellectual sense that we all thought alike, but in the sense that we were the most dominant. This wasn't because it was 'better than anybody else'. But we were in fact the biggest and most powerful archaeological school in the country. The Institute of Archaeology was in its early days and only giving postgraduate Diplomas. It didn't begin to teach under-graduates until just before I moved there. Oxford had people, but really no Department. The new universities were only just setting up. Cambridge was statistically where most people were. It was a big Department and a lot of the people who went into it, a lot of Part Ones came and those who went on to do Archaeology at Part Two level, mainly did so because they wanted to be archaeologists. Most of them made it. A lot of good people every year were coming off the assembly line. It was just at the time when archaeology was opening up in places like Australia and New Zealand, and just when the African Colonies were thinking about Independence and looking to set up a local school. So really Cambridge people went every-where. You know that article 'Cambridge in the Bush'? Well it is true. It was like that. If you look around now, Cambridge dominance is no longer as marked as some think. There are people of good quality coming from everywhere. Cambridge had by far the 'critical mass'.

What was happening in Ireland?

What I remember was a long pub crawl in Ireland.

Who was there?

The ones I knew were George Eogan and Michael Herity. Going around with Michael Herity was an experience, because he had his own radio show, so everybody knew who he was. You couldn't stop in any village without people saying "Ah, Michael, come have a drink and bring your friend." We had a very good time. And Brian O'Kelly was still in Cork. He had marvel;ous stories about smuggling and Spanish trawlers. It was a strange world there; rather wild.

[I say something inaudible.]

Yes. Irish Megaliths. I never really soaked myself in the prehistory of the British Isles at all. I worked on the Copper Age in Sardinia. I have always been more interested in Continental Europe. Once I got the Part Two ex-aminations out of the way, I never seriously read British prehistory.

What about the Department?

There were people working all over the place. Glyn knew everybody on the Mediterranean circuit. Glyn was certainly very Europe-minded, and if you look at Grahame Clark, all the economic work was on European prehistory. His excavations may have been here but he wasn't a British archaeologist, focusing entirely on that.

What about Clark?

Remember, Clark always did see Britain as part of a European phenomenon. This is in all his books. If anything, the emphasis was on Europe. I don't remember detailed courses on just Britain. It was a very cosmopolitan course. Inevitably people did get jobs.

This makes sense.

Brian Fagan and people like that were going off to Africa, Wilfred Shaw-cross to New Zealand. All the people in my generation went everywhere. We were everywhere at that stage anyhow. Remember Grahame Clark's book on World Prehistory. That is really where he was. His fieldwork opportunities were in Britain, but he would be mortified if you just wrote him off as a British archaeologist. In later life, when he got pupils every-where; he came back enormously enthusiastic from his tour of Australia. You see how you get people like Chris Chippindale when you have people like Grahame Clark. There were people who were doing these things, environmental science. He realised that the sorts of things he had done in Prehistoric Europe were being done all over the place, and he got a great delight out of this.

And the teaching?

All sorts of things happened while I was back and forth to Sardinia.

And where did the teaching occur?

There were lecture rooms and old-fashioned lanterns and slides in the Museum. Bushnell was a 'hands on' Director and encouraged people to handle things. The Museum was very much a part of what I was doing. You could go out of the lecture and see what had just been talked about.

[Inaudible remarks by me about the difficulty of getting jobs.]

It was being said. I remember Glyn Daniel telling my father that it would be fine to be an archaeologist, but that there wouldn't be jobs in it. Most of the people still teaching there, though they were very professional about it, gave the impression of having some kind of money behind them, not doing it as a hobby exactly but possibly being able to support themselves. I was there just at the switch. Archaeology became popular. A lot more people came into it and a lot more came out. The other side of the popu-larity was that there were more jobs. This was certainly the situation in the former Empire, as we have said. Over a short period, new universities were opening up with their new university Departments. It was becoming feasible to make a professional career in archaeology. Most of the people who were contemporaries of mine were in that position. I was very near the beginning of that.

That would be when?

The very early sixties. Nearly all my contemporaries were people without serious private money who were looking for a paid career in Archaeology and got one.

I say something about jobs.

In a way, one of the things that begins to creep in is that little edge of desperation that if you don't, you will die. There was one person who desperately wanted to be an archaeologist, and never was. It made people intense about archaeology. I came into Part One Archaeology with no intent of being an archaeologist. I was going to get my degree and then go out into publishing or whatever. My closest College friends were in something else. At that stage, I had no intention of making it a career. In a way, this made it more fun. I didn't have that edge of earnest desperation. It was at the beginning of the end of the private income era.

What sort of courses did you have?

We had all sorts of things in Part One. Looking back on it, Part One Arch and Anth was regarded as a sort of ragbag thing that people went into on a not very serious basis. It was a mixture of people who were serious and the other half, very bright, but not archaeologists. They were good at what they did, but they haven't come through Archaeology. At the end of Part One, the split came. They were a diverse and interesting lot of people. It made for good fun. How are you on the social politics of era? Because —

End of Side 1

The philosophy at that time was that basically anyone capable of university entrance should be allowed to go to university. If you came from a hard-up family, you received a full grant, and if you came from a richer family, you got less. It was graded, but the Government's intention was that anybody capable of going to university should not be barred financially. So a lot of people who otherwise would not have come began to come to places like this from straightforward, non-private-income backgrounds with the need to get jobs at the end. Of course, there were no jobs guaranteed at the end. They guaranteed your entry into the university system. It did make it possible for a lot of people from perfectly ordinary families to come up and to be archaeologists in a way that it wouldn't have been in the period you are primarily interested in. There was social as well as intellectual change. Many of us are part of that.

Do you think that had something to do with the War?

It started there, with grants to returning servicemen. They tended to be older. Strangely enough, my next door neighbour from Sheffield was a university lawyer and Jack Golson was the Best Man at his wedding. So, I heard a bit about Jack Golson. Then, you had nothing to fall back on if you didn't make it as archaeologists afterwards.

Some have said to me that Grahame Clark was a 'scholarship boy' because there was that 'rawness' about him. Mary Cras'ter said this to me. Even though he went to a top Public School.

I didn't know this but I am not surprised. I don't think that you can categorize all people who went to a Public School as rich. Sometimes families scrimped and saved to send somebody there. Some went on scholarships. It is not the Public School as such, but rather real wealth versus not, and the two categories don't always coincide.

[Something about Clark was in a hurry.]

I think in a way I see what Mary Cras'ter was getting at. I was born and grew up in industrial Lancashire — my first ten years or more were there, where there was a tradition of coming from nowhere and becoming a self-made businessman. Whatever the financial situation was of Grahame Clark, he was very much a self-made businessman.

He was an intellectual entrepreneur.

T.S. Eliot's The Wasteland crack about the 'silk hat on a Bradford millionaire', it was that sort of slight sneering attitude toward those who had made it themselves rather than inherited it. Mary Cras'ter is from a moneyed background. Mary was very kind to me.

Mina [Lethbridge] always calls Clark 'rude'.

Grahame could not empathise with people. Other archaeologists from backgrounds either better or worse could. I think it was his personality. You can not put it down to background. He was a very self-focused man. He was focused on his career, and sometimes couldn't see far beyond it.

I think that Mary's statement says something about how he pursued his career. I have often heard people refer to him as a 'Nazi' but in fact during the Thirties he was quite left-wing. Such terms describe how people perceived his personality rather than his politics.

He actually wrote in detail against Fascism. He didn't believe that everyone was equal but he did believe that everyone should have a chance.

Yes, I thought those statements address how people perceived the way he acted and were somewhat unfair.

He believed that the successful élite had the right to take decisions for the unsuccessful. Remember that late book of his? That reflects the attitude he had in his later years. The élite had rights and responsibilities.

[Inaudible comment from me.]

Another thing about British culture, not so much now but it certainly was in my childhood days, you may have noticed as an outsider from Canada — who are our heroes? They are gifted amateurs like Sherlock Holmes who have a natural genius. They do things casually. They don't stay up all night reading the small print and checking out Museum labels. If you have done that, you pretend you haven't.

Why is that?

I have no idea why. It is a sort of cultural thing and Grahame wouldn't do it. He wanted his A for effort.

Yes!

He was serious. He did what was necessary but not tactfully.

Why is it considered bad taste to be hard working?

It is changing anyhow. It used to be rather bad taste.

Bad form!

It may come from the fact that for certain people who were in charge, they were mainly moneyed.

[I say something about Clark's push to 'professionalise' archaeology. Inaudible section follows.]

One point — if you read his books as a piece of writing, they are beautifully written. He doesn't let the effort show there. When you compare the literature since, the effort does 'hang out'. He was reverting to the great British tradition of being literate! That I liked about his work; no jargon. As a piece of presenting archaeological argument, both Garrod and Clark had clear minds. They produced clear books.

Unlike Burkitt.

I haven't read him since Part One year. It is a battle with students to get them to write as clearly as they talk.

Ph.Ds were considered vulgar [inaudible portion] When I was writing my acknowledgements I had to be careful not to insult people by calling them 'Dr'.

Yes, I knew people in academic life who thought that it was vulgar to be one; sort of pushy and a show off. And now you can't move without one.

Burkitt works hard to give the impression of a man of leisure in archaeology.

Burkitt gave the impression that he was very much at ease with himself.

[Inaudible bit.]

He must have known he wasn't up-to-date. He probably felt that he was doing a good job in the kindergarten part of the Department and he was. He was very good for beginners.

[Inaudible.]

There weren't textbooks for courses. Remember you are concentrating on the academic part of the discipline. Even in my day, there was more archaeology going on in local societies then there ever was in universities. Every county had its society. The world was full of amateur archaeological societies. This was before the professional organisations. When I went to Sheffield, I found that the local society knew everything there was to know about what had been found within a bicycle ride from Sheffield, and very little about anything else. So, there was a world of archaeology but academic archaeology was new. When I was up at Sheffield, an excavation on an Iron Age Village had been done by a miner who had dug it to fully professional standards. Unfortunately, he didn't have the literary skills needed. He invited Wheeler up to see it and Wheeler liked it; no formal education; no formal links. There were a lot of very good technicians out there who learnt to dig and knew their own local area very, very well. One of the differences between Britain and the States, one of the main roots of archaeology in Britain is geology. So there were people who understood about soils and stratigraphy. Most of what we as academics did was irrelevant. There was more stuff coming out of county journals than the Proceedings of the Prehistoric Society, in the statistical sense. I am not mocking the academics, but statistically more was getting done day-to-day by amateurs. It puts us in our place. There's a parallel world out there at least in the early days.

Clark realised that. He was part of the Sussex Archaeological Society in the 1920s.

Yet Clark seemed to have realised that in order for archaeology to progress, particularly at the intellectual level, you had to get beyond the amateur weekend dig; those who would just dig and describe but who never got the big picture. This is where university education came in. You could understand the history of Yorkshire in the context of Europe, something that an amateur archaeologist would never have the time to do.

I think that was Clark's goal in the 1930s; to go beyond the local.

Clark was interested in changing the PSEA to the Prehistoric Society; to make it a national and international organisation.

[I mention my Proceedings *article on the 'Coup'.] Let's talk some more about your career. You have your Ph.D. You are in Sheffield. How did you change to Latin American archaeology?*

These are parallel stories. Lots of Cambridge people went off on undergraduate expeditions. I had been looking around for something to do and then at a party of Glyn Daniel's, and by 2.00 or 3.00 in the morning, everyone had drunk quite a lot and were relaxed. A man called David Orr, who was the son of Robin Orr, the musician and composer, who was a great friend of Glyn's —

And Robin Orr was in the same Photographic Intelligence unit as Dorothy Garrod during the war.

Yes. David Orr was Glyn's godson. He came over in the morning and said "There is an undergraduate expedition which wants to go Colombia, but we are not going to get anywhere unless we have someone along with an archaeological degree." I had a Ph.D, with nothing to do. So I signed up for it. I went, and we had a marvellous time. But this was meant to be a 'one off'. Lots of people were there. Then I went up to Sheffield but I had already fallen in love with Colombia, and Colombian archaeology particularly, because nothing had been done. I get more intellectual kicks out of being first and roughing it out than being the last in and doing the 73rd Roman villa. I liked the landscape and the people and the work, and I could see what we ought to do next. While I was up at Sheffield, I said

"Could I go back and have one more go?" Although I was then teaching European Archaeology, they said "Yes, go and do it". So I went back, and this meant I had been twice and everybody else had been only once. I carried on very happily at Sheffield [inaudible bit] and it happened that someone connected to the Extramural Department, a man called Harold Blakemore, a Chilean historian, had been invited down to become the Administrator of the newly founded Institute of Latin American Studies in London. There was a time when the Government felt that Latin America was being neglected and centres around the country were started for Latin American Studies with earmarked Government money. In the bar at Sheffield he was telling me about this, and saying that "I think that we ought to have archaeology. Let's see if we can set up a joint cost-sharing programme between the Institute of Latin American Studies and the Institute of Archaeology which would have a world-wide scope," and this came to pass. So quite unexpectedly —

The bar — you met this man in the bar?

In Cambridge it was definitely the tea and coffee shop, and David Clarke would tell us his thoughts but — it never occurred to me that I might get this. I thought long and hard whether to leave. I enjoyed Sheffield but did want to get into Latin America. Since I was the only British person who had been twice to Latin America, I got it. It would never happen today. It was virtually being kept warm for a married couple who worked in Mexico, but they did not put in. So I got it. If it had been a strong competition, I never would have got near, but it was not fashionable to advertise for an American Americanist. I started in April at the end of our five-year plan and there were no courses going. So I said, "Look, we have all this money we have to spend. If we don't spend it, we have to give it back. I would like to go for three months to Mexico". So I was sent off to make contacts. It was a very small world in archaeology then. I knew an awful lot of people. I got my network in place. Then I stayed a lecture or two ahead in the course, the first year. This was when I moved to London. There was a year where I was doing both before they could find a replacement for me to teach Eastern and Western Europe. There was a time when I was doing two days a week down in London teaching American and back to Sheffield to teach European. I never really had a planned career.

The era seems so different.

You couldn't do it these days. Everybody is super-specialised. There was less to know. For a period of about five years, I knew most of what was to be known in European, and you certainly couldn't do that now. There is still hardly anybody on the American circuit who taught the whole of Latin America. You tend to be a Mayanist, or whatever. I am a product of a slightly different era.

[Inaudible comment by me.]

There are two overlapping things going on. One is that you no longer can know all, but the other thing is that the profession has specialised. I have always been a generalist by inclination rather than a narrow specialist. I was happy with this and did my best. Most people seem to prefer to hyper-specialise. This is what the job requires today. There are now very specialised people coming out, whereas the earlier generation, myself and Norman Hammond, we were self-taught. Norman was the first person in Britain to do a Ph.D in American archaeology since Geoffrey Bushnell. Perhaps the beginning of the change comes between him and me, in a very short time.

You were Norman's Examiner?

Well, there wasn't anybody else. Geoffrey Bushnell and I did it, because we were the only people in Britain. The situation I have just been describing was a joint appointment between the Institutes. The Institute of Archaeology wanted me to teach archaeology, but the Latin American Institute wasn't archaeologically based. It was mainly interested in sociology, economics, history, literature and the world of development and politics. Archaeology was a fringe thing for them. Anybody coming there as a student had to speak Spanish, whereas there was no Spanish required at the Institute of Archaeology. For one, I had to teach what could be read in English, and for the other, I had to teach what could be read in Spanish. So to avoid getting bored and teaching the same thing twice, I did courses on Archaeology and Latin American Archaeology in general for the Institute of Archaeology and one on Aztec Ethnohistory, where the main contributions were made by Mexican scholars in Spanish, as a complement. Generally only people from the Latin American Institute who spoke Spanish took that one. I taught these two courses until eventually the Institutes split. The Institute of Archaeology had begun to take undergraduates a few years before I cameu but the Institute of Latin American Studies was a postgraduate Institute, so I was teaching some of both.

Were you the only one teaching this?

There was really nowhere else to go for that. There has been a bit of a boom in the art. There are art historians in Latin American. There are a few general archaeologists elsewhere, but the Institute is still teaching the only specialised American archaeological course in Britain. I got another colleague a few years before I retired, José Oliver, who teaches South American archaeology. My replacement is Elizabeth Grahame, Canadian. For a very long time, I was alone.

What was the Institute like?

The Institute was a happy place to work. I was personally always very happy there. It was a bit lonely intellectually, but once we began to build up a few Ph.Ds, that made life much more exciting.

May I ask you to say something about David Clarke?

I knew a different David Clarke from most because when I first met him, he was an undergraduate. As you were saying, coffee used to be the thing in those days. We would all go for coffee in the morning to a Café that did coffee, sausages and mash. We used to have long talks. The archaeologists were on one floor and sometimes the geographers, we would have long coffee-breaks there. It was mainly my year and the year above, but somehow David got in on this group. It was hilarious. He had a tremendous sense of humour. He was a person who things always happened to. There was one that took place as he came out the side door of the Museum and trod on a dug-out canoe. He rocked back and forth for a long time and ended with a crash. He was accident-prone and very, very funny; obviously very bright and thoughtful. This was just at the stage when he was gestating the ideas that went into his great theory book. Remember his Ph.D was on Beakers. There was nothing particularly special about that, but he was already beginning to converse about the things that went into the book. That was badly received in some quarters, and well in others. I think it is one of the great, formative books because it is entirely individual, almost entirely self-generated, genuine and original, grabbing from other disciplines. It doesn't owe anything to the American stream. It was a great book. People began to take him seriously. And he became more famous and rather less fun. He began taking himself more seriously. You see what Cambridge does to people. He become a grand young man.

Thank you so much. Few people have memories of him.

I should say something about Geography and its influence.

But we are running out of time and you should say something earthshaking about yourself first.

If I die tomorrow what would I put on my tombstone? "He always returned his library books." I was always there at the right time. Back to Geography, almost at the same time that David was working and not entirely independently, the New Geography with Peter Haggett and the use of statistics happened in Cambridge. There was quite a lot of cross-over between that and David's work. They knew about each other and talked, perhaps through a College connection. Just after that, when I became a postgraduate, I shared a flat with one of my colleagues, David Harvey, who became the guru of American theoretical Geography. And he influenced David Clarke with his book —

End of tape, unfortunately.

The late Professor emeritus J. Desmond Clark

18 April 1996, recorded at Corpus Christi College, Cambridge, by Pamela Jane Smith   pjs1011@cam.ac.uk

Yes, unquestionably Grahame was a major influence in my life when it comes to archaeology and prehistory because when I came up to Cambridge, I had always been interested in archaeology and history and I read history for two years and enjoyed it but realised that I was not going to get a First in history because you have got to be able to write as well as know the data. Then there was this opportunity of joining Archaeology and Anthropology which is what I did for Part II. I enjoyed that very much and got a First in it, and then the two people who influenced my professional life were Grahame and Miles Burkitt. Grahame, as I was saying to John Coles this morning, produced all the basic hard data on which his hypotheses were developed which he did very successfully and of course he was the first person that I realised, that sort of registered with me, he was the first person to look at environmental evidence for trying to understand the behaviour of the prehistoric populations.

Are you referring to his work with the Fenland Committee and Godwin? Are you referring to pollen analysis data? Were you exposed to that?

I never went out there to — what the hell was it called?

Shippea Hill site.

Yes, I had just met Godwin. That was very crucial and it was going on just about that time.

I wondered, did Professor Clark teach you that in his courses? Did you have him as a teacher?

Oh. Yes, indeed we did, yes. There were about half a dozen of us that year; may have been a few more; one of whom was Charles McBurney.

I have the class list.

Who were the others?

In your year there was —

There was a girl named Hey, came from Yorkshire. My wife comes from Yorkshire.

Well, here is 1935. I would really appreciate if you could tell me who they are and if any of them are alive.

OK, which one is that?

You could start at 1934 and '35 and here's '36 and '37. Shaw is on the list and Rainbird Clarke.

Clarke was before me. That's right. It would be 1937. Somebody called Powell, Terence Powell, let me have a look. Terence Powell was a delightful Irishman and I remember we brought him the results of the Tripos and he was propped up in bed in his digs. Oh, I see it is by classes. And, there's McBurney, Charles. I see, got a Second. Who are all these other people? I have no idea. Oh, there is Terence Powell, yes. He got a Third. Some of the other people don't register with me. That's funny; Wakefield, that's the chap, Wakefield, got a First. He may still be alive. He went as a Curator of the Victoria & Albert Museum and you may be able to find out there.

How many courses did Grahame Clark teach you?

He taught Mesolithic, Neolithic, Bronze Age. Miles taught us Palaeolithic, and Miles did the general introductory lecture as well. You have to go back and look at the syllabus but it was from Grahame that we learned the really essential way, the scientific manner in which you carried out an investigation. First of all obtaining the data with archaeology, digging in the ground or collecting stuff; then looking at it all to see how you interpret it and then, of course, in those days interpretation depended on how good the basic information was. If you had a whole lot of data concerning context, in other words, if it was well stratified, if there were associated animal and plant remains, the nature of the site itself, settlement or road gravel, then when you had a reasonable amount of data, you could start thinking about what the archaeological material might mean. And, in those days, of course, one's interpretations were essentially subjective interpretations, based upon what one thought, based upon one's experience. Whereas these days, and this is something that came, I suppose you could say that it came, initially with the Eoliths controversy. Reid Moir who was made a Fellow of the Royal Society, believe it or not, on the basis of this nonsense about rostro-carinates and the Red Crag, etc. And you've got some people saying, no, we need to look, as indeed Lyell, the famous geologist did, we need to look at the present to see how to interpret the past. That, of course, is something Grahame always did. When it came to the stone artefacts, you have to see what went on, how nature broke stone. People like the Abbé Breuil used to look at concrete mixers to see what they did and on the basis of that you begin to build up some comparative data against which you can examine the data you have. This is most important when it comes to stone artefacts today because of all the replica work that there is. You can see everything that results from trying to make a chopper or trying to remove flakes from cores. First of all, you get all sorts of information about the spread of this stuff. You get information about the size, range, and you look at your archaeological assemblage and you can see that a whole lot of things are missing that should be there. And all the studies of animal behaviour, plant studies and climatic change —

And you feel that that began with Prof. Clark? Was there something quite different about him than with Burkitt?

Miles was not interested in that in particular. Miles' interests were more specifically with the Palaeolithic but also with what his students were doing in other parts of the world, largely in Africa, like Louis Leakey and John Goodwin, and that was before Grahame was teaching. John must have been a contemporary of Grahame's. But Miles was a frightfully good teacher and he filled one with enthusiasm for the subject which was increased by all the various little anecdotes he had about all the people one read about, the Abbé Breuil and Count Bégouen and the people in Spain with rock art, Obermaier, Castillo. That's about the only bit of excavation that Miles ever did and that wasn't frightfully good, but he had a great ability to make people widely enthusiastic and of course he had been out in Africa in 1927 to see what John Goodwin had found, and then he wrote that book South Africa's Past in Stone and Paint. So, we had always kept up because he was interested in Africa and I went out to work in Africa. I always returned to see Grahame and Miles.

Did you think that Prof. Clark influenced you when you came back when you were writing your dissertation?

Not so much because Miles Burkitt was my Advisor and Grahame was never particularly interested in Africa but I suppose with conversations that I had with him which weren't all that many because I was sitting down in Miles' study with stuff piled around me in boxes and on tables trying to work my way through this stuff before I had to go back to Africa. But, yes, reading the two major books: The Mesolithic Settlement of Northern Europe and Prehistoric Europe, the Economic Basis, and World Prehistory as well. Grahame was invited to give the Hitchcock lectures in Berkeley in the early 1970s and he was out there with Molly. We saw him around which was good. That is where Grahame gave these lectures where he proposed the terms, a series of modes in prehistoric technology through the stone component of an assemblage. So, he got it through mode one which was Olduvai, mode two the bifaces and that is still used in America by quite a lot of people. I don't think it is used over here.

When you start to use seasonality in the 1939, would you attribute that to Clark?

Yes, that is what got me interested you see, yes.

That's quite a distinct influence.

Oh, of course it is.

You also speak about — you can also tell in your early work that there are many other influences with Peter van —

Peter van Riet Lowe, yes.

And with Goodwin and Leakey.

Yes, exactly, yes, very much so. I must send you a copy. I did a thing for one of those, *Anthropological Review*.

Yes, I've got that. That was the first thing I did, I went and got your personal memories.

There was one in Antiquity that they published, a whole ten together. No, this was absolutely true when it comes to Grahame and my interest in Palaeoenvironment and seasonal movements of population, seasonal of movement of game. Why Mumbwa Caves was in an isolated collection of rocks overlooking the Kafue Flats which was a huge area of grasslands, whereas Mumbwa itself and everything in back of it was woodlands. So, you are in a different habitat. And what I was interested in was whether the wildebeest, there were wildebeest that migrated, whether we could see any evidence for this. I couldn't get any proper information because the Game Department didn't have any. Nobody was interested in that at that time. But there was . . . you could make the suggestion. Now of course there is much more information. The young people are very conscious of the importance of seasonal occupation and the movement.

That is interesting because it is well before Star Carr, well before 1949. I suspect that Star Carr had something to do with the great explosion of seasonality interpretation.

Yes, I am sure it did. That was after the Second World War, wasn't it?

Yes.

Yes, that is right.

I was very impressed with your dissertation on the Horn of Africa and also on Northern Rhodesia. I must say that was enormous amounts of work.

I shouldn't have done both of them. I should have done one and not the other. I had to work like hell to get the other one. Yes. It was interesting actually. It was one of the things that really kept me interested during the War so far as the Horn of Africa was concerned.

Have you ever done an autobiography?

No, only those two things but we were thinking that we might do something. Have got to finish up the third volume on Kalambo Falls for the end of June.

Even Kalambo Falls to me seemed very in keeping with Star Carr.

Oh, it is. Yes, it was essentially Grahame who raised that interest in me.

Amazing, because you knew him for a short time before you went to Africa.

Yes, it was.

And people always speak of Burkitt as if they really did love Burkitt, and Burkitt was the person who helped them become interested.

That's right.

But Professor Clark was the one. They don't speak of Professor Clark as if they loved him, but they do speak of him with respect.

Yes, I think you got it exactly. Grahame was not an easy person to talk to. He was devoted to his research. He was not all that particularly interested in, I suppose, in his students.

And yet people really found him influential in the way they thought.

Oh, tremendously, yes!

Very interested. There is a theory that to be a leader or founder of a research school you have to be loved. With Grahame Clark, it doesn't fit the model.

He was remarkably influential. I would have said that he and Gordon Childe were the two most influential people in the way people who were prehistorians thought in the greater part of this century. And the other thing was, of course, that Grahame developed the Cambridge School in a way it had never functioned before and it is still carried on in that tradition today and it is quite remarkable.

It is remarkable. It is quite shocking to me that it has never been studied.

I think it is due to the fact that Grahame did tend to keep himself more remote. He was devoted to his research. He produced a book a year. It is absolutely fantastic what he was able to do. And he had such a broad and deep understanding of the whole field of prehistory. Not only in one part of the world but right through; he had that World Prehistory which is very remarkable.

Did he stress that you had to do field work?

Yes, indeed he did.

Was it his idea that you work with Wheeler?

Yes, it was.

But it was Wheeler who taught you how to excavate?

I suppose you could say that. Wheeler was rather like the Brigadier who came around on his inspection once a day, looked over the edge. It was John Waechter who really sort of took me in hand, a raw undergraduate. I greatly enjoyed and am very grateful to John for that.

How much more time do you have?

Five or eight minutes.

If there is anyone you can think of that is still alive that I should interview as well —

You could try this man Wakefield. Let's see. 1936. Amazing. Hudson, I learned Anthropology from Hudson. Ellis Minns who talked to us about the Scythians. Miles Burkitt and de Navarro, I knew well. Driberg who became a Greek Orthodox. Grahame, Hutton, oh, yes, the Headhunters in Assam. He was great, actually. Evans Pritchard was teaching there a year, interesting. [Comments made by Prof. Clark while looking at the Class lists.]

Also Leakey was there. When you read the Faculty Minutes, Leakey keeps bursting on to the scene and I don't think that people knew how to handle him. In the Minutes there is this shock evident when Leakey walked in.

[Prof. Clark answers while looking at the Class list.] I think that's right. Fascinating really are the women. J. Carter, Girton, probably the girl, Hey, that is the girl I remember. She came from Yorkshire and Peggy Burkitt knew her family. I do remember that she always used to wear scarlet shoes with slightly high heels. Do you know Gale Sieveking? You ought to see them. Then, Haddon was there. A.C. Haddon.

Did he influence you?

Not really. I just met him once. A shock of hair, bushy eyebrows. He had retired. He would come into the Museum for tea. You would just see him and say "how do you do".

In Africa, did Leakey's 1936 book on Stone Age Africa, did that influence you?

Yes, it did.

Did he speak about seasonality?

No, but he did speak about climatic change and that was the time after Wayland had produced this work on rivers in Uganda, pluvials and interpluvials, and Louis built on that. Then there was a Swede, E. Nilsson, who did work in the Nakuru/Naivasha Basin and did some very good work and Louis built on all of that. The interesting thing about 1936 Stone Age Africa, the Monroe Lectures which he gave in Edinburgh; that was the first book to bring the whole of Africa into a new stage continent-wide. Of course one of the most important things was the Pan African Prehistory Congress that Leakey got organised in 1947.

One of the things that fascinates me is that you were very isolated —

Oh, completely isolated, yes.

And you developed your own 'indigenousness'; it wasn't that you were just Cambridge transplanted, that you were very much a part of what was going on in Africa during the 1930s and '40s.

Yes, also we went out on what were called tours of three years and later two and a half years that you spent in the country and worked there and at the end of that time based

Side two. Professor Clark continues:

at the end of that time we would come back and find a cottage somewhere in the villages around Cambridge. And we would sit around together. When I was writing the Horn of Africa we were living in the White Cottage in Grantchester.

The Burkitt family is still there.

I did keep in touch with his daughter. Miles and Peggy and his daughter, they came out to the Livingstone Pan African Conference, the third one when I was there. I think I should go if you don't mind.

Thank you.

14 July 2000, recorded at the late Mrs Anne McBurney's house in Cambridge, England, during the SAfA Conference, by Pamela Jane Smith, pjs1011@cam.ac.uk

Professor Clark, may I ask you a few questions about your early life at Cambridge and why you came to Cambridge?

Yes.

Why did you decide to take the second part of the Tripos in 1936?

Because I was always interested in history and when I came to Cambridge, I for two years took history. I realised at the end of those two years, unless you are very good at writing an English essay with the factual historical data in it, you would not get a First. I knew the data. What we were taught was not political history. We had economic history. We had political thought; constitutional history and of course you had to read anything from Mediaeval Latin to Mediaeval French into the Early English which I greatly enjoyed. I got all the factual stuff. The European history from about 400 AD up to 1480, that was so crammed full of data. Of course, what one had to do was to make quite certain, because of the range of countries and histories, be quite certain of three or four questions in the exam in which you may have had eight or nine questions. So you couldn't do anything, maybe Scandinavian history, Russian history. I was distinctly interested in Byzantine history but you could never be quite certain that you were going to get a question in it. This was where you had to cut down. It was the question of being able to write a tip-top English essay full of the history and interpretation. And I was always much more interested in the earlier period, Roman Britain and before. I then went into Archaeology and Anthropology and thoroughly enjoyed the year I had. Point of fact, I had summer vacation of '36 and whole of '37 and it was great fun. Thoroughly enjoyed it. We had Miles Burkitt lecturing who was a very good lecturer indeed. His field work was fairly minimal but he knew lots of people. Particularly, he was interested in the Palaeolithic. He knew so many of the French and Spanish archaeologists, and Czech and German as well, that we got a lot of very interesting associated data with the straightforward archaeology. And, then, of course, we also got what was going on elsewhere, particularly in Africa, because Miles had started teaching in 1919 and he had trained a number of people who were going into the Provincial Colonial Administration and one or two subsequently did very interesting work in connection with this. And then, of course, there was Grahame and Grahame's really fine hard data in association with all that work he was doing in the Fens really brought home to one the essential nature of precise stratigraphic information in relation to the various archaeological units that you find and the need to date these in terms of environment and climatic change and there, of course, on the basis of that and Grahame's emphasis on the importance of ecology and environment, that set me off when I went out to Africa. I enjoyed it immensely. Charles McBurney was a fellow student. I did better than I thought I would. I got a First. Then you looked around to see where you might find a job. There were virtually no jobs in England at all. There was one in the British Museum, that's true. I think it was sort of preordained as to who was going to get that one but the only question that I was asked when I went there was "What do you know about Byzantine archaeology?" I said nothing very much. "Oh," they said, "we've got a lot of it, Byzantine material". So, that was that and thank God. Otherwise I would be dead by now if I had got that job.

Did you work with Wheeler?

Yes indeed, that's where I got my excavations, my fieldwork, two seasons, well, the better part of two seasons, which was absolutely essential, at Maiden Castle.

Was Isabel Smith there? Who was your foreman?

Yes, what was her name? Alison, oh, she was excellent and also I had John Waechter and we got on extremely well. Mortimer Wheeler, of course, wasn't interested in the Palaeolithic. He thought that they were curious people who sort of sat in caves and so on, but he was absolutely precise in his fieldwork and that, of course, is essential if you are going to do anything anywhere. That is basically where I learned my field techniques which over the years we improved on as new methods and new ideas came. Particularly when it comes to the Palaeolithic, Mary Leakey's identification of land surfaces with concentrations of Acheulean and fauna together with other features revolutionised Palaeolithic archaeology. You see, when I went out to Africa in the beginning, well I left on the 17th of December 1937 and I got to Livingstone about the 6th of January 1938 and that's when I started off and indeed have never regretted it! It was a great training opportunity, to learn to walk through the country even through fairly minimal roads. Originally we did it all with carriers. And talking to one's African colleagues sometimes through interpreters, sometimes not, I learnt a little about plants and animals and their relationship to them and of course, most important of all, water.

I've been interested in your work that you deeply believe in archaeology as a science — that systemisation of information and data.

Of course it is. The whole basis of what one can say about the way in which people lived, behaved, organised their groupings depends essentially on sound, solid, hard data that comes from excavation and sometimes perhaps as well from surface collections. Basically it is the data with the archaeo-

logical units in their context that you can date in association with what you can learn about the ecology; sometimes, very rarely, in association with plants, more often in association with animal bones and the way in which these resources were treated, processed, give us an understanding of the way in which the group might have behaved. If you have a lot of sound data well dated, then you are in a better position for making hypothesis to form models or scenarios which have some validity. The lack of this will produce all sorts of fanciful interpretations; some of them may be not far from whatever eventuates on the basis of further work.

Professor Clark, that does seem to be something that's innovative of the '30s at Cambridge, that Grahame Clark is beginning to believe that science must be systematised to be science and that does seem to be quite different than some of his predecessors.

Oh yes, indeed, of course it was realised, you see. One of the first people to deal with this was Louis Leakey. Louis, when he organised the first Pan Africa Congress in Nairobi 1947, he brought to it geologists, palaeontologies, archaeologists, people dealing with climate. I don't think there was very much we could say about vegetation, about chronology, at that time except in a purely relative way. We had this pluvial/interpluvial hypothesis that first of all E.J. Wayland and later Louis jumped on to, that ended up to be quite nonsense. That was knocked on the head by Basil Cooke in the 1955 Pan Africa Congress in Livingstone and subsequently by Dick Flint who came out and looked at a whole series of sites. The problem with that hypothesis was it was based on the most unstable part of the whole African continent, the Rift Valley. Following from all of that, we had the Conference which went on for three weeks, the longest one they ever had, where we had groups of palaeontologists, geologists, people working on dating. By the time there was radiometric dating, potassium argon 1960, radiocarbon before 1950, and the archaeologists, and the outcome of that was Background to Evolution in Africa that Bill Bishop and I edited, which still is extremely valid so far as to what people need to understand about methodology and the ways in which cultural entities were set up, faunal zones, and the way in which we need to look at our archaeology and the faunal so far as more precise dating and via good sound stratigraphic sequences into which the archaeology and the faunal can be precisely set in their contexts and on the basis of that with the ways in which formations are built up. Then that is the basis of building-up of the Palaeolithic, certainly until you get to the equivalent to the Upper Palaeolithic in Africa.

That's where also you agreed upon typologies?

Oh yes. If you are going to do anything with lithics then you have got to understand the way in which lithics are worked, processed right from the original sources of these, the whole process from beginning to end. You have to be able to by experiment understand how this all comes about and what the products of all this flaking are going to be. Archaeological assemblages in their primary context, maybe some secondary as well, they do not have all the flaking waste that you get if you sit down and flake away for half an hour; all the small stuff, everything below one centimetre, often below two, has gone away as well as larger pieces will have been removed as you got at FXJJ50. The cores or choppers were not there but they were able to refit the flakes.

Professor Clark, how important was it to African archaeology that you had local terminologies? Goodwin had discussed local terminologies rather than following European stereotypes.

It is very, very important. Firstly, as you say, Goodwin and Lowe in 1929 said that we are not going to follow the European, because we have no idea at all whether there is any connection whatsoever, and they went to what geologists do, and that's why we emphasised in Background to Evolution in Africa, there it is all set out, and John said we are going to use our own terminology. which they did. After a while, when it comes to the lower Palaeolithic, that was subsumed under the term lower Palaeolithic or Earlier Stone Age which is OK. We did away with Stellenbosch and things like that. But it is absolutely essential to have the regional terms. When I did Kalambo Falls —

Is that for accuracy?

Yes, exactly. What we had was what there was at Kalambo Falls. If you've got, I forget what we called, Kapaswe, that was the later Stone Age Mesolithic. That's what there was at Kalambo and if someone finds something else somewhere and compares it and compares the technology and typology, you can see if it was similar. OK, maybe you could find something in the area, something similar, so you could extend the use of the term Kapaswe, but what it enables you to do, we have this, here is the precise composition of the entity and it enables people to look at their own material and see to what extent it is similar or different and they will use a different name.

I wonder about Goodwin and Macrae and some of the others who would have been considered amateurs?

No, Goodwin was the first professional trained at Cambridge by Miles and he must have had geology courses here; and when he went out as Lecturer in archaeology to the University of Cape Town he set about using the basic knowledge that he had, techniques and methodology that there was, and developed this superb basis for description of South African prehistory. Goodwin also emphasised regional entities, looking to see why regions differed, rather the archaeology of regions differed, was it due to different raw materials, due to time, due to environment.

May I ask you about Burkitt and Goodwin because, as an historian, people always say to me to that Burkitt plagiarised Goodwin and I have never found any evidence in the correspondence. They are discussing South Africa and art.

Miles — it is incorrect to say that Miles plagiarised what Goodwin did, because Goodwin had not written it at the time that Miles wrote his South Africa's Past in Stone and Paint. Goodwin took Miles to a whole series of sites and showed them to him as well; perhaps it was a little, I don't know if there was a need for hurry for Miles to get out his volume in 1927, but I think that upset John Goodwin a little. As far as I can remember he gave John the credit of finding these sites.

There is no evidence that there was difficulty in the correspondence and yet there is this constant thing when I am investigating the history of archaeology, people are constantly telling me that Burkitt —

No, that is not true. As I say, to plagiarize something without reference, quote from what people have written, and Miles did not do that. Something on Vosburg may have been written before but I don't think anything else.

What was your opinion of some of the other people who were working in the field prior to you? Were others in Rhodesia working there before you?

There was Neville Jones, of course. Neville was very good. Neville was an amateur archaeologist who taught himself a lot of archaeology. He started at, what was it called? I think it was in the northern Transvaal or may have been at a mission station [Tiger Kloof] there because he was a missionary for a long time, I think a Baptist missionary. Then he went to Hope Fountain Mission near Bulawayo, just outside Bulawayo. Then he went around there, after having artefacts including Acheulean bifaces down in what was that site down in South Africa. He continued searching in the Bulawayo area and found a tremendous amount. He found Acheulean. He found cave sites and he did some very good excavations, good for the time and carefully dug stratigraphically. His last paper on Bambata was particularly good, actually, because you can see the two divisions of the Middle Stone Age very clearly there, the two main divisions. Also, he worked at Victoria Falls and found material there. I enjoyed Uncle Neville, as we called him, very much. Good ethnographer as well, and he did quite a lot about the Hope Fountain Culture. But he did pretty well. He shouldn't have retired when he did, and he died three or four years after he retired, which was very sad. He was good. In 1929, that was when the British Association had the joint meeting with the South African Association of Science in Pretoria. Lesley Armstrong was asked to dig Bambata which he did, published in the Royal Anthropological Institute Proceedings, which

was also good. But apart from that there was no one else between John Goodwin, Neville Jones and Louis Leakey, with the exception of a man who none of us got to know who done remarkable work, Jean Colette. Have you heard of Jean Colette? Remarkable work in the Congo, in particular his excavations at Gombe Point in Kinshasa. He did statistical analyses of all that material which was way ahead of its time. Archaeology then, what happened was, you excavated, you got your bucket full, you looked through it, you picked out half a dozen pieces which you thought would be good, representative, some of it good for illustration, and you threw the rest away. Some of these sites were, particularly one I know in the Desert where Carl Coon excavated, you can find superb material on his dump. That is not an exception. It wasn't really until after the War that people starting getting into total analysis of all finds.

At Wheeler's Maiden Castle, with John Waechter, was he doing total analysis?

No, we were excavating. John was never really interested — I don't know what you mean by cultural analysis.

Total analysis of the remains is what I meant to say.

He was more interested in the typology and its relationship to established archaeological units and the way in which some the material might differ as well. He was a very nice person. I greatly enjoyed John and he knew a lot about the Levantine Palestinian archaeology of those times.

Do you know how John Waechter came to Cambridge as Garrod's student?

I don't know. He wasn't there when I was at Maiden Castle —

He came to Cambridge after the War and studied with Garrod as a Ph.D student.

They were interested in the same area.

I wonder, Professor Clark, when you went to Livingstone, the Wilsons were there — Monica Wilson? Later Gluckman, well-known anthropologists —

I was the first one to get there. They wanted me out as soon as possible to get organised with the Museum. I was also the Secretary to the Institute. And then Godfrey and Monica arrived from southern Tanzania where they had finished their work. Yes, we got on very well indeed with them, and for a long time we kept up with Monica after Godfrey had died. We saw a great deal of them. Then in 1939 or so Max Gluckman came out, and he went off to study the Barotse and did an extremely fine piece of work, that one on the Economy of the Central Barotse Plain; very fine piece of work.

Did you know Audrey Richards?

Oh yes, I did indeed. I greatly enjoyed Audrey. She did extremely fine work with the Bimba, very good work with the Bimba. We saw her, it must be almost the last time I saw her. We were back on one of our leaves, six months leave after every three years or two and a half years, and we had a cottage not far from Huntingdon and she was living nearby and she came over for lunch, and our daughter opened the front door and Audrey looked at her and said "My dear, you have worn well". She was a fine ethnographer and they're so few and far around these days. They've got all this nonsensical post-modern stuff.

It was quite a group of people you have, the Wilsons, Richards, yourselves, Gluckman. These are very important people.

Yes, Max did a fine job with the Barotse and then he was, I'm not certain if he was the Director of the Institute, I don't think he was because after the War, Elizabeth Colson came out. Max was probably there for the first two or three years and then went back to Manchester and founded the Manchester School. I see Elizabeth Colson most regularly, she's in Berkeley, for lunch.

When you went to Berkeley that was a great help to your research, because then you could come back.

Tremendously. When I left Livingstone, I was about 45. Round about that time you get a bit of itchy feet. Are you going to stay here all the time or are you going to go somewhere else and at that time, there was nothing in particular that I heard about. Sherry Washburn wrote and said "Would you like to come to Berkeley?" And we had no particular desire. I got to know Sherry quite well at the Pan African Conference in 1955 and then he came out for two years. Most of his fieldwork was done in Zambia and Zimbabwe and we had a lot in common, and nothing in England turned up at that time. After three months, we said "yes, we would like to go to Berkeley" and so we did, and indeed we have never regretted it because one of the great things — although I had to start teaching from scratch, other than the kind of few lectures one gives from time to time in our little window school — I had done no formal teaching whatsoever, which to begin with was a little problem — but the great thing was, if you had a good project, there was plenty of funding through NSF and Wenner-Gren at that time, and we were able to get back and do all sorts of work that we otherwise would not have been able to do. Shortly after that I was offered the Pitt Rivers Museum and decided definitely not to take that and then after we had been in Berkeley about maybe 3 or 4 years I got this offer for the Disney Professorship when Grahame was retiring. That would have been for 10 years when I would have had to retire. And, I wouldn't have got a pension, or nothing very much. What we get for having worked for 23 years in Livingstone is about 23 pounds and 6 and 8 pence a month. Well, is it pounds at least not dollars. More or less start from scratch.

Yes, Professor Clark mentioned that he wanted you.

Well, you see, what he wanted was somebody to do a lot of administration. There is no doubt about it, he didn't do very much administration himself. He was interested in the research side and did remarkably well with all of that, and I was interested in research and having spent 23 years on administration as well as being able to get into the field, and since I was in Berkeley, I've done as little as possible so far as administrative work. As a result we were able to do quite a lot so far as fieldwork and publications were concerned. Getting labs; nobody ever uses a lab these days. I don't know what it is.

It is wonderful to hear these comments about the present.

They must have good labs here. Certainly in Berkeley nobody ever teaches lithic analysis. Nobody teaches Palaeolithic these days. Quite dreadful.

Mrs McBurney would like you to get a break. I just wanted to tell you how wonderful it is to speak to you. It is a joy to speak to you. Everyone greets you with respect and admiration.

I've enjoyed the conference. I've heard some first-rate papers, particularly later this morning. Linguistics, we've had a couple of linguistics papers, and there is nothing you can anchor it on. Linguistics by itself, it has got to go with the archaeology, and they've got to be archaeologists and linguistics together in the field working, otherwise it doesn't work. In the old days, the geologists would get sent specimens, the palaeontologists would get sent specimens, and the archaeologists would do their own work and they would go out and collect their own, but there was no association, no teamwork. It has got to be there in the field. They have to talk, discuss, that it is the only way they were going to do it.

Wonderful holistic concept. You did that — you had interdisciplinary teams.

Been first-rate. We had all sorts of people in the field.

You have had such an inspirational, enjoyable life.

It has been so very enjoyable. Every moment I was in Africa I think I have enjoyed. Sometimes I'm not, increasingly of late where you've all sorts of nonsensical bureaucratic nonsense, but as far as our later work in Ethiopia is concerned, that hasn't been at all bad. But, in some places, quite dread-

ful, but I think it is getting better now. And, one of the major problems for getting anything done, the Livingstone Museum roof collapsed. Did you hear about that? Quite dreadful. Totally dreadful. The EU has voted $400,000 for the repair of the roof.

Second side of tape:

Said to last about 30 years. Well it is now 40 years and there are cracks in it and nothing was done. It was leaking in 1988 when I was there. Petrol cans were put under to catch the drips. Well, after these heavy rains, all the water collected on the ceiling. The ceiling collapsed, all the water all over books. And we don't know what has been saved and what has been lost, or will be lost. The money has got to get to the Livingstone. I wrote to the President, I wrote to the Secretary of the National Museum Board, I wrote to the Heritage Commission and to the Director of the Museums as well. Apart from knowing that my letter to the Secretary, who was one of my students, got there, I have heard nothing from them at all. I sent them e-mail messages. Nothing has come out. And to me that smells of corruption. Elizabeth Colson was telling me, about three weeks. It does reach quite a long way down. One of the villages she works in, they wanted to build a primary school and the local people got together and made the bricks and in due course, money came down from education for this. Well, the contractor sold the bricks and the chairman of the local thing pocketed the money. If it goes as far as that, you really wonder, but I think we are getting around that now by putting the money into various international organisations that will see it through. Otherwise it gets disseminated. Nothing gets there.

Thank you so much.

Professor Graham Connah

15 July 2000, recorded during the SAfA Conference, at Peterhouse, Cambridge, England, by Pamela Jane Smith.   pjs1011@cam.ac.uk

May I ask you how you got involved in archaeology?

I suppose anybody asked that question has difficulty answering. If I reflect on it I suppose I was always involved. I grew up into it. It was the only thing I ever wanted to do from about the age of eight, when I discovered in an encyclopedia somewhere that what I seemed to be interested in was called archaeology. I was involved in excavations, helping out, being probably a damn nuisance from about the age of 14. Of course, this is now over 50 years ago. I am now in my mid sixties and am supposed to be retired.

I've been involved in the subject for a very long time. As to what got me into it, as I say, it was the only thing I wanted to do. Why was one interested in such a thing? I suppose because I've always been fascinated by human society and one of the means of understanding human society is not merely from documentary records but from the things that men and women have made and used in the past. The study of physical evidence has always been a thing that has attracted me even in this post-modern day where post-processualist, symbolic archaeology, whatever you like to call it, has almost tried to down play that aspect of archaeology. To me it is still the one that really matters. It is what makes archaeology so different, that we claim to be able to extract information from things.

I wonder, are you from Cambridge?

I am part of the Cambridge scene in the sense that I was a graduate from Cambridge. I was born in the north of England in Cheshire, in a place called Bromborough in the Wirral Peninsula. My family was, as many British families in the 1940s were, a family where nobody had ever been to university at all. It just didn't happen. I eventually won a State Scholarship to take me to university and gained entry to this University, came here and read History and subsequently read Archaeology as well. Yes, I was a Cambridge product.

How did you switch over? Did you take Part II?

I took Part II in one year. I attempted what in those days was three years' work in one year in addition to having done a Part I in History. The attitude of Grahame Clark, who was the Professor at that time, was that he didn't mind people doing Part I in Archaeology, and in those days, and perhaps still, you could put together two Part Is for a degree, so you could get a one Part in History and one Part in Archaeology. But, I had quite a lot of practical experience by then, working not only on excavations but working in museums. I was in my, almost in my mid twenties, I had been in the armed services as well. I insisted that I wanted to do the finals and do it in one year, and that is what I did, extremely difficult but not unknown. There have been others who have done it as well.

What year was that?

That was 1959. The same year as Brian Fagan, Richard Wright, who you may not know of, who eventually finished off in Australia. All together I think there were nine of us. Harriet Crawford, Browne before her marriage. There was another. I can't remember some of the others. Stanley West was one, went into Museum work in Ipswich. Four or five other people who vanished from the professional point of view, either didn't enter archaeology or were lost as far as my awareness was concerned, but then I didn't stay in Britain, spent my professional career working in Africa and subsequently in Australia.

Even to have two or three or four well-known names within a discipline out of class of nine is an accomplishment. To me that shows the importance of Cambridge in educating archaeologists.

At that time, it was about one's only choice. It is not quite true. When I was looking to enter university as a student and I wanted to study archaeology. Pressure was put on me by almost everybody not to do so. There were

no jobs in archaeology, whereas if you read history you could eventually become a school teacher, of course. This was the attitude of one's family, friends, contacts. At that time, the only places in Britain to do a full degree in archaeology were either Cambridge or Edinburgh. Cambridge had something of a world view in a way that Edinburgh under Stuart Piggott didn't quite. Edinburgh was very, very good but its emphasis was Western Europe and Western Europe in Prehistory. Cambridge had a broader view, which of course eventually developed with Grahame Clark writing the first attempt at World Prehistory in 1961, a book by that name. This is what attracted me. There were other universities where you could do a bit of archaeology with other things, Liverpool was one. There were probably others. I have forgotten now. Of course there were universities where Classical Archaeology was taught as part of Classical Studies. This was about the choice; Cambridge or Edinburgh, even London then was not giving a first degree. They didn't give a first degree in Archaeology until 1958. What they had was a postgraduate diploma where people who studied under Mortimer Wheeler, Gordon Childe and Kathleen Kenyon and that sort of group during the 1950s — those people were graduates in some other discipline from another university. They were geographers, historians, classicists or whatever, and then they would go to London, and I think it was a one- to two-year Diploma in Archaeology, and this is what the Institute had built its reputation on from the 1930s. In 1958 when they moved to the present building in Gordon Square in London, they then introduced a proper degree course. That was after Gordon Childe had retired and, as we know, committed suicide. He died in late 1957.

So this was largely why I came to Cambridge; the attraction was that the archaeology school here was one of the strongest in Western Europe at that time. Also, looking back on it, I think the influence of Grahame Clark was extremely important. I had read a book by Grahame Clark, I think he wrote in 1940. As early as 1948, at the age of 14, I had read a book of his called Prehistoric England. Here was a book that didn't have any of this nonsense about the Iron Age, the Stone Age, the Bronze Age, nonsense we have still been hearing in the African context at this recent conference. Here is a man writing about people in the European prehistoric past as if they were real people doing real things. The chapters weren't bound to that 19th-century tradition of epochs. They were concerned — the titles of the chapters were 'Settlement', 'Housing', 'Communications', Trade' and this sort of thing. He then went on in a book which is sometimes now forgotten, which is extremely important. A thing called Prehistoric Europe: the Economic Basis, published in 1952. This was absolutely a ground-breaker. You read this book and you don't find any of the Childean approach to Western Prehistory in terms of looking at sequences of technology. Again, it was very much an economic approach to the subject. This was attractive to some of us, as it remains.

I have heard a lot of people say that about that book: that they admire it.

It was very, very important. I remember as an undergraduate reading it, at the same time reading Childe's The Dawn of European Civilization, originally 1925, by the time I was reading it, it was the 1957 edition. It just for one thing, you couldn't equate the Childe approach with what Grahame Clark was doing. The Childe approach, interesting though it was, its emphasis was continually on this cultural categorization, the Beaker Folk and this sort of thing. The world was then changing, and changing quite rapidly, and one of the things that was changing it, of course, was the first of the really important radiometric dating techniques, that is to say radiocarbon dating, 1948, Libby in Chicago. I remember the first I heard of it was the summer of 1950, when I working on an excavation in the north of England. I was still a schoolboy at the time, and people were talking about this new dating technique, and as the 1950s wore on, enough dates began to appear for people to realise that you didn't need to take this rather artificial approach which had formulated European prehistoric archaeology for so long, right back to the date of Christian Thomsen in Denmark in the 1820s or whenever. You could at long last have freedom from the epochal sequence of technological ages. You could actually start to date things and locate people in time as well as space. This was in a sense giving us an opportunity to break away and do different things. It then started to happen in the 1960s and we get this rather arrogant period of the so-called new archaeology, very arrogant in a way. The attitude was almost as if it was rediscovering the wheel, and now people look back on that in a critical attitude. Nevertheless, it did some very important things and I suppose if I had to reflect on my own attitude to archaeology, I would still think of myself somewhat as a processualist. Certainly not to the point of looking for all controlling laws of human activity as some of the people in the 1960s might have attempted to do. The business of human societies adapting to environments and coping with them in different ways at different times is a fascinating subject, so process in that sense, in a wider sense, has always interested me. When I worked in Nigeria, particularly when I worked around Lake Chad, I was fascinated by the fact that here was a harsh environment with little rainfall, particularly at certain times of the year, very hot at certain times of the year, very difficult to live in in many respects, but one to which human beings have adapted by picking out the opportunities offered. You get this interesting interplay of restraint and opportunity, and this is what I wrote about in a book of mine in the early 1980s called Three Thousand Years in Africa. I wanted to look at this interplay over time and the fact that the traditional agricultural systems in that area had evolved over probably 2000 or 3000 years at least, in a way that I suspect many developmental scientists and experts never appreciated. They tended to go in and say "Oh, what we need here is a really big rice field, and we'll bring the bulldozers in and the machines and the rest of it", and they never stopped to think how these people succeeded in this damnable environment for so long. I think perhaps people are a bit more thoughtful about those things now than 30 years ago.

I wondered — was it your choice to take the Part II?

I chose to do it myself and went looking for Grahame Clark, I remember, and found him in his room on Downing Street lying on his back, stretched out on what was a sort of bench in the window. It was a sort of wide window ledge, and he explained to me that he had slipped a disc and therefore had some difficulty with his back, but there he was at work, lying on his back. So my first conversation with Grahame Clark was him lying on his back looking at the ceiling, saying "Do you really want to do this?"

Was he one of the people who told you that it would be difficult to get a job?

Clark was always — to be honest about it — in the 1950s, it changed as he aged, I and others of my age would remember him as a fairly distant and cold man. We had great respect for him and with what we had read in the literature some of us would have realised that he was one of Europe's leading scholars in his field, without any doubt at all, but you felt you could never get very close to him. One suspected all the time that he didn't know who you were anyway, although he had a small number of students and he was generally discouraging of people. I mean, there was one man I knew, should remain nameless, is now dead anyway, who went to Clark to ask whether Clark would support him in application for a postgraduate award to study for a doctorate; that was difficult in those days to get ,and many of us didn't even do it, because there was no money. This man went to ask him about this and Clark said "What do you want to do?" So he told him what he was thinking of doing research on. And Clark's comment was "You know, there's some very good jobs in industry." He's said to have once referred to postgraduate students around the Department as "The crows on the wall. They hang around here."

So, this was Clark. No doubt these stories are exaggerated, and some untrue, but he was a rather distant man. I worked with him in the field in 1957 at Hurst Fen. Clark was not a good excavator in my view, and I didn't think at the time he was either. I had worked with quite a few people by then. I started helping at excavations at the age of 14. By the time I was in my early twenties, I was working as an Assistant Director on government rescue jobs and being paid for it during Long Vacations from University. So I suppose I knew a little bit about excavation by then, and I found Clark was disorganized, and yet one was aware as a scholar he knew what he wanted. He knew what he was after at the site, and some excavators don't, however well they might excavate; they don't have an idea of what they are doing it for. Clark knew exactly what he was doing it for, and the end product was pretty good. We're talking about the man who did things like Peacocks Farm in the 1930s — very, very important development out in the Fens, and Star Carr. I remember meeting people who worked with him at Star Carr, and he had remarkable results and he published them well, but to actually work with him as a student was a little

bit chaotic. You'd be doing whatever bit you were trowelling and suddenly Clark would appear and say "What are you doing that for!?" You'd say "This is what you asked me to do, Sir." "Did I? Oh, you should be doing" so and so. There was this incredible story, which was invented probably, but epitomized Clark's excavations, that he buried his plans. He had a roll of plans and he was forever getting people to move spoil dumps because they were in the way. He wanted to extend this cutting and the dump's in the way, so "shovel it over there." One occasion it was said, although I have no evidence, on one occasion it was said that he couldn't find his plans and it was discovered that several students shovelled the spoil dump on top of them because he laid them down on the ground. He wasn't the best excavator. But he was nevertheless interesting to work with, and in our own way we felt rather privileged to be there. By the 1960s, by which time I was working in West Africa, I would come back to Cambridge when I was on leave in Britain and if I ran into Clark, he by then had become much warmer. Either it was because he was getting older or because he was dealing with people involved in the profession, I don't know. I can remember running into him in the Department on Downing Street and being invited to lunch at Peterhouse, which you would never imagine Clark doing that years before, and that happened several times, so he changed with age.

As he aged was he more receptive to your work?

I think so. The last time I saw him was at the celebration of 50 years of the Prehistoric Society in the University of East Anglia in 1985, and they had a conference to celebrate this affair and they invited about 15 speakers from different parts of the world, and I was pulled in to talk about Africa, which was nice — Lew Binford was there and Flannery and all sorts of people far more famous than I've ever been, so one felt a bit privileged to be there. Clark I remember, after listening to the paper I gave, was very friendly, very complimentary, but by then he was quite an old man. We used to say as students if you went to a social affair with Clark present, he lived in those days on Wilberforce Road, he was quite generous in inviting people, in inviting groups of students, inviting to his house to sherry or afternoon tea or something, and there'd be a group of us standing there with glasses of sherry or whatever and Clark as he went around would be upsetting everybody. You know, "So, you think you've done well in the exams, I suppose." Then his wife would go around being nice to everybody. She was an absolute darling. She was a very nice person. It wasn't that Clark was a nasty person. He was just, I think, rather insensitive, distant in those days in contrast, of course, to Glyn Daniel.

Glyn was incredibly hospitable. Although he had his sort of coterie of students that he was particularly friendly with, and I certainly was never one of them, most of them were St John's men, although that was the case, nevertheless he was always generous and friendly. I had him as a Supervisor for a while and you would go to a Supervision, and you'd arrive at the appropriate time and on the appointed day, and he wouldn't be there, but there'd be a notice on the door saying "problems with some TV programme" and he'd gone to London, "could you come back three days later at such a time". So you'd turn up a few days later. On one occasion it happened that he wasn't there the second time either. So we went back a third time with our essays, showing up, and he was there on the third occasion. This was 10 in the morning and he was very apologetic and said "Well I've got this very good Bordeaux, you must try this, you see." And, he reaches this bottle of wine out of his store and takes the cork out of it and we all sit around drinking red wine at 10 o'clock in the morning. This was Glyn. One of the earliest things I published years ago was with David Clarke, he was younger than I was, but David and I had done some work and we wanted to publish it in Antiquity. So we sent it to him. It was published in 1962. It was all to do with magnetism and Beakers. I was working on some magnetic research here in the University and I was employed by the University to do this, and David was doing his doctoral research on Beakers, and so we got together and played around and wrote a paper and sent it to Glyn or dropped it in his mailbox at St John's. David belonged to Peterhouse here, and I was a Selwyn man, and we got a message from Glyn, "would we meet him", typically "would we would meet him in the Buttery in St John's at 12 o'clock" on a particular day. It was a weekday. So we went to meet him and he said "Oh, I want to talk to you about this paper." And we say "Oh yes, yes" and we sit down in the Buttery and he said "The draft Guinness is very good in here." So, we each had a pint of draft Guinness. I mustn't exaggerate, but I think after we had finished two pints of draft Guinness each, and this is at lunch-time, we all agreed that the paper needed to be revised. We took it away and cleaned it up and subsequently he published it; although I think by the time he published it, I was already in Nigeria.

May I talk about your experience as a very young man in Northern England? Who were you working with there?

As a schoolboy at the age of 14, because I lived about ten miles from Chester, and there was a man who has been long dead, rather curious individual in many ways, who obviously identified my interests, he said "Look, they are excavating in Chester. I'll take you there in my car and we'll see what they are doing." I finished up helping out on an excavation at the age of 14. I was very fortunate. It was being run by Graham Webster, who I think is still alive, who subsequently went to the University of Birmingham, I think, and then after retirement for a long time had written a lot about the history of the Roman Army. In those days he was the Curator of the Governor Museum in Chester. Graham Webster was a good excavator in the sense that he was a man who was a stratigraphist. He understood how to anatomise complex archaeological stratigraphy and its interpretation and recording. He was very good at it. Of course, in those deep urban sites that is very important, a site like Chester, York and London where you've got 20 feet of deposits in some places with your Roman stuff at the bottom, and Mediaeval and Victorian, and everything. It was a very good start. Here was a good excavator. I had the opportunity to help out as a schoolboy. Then from that I helped out at various other sites in and around Chester, some of them not done so well. I won't say who, I don't think I should. And then luckily in 1950 I ran across Terence Powell, who was another product of the 1930s in Cambridge here. He was a contemporary of Glyn Daniel. Terence Powell was Irish. His real name wasn't Terence at all. He was at the University of Liverpool where they taught some archaeology as part of a degree course, and he was excavating in the Pennines and working on a Bronze Age site, and I went and worked with him that summer for three weeks or so; and the following summer he was working in North Wales and I went and worked with him, and so on, and from that I branched out and by 1953, I was working down in Cornwall in a settlement site there with a woman called Florence Patchet, who in those days was known for her studies of Bronze Age pottery; and then the following year I joined the Royal Navy and went to sea, in destroyers in the Mediterranean largely, and was out about two years later and then ran across Paul Ashbee. In 1956, he was excavating on Salisbury Plain, and I worked with him there and subsequently worked on Fussell's Lodge Long Barrow, which is one of the classics of British prehistoric archaeology, or at least it was. Then in 1958, Milton Hill, and in 1959, Windmill Hill, another long barrow. It was a long barrow on the side of Windmill Hill. Isabel Smith and Paul Ashbee, and I was their Assistant, and we had a group of students and paid labourers. It was basically a rescue job. That was very good experience. Ashbee had been trained by Gordon Childe. He was a far better excavator than Childe had ever been, I suspect. His scholarship, I think, he always wrote in a rather laboured fashion, but he wrote a lot and he published promptly, and his real strength was in the field as an excavator; and you drew sections with Paul Ashbee and organised the logistics of stratigraphic excavation with Paul Ashbee, then you knew something about it. He was a good person to work with. By 1961, I was excavating myself, excavating a causewayed camp at Knap Hill in Wiltshire, and that was published subsequently, and soon after that I went to West Africa and never had any more to do with British Archaeology.

Could you say something about your relationship with David Clarke, who was very important . . .

Yes, he was. He wrote a rather unreadable book called *Analytical Archaeology* in the late 1960s. I challenge anybody to really demonstrate that it is readable, a difficult book. I knew him as an undergraduate. He was at Peterhouse here. He was maybe two or three years junior to myself, although I think he had been in the Armed Services also. Most of us had. There was National Service in Britain, just coming to an end, but it did mean that that generation of people to whom I belonged were really ex-service unless they had some frailty. David Clarke came from somewhere in Kent, if I remember rightly, in fact with some connections to Down

where Darwin's house was; that sort of area. As an undergraduate, my principal memory was that he had an incredible conversational capacity, particularly when it came to rolling puns off. In those days, opposite to Emmanuel College, there was a little Café. The 1950s was a time of little coffee houses all over the place in Cambridge, and there was a place opposite Emmanuel. There was a cake shop on the ground floor — Hawkins, it was called — comes back to me. Hawkins was a place where you found groups of people from the Geography Department, I think the Psychology Department, and the Archaeology and Anthropology Department, as it then was. Such groups always gravitated to the top floor in more or less an attic situation in this rather run-down little cafe and for an hour or more every morning you would find groups of people drinking coffee and eating rolls and butter and so on. David Clarke would always be there. I was nearly always there as well. Various other people, I've forgotten. Bernard Wailes was one I remember. He finished up in the University of Pennsylvania, I think. Clarke would sit there and whatever the conversation, he had this capacity to pun in a way which was quite remarkable. Other than that, one of my memories of him as a student was going around to his lodgings. Although he belonged to Peterhouse, many people lived outside the College in those days, because there were more people than space. He lived in lodgings off Tennis Court Road, there somewhere. I remember going around to see him for something and being impressed by the fact that he had lecture notes laid out. Whatever people might think about his revolutionary role in archaeology, he undoubtedly knew his conventional prehistoric archaeology. I remember seeing these notes in impeccable order, beautifully organised, very systematic, and clear illustrations sketched in them in a way which — most undergraduates didn't do anything like that. His knowledge of the traditional subject was probably very sound. He went on to do rather different things. In a curious way, although were he alive today, he might dispute the fact and say his memory was different, I suspect that one of the reasons that he got involved with matrix analysis for his work on Beakers was because of a friend of mine whom I was sharing a flat with, a man called Bill Easterbrook, who was a physicist and a Selwyn man, as I was. Bill Easterbrook had finished his degree in Natural Sciences, physics mainly, and was actually doing a postgraduate Diploma course of some sort on computer programming. Now we are talking here about 1959–60. So computer programming at that time was a very new thing, and I was sharing a flat with this guy and talking about one thing or another, he had mentioned this business about matrix analysis. "Why aren't you archaeologists using this?" And trying to explain it to me, and I'm very stupid mathematically, trying to explain what matrix analysis was. I'm convinced from my memory that at some stage, sitting in Hawkins talking to David Clarke, I must have mentioned this, and he went and talked to Easterbrook about it, but that is my memory, and memory can be an awfully deceptive thing.

Also it does make sense that important ideas were exchanged over coffee.

I think, and I have always thought, this is what universities can mainly contribute and having at one time or another worked outside universities as well as in — I've been in universities as a student, as member of lecturing staff, as a fairly senior member of lecturing staff, as a professor, as a person running a Department, or chairing a Department as you would call it in the States. I did that for 20 years in an Australian university so I have seen many aspects of university life and in Britain, in Africa and in Australia, perhaps a little bit in the States as well, and recently in Sweden at Uppsala; but to my way of thinking one of the things that universities are now failing to do is to provide that sort of informal interaction which is so important, and no amount of persuasion will convince me that you can replace good university supervision with the use of the internet. Sure, that has something to contribute, very important, and I am the first to use whatever new technology is available, but the business of people actually sitting and talking, and arguing and disagreeing, and swapping references and "have you seen such and such a new book — it is awful — or it is good".

Well, I can remember in 1960–61, again sitting around drinking coffee, and somebody said "What's the old man up to now?" We were asking about Grahame Clark. "Oh, he's writing a prehistory of the world", and everybody laughed. "How the hell can anybody write a prehistory of the world?" Clark knew you could by 1961. So he does it, and it goes through three editions up to 1978. But it was the first time anyone had ever tried it. This is a very important thing about Clark. Everybody said it. They have said it in print and said it verbally, but it was true that he realised that there was a big world out there. So you finish up with the big joke that Clark was painting the archaeological world a sort of light blue, putting Cambridge people around the world. Yes and no! I think it was more an accident, due to the fact that he had produced a whole squad of people about the right time, when the subject was beginning to open up in many areas. So, you get Jack Golson originally in New Zealand, then in Australia. You get John Mulvaney in Australia. You get Isabel McBryde in Australia. You get Peter White in Australia. These are all people who were in Cambridge at one time or another, for one stage or another of their studies. In Africa you get Pat Carter, Thurstan Shaw of course from an earlier generation. Myself, Brian Fagan, Steve Daniels although he is now out of archaeology completely, David Phillipson of course, earlier on Desmond Clark, Ray Inskeep in South Africa for a long time, and probably others I've forgotten. These were all Cambridge people. There was no great plot I think. It was just the way it fell out.

Of course, Clark was always keen to support his own people. He may or may not have shown interest in people, but if you were applying for a job and you asked for a referee report, for backing, you got it. In my experience you got it. He was good that way.

When you came through the Tripos, what happened next?

I got a job with the University. I was employed by the University of Cambridge to work on their archaeomagnetic dating project, which at that time was centred in the building we have just been in for the Conference. It was then the Museum of Classical Archaeology. It says so over the door. It is no longer. It is now down Sidgwick Avenue. From 1884 to 1984, that was the Museum of Classical Archaeology. I assumed that what happened was that it was leased by Peterhouse to the University for that purpose, and when the lease ended after 100 years, Peterhouse took it back over and it is now lecture rooms, and library as well, but I worked in that building. I had a magnetometer in the basement to measure David Clarke's Beakers on, and various samples that I collected, not just from Britain but from across Western Europe, parts of Germany, Belgium, France, across England, Wales and Scotland. We were mainly interested in Roman and Mediaeval sites because there we had some chance of getting independent dating from pottery sequences or documentary sources or whatever, to try and build up a magnetic database, to then use the technique for dating purposes. This was using both declination and inclination. It was work mainly organised by John Belshe, who was in the Department of Geophysics and Geology, as it then was, and by a Classical archaeologist called Robert Cook, and hence my presence in that building, as they found me space to work.

I had a little room over that door in the corner there which looks down Little Saint Mary's Lane, a tiny little room, and I worked in there as well. It was out of that window that I first saw Bernard Fagg, who was the means of my going to Nigeria, and he stood in the road outside and yelled, it was a summer night, and he yelled up, he could obviously see me in my room, "I'm looking for somebody called Connah." And I stuck my head out and said "That's me." And he said "You better come down. I want to talk to you." That was Bernard Fagg: the great sort of almost circus manager of Nigeria archaeology and museums. A very important man, and I think often forgotten now, because Bernard didn't publish so much, but he had a very, very important input, particularly in developing museums.

Why was he looking for you?

I had been an applicant for a job as a Research Archaeologist in Nigeria with the Antiquities Department that he ran. And I had been interviewed by the appropriate committee of Nigerians in London. By then Nigeria was independent ,and they decided to appoint me, and this news must have got through to Bernard. So he wanted to know who and what I was. So he turned up. He must have been on leave. In those days he had a house near Cambridge. Subsequently he had a house in Oxford.

Why did you choose to apply?

I had this curious ambition to be able to eat and drink. Make no bones about it, archaeology has never been a particularly easy way to earn a living,

and now I think it has become the great entrapment for younger people entering the profession, because they think they can go out as consulting archaeologists and actually satisfy their ambition to work in archaeology. I am not sure in many cases they are able to do that. Although there are lots and lots of jobs in consulting now, it is not the sort of research and publishing, scholarly aspects of the activity, that attracted people like me. I am essentially, and always have been, a research worker and teacher, running the Department as well, and a writer. I like writing. So, it still is a difficult profession to earn your living in if you are really going to have flexibility of choice, and many people in consulting work do not have flexibility of choice. They do whatever comes along on the next job, and then they don't have time to write it up, or they don't think it merits it, or whatever. Archaeology has never been an easy way to earn a living, and certainly in the late 1950s it was very difficult indeed. There were very few posts in prehistoric archaeology, even in Britain. There were Classical Archaeology posts. There had always been some of them around. For people with training in prehistoric archaeology, there were very few opportunities, a few things, but very few. Mediaeval archaeology was really only just getting off the ground. Nobody had hardly heard of industrial archaeology at that time. But Africa — perhaps I neglected to say that one of the things that was happening in the 1950s was that Africa was being discovered by archaeologists who were relatively early in their careers, and who were interested in later human societies, what you might call the Iron Age. The Iron Age in Africa was the interest. Hence Brian Fagan goes to Zambia and works on the Kalomo Culture and all those things at the end of the 1950s. I imagine that it had something to do with Desmond Clark, who was in Zambia in those days and was looking for somebody.

Brian Fagan went to the Livingstone?

I think so. He was there for six or seven years and then went to the States. He went to Santa Barbara. It was a period when people were beginning to work on Iron Age sites in Africa. Ray Inskeep was one of the earliest to do that. In West Africa, Frank Willett was already working at Ife in the late 1950s, and Bernard Fagg was running the Antiquities Department; had Frank Willett and one or two other people and was looking to appoint one or two more archaeologists. Another one who went soon after me was Robert Soper. He went to Nigeria and was there through the 1960s, left towards — no, left in the mid sixties and went to Kenya and was with the British Institute in East Africa as Deputy Director, and then went back to Nigeria and took the Senior Lectureship that I left when I left in 1971. He got that same post. He stayed there in the 1970s, and then at the end of the 1970s, went to Zimbabwe and remained there. So Bob Soper has crossed the continent several times. He is another Cambridge product. A number of the people who earned their Ph.Ds from this Department were Innocent Pikirayi and Gilbert Pwiti, perhaps one or two others.

Professor Connah is now going to reflect upon other people he knew in archaeology in that era in Britain before he talks about Africa again.

I suppose it is relevant to remember some of these things. I always regretted as a young man I never met Gordon Childe. I didn't. He was in London and I was at Cambridge and there wasn't that much contact between the two really for some of us at that time. But I did meet quite a number of other people; one of whom sticks in my mind particularly was O.G.S. Crawford, the founder of Antiquity, who several times visited excavations I was on in 1956 and 1957. He died in 1957, not so long after I saw him the latter time. Crawford was a very interesting man and I always had the memory of his notion about Antiquity as an Editor. Here was a journal which was intended to interest a wider public than just professional archaeologists. It had to, of course, in those days. He had almost a journalist approach to the journal, and the last time I saw him was at the Fussell's Lodge Long Barrow, and he had come to see us and brought his sandwiches, and sat on the ground with the rest of us at lunch-time and ate his sandwiches and talked to various of us. He asked me what I was doing, and I told him. So he pulled out a little notebook and a pencil and wanted to know who I was and to write it down, and after he had gone, Paul Ashbee said, "Ah, you are in his notebook now. That's the way he works. He likes to know who is doing what and he goes looking for things for Antiquity." Interesting character, was Crawford. That was 1957, probably only a few months before his death. He died of a heart attack in October that year. Who else? Terence Powell I have mentioned. His initials were T.G.E. Powell. Of course, he wrote on Celtic art and wrote a book which stayed in print for many, many years. Powell was a good scholar and a man for whom I had a great respect. He wasn't much of an excavator. I don't think he founded the Archaeology Department at Liverpool. I don't know whether he was the first person holding —

Second side starts very briefly and then stops — then picks up in mid-conversation:

I don't know the history of archaeology at Liverpool —John Garstang excavated Meroë and didn't publish it properly. It was done by someone else long afterwards. That is old history. Garstang was certainly dead before I knew anything about that.

Terence Powell was the first to teach prehistory at Liverpool as a Lecturer, I am quite sure.

One of the people who was a product of Powell's was a man called Forde Johnson, can't remember his first name now, who spent most of his career I think in the Museum of Manchester University. I can't think off-hand of anybody else that I knew of who might be of interest. Isabel Smith, who published Windmill Hill and Avebury. She was employed to publish it by Alexander Keiller's widow, sometime in the early 1950s. She spent many years trying to get all the data together and reorganise it and so on, and produced a monograph on it, in which there is an air photograph I think I took. Air photography is one of the things that interested me, a long time ago. So, Isabel Smith who — my memory was that Isabel Smith had at one stage, at the end of his life, had worked as a personal secretary for Gordon Childe. If she is still living in Avebury, she would be worth talking to. I am trying to remember anyone else, I remember meeting Basil Brown years ago, who is the man who found the Sutton Hoo site, but somebody stopped him; but I think they were probably wise to do so. I only knew him years later, round the late 1950s, early 1960s. I wouldn't have thought that he would have excavated well, although I never saw any evidence.

I heard that he was fine but Cambridge wanted to control it [Charles Phillips wanted to].

It's a good job somebody did —- a very, very important site, literally as the Second World War was breaking out.

It is true that Piggott and Phillips did a great job.

If I hadn't gone to Nigeria, which I must talk about in a moment, I remember one of the last things I was interested in before leaving Britain, and then breaking off contact with British archaeology very largely, one of the last things, having excavated Knap Hill, which had been originally excavated by the Cunningtons in 1911, not terribly well; I was in a sense doing a re-excavation, having interested myself in that sort of problem, one I had my eye on was a place called the Wexcombe Long Barrow, and Wexcombe sticks in my mind as principally significant because it was being excavated just as the First World War was breaking out, rather like Sutton Hoo later, and it was being excavated by Crawford. Crawford and somebody else were doing it, and the War broke out so they filled it in, walked away and never went back to it; and I was interested in the site, and I remember talking to Grahame Clark about it because Clark had in some way contact with Crawford's papers after his death, and Clark told me that as far as he knew all the papers to do with that had been destroyed in Southampton in the Blitz, because the Ordnance Survey was in Southampton when it was bombed.

I heard rumours that a lot of Crawford's stuff was destroyed.

Let's turn to Africa. I went to Nigeria first in 1961, stayed there working there continuously for ten years. I had the title, Archaeologist, Federal Government of Nigeria. I was literally a Government-appointed research archaeologist. So was Frank Willett, so was Bob Soper later, and that was about it, I think. There was also Bernard Fagg, who was running the Department, Cambridge-trained in the 1930s, but had been in the Colonial

Service through the 1940s and then moved into the Antiquities Department as a result of the influence of a man called Kenneth Murray, who was the person who really started the Museum Service in Nigeria, way back. Kenneth Murray had been, I think, an Education Officer of some sort in the Colonial Service, and in the late 1930s he had written a letter which I remember referring to occasionally in print; I don't know where it went now, but he published a letter saying "Look, Nigeria should have a National Museum." No attention was ever paid to this, but after the War, by about 1947–48 , there was a change in policy, he then becomes the person who organises the first museum collections and subsequently the first museum, etc.

Dr Eyo was telling me that he was interested in archaeology through Kenneth Murray.

That would be the case, and Ekpo Eyo, I am right in saying that he came here to Cambridge, and that would be about the time that I was first in Nigeria, that he was a student. But anyway, I went to work for the Federal Antiquities Department, and Bernard Fagg was very good in many ways. He was one of these people who was almost like an archaeological circus ring-master. He liked to organise things, get things done. He had all sorts of ideas that many people thought were crazy, but looking back on them they really weren't. He collected steam engines and old trucks and all sorts of things that most people thought were junk, because he foresaw that these were part of the heritage of a country like Nigeria, even if they were from the 20th century. So in the Jos Museum, he collected these together. Bernard Fagg's attitude to someone like myself coming out to work in Nigeria as a Government Research Officer — I sat with him in the Blue Boar at dinner the same night he yelled at me from the street and he said, "What do you want to do when you get to Nigeria?" And I didn't bother to ask whether I had a choice or not. I thought "Right", if he is going to ask me that sort of question, "I want to go to Benin City." He said "Benin?" He said "Why Benin?" I said "Nobody's done anything there and it is clearly important." These bronzes all over the world in their museums. Nobody has done the archaeology there. Well, there had been a little bit done by A.G.H. Goodwin from the University of Cape Town. He had done a bit in the late 1950s for two or three seasons, because Bernard had got him there to do it. But then the man got, I think he got lung cancer. He died in 1959. Apart from the odd small paper, it has never been published. So here was a major urban centre in West Africa that nobody had looked at. So I said, "I want to go to Benin." Benin was a place that for people of the British Colonial Service background had — its reputation wasn't good. It is an awful climate. Historically, the British Colonial people thought Benin was not a pleasant place. It was — 1897 — you know the history. So, I said that I would like to go to Benin, and Bernard said "Well that's a very good idea, yes, good, right." So I did.

Please mention something about the history.

Very quickly, well, how does one sum it up — in 1897 Benin was in a position where, through no fault of its own, it was at the edge of the expanding Colonial interests of Great Britain. And a young Colonial Officer called Phillips decided to take some sort of a mission, trade mission, whatever, diplomatic mission to Benin City. He was one of the people working, I think, in what was then called the Protectorate, one of the early Colonial areas on the Nigerian coast. So he sent a message to the Oba of Benin that he was going to come with this group of Europeans with African bearers to visit, and the Oba sent him a message back saying, "Don't come. This is a period of our main ceremonies;"End of December 1896, beginning of January 1897. Phillips ignores this. He is a young man of 22. His senior has gone on leave and away, and one can imagine or guess that he saw a chance that he could succeed where others had not tried as hard. So he sets out and walks from Gwatto towards Benin, and is attacked by an armed party of Bini, and all the Europeans except two are killed. I can't remember the exact number, about a dozen of them, and two escape, a man called Locke and another called Boisragon who subsequently wrote a book about it called Benin, the City of Blood or some such title. Anyway, Phillips himself is killed and lots of the African bearers and some, perhaps 100, lots of them who are walking are killed or taken captive. And the British government responded to this by sending what at the time was called a punitive expedition to deal with Benin. They sent up a Naval force from

South Africa, a fair lesson for people organising things like the Gulf War, the British had got their Naval Force from South Africa up on to the West African coast, cut inland with a mixed force of Blue Jackets and mainly one of Hausa Troops from the Niger Protectorate Force, and taken Benin, all within about 6 or 7 weeks of the massacre. This is the story, a misunderstanding, a lack of cultural understanding by a young Colonial Officer who was being aggressive, if not foolish, taking the risk, goes wrong, he and others get killed because of it, the British government reacts. There was a massive reaction in the British Press and British society generally. They regarded it as a barbarous act. And so then there is this punitive expedition involving the attack on Benin, and it is taken by sailors and other troops armed with what were then modern weapons. That is the story, and of course after, when they got into Benin, apart from finding quite a lot of evidence of human sacrifice which very likely had escalated because the Benin saw this dreadful coming cataclysm on themselves, so you get this fantastic reaction to that, but of course to the British Officers this was an appalling way to behave, sacrificing people, hanging them from crucifixion trees, and there are graphic portrayals of this as evidence, some which is photographic, which survive still. So they take over Benin. A day or two after they take over, a supposedly accidental fire breaks out which destroys quite a lot of Benin, but the British invading force has grabbed a whole lot of works of art which are on the shrines, in the houses, in the palace, and in various places in Benin City. You have these household shrines, down to recent times. They assemble all these carved ivory tusks and the bronze heads and the wooden carvings, and everything else, and it is taken away officially as spoils of war; and then auctioned in London. Auctioned, so much so that Charles Reed in the British Museum, I understand, had to — in fact if you look at the publication that came out of the BM at the time about the Benin antiquities, nice to get a hold of, published in 1899–1900 — Charles Reed has a Preface to that book about the items collected by the BM, saying that he thought it was a very wrong situation, as he saw it; as the BM they should have been offered this material, but they had to go out and buy it. It goes to museums all over the place, and one of the people who buys a lot of it is Pitt Rivers, the famous general who was supposed to be so important, according to Mortimer Wheeler, also a man I knew, I forgot about him; according to Mortimer Wheeler we were always told, in print and otherwise, that Wheeler saw Pitt Rivers as the person who revolutionised excavation technique in England. General Pitt Rivers bought a lot of stuff, and one of the last things he published in 1900, before his death, was a study of the Benin antiquities he had acquired for the Museum in Dorset, but the antiquities from Benin ended up all over and had an immense impact on people, because they had not realised that there was African art of that quality, of that technical quality, whatever they thought of the artistic style, which must have taken some of them aback. Nevertheless, the technical quality was immediately acknowledged. Then of course this was before Frobenius starts to find works of art in Ife. That's happening probably nine years later. 1897, this stuff comes onto the London market and is brought back by the expedition; and by the look of it, although one never really knows the full story, individual items just finished up as kickbacks for officers or some of the service men as well. Years later some of it came back onto the market as some of the families sold off granddad's Benin head or whatever.

Interruption. 16 July at Peterhouse.

We were interrupted yesterday. Prof. Connah is going to go on and talk about his experience with Bernard Fagg and when Fagg asked him exactly what he intended to do.

Yes, well, as I was saying, I chose to go to Benin City largely because nobody else had been there but it was a place that with British Colonial individuals had been an unpopular place because of the ideas associated with its early Colonial history, and I touched a little on that. However, my concern with Benin was that here was clearly a major urban centre which was already extant at the time that the earliest Europeans travelled around the west coast of Africa. Somewhat before Columbus set sail to the later called Americas, I think something like the 1470s, you have Portuguese actually reaching that part of the west African coast, and even at that stage they were describing a developed urban centre with its own ruler and series of chiefdoms. My concern was here was a place that had been known for a long time in the historical record, had produced one of the major art

forms in the world of considerable technical excellence as well as artistic interest. Nothing was known of its archaeology. That is to say, we could pick up pieces of pottery from building sites in Benin and we had no idea how old anything was at all. So my task in Benin for three years from 1961 through to 1964 was really to construct a chronological sequence for the place. As is so often the case with later African sites, that meant constructing a pottery sequence and keying it through to a stratigraphic sequence with radiocarbon dates and imported trade goods and so on. That occupied three years and eventually was published, not only in several papers but in a book called The Archaeology of Benin which came out in 1975 from Oxford University Press. But during that time, although I was working for the Antiquities Department, Bernard Fagg was a very long way away. He was up in Jos. Every so often we would communicate in a somewhat acrimonious manner, as he tried to get me to do things that I thought were things not really worth doing and which were really not my affair, but I won't go into those details. Bernard is a very interesting man, I think very important for his pioneering work with the museums. Very important indeed, and I often feel he really didn't get the credit he deserved. He subsequently became Director of the Pitt Rivers Museum in Oxford and had great plans for its development, but had a stroke and spent the latter part of his life in a wheelchair, and retired from the Museum after a while. So that it was a pity really that he didn't manage to accomplish more in Oxford. There was him and a man called Hamo Sassoon who was one of the well-known Sassoon family, poets and others. Hamo Sassoon was the Deputy Director of Antiquities in Nigeria, had been a Colonial officer, subsequently went to East Africa and worked there for a while. As I say I was in Benin. Frank Willett was working in Ife.

By 1964, I felt I had done enough excavations, three or four different sites. A lot of cuttings, 30 or so sections we had excavated in that time with quite a reasonable size labour force, and I had also surveyed quite a lot of the Benin City walls as they were called, perhaps wrongly. They are really a series of earthworks, and we found that there was a very extensive network of them which Patrick Darling in later years, ten or fifteen years later, was able to add to a great deal in his work for his Ph.D.

So in 1964, my interests turned to the African Savannah. I was principally driven, as were other archaeologists working at that time in various parts of Africa, by the necessity to construct chronological sequences. We needed to have dates. We needed to have sequences, chronological structures on to which we could hang particular sites, settlements, activities of the past, and we hadn't got those, so the question was, how could you get them in an African situation where quite often sites were shallow and appeared to have been transient? This was because of the nature of rotation or bush fallow shifting agriculture in much of Africa, no matter if it is savannah or rain forest. Because of that, the urgency by the 1960s was to find deep stratified sites. Thurstan Shaw agreed with me about this, and his direction was, because of his background and experience previously, his direction was towards rock shelters, and so he did the excavation at Iwo Eleru in the 1960s where he got a long sequence in a rock shelter. My interests were later in date and concerned with metallurgical societies rather than lithic ones. So I went looking for settlement mounds in the north of Nigeria where nobody had ever looked properly, and reports had reached me that there were quite a lot of enormous mounds covered with broken pottery in the northeast in what is called Bornu, near Lake Chad. This indeed proved to be true, and of course when one examines the literature it was obvious that some of the French archaeologists had long known this, across in Cameroun and Chad. Jean Paul Lebeuf, for instance, had investigated some of these mounds in these countries. But their interest had been more in art than in chronological sequence, and quite often, when they presented a series of radiocarbon dates it was quite often difficult to relate them to anything. So my major aim in going to Bornu was to construct sequences. Hence the excavation of the mound at Daima [1966], which was over 12 metres high and took us something like seven months to excavate, with a labour force of nearly 60 men at times. I was in what was at that time quite a remote part of the northeast of Nigeria out on the firki clay plains, but I also excavated at other places; at midden mounds up on the Yobe River on the northern Nigerian border near Lake Chad, at a place called Yau, at the site of the urban centre of Birnin Gazargamo which dates from the late 15th century, at one or two other sites also, but all of this was trying to put together pottery sequences, trying to relate other cultural material to those sequences, and indeed trying to produce a record of human activity and adaptation responses to that particular environment over the course of some 3000 to 4000 years. Hence, in 1981, I was actually guilty of writing a book which had the rather silly title of Three Thousand Years in Africa, silly to European eyes or ears but I intended, when I gave it that title, to mean something to many Africans. A notion that you could demonstrate that you know that here was a record of events for 3000 years, coming from non-written sources, from non-oral sources but coming from material evidence, hence the title.

Then by 1971, I'd then been in Nigeria for ten years and, of course it's going a little off the track, but you and I were talking about Mortimer Wheeler, I had known Wheeler for some time and I had him visit my excavations in Benin City in 1962 at an early stage of the excavation. So I did have some contact with Wheeler off and on, and quite frankly for people of my generation, I suspect Brian Fagan was another from the things Brian said to me years and years ago, Wheeler's excavation skills had quite an impact on us. I remember even as a teenager somehow getting hold of a copy of the publication of Maiden Castle, the 1943 publication from the Society of Antiquaries, and being incredibly impressed by this work, not only by the immaculate photography and the beautiful drawings, but the way the sections had been recorded, the way the text handled, the information and the argument and the interpretations; and I think that sort of field research skills, and the real skills of excavation that Wheeler had demonstrated, were ones that many of us felt were, well, we felt it was important to try to emulate them. There was discipline, a rigour, a cleanliness and an order about the way he went around things and did things which was impressive; and I sometimes think that looking at the work of some younger scholars nowadays, and they rather sneer at the whole business, "Oh, you know, neatness and all that sort of thing doesn't mean that much, I know what I'm doing", and there has been this attitude particularly in the post-processual period; they don't realise that if in fact we are going to extract evidence from the ground, then we have to be absolutely assured that we have done so in a controlled manner so what we say comes from a particular stratigraphic horizon, really does come from that horizon, and not merely appear to come from it because we had sloppy recording or sloppy excavation. Wheeler was very important, very influential to some of us of that generation, even though many people probably wouldn't admit it or perhaps won't care to be reminded of it. He was an interesting and quite an incredible character, and one could tell perhaps a few more stories about that, but perhaps it is not appropriate.

By 1971, I'd been in Nigeria for ten years. My wife had been there rather longer than myself, because she was there training midwives in hospitals; and we had three young children and we came through the Nigerian Civil War and the rather difficult period immediately after it, and so we decided to move. At that time, there was really no interest in British universities in African archaeology. I went to Australia, to the University of New England, simply because they had a broader view of the interests that archaeologists might have. I don't think they were particularly concerned whether I knew anything about Africa or not, but they wanted somebody who was far more a generalist than many British prehistoric archaeologist by then had become. My joke in those days was when I was looking for a job around 1971, I remember reading one advertisement in the Times that said something like "The University of Exeter is to appoint a Lectureship in prehistoric archaeology", and one thought "Oh yes, good", and you read further and it said "must be a specialist in South West England, particularly the Bronze Age in Cornwall". When things got that narrow and that specialised, obviously many of us were just completely excluded, so Brian Fagan finished up in California, Nic David eventually finished up in Calgary, Merrick Posnansky finished in California, so did Desmond Clark, of course, though he was an earlier generation, and I finished up in Australia. You could repeat this story with people scattered all over the place.

I went to the University of New England in Australia, where I founded the Department of Archaeology; the only time I have been in a Department which for a few months consisted merely of myself. That was in 1974; by then I had been there two or three years in another Department. The groundwork there had been done by Isabel McBryde, who subsequently moved to the ANU, but during the 1960s she had established a very good base on which one could create a new Department, but she had been there on her own as well. Once I got going, we then appointed more staff, and by the time I left that university to retire in 1995, I think we had about ten or a dozen people, of whom seven or eight were academics and the rest were support staff. So it really did grow, but then that was really on the

basis of the fact that we taught archaeology to a lot of students; and very early on I became convinced that no archaeology department should be in university merely for training other archaeologists — that archaeology, just like history or philosophy or any other subject, was in itself an educative medium that at the university level had value. You know, you don't expect everybody who does a degree in history to become a historian, but there seems to be a notion in some archaeology departments that everybody who gets a degree in archaeology will become an archaeologist, and heaven forbid; we don't need that many, but if one can use it as a general educative, medium particularly if you are in a more general degree structure as is usually the case in Australian and New Zealand universities, then your students will probably be doing courses in history and courses in geography and courses in archaeology as well, and putting the discipline with other related disciplines. Some choices are foolish ones that don't relate to archaeology at all; but because they have free choice, some will choose more wisely than others, but as a subject within a general degree structure, we would teach archaeology as perhaps a quarter of what a student was doing in their first year, a third of what they did in their second year, and if they still stayed the pace and were interested in continuing in that subject rather than going into another, by their third year it would be half of what they were doing; and because we had a fourth year honours degree system, a very small percentage, probably only two or three percent of your graduates because they graduate after three years, would then go on to do a fourth year honours degree in a way which people in Britain never understand, apart from some older Scottish universities. The Honours Degree in Australian and New Zealand universities is probably one of the things where standards have been held up best over the years. It is quite rigorous. It is often done with a mixture of course work and thesis, but the Department I ran, we did it purely by thesis.

So here were a very small percentage of our overall students having the opportunity to go on in a fourth year and try their teeth on their first bit of real research and produce a thesis of 20,000 words. It usually wasn't that long, but they had a year or less than a year to do it in. Those people who got an Honours Degree in Archaeology then, as indeed now in that situation in Australia and New Zealand, would be the people who would be most likely to go on professionally, increasingly into contract archaeology, into heritage management, perhaps a bit into museums, simply because the number of posts in universities has never been great, and if anything since the late 1980s has shown some tendency to stagnate. I was about to say shrink but probably stagnate rather than to shrink.

In Australia, of course, I got involved with Australian prehistoric sites, and for some years I excavated a series of shell middens on the New South Wales coast, partly for research interests, very largely for student training purposes, however. We used to do a site every year. I've excavated a site with Diprotodon bones in it, in other words with Palaeofauna in it, and as time went on and Australian prehistoric archaeology became increasingly specialised, where I had colleagues who did nothing else but that, whereas I was still doing African archaeology in my spare time and still going back to Africa, working in Nubia in the mid eighties and working in Uganda in the late eighties and through to the mid nineties off and on and publishing on that. Most of my colleagues were purely Australianists and so I gradually moved out of Australian prehistoric studies, which increasingly anyway had become so involved in sociopolitical complications that for anybody to work in that field they really had to specialise in it and not do anything else. A great deal of liaison with Aboriginal communities was necessary, and involvement of Aboriginal people in excavations and field work.

So, I moved sideways and then became — or so they tell me — I was one of the pioneers of historical archaeology in Australia. Not quite true because there were others who had done work before myself, particularly Judy Birmingham in the University of Sydney who was looking at historic sites way back in the 1960s, when for her pains she often got laughed at by her professional colleagues. She worked very hard to establish an interest in the archaeology of 19th-century Australian European sites, and I got involved with that by about 1976 and spent time over the years looking at the social economics of domestic situations, in other words, the remains of homesteads, of houses and so on; I also at some length researched a water mill and looked at the subject of technology transfer from Britain to Australia, and indeed published on that. In the late 1980s, by '88 I think it was, I published a book which has gone through two versions. Its present title in paperback is The Archaeology of Australia's History, which tells you what I was on about.

That pretty well concludes down to the present time, when as a person who is retired I am now an Emeritus Professor at the University of New England but attached to the ANU as Visiting Fellow, which means I do a little teaching for them and have the benefit of using their address and a room in the University which I sometimes use; and a few little advantages of that sort, including access to their really very good libraries. My main interest nowadays is not only a certain amount of field work; I still have a big research project which is funded by the Australian Research Council which involves excavation for three years, of which the present year is only the second; but not only that, I am particularly interested in writing and at the moment I am working on ideas of trying to reach a far wider audience in Tropical Africa by writing a brief account which can be sold cheaply and widely, and hopefully made available in a number of African languages as well as in English and French. This is a fairly large ambition and it will probably take about four or five years to really work that one out.

Is that your work in Benin?

No, I would like to write about Tropical Africa as a whole by taking a series of case studies; what do we know from archaeology, except, in this sort of book intended for the last year or two of schools and the first year of university, one doesn't use the word archaeology at all, one leaves it out because you have to explain it, but what we know from the remains of people's life and activities in the past. So you can have little chapter on Great Zimbabwe and another on the stone ruin sites on the Swahili coast, and a little chapter on Aksum and even perhaps earlier ones on the Klasies River Mouth Cave, early Homo Sapiens, perhaps even one on Olduvai Gorge. With some fifteen or so brief chapters written in simple straightforward English and made as interesting as possible. We need to reach a far wider audience in Africa, audiences who have not got the money to buy the sorts of books that many of us write as research monographs or textbooks; and even if they had the money they won't know the books existed in some cases, and probably in many cases won't understand the material anyway without some prior training, if they were actually studying archaeology. I think there is a interested people there, interested in their own heritage, who deserve to be served better than they are being served at the moment by archaeologists working in Africa. I have just been at a Conference where much of the material given in the papers was, if one could sum it up, one could say that it was particularistic, including the paper I gave myself, which was all about a pottery analysis in the northeast of Nigeria. People were looking at very specialist areas in time and space, and rightly so. But the time is now overdue for us to sort of pause a bit and say — right, let's not only write general books about Africa, as I have done and David Phillipson has done, for a reasonably specialist audience, but to write books which will reach a wider readership — there is no such thing as the 'ordinary reader' — I think in this case the market we want to aim for is the last year or two of school, the first year of university, the school teachers. These are the people who, presented with the opportunity to buy a fairly cheap paperback even we can produce such a thing, I think would do so, if it is of use and of interest to them. This could prove to be a very difficult ambition to meet.

Seems admirable because a lot of the African scholars I have spoken to want to make their archaeology relevant to their own people.

I think we have to attempt it, and they would be in a sense more appropriate people to do it than myself. I am not a Black African. I am of European background, but I would like to try anyway, and in trying what we will do is not only produce in English and hopefully French, but see if we can get translations into the main African languages: Swahili, Arabic, Hausa, some of the main languages, but that means obtaining funding that can pay translators, because translation is a very laborious business, particularly to do well. Therefore one needs a good translator, and these people have to earn their living; and we also want an African illustrator who can draw simple pictures which will mean more to an African readers than would be a case if they were drawn by a British or American or Australian artist. This is the idea.

We have about four minutes. Where you associated with museums in Nigeria?

Well, in the sense that whilst in Benin City amongst everything else I was supposed to be the Director of the Museum, such as it then was, as well as running a major excavation and doing other field work. Yes, in that sense, and I had had some background in museums very largely as a semi-voluntary worker both in Devizes, Wiltshire briefly with Nic Thomas when he was there, but also more extensively in Liverpool Museum and that is going way back into the mid 1950s. I helped out in all sorts of things, conservation. I once spent about three or four months sorting a collection of firearms, for instance, for the Liverpool Museum, because Liverpool is one of those tragic cases in Britain in which, there were fortunately few, where the Museum was bombed and basically destroyed in the Blitz and so by the 1950s — they were beginning to rebuild it in the 1950s — it was a long delay before it was rebuilt, because there were far greater building priorities after the War. During those years such collections which hadn't been destroyed, like most museums they had moved a lot of their stuff out into storage, it had been hidden in caves in north Wales; but some had not been moved, and so when the place was bombed they lost quite a lot, particularly some of their archaeological material, I was always told, and they lost records. I can remember spending the whole summer of 1956, when I had just come out of the Royal Navy, helping out at the Museum and they said, one thing you could do is sort out this collection of firearms, the records have been destroyed, can you do something with them? I had an assortment of muskets and pistols and swords dated over something like 300 years, and in an awful state. A lot of it was red, rusty, and I spent three or four months going through it and listing everything as best I could, and doing emergency cleaning. So, I have a bit to do with museums. I think at that stage I probably thought that if there was any job to be had in archaeology that one might well finish up working in a museum, but I never have in a proper sense of the word.

Interruption.

We were just talking about the museums and how they involved indigenous peoples.

Yes, so thinking back to Museums in Africa, I mentioned Bernard Fagg before and Bernard's role in getting the Museum Service going in Nigeria. He didn't originate it. It was originated by Kenneth Murray, it is true to say in Lagos for the National Museum, but Bernard, from what I could gather when I was first in Nigeria in 1961, Bernard very nearly built the Jos Museum with his own hands; certainly he had a very, very close role in supervising the construction of the place and in getting around all sorts of difficulties by networking, getting favours done by people he knew, to get the job finished. In doing this the interesting thing about Bernard Fagg was that outside his museums in those days (it was the same in Benin and Ife as well as Jos, by the time I was there in the early 1960s there were a number of other museums), outside the museums was a notice that read what the name of the museum was and underneath it said "Open All Day, Every Day." He meant it. When I was in Benin, I remember I used to go down to see the Museum Curator on duty Christmas Day morning, usually to give him a small present or just to talk to him because the man was there. It was open on Christmas Day. I am sure that hasn't happened now for many years, but this was Bernard's notion, that if you had a museum, it must be open. It must be available for ordinary people, and of course they were free. Nobody was charged to go in them. The other thing that Bernard did, that I failed to mention before but took a lot of his interest and time and enthusiasm, was that he created a zoo. He had a zoo attached to the Museum in Jos, very much an open-air zoo with African animals, and the reason he did it was largely because he wanted to interest Nigerian people not only in their cultural heritage, but in their natural heritage, the animals. He thought to do that, people must see these things, so he had a zoo, and again I think it was free of charge. It became quite an attraction. It was probably the first zoo in Nigeria. It was already going by the time I first went to Jos in 1961. I think it would be true to say that Bernard Fagg, ex-Colonial Officer though he was, that his view of his role was that museums were not just for the few expatriates who happened to live there, or even for visiting tourists, and West Africa has never really had that many tourists anyway. They were to serve a purpose to do with the local indigenous people. They were to interest people in their own history and their heritage in all sorts of ways. Bernard could be quite a nuisance in this respect. For instance, one of the many things he wanted to do was put up a whole lot of traditional buildings, so he would get hold of build-ers from different parts of Nigeria to build. "I want a Nupe Hut. Build it there!" and he'd pay them to do it. At one stage he wanted to build a Benin building. Well, Benin traditional mud architecture is bright red, because of the nature of the Benin soils, but the available soils for mud architecture around Jos are a completely different colour, so I get a phone message from Bernard Fagg, I'm excavating in Benin City, and Bernard rings me up and says "I want some red soil!" So I said "Oh yes, Bernard, it is only 800 miles away. How am I supposed to get it to you?" "I'm sending a truck next week. Get it filled." And he did. He sent around a driver with a Department of Antiquities truck, and we loaded up the red soil, probably from the excavations if I remember rightly, and it goes back to Jos and this mud building is put up, which is a nasty grey colour; and he has it surfaced in red mud so that it looks like a Benin building. He then has the walls fluted with horizontal grooves in the proper manner and he turns it into a restaurant, the little restaurant of the Museum, which he actually called "The Bite of Benin". It was a restaurant. Bernard I think knew that museums had to serve the majority of people in the countries in which they were situated, but I think he was perhaps before his time in that respect. There had been changes going on in museums . . .

Tape abruptly ends

Professor Ekpo Eyo

15 July 2000, recorded at Peterhouse, Cambridge, during the SAfA Conference, by Pamela Jane Smith

Professor Eyo, would you tell me a little bit about how you became interested in archaeology?

Well, I became interested accidentally. When I left the high school, I did not think about archaeology because I didn't know about it. My intention was to become a Customs Official or Produce Inspector which had some uniforms which I really admired, nicely well-ironed, starched uniforms, and that was my intention because I had a brother in one of those serv-ices. But then after leaving school in Calabar, which is my home town, I went to Lagos, the capital of Nigeria, to look for work, and I went to the beach where I met an Englishman called Kenneth Murray, who was then Surveyor of Antiquities in Nigeria, and he was a very eccentric person. He wasn't married, or rather one would say he was married to his work, and he always appeared naked, or not naked but always had some pants on, and he was walking along the beach and was friendly with the fishermen there. And he was really a phenomenon and anybody who was at the beach was interested in what he was doing. So, I had a small camera, Brownie camera, which I asked to take photographs with, which I took photos of Kenneth Murray; and I asked him, if it comes out what should I do with it, and he gave me an address in Lagos where most Europeans lived. So, the film was processed within a week and I took it down to the address and I when I got there, the same thing. He had pants on and nothing more, and I knocked on the door and he came out to open the door and smiled at me and then he asked for time to get ready to talk to me. But he was arranging a series of carvings, carvings of twins, and he was moving from one end of the hall to the other, picking up carvings and putting them the other way and then bringing some that way and putting them that way, and it was all very confusing and very, very funny. I asked what he was doing and he said that he was trying to organise them into types. Small wooden carvings. But the way he was involved in what he was doing, he did have a very intense interest and he was very, very focused and most of the time while he was talking to me, he would still be arranging these, moving from one end of the hall to the other, and I was fascinated by that. I was fascinated, not because I knew what he was doing, but because of the spirit with which he was doing it. It was that kind of thing, that spirit of commitment and involvement, that really made me ask him if I would find a place in the office he was running and learn more about what he was doing, and find out why he was so interested in what he was doing. And he smiled and then gave me job, what he called an Antiquities Assistant. That is to say, somebody who would be assisting him and doing what he was doing. This is how I got involved and I must say that for about six months after my employment there, I didn't know what it was all about, except that I just wanted to see it because I am one person who doesn't want to like to tread where others have trod and always like to open my own way, and so in many ways I am a learner. I like to strike out where other haven't been and so, because he had no other Nigerians there, I felt very proud to be the only Nigerian involved in collecting and arranging antiquities. I worked for Kenneth Murray for about two years and then he suggested that I should need some training in England, so as to become a senior officer and get more involved and understand what I was doing. He tried his best to explain to me, but it didn't quite make sense. However, he then asked me to go on scholarship. So I came to the University of Cambridge to study Archaeology and Anthropology, and when I gradu-ated here at Cambridge, I went to London to study Archaeology, and so I returned to Nigeria and started working in the Museum and I have not left that service since then because I have discovered why Mr Murray was so involved. I think things of the past had a great fascination for him and he knew that the present can not be appreciated without a knowledge of the past. That has occupied me. I got hooked on it and I am still doing what fascinated me 35 years ago.

So whatever happened to Kenneth Murray?

Eventually, he was a known man although he died prematurely. He retired, but when I returned from England and worked in Nigeria, he had retired then, and another Englishman was in charge of the Museum Service,

Bernard Fagg, who was also trained here at Cambridge. So I worked with Fagg for about two years, and then a position opened up at the Pitt Rivers at Oxford and Bernard left, and so I found myself responsible for the entire set up of the Department of Antiquities which was dealing with museums, ethnology, archaeology and all administration, of course. So I got to stay so long in the Museum and I was practising Archaeology and Anthropology. The kind of thing you have in small museums. One man has to do many professional roles in one. I was there for more than 30 years, and when the political situation in Nigeria became a little bit stifling, I thought it would be good to move out and not be suffocated by the political system. Fortunately I had a position at the University of Maryland to teach art history which I hadn't really studied, but having worked in Museums for a long time, I knew the principles of it and so went to Maryland in 1987, and now I have a great opportunity to do field work which I wanted very much to do. It was not possible as Director of Antiquities. I've been researching on art history until a few years ago and then I returned to archaeology because of recent discoveries I have to make. I started excavating at Calabar four years ago with graduate students from the University of Maryland and we have made fascinating discoveries of a civilisation hitherto unknown which started from the 5th ad and lasted to the 16th century. We have only done three or four sites but we are continuing to do that. We don't know what to expect in the future, but we have got so far is really outstanding, and when I gave a paper here at this conference, everyone who heard me and saw the materials which we excavated, they were happy. I think it is going to be a great aspect and period in the archaeology and art history of Nigeria when it is all done, and it will take many years to accomplish this, but already we have started to make our mark.

I wonder about the dates, to get the chronology correct.

I met Kenneth Murray in 1951 and then I came to Cambridge for my first degree and did my MA at the Institute of Archaeology and then went back to Nigeria because I had spent six years on Government Scholarships. Initially I was asked to come for three years, and so after six years, they wanted me to get back to understudy the Englishman who was there at this time, Bernard Fagg, because Bernard was going away. So I did not do my Ph.D. I didn't complete it. I went back to Nigeria and had to take it through an external degree and had to do fieldwork and write it up for the University of Ibadan which was then part of the University of London.

At that point who was at Ibadan? Was Thurstan Shaw?

Yes, Thurstan Shaw had come as a result of the excavation which was then the oldest site in Eastern Nigeria, the site of Igbo-Ukwu, which had remarkable bronzes. There is no comparison elsewhere in Nigeria, or elsewhere in the world, that can match the Igbo-Ukwu materials. The Governor of East Nigeria was very impressed and it happened that the Vice-Chancellor of the University of Ibadan at the time came from that area. So, he was able to support archaeology at Ibadan and Thurstan Shaw became the first Professor of Archaeology there, and as you know Thurstan Shaw trained here. He is a Cambridge product, and so he started approaching staff and Faculty from all over the world and then by the time I submitted my dissertation, it was a fully developed Department with a person from Oxford and by the time he left, retired and returned to Cambridge, the Department had been very well established and had some good — you know Nic David who is the President of SAfA, I was part of the team that hired him to become a Professor at Ibadan.

What was the relationship between your position and the University?

The Universities did the theoretical work and I did the practical. I thought couldn't employ anyone as an archaeologist without the knowledge. So I encouraged the University of Ibadan to train people because we have a law in Nigeria that before permission is given to excavate, they must demonstrate the ability to handle a site properly, because all excavations are systematic destruction of the evidence unless it is properly recorded. So we are very particular about giving people permits to dig, because once the evidence is destroyed, you cannot get it back. I insisted on taking a degree and one year more of practical year in the field, so when you are qualified as an archaeologist, you can handle a sites properly or it would be a disaster.

That was all in the 1970s?

Yes, late 1970s.

It sounds like a very hopeful time, the 1950s, '60s.

Well, it was time for the expatriates. There was no Nigerian in the field. That was the time of Frank Willett, Thurstan Shaw, Graham Connah who is now in Australia, Robert Soper, Steve Daniel. There are all people who originated from Cambridge and came down to work in Nigeria.

Did that help?

It did establish a standard, a reference point because archaeology is a discipline in the West and much newer in Africa, so when people don't know exactly why people go to dig the ground and the usual question is, "why do you go and dig there?" "Did you know something was buried there?" Well, that is something that comes with training. They have to spot sites, and of course there are many ways of doing that, and if you are not trained, you won't be able to handle — you don't dig anywhere and everywhere, you have to be attracted. You have to have evidence and hope in a particular site and then you try to find out if it has anything. That is one. Two is to be able to handle the site. All this, you need practical experience. You need standards. It is not like anthropology or ethnography where you can collect things and then take then to a museum to study. Archaeology begins with study in the field and one has to have the competence to handle a site. It is much more particular, comparing to other disciplines connected with the past. And so this office set the standards, how to record, how to interpret and how to preserve the objects in the field and in the museum and so on. It may sound so little, but it is really a great responsibility that an archaeologist has when he handles a site, and so we needed people who have done it before to pass on the standards to us.

And that standard when it was passed on, that was in the '60s?

Yes, I was still here. I was in England. I went to England, and then I only managed to do one excavation, because then I was saddled with the responsibility of administration, and looking after 5000 people all over a big country is not an easy responsibility.

That is how many people you had in your Service?

Yes, you had museums all over. By the time Bernard Fagg left in 1964 or '65, there were about seven museums in the country, all under one Administration.

You had to be in charge of all of them?

I had to be in touch with all of them and it was also more difficult because people who were employed in the museums, most of them have no training. You have to train by asking them to do things and supervising them, their actions, their decisions, their execution of decisions and so on. So it wasn't that easy. I had just managed to excavate Ife and a site which was a Palaeolithic site and Mesolithic with art and stone and barbs for arrows and spears. Like I said, this had been done mostly while out of the country from 1986. I didn't have that much time to excavate when I was in Nigeria. I think I have done more fieldwork in the past 14 years than I had done when I was in the Nigerian Civil Service.

Was it a help to get to the University of Maryland and your position allowed you to be more active in fieldwork?

In general research, whereas in Nigeria there was merely administration.

You are known as a top-quality administrator and that you were able to keep very little corruption.

Well, I think that what has happened with that — at the time I got into the Civil Service there were still standards. We tried to imitate what the British did. Although I am not saying that they are not corrupt, but the degree of corruption is nothing to write home about. All the people who got into the Service when the British were there, carried on in the British tradition. After independence, people gradually — gradually people started departing from the standards which were set and then now, of course, it has got out of hand completely. Now if you put someone in a position of authority, the first thing nowadays is you have to make your money. You have an opportunity. You have to make your money. Otherwise, if you don't make your money then you're a fool because everybody else is making money. That was part of the problem. I got suffocated in atmospheres like that. [Inaudible sentence] — I am one person, when I go to sleep, I don't want someone to knock on my door and ask questions. Maybe I wouldn't be like this if I got into the Civil Service much later than I did. You find that people who got into the Civil Service before me and during my time and perhaps a little bit later on, there is a good standard of decency, honesty, commitment. Everyone wants to do something to justify the confidence placed on them and their positions, but nowadays the politicians in particular, the army — what is happening now in Nigeria has been the result of the policies being controlled by Nigerians and everyone wants money. It is money that becomes the target. The soldiers didn't help things at all. They became more corrupt now and so if you don't have the [inaudible bit], you are an odd person. So that is the situation. I think they are doing something about it. We are determined. We are not a poor nation, but very poor in the general world.

I wondered about your education in England? Who influenced you?

Well, here at Cambridge, I had, my personal Tutor was Jack Goody. And I admired people like Grahame Clark who was then Professor of Archaeology and I also admired Meyer Fortes who was the Head of Anthropology. Of course, Edmond Leach was very inspiring, very inspiring teacher who knocked down everybody's houses and tried to build his own. But he admitted that was his responsibility to knock down, even if you can't build one to replace, but he was very, very stimulating kind of person. He was well liked. If he had a public lecture you had to go there very early. I mean the way — he was not always correct but he was stimulating. And in London I had a Jewish German Professor Zeuner who had written the book on dating and geochronology, and when I got there he was one person who took me in personally and helped me. That is why I took Prehistoric Archaeology in London and then I had conservation which I had had already one year at London. I had a woman called Irone Davie [inaudible bit] a very, very motherly woman who took me in. So I had a good time in London and had a good time in my College and that also influenced my life, because I tried to see things in more than one way, and not necessarily in an argumentative way, but trying to question what I and other people do. That has helped me, put me straight. You may disagree and if you have the basis for doing this, it is not as bad as disagreeing with somebody and not be able to say why. That has helped me a lot. I made many friends and kept most of them because of the way I have related to them.

As a person from Nigeria in England, was that difficult? You said that the people greeted you with gentility, Jack Goody and Meyer Fortes. Was that true generally? Was it comfortable to be here?

Oh yes!

And when you went back did it feel — it interests me — this tradition of Civil Service and how that was very important for Nigeria and for the development of your museums.

Yes because the Civil Service was to serve the public, to serve Nigeria, the public service.

And that was a British import.

Yes, that is a British import.

You felt that worked for your country?

Well, yes, it did work and I think, I don't know what would happened but I hope that it will find its level. All of a sudden Nigerians find themselves in a position of authority. They have control over the wealth of the country. The

wealth they never had access. So this money I haven't seen, I haven't had before, now I have the power to control it and very few people will resist that temptation. I would be surprised if it were the other way and when the British left and then you find some people carrying on in that tradition. The British who were sent to Nigerian have had a long history of development. They came from very established homes and a very established service and had also Britain was overlooking and seeing what they were doing. If they messed up, they would be recalled. So there was a force which they had to defer to, if they did wrong but you then leave a country to Nigerians who didn't have anyone to report to but themselves. It is a great thing to overcome that temptation and once you have started doing it, you cannot stop and I think it has come down one generation now and I keep on saying that it can not remain like that forever. Something will happen to straighten people out. It cannot continue like that because people will be fed up with money. The time is coming, perhaps sooner than later.

It is complicated too by the international companies which have became involved and there is complicity in offering lots and lots of money suddenly.

There is corruption everywhere. It is easier for Western people to practise corruption in non-Western countries than in their own home. It is as simple as that. I don't think that Nigeria can be singled out as the worst because they didn't have something to guide them. If you let loose a British person out of this order they might behave differently. When you are in this country, everyone stays in a queue. You don't jump a queue. But, when they go outside these situations, they would probably behave much worse than others. Once I was in London in a taxi trying to get to the airport and there was one accident. There was a hold-up. The British are not used to that situation. They are used to the situation where, if they leave from work at 5 o'clock, they know exactly when they are going to arrive at home and they can arrange their lives and meetings. But, when they are held up by traffic for two hours, which is a common thing in Nigeria, their behaviour is much worse than Nigerians. Then they also jump the queue.

We didn't have the mechanism in place to control this situation. There was a time in Nigeria, there was an attempt, an effort, to say that, in effect, 'everyone should queue up'. They do 'queue up' but if something happens to break the queue, that's it. People can go wild. For example, you buy your ticket for a local flight in Nigeria and maybe you didn't get there in time, you want to jump the queue and pay a bribe or whatever. Everyone was responding to this as if it were like standing in queue. May I suggest that it is not enough to ask people to stand in a queue. You have to help them to stand in a queue. Then you have to support them even to set standards. Even if somebody is then anxious to get in front, they won't because it would be considered very strange by their colleagues. So people will stay there but if you leave people and if they keep on crowding in, they change positions. Some people will be smart. They will be clever in how to pass you but you have to 'herd' them. That is what I am saying. You have to have consented rules and restraints to develop their 'natural' instincts. You have to have some kind of mechanical thing to help.

It is very interesting what you are saying that there was an imported system of societal structure in the British Civil Service and then when that changed there was really nothing which replaced that.

They had a tradition, a long tradition. Now, there are people trying to find ways of coping with that change.

It must have been a very dramatic change. It sounds like almost a revolution socially.

It will find its level but it comes on like that. At first when politicians started messing up, everyone wanted the soldiers to come in. Then the soldiers came and at first it was OK but then they relapsed into the common pool of corruption. Now nobody wants to hear about Army rule in Nigeria. I can tell you if the civilian government messes up, the Army will have to come back. Now the politicians are going to behave themselves if they want to keep the Army away. There must be some kind of tradition. You are building up a tradition. It is not something where you wake up in the morning and it has happened. We are all human and I think that human beings all over the world are in some ways same. If you look at the history of Britain, for example, all those things that have happened in Nigeria, happened. People got rich.

It is still happening.

So more stability will come in Nigeria.

I think that Britain and Canada are fortunate because the change has been very gradual. There has been a social change that would have upset —

You know how many years they had to fight. The goal was just to dominant for a long time in England, to keep what you have and to add more if possible — for centuries.

How has all of this affected archaeology?

It affects archaeology in the sense that if you do something else you can retire. I wouldn't be working today — after being Director of Antiquities for 17 years. I won't be working today. But there is a necessity because the family system in Africa, we have extended families. So long as I have the energy, I have to work as long as possible but today people won't wait. People today want to make all their money within five years of being within the Service. That is what is happening. The top Civil Servants see how other people make money. There within a short time utilising opportunities. If another person sees that perhaps would do the same thing. People of my generation in the Civil Servant have retired into poverty because they didn't make the money. There is no guarantee in the social system that when you retire you will live comfortably as they have in the United States. There is nothing like that. When you retire, things that you used to enjoy as a Civil Servant [inaudible bit] in one way you can justify the actions of the present generations of Civil Servants because when they retire there is nothing.

Then they can't support their extended family?

There are all kinds of things at play here but that doesn't justify the greed which exists at the moment.

Today what do you see, what are the answers with archaeology?

I think we shouldn't pray for revolution. We should pray for evolution. Gradual change, talking and arguing and — condemning and praising until something emerges. People are ready to die just to get money so that my I can have my life, so my children can go to school. This is very logical thinking, to have things to help the children and the family. So when you are in a position of authority, you can make money and you don't care. There is no answer. I don't believe that there is an answer but to condemn it and hope that people will have, as a consequence of greediness, that people will learn lessons. But I don't think that anybody can prescribe anything and if some people try to be honest in a position of power, they will be tempted not only by other Nigerians but by foreigners who want to make money through Nigerians, through Africans. There is no local solution. Most of the money that is stolen in European banks and they know it is there. They know it is illegal but they keep it to become richer. If the European banks did not accept the money, there would be no place to keep it.

All of this change in values and social structure and all this loosening of things that people depend upon to know how to behave, all of this — you talk about this very vividly.

Abrupt end of first side of tape — some bits of conversation are lost.
We go on immediately on SIDE TWO.

Did archaeology suffer?

Yes, because now you can money easily elsewhere. Archaeology is not the easiest life, to sleep in a tent in the bush and to really work hard. To produce one report, you have to study material, there is the physical aspect of the labour, there is the mental aspects and then you have to write and

yet you are not paid. As an Administrative Officer, one gets $1000 for his signature. All you have to do is sell the signature. So, from that point of view, not [many] people would do archaeology. You can't live on the money paid unless of course you dig and sell but then the Western world comes, the public, and then you are in trouble.

The wider academic public, you mean.

Well, when you get into archaeology you must know that there is no money. We trained many, many archaeologists in Nigeria who have no jobs now. But some of them after getting a degree, move out into areas that they will make money. I remember when I recruited a group of youth corps graduates and the government had the responsibility of finding work for them. So they would appear at a time. I had a Youth Corps service sent over by the Public Service Commission and then I remember one of them telling me that I'm not looking for money but I sometime in my life it would be OK to work for money. It was a joke but it was true. She was speaking her mind. They would get contraband to get money. I haven't done that yet, thank God, because I can still contain my needs.

I realise that it has been a very long conference and you have been in great demand and I don't want to tire you too much. We have maybe five minutes. If you have something that you specifically want to say?

What can I say?

You have a lot of feeling for archaeology and for the changed in Nigeria and have little anger. You are at peace with yourself. That is wonderful because you have seen so much change and it has been painful.

I think the purpose of life is to look for happiness and satisfaction and money does not always insure that. I am happy in my station today. I don't have a lot of money and I don't complain. Maybe if I had a little more I would be more comfortable but if I don't have I am still comfortable. So, one thing I want to leave behind is when you read the history of Africa, take any book on the archaeology of Africa, you will have seen that here. The history of a country is interpreted by foreigners. In my opinion the best people to write the history of Africa which is something that you have to study. In the writing of history, people always write from their personal point of view. I remember sitting in the class here in the Museum of Archaeology and Anthropology and Lecturer after Lecturer would come in and talk about "primitive society" and "primitive man". They would talk about "primitive people" and "primitive economic", "primitive technology" and I was sitting there. Each time they would mention "primitivism", there was an example of "primitivism" in the class. I was the only person and I got used to it but every time they would say "primitive", the other students would turn their heads around to see a living example. That is the sort of thing. Why should somebody talk about another society as "primitive"? That is what the students were taught. They were taught the geography, the history, the economics, the government, whatever, the technology of "primitive" people. No African, no Native American, no Pacific Islander would come before anybody and talk about themselves as "primitive people". They wouldn't call themselves that. So, if you can see that if you do something. If you have gone through this experience I have gone through, you feel that if you are capable, there is nothing more satisfying than trying to change this notion of "primitive man". Why "primitive"? Is it because of advancing technology but before the industrial revolution, everyone was sacred. To explain that point to people, who would do it for us? Who would do it for us? If you come into the lecture room here, they are working in Nigeria or they are working among the Luba people, but you don't find any Luba there. You don't find any Nigerians who would talk about history from his own point of view. He knows about it. It is very difficult to practise these kinds of studies to be fair. It is very difficult for one, in the first instance, to get out of his own cultural context and even much more difficult then to get into another. So there are two impediments in the way; to break away from their own tradition, become neutral, and then to penetrate other traditions. So all these are not usually conscious. So I am glad that I am one of those. I am among the first Africans to be part of archaeology. I can put my own interpretation into archaeology and to intervene in cases where I see bias and don't see fairness. To understand what happened in the past, you really have to know the philosophy. Why these things were made the way they were made. You wouldn't call them "ritual objects". You wouldn't call them "primitive objects". The people who made these things. It was a way of conquering life, of making use of their life in the environment which they had. If you live in the desert, you don't have to build igloos, you don't have ice. You don't have to build stone houses because you can't cool them. You can't build houses with wood because there is no wood. So you can see how other things from other countries can be compared to the US and England and Germany and so on, where the environment is not the same. The people we study are people who make use of their environment. To have a balanced view, you need people from outside and you need people from inside. Let them talk and in my opinion that is the only way to have the best of African history and non-European history. I represent one of those — it is just a beginning to see and to describe history from an African perspective.

You teach us. It is your turn to teach us.

No graduate student should take a degree in African studies without seeing the Africans and see how they respond to the environment. They have as much pleasure as millionaire in the United States and that is the goal of life.

It is a very important message. This is what you teaching us.

If you take a man from a village and put him in Buckingham Palace, he wouldn't know what to do with it. He would be the most unhappy person with all the luxury around that, it would be a strange environment. If we brought our mothers and fathers to the United States from Africa, they would want to go back. They would cry to go back. It is a good thing to have many more Africans get into the interpretation of their own culture and own civilisation. They have a special angle. They have a lot to offer. That is why I stayed. As I got into this Service, I was convinced, I dedicated myself, thanks to the fact that I met Kenneth Murray, because although I didn't understand what he was doing, I really appreciated his sense of commitment and involvement.

My great pleasure to talk to you. I hope many people listen to this tape.

Professor emeritus John Evans and Mrs Evans

17 August 2000, recorded at the Evans's home in Shaftesbury, England, by Pamela Jane Smith pjs1011@cam.ac.uk
Evans, who graduated from Cambridge in 1950, succeeded Gordon Childe in the Chair of European Prehistoric Archaeology at the Institute of Archaeology in London. He later became the Director of the Institute.

Professor Evans, how did you get into archaeology?

It is a long story. It was really I suppose being interested from an early age, reading things like Woolley's Ur of the Chaldaea in the 1930s but having no idea at that stage of how to get into archaeology. You couldn't if you weren't —

I should have asked you when you were born?

1925.

Are you English?

NO, I'm Welsh. I was born in Liverpool but my family are all from North Wales. Yes, I would accept 'British'. I was born in Liverpool and went to the local high school which was the same school as the Beatles'; not at the same time. They were a good deal later. John Lennon and Paul McCartney later bought up the remains of the school and turned it into a Institute of Performing Arts. In my day, it was known as the Liverpool Institute, and it was known as the Liverpool Institute because it started in 1825 as a mechanics' institute. They set up a whole lot of mechanics' institutes around the country. It was a sort of 'work as an education' idea. This was the same origin as Birkbeck College in London University.

Did they have any archaeology?

Oh no, no.

Did somebody in your family recommend that you read Woolley?

No, I found it myself. I was interested in books. That was the essential thing. But at school, no, I was doing basically History and English Literature and eventually I went to Cambridge to read English. It was December 1942 when I got a Scholarship to go to Pembroke, and I had the choice, I was 17 then so I was due for call-up at the end of the school year, I had the choice of either staying on at school or going to Cambridge and then being called up from there, and naturally I took the choice of going to Cambridge. I didn't know at that stage when you would get back.

What happened?

I was going into the Air Force, but while I was in Cambridge, my Tutor sent me along for an interview with someone who was recruiting, and I was inducted and it turned out to be Bletchley Park, the code-breaking establishment. I didn't know where I was going.

What did you do there?

Well, I was working on the Enigma codes in German Army and Air Force. We worked with a very early version of a computer. These were enormous things that were the size of a house, practically, that did one thing which was to go through all the positions of the Enigma machine. What you did was, you had to try to guess what a certain number of words were in a coded messages, and you made up what we called a menu from that which was — if this is correct — then 'a' goes to 's' and so on and so forth, and you drew it out and passed it over to the people who ran the machines and they sent it through the machine, and if you were correct, eventually came up with the position, and they began to be able to decode the message of that day.

Did you have to do that every day?

Yes, because the code changed every day. They changed the position being used every day but the Air Force code usually came out by 4 o'clock in the morning each day. Yes, we got there early. The Army code tended to be a bit more difficult, but on the other hand you got a lot of information about the Army's movements from the Air Force missions. There are one or two books that have been written about it in the last few years. Everyone was called up at 18.

You had six months at Cambridge, but were you in Archaeology?

I was interested in archaeology, but I was doing English and I had no idea of how to get into Archaeology, no contacts with the Department. I didn't know anything about the Department at that stage. It was only when I came back from War Service in 1947, I read English for another year and then I discovered in the course of the year that I could in fact transfer to Archaeology for the second part of the degree and that you could do Part Two of Archaeology and Anthropology in one year, so that is what I did.

Were you involved in any amateur archaeological societies?

No, not at all. I had no contacts with archaeology of any kind. Of course, there wasn't all that much in Liverpool.

How did you find out about the Tripos?

I remember that I did get the information and then went along to see, I made an appointment with the Professor, who was still Dorothy Garrod, of course. I went along to see her and was duly accepted and sent to Glyn Daniel as a Supervisor.

What were your impressions of Dorothy Garrod?

Oh, well, rather withdrawn person in a way. Didn't get much contact at all. She interviewed me formally.

And then Glyn Daniel?

Oh, well, quite different of course. Really forthcoming, yes. That was 1948. I got back in 1947 and did a year's English Part I and changed over for 1948/49. Glyn, of course, was a very informal character. He used to conduct his supervisions in the nearest pub mainly. He preferred that atmosphere.

Were you both in the same class?

No, not at that stage. Eve came later, a few years later to Cambridge.

How did you get interested in archaeology? [I ask Mrs Evans]

Mrs Evans:
I had been interested since I was a child because I was so surrounded by it that I knew all the people who were working on it at that stage, Roman archaeology especially.

Did you know Charles Phillips? [I ask Prof Evans.]

Prof. Evans:
Oh, yes, indeed. I think from Cambridge. Certainly did meet him.

Who else was in that class?

Gale Sieveking — it was a very small class. Names escape me. Before John Hurst, before almost everybody. There was a man who went into the Welsh Commission, Christopher Holder. He is alive and must be retired by now. There was the great man of the Department — what was his name — Dauncey. He went off to Manchester University. He went to be a Public Relations man or something.

He was interested in Mediaeval history and was at that meeting that Grahame Clark organised at Peterhouse with Steensberg, in 1948, I think.

It was a very small class. There were about half-a-dozen of us, plus anthropologists. There were quite a lot more people doing the full Tripos. I went straight into doing Part II and some of the people in the class were people who had done Part I in Archaeology and come on. There were only about half-a-dozen of those as I say. There were rather more anthropologists who were by then doing Part II Anthropology.

Who would have been there? Do you remember Maureen O'Reilly or had she retired by then?

No, I don't remember her.

Who was the Curator at that point, Bushnell?

Bushnell, yes. Mary Thatcher was there as the Secretary.

Did you have your courses in the Museum?

The lecture rooms were in the Museum at that stage.

Reo Fortune?

Oh, yes, indeed. Oh, yes, Reo Fortune, over a number of years. Later on, when I was back as a Research student and Fellow, he used to buttonhole me and go on to me about the sins of archaeologists. All rather bad.

There is that famous photo of you at Star Carr.

I was there one season, the last season. I was looking at one of the antlers. He included it when he did the revised version of the report, the modular reassessment of Star Carr. He told me that he was going to put that in.

Were you both at Star Carr?

No, Eve didn't go to Cambridge until 1952 or so.

Mrs Evans:
I worked as a Librarian and went up as a mature student scholarship. Nobody in my family had gone to Cambridge.

Some said that Miles Burkitt didn't encourage people to go into archaeology unless they had a private income.

Prof. Evans:
Yes, he said that very strongly; that it wasn't worth it unless you had a private income.

Was that still true in the 1940s and '50s?

Yes, there were very few opportunities really.

So, how do you explain yourselves?

Things began to open up, you see. Although I think my success was due to luck in various ways. First of all being able to get a Fellowship, eventually a Research Fellowship at my own College. That was the first thing. Then, I thought, having got to the third year of that, with no prospects of anything further, I began very seriously to question if it was worth carrying on and I nearly gave it up. I did in fact enter for a competition for the Foreign Office, the Foreign Service. They had, this was a few years after the War and they were having, decided that they might get some people who were mature people, so they had a competition for this and I went for it and was accepted in fact, and it was so — really Grahame Clark who persuaded me not to. He was very good over this. He really was remarkably good. He invited me to dinner at Peterhouse and after dinner, he sort of marched me up and down and talked to me about his own experiences when, quite extraordinary there, he said that he had thought the same thing when he was at my stage and he had very nearly gone into, I think it was the Coal Authority, or something of that sort. Coal definitely. He nearly went into that rather than completing a Ph.D, yes, which I think few people would know. I am sure that he didn't talk about it very much. That certainly influenced me in deciding not to take up that career.

But you had already begun to publish your material in the Proceedings.

Yes, I had.

Did Grahame Clark approach you for that?

Well, I think it was a joint thing in a way. I think Stuart Piggott and Glyn Daniel had told him that it was something that was worthwhile, and he approached me on that basis.

How did you choose your specialisation?

Well, again, I suppose that was Glyn Daniel in a sense, who pushed me into it. I was really willing because I was interested in the Mediterranean archaeology. Glyn suggested that ,after I graduated, that I should do something on, well, he suggested a subject that stemmed from Gordon Childe and Gordon Childe's views of diffusion. Childe had suggested that, what now seems quite fantastic, that a Bronze Age culture in southeastern Spain might have actually come there from Asia Minor, because there were certain resemblances in the burial customs and the equipment, and I took this up largely because, well, it sounded intriguing, but also because it gave me an opportunity of travelling. It meant going to Spain first and it meant going to Turkey. This was 1949. I spent another year at Cambridge before going, after graduating, in order to fill in on all the things that I had had to skimp during the single year, and then I went to Spain, to Madrid University, in 1950. Glyn had partly suggested this to me because he knew I knew Spanish, which I had done at school and taken an interest at Cambridge, belonged to the Spanish Society. So I had a very fascinating year in Spain, but a difficult one because Spain, at that stage, it wasn't many years after the Civil War, it was very isolated, and also of course things hadn't got going in a way, so all the material I needed to see which had been in the Siret collection (Siret had done a lot of work in the 1890s and the early part of this century on the Spanish prehistoric culture of southeast Spain), all that material was in Museum vaults, most of it in Madrid, part of it in Brussels. You couldn't see it in either place, because there was a lawsuit going on with the family. The National Museum of Madrid claimed that he had actually given the material, or that was the understanding, that he had given the material to the Museums. The family said that he hadn't, he intended to sell it, and so there was a great lawsuit going on. So I never saw the Siret material in Spain. You couldn't get at it; and I went to Brussels after that and spent three days there. I talked to the officials, and again they couldn't let me see it, owing to the lawsuit. That was a difficulty, but I did travel around Spain and saw a lot of other material in the southeast. I had some background, and then I was able to get the Fellowship at the British Institute at Ankara and went out to Turkey and had, I must say, a marvellous experience there, travelling around Turkey and going on excavations with the then Director, who was Seton Lloyd. We went to a place called, quite unrelated to the one I was doing, Sultanpepe, he was excavating then. And I went to, in the winter when nothing was happening in Anatolia, I went down to join Kathleen Kenyon in Jericho excavation.

Were those your first excavations? Was Star Carr the first?

No, the first excavation I went on — I hadn't been to Star Carr at that stage, that was after, the first excavation I went on was with Grahame Clark. It was a Roman site at Cottenham. It was an extraordinary thing to think of Grahame excavating a Roman site, but he did it on weekends. That was 1948 and '49. It interested Grahame because it was a Roman site, but it was an industrial site and they had a canal, a Roman period canal, that they seemed to have been transporting coal. The buildings — there weren't any buildings — there were just postholes. It was a very interesting introduction. It made me realise right away that I didn't know anything about digging at all and couldn't see anything. It took time to develop an eye. That was really instructive.

The course work itself wasn't practical, was it?

No, there was no practical work. You were recommended to go on a

weekend dig with somebody and Grahame's was the one that was offered at that stage.

What were the courses?

I did a mixture of courses. I did some in that year which were Part I courses; Burkitt on the Old Stone Age, and then apart from that the second-year courses I went on, I remember Dorothy Garrod, Palaeolithic, which was a very academic course indeed.

Several people were in that course. Some were already research students. I remember Charles McBurney gave lectures and then for the later periods, it was of course Glyn Daniel and Grahame Clark giving the Neolithic. Glyn did the West megaliths and Grahame Clark did Eastern Europe, lecturing on Rumania, etc. DeNavarro was doing the Bronze and Iron Age, which was a quite complete contrast to the others. You spent your time simply scribbling notes, because he had his notes which he read out and you just tried to copy them down verbatim. They were so full of material, and at the same time, he never put any of his illustrations on slides. He just had books and there were masses of these big tomes, and you had to pass them around while you were trying to scribble notes. You, of course, ran up against that later too [addressed to Mrs Evans].

Was he still there when you were there [addressed to Mrs Evans]? *And, Tom Lethbridge?*

Yes, we remember going to both.

Was there an encouragement to get practical, survey experience?

Encouragement, yes, but there were no facilities for it. There were no practical classes. It was all on a very theoretical level. There were lectures about technique and about excavation technique, air photography, but the practical side of it came after that.

Who do you think was the most influential lecturer in terms of ideas?

I think undoubtedly Grahame Clark [both Mrs Evans and Prof Evans say this simultaneously]. Some of his ideas sounded very strange at that time, but he certainly was with the environmental and economic approaches. This was really something that was the cutting edge. I think we all realised that. Grahame was quite an eccentric character, more so then than later, actually. I think he was a bit of a disappointed man at that stage. He thought he ought to be at a higher level than he was in the Department because he obviously felt that he had the ability and the ideas to really do something, and he was just a Lecturer in the Department.

He was waiting for his Professorship?

Yes, he never said anything about this, but one felt that he was unfulfilled. He wasn't fulfilled before he got the Chair.

Getting back to Glyn Daniel and how he influenced you to work in Spain. What happened after that?

Well, you see, I was trying to establish the link, supposed link, between Spain and Asia Minor, and of course before I had been very long in Turkey, I realised that this was just not on at all. You couldn't go that way. What you had were similarities, certainly, but they didn't imply any direct contact at all. This came out rather strongly.

Where did Childe introduce that?

I think he mentioned it in the *Dawn* and later — certainly he had put it forward once or twice as remarkable parallels. There might be a link there, thinking in terms of long distance. In a way I was in a pretty desperate situation at that stage. I realised what I had been working for two years was really getting nowhere, and it was very fortunate that I was sent to Malta after that. I came back from Turkey with no thesis, as it were, and with my research grant running out; and Glyn Daniel said "Well, there is some money that has been given to do a survey of prehistoric monuments and Stuart Piggott is one of the Commissioners [the other one was the Director of the School at Rome] and they want someone to appoint an assistant to do the work. So, why don't you try. Ring Stuart Piggott," whom I had never met. So I did, and he agreed to take me on. I suppose Glyn had talked to him about me beforehand. He took me on, and I went out to Malta that year. That was 1952. I went to Spain in 1950, Turkey in 1951. Well, for the start, the basic thing was to go over and prepare for publication all the material that been gathered on Malta previously. It was essentially a sort of corpus that was in the Malta Museum but, in fact, after a little time, I began to see some light in Malta — Malta had been one of the great mysteries, you see, great megalithic temples. They'd been studied for quite a long time. The Zamit Temple had been excavated, and others as well, but they hadn't come up with any real chronology for the whole thing. Basically what they said then was Neolithic 3000 BC, Bronze Age 2000 BC. After several months I began to see that I thought I could arrange the Neolithic in some sort of order, some sort of stages, and that I could see a possible development in the temples that would correspond to that, and so this essentially is what I wrote up for the Prehistoric Society.

Was Grahame Clark helpful in terms of editing?

Oh, well, he was the Editor, so he was the one who accepted it and sorted through it.

[I ask something inaudible about who had influenced him to think as he did?]

I suppose the course generally — part of the basics.

Were you a bit on your own in Malta?

Yes, I suppose one was left to one's own devices. Yes, I was alone. Well, I was working in the Museum and employed by the University, but in fact I was just doing it on my own. New plans for the temple were being prepared with the money which the Interuniversity Council for Higher Education in the Colonies had been given to Malta University for architectural students of the University so I had that help; and I had to look at the drafts of the plans and correct them, putting in the significant details and take out everything that they — the architectural students obviously knew nothing about archaeology and ended up doing what they saw on the ground, and I had to go in and sort it out from the archaeological view point of view.

That seems like a good time to be entering archaeology.

It was, because nobody took majoring in prehistory seriously, because the techniques employed by Mediterranean archaeologists at that time were fairly rudimentary. Most of them were Classicists, mainly interested in the Classical, and those who weren't Classicists were dealing with the Palaeolithic and cave art and things like that, and everything in between, you hit a pretty low priority. In Northern Europe there was a tendency to look down on it — "Well, that is not serious". Only Northern European prehistory is serious. This was because technically it was so much more advanced. So in a sense I was in a vacuum. And that was an advantage, in the end, because I was able to get something of a reputation, you see, as somebody who knew about Mediterranean prehistory. There wasn't anybody else.

Did that happen almost by chance?

It wasn't plotted or planned, but I supposed they realised that it was an opportunity.

[I ask something obscure about the opportunity.]

I did indeed. It was a great opportunity.
     I also came back from Malta after that work and had my final year in Cambridge, in which I wrote up the thesis, where I managed to bring together pretty well everything I was supposed to be doing before. Malta allowed me to sort of put the other things together, so I was able to bring in Spain and Turkey in what I suppose now would be looked at

as a rather diffusionist interpretation of the Neolithic and Bronze Ages, but from the point of view, whereas you couldn't — my attitude to this was that you could not link the ends of the Mediterranean and think of people over enormous areas, but if you started thinking of it in terms of what is referred to as 'culture creep', smaller movements, then there was a continuous link across the Mediterranean and this was what I argued in my thesis and subsequently in my inaugural lecture at London.

Was that your term?

No, not my term. It was a term used by anthropologists at that time. I had heard it in the context of anthropological discussions. It was something that American anthropologists tended to talk about. The Americans were dealing with the diffusion of traits from one cultural group to another and it was in this context that they talked about 'culture creep'.

[I say something I can not hear well enough to transcribe.]

It was the first time that I was getting somewhere and really doing something. I was lucky in the sense that, having spent a year, the first year, in Malta and got the results I got, I was able to use that as part of my application to Pembroke College for a Research Fellowship for three years, 1953 to '56.

After Star Carr.

Star Carr came, perhaps it was 1950. I remember going out there. I was back from somewhere, probably when I got back from Spain. It was when I was mostly living abroad, but I was back for the summer.

What did you learn from Star Carr?

Well, obviously, it was a model excavation. It was the sort of excavation that hadn't happened before, particularly in the use of all these environmental techniques, and having specialists, like having the British Museum specialists on the spot with their pressure chambers to deal with the antler and bone that was coming out, and the pollen people taking samples. It was something very new at that time and one certainly learned a lot from that but not, unfortunately, the sort of thing that I could use in the Mediterranean at that time, because the conditions were wrong. Mediterranean climate makes it very difficult to do, particularly collect pollen or anything of that kind, and also the facilities were lacking. So, it was a great sort of experience for the future, but immediately it wasn't an immediate relevance. I had to continue doing it essentially the hard way as it were, the pottery and the stones.

End of side 1

Yes, well, of course Malta was a great experience. The feeling of having been able to achieve something is a great thing, you know, but then of course I came back to the question of having to find a job.

What year again is that?

I was working in Malta in 1952 to '54. I got my Fellowship in 1953, and I spent part of the time in Cambridge and part of the time in Malta. Then 1954 and '55, I was back in Cambridge and doing some teaching for the Department. I gave a course in Mediterranean prehistory. That was a thing they hadn't got. Grahame asked me to that.

[I comment that the Institute today has such courses but Cambridge still doesn't (or something to that effect). I ask Mrs Evans about her experience at Newnham and her interest in archaeology.]

Mrs Evans:
There wasn't at that stage any possibility of going to university.

Prof Evans:
Really there was no way of getting to university. It was really the same for me. I was quite surprised to end up in university. We came from backgrounds where you didn't expect it. I belong to the first generation of my

family to have more than an elementary education. Things have changed enormously in the course of this century.

Mrs Evans:
Girls didn't go on to university.

How did you come by your scholarship?

Prof Evans (to Mrs Evans):
You were a Librarian in Shrewsbury at that time.

[I can't hear the answer — something about people disagreeing or not understanding even a university education when she already had a job. I mention how extraordinary the few women were who ended up at Newnham, how exceptional they had to be.]

Prof Evans (to Mrs Evans):
Well, you could have gone to the Institute in London. You had the choice of two and you turned the Institute down.

Who was your Tutor?

Mrs Evans:
Glyn Daniel.

Prof Evans:
Yes, you see Glyn was Tutor for a lot, he was the Director of Studies for a lot of Colleges because most Colleges didn't have an archaeologist, not a prehistorian. So he came to be the man. You see there was no Director of Studies in Pembroke in Archaeology. That was why I was sent to Glyn Daniel. He coped with Pembroke, with people.

Mrs Evans, did you choose the Tripos?

Mrs Evans:
Yes, I had done Roman archaeology you see before I came up. I wanted to continue.

How did you meet?

Prof Evans:
We met in Cambridge, in fact. She was in my Mediterranean courses.

It must have been a very exciting course and Tripos.

I was only giving one course. I never had a post in the Department. They simply took advantage of the fact that I had a Research Fellowship at Pembroke and was available.

Were you one of the first people to take the full course?

I didn't take Part I but you could take Part II without taking Part I still but a year or two after that, they changed it and made it necessary to take the full course. Well, I think after that you could take Part I but you couldn't skip Part I and take Part II. They changed it. Part I ran for two years and Part II one year and then they changed it to Part I one year and Part II two years which was really the best, the logical way around.

Did anybody discourage you from going into Archaeology?

Oh, indeed yes. [They both say this!]

Mrs Evans:
A lot of people were horrified. There were no jobs.

Prof Evans:
It is not a Profession .

Your family?

Well, my parents, they were very good and they supported me over this,

but they were very worried because they didn't see what I was going on. Some of their friends whose reaction was "What is archaeology?"

Did you have that reaction as well? [I ask Mrs Evans].

Mrs Evans:
No, not quite.

Prof Evans:
In Lincoln you won't.

Mrs Evans:
I had taken my exams for Librarianship and then going on to another subject you see, people just didn't see the point.

What was it like at Newnham in the 1950s? You were full members of the University by then.

Prof Evans (to Mrs Evans):
You lived in a separate house at Newnham. By the time I got to know you.

[Inaudible bit]

Did you still have very small classes?

Mrs Evans:
Oh yes, very small. I think there were about three girls. [Inaudible bit]

[Inaudible bit about Glyn Daniel and Grahame Clark as lecturers]

Prof Evans:
He had a rough exterior at times.

Mrs Evans:
People were frightened of him.

Prof Evans:
Yes, they were, he was formidable. Even when he wasn't Professor.

[I ask if Clark was helpful or something to that effect.]

At that stage, no, much more so later, I think. He was really tied up with his own work, and as I say was not feeling totally happy about his position.

Once he got the Professorship —

It made an enormous difference and he began then to expand his interests. He always gave the impression, I don't think that this is true, but he always gave the impression that he was really sort of buried in the Mesolithic in Northern Europe when in fact his interests were broader, but it didn't show that much at that stage.

Did he ever talk to you about his philosophy about how archaeology should be taught at every level of education, as something good for humanity? Because he does in his published work. Did that come through in his teaching? About the social value of archaeology?

Yes, he does in his published work. I don't know that he talked very much about it in lectures.

Did either one of you feel intellectually influenced by him?

Oh, yes, indeed, he was challenging. It was the approach to archaeology. I don't think that I got much about the cultural value of archaeology from his talks, from his books, yes, but from his lectures and so on it was mainly the intellectual stimulation, the feeling that he got over that things really were going ahead and exciting things were happening — the link with Godwin, of course, and the pollen side of things, and the link with zoology, and all the environmental background, which was something that seemed very new then; and in fact he and Godwin had pioneered this in the 1930s with the Fenland Research Committee, but this came over to us as very stimulating.

You were saying in the car earlier something about Miles Burkitt and how he differed. Would you put some of that on tape about his attitudes?

To students, yes. Well, I think that Miles Burkitt's attitude was very kind indeed and very, very helpful. I mean, he threw his library open to any of us who wanted to use it. But it was, in some ways it was like a throw-back to the 19th century. It was the moneyed man with leisure pursuing his interests, and sharing his interests with you, but regarding the whole thing as something that was not a profession where people could earn your living.

He would talk about that to his students, that it was not a formal thing.

Yes, it was absolutely that sort of thing. You got this atmosphere — it was very much on the informal level, and his lectures were very much on the informal level too. Whereas with Grahame it was a very much more professional approach. As I say, I don't remember him talking very much about values as such in the general way, but you got the seriousness of the approach and the professional standards of the approach. That, I think, came over, and I found this very much a contrast when I went to the Institute. I was — I found that a very different atmosphere because at that stage the Institute's attitude was, seemed to be, that it was training professionals. I think this was Wheeler. Of course, this was the Wheeler legacy. It didn't apply to Gordon Childe, obviously, but the Wheeler legacy was very much there. If you were going to train a few people who were going to become professionals, and it was a limited business, and this reflected itself in the attitude that you shouldn't do this at first degree level. That was why they had a postgraduate diploma. This was something that Wheeler had opted for, and it was an attitude very much shared by Kathleen Kenyon and others on the Institute staff, that this was an Institute for training professionals in the sort of narrow sense, people who were going to be diggers, excavators and who were going to have jobs, yes. So you won't train too many of them. You would just take a small number, and I think that is the contrast to Clark's professionalism. His was much more academic in a sense. And much more linked to academic values. I found this interested me, because in a sense I felt it was a theme that went right through my time at the Institute; because I felt first of all that it was important to establish archaeology as a profession. Something that had the respect as a profession, but at the same time if you went on down that road entirely and you just trained professionals, a small number of professionals, then archaeology was useless, and to change attitudes on the part of people that the appreciation of the immense length of human history that is only known from archaeology is something you have to get across. So this was really, I suppose ,what I felt most strongly that one had to do, and to do this you had to change the postgraduate diploma at the Institute to a degree course. You had to have a degree course, and this took years.

Was that your initiative?

Well, I was certainly behind it. Yes, I certainly pushed it very strongly before I became Director, and after I became Director, it had — already the battle had been won, but it wasn't until 1969 that we were able to get a degree course, a first degree course, at the Institute, and partly it was you had some people on the staff who were very much against it, like Kathleen Kenyon, but also, and Wheeler himself, who was a member of the Management Committee for the Institute at that time. But also you had a fairly widespread prejudice against it, against the idea of a first degree in the university at large, you know. I think these were mostly people who had taken their cue from Wheeler himself, but in fact it was very difficult. Whenever you raised it in any committee in the University, it was always "Oh, but Wheeler opted for a postgraduate diploma and that is the right place, archaeology as postgraduate activity." It took — we tried when quite soon when I was there. Peter Grimes, who was the Director then, put it forward in the university that he would like the course and it was slapped down, and he never dared to bring it up again for years.

Did Grimes come out of Cambridge?

No, he came from Cardiff University. In fact he was a pupil of Wheeler. And he followed Wheeler in his jobs right through. Wheeler was in the National Museum and taught archaeology at Cardiff or the University of Wales, and Grimes was a student at that stage, and then succeeded him in his post when Wheeler went to the Museum; and then Wheeler, when Wheeler left the Museum of London, and Grimes became his successor there. And then his successor as Director of the Institute. Right through!

[I say something about Grimes being critical of Wheeler's work.]

Oh, yes, he was. There was no love lost between them.

[I say something inaudible about Grimes.]

No, I don't know what his first degree was in, but it certainly wasn't archaeology. Cambridge and Edinburgh were the only places.

    You see the Institute in London began, it opened its doors in 1933. It didn't have any doors in 1933 because it had no locus but it started teaching as a notional institute at that stage, with its two first students being Lady Mallowan (Barbara Parker) and Mrs Maxwell Hyslop.

[I mention that I believe (Barbara Parker?) someone (inaudible) had died.]

Yes, I thought perhaps she had. I couldn't quite remember. They were the first students.

[I mention that I will try to reach the other.]

That would be useful.

How did you get to the Institute?

That is a curious story. Gordon Childe was retiring. He had been Director of the Institute and Professor of European Archaeology, the number two post, in one, and he had been elected as Director in 1945, perhaps even before then, at the end of the War, but began functioning really in 1945. He had reached the time in 1956, well he hadn't quite, rather magnanimously because it was his whole life, he decided to retire a year early, because he knew that the Institute was about to move from Regent's Park to the new building, and he wanted to allow the new Director the chance to make all the arrangements, so he almost condemned himself to death; because he committed suicide a year afterwards, saying that there was nothing left for him. So the post came up in 1956. I wasn't that primed for it — Gordon Childe, a great man — the Professorship. I hadn't held any teaching post at all. Suddenly Glyn Daniel said to me one day, "Why don't you apply?" I said, "I can't do that! This is ridiculous." I wasn't even a well-established archaeologist. And he said "Well, try. Have a word with Grahame." Grahame Clark was on the Committee. So I went to Grahame and said, you see, "Glyn has suggested to me that I apply and I consider that to be crazy and I can't possibly do this." He said "Well, I don't know. You might" and encouraged me to do it. Finally I did make an application out in great trepidation, and I left it so late that it was the last day, more or less, and I had to travel up to London with this application and hand it in at the Senate House, which came as a great shock, getting into the Senate House, I thought I had gotten into a bank. It was so unlike any building in Cambridge. Anyway, I handed this thing in and, well, it went on from there.

I wonder who competed with you?

Well it was, I felt quite embarrassed about it because it was, several of us were interviewed. And there was Richard Atkinson, names escape me, Humphrey Case and Terence Powell.

[I ask something about Terence Powell — was he from Ireland?]

Yes but he had been in Cambridge, of course. He was a student of Grahame's. He was in Liverpool, and I had been sent up by Glyn to talk to him when I first started to read archaeology, being from Liverpool.

What was your impression of him? I don't know anything about him.

Oh, he was delightful man, quite small, very Irish and great sense of humour, and a great deal of knowledge, too. In fact, I actually had worked with him. I think it was the same summer I went to Star Carr. He was doing some barrows up near Bolton.

The Professorship — that was your first job?

Yes, that was my first job. And then I stayed at the Institute for the rest of my career.

At that point when you got the Professorship — how was that?

Ah, yes, well when I took over, I had to take over my first year the whole of Gordon Childe's lecturing commitments, which I think amounted to about 120 lectures. Having never given lectures — only gave the odd course in my own speciality, it came as quite a shock. I found myself giving an introduction to Social Anthropology because Childe had done it.

Did he leave you any notes?

He left some notes, yes, but they were written in a very Childean hand which you couldn't read. They weren't all that useful. At the Institute there are some notes.

What did you do?

Well, I had to just scramble through the best I could, which was quite an ordeal; but I got through it and then gradually I modified things a bit to my own taste, but still giving a very wide number of lectures.

[I ask something about his teaching, his specialisation — inaudible.]

Well, not really, no. I didn't really give a specialist course on Mediterranean prehistory until I became Director and gave up the more general teaching, but what we did start doing was expanding the staff as soon as we could. Because when I went to the Institute, it was all chiefs and no Indians. It was very much, it was four Professors and practically no Lecturers.

Who were they?

Oh, I was the Prehistorian and then Kathleen Kenyon, Max Mallowan was Professor of Western Asian Archaeology, with Kathleen Kenyon as his Lecturer, Roman archaeology. Wheeler had retired the year before and was succeeded by Shepherd Frere, and then Zeuner was the environmentalist.

When did Zeuner come, do you know?

He came before the War. He actually came over as a refugee from Germany, because his wife was Jewish. He wasn't Jewish, but his wife was. And he was dismissed, he had a Chair, Professorship at Breslau, and he was dismissed and came over. He was provided with money by the Refugee Council. There was a British Academic Council for refugees which provided money for academics to allow them to continue teaching, and Wheeler, who was then trying to get a staff together for the Institute with practically no funding, took Zeuner on to teach what then was called geochronology. That is how he started before the War, and he went on, and then after the War, they created a Chair for him. They created several Chairs at the Institute. Childe's Chair as Professor of European Archaeology was created then. Max Mallowan's Chair as Western Asiatic Archaeology was part-time then and that was created, and also one for Wheeler. His was Roman, well it was interesting, it wasn't Roman Archaeology as such, it was the Archaeology of the Roman Provinces; and the reason for this was peculiar to the London situation, that the University College had a Professor of Classical Archaeology, Robertson, in fact the oldest Professorship of Classical Archaeology in this country, and therefore, the Institute was founded on the basis that it wouldn't encroach on anything the University College already taught, so Wheeler had to invent a title for his Chair which didn't appear to encroach on Classical Roman Archaeology, and so he chose Archaeology of the Roman Provinces. Now, of course, since the Institute has gone back into University College, the Yates Chair, which

was the University College Chair, has been succeeded to by the Professor of Roman Provinces at the Institute, so the whole thing has been unified. It is very curious indeed. I think it is very appropriate and a very good thing that the Institute was in a sense forced by circumstances to combine with University College, because it resolved the anomalous circumstances. Classical, Egyptology, Mediaeval Archaeology, which were all taught in University College, have now become part of the Institute too, and covers the whole range.

The curriculum for the Institute is very broad .

Oh, yes, we, that is partly due to Peter Grimes and his attitude, backed up by me and others, of expanding as fast as we could when the going was good in the late 1950s, 1960s and the beginning of the 1970s; because, as I said, the original staff was very unbalanced. There were four Professors and only about one or two Lecturers, and what we did was to expand during that time and build up the Faculty so that it became much bigger than Cambridge. Cambridge was always relatively small.

Why was it kept small?

This, in a sense, was Grahame. This was where Grahame was, Grahame's weakness. He rather despised that sort of development. We are the best. We are the best academically and we don't need to expand, and that was rather his view and he didn't push development, which I think was a pity.

And Clark thought of archaeology as prehistory.

And, of course, in Cambridge it is a bit more, there are problems also because Western Asia is separate, in a separate Faculty. So is Classical Archaeology, and I think that is a discipline issue there. This is something that obviously Grahame didn't feel he needed to do.

Institutionally, Cambridge is prehistoric archaeology.

Yes, he really was the person who moulded the Department.

Yes, I think so. [I ask about his work in Malta.]

Yes. I had really finished my work in Malta by 1956, so I was looking around for something then; and I was approached by Sinclair Wood, who was then Director of the British School in Athens, who said that he would like to begin as part of his programme of excavation at Knossos, he wanted to begin doing a Neolithic excavation, and he wondered if I would take it on. So I jumped at that, because Neolithic Greece was what I always wanted to do and I hadn't had the opportunity to do it so I went — we [Mrs Evans agrees as to the date] went out for the first time in 1958. From 1958 to 1960, we worked there and published the results in 1964. Then, after finishing that particular work, which had been very interesting because, you see, we were able to, for the first time, show what the Neolithic culture was like there. We knew it existed, because there had been a few samplings, but all there was, was a sort of pottery sequence, which we were able very much to define and also to show the development of the settlement itself and to show that at the bottom there was actually an aceramic level, which was something that hadn't obviously been suspected before.

This was in 1959?

This was '58, '59, '60. And then I was occupied by the writing up of it, and the British School then approached me to, said that one of its bright students at the British School, by the name of Colin Renfrew, had been working on the Early Bronze Age but had discovered a Neolithic site which he wanted to excavate, and they thought he ought to have someone associated with, well in fact he had to have someone associated with him, because the Greek authorities insisted that you had to have someone senior from the university; a doctoral, working on his Ph.D couldn't do this alone. So I said yes. Colin and I excavated Saliagos in 1964, '65. Then I felt unhappy that we hadn't really fully explored Knossos Neolithic, so I put up a project to go back to Knossos and do some more work, particularly on the West Court, which hadn't been touched before, and we did that in 1969 and 1970.

Who was we? [I expected a long list.]

Mrs Evans and me [laughter]. We were a team.

You worked together from the beginning?

Yes, we did.

Did the Tripos prepare you? [I ask Mrs Evans]

Mrs Evans:
Yes —

Prof. Evans:
She had already done her own excavations before going to Cambridge.

[I say something inaudible.]

Yes, she had experience. Actually, as a Librarian, you were also in charge of a Museum [to Mrs Evans].

Mrs Evans (quietly):
Yes, I was the Director of the Museum.

How did that work with your work at the Institute? [I ask Prof Evans.]

I had vacation, which was the only time you could get the students to form the team.

[My question is inaudible.]

I think we were very lucky with these opportunities coming up. One thing followed from another. The point was that Sinclair Hood approached me because he knew my work in Malta, and that I was interested in Mediterranean prehistory which — there really weren't many people around at that stage who were, and I was the only person he could approach.

You were the specialist. Did you train Colin Renfrew?

No, no, he had done his degree at Cambridge already and was doing his Ph.D, his research. But he hadn't done his own excavation before. So we all worked together on that, with a team partly London and partly Cambridge, partly others as well.

It is a small world [inaudible bits here]. Was Jane Renfrew there?

Yes, she was on the excavation. I can't remember what stage she was at then. I think she just finishing her degree, or just finished and hadn't started research, but she was just about to.

Tape 1 side 2 ends

Tape 2 side 1
[17 August 2000 continued, recorded at his home in Shaftesbury. Mrs Evans was not present for the second tape.]

Professor Evans, you were just discussing your experiences at the Institute.

Well, I think we had a favourable situation at that stage, because universities were the flavour of the decade. Money was coming for universities and university expansion. This began after the War and accelerated very much in the sixties and the seventies, well fifties and sixties really. The seventies was when it stopped. I think Peter Grimes' policy was very much to expand as much as possible, and I and others had backed him up in this. This is what we did. We thought we had to get the infrastructure. That meant developing the Departments, getting more people in at the more junior level, lecturers, assistants. And, then eventually we got down to the question of back-up staff, other back-up staff too, technical assistants and ultimately secretaries. We just got to secretaries when the tide turned. In

the 1970s things began to get bad and difficult. And the government at that stage, it isn't often remembered, but it wasn't the Thatcher government that started the cuts in universities. It was the Labour government previously. I remember this very well indeed. They didn't do it in the brutal way that the Thatcher government did, but they had to. The economic situation was bad and they thought they had to cut down on universities, but of course the animus came in with the appearance of the Thatcher government, who really were intent on giving universities a bad time, I think, as part of their general programme. I felt I came in just at the wrong point, really. Peter Grimes had all the expansion. When I came to be Director in 1973, we were just facing the beginning of cuts which went on right through my time, getting worse as they went on. The Institute, of course, from 1980 and beyond, the Institute suffered very badly. This was one of the reasons why we came to eventually to consider proposing joining with University College, because we had a large number of foreign students, particularly students from Third World countries. We had the tradition of taking these to train them. We'd take them on the recommendation of their Departments of Antiquities or universities and train them, but of course they couldn't afford the fees, when the fees came in; and when the Thatcher government came in, of course they — the previous government had already introduced fees for foreign students, but only at a relatively low level. When the Thatcher government came in — they said immediately they were going to estimate the full amount of fees that should be paid by the foreign students at any particular university or college, and they would then deduct that from the grant given to that institution. Now we were a small institution, with a turnover at that stage of about maybe a million a year, and we lost several hundred thousand pounds this way. It was something that was very difficult to face up to. Well, we did actually manage to replace that money, but only by taking people who could afford to pay fees, and that meant taking on a completely different range of students and not necessarily the ones that we have given priority to, set by their departments. But we did manage to replace that; but then again, at the same time, we were getting progressive cuts from the university, having to cut us down because its funds were getting cut, and getting very savage cuts from that and I was told at one point, "Well, you're going to have to lose a member of staff a year". I said "Well, we can't." It was impossible because if we did that, the Institute would be ruined in a very short time and won't be what it pretends to be at all. You wouldn't have the range or anything, and that really was the stage at which we thought we'd better open negotiations with University College to see if we can come under their wing. As a small institution we simply can't face up to it, whereas University College, you see with its size, it had provisions for helping Departments which did well at the expense of Departments which were going downhill, losing staff and so on. You had a flexibility, compensation. So we did join University College, and by the time I left we were in balance. Of course it had the added academic benefits too, that it was possible to bring together the specialist Departments of Archaeology in University College with the other Departments in the Institute. The whole thing, I think, has had a good — very beneficial all around, coming out of the troubledness of the 1980s.

Was that the most difficult time?

That was absolutely the most difficult time. The period from when I went to the Institute up to 1970 was the period of prosperity and expansion. We always knew that we were going to get enough to cover our costs for the year, and probably a bit more as well, so we could think in terms of some sort of expansion, but then the whole thing changed and we were being cut down, having to cut down all the time.

Could you say something about how you were elected to the Directorship?

Yes, well, this was curious. One would expect the post to be generally elected, but in fact it was not. The then Principal of the University said that it should be [inaudible] but in fact they went around and checked with all the Heads of the Departments and asked if they wanted the job and they turned it down. And he came to me and I said well, I would, yes, because the Institute had been my life at that stage, and I had very strong ideas about the way the Institute should go and so I was prepared to do it, although I knew that it was going to be difficult, academically.

You came after Grimes, and who took your place in the Professorship? Or did you keep it?

No, I didn't, no. I couldn't keep the Professorship, because the post was divided after Gordon Childe retired, because they said it was too big a job. The Professorship was then advertised, and Roy Hodson, who was in fact my second in the Department, got the job. We had quite a brilliant field, but he got it, to my great pleasure.

After you worked with Colin Renfrew, what happened?

That was the mid sixties, but then I went back to Knossos for seasons in 1969 and 1970 and more or less brought the Knossos excavations to a stage where I thought they couldn't be taken further without massive financial support and quite difficult logistics, and so I left it at that; and then of course when I became Director, I wasn't in a position to do a great deal of excavating. I did do some in Portugal in 1972, and the Segovia evaluation, but after that I didn't really do any excavations.

How long were you at the Institute?

All together from — it was over 30 years, 33 years. One thing which I was very pleased about after I became Director, again it was a stroke of luck in a sense, we had always run field courses which had been run by various people with students taking part in various ways, but at that stage in 1973, they were just setting the rescue archaeology units in the country, various rescue, local units in the country, and one or two universities had a link with this; and Geoff Wainwright who was then running the — who was fairly senior in the English Heritage, it wasn't English Heritage at that stage, but in what became English Heritage — suggested to me that we might take up a unit of this kind, and I was rather anxious to have one, in fact, and I said, yes, indeed. He said he got somebody who was an excavator with the Department at that stage and he would be a very good person to have, so, yes, indeed. So we set up the Sussex Archaeological Field Unit with Peter Drewett as the Head of it, so that was, it started as the Sussex Archaeological Field Unit and then gradually developed. It became eventually the Institute unit and was doing work in lots of places besides Sussex, Hong Kong and Barbados and various places, and that of course still goes on. That was very nice, because it took care of what before was more difficult to arrange. We had always run field courses because we felt that it was part of the Wheeler tradition and it was necessary to have field-trained students. But this provided us an excellent way of getting that, and we had very happy collaboration with the local Sussex archaeologists, with the Archaeological Society there, which was very well endowed, and with the museums and county archaeologists.

It is one of the oldest Societies.

One of the oldest and one of the richest, yes, Societies. They had a lot of means, various bequests. So that worked very well indeed. Of course, it eventually something very spectacular, in Boxgrove man.

Oh, I didn't know that!

Well, it was done essentially by the Unit. Eventually it was set up with a unit of its own, but it was started with our unit and then went on to become a unit of its own, with one of our ex-students in charge. That was Roberts, who worked there.

When you were talking about the Institute, from my observations when I visited there, was the internationalism of the student body and that it cuts across class. When I first visited England it was for the Childe Conference at the Institute, and I was struck by that.

Oh, I know, yes, the Childe Conference —

Is that a conscious policy?

Yes, I think it is. We attempted to be very cosmopolitan. Our Admissions Tutor was very keen on keeping that.

Is that unusual?

I don't think so. Certainly not in London. Certainly not at places like University College, which essentially was founded very much on the principle of education of all.

[I say something about the Cambridge comparison — inaudible bit.]

Yes, different, although I must say I find a lot of the fuss going on now about this discrimination in entry to Cambridge — I mean I had no difficulty in getting in, and as far as I could see when I was at Pembroke they did their best.

I find that at Lucy now.

The real problem is, of course, you see, with places like Oxford and Cambridge, they are relatively small. After all, London University has about 30,000 people. Oxford and Cambridge don't have this, but they have the prestige. So naturally the competition is great. [One sentence inaudible.] There was no reason in my own case that they should have taken me, except purely academic reasons.

[I mention that after the War there were a number of people coming in from the 'working class' who had come to Cambridge in the early 1950s, Merrick Posnansky, John Hurst — no, not John Hurst.]

No, not John Hurst.

Jack Golson, Sylvia Hallam.

Yes, there were a lot of people. I think from what I saw at the time after the War, the mix was considerable.

The War?

That must have helped, because a lot of people came back who had been there before or who may have been sent on short courses by the RAF or something like that ,and came back to finish there. It had some effect. I don't think it was overwhelming. I think there was a mix anyway. I certainly got that impression when I went up during the War. Actually many people were taking off after their first year, but they were coming up in preparation, and certainly there was quite a variety at that time.

There is a major change recently. [Inaudible]

I mean I think on the whole, it was, can't say exactly, it was opportunity in a sense, in my day there was still hardly any posts, very few posts, so you weren't going into it necessarily with the idea of becoming a professional. You couldn't do that, and you were told that. But then there were very few people in the Department, very small Department, but then the expansion went hand-in-hand with the expansion of jobs. The money for universities was symptomatic of what was happening. Universities were expanding, and university departments expanded, and therefore jobs in universities expanded. The Ministry of Works and Directorate of Ancient Monuments expanded too. Museums expanded because there was money for it, and so on. Things worked together. Obviously, as you add more jobs and more departments, you got more coming up.

In 1950, you didn't know if you had a future.

No. Oh, no.

So what motivated you?

Well, hope really. There was a feeling that you would probably end up in something else.

But —

But this was your interest, so you went on and hoped to get somewhere. As I was saying earlier, some times you got very despairing. But I think there was a process after the War; and also you must take into account in thinking about the popularity of archaeology, Glyn Daniel and Mortimer Wheeler's show Animal, Vegetable, Mineral. That had an enormous effect in increasing interest among everybody, but among young people in particular.

Somebody should do a biography of Glyn Daniel.

Yes, somebody ought to. He was significant, and could have been more significant. Glyn, by the way, was very proud of the fact that he had come from a fairly humble background and made it. In the context of what Burkitt was saying to us all at that time, I mean, it was interesting that Glyn had come up earlier than this, in the beginning of the 1930s, and had managed to make it into a job. Mind you, well, there was the War between and he had become a very exotic Wing Commander in the RAF in the meantime. Still, it was something to end up in any archaeological post.

Interruption in tape

Prof. Evans will now talk about international cooperation.

Well, something I was led naturally into by my interests and contacts with other countries; but during the time I was Director I began to get involved with various international initiatives, partly through Grahame Clark; because, for instance, Grahame Clark was invited on to a committee about 1973–4. The European Science Commission established archaeologists for the limited job of surveying scientific cooperation in Europe and the facilities for it, and Grahame was busy with other things so he didn't want to stay on it, and he suggested me, and asked me if I might do it. I took it on, and found it extremely interesting, stayed on it in fact until it broke up.

Who sponsored this?

It was not the European Union, but the Council of Europe. It was their Science Foundation, which is a permanent body they have, but they established an archaeological committee for a number of years for this specific job, and I found that extremely interesting; and also I'd been with the International Union of Prehistoric and Protohistoric Sciences, eventually became the President of that in the 1980s.

That was very much in line with Grahame Clark's work.

Yes, very much indeed. I suppose in a sense, although I never specifically was a Cambridge student of Grahame's, except going to his lectures, in a sense I suppose he has been very influential, looking back on it.

Yes. I wonder, was your wife involved all this time as well?

Well, when we were excavating, yes. She was also very much involved with the students. We had so many social things to organise, entertaining lecturers and that sort of thing.

You would have had people from all over the world.

Yes, we had people from everywhere, well, visitors for scientific reasons, also people coming to lecture. The university sponsored some lecture courses which we ran a number of years, until the university became too poor to do it any more, but we still got lots of visiting people, of course, who were interesting.

I notice how broad the Faculty is.

In the Institute. Yes. Well, we tried to keep that. Of course, the basis was there in the founding of the Environmental Department with Zeuner, and of the Conservation Department.

Zeuner worked at a Department as well as in the Institute?

Oh, no, he was in the Institute. His Department was always part of the Institute. Yes, it started as geochronology, and then it became the Department of Environmental Archaeology.

He was a very important man.

Oh, Zeuner, yes, a key person I think, absolutely.

He worked with Desmond Clark in Africa.

Yes, he worked widely.

Did he and Grahame Clark know each other?

Oh, yes, well in archaeology, you couldn't not, in a sense. It was still such a small world. They couldn't help to know each other pretty well.

When I was interviewing Stuart Piggott, he said "Oh yes, we all knew each other. We were all friends — or enemies."

Yes, that's right, and everyone knew everyone else and in a sense tolerated everybody else.

It worked.

Yes. I think this must have helped.

Did it help advance archaeology, to have it that small? Was there something in the smallness that —

No, I can't say that. I don't think so. Well, at least, the close cooperation between the people involved did help to advance it, but of course the very restricted financial base, which was the reason for it being so small certainly didn't help to advance archaeology.

Was it very competitive?

No, I am really thinking that it restricted what people could do. The excavations were often very inadequate, very small, because you hadn't got the funds. I mean, after the War this was the case. When I put up my ideas about Maltese prehistory and Stuart Piggott and the Director of the British School at Rome were both keen to see some excavation, I said I thought excavation could prove or disprove it, and John Ward Perkins, who was the Director of the British School at Rome —

Ward Perkins — he must have been quite elderly?

No; he was older than Stuart. He had been through the War.

Was he older than Grahame Clark?

No — but anyway, Ward Perkins was very proud of himself because he managed to persuade the BBC to produce £250 pounds so that I could do some excavation on the basis that we, he and Stuart Piggott and I, all gave talks for a programme, which we duly did. You see, that was the situation. There was no money for excavation then. The British Academy had no funds for research. Wheeler created the British Academy Research Fund later, in the beginning of the 1960s.

How did he do that?

He went to the Gulbenkian Foundation, and he managed to persuade them to give him some money for a trial to see, believe it or not, if there was a market for research in the Arts, which they did; and in three years he was able to show the government that there was. You see, before that they just said, "Well the Arts, you know, all you need is a seat, a library, paper and ink".

So he began that.

Yes, British Academy grants, yes. Most of the people in the British Academy at that stage were quite content with paper and pencil and a seat in the library. It was the archaeologists who wanted the money, and of course took the money, which didn't make them altogether popular with the British Academy.

It is good that we have that on tape, because Wheeler is very important.

Very important. Have you read his book on the British Academy, on his time at the British Academy?

No, what is the name?

It is one that isn't known very much, because it is published by the British Academy and not circulated. I'll look it up.

In the 1970s?

Yes, it was published in the 1970s. It is a very candid account of his time at the Academy and what he did. He said when he went there, the Academy consisted mainly of old gentlemen whose main occupation was keeping other old gentlemen out of the Academy.

I'll read that with interest.

It was a very good effort altogether, and he was able to sort out the funds for the British Schools and Institutes, because they all came through different, he found that they all came through methods. One came through the Foreign Office and another came through the Colonial Office, and very peculiar arrangements, and he was able to unify this and get it given to the British Academy as a block grant, which was then distributed by them to the Schools.

I was going to ask you — also we don't have much time. So, one final statement?

That is difficult, my life in two minutes —

Time runs out.

Professor Norman Hammond

23 August 2000, recorded at the University Museum of Archaeology and Anthropology, Cambridge, England, by Pamela Jane Smith pjs1011@cam.ac.uk

I started doing archaeology in 1958 when I was thirteen, because a local group was digging an Anglo-Saxon and Mediaeval habitation site about a mile from where my parents lived and because my mother had taken me off to look at churches when I was even younger. I had got into things like brass rubbing. Local people knew that I was interested in the past, so someone told me that there was a dig. So I went and said "Could I take part?" I then joined this group, which was called the Rocky Clump Group and belonged to the Brighton and Hove Archaeological Society, and worked with them at weekends for probably three or four years, and I then realised that it was possible to study archaeology at university; and I got that idea, I think, from reading Kathleen Kenyon's book Beginning in Archaeology, which was in the local library. I had originally intended to read medicine, but reading medicine in those days meant that you had to get A levels in Chemistry and Physics and Biology, and I was no good at either Maths or Physics and got thrown out of both of them, so I decided I had turn my attention to the dead rather than the living; and so I was doing A levels at school in History, Geography and English Literature, and Chemistry, because I could do Chemistry, all of which have proved to be enormously useful: Geography because it enables you to understand how people fit into the landscape; History because it teaches you to understand documentary sources; English Literature because it teaches you to write clearly and to introduce the idea of style, and after all, if archaeology isn't well written, then nobody reads it, and it might as well never be published; and Chemistry because even at A level it gives you an idea of the language of science; and it means that you can cooperate with scientists by talking to them in language that they understand, and you can understand enough of what they're saying to collaborate, whereas they may not know the technical terms of archaeology. So it turned out to be an incredibly useful set of A levels to do, although that was pure accident, as was the fact that I did a Geology O level at the same time — again just because it seemed interesting, but now I can tell different types of rocks apart and, more to the point, I can tell when I can't tell what it is and I know who to go to and ask, and this has been very useful when doing things like characterisation. Anyway, the only universities that did archaeology at degree level back in the early 1960s were Cambridge, London, Edinburgh and Cardiff. London wanted me to sit an exam and sent me the papers too late to take it. Edinburgh demanded that I have an A level in Modern Language. Cardiff I don't think I knew about, and I had sort of assumed that I was going to go to Cambridge through sheer ignorance. And my school hadn't really been frightfully keen. In fact, my sixth form Master told me that I wasn't fit to go to university, so nobody had done anything to prepare me for this. The change came when I travelled around Europe in the summer of 1962, and visited among other places the Roman ruins in Trier in Germany. I came back and was in my sixth form class room and came across one of my fellow pupils sticking pictures of what I recognised as the Porta Nigra at Trier in a notebook, and simply said in a friendly manner, "What are you doing, Johnny?" And he said he was doing a thesis for a Trevelyan Scholarship and I said "What's that?" He showed me this form which was an application for a scholarship tenable at Oxford or Cambridge, worth £500 a year which in those days was 30% more than the student grant, and it said that, while it didn't carry a guarantee of a place, nevertheless the Trustees would use their influence if somebody didn't get in by normal means; and what you had to do was fill in a form, get a recommendation from your Headmaster, and write a 5000-word thesis; and the deadline was ten days away. I had been doing some independent research on pre-Reformation Chapels in Sussex for sixth-form project work, and I had been doing project work in order not to have to be in the cadet corps because I couldn't think of anything more boring than standing around on a Friday afternoon in a sweaty uniform being shouted at by the prefects. So I had been doing this research, and I was able in ten days to turn this into a thesis, "Pre-Reformation Chapels in Sussex". The Head Master, who was almost the only person in the school who thought I had any ability, agreed to write a recommendation, and the result of this was that I finished up with a Trevelyan Scholarship to Cambridge, although at that point no actual place. I didn't do well enough in the Cambridge Scholarship exams, which were the only things that I could put in for at that late date. I didn't do well enough to get a place on the basis of those, but Peterhouse decided, after seeing that I had got a Trevelyan, to let me in anyway, so I finished up at Peterhouse, where Grahame Clark was Disney Professor and where I was given David Clarke as a Supervisor. Really the first great influence on my thinking was David Clarke and his interest in theoretical structure in archaeology, in which he was talented and I wasn't. The other influence was probably John Coles, who supervised me in my first year, and made me go and read lots of sources in German and was prepared to criticise essays in an extensive way. It was the impact of those two in my first year that made me decide to do the Neolithic/Bronze Age/Iron Age option, that is the post Palaeolithic-to-pre-Iron Age/Roman/Saxon option for Part Two. I did that with both of them supervising me, and also with Eric Higgs, who was a very annoying man, who would provoke you without then providing any real instruction. He told you to go and work for yourself, at a stage when most of us weren't yet ready to work for ourselves in the way that Eric needed. The end result of this was that I finished up with a 2.1 in each of the three years, and Tim Potter and I at the end of our third year just missed Firsts. They didn't give Firsts that year, but by the time I had got to my third year I had run my first independent project in my first Long Vac, tracing Roman roads in Libya and Tunisia, and in the second Long Vac had gone and dug with Eric Higgs on his Palaeolithic Cave site at Asprochaliko in Greece, and also worked with Brian Hope-Taylor, who was then a Lecturer in the Department, on the Saxon Palace site at Doon Hill at Dunbar, East Lothian, in Scotland. Higgs taught me that I wasn't interested in the Palaeolithic, but that it was possible to run a project in an exotic part of the world on very little money, and that it was much more interesting digging abroad than it was digging in England, where it was far too wet and cold and crowded. Hope-Taylor showed me what really good excavation technique was. He is probably one of the best excavators still alive, although his lack of publication has screened this from people; but if you look at The Anglo Saxon Palaces at Yeavering, his great book of the 1970s, it's a standard of technical excavation matched by few people: Mortimer Wheeler, Martin Biddle, Philip Barker, but not many others. Working in Greece with Eric Higgs and working in North Africa for myself, I realised that there was a large eastern-Mediterranean-shaped gap in my education. We didn't touch on Greek or Roman archaeology. We didn't touch Greece after 6000 BC, and I decided that Classical Archaeology interested me, and I decided that what I was interested in was going and looking at the Greeks in Asia, specifically in Afghanistan; in my third Long Vac I ran an expedition to Afghanistan, doing survey, which in fact finished up with more Islamic prehistoric and Islamic sites than it did with Classical Period ones; but this confirmed to me again that I was interested in working overseas, and because of the publication of the North African work, I was able to persuade the Classics Department here to let me in to read for the Diploma in Classical Archaeology, despite the fact that I didn't have any Classical languages beyond O level Latin, and I didn't have a degree in Classics, which was the normal baseline; but they passed a special Grace in the Senate to let me read for the Diploma and I simply avoided the Epigraphy paper, which was the only paper in which you needed to know the languages. I passed that in 1967, again I gather just missing a Distinction, but by that time I had been seduced sideways into American archaeology; and that happened because Grahame Clark called me into his room when I came back from Afghanistan in the summer of 1966, and he said to me "How would you like a job?" and I said "Yes, please, what is it?" "Well, we have a Research Fellowship in American Archaeology. The Parry Fund is sponsoring a revival of research on Latin America and we have an Archaeology Fellowship", and I said "I don't know anything about American archaeology", and he said "Well, neither does anyone else in Cambridge except Geoffrey Bushnell. We've got the money, do you want the job?" and it seemed foolish to turn down a job just because I didn't know anything about the subject, so I agreed to accept this Fellowship on the proviso if after the three years of the Fellowship, I wanted to go back and work in Asia I could do so without any hard feelings on anyone's part. So, as soon as I finished doing the Diploma in Classical Archaeology — which I continued to do for a year, because people had made an effort to get me into it, and I felt that I had an obligation, and also the subject genuinely interested me — but as soon as I finished in the summer of 1967, I took a month to go and dig with Eric Higgs again, at Kastritsa, to learn how you organise and run a field project with limited funds, and also dug with John

Coles at Somerset Levels. I then started work in the Centre of Latin America Studies; at the same time The Times offered me the job as Archaeological Correspondent. I'd written a couple of pieces for them on the North African work. Derek Roe, who was their previous correspondent, had just landed an academic job at Oxford and decided that he couldn't combine academia and journalism, and he knew that I was interested. I had written a lot of stuff for the local paper down in Sussex as the Press Secretary for the local archaeology society, so he suggested that they offer me the job; and so that is how I became first an archaeological journalist on the first of July 1967. Then on the first of October, I took up my position in the Centre of Latin American Studies; and the first thing that Geoffrey Bushnell, who was Curator of the Museum — he was the only American archaeologist in Cambridge and one of only two in England — did was write to his old friend at Harvard, Gordon Willey, to see if Willey had any idea as to where I might get some field experience in the Americas. Willey turned out to being running a project on a Maya site called Seibal in Guatemala, and he had space for a graduate student. So he told Geoffrey to send me along to work with him, and that is how I acquired both the next major influence on my career, and set the direction I would work for the last 30 years. If I had been sent off to work in Peru , I would probably have found something interesting there. As it was, Seibal proved to be extremely interesting. The Maya were intellectually interesting, not emotionally interesting as one's own ancestors are, but they presented intellectual problems: how did a society adapt to a tropical rain forest; how did a civilisation emerge and collapse in what is seen as an unfriendly environment? I was put in charge of excavating a large chunk of the surrounding settlement. I found that none of the previous graduate students, who had worked the previous four years, had the faintest idea about stratigraphic excavation; in fact I was horrified on my first day there to be told to take five workmen and a 20-centimetre length of stick, and to set the workmen digging two-by-two-metre pits and to give them the centimetre stick and tell them to dig down 20 centimetres; put everything they had found in a paper bag, go down another 20 centimetres, and put everything into another paper bag; and I asked Gordon Willey, "What about the stratigraphy?" And he said "Oh, it is all right. We have to reconstruct it from the sections afterwards." I thought this was probably not a good idea, and I dug a couple of pits by their method and then expanded them sideways and took down an equal area using natural stratigraphy, and showed this to Gordon Willey and to Gair Tourtellot, under whom I was working, the settlement pattern analyst, and they agreed since I seemed to be getting useful results and could clearly do the stratigraphy, that I should do a stratigraphic excavation for the rest of the season. I had the luck to come across some Preclassic temples, which I stripped in their entirety. Gordon Willey was impressed enough by what I had found and how I had explained it that he agreed that he would take me on as a supervisee. So I finished up with a research supervisor at Harvard, doing a Cambridge Ph.D, and the question of what I should do came up; Gordon suggested that what I should do is go to British Honduras, which was then still a Crown Colony and do some work there, because he thought as a British citizen I would get better co-operation from the Colonial Government; he sent me to a site called Lubaantun, which had been investigated by the British Museum back in the 1920s, but no really satisfactory reports had come out of it. The architecture was intriguing. There was megalithic architecture. No one knew the date of the site. It didn't have any carved and dated monuments so nobody knew very much about it, except that it was intriguing. So he sent me off there to do a season's excavation. He gave me some money, the Crowther-Beynon Fund here gave me some money, and Mortimer Wheeler, whom I had known for a number of years at the BA, gave me some money, and Kathleen Kenyon whom I knew at Oxford gave me some money from there, and I had about £10,000. The British Museum gave me some money because they wanted their former work checked up on and clarified. So, I finished up with about £10,000 for a four-month season. I had a staff of four myself to run the excavations, Kate Pretty, who is now the Principal of Homerton, to run what is called in American archaeology the Lab, here the finds shed, to do the drawings, a man called John Hazelden, a geologist, to do the environmental survey, and an architect called Mike Walton, who was keen on archaeological mapping, to do a map of the site; and the four of us lived down in the bush in southern Belize for four-and-a-half months, along with my Maya assistant surveyor, a man called Basilio Ah, who gave us a lot of help with the environmental assessment and also collecting local information about the use of local resources. The

146

results of work at Lubaantun showed in brief, instead of having a long history from the Preclassic to the Postclassic like Seibal, it had a very short history of less than 200 years; when I first reported this to Gordon Willey I was rather disappointed, thinking that I didn't have nearly enough material to actually do a dissertation. I remember the letter that I got back from Willey which said, "You seem to have made a negative discovery of importance." And he suggested that I now confirm that we had no Preclassic, no Early Classic, no Postclassic and that what we had was a site that appeared to mushroom up in the early 8th century and died before the end of the 9th. We were able to confirm this. He liked the results enough to offer a publication through the Peabody as one of their monographs, and he recommended to Cambridge that I be given a Ph.D. He didn't understand the sudden-death method of examination at Cambridge for the Ph.D, but Geoffrey Bushnell and Warwick Bray as Examiners seemed to take his assessment fairly seriously and didn't give me a hard time. So I finished up in early 1972 with a Ph.D (viva April 1972, Ph.D confirmed July 1972) and my Research Fellowship at the Centre for Latin American Studies had run out. There weren't any jobs. Grahame Clark had originally suggested that the Fellowship would turn into an Assistant Lectureship in American Archaeology here; but by the time the Fellowship had come to an end, there had been a downturn in academic fortunes in this country, and no new Lectureships appeared. What I was able to do was to think of something else to do, to survey Northern Belize and to look for the origins of Maya civilisation; to try to understand the Preclassic which no one had done. I got the Levelhulme Foundation to provide me with a salary as a Fellow, on condition that the British Museum put up the money for the fieldwork. I persuaded the British Museum to put up the money for the fieldwork in exchange for being able to obtain legitimate archaeology material as a gift from the Belize Government, and I persuaded the Belize Government that they would do well to gift some of the material to the BM because it was a way to acquire material legally rather than go out and buy stuff on the art market, which they had just started doing, which I and many other people disapproved of them doing in the 1970s. So Leverhulme provided me with three years of Fellowship funding, the BM provided two years fieldwork funding, and the Northern Belize survey was the first regional project in lowland Maya archaeology. What it did was give us a broad background to see the emergence of the Pre-Classic out of early village occupation. We found a number of sites: most notable was Cuello. When we tested it in 1975, it produced the first pre-1000 BC radiocarbon dates for the lowland Maya. It suggested that there was an undiscovered Early Preclassic there, and also excited people like the National Geographic Society. This was a stroke of luck. The early dates enabled me to persuade National Geographic that they should provide sponsorship for three years of excavation at Cuello, because this would be the first serious excavation of a purely Preclassic site. In the middle of all this in 1974, I had acquired a job (helping to set up a Department of Archaeological Science) as a Senior Lecturer at the University of Bradford, which I began in early 1975, mainly because I had got interested in analysing Maya jade, to try to track it back from its sources; here I was really progressing onwards from my work on Maya obsidian analysis that I had been doing based on the Lubaantun and northern Belize material, and that research took off from what people like Colin Renfrew had been doing in the Mediterranean. Nobody had done serious work on Maya obsidian trade and the two-page paper in Science that I published in 1972, put forward a model for Maya trade, is probably still the most cited paper I 've written, although it is mainly cited because people keep trying to prove it wrong. 'Obsidian Trade Routes in the Mayan Area', 1972. The work at Cuello had one other advantage, because while I was at Bradford helping to develop a new department of archaeological science, it became very quickly clear this was not an academic environment in which I was likely to flourish. The Head of the Department, Professor Gordon Brown, didn't want people doing fieldwork outside West Yorkshire and thought that the way to do archaeology was to be at the office at nine in the morning and go out and do fieldwork and then come back to report to him at 4 o'clock in the afternoon; so I became relatively unhappy relatively quickly; when the University of California at Berkeley invited me to go there as a Visiting Professor in 1977, I decided that I would resign my Senior Lectureship and look for a job in America. When I was teaching at Berkeley I was lucky in that some of my research on Cuello was published in Scientific American (1972 'The Planning of a Maya Ceremonial Center', 1977 'The Earliest Maya', 1986 'The Origins of Maya Civilisation') which was a

very public forum, and it excited people. A number of universities immediately offered me jobs, and the place that offered me the firmest job quickest was Rutgers University in New Jersey. So I moved permanently to work at Rutgers and live in Princeton in 1977, stayed there until I moved to Boston in 1988 and continued to do work, first of all at Cuello and then at the nearby site at Nohmul, thirteen miles to the north. Again the reason I moved to Nohmul was that National Geographic, after funding three years in Cuello, said "That is enough, but we like the results; we won't fund you at Cuello, but we will fund you somewhere else". So I thought up a project at Nohmul, which was the largest site in the region and which we had touched upon briefly in 1974; and once again NG funded what was the first explicit study of a medium-sized Maya centre which ran from 1982 to 1986. There had been a lot of study of rural settlement patterns by people like Gordon Willey, a lot of studies of major centres like Tikal, but no one had looked seriously at one of the much more typical medium-sized cities in between. So Nohmul, although the results were not earthshaking, nevertheless was the first serious study of what looked like an average Classic city. Of course it turned out to be not a Classic city at all, but a large Preclassic city abandoned for most of the Classic and reoccupied during the Terminal Classic period. So it proved to present much more interesting intellectual problems than we had first envisaged; but at the end of four years of funding for that National Geographic said "Well, you've had enough money", and I said "Well, I have a few more questions to ask about the Maya Preclassic at Cuello". So they said "Well, OK", and gave me some money to go back and answer some more questions about the Maya Preclassic at Cuello; and at this point it became very clear that the very early dates that we had been getting at Cuello were increasingly at odds with the much later dates that other people had started to get at other Preclassic sites, as our dates — which were for seven or eight years the only dates — started to be challenged. I thought we should go back, get some more samples and try to examine Cuello dating from other points of view, and the way to do this was to date, not the occupation from radiocarbon samples of charcoal from middens, but to date the people themselves, using bone collagen dating on the skeletons. As a result of that we were able to date the grave goods precisely, and to obtain a cultural sequence by dating the people themselves, and we went back and acquired a lot more info and it became clear that our original dates were 1000 years too early. We bit the bullet and acknowledged this in American Antiquity, and at the same time it became clear that the key to the rise of Maya civilization wasn't at the beginning of the Preclassic but in the period between 700 and 400 BC, what is called the Middle PreClassic and so we concentrated our work at Cuello, from the late 1980s through to the early 1990s, on excavating the Middle Preclassic deposits and building up a picture of a society that developed a stage of preliterate complexity, that is equivalent to Chiefdoms in the Europe and the Middle East, in the period before the emergence of the first Maya cities in the late 1st millennium BC. So all of these themes have more or less run into each other, in most cases generated by discovery. I don't think that I ever went out with a theoretical model to test. My colleague Will Andrews, in his evaluation of the grant proposal at Nohmul, said "Hammond has submitted an entirely atheoretical proposal but give him the money anyway, because he will come up with some theory by the end of the second season".

What has been a connecting theme has been an interest in the rise of the Maya civilization, partly because of my training as a prehistorian in the Old World, and the fact that I was interested in the preHellenic civilization rather than the pure Classical civilization in the East Mediterranean, partly because as a non-epigrapher I gravitated naturally toward the periods prior to those illuminated by written texts, partly because the Preclassic represented a challenge. Nobody had studied the Preclassic seriously and explicitly when I began work on it in the early 1970s, and by the time I finished work at Cuello in 2000 it was generally recognised that the Preclassic was one of the more important and interesting areas of Maya culture. Other things slotted into that as I went along, so that my work on obsidian characterisation began because I had lots of obsidian from Lubaantun and wanted to know where it came from, and then I had to look at other sites where there had been one or two bits of obsidian characterised, and gradually built this into a model; and then I moved on to trying to characterise jade, and track jade artefacts back to their sources, to look at a precious instead of an everyday material. I became interested in the application of theoretical models of organisation in the landscape — the application of things like central place theory — because in writing up

Lubaantun for my dissertation I had to put it in the context of both its natural and political environment in the Maya lowlands, and I found the work of Peter Haggett on location analysis in human geography very interesting. I took Haggett's ideas and applied them to the Maya lowlands — things like Thiassen polygon networks had never been applied to the Maya — and I was able to place Lubaantun within a network of such polygons showing the likely territory attached to the site and the likely range of exploitable resources within its area of political control, and then expanded that into looking at the network of territories across the whole Maya lowlands from all the sites that had yielded texts, that is everything that was a centre with an apparent degree of standing; but even at that point I didn't think that the centres were of equal status. There merely wasn't at that point decipherment of texts to show us where one was more important than the other. What happened not very long after that, we started to get the decipherment of texts, we started to get ideas of subordination to superior centres and therefore hierarchies of cities within the Maya landscape, and for the last 25 years we have all happily worked with the idea that some cities were more important than others, although I'm still inclined to the small state model of a mosaic of centres which are autonomous — some of them large, important and autonomous like Tikal and some of them small and much less important, but still autonomous, like Lubaantun. I've stuck to this point of view in the face of competing models such as Dick Adams' view that there were only six regional states in the whole of Maya lowlands with capitals at places like Tikal, each of them ruling a dendritic tree of smaller but still inscription dedicating centres. I now think the truth is somewhere in between, but closer to my side. It is now clear from the work of Simon Martin and Nikolai Grube, these large regional states or regional alliances with a single centre at the head of the alliance did in fact emerge over short periods of time, I mean over a century, and then crumbled and dissolved back into their constituent autonomous units, a bit like Egypt dissolving into its constituent nomes during the Intermediate Periods; a bit like the apparently autonomous palace economies of Crete, where Knossos may well have been just a primus inter pares. So, I had some impact on how people have debated the political organisation of the Maya lowlands, but the contributions I have made have been overshadowed by what I have done in other fields, and therefore tend to be unnoticed compared to with the work of people like Kent Flannery or Martin and Grube, or the people who have made truly important discoveries in decipherment which have enabled us to outline what the political situation in the Maya lowlands was.

The current project I am working on, apart from going back and answering a few more little questions at Cuello, is a large Classic period site called La Milpa deep in the rainforest close to the Guatemalan and Mexican borders; the reason I am working there is pure romance. I decided that I hadn't worked in the tropical rainforest since Seibal, I liked living in the rainforest and that I would like to do another major site while I was still energetic enough to tackle it; and the Belize government was nice enough to offer me La Milpa, the second largest site in Belize after Caracol, and we have been attacking that with a variety of investigative techniques, including mapping it and mapping onto a GIS that enables us to make predictions about the nature of the political landscape. It has enabled us to apply viewsheds and look at the dynamic organisation of a minor centre within the territory of the city. We have been doing standard archaeological mapping, stratigraphic excavation to build up a picture of the city's history — like many other Maya cities of the Classic period, La Milpa collapsed. Unlike many other cities we have a very clear picture of that collapse occurring very suddenly, so that we had buildings unfinished in the middle of a major royal development project and we are able to say that La Milpa went out with a very sudden whimper, rather than an occupation with squatters living on for decades or centuries as happened at Tikal. Yet again we found a site, starting out to work on it without theoretical preconceptions and without theoretical models to test, we evolved a set of models for testing on the basis of what we found on the ground.

There are two things. You are an entrepreneur.

I am an entrepreneur to some extent. Basically I do archaeology because it is fun. If it wasn't fun, I wouldn't do it. I do it abroad because I like to travel. I work on the Maya because I find them intellectually challenging, although not really emotionally involving, and I like to set myself problems and then to resolve them.

Yes, there is something quite different about you than the generation I have interviewed. It is almost like you are not following preconceptions. You didn't come up to Cambridge because somebody had you plotted for Cambridge. You didn't — you are your own agent. Do you think that is generational thing?

I have wanderlust and I found that archaeology is a very good way of travelling to places and doing interesting things and making some intellectual contribution. I am not a theoretical thinker. Grahame Clark said to Charles Higham on one occasion, about me, that I had never had an original idea in my life. He was absolutely right, but rather like Colin Renfrew, although Colin does it much more successfully, I can see that other people have original ideas and can see a way that these ideas can be applied to resolve problems that I am prepared to examine.

Vintage Clark. You are original because you go out without preconceptions and develop a point of view. That is original work.

I never had money from the National Science Foundation, because I am constitutionally incapable of developing a Hypothetico-Deductive Nomological Hypothesis for testing.

Which has fallen apart anyway.

I could have used their money. Grahame Clark's nick-name when he was in the War was 'Sweetie'.

[I mention Mrs Daniel's comment about him 'always wearing pink trousers'.]

He may have been an oarsman. He may have elected to 'Leander', which is a boat club. You wear a pink hat and pink socks. May have been that. The point was, Grahame was brilliant. He created was original, created ecological archaeology. The other person that I can think of who had a broad spectrum idea was Manuel Gamio in the Valley of Mexico in 1911, looking at the totality of an environment both human and natural, political, geological, botanical. There is an article about him in Tim Murray's volume. He was the predecessor of MacNeish and Willey as a multidisciplinary scholar, rather interdisciplinary. He saw that everything had to be done, in the way that Grahame did in European prehistory.

The implication about what Mrs Daniel said was that Grahame Clark didn't fit in on some level, wasn't quite acceptable to her.

Yes, but you have to remember that Glyn hated Grahame and Ruth hated Grahame. Grahame was the person who got elected to the BA early. Glyn only got in after he retired. Grahame was the person who became Disney Professor. Glyn didn't. Glyn was the person who got the Starred First and Fellowship early and Grahame overtook him. Glyn was the person who finished up with a high rank during the War and Grahame didn't. I think that Glyn saw that Grahame was his intellectual superior and he would be the person that eventually made it into the history books. Glyn is underestimated, not as a prehistorian, where I think that the anonymous Times obituary had him pinned pretty well. The history of archaeology started off as a major subfield, which he [Glyn] started in the 1940s and with his book in the 1950s, and was brought to fruition by Bruce Trigger's book The Intellectual History of Archaeology in 1989. That was Glyn's major contribution. His second contribution was that he was an Editor of genius. He made Antiquity into a more interesting journal than Crawford had done, but he maintained it as an independent voice.

Second side begins here on copy

He also had the talent to see that there was room for popular books and his alliance with Thames and Hudson, with the 'Ancient People and Places', meant that T&H were producing a string of very good archaeology books for a popular market at a time that archaeology became a subject of popular interest. He ran Animal, Vegetable, Mineral on the television with great panache. He helped to make Mortimer Wheeler's popular career, though Wheeler, of course, made his own professional career as a prehistorian. Most of Glyn Daniel's work was superseded even in his own life time.

His work on megaliths was no better than average. In fact, by his insistence of analysing mainly the plans of megaliths, he may have actually held the subject back.

Second side begins here on original

As Disney Professor he continued to promote Johnians over anybody else. He failed to make the leap into hyperspace and to be able to act as a Department Head. He did, on the other hand, make the Department grow far more than Grahame had. He did get the job created that David Clarke finally got. On the other hand, he chose to have John Alexander as a full Lecturer in the Department rather than David Clarke when a vacancy came up, and John Alexander was/is a very nice man but of no intellectual achievement and indeed with a greater backlog of unpublished excavation than almost anybody else. I suspect that, to put some positive spin on it, that the reason why Glyn did hire John is that every Department needs an Uncle, and that Brian Hope Taylor had been the Uncle, the person who goes out and drinks beer with the students and is universally approachable, and that Glyn may have seen that with Brian's retirement there wasn't one, although I think that John Coles was very approachable. But it did mean that David Clarke was kept down at a point when a broad-minded Head of Department would have promoted him, given him a job and allowed him to flourish, instead of letting him labour away just in Peterhouse and, of course, in the wider world, no one could understand why David wasn't himself the Disney Professor. Right, I have to go.

End of tape

Mr John G. Hurst

20 July 2000, recorded at Cambridge University Museum of Archaeology and Anthropology, by Pamela Jane Smith   pjs1011@cam.ac.uk
One of the founders of Mediaeval archaeology in Britain, Mr John Hurst.

How did you become interested in archaeology?

I was born in Cambridge in 1927, where my father was a Fellow-Commoner at Trinity, and he was a pioneer geneticist, and my mother also was a botanist. When I was quite young, in fact about five I think, when I was taken out for walks, I suppose in a push-chair, I was taken to the Fitzwilliam Museum, which was really quite close to our home in Brookside; and I became fascinated in the collections there, particularly the lower galleries with their hundreds of objects, which my mother tells me I wanted to go back to again and again. How I first got into the Fitzwilliam, I don't know. I expect my mother, just out of general interest, because neither of my parents were interested in archaeology, just took me to the Museum for something to do, but I became so fascinated that I wanted to go back again and again, and I have never really looked back since that time.

In 1936, we moved to Leicester and that was the time that I first visited various ancient monuments, and also the Museum, which fascinated me at the time. In the 1930s, of course, the most popular subject was Egypt, with the recent discovery of Tutankhamen. I was fascinated, and there were Egyptian collections in both the Fitzwilliam and the Leicester Museum. Not very much happened during the War, when I was at school at Harrow, because it was very difficult to get around; but in 1945, just after the War, I did my National Service, and this took place in the Middle East and I was in Palestine, Egypt and Greece, and of course that doubled my interest in archaeology, and I was very lucky being able to travel about quite a lot, as the War was over and it was easier to get about.

I left the Army in the summer of 1948, and I came up to Cambridge, to Trinity, to read archaeology. At that time, I was interested in prehistoric archaeology of Europe. I am not quite sure why I changed, because I could have done either Classical or Mediterranean archaeology here. But I chose prehistoric archaeology, and I was forced to specialise in the Palaeolithic under Dorothy Garrod. At that time, in the late 1940s, there were very few students. There were, in fact, almost as many students as there were lecturers. Grahame Clark, who was my Supervisor, recommended that I took the Palaeolithic course under Dorothy Garrod, because nobody else really wanted to do it. Therefore, I was rather stuck with it. It was rather a difficult course, because Dorothy Garrod was a very shy person, and I am a very shy person myself, so it was difficult for us to get on with each other. The worst thing, really, was that her lectures, and I say lectures advisedly, because although I was the only person in the room with her, we never really had any get-together. She just lectured to me as though there were 100 people in the hall. She wasn't really very good at explaining things, either. I had great difficulty with the sequence of the Somme Terraces, for example. I had to go to Charles McBurney for supervisions, to try to understand what these were all about. So it has been rather surprising recently to hear about [the] other part of her life, where she seems to be much more out-going and did much more general things than was apparent really when I was here at Cambridge.

The other point about Cambridge was that, in the 1940s, there was actually no practical work at all here, no teaching of excavation techniques, no fieldwork, and very little on objects. In fact, those of us who wanted to do excavation, we had to teach ourselves, and even so we had to go to the Engineering Department to learn how to survey. In my case, the reason I got interested in Mediaeval archaeology was that, together with Harry Norris — who is now, or was until he retired, in the School of Oriental and African Studies — we paired together, and as he lived at Harrow in Middlesex, we chose a Mediaeval moated manor site at Northolt, only a few miles from his home and easy reach of London, where we started a trial excavation, really teaching ourselves how to excavate; and, in fact, I went on with that for 20 years until 1970, and we fully excavated the central part of the Manor House. It was at that time, in 1950–1951, we were producing large quantities of Mediaeval pottery from this Manor House, and of course something I knew very little about, as I specialised in prehistoric archaeology.

I contacted Gerald Dunning, who was the pottery expert, the only person who had worked on Mediaeval pottery throughout the 1930s and 1940s, and he came out to see my pottery and he encouraged me to do more work on pottery; and when I finished my degree, when I graduated in 1951, he persuaded me to do postgraduate work for a Ph.D on Saxo-Norman pottery in East Anglia, that is to say, pottery from the late Saxon period going through to the 12th century. I worked on that for some years, but not as a Ph.D, because at that time one had to have residence, not like nowadays when you can do it more generally. It was through Gerald Dunning I got my first job. My real job, I spent 35 years in the same job, Gerald Dunning persuaded me to apply for a post as an Assistant Inspector of Ancient Monuments in the then Ministry of Works, and I was lucky to get this post; and my responsibility was to help Gerald Dunning, who at that time, with the surge of rebuilding activity and increased agriculture after the War, was responsible for rescue excavations. Excavations on sites which were going to be destroyed by various activities. I was his Assistant, and when we expanded a year or two later, the work was divided. There were four of us: Sarnia Butcher who looked after Roman excavations, Robertson-Mackay prehistoric, I was allocated to Mediaeval excavations, and therefore for most of my working life, certainly at least the next 20 years, I was responsible for organising rescue excavations on Mediaeval sites.

My interest in pottery was very much to the fore in these activities, and during those years I became very — I tried to see all the Mediaeval pottery being found all over the country, something of course not possible now, with so many excavations taking place. The other aspect of my work was deserted villages; pottery and Mediaeval settlement generally were my two main interests. It was through Jack Golson that I slightly changed direction, although I always kept up pottery. Jack Golson was reading history at Peterhouse under Prof. Postan, and he was interested in archaeology and he came to the Faculty of A &A in his final year, about 1950–51. He was extremely interested in getting excavation work going on the deserted villages. Prof. Postan had tried to start this off in 1948 when he called a very important meeting in Cambridge including Mediaeval historians, Professor Grahame Clark, of course, leading it from Peterhouse; and they brought in William Hoskins, who had been working on deserted villages in the Midlands, and Maurice Beresford, working on Yorkshire deserted villages, and other economic historians and geographers. They went out to visit sites in Leicestershire, and the most important person in that party really was Axel Steensberg, from Denmark, who had been working through the 1940s on deserted villages in Denmark at a time when nothing like that was happening in this country. He had been working under Prof Gudmund Hatt, who in the 1920s had pioneered the open-area excavation which was necessary on the Mediaeval sites. Over most of Europe in the 1920s and 1930s, excavations were carried out either by trenches or by grid method with baulks in between, a method particularly associated with Mortimer Wheeler on Roman sites in this country, but really universal through most of Western Europe; and on these sites in Denmark where you have peasant houses of the Mediaeval period, which were very flimsy and therefore if you put a trench across it you really find nothing at all. It would just be the odd posthole where posts had been put or various marks in the soil.

Professor Hatt developed this method of clearing the whole site layer by layer, and planning it, and planning all the finds, to get a general picture which would not be possible from all these small grids and baulks, which were of course all right for a Roman villa with stone foundations. His student in the 1930s was Axel Steensberg, and Axel became interested in Mediaeval — I'm not quite sure why, but like myself he changed from prehistoric to Mediaeval, partly I think because he was interested in farms. He was himself the son of a farmer, and this was very important for his whole career, because he understood harvesting implements, which he particularly worked on, were found, he knew what they all were and how they worked, from his personal experience as a farmer in the early part of the century. He was on the farm for the first 25 years before he went to the university. I think this must be the reason why he changed from the prehistoric to the Mediaeval.

Jack Golson and I met Axel Steensberg in August 1951, at the Edinburgh meeting of the British Association for the Advancement of Science. I, of course, was interested in pottery at that time, as I said, and Jack Golson was interested in the excavation of villages themselves. So it must have been between 1951, when I graduated, and 1952 that we got together and suggested that he would excavate Mediaeval villages in this country

and I would help him by looking at the pottery. This was all changed by chance, in fact the whole of this business has been chance I think, because Golson went over to Denmark and spent six months excavating with Axel Steensberg, leaving me here in England still working on pottery. Donald Harden (Museum of London), who I had also known through the British Association, asked me to give a talk on deserted villages to the British Association at Belfast in 1952, and I had to look up a lot of the work that Golson had done because I was not familiar with the literature. I had a lot of help from Jack Golson. I gave this lecture in Belfast in 1952, and Jack Golson came back that same Autumn from Denmark, and we managed to get as many experts on Mediaeval settlement as possible; and we formed the interdisciplinary Deserted Medieval Village Research Group in October 1952, with the aim of coordinating work on Mediaeval rural settlement, a subject that was entirely new.

Before the War and back into the 19th century, all work on the Mediaeval period was concerned with the upper classes, with churches, abbeys, castles and manor houses, and even there it was mainly architectural. They were interested in the surviving buildings, not in the excavation. There was some very early pioneer work in the middle of the 19th century, the time when the Romanticism of the 18th century was changing to the scientific foundations in the second quarter of the 19th century, with the understanding of the principles of geology and basic science coming into the fore, leading up to Darwin in the middle of the century. In the 1840s, there was a great surge of archaeological interest. Archaeological societies were formed all over the country as part of this general process, and very much increased by the building of the railways, which made it practical for people to attend meetings at some distance; that is to say, the Society of Antiquaries of London had always held weekly meetings in London, but in the 1840s, the Archaeological Institute and the British Archaeological Association were both founded, with monthly meetings, and with the railways people were able to come from all over the country to London for these meetings, and there was a great surge of archaeology generally and particularly excavations; and it was at that time, that the first excavations were carried in a very primitive way on deserted villages, particularly at Woodbury in Oxford, by Reverend Wilson of Trinity; but then suddenly the whole thing seemed to change, and throughout the second half of the 19th century there was no interest in Mediaeval rural settlement. Interest seemed to be entirely concerned with the upper classes, as I said, with the castles, abbeys and churches.

It wasn't until the 1930s that Mediaeval archaeology really took off, and this happened in Oxford with several undergraduates who graduated in the 1930s. There was Rupert Bruce Mitford, who carried out the first urban excavation in Oxford on the Bodleian site, or at least he didn't excavate so much as watch the building of the new Bodleian site, and he formed a sequence of pottery for the Oxford region which still stands today. It was remarkable as a piece of work. And then there was Martyn Jope, who was a chemist. There were no archaeology degrees at that time. All these people did other subjects. There was Martyn Jope, who was also interested in pottery. It was he who excavated one of the first Mediaeval peasant houses in 1938, at Great Beere in Devon. Then there was John Ward Perkins, who was interested in objects, and he worked on these, particularly material in the London Museum, and published the famous London Museum catalogue in 1940, and this was the first assessment of archaeological finds from the Mediaeval period.

The War years prevented any more work from happening. It was in 1948, which was really a most remarkable year and the founding of Mediaeval archaeology, not only with this meeting of Postan's, but Rupert Bruce-Mitford made a plea in the Archaeological Newsletter, the popular periodical of the time for Mediaeval archaeology, and suggested that it was time to pay attention to how the ordinary people lived, and not just the upper classes; and it was also the same year that Dr St Joseph, here in Cambridge, started his aerial flights, taking aerial photographs. And it's really aerial photographs, together with the historical work by Maurice Beresford and William Hoskins, that really made it possible for the Deserted Mediaeval Village Research Group to work on Mediaeval settlement, because the historical evidence showed that there were these deserted villages which, incredibly, despite the large number of earthworks on the ground, had been denied by historians. In fact, only in the 1940s, there was an economic history of England which stressed that this was all Elizabethan propaganda, that there weren't any deserted Mediaeval villages. When Maurice Beresford produced his Lost Villages of England in 1954, a lot of people did not really believe that there were as many as 1500 deserted villages in this country. The historians had never got out onto the ground. It was really Dr St Joseph with his air photographs, his remarkable oblique air photographs showing up the regular nature of these earth works. You could walk over these sites and they are really just humps and bumps in the ground. It's really only when you get up in the air that you can see the layout of these villages.

So, the Deserted Mediaeval Village Research Group spent a large number of years visiting these sites, particularly Maurice Beresford and myself. Over a period of 20 years we visited some 2000 of these sites, of which some 3000 are now recognised. That was one part of the work, but perhaps the most crucial work was the excavations which we carried out. When I first met Maurice Beresford at the end of 1951, he had been doing some trial excavations at Wharram Percy, in the East Riding of Yorkshire, on the chalk wolds, and he asked me to come and have a look, and this I did in April 1952. He was excavating on house 5 (the earthworks had been planned and the various earthworks given numbers), and he had dug around the chalk walls of the late Mediaeval peasant house. The village was abandoned about 1500, but he had no expertise in archaeology, and what I did was to excavate a square in the corner of the house, and we dug down below the standing chalk walls and we found a wall underneath on a different alignment, and underneath that a pit which turned out to be a chalk quarry; the chalk providing the building stone for the peasant houses. So on that very first weekend when I joined Beresford, we had shown that there were three different periods on this site at Wharram, and because of facilities on the site, there were some cottages which had been abandoned, labourers' cottages, and because of the fact that the site belonged to Lord Middleton who was very sympathetic to archaeology, the DMVRG decided that they should carry out excavations at this chalk site of Wharram Percy and also to try a site in the Midlands at Wolfhamcote, Warwickshire. Clay sites were very difficult in that time. You can't see where the peasant houses are, because they were built of timber which had decayed, and therefore you have a 200-foot square enclosure with no idea of where to find the house. It was a very hot summer indeed in 1954 when we started there with my wife, and unfortunately we didn't find any structures at all. But at Wharram Percy we had found a tremendous amount of evidence on house 10, the area we had decided to excavate, and we therefore suggested that we should concentrate our efforts at this one site at Wharram Percy.

It was not possible to do more, because at that time there was very little money for research, and Maurice Beresford and myself each took time off without any financial help, and we relied on volunteer students coming to help. In the 1950s, students were happy to come on excavations and offered to pay for themselves. There was none of the situation now where nobody will really go excavations unless they are paid to do so. We were also very lucky in the fact that Professor Darby, Professor of Geography in London, and of course geography is a very important aspect of the deserted villages, contributed his geography students to the Wharram project, and over the first 20 years or so we had about 30 students excavating at Wharram. Not just history, but others from all over the country and from abroad, from America, Canada and elsewhere. We were only able to excavate one site at a time for three weeks each July. Three weeks was the longest time that either Maurice Beresford or myself could take leave from our work. During this first period in the 1950s, we completely excavated the area 10 peasant house and we found a whole sequence of periods which was very difficult to understand. We had very flimsy remains, and therefore we formed the idea that the peasant houses were rebuilt about every generation, and therefore they must have been very flimsy, but we should have been aware even at that time that it was not as simple as that, because we had been finding keys which presupposed solid wooden doors; and therefore the houses are unlikely to be very unsubstantial. And incidentally it does show that even in Mediaeval times people had to keep their properties locked up.

It wasn't really until the 1980s that Stuart Wrathmell of [West Yorkshire] Unit suggested that in fact we had more solid peasant houses than we had supposed, and the houses were in fact cruck buildings, that is to say, the main structure with two curving timbers joined together at the top, which formed the superstructure, and in between there were just very flimsy walls, not any solid load-bearing walls, and therefore what we found were these flimsy in-fillings between the major timber structures which have to be renewed every generation. So the actual houses survived over a longer period of time. But nevertheless we still had two or three

major periods during the 13th, 14th and 15th centuries when these peasant houses were rebuilt, and we therefore learned a great deal about how the Mediaeval peasant lived, something entirely new. The typical type of house, the long-house, in which the people lived at one end of the house, a cross-passage at the middle and then at the lower end, the byre where the cattle were stalled with their drain; all part of the system, everybody living together. The general heat generated was very beneficial for the English climate. We went on in the 1960s again with the small number of volunteers to excavate another peasant house, area 6.

Then the situation completely changed in 1970, when I managed to persuade the Department of Environment, as it then was, having gone through various different bodies from the Ministry of Works in the 1940s, to take guardianship of the site. Again, we were very lucky that Lord Middleton was willing for this to take place, and therefore between 1970 and 1990, we had a 20-year programme looking at as many different aspects of the village as possible. We had already quite by chance found the undercroft of a 12th-century manor house underneath the peasant buildings in area 10, but we went on to completely excavate the church, to excavate the site of the Mediaeval mill and then look at the boundaries of the village as well, which showed that the village had been laid out in late Saxon times on the Roman fields of an earlier Iron Age and Roman settlement. This was one of the most important developments, which had also been found elsewhere in the country. I persuaded the Ministry of Works, in my function as rescue coordinator, to look at individual peasant houses in the Mediaeval villages which were being destroyed through agriculture in the 1950s. We excavated a number of single peasant houses in different parts of the country to get an idea of how these varied, with the idea that Wharram Percy would be the main excavation where large-scale excavation would take place.

Concurrently with the excavations, the work going on in other parts of the country, and gradually it developed that the whole understanding of Mediaeval settlement had been wrong. Historians had assumed that when the Saxons came over in the 5th century, they laid out these villages, and in fact they cut many of them out of the primeval forest which had not been cleared; but work of prehistorians had already shown by 1970s, '80s that certainly by Roman times, the whole country had been cleared of forests and was very fully settled. Our work on the Mediaeval settlements showed that none of these nucleated settlements were earlier than the 8th or 9th centuries, and the Saxons had come over here and lived in scattered farms, very much the same as throughout the prehistoric and Roman period. I think that was the most fundamental discovery of the work of the DMVRG at Wharram Percy and corroborated by all these other excavations all around the country, which showed that the Romano-British and Prehistoric scattered settlement remained throughout the early Saxon period, and it wasn't until the 9th and 10th Century that most nucleated settlements were formed. These, of course, were what we had been excavating, and it was the further development that we learnt a great deal about how these people lived and about how the Mediaeval peasant lived, as well as the upper classes.

Interruption

Would you be willing to discuss some of the other personalities involved, such as McKenny Hughes and Lady Fox?

McKenny Hughes was a very remarkable Victorian who was in many ways a pioneer of Mediaeval archaeology, although he had wider interests in the Romans and in prehistory. He was Professor of Geology here at Cambridge, and in the 1880s and going on into the 20th century, he watched a great deal of building work in Cambridge, and I think it is fair to say that it was the only town in the country where this sort of work was going on at that time; and he also carried out a limited amount of excavations, trying to determine the line of the city ditch. He took notice of the stratified levels, which of course was very early for this type of technique, which was being pioneered by Pitt Rivers at the same time in the 1880s, and this was the first time it was applied to an urban situation. I came across his work when I was doing my thesis on Saxo-Norman pottery in East Anglia. The first thing I did was to go through all the collections here in the Museum in Cambridge, and it was remarkable what a pioneer he was, because after the early part of the 20th century, no more work was done on this material until I came along in 1951. The most incredible thing of all was that the boxes were still packed in [contemporary] newspapers and it was clear that nobody had looked at the material since McKenny Hughes had packed it away. He was certainly a very important early pioneer for both Mediaeval archaeology and urban archaeology. Of course, I never knew him. I think he died during the First World War [1917], but there are some other pioneers that I did know, and in fact still do.

Sir Cyril Fox was a very important pioneer here in Cambridge with his survey of the Cambridge region, one of the first archaeological surveys of an area, and his wife was Aileen Fox; and in the 1930s they did carry out, at Gelligaer Common in Glamorgan, one of the first excavations of a Mediaeval peasant house, at the same time that Martyn Jope was working from Oxford. I came to know the Foxes in 1952, when Jack Golson and I were making a list of people interested in Mediaeval settlement to join the Committee of the DMVRG, and of course Sir Cyril Fox was one of the first people to come to mind, because of his early work, and we brought him on to the Committee and he was extremely helpful and friendly. Lady Fox was mainly working on Roman Exeter, after the bombing, but she was of course still interested in Mediaeval settlement. I arranged a Mediaeval excavation for her at Dean Moor on Dartmoor, of a Mediaeval farm which was being threatened at that time, part of my arranging of rescue excavations in different parts of the country.

At Cambridge, two important people were Miles Burkitt and Geoffrey Bushnell. Geoffrey Bushnell was the Curator here in the Museum, and of course mainly an American archaeologist. He was interested in a very wide range of materials, and when I started my research on Mediaeval pottery here in the Museum, he worked with me on a special type of pottery made here in Cambridgeshire, sgraffito ware, in which the decoration was scratched through the pottery. We did an article together on this, and he was really most helpful in all my research here, getting the pottery out for me and helping me on my research, which never led to a Ph.D, as I said, but nevertheless I did publish three articles in the Proceedings of the Cambridge Antiquarian Society. Miles Burkitt was doubly known to me by the fact that he was a leading member of the British Association for the Advancement of Science, and my parents had always attended the Association from the 1920s and in the 1930s. I went to BA for the first time in 1936 when I was only nine, but I was just taken along there. It was the earliest time they thought I could go. I am not quite sure what I did at that time, but I next went, or tried to go, in 1939; but that was cancelled because of the War. But from 1948 I was a regular attender, and I knew Miles and Peggy very well from the British Association, much more socially than I did here at the University, when I was just being lectured to by Miles. They were both very close friends of my mother from the 1930s, and therefore when I came up here to Cambridge, Miles was very friendly already, being a family friend.

Could you mention some of your memories of Miles Burkitt, since he is deceased?

He was a very jovial, outgoing person. I must say my main memory of him was he always wore an overcoat when he was lecturing. I am not sure if he did this through the summer, but my impression was that he was always wearing this overcoat. I am a bit hazy as to what lectures and courses I really had 50 years ago, but he gave general archaeological background lectures and I found these fascinating. He was certainly a very good communicator indeed, certainly a very marked contrast to Dorothy Garrod.

I wonder about his contributions intellectually. Do you think that he was primarily — he worked with Breuil — do you see as an original thinker or someone who more synthesized other people's material . . . ?

He was very much a synthesizer. He has been criticized. I mean, his book on Africa, for example, people say he just went down there and sort of wrote up everybody else's work. That may be the case, but I think that they are very brilliant syntheses, of course out of date now, but the series of books he wrote based on his lectures here were certainly ideal for university students and the best way of getting the information to them. I think he was very good in that way.

I have been told that many — Jack Golson took his The Old Stone Age *to New Zealand and used it as a text.*

I don't know how much original work he did. He was certainly a very brilliant synthesizer.

I wanted you to comment on how revolutionary the open-area excavation techniques were.

It was certainly a very remarkable development, because there is no way that the Mediaeval peasant house, with its flimsy foundations, could have been understood by digging the grids and trenches of the Mortimer Wheeler school. By opening the whole site at once and seeing each period in its entirety, and then peeling off to the next, it was possible to understand these very slight foundations of Mediaeval buildings; and this has now become the standard method of excavation throughout England and, in fact, most of Europe. It is now applied not only to rural sites, but also urban sites and other sites in general, because it has come to be understood that looking at the entire level of any one period, whatever the circumstances, is a much better way of doing things than digging trenches or opening up small squares, the great fault of which has always been that you excavate one square while the other square, two feet away, is totally different and bears no relation to the previous one. This is fine for major Roman stone buildings, but is really useless for these slight traces in the soil, just different colour marks in the soil, which are of course usual on the peasant house, which without the major building stone and architectural fragments of the castles and abbeys which had been previously studied before.

I wonder about Bersu's work?

Indeed, the same sort of technique was being developed in Germany. The excavators at the Neolithic site at Köln Linderthal, near Cologne, were doing this during the 1930s, and again Bersu was obviously a part of this German school and he came over here.

Tape cuts off

Side 2

You were saying about Bersu and his excavation in the 1930s?

Yes, he excavated Little Woodbury, Wiltshire, which first brought open-area excavation to this country in the prehistoric period and then during the War he was interned. He dug a very important site at Vowlam in the Isle of Man, where he had a site which was entirely different marks of the soil without any stone at all, a site of the Viking period. This he excavated in a very remarkable way. Really, the whole process of archaeology has been changed by this method of open area excavation, which has enabled excavators in the second half of the 20th century to produce very much more remarkable results than was possible in the earlier time.

Does it also permit better pollen and soil studies and other types of scientific enquiry?

I am not sure it does in that way because you really need sections for pollen and that sort of analysis. The main trouble with Mediaeval sites is that you very rarely get any pollen or ecological samples at all. Wharram Percy was on the chalk; of course nothing survives there, although we do have some deposits in the valley bottom, underneath the mill dam. It is one of the main needs for the future of Mediaeval rural archaeology. We do need to try to find a water-logged site which will give us better evidence. The surviving materials, the pottery and the bone, are only a very small aspect of Mediaeval life. We have lost all the basketry and the leather and all the other things which don't survive.

But it did allow you to think about the economic arrangement of houses?

Well, yes and no. The animal bones are the most important find that you get, after pottery, and to a lesser extent metalwork. We have done a lot of studies on the animal bones. We have rather different evidence from different sites. At Wharram, the largest number of bones are sheep and slightly less cattle, but because of the size of cattle it is likely that the cattle provided the larger proportion of the meat diet than the sheep. We have very few pig, which is surprising, even from the Manor House, because it is supposed that in Mediaeval times the upper classes ate a lot of pigs. In the later Mediaeval period we get quite a lot of old sheep, that is to say, that they were not killed for eating but kept for a long time for wool, and this is one of the major changes in the later Mediaeval period; that people, or rather Lords, found it much more economical to increase the numbers of sheep and cut down on the arable land, because the price of wool was very much higher than the price of corn. With this great export, England was famous for its exporting wool to the Continent.

It was because of this very fundamental economic change in the second half of the 15th century that some 1500 of our 3000 deserted villages were destroyed, with this changeover. The landlord found it much more profitable to have a single shepherd and his family looking after sheep over 1000 acres, rather than having some 30 families growing corn, which would not bring him quite so much profit. This is the main reason for the desertion of villages like Wharram Percy, which was deserted about 1500 AD. Quite a large number were deserted at other times, going right back to the 12th century, when the Cistercian Monks came over and they wanted to put their abbeys in solitude and quite a few times they had to clear away villages for this. During the 14th century there was an economic decline and a lot of marginal land was abandoned. Only half-a-dozen villages out of the whole large number were destroyed by the Black Death. It is a popular fallacy that the Black Death was the main cause of the deserted villages. If a village was decimated by the Black Death, it still survived, because people came in from other sites, from the marginal land, and this is quite clear from the Mediaeval tax returns. When you compare 1334 AD to 1377 AD, you find as many people in these villages as there were before the Black Death, despite the large numbers of deaths, because these people come in from elsewhere. It wasn't until later in the 14th and particularly in the 15th century you get these other economic changes which caused the desertion of villages. Finally in the 18th century, you have the clearance of villages to create the 18th-century parks around the great country houses of the period. In Mediaeval times, as at Wharram Percy, the Manor House would be in the middle of the village. In the 18th century Romantic situation, they wanted to clear all the nasty villages away and just look over their lawns to their Capability Brown parks.

Perhaps we could just say some concluding remarks? It does strike me that this is an interdisciplinary approach. You are using historians, as well as economists, as well as archaeologists.

Yes, indeed, that was the main reason for the forming of the DMVRG. It was basically comprised of historians and archaeologists, and also particularly geographers, because of their importance in doing this, in particular Professor Darby, because his impressive volumes on the Domesday which linked in the early part of the evidence that the historians had. We always had very close contacts with other people. The physical anthropologists, for example, we haven't mentioned that, we excavated sample areas at the Wharram Percy church. We excavated some 200 burials north of the church and a similar number from the west. Simon Mays has some very exciting results, with the examination of these burials producing a lot of evidence on disease. For example, he has completely debunked the modern idea that osteoporosis in women is due to the modern life-style with smoking and things like that, because quite a large proportion of the Wharram Mediaeval peasants also had this disease, so it can't have anything to do with the modern way of life. Other interesting things he has found out is that there are more men than there are women, while if you go to York, you have more women than men, and this confirms the historical suggestions that peasants were not completely confined to their village but the women, or quite a lot of the women, went to the towns to do menial work, and therefore you get this larger proportion of men in the countryside and a larger proportion of women in the town. Other interesting things have been found out from this work, which has been going on for a number of years and still is not published. I hope it will come to fruition in the next two or three years. We are in the process of publishing a large number of monographs on Wharram Percy. The eighth volume has come out, on some of the Saxon occupation, and another volume is nearly in the press, and then we have three or four other volumes to complete the work.

I thought it was interesting you brought up Darby because Darby was here during the 1930s and he worked with Clark on a number

of committees for the investigation of the Fens.

Yes, yes, indeed, the Fenland Research Committee is one of the most important things in British archaeology. It was the first time that an interdisciplinary group was formed to study a subject. It is quite clear, I think that Jack Golson and I had this in mind when we formed the DMVRG, because Grahame Clark had lectured on this during his courses, obviously. We actually had had a visit to the Fens, and with Major Gordon Fowler, who was one of the prime local people in that study, and we went out and saw some of the roddens, the extinct water courses which have been the main part of this project.

I wonder could you comment on Star Carr? Were you and Jack Golson both there?

Yes, Grahame Clark carried out excavations each summer. In 1948, before I went up to Cambridge, he invited me to help him at Cottenham, a Romano-British village just north of Cambridge, and that was one of the first excavations I helped at, although I had been down to Chichester with Dr Wilson, working on the urban site there. I was very lucky, because it was the three years 1949–51 that Grahame Clark excavated at Star Carr each summer on the Mesolithic site. I was very, very privileged to be at Star Carr and be excavating this very important trench with these remarkable artefacts from the Mesolithic period.

Could you say something about the working conditions there? People said that it flooded every day . . .

Yes, it was not only water-logged, but all the wood was very fragile, and we weren't allowed to actually stand in the trench. We had to work from planks which were stretched across. We had to lie on these planks and lean over, excavating the levels underneath, which again was very difficult, because things like the birch bark was very fragile and you couldn't trowel them with a normal trowel. You had to use blunt instruments. But it was certainly a very exciting experience to be part of that excavation which, of course, all the archaeological students attended each year.

Thank you, Mr Hurst.

Professor emeritus R.R. Inskeep

11 August 2000, recorded at the Oxford home of Professor Ray Inskeep, Professor emeritus of Archaeology at Cape Town University, by Pamela Jane Smith   pjs1011@cam.ac.uk
Tape I side I

I was born in 1926, 18 November at Brighton or just outside Brighton and spent the first four years of my life there. Although it was a long time ago, I was four when I left, I can still remember a great deal and even went back and found the house after returning to Oxford in 1972. From there the family moved to a little village called Hampden Park [just outside Eastbourne]. Father was the manager of a typical seaside town shop which sold photographic equipment, sports equipment, toys, you name it. We were a family of six children, four brothers and a sister besides myself. One has to say that it wasn't a very well-off family. It was not a household where there were a lot of possessions and one of the things that was missing, I am well aware now, was books. The books we had were annuals which came at Christmas as Christmas presents, boys' annuals and various magazines that came throughout the year. But mother loved reading. She used to read to us a great deal. We loved it. We used to love to sit around and listen to her reading. She collected [borrowed] books from the library and read to us. This is something which goes back a long way in her history, because she was orphaned when she was a child and many years in an orphanage. She used to read to the other children there while still only a child herself and developed early on a love of reading.

Very soon after the outbreak of war in 1939, we were evacuated, at least my sister, youngest brother and I were evacuated. My two oldest brothers were in the Forces. We were moved to Hitchin in Hertfordshire. My sister was at the High School at Eastbourne. I was put into a church school and soon after I arrived there, they came to me and said "Would you like to be moved to the boys' grammar school?" "No," I replied, "I don't think my parents could afford to keep me there." One would need things like sports clothes, tennis racket, and things like this so I stayed at that [church] school until I had just turned 14 [when I left and went to work].

I sometimes wonder where the interest in archaeology came from. I suppose if you spoke to most archaeologists they would say yes, they had always wanted to be archaeologists, or at a certain age before they went to university, they knew that they wanted to be archaeologists, but I can't do that. I do know there was a sort of curious interest in things mysterious and old when I was a youngster. Perhaps nine, ten years old in Eastbourne, one of the favourite places for myself and my friends to go to was Pevensey Castle. We walked along the ash path, then off along the coast, stopping off to climb around the Martello Towers and then crawl all over Pevensey Castle and eat our sandwiches there. Then come back. That was about nine or ten miles, which was nothing to us then. I also recall that on the playing fields, it was a hay-field really; in the summer when the hay had been mowed it was used for cricket for the local village, but in the next field there was an earthen mound, which I now would dare say was a barrow, which we used to go and put our ears to the ground and it was claimed that you could hear marching feet. We all believed it.

I also remember another of our favourite walks was up on to the South Downs, across the fields from Hampden Park to Willingdon and then up the drove path, a shepherds' drove path, and up on to the top you would come across a beech wood. In that there was what I have no doubt at all was another barrow that somebody had already scraped into, and there were flint nodules lying around on one side of it where people had scuffed things out. I supposed a Bronze Age barrow which someone had tried to dig into. These were just mysteries, things which you dreamed about.

When I left school in Hitchin, my job was to work as a junior shop assistant in a small family business of gents' outfitters. My chores were to scrub the mosaic pavement in the front, oil the black stone [surround below the windows], polish the windows and polish the floor inside. I eventually graduated to selling collar studs. It was a father and son business and the son was quite a nice chap and had an interest in things, local history and on the one afternoon a week when the shop was closed, Wednesday afternoon, he and I would go off with a chap called Latchmore who was the photographer in Hitchin and we would walk all over the countryside. Latchmore, who was a keen local historian and antiquarian, knew a lot

about things of historical interest. I don't recall anything archaeological: churches and so on — as we walked around and looked at all these things together. I suppose this probably gradually fed into a developing interest in things archaeological.

Egypt figured in all of this because one of the books I recall Mother reading, as small children, was one of Haggard's books. I've never been able to discover which one it was, but I do remember a page in this book which showed a view across open water with a cliff on the other side and a ledge with hieroglyphs above the ledge and an Egyptian priest standing there. This intrigued me so much that at the age of probably nine I went over to the local library and found that they had an *Introduction to Egyptian Grammar* which I carried home and kept for a fortnight. This was an indication of the way the imagination wanted to go; where the interest wanted to lead.

Then the house at Eastbourne was damaged by a bomb. The family moved up to Stamford, which was my mother's home town, and father found work there. Stamford became the place where one went for a weekend. The time came in Hitchin when I had decided that I wanted to go into the Forces and therefore wanted to spend some time at home. So, I left Hitchin and went to join the family in Stamford, and oddly enough I couldn't get a job in Stamford. I think a lot of young men had gone off to the War and women had replaced them and I couldn't find a job, but I joined the Air Training Corps. One of the things I had a flare for was the Morse Code and one of the two men running that Corps had worked as a telegraphist at some time in his life. He was very keen and found me a good pupil. We used to have sessions and he would get me further on until I was receiving over 20 words a minute, 26 at times, which was quite something, but jobwise that was difficult. One of the other people involved in the Corps was a local builder, and he said I could work for him, which I did. I joined his firm for a while and did some work on Air Force barracks that were occupied by the Polish Airborne Regiment, a Regiment which played a major role in the Arnhem raid which was rather disastrous. I did various things there but then I managed to find an old retired undertaker, about half a mile from home, who had a large workshop, and I banged on his door and asked if I could rent a corner of his workshop, which he agreed to. I think I paid about 7 shillings and 6 pence a week. I then used to get such wood as I could. I used to go to local auction sales and buy odd bits of furniture and break them down and make up things that people wanted as commissions; ironing boards, a garden gate, gift boxes. I had learned this at school. This kept me going for the major part of a year until I could get into the Forces.

I had wanted to go into the Air Force and I had got myself down to be an Air Gunner but at that time they were then running down the Air Force so I ended up in the Army. In January 1945, I went off to Bodmin and did training there and ended up going out to Egypt in December 1945, where I spent the next four months. Most of the troops I went out with, we all went into a transit in El Maza which is just outside Cairo, moved on fairly quickly. I got hung back because they wanted me to go through a War Office Selection Board for a commission. I stuck around in that transit camp from early December until well into March. During that time I joined several — apart from the army exercises that we were doing, I was then a wireless operator and a driver. This took us down to places like Memphis and Sagara. I remember going on one trip to the Pyramids and not even seeing the Sphinx or getting around the Pyramids because I was stuck on the back of the truck operating the wireless. I went on one or two education excursions to Sagara. I was absolutely thrilled at Sagara. I fell in love with it. I loved the mystery of it, looking through those little holes at stone effigies. The whole thing fascinated me. It was another one of those things that keyed in to the growing interest in things archaeological, but along with this there was an interest in geology.

I decided not to go for the War Office Selection Board, because to do so I would have had to agree to sign on for an extra two years. That was scrubbed and I simply went with a contingent across the Sinai Desert and into Palestine to join an artillery regiment in Palestine. That was a wonderful experience after spending three or four months in Cairo, which reeked of urine and goodness knows what. To go across the desert, which smelt of nothing but the lorry fumes, and then arrive into the south of Palestine in March, when the first orange harvests were on the roadside in great mounds and the fresh blossoms on the orange trees, so sweet-smelling — really quite wonderful. In Palestine, I served two years. Left there in 1948 and came back to this country. I do recall seeing the Mount Carmel caves, though I didn't know what they were. I could see the holes in the mountain-side. We were visiting various places where there were ruins. I recall being taken down with a group of soldiers to swim at Caesarea. It was in a sense quite thrilling, because we weren't told that there was anything to be seen there, and there wasn't very much to be seen, but I do recall seeing great columns lying on their sides in the reeds and mud. I went back about seven or eight years later, on a return visit to Palestine with my wife, and we went down to Caesarea to bathe again. It is a great tourist attraction now, with many of the columns set up. There is a great concentration of Roman ruins there, as well as Mediaeval, but none of that seemed to be visible when I was there during the War. I remember too being sent on a detail from camp at Zikron Yakov, 10—20 miles south of Haifa, to dig a hole in the hillside for a great rubbish pit and coming across part of a lead coffin. I finished my two years there.

Before I left the Middle East, I was sent down to the Canal zone to attend a 'demob' school where we could opt to attend various courses and lectures in subjects, I suppose to get us orientated to returning to a civilian life. It wasn't so much returning as starting, because I had not much of a life before that. The only thing I can remember doing there was a long and rather tedious course on European civilisation by a German with a very heavy accent, but I don't recall very much more. I was already reading a geology book in Palestine that I took out from the library there, Holmes' *Introduction to Physical Geology*; at Tel Aviv, when I was stationed there, I found a book shop with Holmes' introduction to geology and I bought that. At the Canal Zone — it was rather interesting — whilst in Egypt, just outside Heliopolis, before I got posted up to Palestine, one of the people who came to that camp, and I found myself in one of those big tents that sleeps 12 people, with a man who I found I could talk to in an interesting way. He was an older man, a sniper, who had had some sort of breakdown and had been sent there to recover. He was very interesting and he started to interest me. He was one of the first people to get me thinking about what I was going to do when I left the Army. He wanted me to go on and get a commission, and he promised to give me a handgun when I got my commission. I can't remember quite how, but I got involved. I remember borrowing from the Library Bannister Fletcher's *Introduction to Architecture on the Comparative Basis*. What I was interested in then was finding out more about Egyptian buildings. There was a whole section on Egyptian architecture. That was one of the milestones.

I call it 'pin-balling' through life if you like.Quite by chance bouncing off people who contribute something to your life as you go along, and he was one of them. I call it 'pin-balling' because it is a bit like a pin-ball coming down the table, bouncing around, not with any sort of planned trajectory but moving rather by chance.

Well, two years in Palestine and then demobilisation and back to England without any qualifications, but this man, whose name was J.E. Paul Butler, he said he came from Sevenoaks in Kent. One of the things that he had suggested to me was when I got back, I should try to get into a teacher-training college. The family was now living in Newark in Nottinghamshire, so I went there to live with them. I went off to the labour exchange to look for a job and they offered me two things: working in an iron foundry or working for the Forestry Commission. I said Forestry Commission. I found myself working about six miles from Newark cycling up early in the morning to be at work at 7 a.m. chopping trees, burning mountains of vegetation.There had been a forest there and the oak trees and various other trees had been cut during the war for the war effort, and it had been left to go wild since then and was heavily overgrown with all kinds of scrub vegetation, including huge mounds of rhododendrons. This all had to be cut, chopped, burned and so on. Various other jobs that one had to do. That I did for four or five months. I used to do fire-watching duty at weekends because I liked the quietness of the place. There were books there to read, but I didn't want to stick with it. A job came up in town at a local maltster's office, a job in an office there. There were only two of us, the man in charge of the office and myself doing the dogsbody jobs. In a short while, the company's secretary — it belonged to a company in Ipswich in Suffolk — came up and asked me if I would like to go down to Head Office and spend some time there, to get the feel of what the business was about and start maybe studying for secretarial work. I went down to do this and then came back and enlisted with a correspondence college to do secretarial practice, accountancy and economics for a while, but I had already put my name down to go on an emergency teacher-training course. I waited quite a long time for that. It eventually came up, so that let me out from the office work.

Off I went to West Kirby, near Liverpool, to the last year of emergency teacher-training programme, where I found myself with a relatively small group of people of all ages from mid twenties — I was then 23, 24, I can't remember — people up into their fifties. Some from the Army, some from industry, some from commerce who had decided that they would have a go at teaching. We attended various courses to make sure that we knew something about what we might be teaching eventually. We did our teachers' training course, practice in schools at Liverpool, and then I came back to Newark where I got a job first as a supply teacher at a little village school outside Newark, which was really quite amusing. It was a school with only one class of children of all ages from 8 to 15, about 12 children and two teachers. I was one of them. We spent an awful lot of time playing rounders under the chestnut tree and then I was asked to take all these children off to the swimming pool in Newark, which I did — holiday time. The bath was absolutely crowded with schoolchildren and when mine got all their clothes off and into their swimming costumes, I could no longer recognise them. We had to catch a bus back at a particular time and I eventually in desperation found one that I recognised and she found the others. I then got a job in a school in Newark where I worked for two years and had wonderful times there, teaching and taking some of the children camping in the summer holidays up to Wales and Derbyshire.

But it was during that time in Newark for two years, I was out cycling one Sunday with my brother, and going up the hill near East Stoke we saw in a field on to the left a group of people stripped to the waist wielding shovels, and I said, "Those must be archaeologists. Let's go and have a look." So we dumped our bikes and went off into the field, and sure enough it was the local archaeological society. They were cutting a trench across the mound, a sort of ridge that ran down into the field, which Maurice Barley was in charge of that exercise. He was a local man. He was an historian, primarily a local historian working in the Extramural Department at Nottingham University; he lived in a village near there [subsequently he held the Chair of Archaeology]. He and the man who was Principal of the local technical college, a man called Bowen, had started the Newark Archaeological Society. They were cutting a trench there because they thought that it might be a Roman road, because it was pointing straight down at a known Roman posting station. Well, they never found the Roman road, but I joined the gang and spent the weekends digging with them on all sorts of sites. Apart from attending WEA classes, some of which were Maurice Barley 's classes on local history, he organised a class in archaeology which was given by a man called Dauncey, K.D.M Dauncey, who was a Cambridge graduate who was teaching at Birmingham University. He used to come over. He was a brilliant field archaeologist and brilliant lecturer and teacher. I learned a lot of archaeology and a lot of the approach to archaeology, the attitude to archaeology, what archaeology is about, what it is trying to do and how it worked, from him.

What class was he in? How do you spell his name?

Dauncey. I don't know — during the War   he must have been a very bright chap. He got a job in the Admiralty I think in London and was doing something quite responsible. He was still a very young man when I came across him. I got the chronology wrong there a bit. Barley, Bowen and Dauncey came into my life during the two years I was working before I went to teacher training. So, we set that back a bit. I came out of the Army in January 1948 and went off to Teacher Trainer College about two years later and it was during those two years that I met up with Newark Archaeological Society and Maurice Barley and Kenneth Dauncey. Barley was a very important influence in my life.

[I say something about Dauncey, most likely about his involvement in the Mediaeval Deserted Village projects.[

Cambridge, he must have been — you see he had a job during the War in London so he must have been at Cambridge in the years immediately before the War. Well, Teacher Trainer College — back to Newark. These courses were not very long, about 13 months. Then after the temporary teacher job, I got a post in a junior school, teaching seven- and eight-year-old children. Interesting challenge there, because the class I was teaching was a class of 63 children. Sixty-three in one class. At one end of the spectrum there were children who didn't even know the alphabet, and at the other, there were some who could read straight through the Schonnell reading test. It was a very interesting challenge to control a class that size and teach them something as well. Back in Newark, I got back in touch with Maurice and the Archaeological Society, I could remember after an evening class going to the pub with Maurice Barley and another friend of mine, Doug Hurrell, and Maurice saying to me, "You know, Ray, you ought to do something more with your archaeology. You ought to apply for a government scholarship to go to university to read archaeology". Well, he looked at that and found that I couldn't do this, I wasn't eligible because I had had a government grant to do the teacher-training course, but there was one other possibility. That was Cambridge University, which offered Adult Bursaries through their Extramural Department, two a year, not in archaeology but in any subject, and you had to submit a piece of written work in the subject that you wanted to pursue.

Meanwhile, during the two years I had been teaching at Newark, I had also been working on that Roman site at East Stoke where it all started, with what was possibly the road leading down into the posting station which was known from air photographs. Adrian Oswald had excavated in it before the War back in the 1930s, but I spent some time there with Doug Hurrell, probing with a steel probe to locate ditches. It lay — the road from Nottingham to Newark ran approximately parallel to the River Trent and ran into Newark, and the major part of the posting station lay on one side of the road. On the river side [the air photograph revealed] there was nothing because it was a rather narrow pasture field with cattle and a bank [close to the road] which Oswald had mentioned in his report as being a [natural] bank of gravel. I happened to notice that in the rabbit scrapes on that bank there was dark soil and stuff that looked like occupational debris. So I said "this bank parallels the far side of the posting station and maybe it is the other side of the posting station". We cut a broad six-foot trench through there from the hedge by the road towards the river and got a lot of very interesting information out of there. We found evidence of an early Roman site with Claudian pottery and foundation trenches of timber [structures], but quite by chance. The trench had run pretty well down the middle of what was obviously a road out of the camp on that side towards the river. On the one side we got a set of massive post-holes, and we cut through the remains of a rampart which had had a checkered history, at least two periods of building, and then, in the front, a stone wall had been inserted. Clearly what we had got was the massive post-holes associated with a gateway. So we got a lot of very interesting information out of that. I wrote it all up and sent that in with my application to Cambridge. I was told that there were 300 applicants. They were whittled down to a short list of about six or eight who were called up for an interview, and during a sort of nightmare 24 hours we were there. The first night we arrived they arranged a cocktail party for us, where we met the other applicants and some people who would interview us. I remember being sort of terrified. There were three large gentlemen from Oxford who had studied at Ruskin College, which is just down the road from here. Ruskin College is a working man's college, started really for people who were going to try to pick up some sort of education later in life. There were three applicants from there and they were standing around talking about Proust ,and I had never even heard of Proust, and I thought "Oh God." Anyway, I went into the interview room the next day. Dame Myra Curtis, who was then Principal of [Newham] at the time, was at the far end of the table. People were all around, and the one archaeologist there was Glyn Daniel. They asked me all sorts of questions. Glyn asked me had I read Kenyon's little book which had just come out, *Beginning in Archaeology*. I said "No, I hadn't." And he said that in that book she says she believes that archaeology is a subject which should only be read as a post-graduate subject and he said "What do you think about that?" I thought very quickly and said I did not believe this was a view that was held in Cambridge, otherwise they wouldn't be teaching undergraduate archaeology. That seemed to be the right thing to say. They asked me, if I were given this opportunity, what I proposed to do with it at the end of it. And, I said "Well, I would propose to go back to teaching." They asked why would I want to read archaeology and I said because I was interested in it and fascinated by it and wanted to learn more about it, but I expected to go back to teaching and that was that; and I got the bursar — one of the two Bursaries. So I read my Archaeology and Anthropology. I loved the Archaeology and thrived on it, but Social Anthropology, I never understood what it was about, and I think this was —

SIDE TWO on duplicate tape starts here

— they assumed too much prior knowledge. That was 1953. Meyer Fortes, Reo Fortune, G.I. Jones, West Africa, lots of circles on the blackboard and diffusion. Leach was fascinating. I had an association with Leach later on [we collaborated on a teaching project]. He had just come to Cambridge. His was the first lecture I went to when I was at Cambridge, and I sat through that lecture on "Time and Space in Primitive Society".

SIDE TWO on original tape starts here

Edmund Leach talking about time and space — sitting there with my notebook and not getting a word on the page because, although I was fascinated with what he was saying, I couldn't really — I just wasn't up to making notes. Never in all my life had I written an essay, you see. Well, apart from limited written assignments in those years I was attending Worker's Education Extension classes with Kenneth Dauncey. We had to do little bits of written work for Dauncey, but they were on a very limited scale. I was feeling very nervous about that because the chap next to me was filling his page. I never really understood what Social Anthropology was all about, and I ended up with a 2:2 and suspect that I was pulled down on the Anthropology papers. I didn't like it. It didn't seem relevant. It certainly wasn't relevant the way it was taught at Cambridge in those days. You wouldn't expect any student of archaeology today who was asked to combine a bit of anthropology with archaeology to concentrate on the sorts of things that were talked about. In retrospect one recognises the essence of what Leach was talking about. The sort of thing I couldn't understand the relevance of was the importance of distance measured in Burma by teahouses. That was Edmund Leach.

What did Meyer Fortes teach?

Almost certainly kinship relationships. The ones that froze me absolutely rigid were the Australian ones. I was set to read in that first year by the woman who supervised me, she was a Fellow of Girton but she didn't have a teaching post in the University, but she did supervisions, Doris Wheatley.

She died very recently.

She was a very nice person and a very good Supervisor. I was in St John's. Glyn Daniel was at John's. He wasn't my College Tutor. My Tutor was a man called Claude Gillebaud, who was an Economist. He wrote about peanuts in Tanganyika, I discovered a few days ago. Wheatley was my Supervisor in Part I and I was set to read things like Evans-Pritchard's — he did a series of radio lectures on anthropology and they were published as a book. I was sent to see Doris Wheatley before Term started, and she sent me away back to Newark with instructions to read Evans-Pritchard's *Introduction to Social Anthropology* and Radcliffe Brown's — what was the title? These two books seemed to be saying very different things — *Structure and Function in Primitive Society* — what a thing to start someone on! It was heavy stuff. I couldn't like it. I couldn't understand it. It wasn't what I wanted to do. Once we got back to a supervised project, things got a little more under control. I dutifully wrote my little essays. She would say to me, "Ah, that is an interesting statement. Where did you get that from?" "I can't remember," and she would say "Well, tell me next week when you've found out."

[I say something inaudible about Meyer Fortes.]

Reo Fortune was interesting. I sat right through his course of lectures in first or second term. We started with a class of maybe 20 people, and at the end of it there were three of us. He would come in with a pile of books with little bits of paper sticking out. He would start lecturing with the intention of referring to these, but he never did. He used to wander off and suddenly stop talking for, oh, seconds and seconds, which is a very long time, perhaps even a minute of absolute silence while his gaze sort of wandered around in space and then he would start again on a completely different tack. He was a very strange man. I liked him and we were colleagues later on, but he was not a gifted teacher. He might have been a gifted anthropologist.

I ask about Lindgren.

I don't remember that name. Before I went up to Cambridge, I had been doing mostly Roman archaeology. I had excavated a Roman Villa for the Ministry of Works in East Anglia. I had started to excavate another for the Ministry of Works at High Wycombe, which I was unable to complete because it turned out to be a huge villa. That's right — I did that during my first Long Vac at Cambridge and had to hand it over to Brian Hartley. I worked before I came up on several Roman sites. I then had to decide what I was going to do at Cambridge. The first year, you don't have any choices. General introductory, you do a bit of Palaeolithic with Miles Burkitt, you do some Neo and Bronze Age with Glyn Daniel and get some Iron Age with Tom Lethbridge. Yes, he didn't have a post, but was in a sense a Visiting Lecturer, used to do regular courses and lectures on the British Iron Age and on Anglo-Saxon. He used to appear in ginger plus-fours, a very large and imposing figure, wonderful character who used to produce the most superb blackboard work. He'd be talking, and whilst he was talking great big beautifully drawn Saxon square-headed brooches would appear on the blackboard, and other things, lovely Celtic pots with decoration. Toty de Navarro wasn't teaching Part I but teaching course II people. De Navarro did a Part Two course on the Iron Age, which I attended. Yes, indeed, eight lectures. McBurney was teaching Part Two Palaeolithic courses. I had to make the choice, not in the first year because we had all that general stuff and Social Anthropology, but for the second year you had to choose. You could do Roman or post-Roman or NBI or the Palaeolithic, and I hadn't decided to do the Palaeolithic at that stage but I was very, very conscious of the fact that if, for instance, you wanted to understand Roman Britain you had to know about Iron Age Britain, and it seemed to me if you wanted to know about Iron Age Britain, you needed to know about the Bronze Age — the sensible thing to do was to go back to the beginning and start at the Palaeolithic. So, I opted to do Palaeolithic in Part Two, and that is what I did. Interestingly, at the time they were making changes in the Tripos. They had just introduced new Tripos regulations. What this meant was that Charles McBurney was teaching a special Palaeolithic course for Part Two people, and that was the first year. The half-dozen of us who were doing it sat through those classes with McBurney, and come the third year, Charles was giving effectively the same course, and I can remember going to him saying "Charles, I think I am not going to sit through your lectures this term. I'm going to attend lectures in Botany, with Godwin and West, and in Geology." I have forgotten the name of the person who was teaching a course in Quaternary — King — probably King. So I did those two courses outside the Department and came back in the second term just to get refresher notes from Charles.

Can you say some of your impressions of Burkitt in Part One?

Burkitt, I recall — he always insisted on lecturing at 9 a.m. in the morning. I think this was probably so he could get away at 10 a.m. and spend the rest of the day attending his committee meetings, which he loved to tell you he sat on so many of. But I remember him. He had a very rich, plummy, booming voice, which was in a sense a comfortable, friendly voice. You had no difficulty hearing what he was saying. He was a thorough teacher. You had no difficulty in getting some notes down and following what he was saying — well, I have described him formerly to you. His habit of sitting on the large table in the middle of the back of the lecture room on which he had this giant epidiascope, showing his 4-inch by 4-inch slides. He would have his notebook open and he would sit there talking away in the dark. Always the lights were out and the epidiascope always on, and he would talk and turn the page, and talk and turn the page, and walk up to the front of the room, and point out some features of the current slide, and then walk slowly back, and then sit on the table and push the next slide through, and turn the page and carry on talking, and so on. I remember him once going to the front and walking slowly back, and there was a student two rows in front of me, his head was down on the table and he was fast asleep. He obviously had a late night and Miles just came down and sat on the end of the table beside him and boomed into his ear a minute or two until he woke up, and then he came back to his slides. I think he was a good teacher. I remember [recall] sitting in a supervision once with Doris Wheatley and another student, Tony Baggs, who ended up as quite an eminent figure in the Historical Buildings Commission. Doris was asking us how we were getting on with our classes, and Baggs made very disparaging remarks about Miles Burkitt, I think being over-simplistic in his teaching, and Doris Wheatley reacted very badly to this — rather cross

with him. I think rightly so, because Tony Baggs knew about as much as I did about the Palaeolithic, and I think probably what he was reacting to was the rather teacherly, school-teacherly approach of Miles. But I think, subsequently when I went back to take over his post when he retired, and I came back from Northern Rhodesia to take over his teaching of Part One Archaeology, the Palaeolithic, one of the things he said to me was, "You should remember," he said, "everything you teach, you should tell it three times, but not so that they notice it." For introductory people doing a strange subject, where you are hoping to get them to absorb some of what you were saying, this is not a bad thing, that you somehow refer to the same bit of information more than once in slightly different contexts, to be fairly sure that the message is getting in. I think that there is nothing wrong with that.

In my subsequent years of teaching in Cambridge, Cape Town, Harvard, Oxford, I often come across young people just starting a teaching career in university, and what they want to be teaching their first-year students is the kind of level they reached during their Doctoral years. They somehow feel that you have got to throw them in at the deep end, "This is what it is really all about, this is important stuff, let's get them to grips with this right away," and the students don't know what's going on. I believe in starting right at the bottom, assuming nothing and build up. The other thing that is very important in teaching archaeology is to get people to grips, right at the beginning, with the actual artefacts of the periods you are talking, whether it is Roman pottery or Bronze Age bronzes or Palaeolithic stone implements, you've got to not only talk to them about these things, about how they were made and what they were made for, but to get them to handle these things to get the feel of them. At Cambridge, when I was teaching Part One Palaeolithic practicals (I don't remember that Miles, I don't think we had practicals), I think I introduced them for Part One people [as an innovation]: I used to get out trays of material and have small classes in at a time, and get them to handle these things, and ask them, "OK, tell me what that is?" "A scraper." And they were right, and I would say, "Why is it scraper?" They couldn't tell me. I realised that there was this gulf between the image they had seen on the screen or in a book [and the real thing]. They could recognise it, but they hadn't understand about secondary working, things like this; what made it a scraper.

Burkitt would talk a lot about the stone tools, about typology. It comes out very strongly in his book *The Old Stone Age*, but I think those descriptions of tool classes and families are very good of course for first-year students. Our lectures were in the North and South Lecture rooms and we were taken into the Museum to see specimens in the showcases by Grahame Clark; to look at Mesolithic things. Audrey Furness used to take us in to show us some of the Neo/Bronze Age/Iron Age and Roman things, and she would occasionally get something out of the case. I remember one terrifying occasion when she got out the Grunty Fen torque. The Grunty Fen torque is a gold arm ring, which has two terminals coming out at the ends, and made from a sort of cross twisted and coiled around. It is about a foot long, and coils are about five inches, and she got this out and passed it around for us to get the experience of holding it and one chap took the two ends and did concertina with it. She nearly fainted. I think Grahame and Audrey did this sort of thing. I don't remember Glyn Daniel taking us in to see things in Part One, and Miles I don't think did.

Glyn was entertaining?

Not greatly entertaining. He wasn't greatly humorous. He would stand in front in his gown, always wore a gown when he lectured. Grahame, I think, also wore a gown when he lectured. And Glyn would stand there holding the sleeves and swinging them. He was quite interesting but not outstanding. Miles was a pleasant, good, not a vastly inspiring teacher. He would wander off with little anecdotes.

Break for a minute

Back to Miles Burkitt: from my undergraduate days, I don't think I can enlarge on him as a teacher. He clearly loved the Old Stone Age. In particular, he loved the Palaeolithic art, and there he really got some atmosphere into talking about the sites, going down the long, gloomy passages of the caves, the boom of the water drops falling from the roof in the silence of the great caverns. Yes, his presentation of the art was entirely in the style of thinking of the Abbé Breuil, it was concerned with the typology of the drawings, the superpositions and sympathetic magic. They were memorable introductions to Upper Palaeolithic Art.

Since we are talking about Miles would it be all right if I jumped, because he then went out of my life until I came back to Cambridge to teach when he had retired, and I applied for and got his post. He had it as a Lectureship. I got it as an Assistant Lectureship. I decided to come back, very tempting to get back to Cambridge. Miles and Peggy kindly invited me to stay with them for a few days in January '59 until I found somewhere to live. During that time, Miles showed me some of the treasures he had, including that little Magdalenian palette with the bison licking its flank, and we would talk about what was I going to do, and he would say "Always remember that nature proceeds by evolution, not revolution." There would be some changes, but he was saying that I should not go off the deep end into teaching advanced archaeology to first-year students ;and he produced this message that I had almost forgotten, about always making a point three times, not so they notice, and he offered me, one evening as we were sitting in front of the fire, his lecture notebooks. So I took them into my room and had a look at them, and it was perfectly clear that these were the chapters, almost word for word, of *The Old Stone Age* book. No doubt at all that those were the lecture notes that he had built up and put together. The book came out of that, and the notes continued as the lecture notes. For all these years of teaching, and all the thoroughness with which he knew it, he still sat there and turned the pages, one after the other.

We used not *Prehistory* but the *The Old Stone Age*. *Prehistory* was a little bit earlier, didn't have all the detail about tool types in it. I can't remember being told to read anything else on the Palaeolithic except *The Old Stone Age* in that first year on the Palaeolithic. My Supervisors in the first year were Glyn Daniel and Doris Wheatley. If I wrote anything on the Palaeolithic, it was for Glyn Daniel. I don't remember what it was.

[I ask something which is inaudible — something about who was the best at teaching?]

Hard to say. I went in with a very positive interest. I wanted to know as much archaeology as I could, and if there were people there who could stand up in front of the class and tell me, it didn't matter if it was Miles Burkitt on the Old Stone Age, Grahame Clark on the Mesolithic, or Glyn Daniel on the Bronze Age, round barrows and long barrows. I was fascinated, and I wanted to know, and I got my nose down and made as much of it as I could for the tutorials I was set by Glyn Daniel. Thinking of the four principal archaeologists whose lectures I attended, that is Burkitt, Daniel, Clark and Lethbridge — I suppose it is difficult to say. I think in terms of what I was getting from them. They were all very much on a par, because they were doing very different things. If two different people were giving lectures on the same subject, you would know to say "Yes, that one is doing a much better job than that one," but I felt that I got a good introduction to the Old Stone Age with Miles and learned some fascinating stuff from Grahame. He was newly appointed Professor, very interesting, because all sorts of things have been said about Grahame being aloof and rather haughty.

When I came up for interview for that Adult Bursary, they had arranged for me to meet Grahame Clark and here was I, a complete nonentity who was hoping to get an Adult Bursary and read archaeology, and he talked to me in his office and took me all around the Museum, all the rooms of the Museum, and pointed out the major things of interest to me. That was not the action of the kind of man who deserved the reputation of an unapproachable person. I was always grateful to him. He asked me, I may have made some reference when talking in his office to having read with very great interest his book that had just come out on *Prehistoric Europe: the Economic Basis,* and I can remember him saying to me, sort of smiling somewhat, "Yes, it's enjoyable to read books like that, but you will enjoy it much more writing your own." Even at that stage, before I got the Bursary. One of the things that he felt he should say to an aspiring archaeologist, that this should be the ultimate goal, to be writing your own book. I had to rate them different but equal.

I mention the tradition of Tea at Miles' in the 1930s.

I don't think that we ever went to Miles Burkitt's for Tea. They had supervisions with Miles, you see. I didn't. I don't think he was supervising

students in those days. Burkitt talked about Thurstan. He talked about Desmond.

I remember when I first arrived in St John's, I had to go to see Gillebaud, my moral Tutor, a very nice sort of fatherly gentleman, and he asked me if there was any problem that I was concerned about and I said, "Yes, I was slightly concerned because coming up through rather strange channels to Cambridge, a very strange experience to me, and one of the things I certainly don't see myself doing is things like rowing, playing cricket or football, not part of my life." "Oh", he said "You don't have to worry about that," he said. "Before the War anybody would have been expected to do things like that, but now that's gone," he said. "You do it if you want to, but if you don't want to, you don't do those things any more." Things had changed after the War with the influx of people who came out of the Army and found their way in to university for various reasons. But in fact someone came along in my first year, there was a group of us in Second Court in St John's, and said, why don't we make up an eleventh boat, and we did. One man had rowed before, and he was going to be the coach, and I was going to be the cox until they found that I turned about 11 stone 6 then and was heavier than the chap in number 8. So I was whipped out of the cox's seat and put into number 8, and we rowed mightily. We turned out early in the morning, like all the others, and worked in the tubs and on the river — a lot of splash. We tried very hard. Dave Grigg was our cox. He then became a Lecturer and Professor of Geography at Sheffield, and we are still in touch. In the May bumps, we went down four places. That is as far as you can go in the May bumps. But on the final day, we were rowing like hell up the side of the river, and I think we had been bumped, so the object of the exercise was to get out of the way of the other boats. And Dave gave a strange order which we all obeyed and we ended up with the prow of the boat in a ploughed field — shot up the bank of the river, and that was the end of my experience, but we did row. It was good fun!

I mentioned doing Palaeolithic with McBurney, and in that third year cutting his lectures in the first term and going on to Godwin and King. It was in that final year that we went off to the Haua Fteah to do the final season in that big cave, and I think that I played a fairly major role in that because, I am sorry to have to say, I don't think that Charles McBurney was particularly a field worker. He did a lot of field work, but he wasn't a born field worker. He had already gone down about 28 feet in this cave. There was this great trench, so many feet wide, and he said he wanted to go much deeper. Fortunately, he had cocked-up the arrangements with the Administration in Cyrene over Arab labour. He had written and asked for a labour force to be got together, and when we arrived it wasn't in evidence. So he took on local Arabs who were just wandering around. Pitched camp and took these Arabs on, and then the Arabs who had been taken by local authorities in Cyrene, told that they had work, were very angry, and there seemed to be the prospect of a fight. Charles McBurney said that first night, "There may be trouble," he said, "There may be trouble. If there is, beat them off with pickhelves.". We all had pickhelves next to the bed. Nothing happened, but Charles had to spend three or four days in Cyrene sorting out the administrative problems, and meanwhile I simply assumed responsibility for deciding the size of the cutting. I thought, if we are going to go much deeper than he had, then we needed a large cutting to make it safe, and I laid out a very large cutting. Charles was a bit surprised when he came back and saw it. We laid out the cutting. We cleared off all the sheep dung for about 10 feet around this cutting, because when you walked into that cave wearing shorts, the fleas ran up your legs because it was still used [to pen livestock] in the winter. So, we cleared this huge area of dung to reduce the flea problem. It was understood that I was going to draw the sections, but I wanted to use a dumpy level and staff to draw the sections, and Charles had agreed. I took these along on the expedition and set up the dumpy level at one corner of the cutting to draw the profile. Charles came along and we swung it through 90 degrees and, of course, when you swing it through 90 degrees the bubble goes out of true, and you just use a screw adjustment to bring it back to centre. "No good, no good" he said. "It's inaccurate. We can't have this." He didn't understand that the bubble automatically goes out and you just have to adjust it. He wouldn't allow me to do this, and I just had to use the old string [and spirit level technique].

END OF TAPE I

Tape 2 side I

Back to Miles Burkitt; one of the things he would love to say to us as first-year students doing the Palaeolithic course, "Some of you will no doubt end up in the Colonial Service," he said, "overseas." He said, "I want you to remember, when you find those stone implements lying around the camp site where you are and you are administering justice under the Juju tree, never let the sun set on an unmarked implement." But he spent a lot of his retirement in his office (I know because I shared his office with him when I went back to Cambridge), marking stone implements.

May I ask you, did he still have a library that he would let students come to in Grantchester?

I never had knowledge or experience of that.

It may have been transferred to the Haddon?

No, no, it was still in his house because after he died, I think a lot of the books, after he died it is possible that the bulk of books went to the Haddon, but for a long time they sat at Grantchester and Peggy, if people came to see Peggy, who were former students or colleagues, she would always invite them to take a book. She did so when I went to visit her with Adi, when we came back from Africa in 1972. There were relatively few books left on the shelf then. I don't think they had been all given away. I think most had gone; the Haddon had promptly taken what they wanted, without taking duplicates. But I was asked to take a book.

Where was the Haddon?

You reached the Haddon by going up the stairs in the Museum; on the first floor were the lecture rooms, and then on the top floor you went through to the Haddon.

When I last saw the Haddon, you didn't go into it that way. You went into it through the Downing Street court, but when I was a student, the Haddon was upstairs and very convenient.

I did go back there to talk to the Librarian two or three years ago to see if they were interested in my books. They said they were interested only in books they may not already have. My guess is that they already had a lot of them, but I didn't want the collection broken up. There is a lot of natural history, early travellers.

We discuss Grahame Clark's library.
Interruption — to continue about Charles.

Charles had this problem with the labour, and in his absence I was able to lay out this very large cutting. I had wanted to draw the section using a dumpy level and staff as the cutting went down, but that was not to be because he didn't trust the implement, so I simply spent most of the time excavating. I did an awful lot of excavating on that site whilst other people were doing various other things. There were usually two of us working at the same time, and two people could keep the sorters busy; people who had to sort and deal with the bone and the packing and the labelling and so on. I seem to recollect that I spent most of my time in the cutting, and then at the end of the excavation, when Charles had got everybody back at the base camp with all the equipment and all the specimens and so on, I was still drawing the section. I'd drawn the upper levels whilst some of the work was still going on, and the clearing up, and then this perilous business of drawing the next stage, which is the very deep stage, about 28 feet if I remember rightly, which I had to start by hanging over the edge and putting in nails and a string to get a horizontal line, then working off a ladder to draw the thing from within the cutting. Finally, the deep sounding which went down to a depth of 43 feet, and I was down at the bottom of that at 43 feet still drawing that when the Arabs were filling in the cutting behind me. The soil was just coming in a great swell towards me, and there was nobody but those Arabs and myself at the cave at that stage.

I came up for a break during the middle of the day and there was an Arab woman who had just come in to the cave with a great flock of goats. So I went over and sat down by her. She couldn't speak any English and I couldn't speak any Arabic, so we had a slightly stultified conversation, but she clearly wanted to ask me if I wanted a drink. So, I said "Yes."

She looked around, saw her favourite goat, grabbed it by the head, pulled it to her, kissed it on the head, then milked it into a tin can and gave me a drink of nice warm goat's milk, straight from the goat, wonderful!

I finished up then, and Charles came up late in the afternoon and collected me, and that was the end of the excavation. Let me say this about Charles, he was a superb teacher. He absolutely emanated enthusiasm for the Palaeolithic. He had a tremendous knowledge, and taught us everything that he knew. There was never a boring moment. One really learned an immense amount from him, and he did have parties for students, he and Anne. I can remember going to their house on a number of occasions, probably in the summer. They were very generous in that way. But I just felt that, from that experience with Charles then, and from one or two other things that happened, that he was not a born excavator. He excavated because he knew that there was information that could be got out, and he wanted it out, and he got it out as best he may. He got a lot of good information from the sites that he dug, and wrote some extremely important papers, but, for instance, at one stage before we got down to the Neolithic, when we were working down through Mediaeval Arab stuff, emerging at a slightly diagonal line from one of the long faces of the cutting, there was a double row of big slabs of stones on edge, sticking out parallel on edge, with rubble in between them. As soon as we picked up the tops of these and started cleaning out the stone and soft soil on either side, I said, "Charles we have a building." And he came along and looked at it and said, "No, no, those are slabs which have fallen from the roof." They were part of a building. I got him to leave them there. We cleaned, worked around them and left them '*in situ*'.

Whilst we were there, Richard Goodchild came up from Cyrene. Richard Goodchild was Director of Antiquities in Cyrenaica at that time, and he was based at Cyrene. I said, "We have a building here. Come look at this". He stood at the edge and looked and said "I can't see any building." I think this was because as a Classical Archaeologist, he wanted dressed stone. Something very interesting going on there, because there was no question about this. Associated levels, appropriate levels, we were getting Greek material. We got Greek figured pottery and bronze, and I think there was a coin, and those are not the things you find in a cave in the country-side in the possession of shepherds using those caves for their sheep, just as the modern shepherds do. I believe that rough stone building was probably part of a shrine.

I can't remember what Charles says about it in the Haua Fteah. The material is there [in the Museum]. It has not been repatriated. Eric Higgs and Richard Klein did something. Eric Higgs did the faunal remains and subsequently Richard Klein and [Cruz Uribe] did a re-examination and reassessment of the Haua Fteah faunal, but the archaeological material has not been worked over. I believe there are three applications in to Libya for permits to re-dig the Haua Fteah. I know of one of them, an Italian group, and I think there are a number of leading Palaeolithic archaeologists of North Africa who realise that this is a gold mine waiting to be redug with all the modern techniques of recovery and analysis which couldn't be brought to bear in 1955. One hopes that it will be re-dug but it won't be an easy job.

We came back from Haua Fteah. On the way back, a small group of us did a very nice tour around some of the French and Spanish painted and archaeological sites. Jacques Nenquin, Eric Higgs, myself, Eric Higgs' first wife, and there was somebody else, a group of about 5 or 6 of us. We went along the south of France, up the Pyrenees and crossed to the [border near Biarritz] and along the north of Spain, then down into Pamplona and back to France and across to Calais. That was very good to see. We got into Altamira, for instance, and into Lascaux and some of the other painted sites in [Spain and] France. It was interesting and then, of course, shortly after that, there was the Tripos.

Eric Higgs and Tony Baggs had got together between them and had beavered up on all the publications of Kenneth Oakley because they had all been speculating about who the External Examiner might be and they were quite sure that it wouldn't be Zeuner because McBurney didn't seem to like Zeuner very much, so they thought that the only other person it could be was Kenneth Oakley. They had boned up on Kenneth Oakley and used Higgs' high-tech tape recorder to record bits and pieces. Lo and behold it turned out to be Freddy Zeuner as the External.

I can't remember whether I was actually writing the finals or whether it was just after or before we wrote the finals. I was going up from the ground floor of the Museum to the next floor and met Grahame Clark coming down. He stopped me on the stairs and said [quite casually], "Oh, Ray how would you like to go to Tanganyika and do some work there?" And I said "Oh, I'd love that. That would be fine." He said "All right, I'll put you in touch with Mortimer Wheeler, arrange a meeting with Mortimer Wheeler." He told me that Mortimer Wheeler had been out with Gervase Matthew looking at archaeology in those East African territories: it was all tied up with the establishment of the British School in Nairobi. One of the things that had emerged was the concern of the Tanganyika government of the day, the Colonial government of the day, with the Rock paintings in the central district, in the Kondoa district. They had asked for somebody to go out to advise them on the desirability and practicability of preserving the paintings; Grahame told me this much.

Eventually I got the appointment to go to see Mortimer Wheeler and I can't remember if I had written to him but I had said if the funds were adequate, would there be any objection to two of us going, Eric Higgs and myself, because I had struck up a good relationship with Eric Higgs. I was a rather mature student and we saw eye to eye on many things. That was all right, he said. We were to go up and met the Great Sir Mortimer, I suppose in Burlington House. Eric and I arrived in London and got there early with half an hour to spare. Meanwhile, before all this happened, we had gone around Regents' Park Zoo to take a look at some of the animals we might meet in East Africa, particularly the snakes, because the only bit of information on this area was Sonia Coles' Penguin book, *Prehistory of East Africa*. She had described the rock paintings and said that any moment you may come face to face with a rhino on the foot path, poisonous snakes [were everywhere]. So, we went and had a look at a rhino and went and had a look at the snakes in Regent's Park Zoo; trundled along then to Piccadilly. As I said, we had a bit of time in hand. So, I said, "There is a gunsmith's down here. Let's go and find out what sort of gun . . . " We went into the shop and a smart man in pinstriped trousers and a black jacket [enquired] "What can I do for you?" I said "What sort of a gun would you need to shoot a rhino?" "Oh, thick skin, heavy game, you'd need a four oh four, Sir." "Could you show us one?" He took a gun down from the gun rack and offered it to me stock first and I took this thing and nearly fell over, it was so heavy. We enquired about the price. I think it was about £100 sterling. He said they could have the cartridges packed [in grease] for us to travel. We then went off to see Mortimer Wheeler. We progressed through the interview and he told us what it was all about and what one was required to do, discussed the question of Eric Higgs. And he said "Well it is up to you. There is about £1000 Sterling." Then I said "What about a gun? According to Sonia Coles, any moment you might run into a rhino. I've no desire to go around shooting game but one would like to defend oneself." He paused a moment and twirled his moustache and said "A gun!? A gun!?" he said, "Don't irritate the game!!" "If they think it is dangerous, they will send an *askari* with you." Which they never did, of course, because it wasn't dangerous. [I went on my own.] We never saw anything bigger than a guinea fowl, except when I went to Olorgesaillie with Louis Leakey and Merrick Posnansky and saw a semi-tame rhino.

When we left Wheeler, came back to Cambridge, it was quite apparent that Eric couldn't come along on £1000. There just wouldn't be enough. So, I went on my own. That £1000 had to cover everything, the airfare, all the expenses, the expedition. I flew out to Nairobi where I was met by Louis and Mary Leakey, who took me home and talked to me about Kisese and showed me things in the Museum and their home. They said that Kisese was the only site in the Kondoa district where they found deposit of depth. They had cut a trial trench at the rock shelter and showed me some of the specimens they had got out, and said if I would like to do so, I could take over the excavation and that could be my site. That was a very wonderful thing. Mary Leakey took me around the game reserve at Nairobi, the game park where we saw lions and other animals. One of their sons, I think it was Jonathan, small boy, a keen snake collector, was with us and on the way home, it was getting dark when we drove back to their house outside Nairobi and all of a sudden, he shouted something and Mary slammed on the brakes and Jonathan jumped out of the van. There was a snake. He caught this thing by the head and brought it back to the Land Rover. [I kept a nervous eye on it the rest of the journey]. He collected snakes.

I think it was the next day, I flew on to Dar-es-Salaam where I was met by a District Officer and taken to accommodation and to see the Colonial Governor who was from the Attenborough family, brother I believe of Richard and David Attenborough. We talked about what I

was going to do. I was kitted out with some sheets and pillow cases at the local hospital, put on the train to Dodoma in the Central District and stayed there for a couple of nights [with the Provincial Commissioner]. There I was kitted up. One of the geologists from the Geological Survey had gone on leave to England so his survey team consisting of three or four Africans, two vehicles, Land Rover and a 13 hundred-weight truck, and drivers and I was given this crew and kitted up with tents and other things I would need and off we went to Kisese with the District Commissioner's son, who was on holiday from school. After a few breakdowns on the way, eventually arrived up at Kondoa where I stayed for a couple of nights in a rest house whilst I decided where I was going to make a base camp. I drove up the Kisese area, which was just below the Masai escarpment, and the problem was whether to camp at Kisese, which was rather out of the way on a little road and then a dirt track going up to the Kisese Rock Shelter and a couple of miles back on one side there was a mission station and a couple of miles further on the other way was a little village, where there was a house which had belonged to the Colonial Administration. It had been used by the Tsetse control people but it hadn't been used for years, and the question was that I might stay and make the trip to the cave each day. We went up to look at this and I was tempted, because of the security and comfort of being in a house rather than in a tent. This was my first experience in Africa, apart from Haua Fteah. I was a little uncertain about things. We couldn't get into this place. We didn't have a key. We went around back and broke the fly netting on the back door, got the hand through and opened the door, went through a corridor to the front. At the front, there was a room on the right and a room on the left. I went into room on the right. It was a small room and [at the front] there was a window and a table and a chair, another window on the side. A pile of mattocks, long-handled hoes, stood in the corner, heavily rusted. Behind me was a red ant heap which rose up from the floor in a column to the ceiling. On the table was a pile of papers. They were eaten away on the edges by ants. I picked them up to have a look at them and a lot of it just fell to pieces. These were control officer reports, carbon copies of reports, and they stopped abruptly about 20 years previously and I [guessed] that place hadn't been used for about 20 years. The local Africans down in the village said it was haunted. Putting together the rather creepy feel of the place, I said "no" and we set up camp just below the rock shelter. I had quite a big tent to myself with a sort of half round at the back for a little canvas bath. The crew had their tents a little way away on the side. I think we had better stop here . . .

We have decided to stop at 1956 and I will come back at a later date to record another tape with Professor Inskeep.

Was this the first dig on your own?

Yes, alone, the only white man. The District Commissioner's son had to leave to return to school in the few days. One felt lonely at night, sitting there in the dark, with perhaps just a little lamp going, making up the notes for the day and sorting specimens and writing letters home.

Did the Africans understand?

I had one man who really did. That was Heslon who was Louis Leakey's right-hand man, whom Louis had lent to me. Heslon had come down and joined me. Louis Leakey came down at the end of the dig and collected him and [the skeletal remains I had recovered and I returned to Dar es Salaam.]

Thank you. [To be continued.]

END OF TAPE 2 SIDE I

Professor Pierre de Maret

14 July 2000, recorded at SAfA, Peterhouse, Cambridge University, by Pamela Jane Smith pjs1011@cam.ac.uk
I am speaking to Professor Pierre de Maret from the University of Brussels and the Museé Royal de l'Afrique Central in Tervuren, Belgium.

Could you first discuss some of your early influences and why you are in archaeology?

While as a child I was fascinated by archaeology and as a matter of fact we had a country house in Belgium and I ended up finding some interesting flint tools. I gave them — my best friend's father was a Curator of a major museum in Belgium and I gave them to him saying, "Would that possibly be a prehistoric tool?" Indeed, after a couple of weeks, the answer came back from one of the great Belgium specialists that they were Neolithic stone tools. They thought 4000 years old. I was very excited. I was not even ten years old and I decided that day that I would become an archaeologist. My parents were not very convinced, because the job market was very, very poor and the prospects of making a living out of being an archaeologist were not good. So initially I started to study science in secondary school and was about to become a medical doctor, enlisted in pre-med, when I discovered that I could combine — another of my interests was the study of traditional life in ethnic and tribal groups in the world, what we call social anthropology.

I had a Grandmother who was an artist and very close to the Surrealistic group and a major intellectual. She was a sculptress and was influenced by African sculpture. When I was small, my parents divorced and she raised me for several years and took me to the very early exhibit of what was called at that time 'Negro Art'. I was absolutely fascinated by it. She, being a very prominent intellectual, had many friends. She went on trips with René Magritte, the famous Surrealist painter, and many of the major intellectuals in Belgium and France. She knew a Professor of Social Anthropology, Professor Luc de Heusch, who became very famous in social anthropology and was teaching at Brussels University; and he told me that maybe I could combine my interest for archaeology, at that point it was not merely African archaeology, with Social Anthropology. He was Professor and researcher doing field work in the Congo because, of course, the Congo being a former Belgium colony, a lot of research was being done there. In the suburb of Brussels, we had a beautiful museum, a huge museum, built between 1901 and 1908, and it happened to be a very old looking museum, which is a dream museum where all Belgian children go on school trips to see elephants, giraffes, rhinos and crocodiles and dream about the wilderness in Africa.

I started at university combining, the Belgium university system is quite strict, it is very difficult to combine different interests, so I had to enlist simultaneously in two Faculties and do both social sciences and history of art and archaeology which were joint in our curriculum. I ended up taking as optional the matters, the lectures which were mandatory in the other Faculty and eventually I managed to achieve both being very interested at that time — my major Professor, Luc de Heusch, was very much into Structuralism, so I was very interested in structural anthropology, and at the same time I got interested in material culture and mostly on iron working; and I did my MA research on the blacksmiths in Bantu Africa from a symbolic, social, economic and technological point of view. Meanwhile, I was doing my MA papers, essays in archaeology on the potsherds collection from the lower Congo, because at that stage I was looking at the map of Africa as a whole and realised that everybody was speaking at that time about the great Bantu expansion which was a major phenomenon in the history of Africa and eventually in the history of the world. There is hardly any other example of such a wide, long-range population movement documented in the whole world except with some obvious comparisons — the older Indo-European movement which is still open to much debate and eventually the whole of the Pacific Ocean got colonised by the Austronesian people.

I wanted to start looking into the archaeology and combining my interests for social anthropology and archaeology in looking at what was being said to be the homeland of the Bantu people which was situated on the west part of central Africa, the northwest central Africa along the coast between the Cameroun, Gabon and what was at that stage called the

Congo, eventually to become three years later Zaïre and then Congo today. So, I started to be interested in that and I managed to find a collection of potsherds which had been collected in preparation of the 4th Pan African Congress, was held in Leopoldville in 1958 if my memory is good, and one of my Professors at Brussels University was the organiser and the Editor of the proceedings at that Congress and he, during the survey for the excursion, collected archaeological evidence in an area that had previously been hardly surveyed. That was the topic of my MA essay.

Well, I passed that with what was called in Belgium 'Summa Cum Laude', and then it was the upheaval in 1968 and somebody who was a bit older than I and very stimulating and an extremely bright archaeological researcher was Daniel Cahen. We were dreaming about reorganising the whole prehistoric Department in Brussels University in the heat of '68 upheaval in Belgium and in France, and we got to know each other very well and he told me at the end of that year "You know, I am off to the Congo, in Katanga, I am planning to excavate for my Ph.D a major Acheulean site. Would you be interested to come with me?" It happened that my stepfather was working for Sabina and I had free tickets around the world, and I jumped to the occasion and off I was to the field in Africa with him.

It was a very interesting experience because his father was the Director of the Tervuren Museum at that time and he had very good connections there to the old Colonial major enterprise, was the Union Minière, mining the copper in the copper belt on the Congolese side. Off we went with a truck full of what we needed for excavation, tent and everything, and eventually the truck dropped us in the middle of the bush and left us without anything else and we were two White men all by ourselves in the middle of the Congolese Savannah; and I stayed there for almost two months and Daniel for another couple of weeks, and we excavated and surveyed the site, which is still one of the major prehistoric sequences in central Africa.

After that I was really very pleased to be able to combine both my interests in African archaeology and in anthropology; and as an old Boy Scout, like many of us, I enjoyed camping and being out of doors, and when I went back to Brussels eventually Daniel Cahen, and the Head of the Department at that point was Francis Van Noten, said to me "Well, we are willing — we are planning to establish a new real Department of African Archaeology in the museum". Van Noten would be the Head, or was actually already the Head of that Department, and he would be working on the Late Stone Age and on the transition from Late Stone Age to the Iron Age. Daniel Cahen had a keen interest on the Early Stone and Middle Stone Age, and they said "Well, we need somebody for the Iron Age and seeing the connection between the social anthropology and the oral tradition and the Iron Age, and would you be interested?" And I said, of course, "Yes." I got a National Science Foundation, which is called in Belgium, Fonds Nationales des Researches Scientifique, four-year grant to my Ph.D on this wonderful topic. That's how I started to be involved in the museum.

Yes, please carry on.

Basically as I said I was first — I went with Van Noten to Nigeria to collect in fact the remains of a major Belgium archaeological enterprise, the Benin Valley Expedition, which failed due to, I think, two factors: they never got any very significant site, and they got very frustrated that the money was being spent for very little results; and the fact that some of the major researchers of that expedition could not get along very well, and started to fight each other. Fortunately, I was not part of that ill-fated expedition and I eventually went with Van Noten to collect the pieces what was left of that expedition, across Nigeria. That is where I learned to drive a Land Rover, four-wheel drive, the old Land Rover type where you have to fight with the clutch, and I ended up — my first minute was in a traffic jam in Lagos with a Land Rover which had not been driven for two years. The tire exploding because they had been completely rotten under the sun, the old engine full of dust, insects, and it was quite an accomplishment to drive; and to drive on the wrong side of the road for a Belgian like me was quite a challenge in Lagos. Eventually we crossed Nigeria. I was hoping to do my first professional survey on my own in Nigeria, but I had to wait for a Nigerian colleague to join me to supervise me, and eventually he never came, and I got stuck in the middle of the Plateau waiting for him for a week while Van Noten was horse-back riding with his wife-to-be and doing some survey.

After that we both left, and we drove in a caravan of three very old Land Rovers all the way through Cameroun. After Nigeria, which was already a very challenging and harsh ambience, I was so delighted to reach Cameroun and the dolce farniente à la francaise. We had a very good time in Cameroun, and I always told myself that I would love to go back to Cameroun. That was 1972, and we drove through northern Cameroun all the way to the Central African Republic of Bangui and crossed the Ubangi River in front of Banguis/Zongo; and we entered the Congo Republic and drove through the forest for several days and then reached the famous bend of the river, famous through the book. Van Noten left me with two of the Land Rovers and he took off with his girl-friend, wife-to-be, and he drove all the way to Rwanda, which was quite a drive at that time. I stayed and did a bit of survey in the vicinity of Lisala and then put the two Land Rovers on the boat, which is a kind of floating market that takes days to go down the Zaïre River, like in the good old Conrad stories, and eventually after getting stuck in sandbanks and having nothing to drink and to eat for two days, because we were late and there was no supplies left in the boat, we reached Kinshasa and I started my survey in lower Zaïre.

What strikes me is the excitement! A very exciting thing, and here very adventurous. And you're young. And as soon as you reach Cameroun, it is French?

The Nigerian experience was very frustrating and it was sad to collect what was left of a failure. A lot of money had been put in that. In Cameroun I was starting to be responsible for my own work, and reaching the Congo I knew that I was going to start doing surveys for my own research and Ph.D.

Was it good that the Congo had been associated with your country?

It was ambivalent. Already the Congolese were calling us the 'Uncle', which is a very ambiguous name. They call us 'Noko'. You know, the uncle is a member of the family, and at the same time if you have witchcraft usually it is being sent by the uncle. So it has always been between the Belgians and the Congolese a very ambiguous rapport between love and hate. But up to now the Congolese really feel that Belgium has a responsibility, and I share their view; and myself, since then, I have tried to help and support a country which has undergone so many dreadful events.

We reached eventually Kinshasa, and I started then to do a survey. It was very interesting, because at that stage Mobutu had decided to establish the National Institute and Museum of Congo with the support of the Director of the Museum in Tervuren. He was an extremely bright and entrepreneur person, Professor of Geology, who had written the book, the major monograph, on the geology of the Congo, he was somebody who had a vision, a Director with a vision, which is usually lacking in many museums, and as some of the Congolese intellectuals were starting to say "Well, Tervuren, you should give us back our treasures, our art treasures". There was a famous poem called "Redonner nos masques!" [Give us back our masks.] Lucien Cahen said instead of that, in association with one of the military advisors to Mobutu, he said "Well, instead of doing that right away, what about the Belgian Development Corporation giving you some money to establish a museum to train Africans, local intellectuals to gather as much arts stuff and information that we could, and we will evaluate what we will be able to collect in five or ten years? Then Tervuren will eventually complete what is lacking in your collection, what you won't have been able to find". This was very interesting from a scientific point of view, because we have in Tervuren indeed many, many hidden treasures, but they have been collected during the Colonial time; most of the time at that time, people were just collecting something, putting it in a parcel in the post without any stamps, just writing "Musée Royal du Congo Belge" as it was known and putting it in the mail, and it would reach Tervuren without any problem. So most of what we have in the museum is unidentified. There is no background. There is no ethnographic information. The localisation is very general.

I got involved there and that was really exciting because I was on my own in a whole area that had hardly been — I knew there was rchaeology to be done but nothing had been done before from a professional point of view. I was connected with a major institution, reporting directly to the President. At that stage, many people, including the Belgians, had great hopes in Mobutu's ability. The country was at its peak from an economic point of view. It was 1972, '73, just before Mobutu took his dramatic decision to 'Zaïrenise' the economy, all the shops, giving over to his cronies what was really the skeleton of the economic life of the country. All the shops and all the industries of the local Belgians or other White people working there.

I was on my own and I spent several months criss-crossing the lower Congo, going into caves, looking for a sequence that I was planning to work out. Fortunately I found rock art, I found, I remember on Christmas Eve, I found the first polished stone tools that had been ever found in a stratigraphic context. I knew I would be able to date it. That was a breakthrough, and on Christmas Eve! It was a great Christmas for a young archaeologist. But I failed to find what I was most interested in, the Iron Age. I was finding stuff consistently older than what I was looking for for my Ph.D. So I got a bit frustrated. I managed to publish the first polished tools in Antiquity and couldn't find what I was really interested in. At that stage, my friend Cahen was excavating another site in Kinshasa. It was very funny. It was in the garden in the park of the National Assembly. We were overlooking the Zaïre River's white waters just outside of Kinshasa. It was very interesting surroundings. Once again the layers were quite mixed and we couldn't — it was a sand deposit with a lot of admixture between natural processes and termites, and it was not very promising. At that stage, I learned that there was some looting starting in the major necropolis.

We were smack in the middle of Katanga, which had already been studied and excavated and published in detail by two other Belgian archaeologists back in the late 1950s, Jacques Nenquin and Jean Hiernaux, who had been my Professor of Physical Anthropology at Brussels University. The Director of the museum in Tervuren eventually called me to his office when I was back in Brussels and said, "Maybe you should forget the lower Congo for awhile and go to Katanga and we'll take care of that and it will be very interesting". In fact, the location was very interesting. There was a mass of very fine pottery, jewels, copper jewels, very interesting. He told me "Well, take one of those Land Rovers. If it doesn't work, take one of the — the museum just got one of those convertibles, a beautiful, extremely expensive, white Mercedes, that one of Mobutu's Ministers was trying to fly away from Zaïre with a trunk full of money, was caught at the airport and Mobutu despised him and took his Mercedes and gave it to the museum. My Director in Tervuren was still told, was thinking, could still remember the day when you could drive in a normal car from Leopoldville at that time to Elizabethville at that time, crossing the whole country, which is 1000 miles, even more, a 1000-mile drive with what used to be a normal well-maintained truck. Sensibly, I didn't take the convertible white Mercedes. I took one of my old Land Rovers and off we go with all the archaeological material and it took us ten days just to do what we were supposed to do in two days, because the roads were completely destroyed, and that was already the end of the country [the beginnings of many problems in the country]. There was a saga. It took us almost three weeks to reach Lubumbashi, one of the worst drives I have done, and since then I have been doing a lot of driving through all of Africa. That remains one of the most challenging drives ever. We reached a point that we had to put the Land Rover on a train.

What is happening then, politically, at that point?

At that point, it was really the peak of Mobutu's power and glory. It was just a couple of months before the famous 'Zaïrenisation', and I joined the university in Lubumbashi and that was also very exciting because it was a very intense, intellectual group of White and Black. The Rockefeller Foundation was supporting the part of the university in what was becoming part of the Lubumbashi University, because at that time of the Zaïrenisation they also changed all the names. It was very stimulating intellectually. There was a famous philosopher who was known, a Professor from Stanford, Valentin Mudimbe, was there; Johannes Fabian and a whole series American, Belgian, other European and Zaïrian intellectuals and researchers. That was very stimulating. I was a young Assistant teaching to the students there. That was my first experience as a teacher. Meanwhile, I was working in the museum in Lubumbashi and doing fieldwork for my Ph.D on my own for a long time. I spent two years just mixing fieldwork, intellectual exchange and debate, political discussions. What was also very interesting, going back to the American scene, at the same time, there was a whole group of American younger researchers doing Ph.Ds in Social Anthropology or

History like me, most of them, of course, trying to avoid being drafted and going to Vietnam. That was that time. It was a time when there was a lot of stimulating, intellectual discussions, and we forged a very strong link to a person who was to become a major prominent scholar in Social Anthropology in the States.

Who were some of those people?

There was Tom and Pam Blakely, Jeff Hoover, Tom Yoder, Al Roberts. So, it was a lot of exchange. Major European and American scholars came to visit us: Vansina, people like that. It was really interesting. I was really pleased because my Ph.D was about reworking the old Upemba sequence, starting with the famous site of Sanga, and I was able to work out a 1500-year sequence starting and connecting the history of the Luba, based on oral tradition, with the archaeological finding, and working out the full sequence; which has remained one of the very few complete sequences where you could link and provide a history for local people stretching all the way to the Late Stone Age, with a continuous demonstrated occupation. That also branched into doing some ethnoarchaeology and other programmes of research.

How were the local people reacting to that?

That was quite a touchy and less touchy issue, because not only was I excavating, I was excavating mostly in a village, because the Upemda depression is a very large depression where you have a flood-plain with what eventually becomes the Zaïre River; but there it is still named the Luoloba River, and the Luba people live on the bank on the side of the river and on some mounds and hills, where they remain more or less above the flood or on the side of the depression. As there is not much ground that remains outside of the water, they have used the same place for the village for centuries, and for fields, depending on which period. So I was excavating in the village and we were finding many bones. I was studying mostly the graves, because the occupation layers have been completely mixed by this continuously on-going occupation. Of course, excavating human skeletons in the middle of the village anywhere in Africa is already touchy, but on top of it in that area, people have been known to be quite, I will say, rough, and only six or eight ??? before, they had been killing and eating the missionaries locally, so I was a bit concerned; but to my great surprise, things went very smoothly, because people felt that, well, all those graves are the enemies of our ancestors. So it is perfectly all right for us to play with their bones, because they are our enemies. It was only gradually, when they saw how interested I was, that they started to say "Well, maybe after all it could be connected with our ancestors", and then many strange stories started to circulate about me that nobody could touch me, especially no woman, and that my light was a special telephone to speak to the dead. I was trying to locate graves by doing trenches, opening one full metre and then a metre away, I would do another trench, and the people got the impression that I was always excavating the same skeleton and the skeleton was running away during the night, and that I was chasing the same skeleton because the density of those centuries was just amazing. Wherever, in a certain area, you excavate, you found one at least, if not two or three skeletons in one square metre. It is absolutely mind boggling.

Did they eventually then become involved?

Oh, yes, always. That has always been very much my policy. I have never worked, even if I had all the official papers, I never worked with any military assistance or anything like that. I would always spend whatever time it took to discuss with the Elders and try to tell them and convince them that it was interesting to know more their history. So I never forced anything. I was completely with all the local people, I was completely depending on them, and they were in a strong position to where the young White foreigner was. I established a very, very good rapport with them, and I became to be regarded as very powerful, because I was speaking and working with the dead people. Eventually after that I was not able to go back because of all the problems in the Congo, until much later when I got a grant from the NSF and MIT, and then went back with American colleagues to do a special study on the metallurgy. The memory of going back to the village where I was working, when people recognised me, they started to call out

the major big drums and all the village in the field, the people ran back to the village and it was a feast for two days I had to pay for. I was crying. It was so, so wonderful. So that is a long and lasting memory. It is a pity when I see in what state the village and the places where I have had such a wonderful life, that really became part of almost my family, very close, close friends. They are in such despair, you know. I am receiving letters from people calling for help and seeking and it is absolutely pathetic, and that is why I am still very much involved. I am not working any more in the Congo right now. It is so desperate. But I have been now coordinating a kind of relief effort, trying to launch the African University again. I have been trying to contribute to the revival of the University of Lubumbashi, rallying support and money and sending young colleagues there, and that is already starting to produce some results.

Meanwhile at a certain point, I felt why should I keep working on archaeology when people are so desperate and suffering? Eventually I ran away from the Congo and went to work in Cameroun and Gabon, where the situation is much better, although difficult also. At least in Cameroun, where there was a strong economic crisis. But I think the importance of archaeology in Africa is that you have to realise that in no part of the world the split between the past and present has been so radical as in Africa, because in the African tradition, there was very little stone monuments. In many parts of the Congo basin there is no stone, so there is no way to do that, and when there was stone, the Africans built in stone quite often, Great Zimbabwe. In between the Ivory Coast and Burkina Faso there is no written tradition also, for probably good reason, but that is another story, and so the contact with Europe and the western world was dramatic and almost completely obliterated the very in-depth action of the missionaries and the education and the colonial system.

We obliterated and annihilated most of the heritage and I think that every civilisation needs to incorporate and keep reincorporating their past into their present; as some Africans say, "You need to know where you come from to know where you are going." It is true in America, if you look in a place like Washington DC, everything is incorporated in the Federal Capital to remind you of the past. It is not a coincidence that, for example, the Senate, the Capital, the General Assembly and so on always mimic the neoclassical architecture, because we want to reinforce the idea that the democratic tradition takes its roots in the Latin and mostly Greek tradition. So every civilisation, every culture, every country needs to manipulate its past, and in Africa it is not possible, or there have very little possibilities. It is no coincidence that when South Rhodesia became independent, they called themselves Zimbabwe, connecting to archaeology right away. So I think we need to provide Africans with a past that they could relate to and also be proud of, because they have accomplished and they have had great achievements; and if they didn't develop the kind of urban civilisation and things that we have developed in other parts of the world, it is probably because the local conditions were less harsh, the demographic pressure was less, the weather was nice. You eat something, you throw it on the side and it will grow, in Central Africa. So there the life was, I think, quite easy. There was a very good balance between the environment and the people, achieved quite early. There was no major pressure for that. Now, with the White man coming and the whole Colonial system, the balance has changed, but I think that it is very important for Africa to know its past and to study it and also to be aware; and that is a major concern for me, is that indeed there are people now using the African past, politicians, but sometime they do it in an almost fascist way. And Rwanda blood-bath and the problem in Burundi and some others, and the false stories about the Tutsi and Hutu, and everything, are good examples that if scholars from all over the world don't work and try to bring to the Africans their own story on firm ground, it is going to be demigods and dictators who are going to manipulate and create their story for their own good and their own goals; and that will be a major catastrophe for Africa.

I've noticed every time somebody speaks — all of you are highly political. Do you think that is something specifically because you are Africanists?

I think that you can not be indifferent to what is going on, in that African archaeology developed in the Colonial system in the first place and was quite ambiguous, because the whole science during the Colonial time was being manipulated in a certain way and being incorporated into the Colonial discourse, so the older generation were connected with the Colonial rule, which was not my case. I never set a foot in any of the Colonial places before independence. That is one concern, and the other is that, I mean we are into the Humanities and have been looking into the powers, the symbols and those issues. Recent archaeology looks also at state structures and kingdoms and chiefdoms, that kind of interest. We are certainly politically sensitive. Of course, we are also concerned by the changes and the way archaeology is always manipulated and used for better or worse. So, it is also important to be aware, and at the same time of course archaeological discourse, even mine, is ambiguous up to a certain extent, because we need money to do what we have been doing, and archaeology is a more expensive sport than social anthropology or history because you need a lot of means to be able to excavate and carry the material and the paraphernalia and what you get and the labs and everything else. So we have been indeed more or less quite dependent on funding agencies and government, and so on. So politics is present, yes, indeed.

Another aspect of the political aspect where I was probably influenced was that seeing all those problems and being interested from a theoretical point of view on Bantu expansion, as I mentioned earlier, I started, of course, to think not only from the theoretical, and the very nice intellectual game trying to correlate archaeology, social anthropology, historical linguistics, historical technology, and so on, and the symbolism of that and the theoretical methodology which goes far beyond the small interest in African archaeology; but really a way to interact with major social sciences discipline, but at the same time I came to realise that probably I would be quite willing, and I have been doing that for a number of years now whenever I have been given the opportunity, and as I have been getting older, I am getting those opportunities more often, to give key-note lectures and major political rallies in Africa and places like that. We may want to emphasise trying to fight against those ethnic fighting and deterioration and antagonism, growing antagonism in the cities where people and politicians and dictators are playing on the differences and trying to get people fighting each other for their own manipulative political 'cow', and there is more and more a kind of the political of the 'cows' which is typically African. I saying that the Africans should look more at what unites them, and if they look into the detail and that is one of the beauties probably of Bantu research.

What strikes one after all is that they have much more in common than what differentiates them. Archaeology works on the big picture and in the long term, being not very sensitive to small change to people and places but mostly looking at the major ecological, economical, demographic trends. We provide a background that many Africans can go back to and start thinking "OK, well, indeed we should look back to what was the cradle of the people who fought for African independence, which was Pan Africanism". They were interested in saying that, "Well, we are the brothers in the fight against Colonialism." The whole ideology of Nkrumah and all the major leaders of the independence. I am certainly influenced by that, trying to say, OK, the Bantu, sure there are differences into — at this stage I estimate that we have over 215,000,000 Bantu people, and they all originate from one small area, probably in northwestern Cameroun. Well, they have so much from a linguistic, from a symbolic, so much in common that we may want to stress that much more and say "Please stop fighting for small differences and try to look back at the time and at the big picture and realise that you have so much more in common, that if you united a bit more, it could provide all of you with a much better life, and Africa which has so many riches could really achieve something in the long term". In the long term Africa is in any case going to be a significant part of the world dynamics, just because of the demographics. Even with the catastrophe like AIDS, African demography is still very significant and is still expanding very fast. They have so many minerals and natural riches that Africa ought to have a much better role in the world economy, which is not the case at this stage.

Also something is that really when you start to speak — very few people speak about the long-term perspective and the big picture in African history, at least in French-speaking Africa, students really get very excited and even major intellectuals and politicians and leaders are quite keen and fascinated by when you start speaking about their own history before the White man, and that is only one thing that archaeology can provide. I have had experience lecturing and teaching in primary school and getting all the kids very excited and really one fascinating story, it didn't happen to me; for the longest time we knew of all of the Katanga, and Katanga is two or three times the size of the UK. I mean, you have to

realise how big it is. We had only two or three polished stone tools, although archaeologists have been there for quite a while, and then a school child brought a polished tool to school and the missionary, the teacher said, showed that to the other children and say that is very interesting and so —

Tape interrupts — we lost the end of the story

Side 2

Professor de Maret will continue to speak about globalisation.

Africans, even intellectuals, are very concerned about the global village. Another thing that archaeology could provide, and is also one of my interests, is to realise and to make them realise that Africa has not been all that isolated as people, and even Africans, have a tendency to believe. I mean, Africa has been providing, unfortunately through the slave trade, many cultural influences. The influence of African music on — through jazz and through all the music of the world, has been major. About the same time as jazz, the influence of African sculpture was major, through Picasso, and has also influenced dramatically modern painting and plastic art. But also, Africa was exposed very early to long-distance influences from across the oceans, and one of the most interesting discovery in the last four or five years was the discovering evidence of banana cultivation in the Cameroun rain forest in a village going back to 500 BC–800 BC, which is absolutely fascinating because you have to realise that the banana came from Malaysia and Papua New Guinea, and that part of the world, and it was carried by Austro-asian navigators, who were the all-time sea-goers of the world. The bananas must have reached the East African coast probably at least a thousand years before Christ, which means you have a lot of contact between Africa, India and the Far East, much earlier than we previously thought. So, Africa has been part of the world scene. Indeed, the first modern man came out of Africa, the human kind came out of Africa, and Africa has been interacting over the years, both through the Indian and Pacific Oceans, with the eastern part of the world, and probably in more recent times quite significantly with America. I think through many processes, for example copper exchange, Africa was exporting copper in the 18th century both to India and to Brazil. There is a lot of contact and I think if Africa will come to terms with the past and really root the present a bit more in the past, they will be in a much stronger position to see the future.

Was this your research on bananas?

Yes, that was in Cameroun. You see, the problem was that early in the 1950s Murdock came with the idea that bananas were linked with Bantu expansion in forests, because bananas are the best crop to grow in the forest as long as you don't have manioc. Manioc, obviously we know, came quite later with the slave trade and the contact between South America and Africa. But then, people said, yes, the banana coming from Malaysia, the Far East, there is no way that it could be linked with the Bantu expansion. It was dated at the turn of, around a couple of centuries before or after Christ. So, that was a bit puzzling, but we had many indicators that we had more banana variety in Africa than in other parts of the world. We knew that bananas had been there for a long time and had been manipulated for quite a significant amount of time, but bananas are very difficult to trace in the archaeological record because you have no seeds, you have no wood. It doesn't leave any — there is no pollen. We were trying — there is a very nice opal crystals which were part of the stone skeleton, crystal skeleton inside the vegetal cell called phytoliths. We started to look at phytoliths but lacked a reference collection, so we had to establish first the collection. There is one plant which is a kind of not-banana, a related family called Nsete which grows wild in the Tropics and is also cultivated, and we wanted to be sure that the phytoliths of the Musa, the banana, was not the one of the Nsete. So, we had to go through a very high magnification, looking at phytoliths, to be able to see the difference between the two and make sure that we were indeed dealing with the banana phytoliths. That brought a whole new perspective, because then we discovered that Murdock was right, and that you have indeed fascinating contact between Asia and Africa a thousand years previously than other evidence will testify. But it is not surprising from the botanical, the technological aspects, we have some very significant boats and so on and the linguistic aspect — there is some evidence to confirm this archaeological proof.

And, you did this at your laboratory in Brussels? For many years?

Yes — it was a project connected with all. We did some survey in Cameroun and found many very old villages in the rain forest. Many of my students from Yaounde University and Cameroun colleagues that I have trained know, and a Professor of Archaeology at Yaounde University have been surveying and excavating. Then, I did with some success in lower Congo, a survey of rock shelters. Rock shelters are very important in Central Africa because the erosion due to the rain season, and the vegetation and the animals are very destructive and the soil is very acid, so you look to a rock shelter, but unfortunately everybody looked for rock shelters, even in earlier times, and the deposit in the rock shelters are usually disturbed. So it is difficult to make sense of a rock shelter deposit in central Africa because there is a lot of admixture but I was after several years of systematic surveying in north central Cameroun which is, by the way, absolutely a beautiful area of old volcanoes and mountains and sweeping views and clouds and it is quite dramatic. I discovered at least two very interesting and promising rock shelters and I test-excavated them and eventually, through a whole series of other circumstances, we ended up excavating which has been the largest excavation ever done in central Africa. We excavated for altogether six months with a large team of Cameroun and Belgian and French and some others, archaeologists, botanists and palaeoanthropologists. We excavated this major site which provided us now with the longest prehistoric sequence for most of West Central Africa, with human skeletons going back to 7000 BP and with the whole record going from the early Holocene and even before, going back to 30,000 years up to the recent with all the succession of the upper range of pottery and metallurgy.

That must very exciting for everyone in that area.

It is an easy area because it is huge. You have to realise that Central Africa is larger than West Africa outside of the Sahara and East Africa put together. It is many times the size of Europe. There are a handful of professional archaeologists busy in that part of the world, so we are a very closely tied community with a couple of students we have trained both in the Congo and Central Africa Republic and Gabon and in Cameroun, and everybody knows each other, and it is also still one of the last unknown areas for archaeology. So what you do, which I have always found fun, is that you don't have, as when you work in Europe, whenever you find one piece of pottery, you spend most of your time trying to find parallels to that pottery in other published material. In Central Africa you hardly face those problems, because whatever you do, it is new. You are very much in the state where archaeology was in Europe at the turn of the last century. It is still a kind of pioneer archaeology, much more than what you do even in East Africa or many places in West Africa.

Although you are using very sophisticated techniques —

Sure, but yet funds being limited and the road system being in a apocalyptic state — there is no other word, in many areas of Central Africa, you resort to very basic excavation techniques. It becomes more sophisticated once you have brought everything to the lab, but down to the ground, man power is very cheap, but very sophisticated material eventually jam before you reach your excavation location. So we still use a lot of sieve, trowels and sweat.

Did it make the local newspaper?

Very often people are absolutely fascinated. I remember the first major village that we found in Cameroun was by sheer coincidence. In fact I was going through the local red tape and the bureaucracy was horrendous, and I was fighting through all the layers to get my permit to survey and excavate in the northwestern Bantu homeland, and as I was seeing my funding going down and being stuck in Yaounde waiting for the permit, I spent my weekends and my afternoons just walking around and surveying new developments and places like that; and that's how I refound a site that had been signalled in print in 1948, but was thought to have been destroyed and lost, and I found it and said "Well, as long as I am stuck in Yaounde, I

may as well start sampling and testing this site while I wait for more formal clearance"; and then word spread through Yaounde and it made the headline of all the local newspapers, and the next day I had crowds. I had to fight through crowds, because everybody was coming to look at this crazy white person who was looking at the oldest village of central Africa.

It is a very exciting life.

I think that I had great fun so far. But I am reaching a turn of my life because I have been asked to now embark on a new commitment, and I am going to run my university as of the first of October. At the same time, Central Africa is very demanding, and sometime one feels a bit desperate and sometime it is almost embarrassing to have fun when you see so many people suffering around. Over the years, I have tried, beside archaeology, to keep helping researchers and local institutions, museums and archaeological departments or universities, and I think I could spend some time working in my own university and by that helping universities in the Congo, Gabon and Cameroun, with which we have a close collaborative ties. Eventually, in four years, I will do something else, because meanwhile I was also working on the future of rainforest people in social anthropology, and I ended up managing a major research project for the European Commission involving researchers in Central Africa, Papua New Guinea, Vanuatu and in the Amazon, and that is another whole topic.

Do you want to say something about that?

That is another whole saga. That was also as a kind — just looking how desperate our rainforest people like Pygmies, villagers, agriculturalists in Africa. On one side, the rain forest is being clear cut and logged down and on the other side you have a very strong White ecological pressure, and sometime villagers are desperate. On one side, the forest has been cut down and on the other side, they have been told this is a national park and you are not supposed to set a foot into it any more. And people say, where are we going to live now? You have really — I have seen desperate people along the road. On one side there is no forest, on the other the forest has been completely restricted to them. Then, the archaeological perspective, the long time perspective and the long time interaction between the forest and the people of which I was fully aware, made me think about that. Everybody speaks about sustainable development and conservation and nobody is very sure of what kind of time frame we are dealing with and that, with some colleagues, Social Anthropologists working with Pygmies and other groups, we thought that we ought to try to do something. In order for the conservation of the rainforest to succeed, we ought to put the human dimension into it. There is very strong evidence that the forest has been inhabited for the longest time and that the so-called virgin forest is a misconception of urban ecologists in the West, who have this fantasy about the rainforest being pure and without anybody. In order to have a rainforest which conforms to this misconception we are creating, we are trying to impose on the rainforest a nature against nature, by expelling the people who have been part of the forest and that we could demonstrate at this stage that those people in fact have been enhancing the rainforest. By cutting and by doing slash-and-burn cultivation, they contribute to the biodiversity in a very significant way. Everybody seems to be blaming, and there is a sort of misconception about slash-and-burn agriculture; but satellite photos and every study show that what is restricting the forest is industrial logging by far, and then it is the pressure of the poor people trying to make a living out of the cities and running away from the poorest areas in Brazil, in the Amazon or in Africa or in Indonesia. Those are the ones responsible for cutting, but not the indigenous people who have been living in symbiosis with those rainforests for thousands of years and where indeed they develop a very sustainable way of living with the forest. Even not being solely agriculture, hunter-gatherers, but being mostly agriculturalists but doing very well. That's another story.

Another very interesting feature for archaeology in general is that in Africa you have amazing continuity between traditional life and archaeology and although, of course, it is not the same, people have evolved, there was history, there was change, some of the more crucial technology, iron working, copper working, metal working in general and pottery, which is a major evidence in the archaeological records, have been going on for centuries, if not millennia, and you could still document and interview people still practising the craft. Both from a technological point of view and a symbolic point of view, the place of the technology in everyday life and in the social and in the symbolic life is very important. So, I ended up also to be very interested, that was back to my MA thesis in social anthropology on the blacksmith and the symbolic nature of the blacksmith's work. In many aspects the symbolism of metallurgy is absolutely fascinating in Africa and central Africa particularly. You have two aspects, one is smelting, because usually the smelting is done like it was a woman delivering the baby and the furnace is like a womb. The bellows being like a male genitalia and you have a whole interaction where in certain ways the male tried to appropriate the fecundity and the fertility of the woman and the idea that you are delivering the bloom which is part of a kind of intercourse. So that has far-reaching symbolic implications, one of them being that the king, the sacred king of all the Savannah from the Congo Kingdom to the famous Lubanwana Kingdom, the King is metaphorically associated to being a blacksmith. You have a whole symbolism of when the major coronation rituals, there is a major part of the rituals which is the king-to-be has to hit two major anvils. They are a peculiar form, they look like big nails, and you have to strike them and this part of the ritual is called 'striking the anvil' and the metaphor is that the blacksmith and the King is like a blacksmith. He is able to give life to new bodies, and so it is also part of the initiation rituals. It is very, very intricate and absolutely fascinating.

The same thing also, another interest of mine has been pottery. There also we have come to realise that pottery which has been used consistently in archaeology all over the world as a major indicator of cultural tradition and change; the pottery, we try to work on how to use the pottery as a cultural indicator, and we came to the idea that eventually the shape and the decoration of the pottery are subjected to quite significant change, sometimes on very short notice, because an invasion but also because the trend, the fashion, some inter-ethnic contact, whatever, but what is probably most significant is the shaping process, because the shaping process is something that is learned and used in Africa. Often it is women teaching, mother teaching a daughter or nieces, and the shaping process is something which is embedded in the brain because it is kind of a mother apprenticeship and you have to really master it. It is something which doesn't change too much, so we have a whole research project on how pottery is transmitted, how much flexibility is there in the transmission from mother to children and mapping all the detail of shaping; because you have the moulding techniques, you have the punching techniques, you have the coiling techniques, but those are very general categories. But inside the coiling techniques, you have fifteen different kind of coiling. We were doing systematic survey and putting together what is already the largest by far data-bank on pottery techniques before firing, post-firing, and all that surrounds pottery technology, and we believe that there African archaeology and technology will be a very significant contribution to archaeological theory in general, not only restricted to Africa.

It is a very rich area in every way.

If you look at the technology, and there are so many technologies that are vanishing: basket weaving, bark for clothes, which should be rescued. In many ways, I wish that we will spend more time at this stage trying to rescue the major traditional knowledge of the environmental or technological, because in many ways archaeology could wait a little bit. Of course, there are restrictions, and it is very important that major donor agencies like the World Bank and the US AID and the other European agencies of development abide by the strict rules that they have imposed on impact assessment of major works in the USA or Europe, the same rules apply to what they have been supporting in Africa, which is far from being always the case; but things are improving very much in that. I think that the old remains less at risk as the tradition, the knowledge, what was being transmitted from one generation to the other. As the younger generation are really laughing at what the older generation was doing, there is something of a rescue that has to be done, and there also once again archaeologists have a political role in a larger sense to play, just to show interest, because our interest in the African past is communicative. The youth, seeing the scholars from the outside world coming in and being interested in the stories of the Elders in the village, or how the old mother is doing pottery, or cooking, or collecting plants for medicine, make the younger generation also aware and interested in that, and contribute in many ways to rescuing that before it is too late.

When the knowledge, the vocabulary, when all that is gone, it will be gone forever. We will never be able to reconstruct it. To excavate a site most of the time, it has been in the ground for thousands of years. It could wait another century.

End of tape

Professor emeritus John D. Mulvaney

6 July 2000, recorded at the late Mrs Charles McBurney's home in Cambridge, England, by Pamela Jane Smith   pjs1011@cam.ac.uk

Professor Mulvaney, according to Isabel McBryde, is the guiding spirit of Australian prehistory archaeology and the founding father of Australian archaeology.

This is John Mulvaney. I was born in 1925 in the Victorian country. My father was a schoolmaster and my family had a family of five, and in those days teachers were paid very little. He moved around the country, and during the depression we had very little money, and I left school at the age of 16 — what would be year 11 — and I became also a trainee schoolteacher in the country. This was during the war, and the week I turned 18, I enlisted in the Royal Australian Air force to get away from it all, because I did not enjoy the teaching system and I was just waiting to turn 18. Fortunately for me, I was sent to Canada, where I was trained at Winnipeg as a navigator; and in September 1944 I went on to England where I was fully trained as a navigator, but never had to drop bombs, because the war ended before we were fully trained. I mention this because it is vital to my background. When I came back to Australia, because I had been in the Services, I was entitled to post-war reconstruction training funding, and as a result I decided I would go to the University of Melbourne and assumed that I would become a teacher in secondary school. I was interested in history — being in England, it fascinated me — and I decided that history was the only subject I was interested in. So at Melbourne University between 1946–48 I did an Honours degree in history and specialised in the history of the ancient world, and for a special honours subject I, we, six students, took the study of Roman Britain, and this is how I got interested in archaeology. I wrote an essay during my undergraduate year in studying Roman Britain, reconstructing the economy of Britain at the time the Romans came. And, after graduating, I went on to do an MA degree, a research degree and my Supervisor suggested that I elaborate on the subject of the economy of Britain. So, I wrote a 60,000 word thesis on Britain, and the State Library of Victoria had a remarkable run of 19th- and early 20th-century archaeological British literature. Over 60 journals published in Britain in archaeology were held in that library. Came the depression, they cancelled most of them but anyway, I had a marvellous time going through the files of these journals and getting fascinated in archaeology; and during the course of 1950, when I was writing my thesis, I read Grahame Clark's articles on prehistoric economy, which were then coming out. This to me was absolutely exciting work and I read his book, Prehistoric England, which was a new approach to writing the archaeology of a country and in the same year Glyn Daniel's A Hundred Years of Archaeology appeared and that was one of the most exciting books I had ever read at the time. People criticise it now, but in 1950, it was one of the first books to look at the history and I was a trained historian by that stage with a 1st class degree and it appealed to me.

So, I decided that if there was archaeology in Britain there should be archaeology in Australia and I started reading around at the time and discovered that the only archaeological work being done was by Fred McCarthy, a Curator of the Australian Museum in Sydney who had no training at all. He enlisted, he joined the staff at the Museum at 14 or 15, I think; later in life he did a diploma in Anthropology at the University of Sydney. He published hundreds of articles that, I suppose you'd say they were amateur studies, but they were very important. The other major figure was Norman Tindale at the South Australian Museum, who in 1917 took a science degree at the University of Adelaide, was in fact an authority on moths, and he, over the period from 1921 on, got interested in Aboriginal people and became more or less expert in linguistics and social anthropology and all sorts of things, but at a very elementary level academically but a very detailed level practically because he moved around with J.B. Birdsell. In 1938–39 he spent an entire year wandering around Australia. Birdsell was doing genetic studies really and Tindale was assisting him. He had a such a knowledge of Aborigines that was extraordinary, but he had no theoretical background. Anyway, he and Hale, who was the Director of the South Australia Museum, in 1929 excavated the site Devon Downs which is revolutionary. They went down about 6 or 7 metres and found that is was stratified. They realised it was stratified. They kept the

evidence separately layer by layer and published it in great detail in 1930, and that really inspired me, that here was a site that everybody ignored, just didn't feature subsequently, but there it was. There was archaeology in Australia.

The other person who was working was Edmund Gill, who had been a former Congregational Minister who was dismissed from his church because he believed in human evolution. He was given the job of palaeontologist at the Melbourne Museum and he was working at the site of Keilor in Victoria where he claimed human remains were of Pleistocene age, but he had very little background; but all three of these men, McCarthy, Tindale and Edmund Gill, all published hundreds of papers on all sorts of subjects. Some of them involved archaeology. Well, that was all I could find but it was enough to convince me that there was archaeology in Australia. Fortunately, at that time the Australian National University in Canberra had just been created in 1950, '49–'50. As there was no university but as there was a great brain drain on Australian academics, they were all going overseas, this was founded as a research institution to bring people to Australia or stop them leaving. So they had a very broad and rich scheme for giving postgraduate research degrees. I applied for one at the end of 1950 and by the time I was awarded a First Class Honours degree for my thesis on Roman Britain, I awarded this scholarship but I had to state in my application that although I was applying for a Ph.D scholarship, I could not do a Ph.D because I was not an archaeologist and therefore, if I got this degree, I would only take it up on condition that I was allowed to do an undergraduate degree to learn the background of how to be an archaeologist. Believe or not, they awarded me the scholarship to do an undergraduate degree. I am the only one in the history of the ANU to be so privileged, and in those glorious days, you nominated the place that you wanted to go. They didn't tell you where you had to go. So I said that I wanted to go to Cambridge, and I said specifically that I wanted to work there because Grahame Clark and Glyn Daniel were there doing exactly the sort that I thought an Australian needed to learn, to go back to Australia to apply it. So in 1951 I came to Cambridge and entered Clare College. I was very lucky there. In postwar years, it was hard to get into Colleges, but a staff colleague at Melbourne University who had been at Clare managed to get me in. And I arrived full of great enthusiasm in September 1951 to learn to be a Stone Age archaeologist, and I went to see Grahame Clark, who was my first Supervisor. He had not got his Chair at that stage, and he told me that, in addition to himself, I must go to a young man named Charles McBurney, who was the real Stone Age authority. I hadn't heard of him at that stage and I was very fortunate because I had a degree already, I only had to do Part II of the Tripos and for the two years I was here I was Supervised every week by Charles McBurney; and in the first year I had Grahame Clark for most of the year and then he got his Chair and gave up, and for my second year, I went to Glyn Daniel every week. So I just had a Golden Age and that's how I became an archaeologist. That OK for background?

That's brilliant. Were you supervised in this house?

In those days, Charles McBurney lived in, sorry, to begin with when I arrived here, Charles McBurney was not married and he was a Fellow of King's and I went to the Gibbs building in Kings to his study, which was a marvellous 18th-century building, and he had an enormous grand piano in his study and it was all very impressive indeed; and Grahame Clark in those days lived in Barton Road, and I went to his house in Barton Road for my supervisions. Shall I continue with this? Charles McBurney was of course working in Libya and in early 1952, he invited me to join his party to go to Libya to dig at the Haua Fteah, the enormous cave which he had put a trial trench in the previous season. So in June 1952, I think there were four of us and Charles went out in his utility small vehicle and we drove across France to Marseilles and went by sea to Tunis and drove right around North Africa to Apollonia. The site was about 10 miles further on from Apollonia. The British army was in Libya and we were supplied from the British Army base at Apollonia and very fortunately there was a British Hospital at Darnah (Derna) because I got blood-poisoning or something for some reason or other. I had to have a hand lanced, and penicillin injections, and I got back to the camp and because I only had one hand for a time, I did sieving all the time, or sorting. Then my toes festered, so I had to go back to hospital again. I had to spend a week in hospital. It was very fortunate that the British Army was there. I mention the Haua

Fteah cave particularly because that was the greatest influence on me. The techniques that Charles had developed to excavate a deep site, the year we were there we got down to 27 feet, and he used sieves suspended on stands that he developed, and the way he sorted material separately according to stone, bone, shell and keeping them separately in layers. It might have been standard technique but for me, I had never seen archaeology before in Australia, this was very influential. When I went back to Australia, I adopted his sieves, used angle-iron steel, the mountable sections which could be screwed together which were easily transportable for the frame for standing the sieves on. Also for a ladder that could be put together to get in and out of the trench, and I devised a way of using the ladder so it didn't lean on the wall of the trench and so did no damage, and that was my standard technique. I think that nowadays most people sieve, and I think they use finer mesh than I used but nevertheless it was quite revolutionary when I started this in Australia; that we were using sieves and I had to emphasize that stratigraphy really mattered. This is despite the fact that Tindale had demonstrated that years before, but in Australia there had been very little excavation work and such as there was was just shovelling out deposit. When I returned to Australia — well, could we stop —

Drink of water break

These sieves I really followed McBurney who had quarter-inch and eighth-inch mesh. That's what I had, which of course is not really fine enough to get really fine material. I suppose I was aware of that, but likewise I excavated trenches which today would be regarded as unnecessarily large. In fact, in Australia, we complain that many of the younger archaeologists dig 'telephone box archaeology'. That is, they dig a trench a metre square because they say they mustn't damage the rest of the site, and it does seem to me that that's got some advantages, but doesn't to my mind give a fair cross-section. You've got to understand, when I started excavating in January 1956, we knew very little about the archaeology of Australia and it was first necessary to prove there was an antiquity in Australia because there were many people around, collectors of stone tools in Victoria, for example, who said that the Aborigines haven't been here long and the culture has never changed, and there is nothing that archaeology will find out. Now today this may seem fairly hard to credit or not worth worrying about, but in 1956 it was absolutely essential to demonstrate to Australians that Aborigines had an antiquity, that there was such a thing as cultural change through time, and that there was such a thing as stratigraphy, so that the way to study the Aboriginal past was to dig systematically and separate your material according to strata. So my early digs were designed as, if you like, as academic publicity; that there was this past. I dug areas that would be today larger than necessary, but the number of artefacts found was few, so one had to extend the area to do it. The first site I dug at Fromm's Landing at the Murray River in South Australia. The Murray River is Australia's Mississippi, and Tindale and Hale had dug site at Devon Downs; and I selected this site which was ten miles downstream from Devon Downs, partly because it had been shown to me by C.P. Mountford, who was a distinguished amateur anthropologist. He told me about the site and took me to it, and I decided that it was worth digging. In fact it was. It was about six metres deep, with stratified deposit dated through about 5000 years. I might add that it was tremendous help to me and a coincidence that I started fieldwork in Australia just at the time that radiocarbon dating had been established and was being dated. Not that there were many laboratories. In fact the first dates from Fromm's Landing, the first samples which I collected in 1956, in the first place I had no money. I had no research funds. I was able, through the good offices of Hallam L. Movius Junior, to get four samples dated in the US, free. They were my first radiocarbon dates.

Really, he arranged that?

Yes, he worked in South Australia. His wife was a South Australian. That was a useful contact. I should say also that, when I came back at the end of 1953 from Cambridge with my degree, wanting to do archaeology, there were no jobs in archaeology in Australia and a Professor of History at Melbourne, where I had already worked, offered me a Lectureship in the History of the Ancient World and between 1954 to 1964 inclusive, I lectured in Greek and Roman history and gradually increased the input of archaeology, and history, archaeological theory, and in 1957 he allowed

me to introduce, as a fourth-year honours history option to undergraduates, a course called Pacific Prehistory. That is the first course ever taught anywhere in Australia on the history of our own region, but at that stage there was so little known about Australia that we took Polynesia as our main field and as the years passed added, sort of, added more and more Australian. So I had only commenced my own excavations the year before I introduced this course. When I came back, it seemed to me, well, I am rationalising after the event: I think I saw a situation where I needed to do fieldwork to prove that fieldwork was possible in Australia. I also needed to survey the literature and see what had been done and also criticise it and state what was really known, and I was invited by Grahame Clark, who was then the Editor of the Proceedings of the Prehistoric Society, to write a paper on the Stone Age of Australia. The title was his. Nowadays one wouldn't dare use the word, Stone Age. The Aboriginal people would certainly object to being called Stone Age people. Anyway, so over the years I did survey the literature and published it in the PPS in 1961, and that I think was a useful service. I did survey the literature and criticised Tindale's work quite considerably, because he was making claims that were totally unverifiable and I said, well, you have to verify them before you make claims. I was less critical of McCarthy's work than I should have been, I think, because I didn't know it as well the other thing. The other thing, I was interested in as an historian, but I think it was quite important, over the centuries since the Europeans found Aborigines, they have held various views of them. They became the models of primeval man and the missing link and all sorts of things. So I went through the literature from the early 17th century, when Europeans first saw Aborigines, up till the Devon Downs excavation of 1929; I took as my concluding thing of just how people had interpreted Aborigines, how they saw them in the state of nature. That was a straight historical thing, but I published that as a two-piece long article in an historical journal in Melbourne in 1958. Then I published the Grahame Clark survey of the Stone Age of Australia in 1961, and I published my first archaeological report in 1960. So I had quite a busy time on all these fronts.

What was your first archaeological report?

Well, actually, Fromm's Landing — I excavated at Fromm's Landing in 1956 and '58 and published that in 1960. That would have been my first excavation report. Then I was invited by the Professor of Geography at the University of Adelaide to come back to Fromm's Landing and excavate another rock shelter, because there were six in a row a few hundred metres along. He wanted his students, their interest in geomorphology, and they wanted this, so in 1960 and '63, with the geographers, I excavated another rock shelter. That one turned out to be highly significant because we found, in addition to the stone tools similar to the other shelter, we found the skeleton of a Dingo dog, of about 3000 years old and the tooth of a Tasmania Tiger, an animal which when Europeans arrived only existed in Tasmania and had become extinct probably because the Dingo outhunted it. There they were together in this site, round 3000 years, and the evidence for the highest flood in the history of the Murray River at about 3000 years, and this was what I was really interested in because I had been at Cambridge, which was essentially an interdisciplinary place. I attended whole courses by Harry Godwin, the palynologist. I directed the little student dig with Richard West, who succeeded Godwin, the dig at Hoxne. We went out together. West was doing his Ph.D. So I came back full of this interdisciplinary sort of thing. USE So, to work with geomorphologists at Fromm's Landing seemed to me ideal. In fact, in 1956 I took a palynologist, Sue Duigan, who had done her Ph.D under Godwin here at Cambridge on the Cromer Forest Bed, I brought her to Fromm's to collect pollen, but there was no pollen in the deposit, which was very, very sad.

That is very interesting — the interdisciplinary influences. McBurney in 1952 —

Well, yes McBurney was also interdisciplinary. No, he wasn't looking for pollen, but he had a geologist, Hay, a geologist from Cambridge with him in 1952. It was a great deal of geomorphological work was done on the site. The other thing was in 1952, that was very early radiocarbon dating time, and he was meticulous, and that was another influence on me. In those days one wasn't too sure about contamination. So when we collected carbon, we collected them on silver teaspoons. Our hands didn't touch anything. We put them, from the British Army base there were great jars which had contained, I don't know what, but he was able to get these jars. They would hold five pounds of sweets or something, and samples were put in these jars, but before we used the jars, they were washed out with petrol. Petrol being so old that it wouldn't matter. Then they were dried in the sun. The sample was put in a plastic bag and then it was surrounded in the jar by earth taken from the level at which the sample came, so it would be not contaminated, and then they had to be put in 44-gallon petrol drums and soldered and shipped back to England. The care with which these samples were collected had a great influence on me, and when we worked in Australia in the early years we collected them with silver teaspoons and put them in plastic bags and we didn't need to go further than that. The plastic bags were kept carefully, and so on. We took far more care collecting charcoal samples than people do these days. It does make me rather angry; at least in Australia they snipe a bit these days about how inaccurate the early samples were, largely because the carbon technique has been improved, but technically I believe nothing could have been more careful than the way these samples were collected; and the ANU established a lab in 1966 and the care with they dated our samples there was quite remarkable. So I think it is a bit excessive to say that our early samples were inaccurate.

Did Clark offer you a job in New Zealand in 1952?

In 1953, well, in those days and still people in Britain think that Australia and New Zealand are the same country. They don't realise that Melbourne to Auckland is the same distance from London to Warsaw, and Grahame Clark didn't know much about that part of the world in those days. He came to Australia in 1964 and that was a shattering experience and he was never the same again, but in 1953, he was doing the best he could. I had to, I was to have stayed in Cambridge for a while doing a research project with Charles McBurney on the stone tools from Hoxne site, which is Frere's site, the 1790 site, where he found Palaeolithic tools there and that is where Richard West was doing his Ph.D. Charles had worked there and I was to do something about the stone tools, but in September 1953, after I had graduated, I had met my present wife, Jean. We were engaged. We had visited friends in the north of England and we were in the back seat of the car and we were in a motor accident, and she was very badly injured and I was slightly injured, and when I came out of hospital, I found a message from my parents that my father was dying. So we had to abandon all this proposal of working in Cambridge and went back to Australia as quickly as possible, and as I said, my Professor at Melbourne offered me a job; but getting back to Grahame Clark, I went to say goodbye to him, saying that we had to get back to Australia and he said "Well, oh, I'm sorry you only got a second, but it doesn't really matter does it? You're going back to Australia." It must have been a little earlier than that, he asked to see me and said that there was a job going in Auckland, in Prehistory. It was the Professor there, Professor Bill Geddes, an anthropologist, was interested in archaeology and felt that there should be archaeology in New Zealand, and they had written apparently to the Department at Cambridge to say that there was this vacancy. So Grahame said that there was this job, and if I wanted it, he would tell them that I was the man; and I had to say that I had to go back to Melbourne for personal reasons, and he said "Very well, Jack Golson will go." Jack Golson was at Cambridge at the same time, but was then working in his first year for a Ph.D on deserted Medieval villages and he was the pioneer archaeologist, the first (along with Hurst) to work systematically on a Medieval deserted village — Wharram Percy in Yorkshire. So Jack had to abandon his Ph.D and went out to New Zealand, and he founded New Zealand archaeology, and he's certainly the man to interview if you want the history of archaeology in New Zealand. In 1961, however, he was appointed to the ANU Research School of Pacific Studies, and moved across, and in 1965, he was able to engineer an appointment for me. Or rather I applied for a job, and I was appointed in 1965. That was the first time I was able to work full-time as a research worker in the Australia region. Up to then, I had been teaching Greek and Roman history to over 100 students, and so on. So it was a big thing, but by the time I became a professional archaeologist full-time, I had excavated the two sites at Fromm's Landing and published them. I had excavated a small rock shelter in Victoria at Glen Aire, which was published in 1961, and had finished the excavations at Kenniff Cave. Perhaps it might indicate

just how unsystematical life was in those days, but also how one tried to systematise it, if I explain how I got all of these sites. Well, I 've already said that C.P. Mountford told me about the Fromm's Landing site. That's how that site was discovered, but I realised that it had tremendous stratigraphic potential, and it was near the Devon site, so it was a good way of checking the reliability or otherwise of the Tindale interpretation. In 1959, I was told by a historian, forgotten his name — in 1959, I received a letter from a friend who had been doing a Ph.D at Cambridge and knew that I was interested in archaeology. He was then at the History Department at the U of Queensland, Brisbane and he had been out in west Queensland, trying to trace historical records, and met a man named Reg Orr who was the radio operator of the Royal Flying Doctor Service base at Charleville in West Queensland; and Reg had shown him a lot of slides of rock art that he had taken, and he so impressed my friend that he wrote me a letter saying that this man Orr, if ever I was in Queensland, that I should contact him. As a result, I wrote a letter to Reg Orr, saying that I was delighted to find that there was somebody in rural Australia who was actually recording Aboriginal Rock Art, and as a result Reg sent me a letter saying thank you and enclosing a box of slides; and I projected them and immediately I was transfixed, because one of them was called Kenniff Cave, named after some bush rangers who had camped there once. I could see that there was a flat sandy floor and that the wall of the cave was covered with rock paintings, but I could see that the wall was going down vertically and here was this level sand, all the potential for stratified site. He also showed me another site known as The Tombs, similar. So I wrote him a letter saying that "This was marvellous, if I could come up, could you take me to them", and just at that time I was awarded a grant of £4000 which was an extraordinary sum of money in those days, the first research grant I had had, by the Nuffield Foundation which in those days had very generous funds in Australia for research. This was for three years to do field work. As a result I was able to fly up to Charleville, 1500 miles away, with one of my students, and we went out in Reg's jeep. This is the term vacation in July 1960 and he took us to these places, and we did test excavations at three sites; one was The Tombs, one was Kenniff Cave, collected radiocarbon samples and then returned. I also, from 1961, was awarded a Nuffield Foundation Travelling Fellowship for a year, and I worked at the London Institute of Archaeology. I had made the case that one needed to learn about the conservation of antiquities. That was one of the main reasons. I wanted ethnographic stuff in Museums, and I had a happy year in London doing these things, and I brought radiocarbon samples I had collected with me in a suitcase, and I was able through the good offices of Harry Godwin and others to get these samples dated free at the National Physical Laboratory at Teddington. I did six samples. This is one of the famous stories one tells, so I better tell it on tape. In 1962, back in Australia, I returned to Kenniff Cave, this time driving a Land Rover the five days from Melbourne to Kenniff Cave with a small team and others —

Side 2

— and then the Royal Flying Doctor Base every morning had a session every morning with Reg. He kept in contact with the base and a telegram came through from my wife, Jean, saying that the radiocarbon samples had been dated and that the dates were as follows, and the oldest one was came as 16,000 years, and I didn't believe it. The site was so fresh-looking and the charcoal lumps so large, I thought that perhaps in the telegram they altered it. So I got Reg to send a telegram via the base to my wife, checking, did she mean 16,000 or 1600, and the next morning we got the response saying, yes, 16,000 and that was really an event, because this was the first stratified, demonstrated proof that Aboriginal people had been in Australia during Pleistocene times. Tindale had long claimed it. So had Gill at the Museum. They based it on perfectly reasonable inferences, but they hadn't demonstrated it stratigraphically, where you have at Kenniff Cave one stratum above the other and the deeper you get, the older they got. So that is acknowledged as a significant moment in Australian prehistory, and it was overshadowed almost immediately because people started to get older and older dates. My date in 1962 was 16,000 years, in 1965 other dates became 18,000 to 22,000, in 1969 we got the Lake Mungo remains which were 26,000 to 30,000, in 1973 I did an excavation with Jim Bowler, the geomorphologist, at Lake Mungo and we got a positive date of 32,000 plus or minus about 1000, and then there were clearly older dates then that.

Nowadays, it is disputed rather; the dates are 40,000 50,000 or 60,000, but I'm not going into that, but between 1962 and 1973 we moved from 16,000 to beyond 32,000. Remarkable.

That decade is remarkable in Australian archaeology.

Yes it is. The thing about Kenniff Cave, it did produce a sequence of artefacts which showed that there was change through time, through Pleistocene time, but it was very acid soil and there were no bones preserved and no pollen preserved, because it was very coarse sand and therefore it doesn't quite have the significance perhaps some later sites have, where you've got faunal; but in its time it was highly significant and a very rewarding thing to produce.

BREAK FOR COFFEE (We'll have a cup of coffee eh?)

During my career, there have been enormous changes in the approach to the archaeology of Australia. As I said, Grahame Clark suggested that I write a paper called 'The Stone Age of Australia', which I did. I was trained in Cambridge, where we assumed that Palaeolithic people were dead. It was all in the past, so I was not an anthropologist. I wasn't trained in anthropology and I quite rightly felt, well, anthropologists study the living ones, so in Australia I'm studying the dead. I don't think that the past is dead, but I am studying the past of people who are deceased, and therefore one didn't think you were associated with the living people. On the other hand, Australia was one of those rare countries where Hunting–Gathering people were still surviving ,and Clark was aware of that back in 1938 when Donald Thomson, an anthropologist from Australia, visited Cambridge and he talked Donald Thomson into writing a paper on the seasonal changes of a living hunter–gatherer people and it was ignored. Clark published it and it wasn't until the 1966 'Man the Hunter Conference' at Chicago that work like Thomson's, published 30 years before, suddenly became very important. So one should have been aware, but one still separated the living and the past, and I grew up in the State of Victoria where I was led to believe there weren't any Aboriginal people. There were no Aboriginal people of pure descent, but there were people of mixed descent, who were very proud to identify themselves as Aborigines, but I didn't know that, quite honestly, and I believe I didn't knowingly meet an Aboriginal until I saw some in Queensland when at Kenniff Cave in 1960 for the first trip. Now, I doubtless met them in the street, but I didn't know them as Aboriginal people, and this is perhaps a bit surprising that you could — I would have been 35 before I knowingly met the first Aboriginal, but of course immediately after that I started going up into the Northern Territory, doing fieldwork from 1963 on, and one saw them all the time. So I suppose in my own career, I went from this "I was a Stone Age archaeologist, I wasn't dealing with the living" till I started meeting living people and giving greater and greater credit to work of Donald Thomson, work like that. Then with others, Jack Golson and Isabel McBryde, myself, we were campaigning to have site legislation, protection of Aboriginal sites, because when I started work in the 1950s, anyone who wanted to go collecting stone tools or to dig in cave deposits was free to do so, and it was finders, keepers, and I established I think a fairly unique situation in 1955 when I wrote to Norman Tindale at the Museum in Adelaide, saying I was proposing to work at Fromm's Landing and of course I would give all my finds to the South Australia Museum; and in response he gave me a whole bunch of museum numbers so that I could number my finds according to the Museum. This was absolutely unique. So we were running conferences. As late as 1968, we ran a big conference in Canberra on the requirements for site legislation. You have to understand that, like the USA, Australia is a federation, and each state has its legislation and the Commonwealth has certain overriding rights, but the states have their own rights as regards things like site legislation; and between 1965 and 1975, every state in Australia introduced some kind of legislation to protect Aboriginal sites. It was an even greater struggle to get legislation to protect European sites. Nowadays there is legislation but depending on state, depends how much they get implemented. This has been one of the big changes, the realization there is such a thing that in Australia we call heritage sites that require registration, but, of course, because white people were the ones who led the campaign, the early site registered are all Mulvaney's sites. All his sites are registered and protected and it was only beginning in the 1970s really, not to the '80s, that the Aboriginal viewpoint became more established. They

couldn't care, many of them, about Mulvaney's sites. There are to them more significant sites that aren't archaeological at all. They may just be a rock or a land feature where creation events occurred, or dreaming story of great significance to that particular clan, and they are more important than an archaeology site 5 metres deep. This was one of the other great central problems. These sites are secret and sacred. They don't want people to know about them. Even many sites where male ceremonies occur without female people, would be pain of death to have seen them. So it is all very well to have a heritage list, publicly listed. So we went through a stage where you had to have sites that were not publicly registered, that were secret and sacred. Well, if they are secret and sacred, how do you register? Gradually, led by the state of New South Wales, Aboriginal people were appointed to Administration and consultation. In early '70s, there was the beginnings of Aboriginal activism generally in politics. In the archaeological field, it was particularly represented by the campaign to have the remains of the Tasmania Aboriginal woman, Truganini, who was the last Aboriginal Tasmanian of full descent to die. 1876, I think she died. Her remains, her skeleton was displayed at the entrance of the Tasmanian Museum for decades. Not a very tasteful thing. It was taken away. In the 60s, there was this movement for her reburial. A traditional Aboriginal burial technique was cremation, so there was a campaign to have her remains buried. That was the original thing that happened in Aboriginal activitism towards archaeology.

Were you involved in establishing the Institute of Aboriginal Studies?

The Institute of Aboriginal Studies was begun through a conference in 1961. I was in England, but I contributed a paper to it and in 1964, an Act establishing it was passed by the government and I was elected to the Council at the first election of Council, and subsequently I was elected to the Executive Committee and between 1964 and 1980, I served permanently on the Council. I acted for quite a while as its Deputy Chair and Acting Chair when the Chairman was ill and again in 1982 I was elected to Council and appointed to Chair for two years. I could have had a four-year term, but by that stage Aboriginal activism and the realization by archaeologists and anthropologists that Aborigines must be brought in more, it was quite clear that a very prominent Aboriginal, Ken Colbung from West Australia, was on our Council and it was quite clear that he was more than capable of acting as Chairman. So when my first two-year term ended, I just stood down, on the knowledge that he would be elected, and since 1984 there hasn't been anyone but an Aboriginal who has been Chair and the majority of Council is Aboriginal. So we went from, in 1964, a Council entirely of white academics to a Council of the majority of Aboriginal people. This has met many good things, but it has also met that their emphasis has changed. They are more interested in welfare, health, petrol sniffing is one of the terrible things in central Australia. Young children sniff petrol and it ruins their brains. So it is not surprising that these welfare issues, in Australia, in prisons, it is totally disproportionate. So they are tending to emphasize this and downplay the more academic, and downplay the archaeology, linguistics, the sites I'm interested in, but it is understandable. One of the more important things, there are Aboriginal people now going to the universities. In about 1965, I think there were 70 Aboriginal in tertiary education in all of Australia. By 1975, it had risen to 700 and now it runs into thousands, but tending to go into law or social welfare, not archaeology or anthropology, but there are some. Marcia Langton, an Aboriginal lady who came to our Department at ANU, and did Archaeology and Anthropology but mainly Anthropology, she is the first Aboriginal person to graduate with first class honours in the history of Australia, and she is now a Professor of Aboriginal Studies at the U of Melbourne. That is a revolutionary change. We've have had a big struggle in Australia concerning the reburial or the return of relics and I am regarded as a reactionary in all of this. I think a lot of younger academics have got 'bleeding hearts'. They are very worried about the way Aborigines were treated in the past and so am I and my publications, I have many publications which have detailed how Aboriginal people have been treated, not ignoring it, but it seems to me that it is no good jumping from one side to the other overnight and in so destroying evidence. In the late 1980s there was a campaign in Victoria for the reburial of the Kow Swamp human remains. These date from about 8 to 15,000 years ago and they came from one cemetery and I believe there were about 40 human remains, one of the largest groups in existence from the Pleistocene from one local group. Anyway, there was a campaign for their reburial and I opposed it on the grounds that in the future Aboriginal people may want this evidence, and of course we were just beginning DNA studies then. I said in an article in Antiquity in 1990 that in the future, DNA studies may be very important to land rights. Aboriginal people are claiming land because they have been there and DNA may be one legal means to prove this. So the Kow Swamp people were all buried, their remains are now unstratified and will never be useful again, and I opposed it, and most of my colleagues didn't wish to be identified. I'm retired, so I can speak. They are afraid, and in my most recent addition of my prehistory Australia book, we've presented the case that there is an obligation on all people. We are one human race and there is an obligation and the UN approaches, world heritage approaches, so on, not to destroy evidence. At the same time we quote from Australians who hold totally opposite views. If the Aboriginal people, it is their material, if they want things returned from museums, if they want humans buried, it is their material. My argument is, this may well be in this generation but is it true of 2000 generations back? Because we can now say that people have been in Australia 2000 generations, and it does seem to me to be nonsense to assume that the present people own remains so old. Now that is my view. Other people have other views, and fair enough, but I am willing to fight for this on the grounds that future generations of Aboriginal people are going to say that those who campaigned for the reburial of Kow Swamp were vandals. I believe that, but the point is they are campaigning for political reasons. That is the point. So archaeology in the early 1970s got involved in this, and in 1974, it reached the stage that archaeologists needed to talk to Aborigines and I did a bit of that. I talked to a group of over 100 Aborigines at one stage to try to explain what archaeologists do. In 1975 there was a big conference in Canberra. Isabel McBryde, myself and Jack Golson organised for a group of Aboriginal people to come and discuss as to what one should do. Subsequently in more recent times it has gotten to my mind a bit out of hand. One has to consult reasonably. That's all right, but what do you do at the ANU, we take a student to do a thesis, a Ph.D, who wants to do fieldwork 1000 miles away. They have to consult with the Aboriginal people. They are young, inexperienced, where do they get the money from? Perhaps they have come from overseas. You just can't send them up to talk like that, because Aboriginal people like you to stay for some time. So it has involved a lot of problems, and there is less fieldwork at the moment than in the more 'heroic age' when we didn't ask anybody. Let me give an example, when I first worked in Arnhem Land in 1965, up in the top of coast. That was an Aboriginal reserve, so you might think that Aborigines had some say. Not at all. There were Christian Missions had settled centres, and the system was that you first of all had to get the permission of the particular mission where you wanted to work, and then if they said yes, you had to get the permission of the Northern Territory administration, and then you had have an X-ray to show you didn't have TB, and with that you would be given a warrant to enter this reserve, and never ever ask the Aboriginal people themselves. That was 35 years ago. Nowadays, of course, the only people you would ask would be the Aboriginal people. That is fair enough, but one of the problems, though, is who do you ask in the Aboriginal society. They like to sit down and talk for a long time. Their chronologies are not ours, and they have their ways of doing things, so it has made it more difficult, but as time goes on and there are more Aboriginal archaeologists, maybe they'll be able to resolve it also, but there again there are problems because Australia is a huge continent. It is the size of the USA, and there are many different tribal and linguistic groupings. So an Aboriginal, say, from northwest, west Australia who did an archaeology degree and wanted to work in the top of Cape York in Queensland might find it more difficult to get Aboriginal permission to work than I would. It has made Australian archaeology move from a thing of Stone Age where you just worked where you liked, when you liked, on the past, to a situation where you can never get away from the present and it has made many of us more activist than we used to be, and that is one of the other things that has involved me very much. I have become active in some areas which I never dreamt I would be involved in. One example: in Arnhem Land there is a world heritage property called Kakadu National Park. In that region of some thousands of square kilometres, we have some of the oldest dated sites in Australia, perhaps back to 60,000. We have almost certainly the oldest rock art in Australia, which is undoubtedly of Pleistocene age, but one can't say much more than that.

I regard some of the art there as some of the most significant scenes depicting the prehistoric past from anywhere in the world. It is being analysed now. So it is an archaeologically significant area. It also has tribal living people with their own beliefs and sacred sites, so it is significant in that way. In addition, it is one of the great nature wonders of Australia, a breeding ground for birds. Unfortunately, uranium occurs right through the area and uranium leases were granted before all this knowledge existed; and there is uranium mining going on, and three years ago the Government said that mining could go on at a place called the Jabiluka Lease which is within about, less than two kilometres of one of the oldest 60,000-year-old sites. It is an area that contains significant rock art, and more particularly it is an area with dreaming tracks of great significance to the living people. I was one of those who, acting with specialist knowledge, sworn an affidavit in the Supreme Court case in Darwin on behalf of the Aboriginal people who say the site is significant. We didn't succeed. The mining is going ahead, but there you are, you see, I began as a Stone Age archaeologist and ended up in the Supreme Court in Darwin in 1998, testifying what Aboriginal people were saying is in fact true, not made up, and I quoted from historical literature on this as well as from field evidence.

So it is reconcilable at times?

Yes, absolutely, this has been one of my claims and I hope it gets resolved. Aboriginal people believe in creationism. They were all created at various times. There wasn't just one divine creation. There were hundreds of creations all over the place, and if you analyse the traditions and dreaming tracks, time and time again, you find that they have come from the sea or they come from the north, and in fact there are sacred sites that are under the sea today. One would like to believe that they relate to lower sea levels perhaps, at least 5000 years old, and the dreaming tracks, these ancestral beings didn't just sit down in one place, they moved. So I believe it is possible to say that Aborigines came to Australia from somewhere else and moved across Australia, and this is not in conflict with Aboriginal creationism, but most people don't agree; but it is not a necessary contradiction, but I do not accept and absolutely oppose the view that what Aboriginal say about their oral traditions is absolutely true and must be accepted as holy rite. They don't need archaeology and that, they know it all, and I do not believe that their traditions go back 2000 generations.

How are you for time?

Well, it is all right.

[I ask something inaudible.]

Well, as you know, I was trained in humanities, particularly in history. I do believe that humanities do matter to us. People are thinking beings and one of the, also I am a Christian, one of the papers I thought is particularly important which people have mocked is a paper written by Sir Mortimer Wheeler, I think in Antiquity in 1950, which was called "What matters in Archaeology?" and I used to cite that to my classes quite a lot. Now, what does matter in archaeology? Is it the sort of Binfordian new archaeology, rational statistics, or is it where more spiritual aspects — and that to me is the exciting thing about Aboriginal Australia. The Aboriginal Australians are certainly extremely spiritual all their dreaming tracks. This rock art, art is beginning to suggest interpretations about past belief systems and that seems to me, as a historian, one looks at the society, you don't just describe the kings and queens. You try to present the whole fabric of functioning society, and that is what we have got to do with archaeology and I think that people who are studying rock art in Australia are beginning to do that. I also held the belief that the study of prehistory is a marvellous introduction for undergraduates to anything. It's interdisciplinary, so in the course of the first year course I used to teach, I would emphasize the importance of environmental factors and at the end of the first year, if you didn't want to go on, you could go on to linguistics or geography or history, or many other subjects, with an understanding of something of a background to it, and that I think is its great value. I would almost make it compulsory for first-year students, but it did work and quite a number of our students combined courses of archaeology and geography. So I think the value is very great, but then there is another aspect that we always stressed — just like historians, you are dependent on evidence. You have got to quote your evidence. It is no good speculating. You have to analyse your sources and many of the sources may be historical. This is what impressed me about Grahame Clark's early economic articles. He was going back to early historical literature about bee-keeping or about various things and he was combining historical sources with archaeological sources.

Because Mrs Glyn Daniel has recently died, could you say something about the Daniels?

Glyn was one of the best features of my life in Cambridge. Charles McBurney was one of them. He was great. My trip to Libya was one of the great influences on my career, but Glyn Daniel was such a friendly, jolly man and he had many critics. In fact, it took years before he was elected to the British Academy, and I think that was wrong. When one looks back, one might say some of his work on megalithic tombs doesn't stand up to, is dated, but he was an all-round man and he was interesting in teaching, and I think his teaching method was tremendous to under-graduates. He would give you a lecture in a very informal friendly style. You could take notes on it, and then at the end, and only at near the end, he'd come out with a whole series of slides. Now most lecturers use slides all the time and so many of them get so bogged down with what they've got on the screen they are just sort of describing, but he revised his lecture by a series of well-chosen slides and I think he deserves great credit. He was a great man to go to for supervisions too. I was very lucky that in my second year that I went every week to him, with the man who later became Sir David Wilson, who became the Director of the British Museum. He would give us a glass of port or something. It was a very civilised experience, but you'd do some work; but his great influence on me was his interest in the history of the subject and that is one of the reasons I came to Cambridge, as I explained, because of his Hundred Years of Archaeology. At the time it was quite path-breaking, that he was surveying such a range of literature and so many of his conclusions, even if they are just odd sentences, were very appropriate and stand up. So his interest of the history of archaeology certainly determined me and I suppose is one of the things that led me, when I went back to Australia, to look at how people have explained Aboriginal society through the ages, from the first Dutch experience in the early 17th century on. Yes, he was a very humane man, and he took his students seriously, and he had a very large number of students going through John's, and as an Editor of Antiquity, again I think he did a marvellous job. Later on, as he got older, it tended to be a bit repetitive. He took a view against the New Archaeology which I sympathised with, very much along my views. He published an article by J. Hawkes which I think had a lot to be said for it, but like the article by Wheeler, most of my colleagues derided them as being emotional and subjective. Well, they are subjective, but prehistory and history are subjective things, and it is one of the clichés that every generation rewrites its past and there is no reason why every generation shouldn't rewrite its prehistory. I've done that. I produced a prehistory book in 1969, rewrote it in 1973, published in Penguin in 1975. It was a totally different book, light years different. That was because so much had happened in Australia at that time and I saw the light of beginning to be ethnographic of the living Aboriginal people, the tremendous antiquity in the past of Australia and the tremendous environmental changes, and all this was happening. Now I resisted rewriting it, but with Johan Kamminga, younger colleague, last year we did produce Prehistory of Australia. It is totally rewritten and it is just so different. I suspect that is the last Prehistory of Australia to be written for some time, because to cover a continent in one book is impossible. We had to leave so many important things out because of publishers' space requirements. It would be so very easy now to write four or five regions of Australia and fill a book. You could write one on Tasmania alone.

Your life spanned enormous growth and changes.

It certainly did. Well, to be the only archaeologist to be employed in aca-demic life in Australia in 1954 to now, where I'm not sure — Australian academic life is going through a bit of revision lately. The government is not funding it adequately, but archaeology is now taught at quite a number of Australia universities and consulting archaeology is universal, because under the State legislations now it is necessary to have it done. So there are some hundreds of archaeologists in Australia now.

Tape 2 side 1

I have a few questions. In your MA thesis you discuss the Teutonic influence in the 1930s, and I wondered if you understood why there was this very quick change that you detail, where people begin to say that there is this Teutonic note?

Yes, I think that that was the most significant. I think the fact is that, in the 1930s with the depression, people were greatly influenced by Mussolini's developments in Italy and also Hitler's in Germany. Not only did Italian trains run on time, but in Germany they had roads that were marvellous and everyone seemed to be jolly and this is perhaps the reason also there was a tremendous amount of archaeology fostered. We now know it was the wrong kind of archaeology, but archaeologists were uncovering Neo-lithic villages in Germany. They were wanting to prove that they were the original Aryan folk, but the fact is the techniques being used were very impressive to English archaeologists who had seen so much amateurism here; and men like Christopher Hawkes and Collingwood, I think, they were just influenced perhaps unaware by certain racist, the superiority of the Anglo-Saxon people crept in and it was only when I started reading this literature that one began to realise that they used as self-sufficient explanations that these were progressive Aryan people as opposed to these autocratic Romans.

It is very interesting because it is during the 1930s there is a rebirth of interest in British archaeology, using this German model as an inspiration to become interested in their own Teutonic past.

Yes, I think so, and Grahame Clark in my day was regarded as an extremely right-wing man, but it is a great credit to him that he doesn't use any of this. He didn't stress the superiority of the Aryan race.

But certainly his cohort did. Hawkes and Curwens —

Yes, they did. Curwen was just a local doctor. It was very common in all sorts of things. The whole attitude, the Neville Chamberlain attitude, that you could negotiate with the Germans, they were reasonable people. The Second World War put an end to this, but it is there all right.

I think it began to change in the 1940s.

Oh yes, Grahame Clark's very great book *Archaeology and Society*. I don't think that he has gotten enough credit for that. It was published before the war, and he was showing that totalitarian beliefs had problems. It was the first really good synthesis of what archaeology exactly, what it was, that Archaeol-ogy and Society. That was another book that I had read before I came here. I found a copy in a, second-hand copy in a book-shop in Melbourne.

Did that book influence students of your generation?

I don't know. Well, yes, Grahame Clark's lectures were along those same lines.

Could you say something about the Cambridge connection?

Well, yes, the Cambridge connection in Australia has become something of a vexed problem, but put in perspective we have the situation in Australia and New Zealand where there is no archaeology and if you go back to the 1950s, where were archaeologists being produced? Well, presumably in the USA, but in those days Australia and New Zealand had no cultural contact at the level of universities, very little indeed. So except for the British Isles, we in Australia didn't have much contact. Now, if you examine the departments in England at that time, the Institute of Archaeology in London hardly had anybody, didn't produce very much. Oxford was very inward and did very little undergraduate teaching of archaeology. Edinburgh was producing some students. So if they were going to come from Australia to anywhere, given the cultural ties of Australia, they had to come to Cam-bridge. So I don't think it was necessarily just Cambridge or imperialism or Grahame Clark's imperialism which he undoubtedly had. In a sense he appreciated that there was a great need for prehistory to be done in other parts, and quite remarkable really that undergraduates, particularly British ones, were, if they wanted to go on in research, it was almost "Go west, young man, go overseas, young man, you must do archaeology somewhere else". People went to Africa and became Africanists, from Cambridge. It is quite understandable that the Department at Auckland would write to Cambridge seeking somebody; having done that then there was the Cambridge influence. Jack Golson was there, and Wilfred Shawcross and Peter Bellwood were the next appointments, and then a revolution occurred. Roger Green, an American, was appointed. Once he was there, it established an American axis. Peter Gathercole went to Dunedin. He was replaced by Charles Higham. In Australia, well, I was the first one. I was Cambridge-trained, but I would emphasize that I had two Honours degrees from Melbourne, so I really am a Melbourne person. The next Australian was Isabel McBryde, who in 1968 paid her own way to come to Cambridge to do a Diploma, but already had two university degrees from Australia. The great deluge occurred around 1961. The Australia Institute of Aboriginal Studies was gradually being established, and in 1961 Jack Golson was appointed from New Zealand to Australia, but of course Jack Golson was Cambridge; and Isabel McBryde started teaching prehistory in 1960. I was already teaching it, but then Vincent Megaw was appointed from Edinburgh to the Sydney Department of Archaeology, which is the European, not prehistory. He was teaching Iron Age Archaeology in a Department which is primarily Middle East and Classical Archaeology. He was a graduate of Edinburgh. Then Ian Crawford, who was a student of mine in Melbourne and went to the London Institute in 1960. He was appointed to the West Australia Museum in Perth in 1961–62 as Curator of Archaeology. He was the first Curator of Archaeology in an Australian museum. He was Melbourne and London, and Megaw was Edinburgh. Richard Wright at the same time was appointed to the Anthropology Department in Sydney, to lecture in prehistoric archaeology, so by 1962 we had Golson, Wright, myself, McBride, as Cambridge archaeologists, and Crawford and Megaw as non-Cambridge archaeologists. About a year or so later, John Clegg was appointed to a post in Queensland, moved to Sydney, and then of course we started taking students to do PhDs; and not unnaturally, given the numbers at Cambridge and the attitude at Cambridge that you should go overseas to do research, quite a number came from Cambridge. But then one of them was Peter White, who was one of my students from Melbourne who went to Cambridge, and the other was his then wife, Carmel Schrire, who was the one who produced 20,000-year-old dates from Kakadu Park for her Ph.D.

Sylvia Hallam?

Sylvia Hallam, her husband, Bert, was appointed to the Professor of History in the University of West Australia in 1970. She came out, not in her own right. She came out as the wife, but started work and eventually was appointed to lecture in prehistory in the Anthropology Department, but you know, nowadays we have people from all over the place, American, and John Campbell, an American who did his Ph.D at Oxford.

Did you train a generation in Australia?

Well, a lot of people, in academic life certainly, I had as students. Ian Crawford and Peter White in Melbourne would be two who have gone on professionally, but most of my other students have gone on in history. Greg Dening, who is one of the more notable of the contemporary historians, he was the brightest student I ever taught. He did his MA on the voyaging in the Pacific. Jack Golson was his examiner. He has now gone on to be preeminent as a Pacific historian. When I went to Canberra, I supervised some Ph.D students there, most notable would be Jim Allen who became Professor of Archaeology at La Trobe, and Ian Glover who worked in what was then Portuguese Timor and went on to be a Lecturer in Archaeology, at London, and this was the great moment, wasn't it, when an Australian-trained person got a job at the hub of the Empire; and then Campbell MacKnight became a Professor of History in Tasmania, and he has just retired this year. Ian Glover retired a couple of years ago. Time has caught up on us. Now any other questions? One question.

You have throughout your work, there is this great admiration for human diversity and that somehow through archaeology this is expressed, that there is spiritual value, that it points us to our common humanity and this seems to go through all your work.

Yes, I think it does, and it is because I do believe in the common humanity that I am so worried about the present Aboriginal assertions that they are a separate group from the rest of the world. If, in fact, there were a totally separate creation, the whole thing about rules, about United Nations and how you treat — we are all one human race. Slavery is wrong. When the southern states were defending slavery, they ran the line that Negroes were a separate creation. They had no relation to white society. They were subhuman, and we get back to that unless we accept the rule of a common humanity, and that the best way we can handle it is through the UN; and if you are an archaeologist or interested in history, the best way to do that is through bodies such as UNESCO with its concept of world heritage. Unless you are going to support them, I don't see you are going to get anywhere, and it worries me at the moment that quite a number of archaeologists in Australia are sneering at the whole idea of world heritage.

That is a theme. The other thing that interests me is your belief that historical analysis can teach, that through that understanding how we make our conclusions we can become more self-aware. That seems to be another theme. Do you agree?

Well, it probably is. I'm not really a Hodder-like theorist who write books on how we work but I think it is true, yes. I just say, yes. I don't think I can answer you. I agree, but am not sure what I can say.

Thank you for the interview.

Dr Innocent Pikirayi

14 July 2000, recorded at Peterhouse, Cambridge, at the SAfA Conference, by Pamela Jane Smith pjs1011@cam.ac.uk

Will you please just tell me something about yourself and how you got into archaeology?

OK. Well, I started my career in archaeology 1982. I am a student of people like Peter Garlake, Robert Soper, Gilbert Pwiti and Paul Sinclair. I did my Honours Degree in History as well as my Master's in History with a bias towards archaeology. Then I read for Historical Archaeology at the University of Uppsala in Sweden, graduating in 1994. Since then I have been teaching at the University of Zimbabwe. Now I am also the Head of Department, actually for the last three years. It has been a career of research and administration.

I can hear you on the tape clearly. Can you tell me what your specialisation is?

My interests, as I say, since I studied both history and archaeology, I've tried to find the common ground between history and archaeology and I finally settled for a career in historical archaeology because I felt that I should not lose touch with history which was my original discipline, as well as archaeology which was the specialist discipline that I took for my Honours Degree as well as my Master's. It was logical, in a way, that my Ph.D had to be in Historical Archaeology which combined both history and archaeology. So, that is my area of specialisation. I am actually involved in the research of the last 500 years of Zimbabwe archaeology which involves the Zimbabwe culture, its contacts with the Portuguese and others of northern Zimbabwe as well as the archaeology of the later Europeans. I am talking about the British missionaries, the British colonists, hunters of the 19th century, which is the terminal phase of the Zimbabwe culture. So, it is this kind of interruption between the indigenous Zimbabwe culture peoples and the European colonists in the sense of the Portuguese as well as the British for the 19th century. I am looking at that area too. But I am now also getting interested in what we call cultural losses; the kind of losses that Africans as well as many other people in the world are experiencing as the result of major development projects. I am particularly interested in, we are particularly focusing on the major dams, their impact on cultural heritage. Zimbabwe (then Rhodesia) as well as Zambia saw the construction of one of the largest man-made lakes in the 1950s in the world, the Kariba Dam. It had a tremendous impact on the culture of the indigenous people who were living in the Zambezi valley because these people were forcibly moved. They lost a lot in terms of their culture, in terms of the identity, and they were actually improvised as a result of this major development which took place with the construction of the Dam. So, this is part of what I am looking at now and this is what has brought me to Cambridge. We, Zimbabweans, are now thinking of building another dam to the west of Kariba, just below the Victoria Falls. This dam is going to impact on tourism and indigenous people. I think as archaeologists, we need to sensitize the whole issue of development and cultural losses and dams being so impacting in such a way that they flood huge areas and leading to losses of so many things like our traditional heritage. This is what I am going to be talk about or at least make suggestions as to what we should be doing in terms of the losses that are likely to occur.

Are there rules that you have to do impact studies?

Well, when such projects are done, governments have to follow guide lines from such organisations as the World Bank, or other development banks, the Asian Development Bank, the African Development Bank. They have their own guide lines as to how environmental impacts have to be done. But, the major problem as far as most governments are concerned, including my government, is that of consulting the people on the ground, the people affected by these projects, to see how they think about it. It also has a lot to do with publicity. Most of these projects are done in secret and you only get to know about them when they are in advanced stage. So, it should be their planning process that has to be publicised. It is this process that people have to be fully aware of and also be involved in, in the sense — the people affected have to be participants in these decision-making processes as to

how they want to see their future being shaped. Because in the end they are the ones who suffer most. Our experience in regards to the previous dams is that they are not benefiting from anything. The hydro-electricity is not benefiting the people displaced by the dam. It is benefiting towns 300, 400 kilometres away. The water sports, the fish are not being given to the people displaced by the dam. It is being sold elsewhere. It is being exported to other countries. Many people are displaced by the flooding as well because of the Colonial grand design to carve out huge areas for game as well as water sport. The people affected by the Dam, most lost terribly. The main problem is consulting them to say "OK, this is what we want to do. How do you feel about it? Yes." You know giving them a chance to air their grievances in a way that they are respected and they are taken as part of the decision making process. Part of what we resolved in February, when we met for a workshop in Gainesville, Florida, was that heritage is really a human right. Every body has a right to heritage. There is no heritage which can be regarded as inferior or superior. I am entitled to the little heritage that I feel most about. Therefore, I should be given the right to express myself, my feeling of it, and if I don't want anything to happen to it then I should be allowed to defend it to the fullest. So, this is what I see as the direction of archaeology and heritage in this millennium. Archaeology has to address such issues. I know we are getting so much material in terms of discoveries, stone tools, everything, but as long as we fail to address the genuine needs of the people affected on the ground, I think archaeology will not attract as many interested people as it should. But archaeology has that potential of addressing meaningful problems and issues affecting everybody because it is linked to almost every discipline. So if we try to address ourselves within that angle. I think there is a lot of relevance for the disciplines.

Yes, that is wonderful. Is that why you began to study archaeology, for this hope?

I think, you know, one of the reasons I did archeology was that one of my first professors was Dr Garlake. He addressed the problem of Great Zimbabwe in a meaningful way. Great Zimbabwe is one of the world's famous monuments and it is one of these monuments which gave my country its name. Ours is one of the only countries in the world named after an archaeological site. So, my other Professor was Professor Vella from Malta, who taught me a lot of Roman and Greek archaeology, and he did it in such a way that you could see how archaeology was used to address the problem of Greco-Roman origins which I think even up to today, many people in the Mediterranean world value so much. You can not talk about European civilisation without talking about Roman Civilisation, at least for the Mediterranean, but for Zimbabwe, for example, it is very difficult to revert to our traditional or pre-colonial past in trying to address problems of modern development because of this episode of Europe colonisation. But, I think for us to succeed as a nation we need to address our prehistoric origins. We need to address our past. The past is very relevant to modern-day needs. In fact it is what gives us identity first. So I really derive so much inspiration from what I learn from the past and I think if you try to take away that past from me, you take my identity. You take my essence. That is what I feel about archaeology.

Do you teach that?

Yes. I teach introductory courses to my students about what archaeology is. I also teach prehistory in second year, the origins of Humans in Southern Africa. I also archaeological methods to my third-year students. But for my Part I students, part of what I teach them is the whole problem of heritage management and how do you handle what is brought to you from the past. How do you look at development? What do you think is good about archaeology that you would like to use with modern developments needs, to link archaeology and development? They have to come up with debatable issues. The whole thing rests on whether archaeology is relevant or not. And we all agree that archaeology is so relevant that there is no other way we can address meaningfully the problems of origins, the question of origin. I teach that with so much satisfaction and so much passion.

Yes, I wonder, was your family supportive when you decided to study archaeology? Many people in Britain tell me their families said "No, no, you will never get a job."

I studied the discipline young and got married when I had already started my Master's. My wife was so supportive in such a way that she even allowed me to take four years off in study leave to do read for my Ph.D. So she was so supportive and I am thankful for that. Right up to today, archaeology involves a lot of travel and conferences. I mean I miss my family because I have to spend weeks away from home, leaving her and my two beautiful girls to grapple with the problems at home, but it is this kind of support that has kept me alive. Without that kind of support, I won't be here. I really appreciate them and want to acknowledge them for the way I am.

Were you educated in Zimbabwe?

Yes, I was educated in Zimbabwe. I did my primary in Zimbabwe, my six years of secondary education in Zimbabwe, my BA in Zimbabwe which is three years. My Master's, I did in one year, record time and then in Sweden, I did Ph.D in four years, record time. Normally it takes the Swedish Doctoral Studies takes quite a long time, five, six, seven years.

We were interrupted by someone who wanted us to light his cigarette.

I just said it takes quite awhile for one to study in Sweden but I did it in record time because of family concerns at home. My father and mother are still alive. They are all retired in a rural area doing peasant farming, but my wife is a school teacher and I thought the earlier I finished my study programme the better, because she needed my support and my presence. That is how I came back to Zimbabwe to start on a teaching career and am now part of the University Development Programme. I am now a full time Lecturer there. The University is a sizable community of up to 20,000 students, with over 1000 teaching staff, 3000 support staff including secretarial, technicians and associated researchers. We are a sizable community, the biggest university in Zimbabwe at the moment, but there are other smaller universities that are coming up as spin offs from the University of Zimbabwe.

Do others recognise archaeology as a way to solve problems?

Unfortunately, no. That is the biggest problem. Archaeology is seen as part of history. That is why in Zimbabwe it is taught in the History Department because they think that archaeology is simply the other end of history. Before you study history proper, you have to do archaeology. But that is wrong, in the sense the main culprits are the policy-makers, the legislators. They fail to see beyond that requirement to where the past can be used to address some of the problems of the present. They fail to see how to use the past to solve contemporary issues and part of what they should realise is that Zimbabwe is the only country in the world named after an archaeology site. There are so many stone structures of the Zimbabwe culture that gives Zimbabwe an identity and it is that kind of heritage which we can market successfully. We can advertise. We can play around with that. We can teach our children that this is the past that makes us what we are. That is why we are called Zimbabwe in the first place. It is this fundamental realisation that the policy-makers should be able to see and try to address, but we Lecturers in Archaeology are trying to do that. I think that it is only a matter of time before they have to take us seriously.

This is a very important message you're saying. You are talking about something that is almost of spiritual value for people, their identity. Do you agree?

Certainly! I think any discipline without a spiritual connection is totally devoid of the human element. One of the most satisfying things that I find in studying archaeology and the past is that I am able to see how the humans interacted with their environment. How the humans tried to grapple with their problems and how they tried to solve them without recourse to so much conflict, without recourse to the problems of global dominance, global finance, even what we call globalisation at the moment. I really don't know what we mean by globalisation but part of what we need to do is to look into the past to solve our problems, because in the past I find so much hope, so much inspiration

Could you say something about your methods, your archaeology when you go to communities faced with development?

Well, my simple agenda when I am working in an area with archaeological sites and with tremendous research potential, I have to try to address the people where the archaeological sites are, because without consulting the people, without telling them what your mission is, your project is going to fail. Part of the problem in Zimbabwe is that so many people have been moved around owing to Colonial administration. Many people found themselves living in an area where they are not connected with their past. Part of my task is to try to address this problem, to say one of the reasons you are here is that they were trying to do this, but you belong to this Dynasty, or you belong or are linked with these archaeological sites in this way. This is a Heritage which you need to protect. It tells a long story. It is a story about yourself, about your past. It is this fundamental issue that can lead one to appreciate the value of the past, the value of archaeology in modern-day issues, in modern developmental problems. People start to appreciate you as a researcher. They help you, will even show you more of what you are looking for because if you don't identify yourself, if you impose your wishes on the community, they may choose not to cooperate with you. It is very fundamental in Africa that whoever is coming to do research should get the good will of the community. It is from that point you see what the community can offer including their culture.

Do you see a direct connection between the dynasty, the culture and the beginnings of archeology?

Yes, in Zimbabwe, the main problem is that historians as well as politicians do not see the direct link between dynastic histories and archaeology. They say archaeology belongs to prehistory and dynasties belong to modern history, but as a specialist on Zimbabwe culture, I see the Zimbabwe culture right from AD 1000 to 1900 AD when the last pre-colonial state finally collapsed. I see a lot of these dynasties interacting with monuments. I see them building monuments, building the very past I am trying to study. So it is this link between history and the tangible physical evidence that we see as stone buildings that we should bring to the people to say, "Here is a handbook of the past which you should read which will give you an overview of what history and archaeology are all about." The past is not made up of one discipline but a multiplicity of disciplines of which archaeology and history are only part of the whole issue.

If someone listening to this tape and wanted to be an archaeologist, could you give them an example of what you do, day by day?

Personally I believe in hard work. I wake up very early, 4.00 a.m. I start preparing for my day, preparing for my lectures, just an overview of what I am going to talk about because I am very careful not to just talk about anything. I have to prepare, even if I know what I am talking about, at least doing a preview of what you are going to say opens up a lot more issues than you think. Then I do a lot of reading and writing. My hope is to become full Professor in four or five years' time. I publish quite a lot at the moment. I have just published a monograph on the Zimbabwe culture which will be available on all continents, California, USA, London, Europe.

Who publishes it?

It is Altamira Press, the Editor is Professor Joseph Vogel who is in California and the book is called The Archaeology of the Zimbabwe Culture, which looks at state formation from AD 1000 to 1900 AD. It is a book I look forward to and I would like to invite comments from the general public to see what Zimbabwe is made of.

If an intellectual happens to come and listen to this tape, perhaps you could say something about the more technical part of your work too.

Historical archaeology, of which I am a specialist, really involves trying to use historical evidence to interpret archaeological material. Basically with my archaeology training, I use a lot of history, which I also read as part of my Honours Degree as well as my Master's, to come up with what I call a holistic view of the past. All the methods and approaches that you study in archaeology, I use to understand the past.

One issue that is in the press a great deal in North America is the land issues of Zimbabwe. Could you comment on that?

Land is an important issue in Zimbabwe. But, the main problem with the politicians is that they failed to realise that land is a Heritage issue, not simply an economic issue. The problem with the current political analyses, is that they are failing to address fundamental economic problems like national debt, poverty, and things like that. From an archaeologist's point of view, I see land as an important component of cultural heritage. It is something that we inherited from our forefathers and something that we have a right to. Agreed that there were colonial injustices the way the land was acquired 100 years ago and I think it can be addressed meaningfully without so much politics. But, whoever addresses the land issue in Zimbabwe, must take into account pre-colonial human relationships, how people valued their land rather than what the current politicians would want us to use the land to do. Of course, there is need to feed the people and to address issues of famine, but you can't take all the land and put it into commercial farming. Part of the exercise should be to try to reutilise that land for pre-colonial human land relationships because people always viewed the environment beyond the settlement in a certain way. There are sacred places, places of economic power, places of political power. People saw land in a unique way. The politicians are failing to do that. I just finished writing an article for a journal in the UK called Africa Now where I addressed the whole issue in more detail. Land is a Heritage which the politicians must realise. It is part of the what makes us Zimbabwe, part of the Zimbabwe culture. So unless we put Archaeology and Heritage into it, we won't solve the land issue. It is not just a question of grabbing it for who wants. It is really coming up with a holistic programme as to how we want to utilise the land in the best possible way.

Yes, over and over you speak about a human right to the past and to land and to Heritage, human right to dignity. I wonder how successful you think you will be.

All depends on how the country views itself within the current global concerns and what human rights are, but everybody knows what they are entitled to. At least I am entitled to my own life, the way I want to live it, but I have to respect people, the way they want to live their own lives. This should be the way we relate to each other, mutual respect of what people would like to do and what people believe in. Of course, people don't have a right to interfere with what others would like to do on some other issues, but mutual respect, mutual understanding of one another's feelings, hopes, aspirations, is very important. Everyone has a right to what we call culture. I still don't believe in globalization of cultures. I think we are entitled to lead our lives in a unique way, and it is this uniqueness that makes up the global village. If we are encouraged to look the same, the world won't inspire anybody. It will be a boring world if we don't show our differences, what we are made of, and how we link to the rest of the world.

Do you find the archaeological community such as the Society for Africanists Archaeologists, do you find them to be supportive?

Yes, they are very supportive, but there are limitations on the resources. I think more resources should be made available to support such organisations such as SAfA because they are now slowly and surely trying to address some of the problems I have been talking about; but their major problem is that they are working on a very limited budget. I want to acknowledge they have brought a number of Africans, including myself, to this meeting. They would need a lot more resources. Travel between continents have become extremely prohibitive. The economies of Africa can not facilitate travel let alone other costly things such as accommodation.

I imagine things such as journals, books etc. . . .

Those again are very prohibitive because the cost of journals, books within the last two years have gone up tremendously.

And costs for your type of work is labour intensive, isn't it?

It is. I think the best way to do it is to work in a collaborative way, to involve researchers in Africa more often than what we have achieved so far, and also to involve the researchers in Europe more than what they have been able to do so far. One is to address the issue of resources. It is part of this global economic alliances between rich and poor countries.

SAfA is satisfying in what it is trying to do, but it also needs more publicity. Of course, they have a web site, but they need to publicize much more often. I think the public needs to know that we do exist and we are part of their global concerns in terms of heritage issues, cultural losses, thefts of cultural property, and destruction of archaeological sites through development projects.

Are those the goals of SAfA, to address those very serious problems?

These are some of their key goals. They also are interested in trying to address the simple problems of African prehistory, origins, disseminating information, benefiting African scholars as much as possible. They have done their best, and I look forward to the continued existence, because SAfA has managed to address concerns but within very difficult circumstances.

I am very impressed with your integrity and passion.

It has been nice talking to you. I think that the interview will help others understand what we really think about archaeology. It has changed its face and dimension and has changed focus. As an African studying African archaeology, I think archaeology should be more embracing, more inclusive. It should be archaeology with a spiritual strength involved. It is what makes me as a person. This is how I want to look at it.

End of tape.

Professor Merrick Posnansky

14 July 2000, recorded in Peterhouse, Cambridge, at the SAfA Conference, by Pamela Jane Smith.   pjs1011@cam.ac.uk

Could you just say a bit about your life and when you were born?

I'm Merrick Posnansky and I was born in the north of England. I started life at the University of Nottingham as an historian and geographer and then went to Cambridge as a graduate student, actually to this College of Peterhouse where I did prehistoric archaeology. Later I went back to the University of Nottingham where I did my Ph.D in Palaeolithic Archaeology, looking at the earliest extent of humans in middle England, and in 1956 I went out to Kenya to work for the Royal National Parks of Kenya as the Warden of Prehistoric sites and stayed in Kenya for nearly two years, and then went in 1958 to Uganda as the Curator of the Uganda Museum, where I also looked after antiquities; and in 1964 I transferred to the University, Makerere University College, where I began the teaching African Archaeology at Makerere and designed a programme for the other colleges in East Africa to begin teaching archaeology. We also began a graduate programme. Our first graduate student in archaeology was John Sutton, who received his Ph.D in 1965. I transferred to the University of Ghana in 1967 as Head of the Department of Archaeology and stayed there for nine years before going to UCLA.

I wondered if you could say something about your experiences as a young man in Britain and what drew you to archaeology?

I was led to archaeology, in fact as I think many children in Britain are, as a collector. I collected all sorts of different things. I think as a small child, I wanted to be a street cleaner because I felt that such people picked up coins. They had great machines which cleaned the drains out. I later collected coins myself and wanted to specialise in Numismatics and then I went to University to read Ancient History but while at College, I began doing excavations in my free time and during holidays and dug Roman and Mediaeval sites and progressed to prehistoric sites when I went up to Cambridge, and that is basically what led me into archaeology as a career. In the mid-1950s, there weren't so many jobs in archaeology but there were still opportunities in what we still called the Colonies, and so there were opportunities in places in Kenya where I went. Other archaeologists went out to Australia or New Zealand. Neville Chittick, from the same College, went out to the Sudan and later on to Tanganyika.

Who influenced you at Cambridge?

Well, various people influenced me intellectually. The man who brought me to Cambridge was Grahame Clark who was the Disney Professor. I studied with him and Charles McBurney and also had, for a time, Glyn Daniel as my Supervisor. He was a very inspiring person on the history of archaeology and he broadened my vision as regards the world. One influence on me, though he only taught me one class, was Miles Burkitt, because Miles Burkitt had an abiding interest in Africa and felt that Africa was the place to be and it was he who had sent out many of his former students to Africa, people like Desmond Clark. The middle 1950s was a time of austerity in Britain. I wanted to see the world and I felt that Africa was a place which we didn't know much about and it would be exciting place to go. So off I went to Kenya in 1956.

What was your first impression of Kenya?

My first impression of Kenya, of course it was during the Mau Mau and we drove into Nairobi, had lunch at the Norfolk Hotel and various people were sitting at tables with guns on their tables. It was a slightly scary first impression. The other thing, I slightly felt a fish out of water. I had been brought up in a small town and I was from a Jewish background, had a rather settled life and even at somewhere like Cambridge, most of the archaeologists came from public schools and I felt that people who came from red brick universities weren't quite in the same sort of league. At first I may have felt out of it, but slowly I got into things, and I am a teacher by interest so began teaching archaeology for the extra-mural college, Makerere University College, based in Kampala, and began the

first adult education courses in tropical Africa in archaeology in 1957 in Nairobi, which was quite exciting.

Who came to those courses?

They were mainly, at that time, British house wives. One of the things that appalled me about Kenya was the lack of interaction between the different races. I went to Uganda in 1957 on a project with Professor Richard Flint from Yale, who was writing a Pleistocene chronology of Africa. He was an inspiring person. I went around with him and with someone I had already known from Britain, Bill Bishop, and we looked at many of the Pleistocene or Quaternary sites in both Uganda and Kenya, and this gave me a total overview. When I went to Uganda, I noticed a big difference between the two countries, particularly with regard to the education of Africans. There was much more interaction with Africans. In fact, I had introduction to several people, and so this was the first time that I sat down and had meals with Africans and talked with them on an equal basis, and this inspired me to want to go back to Uganda where I felt that there wasn't that sort of racial tension that there was in Kenya. So when the opportunity came up in 1958 to apply for the post at the Uganda Museum, I did so with alacrity. At that time, Peter Shinnie was leaving as Director of Antiquities in Uganda. He had only stayed a year. He found Uganda rather boring. So I persuaded people in Uganda to combine the control of Antiquities with that of the Curator of Uganda Museum. This was very attractive to me because it meant that I could look after a country. I had a lot of scope, a lot of responsibility. This was one of the exciting things about going out to Africa, since as a young man, I was then 26, one could look after a whole country and design a programme of research. I was very multidisciplinary in my interests. It was exciting. One of the things I think I did well there, which affected many people, is that I began to link the study of oral history with the study of archaeology and began a series of excavations which made use of oral history. So I went from Old Stone Age material which I had studied in Kenya to looking at the development of states in western Uganda.

Could you describe Flint and Bishop and their contribution?

Well, Flint was very important because he tried to look at Africa as a whole and he got rid of a lot of the nonsense that people like Leakey had spread, particularly the idea of a number of great pluvials [or rainy periods corresponding to the Ice Ages]. He attempted to put these into perspective. Leakey and many others had said that when there were Ice Ages in Europe, there were Pluvials in Africa, and they exaggerated the influence of these Pluvials, and so Flint was able to tie in the geological events in Africa with the geological events in America and Europe and provide a universal chronology which was so important. This was the time when radiocarbon dating was coming into play and other types of dating were just being initiated. He was a very fundamental person in this field. Bill Bishop was very important. Bill Bishop tragically died in 1977 when he had just been appointed Curator of the Peabody Museum. Bill Bishop also worked on the Pleistocene, he was a Palaeontologist and he succeeded me as Curator of Uganda Museum. He was also interested in education and did many things with University Extension and that type of thing; and he was a very vigorous Museum Curator and revolutionised the study of Palaeontology and made it much more meaningful, rather than just the study of bones. He related the bones to environments and made these environments live and showed how people interacted with their environments. Rather than Palaeontology comprising collections of fossil fauna, I think he had a much stronger ecological approach. He was particularly interested in the prehumans of the Miocene period.

[Prof. Posnansky is eating lunch. We may have to wait occasionally while he has a bite to eat . . .]
In the meantime, could you mention something about the Grahame Clark story about how he approached you?

This really has very little to do with Africa but I came to Cambridge because at the University of Nottingham, I had started the Archaeological Society. There were no archaeologists and we were doing excavations on Mediaeval tile kiln and Mediaeval well and things like that, and Grahame came as the first speaker to our Archaeological Society; and he asked me what I was going to do after I finished my degree, and I said that I was going to work on a Mediaeval cartulary, doing purely historical work on documents, but also I was hoping to excavate the priory in Lincolnshire [that produced the historical records]. He suggested that I come to Cambridge and get a grounding in archaeology and I think Grahame Clark was very influential in this sense in that he was very much an evangelist, a quiet evangelist, but he liked to bring people from around about to Cambridge and try to do it that way. Many of his successors tried to enlarge the Department. They were more political but Grahame Clark I think was a good ambassador for archaeology, and for Cambridge archaeology in that particular sense. I went to Cambridge and Grahame introduced me to many different people.

Was it one of the few places in England where you could get training?

At that time, the only places you get a training in archaeology were the Institute of Archaeology [University of London] and Cambridge University. There was a Professor Christopher Hawkes at Oxford, but there weren't regular courses in archaeology at the University of Oxford. There wasn't structured training. There was also beginning at that time a training in archaeology in two other places, not of course in England. One was in Cardiff, in Wales, with Atkinson who had just written his book on field archaeology, and the other was at Edinburgh, with Stuart Piggott.

[Break for lunch]

We were just discussing Wayland and Bishop and Flint again.

Yes one person who I think is sadly overlooked in African prehistory was E.J. Wayland. He came out to Uganda in 1919 and the first thing he did was he walked around the whole Protectorate, spent weeks on this great walking tour, and then he tried to get a chronology of the most recent past. He looked at river gravels. He looked at things like terraces. He was the person who proposed something called the Kafuan, the earliest Stone Age, based on the gravels of Kagera River. He did a lot of work. He sort of excavated in the Kagera River on the Acheulean sites, handaxe sites, and he went to Magosi which became a classic site and did an excavation there in 1929. He was the person who proposed the Sangoan. That was a Middle Stone Age industry. In this way, he named many of the Stone Age industries of Africa. He was at his peak in the late 1920s. He helped the young Louis Leakey quite considerably. Louis Leakey took many of his ideas but then Louis Leakey never gave Wayland very much credit for what he took from him. They later became somewhat bitter about one another because they had differing ideas about Quaternary stratigraphy. Wayland was rather a lonely sort of man. He had a rather unhappy married life and lost one of his children in a sad sort of way. He went from Uganda to Bechuanaland, now Botswana, but always had a love of Uganda and came back in the 1950s, perhaps about 1951–52, to Uganda as a consultant. The whole idea was that he was going to write up the Pleistocene chronology of Uganda as Part I of a volume which had been started by Van Riet Lowe from South Africa who had been invited from South Africa to work in Uganda in the 1930s. Wayland never finished that volume and in fact it was written by Bishop later on. Wayland became rather bitter and began churning out large amounts of material but never drew them all together. I helped to evacuate him from Uganda in 1959, helped him to pack up. He went back to England and died a rather bitter old man.

It is interesting because there is so much material from him in the Cambridge Museum Archives. He sent an awful lot of lithic material to Burkitt. Could you say something more about what he was collecting?

Oh, yes, I think the importance about Wayland was that he discovered that in Uganda you had the whole sequence of the Stone Age and he made wonderful collections; some of which he made for a collection for the Geological Museum in Entebbe, and he also sent collections both to the Cambridge Museum and to the British Museum. So some of the type series which many people learnt from later on in the 1920s, 1930s and so on were based on Wayland's collecting, but he was the one who named many of the industries; but he was also tied up of course in this business of trying to work out pluvials and which was a red herring, we found later

on, but of course it was very difficult for people at that time. They would look at river valley sequences. They would then see, in their sections, they would then see gravels. They knew that gravels had to have a lot of water to bring them down. Therefore gravels indicated pluvial periods and so they erected this chronological, false chronological sequence which tended to mislead people for many many years until we got universal chronologies based on radiocarbon and potassium argon dating, etc.

Was Wayland and perhaps Bishop, were they both very much in favour of local terminologies rather than using European frameworks?

Yes, I should think so. I mean many of the — yes you could say that, that they were interested in getting new terms, whereas Louis Leakey when he came out of course talked about Mousterian and many other European industries. He tended to put a European slant on things, and then of course he went on to name things in Kenya and he tried to relate most things to the sequence that he built up what in Kenya. But I think this was the way of most of the early archaeologists. They became Prima Donnas in their own countries.

I didn't realise that Kenya so different structurally, socially than Uganda.

Oh yes, yes, Kenya of course you had the White settlers. They weren't all that numerous, about 60,000 in mid 1950s, perhaps there may have been 100,000, but there weren't a large number of Whites in Kenya. They had these large farms and it is often said that the officers went to Kenya and the sort of subalterns [non-commissioned officers] went to Rhodesia. It was a very structured society with the Whites on top, the Indians in the middle and the Blacks underneath. The White society was very structured in that there was an administrative class, people who had gone to public school, and then there was a technical officers, public works department, people who were often of lower standing. There was a lot of other racism. I was Jewish but wasn't allowed as other Jews to belong to either the Muthaiga Club or the Nairobi Club. As late as the early 1960s, here was a famous Minister of Finance when Kenya was on the way to independence, whose wife was Jewish but he wasn't allowed to belong to the Nairobi Club because his wife was Jewish. He then went off and became the Finance Minister in the new Tanganyika. So it was a difficult society.

And Uganda?

Uganda was a very free and easy society because there weren't the White settlers. There weren't the same number of Europeans in Uganda, only about 10 or 12,000. There were people, teachers, the administrators, and the merchants in the big commercial houses in Kampala, and there were the missionaries. There were more missionaries in Uganda than there were in Kenya, but it was a different sort of world. Europeans weren't allowed to own land and there were the Kingdoms of Buganda, Bungoro [Toro and Aukole]. Africans were much more prominent. There were African mayors of Kampala. You had African Presidents of the Uganda Society in the 1930s. Africans were writing articles for the Uganda Society Journal in 1930s, whereas none of that happened in Kenya.

Knowing the Africans, did that affect your archaeology?

I think so, yes. Knowing the Africans meant that one could make them partners in your research, unlike the excavations done by Louis Leakey. Louis Leakey had a very paternalistic approach to Africans. He didn't like Mission-trained Africans. Most of people he worked with were assistants who had very little education. He taught them but they were a different social group. Most of them were Kikuyu so he excavated with what he called "his boys" and that was a very different sort of excavation [to what was the norm in Britain]. When I went to Uganda, one of the first thing I did was that on excavations we had University students, so that all our excavations were done with Makerere students, both men and women. So I think we were the first people who had African women participants on excavations in the late 1950s. In Kenya, I had schoolgirls, European schoolgirls as well as European schoolboys working on my excavations in Kenya.

Do you know anything about the beginning of the British African Institute?

I know quite a lot about the British Institute. The British Institute was basically founded because of the interest of Sir Mortimer Wheeler. And in fact, his interests stemmed from several visits to the East Africa coast and the interior in the mid 1950s by a remarkable Jesuit historian and savant called Gervase Mathew from, I'm trying to remember the College [All Souls]. I can't remember which College he was at. But anyhow he was a strange and intriguing gentleman. And he came along and in that time in the mid-1950s, there was a lot of interest in African history. This was the time when Basil Davidson wrote his Old Africa Rediscovered. He had said that the view of Africa, that we had got from the old scholars, people like Seligman, were completely wrong. The old idea of Africa was that you had people like the Megalithic Kushites spreading from Ethiopia, teaching the knowledge of building in stone to the local natives, so it meant that advanced civilisation came from Egypt and the northeast and spread throughout Africa and that where you had building in stone this was due to these more advanced people, and so on. Basil Davidson and Gervase Mathew and people like that began to question this idea and said that Africans probably had a much stronger role. Black Africans weren't inferior people but they were the ones in fact who had built Zimbabwe etc. They were the ones who were involved on the East Africa coast and so people were becoming excited about the interior of East Africa, and Gervase Mathew persuaded Mortimer Wheeler to make several trips to East Africa and there were several enlightened administrators in East Africa. One of them was the Governor of Uganda, Governor Andrew Cohen of Uganda, who advanced many bodies like the East Africa Institute of Social Research and the University etc., and so there were lots of people who were supportive of the idea that the British Academy in London, with the help of grants from the British Treasury, should support a school of academic studies in East Africa. This is how the British Institute of History and Archaeology was founded in 1959. The first Director was a man called Richard Goodchild who was based in Dar-es-Salaam. He didn't stay very long. He was basically much more interested in North Africa. He had excavated in Cyrenaica. But his Deputy was a man called Neville Chittick. Neville Chittick was a Peterhouse man, and Neville stayed on in Dar-es-Salaam, and I was recruited in 1962 to be the Deputy Director of the Institute, but based in Kampala. At that time they were trying to decide where the British Institute finally should be based. They were just starting the idea of having a University of East Africa combining the old Royal College in Nairobi, a new college in Dar-es-Salaam and of course the existing Makerere University College. Negotiations were initiated with the Council of the new University of East Africa to have sort of linkage between this British Institute and the University, and eventually the place which offered land and support to the British Institute was Kenya. Kenya offered a building, [?] Lodge and so the British Institute transferred in 1964 to Nairobi, and I left and joined Makerere in 1964 and at the very beginning we had very much an educational mandate. We ran a series of schools. We had a winter school on the model of that Desmond Clark had started at Livingstone, where for a fortnight we brought African students from the three colleges to learn about archaeology. We invited different speakers, people like Glyn Isaac, James Kirkman from the coast, Louis Leakey, Bill Bishop from Uganda. We brought a whole lot of other speakers to give talks. Then we took students on different excursions. That was followed up by a field school at Kilwa for four weeks where we even had students from Zambia. The idea was to provide training. We followed this up by a further training programme in Kenya where the Field Director was John Sutton. We had an interest in promoting the training of archaeologists in East Africa although, after 1964, the Institute became much more of a research Institute with most of the researchers coming from Britain, and the concentration was on building up a library, making this a strong centre for research rather than trying to expand into the training of Africans. At that time it was felt that because there were by then nascent Departments of Archaeology in each of the three African countries, that education was no longer a principal mandate of the Institute.

[Another brief break]

We are back. We are discussing Wheeler's role in the establishment of the British Institute.

I think that Wheeler was essential because Wheeler was Sir Mortimer Wheeler. He had been a Brigadier in the British Army. He was Secretary of The British Academy. He knew all the wheeler-dealers there were at the time. When he visited East Africa, he stayed at Government House. He had the power to do practically anything and during his tenure as Secretary of the British Academy he started new schools in East Africa, Persia and several other countries. He expanded the role of the British Institute with this idea of British research overseas. He was a very, very important person. He held court rather like a sort of diva in the Athenaeum and places like that, where, when people went back from Africa or anywhere, they called on Wheeler. Wheeler also, of course, had been a Professor at the Institute of Archaeology and for a short time Director, before Gordon Childe. He was influential in the University of London and of course, he was a popular person on TV with his "Animal, Vegetable, Mineral" which was one of the most popular shows on television at the time. He also did the adventure series for BBC where he showcased Zimbabwe and other major archaeological sites through out the world. Wheeler was influential and what Wheeler wanted, he really got done.

He is always remembered as being extremely colourful.

Wheeler was a man of 70 when he came to Uganda, and of course he was invited to High Table at Makerere. They invited him to High Table and he finished High Table about 9.00 p.m. and then he decided that he wanted to go dancing. So he went to one of the, practically the most seediest of dance places, "Top Life in Mmengo", and was dancing until about one o'clock in the morning and he got up a bit late, but he still wanted to go to the famous archaeological site of Bigo, which was 80 miles away. He had to catch a plane in the afternoon. So he got me to take him to Bigo from about 10 o'clock. We drove like mad. Bigo is not the easiest place to get to. We were driving over 80 miles a hour and Wheeler kept saying "Posnansky, can't you go any faster?!" and then we got to Bigo and we saw it and we came back and then we raced back and he went on his plane to Dar-es-Salaam. But he was one of those people. He drove himself and he drove others and he had fantastic energy.

Was he was quite self-centred?

Yes, I think many great people are. Louis Leakey was self-centred.

Actually Clark had self-centredness. Could you say something about your archaeology?

At that time, my contribution I suppose was that I did excavate Royal Capital sites in Uganda and I did work on Bigo, which was the centre of a very large cattle-owning complex. And now a lot of work has been done in Uganda and quite a few lectures have been given here about places like Tusi and what used to be called the Bigo culture. One of my approaches, which was very different, was that I was using oral history alongside archaeology. Sites could be located by oral history. Sites could be explained by oral history. So, oral history provided a separate chronology. We could get dates by means of genealogies by talking to elders and chiefs and keepers of tombs. We could find names of people in the past associated with sites. We could then find the same names in other genealogies. So, we could do cross-dating by means of genealogies. And in the oral histories, we could get significant events like eclipses. We could find out when eclipses occurred by using astronomical data. So, this use of oral history was extremely important and my students went on to use that data. Again in Ghana I used oral history a lot. Many people came to train with me. People like Peter Schmidt. He worked in northern Tanzania, using our same methods, and this was very important because he used oral data to get back even 2000 years because he found he could find sites by as it were communal memory. There were myths in which places were mentioned and [scholars had previously] thought that this was just story-telling, but when he came to excavate, he found early Iron Age sites. Oral history was very important. I think this was one of my contributions. My other great contribution at the time was to start off the training of archaeology in Africa on a firm basis. There had been no University courses in archaeology other than in South Africa. The South African courses were just for White students. We started courses at Makerere from 1962. We then laid out a framework which led to creation of Departments of Archaeology or Archaeology in History Departments in

Nairobi and Dar-es-Salaam, and eventually in Addis Ababa. We advanced the teaching of archaeology quite significantly for Africans and this hadn't been done anywhere else, and it was some of our experiences which were important in West Africa. In West Africa [before I arrived] there had been only one student who had taken a post-graduate diploma at the University of Ghana. I was invited to become Chair of the Department of Archaeology in Ghana. We instantly started a BA programme, an MA programme, a Ph.D programme, and that was the first fully integrated programme of teaching in the whole of Africa, and we had students who came from other countries. Our first MA student was a Nigerian [Hudson Obayemi]. We had other MA students who came from places like Zambia, such as Frances Musonda who later took a Ph.D in Berkeley and became a very key figure in Zambian archaeology. So we were, I think, very important. People came to train with us [for short periods]. People like the McIntoshs who on our field schools. We started a series of annual field schools from 1970 at the University of Ghana. Those were very important.

Who did you succeed?

I succeeded Peter Shinnie and he succeeded A.W. Lawrence. Lawrence was the brother of Lawrence of Arabia and was his literary Executor.

Do you know about why the brother went to Ghana? He gave up the Chair for Classical Archaeology at Cambridge.

I think he was just invited. He was interested in monuments generally. And what Lawrence was particularly interested in was military fortifications. Before the First World War, he had been involved in looking at military fortifications in what was then called the Levant, Syria, Southern Turkey. In the 1950s there was a very important Head of Ancient Monuments Commission in Britain, called O'Neill, who had been contacted by the Colonial Office to do something about the forts and castles along the Gold Coast. So O'Neill said that the man to go there was Lawrence. Lawrence went on a fact-finding tour and went around the forts and castles of the Gold Coast, was fascinated by them. So, when the University College of the Gold Coast was founded in 1948, the first Principal was a man called Balme. Balme was a Classicist, probably from Oxford, and Balme went out and the people he knew were mainly Classicists. So when it was decided that archaeology should be a key ingredient of the curriculum, they taught both Ancient History and the Classics on the Gold Coast, it was decided that a good man to bring was Lawrence, who had had experience of the Coast by writing this report for the Ancient Historical Monuments Commission. So, in 1951, he was appointed Professor of Archaeology and he spent most of his time on the forts and castles and wrote two very elegant and distinguished books published by Faber & Faber on the forts and castles of the Coast which are now classics. He then also became Head of the Museum. They had an important museum at the University, a Museum of Archaeology and Ethnology which was part of the Department of Archaeology, and he was Head of that, but it was then decided for independence they needed a National Museum. So much of the collection of the University of the Gold Coast, as it was then, was taken as the nucleus of the National Museum of Ghana. For a short time, Lawrence was both the Director of that Museum and Professor of Archaeology. That was in 1957, but then they decided they needed a Ghanaian Director of the Museum and for various reasons Lawrence felt that he was cut out of the loop. He was a man linked with the Old World and he left in rather a huff in the mid 1950s. There was a vacancy and curiously enough, I was in Uganda at the time and met Peter Shinnie. Peter Shinnie was miserable. He hated Uganda where he was Director of Antiquities and I said "had he noticed that in the Times, they were advertising for a Professor of Archaeology in the new country of Ghana?", and he hadn't, and he immediately applied and got that post. So, by me telling him that, I got his post, and later on when he was leaving Ghana, he suggested that I apply for his position, which I did do. So I succeeded Shinnie on two occasions.

Was the Museum that Lawrence directed, was that the Museum that Shaw was in charge of?

In a way, yes. Thurstan Shaw went out to the Gold Coast to Achimota College. Achimota College was founded by a very remarkable Governor, Governor Guggisberg of the Gold Coast in 1922. It was far in advance of any education institution in West Africa of its time. They did many more subjects. Right at the very beginning, they had an advanced education group which then later on became Achimota University College and Thurstan was brought in in 1936 as a teacher, but also to look after a little collection and to develop a Museum at Achimota, which he did remarkably well [which ultimately became the collection of the University Museum of Archaeology].

SIDE TWO

Shaw stayed on during the War years but then later on probably for his children's education, went back to England. He also trained the first African Curator, who was Richard Nunoo, who later became the Director of the National Museum of Ghana and so this collection then became the nucleus of the Department of Archaeology when the Achimota College was then transferred to a new area which became the University of Ghana, a place called Legon, about two miles from Achimota.

When you came to Ghana, how did you compare that to Uganda for social structure against Kenya?

Oh, Ghana was very exciting to go to. Ghana was a bit similar to Uganda. Similar in some of the plants one saw. It was greener. It was, I was going to say, more African. Kenya was more European, whereas in Ghana there was much more healthy mixing between the races. There was a lot of healthy mixing of races along the Coast, so many Ghanaians had European names like Hanson, Johnson, Brown, Wolf. These were all Ghanaian names which had come from the mixing of Europeans on the Coast. English had been used as a language along the Coast from the 1800s. The first newspapers in English were in 1870s. The first Gold Coast Barristers were from the 1890s, whereas the first African Barrister in Kenya wasn't until the 1950s. That is sixty years later. So there is a much bigger middle class. It was a much more exciting society. The University of Ghana was one of the most exciting intellectual places on the continent at that time. Thomas Hogskin had developed the Institute of African Studies and had been encouraged by Nkrumah, who had been trained in the States. Nkrumah was a great African Nationalist. He promoted different conferences on Africa in Accra. This all rubbed off. It all led to an intellectual excitement in the University. The library was probably the best on the continent. Its African Library was outstanding. Another big difference of going to Ghana was that the stress there had been on the Iron Age, the later archaeology [unlike Kenya where it was on the Stone Age]. There were masses upon masses of finds of pottery, whereas the mass of the material in Kenya was still the Stone Age, so people tended to think in terms of the prehistory and people associated the prehistory with the distant past and not with the present living Africans. I think there was this greater link in West Africa between modern people and past people so that there was so much more vitality. There was art. There were no art objects like carving and brass working in East Africa, Kenya, whereas in West Africa there was, and so this made it exciting, particularly if you were interested in last millennium [developments and creative endeavours].

Could you say something about the archaeology you did in Ghana as compared to the archaeology you did in Uganda?

In Ghana, one of the things I wanted to do — I really wanted to work on the Coast and do historical archaeology, which I had started up doing as an undergraduate in Britain in the 1950s, but the Vice Chancellor, who was a Cambridge man, Alex Kwapong, who had written in the Cambridge Ancient History, a remarkable man, got a triple First at Cambridge. He said that Peter Shinnie had worked in Nile Valley, that Lawrence had worked on the Coast. He felt that the new Professor should work in the Interior and try to find out about the indigenous states of Ghana. So, I started something called the West African Trade Project, which was looking at the development of long-distance trade from the middle Niger area, big towns like Jenne and Timbuktu, going down from the Middle Niger to the area on the northern edge of forest where you had market centres like Begho developing; which were places where gold and cola nuts and hides were traded for beads, brass ware and cloth. This was an ecotone on the frontier between the Islamic world to the north and the forest non-Islamic world to the south. Along that frontier a series of states developed. I worked with my students, many of whom then later on did their Ph.Ds. We worked on the development of states from about 1300 AD to 1700 AD, working on the development of the first states. So you had the city state of Begho which I was working on, probably had a population of 10,000 to 15,000 at the time that the Portuguese came off the Gold Coast in 1470s. That was a big town because none of the towns in the New World, places like New York, would reach that figure until the 1700s. It was an important trade town.

I was thinking about your observations that the structure of the co-lonial administration affected archaeology and how it was done?

Yes I think it did affect — well — first of all, Africans in many countries were just not consulted. They were studied, but they weren't consulted in the same way. Many people had a interest in them. Many people were sensitive to their needs, but they weren't part of the research structure. There wasn't the sort of easy social interaction which leads to joint initia-tives, and so on. The colonialists kept to themselves. The wives did good work, helped their husbands, but the life of many of the White people was built around the European club in the town where they lived. Most of the Europeans went back to England every few years. Many of their children were sent to boarding school in England from about the age of six or seven, to prep school and then to public school. So there wasn't the investment of emotional energy in African countries. There wasn't the building-up of friendships which is important to get firm understanding of the past of Africa. This is something which has changed now with intermarriage of people like myself and Peter Shinnie whose wife is Ghanaian. He is now working on the site of Asantemanso which is one of the Ancestral sites of the Kings of Ashante. This has changed. My wife is Ugandan. Just this social interaction makes a very big difference.

May I back up and question you about Uganda when you said you introduced methods of oral history? Could you talk a little about those methods?

Basically oral history is the history passed down through the ages from Chief to Chief or from father to son, or in West Africa you have matri-lineal societies, so it is passed from mother to daughter, where you have stool histories. You have a very rich history of Africa stretching back often 20 generations, and particularly in the states of Africa which the Europeans found, and this was a rich source of history which wasn't taped sufficiently until the late 1950s. This is when African history comes into its own when you get Africans become involved in writing down their own history. People like [John Fage at Birmingham] Roland Oliver, the Professor of History in University of London began to encourage many Africans to come to London where they often wrote their own histories based on oral traditions.

We have about five minutes. There are two questions, one that many of the people at the Conference are talking about, the looting of antiquities, and I wondered if that had been an issue during your tenure of these different jobs in Ghana?

No, at that time there was no looting of antiquities. There were attempts to bring in antiquities ordinances in the late 1950s. The antiquities ordinance in Tanganyika was about 1959. In Uganda it was the early 60s. In Ghana it was about 1969. People were attempting to bring in ordinances, but there wasn't the commercialization of African Art. It was when African Art became trendy, particularly in the States. I am afraid our own University, with the publication of African Arts, the journal, which started in the 1960s, has helped to lead to this great interest in African Art. African Art became a commodity. It began to increase in value. Local, people, col-lectors came to Africa to try to buy it. They then got local people to try to collect it when they couldn't find it in the villages, they would often find out that archaeologists had dug up interesting pieces, and so they would get people to pillage sites. In the late 1970s and 1980s, sometimes called the 'lost decade' of Africa, when the economies of many African countries plunged so that the wages of people like Customs Officers were nothing — or even of museum personnel — their wages were meaningless. In order to get money to live, to send their children to school, to get commodities like refrigerators or radios, they looked to ways that they could get money. You could either get bribes or you could sell objects. So people began to

loot things from Museums. This process really began in the late 1960s and has gathered steam ever since, and it is really very tragic because a poor peasant can earn as much in a week's digging in a favourable site as he can get in a year of hard work. The trader who then takes that down to the Coast and sells it to a European, can also get a handsome return and the person who takes it to Paris or NY can then sell it to dealers who then get $20,000 to $200,000. So the profits are enormous. It is really like a slave trade, a trade in the integrity, the cultural history of Africa.

We have only about two minutes before Professor Posnansky has to leave. I wanted to give you the opportunity to sum up your life in one sentence.

Fascinating and interesting! I wouldn't have done anything else. I have enjoyed being in Africa. I have enjoyed being there, seeing the changes in Africa from the Colonial times to the great hopes of independence when we thought everything would move very fast, to the disillusion of the late 1970s when there were the military coups, and to the economic depres-sion of the 1980s, to the new hopes of the 1990s and though sometimes it might seem depressing at this time, a lot has been achieved. There is a lot of good education in a Africa. There are some successful Museums in Africa. There are many very good African scholars, some of whom are at this Conference. Now, we do have African women scholars who are making great contributions, who are showing that White scholars have neglected the place of women in African history, women in Africa's past. We are looking at social history rather than just the history of great states. So there has been a big change and many of these changes have been brought about by African scholarship and through the development of education of African archaeology and of African history in African universities.

Thank you, and may I add that at this Conference, Merrick Posnan-sky has been one of the most trusted and respected people. There is a great gentility and respect [shown] toward you.

Professor emeritus Thurstan Shaw

27 July 2000, recorded in Great Shelford outside Cambridge at Thurstan Shaw's home, by Pamela Jane Smith pjs1011@cam.ac.uk

Tape 1 side 1

Professor Shaw is the father of British Western African Archaeology and Professor emeritus of Archaeology at the University of Ibadan, Nigeria. Professor Shaw, I wonder when were you born?

I was born on 27 June 1914.

And what attracted you to Archaeology?

The first time I heard about Archaeology at all was; my father was an Anglican parson and Vicar of the village and he had Sir C.L. Woolley's book about Ur. He was very interested in the idea of Archaeology giving confirmation of some of the bible stories. So I learned about the evidence at Ur in the metres of silt which were taken as archaeological evidence of the Flood as described in the Old Testament. That was the first I heard about Archaeology at all. Then I was at school at Blundell's School, Tiverton, and when I was 15 or so our History teacher suggested various books we might read during the holidays. I was put on to Breasted's Ancient Times and this was an absolute revelation to me about all the ancient civilisations of the Middle East. It just gripped me. It just fascinated me! So when I had a chance to learn more, I was keen to do so. That is how it came my way. After that, I came into contact with what had just been formed, the Devon Archaeological Exploration Society. I lived several miles from Exeter and had heard that there were underground passages in Exeter. My mother had been very good at showing me around all the medieval places in Exeter. Naturally when I heard about these underground passages this was very intriguing to a 15-year-old boy. I went to the information bureau and asked about these. They told me that it was true that there were underground passages in Exeter. The man at the desk said "There's a magazine over there on the rack with an article about them." This was indeed the first issue of the Proceedings of the Devon Archaeological Exploration Society. The passages were a system of medieval water conduits which subsequently I managed to get through by means of a torch and crawling on my hands and knees. It was very fascinating! But the significant thing was that in that same issue of the Proceedings there was an article by an amateur Archaeologist named C.F. Moysey. His article was entitled 'Surface Hunting' — what would now be called 'field walking'. This described how you could walk over the surface of ploughed fields and find ancient coins, flints, implements, arrowheads and things like that. That was the second revelation to me, because as a result of reading Ancient Times and Sir C.L. Woolley, I thought that Archaeology always consisted of digging, and here was a way in which one could get some of the excitement of it and make discoveries without digging, just by keeping one's eyes open walking across ploughed fields. So the next Sunday afternoon, I was out on the nearest ploughed field to my home; here again I was lucky because I happened to be living in an area of Neolithic/Bronze Age activity. This was an area which had no natural flint. The nearest flint came from Bear Head, some 20 miles away, so that any piece of flint that you picked up was an import. In fact, practically all were Neolithic/Bronze Age flint implements. That very first afternoon, I came back with my tail high because I had found a couple of pieces. I remember putting them on the tea-table and showing my father. He confirmed that they were flint. I gradually took to spending more and more time around my home in a 5–6 mile radius and started collecting a lot of these flints implements. Then I took them to show to C.F. Moysey. He was able to tell me which were arrowheads and scrapers. It went on from there. I spent a lot of time and had a lot of boyish excitement finding these things and making a big collection of my own.

I wonder what was Moysey's training?

I don't know what his training was. I think it was entirely amateur. He had lived in Somerset and had discovered a Neolithic occupation site with a lot of flint artefacts on the surface of the ploughed fields. That was a site that was comparable to the one around my home, north of Exeter. In ad-

dition to the flint implements, there was a Bronze Age barrow field there and I was able to discover and record these barrows and send details to Crawford at the Survey. It was rather interesting many years later, when I was working in Nigeria, Lady Fox, who was the Lecturer in Archaeology at Exeter, excavated one of these Barrows. She said in her report that she didn't know where the occupation was and from my field walking as a boy many years before, I knew exactly where it was. So I wrote to her and told her this, and while on leave from Nigeria, we met at a nearby crossroads and I was able to show her.

Did all of that happen about the age of 15?

Yes, it started when I was 15 and went on until I was 22 or 23; all that field work near my home. There were one or two lads in the village who became interested. I gave talks at the school and one or two came out and went 'flinting' as it was called. In particular, one man, John Huglo, who has continued until today as a very, very good amateur Archaeologist. He has made a tremendous collection of these surface finds and has found other sites. When I had to move house, when I was 70-odd and this flint collection had travelled around with me, I wanted it to go to the Museum in Exeter. He was working on the publication of his collection and I added mine to his. He is still working in a very sophisticated way, computer-based, but he still hasn't finished. My things with his are destined for the Museum but it still hasn't happened. I'm just hoping that it is going to happen before he dies.

When did you meet Dorothy Liddell?

I joined the Devon Archaeological Exploration Society, who had lectures and visits to sites in Devon, and derived enormous interest and enjoyment from those. Then, in about 1930, they decided to mount quite a sized excavation at Hembury Fort, a prominent Iron Age fort, but contrary to expectation there was a Neolithic site of an interrupted ditch, a causeway camp underneath. They appealed for volunteers and I went along and camped there, volunteered. Those excavations were conducted by Miss Liddell who was a sister-in-law to Alexander Keiller, who had recently excavated Windmill Hill and later West Kennet Avenue, with which I also helped. So I started working as a labourer but the digging Foreman borrowed from Keiller was William Edmond Vincent Young. He taught me how to use a trowel and a very great deal. We became great friends although he was so much older. That is how I got to know Liddell and Young, who later became Curator at the Museum at Avebury and became locally known because of his initials as WEVY Young. In her book about Avebury, Isobel Smith gives a very nice and well-deserved tribute to him. I did three whole seasons at Hembury Fort.

Could you describe what they taught you?

When I started I didn't know what Neolithic meant. All of that and what had been established about the Old Stone Age I learnt. I once did some excavation there at Kent's Cavern. They taught me about different periods of British prehistory. Of course, at that moment which was very exciting was the opening up of the English Neolithic. I learnt about the Neolithic A, B and C through Dorothy Liddell. But, what I learnt from WEV Young was 'soil sense' and the actual business of excavating. This was very valuable. Miss Liddell had two or three assistants, one of whom was Mary Nichol who became Mrs Mary Leakey and another was Aileen Henderson who became Lady Fox. There was another girl who became a farmer's wife in Cornwall. She and Mary became great friends. They hit it off better than they did with Aileen Henderson but Mary and this person broke it up because Mary was so incensed that this woman and her husband had reintroduced myxomatosis on their farm to keep down the rabbits, but I think toward the end of their lives they became friends again. Looking back on the class structure of the time in that excavation, I took it all for granted at the time, but it is quite interesting. Recently there was a programme on the television about the Battle of Britain and the 'famous few' in the Royal Air Force. The myth has always been that these were all public-school men, the few who were the pilots. This programme showed the class structure in the RAF, that the officers were public-school men but there were a greater number of sergeant pilots who came from different backgrounds, and they took part equally in the Battle of Britain. That same kind of class structure ran through everything in the 1930s and it did in this excavation. Miss Liddell and her assistants stayed in a hotel and had their rooms there. For the first year, Miss Liddell, the General, took her meals in her room by herself and her staff, the majors and captains who were Mary and Aileen, had to have their meals separately and in a 'lower mess'. Her 'sergeant' was Will Young and I was just one of the other ranks at the time. I wasn't conscious of it at all, but looking back on it, I notice it was so.

That is very interesting. So Young wasn't from the middle class?

He was the village blacksmith's son. I have seen some of his father's work; he was a very skilled blacksmith doing wrought ironwork. He made wrought iron gates and so forth. When he came back from WWI, Will Young was unemployed and he was taken on by the local GP, Dr Clay, who was an amateur Archaeologist, excavating sites up on the Downs, and that was where Will Young started learning his archaeology. Then he was later taken over by Keiller when they were excavating Windmill Hill.

Could you say a bit more about Crawford?

I corresponded with O.G.S. Crawford who was at that time either a Communist or expected of being one. And the Russian Secret Police at that time was known as the OGPU. So Crawford was always known as Uncle OGPU. I had very little first-hand contact with Crawford. I met him once. I was encouraged by the Keiller lot, Keiller himself and the young Stuart Piggott and Will Young, and very much Dorothy Liddell. She was very good indeed. I was very sad when I came back to England after the War to find that she had died so young. What a good training that was! More than once when I was talking to Mary Leakey in many later years, who I consider was the better Archaeologist than Louis Leakey. She commented on the fact "what a good training we had with Dorothy Liddell and WEV Young!" There was a rivalry between the Keiller and Wheeler outfits. Alexander Keiller's was entirely private. He used the money that was made out of the marmalade business to pursue his interests. He was one of the last of the amateur millionaire Archaeologists; one of the last, and was very good at bringing the latest developments of Archaeology and the latest equipment. He was keen on motor cars. At Avebury, I remember he had a tracked vehicle as a sort of Land Rover of the day. That was quite an innovation. He was a very arrogant man. I heard all sorts of very amusing tales from Will Young about what his labourers had to say. One of them was that, down at the pub in Avebury, they were discussing him and one of the Wiltshire labourers said "Oh, I reckon he's all right on the whole." And one said "Yes, off the hole, he's a bugger." Wheeler, of course, operating out of London University, he was also an innovator. These different camps were quite rivals. I remember once when we were digging at Hembury Fort, we had an expedition to go over to Maiden Castle and criticize. We wanted to see the excavations but we went ready to criticize. For example, his exploratory trench was only one-and-a-half feet wide. We felt "How can you read the section of the trench which is only one-and-a-half feet wide!?"

What were your impressions of Wheeler?

Here is an Archaeologist digging a very expensive and extensive site. He was operating on a rather larger scale than we were at Hembury Fort and obviously had his own innovative ideas, particularly his grid pattern of trenches. He was also an excellent showman.

I wonder did he himself excavate?

Not as far as I know, any more than Dorothy Liddell did. I mean that would have broken the class structure. I think he was . . . I would not like to denigrate his skill. There were a string of young women who not only did the excavation but also warmed his bed. That story is well told. The women were excellent. I didn't know Wedlake. He was Wheeler's digging Foreman corresponding to WEV Young. He was good. I never met Tessa Wheeler.

I have always wondered about that rivalry between Keiller and Wheeler, was it theoretical as well as personal? Were you approaching Archaeology differently?

I don't think that I knew enough about Archaeology to judge. I was only 18. I didn't know enough. The Keiller method, very meticulous. That was something we picked up; that everything we picked up mattered; the exact position mattered; everything mattered; every change in soil colour might have some information to give. This was drilled into us.

I do know that later in the 1940s, Piggott and Grimes were very critical of Wheeler's methods.

One thing I know that the Keiller School disapproved of was Wheeler's habit of selling off surplus Romano-British pottery from his sites to help raise funds. They didn't feel that no more information could be gained. Keiller was speaking from money. A lot of it was personality. Both Keiller and Wheeler were men who were larger than life. Both were arrogant and ambitious. It was almost inevitable that a rivalry and antagonism would grow between them.

At this point you came up to Cambridge?

I went up to Cambridge in 1933, after three or four seasons at Hembury Fort. In those days you couldn't take Archaeology as Part One, only Part Two. So, for my first time at Cambridge, I was not doing Archaeology. But I managed, at a meeting of the Cambridge Antiquarian Society, there was a lecture being given by a man called Charles Leaf. He was another wealthy amateur who did a lot of Archaeology out in the Fens. Sometimes he would take me, he also had a passion for fast cars, I can remember the thrill of being driven at 80 miles an hour. That was quite a speed. I remember doing a bit of amateur excavation with him. He was not accepted by the Cambridge archaeological, by Burkitt. Ultimately he committed suicide, I believe.

Charles Leaf found Burnt Fen, Grahame Clark's first site in 1932. I know his family.

I went there. I didn't come across Clark until the later time when I was actually doing Archaeology and Anthropology at Cambridge.

What was your impression of Grahame Clark?

He was very exciting and very inspiring. He opened up a whole new range from the Archaeology I had hitherto encountered. His big thing at the time was the Mesolithic; another was palynology and although he was not a good lecturer, rather dry, all he was doing and what came across from his own research was very, very exciting. He was excavating and lecturing at the same time. That was such a contrast to Miles Burkitt. He was a very good lecturer and entertaining but, of course, had done no research of his own. He had an incredibly retentive memory but his work was derived from the Abbé Breuil.

I was going to ask you about the controversy between Goodwin and Burkitt in 1929?

The actual happening was before my time, but it washed over me later when I came to know Goodwin in Cape Town. I was on leave in Cape Town during the War. I think it was 1940. When I got to know Goodwin, he was very good to me and took me as far as petrol and range would allow. I used his library as well the Cape Town University Library, and it was from him that I learnt about him and Burkitt, and Burkitt's book. At that time, in 1940, Goodwin still very, very, very bitter about it because Burkitt came out to see what his pupil was doing. Caton Thompson was doing Zimbabwe. When I was there in 1940, he pointed out to me that he had given Burkitt a 2000–3000-mile conducted tour, taking him to his sites, and gave him his notes to use. Burkitt gave no acknowledgement in the book, except in a footnote, thanking him for conducting him on this tour. Goodwin would say that the book was his notes, his material. Immediately after, Goodwin and van Riet Lowe raced to produced their milestone. There was nothing really until Leakey produced his Stone Age Africa in 1936.

It is commonly understood that Mary Leakey was the superior Archaeologist.

Louis, his great gift and contribution was when he started putting Stone Age stuff on the map. His great contribution was his enthusiasm, passion and that he went out into bush and found things. His other great contribution is that he introduced Mary to it all and for years after all he realised the significance of Olduvai Gorge. The conditions have changed so in African Archaeology —

TAPE 1 side 2

Conditions have changed so in African Archaeology. People nowadays don't realise how difficult things were when Louis and then Mary first started doing Archaeology at Olduvai Gorge. The logistics were extremely difficult; the transport, the supplies were extremely difficult to arrange and they were doing it on a shoestring. They were really strapped for money; so different from today with enormous funds from the National Geographical Society and foreign expeditions and American Universities. It was a totally different world. Mind you, Louis had grown up in East Africa and he rather prided himself, being contemptuous of having efficient equipment with which to operate. The first time he took Mary to Olduvai Gorge, the backup vehicle failed and they got bogged. All they had with them to dig this vehicle out of the mud was an enamelled plate. They were there without food for a couple of days. This was about 1934/35. People forget how primitive things were. In 1934–35, Louis was a Research Fellow at St John's College and I can remember gloating over all his stone artefacts that he had in racks in his rooms in New Court in St John's. He and Mary were living together in a cottage in a village just over the Cambridge border. Sometimes I used to stay with them on weekends there. We used to practice our flint-knapping skills, using soft hammer techniques. Louis was very good at flint-knapping, not quite as good as some of the present generation. He was one of the earliest to do it. There was another Frenchman who was very good; I can't remember his name. I can remember Louis teaching me to make a flint saw by getting a flint blade and then by getting another to take nicks out of the edge.

I remember there was a controversy about them because he was still married.

Oh yes! The Cambridge establishment was very offended by him. He rather enjoyed offending people; he enjoyed offending the people he regarded as stuffy establishment. He was the first to play tennis in shorts in Cambridge, which shocked a lot of people. The only thing for a man to wear to play tennis in was long white flannels. I would never have dreamt of wearing anything else. His first wife, Freda, became disillusioned with life in the bush with Louis. She just didn't like that sort of life. She wasn't that sort. When Louis met Mary, she was very much that sort. I first met Louis at Hembury Fort soon after Mary had met Louis, introduced by Caton Thompson. Mary had brought him down to Hembury Fort to give a demonstration of flint-knapping. There he was standing on top of the rampart with this enormous block of flint which he proceeded to knap into stone tools.

May I ask you one more thing about Goodwin? I am going through all the correspondence at the Museum about him and there is no evidence that he had any feeling about that book, and also it was clear from newspaper clippings that Burkitt had said "I am going to author a book immediately when I get back to Cambridge." He had announced that to Goodwin before he left. There is nothing to corroborate the oral history. You are the only one who has ever told me about the notes being used. There is no other record of that. In his book, there are lot of amateurs being synthesised. Burkitt talks about one person's site, then another etc. They were not Goodwin's sites in that sense. I have to be very clear about the notes because that seems to be a key to Goodwin's bitterness later.

I can't give you any first-hand or documentary evidence about that. I can only tell you, and I am quite clear about this, about Goodwin's bitterness when I met him in Cape Town in 1940. I saw quite a lot of him over a period of two or three months. He was not a bitter man at all, oh no! That was the only thing he felt bitter about. He was critical of Louis also about his breakup from Freda when she was pregnant with his last child by her. He thought that Louis had behaved badly, but no! I knew Goodwin as

a very genial, friendly man. I wouldn't call him a bitter man at all, but over that book he was very bitter. He felt that Burkitt did not properly acknowledge him.

Did he feel that he should have been co-author?

I don't recall him saying that. He felt that he had been pirated. He had been generous in giving Burkitt the use of all his notes and he felt that Burkitt had mined these and used them for the book; wrote it in the fortnight after leaving on the boat to England. I did once check up on this with Peggy Burkitt and I said "Is it true?" And she said "Yes."

I think it is an important point because at the Africanist Conference recently, I heard the expression "Don't do a Burkitt on me." Don't take my research and publish it in Cambridge's name. I don't have it on tape. This showed me that there was a feeling about Cambridge and the Empire and Goodwin was from the Colonies and had come to Cambridge and been Burkitt's student but had gone back. He was originally South African. Whereas Burkitt was British; this was a sort of Colonial exploitation of research done by African nationals who may be white but then were used by the British. There is some sort of intellectual resentment.

I never caught anything like that. It was purely a personal thing between Burkitt and Goodwin.

I think that it has become symbolic.

Could be. You know that I did a note in *Antiquity*. If you are interested you should read that. I can go and check it out.

Interruption.

The Antiquity *article by Prof Shaw is 1991, volume 75: 579–80. We were just discussing Burkitt's relationship to students.*

It is funny the relations of teachers to students after they are no longer students. They have gone out and done their own work. I don't know anything about Burkitt's relationship with Goodwin other than what I have already told you, but I do remember an incident of Burkitt laughing with pleasure when Louis Leakey's Fellowship with the Society of Antiquaries was terminated; I think simply because he failed to keep up his subscription, but this seemed to be to Burkitt a pleasurable put-down to Leakey, who Burkitt I think had felt had got too big for his boots. It may have also been connected to the breakup of his marriage with Freda. My only personal experience with that sort of thing, apart from what Goodwin had to say to me in 1940, in which he clearly also thought that Louis had behaved very badly towards Freda, but I, as it were, met this from the other side. It was Mary who was my friend whom I knew from before she was married. She told me at the time when she became in love with Louis and that they were going to marry. Louis felt it necessary to write to me as the son of an Anglican Parson who might be liable to be shocked at this divorce and remarriage. I remember Louis writing to me and explaining this and what they were planning to do. I do remember that I had this letter and a vivid memory of reading this in the lavatory at home. Of course, when I was an undergraduate and Louis was a Research Fellow at John's, ostracized by most of the establishment at Cambridge. He and Mary were living in the cottage outside Cambridge, I remember going and spending weekends with them. Having been brought up in an Anglican Vicarage, I had that background, but I remember having quite a thrill when I spent weekends there, sleeping under the same roof as a couple living in sin!

I bet they appreciated your humour. I have always heard that Cambridge was very judgmental of them as people. I don't think that has changed.

Moving on from what I was saying about it is a funny business between teachers and students when students go out and do things later, I always found Burkitt very kind, very friendly, very helpful, very interested in later years, whereas Grahame Clark was the opposite. I would dutifully come and see him every time I came home on leave from West Africa and wanting to tell him, bursting to tell him what I was up to and perhaps wanting some advice and I would be allowed perhaps ten minutes for that and then three-quarters of an hour would be spent with Grahame telling me about what he was doing. I and Desmond always tried to interest him in African Archaeology and always had difficulty. We were particularly miffed when he instead shot off to Australia and immersed himself with Australia and with Australian Archaeologists. Someone said to me about Clark, "Grahame does not like colour."

He was reserved. I suspect that anything different, unusual, would have been frightening to him.

I also once had an amusing description from Burkitt of an interview he had had with Grahame's stockbroker uncle, when the uncle could see no long-term profit in a career in Archaeology and when Burkitt was trying to persuade Grahame to take a Ph.D and take up a career in Archaeology.

It must have been a hard decision. There were no jobs.

Well, and something which Burkitt said to me after I had taken my degree. He said "Do you hope to have a career; to make a living in Archaeology?" I said "Well, I would like to, very much." And he said "Well, don't think about it unless you have a private income of a thousand [pounds] a year." That was in 1936.

Burkitt did have a private income.

Oh, he did and his wife as well. She was from a famous Quaker family.

It is such a beautiful house.

The five of us who were doing Archaeology would bicycle out to our tutorials on Monday afternoons and were due there at Merton House at four o'clock. Peggy would give us the most wonderful tea; chocolate cakes and everything, and then after a half-hour of tea we would migrate to Miles' study. We would sit around and he would sit on a wooden bench in front of the blazing fire, smoking a cigarette held in a holder made of a piece of rubber tubing, and would just lecture to us. This is where his memory came so well. He had it all in his head and had no problem in bringing it all out. He would just talk with no notes and had his library all around him; from time to time he would get up and pull out a book, show us a book, an illustration. Towards the end of my time, I would go out on my own because he gave us the free run of his library. Of course he was very, very disappointed that he didn't get the Chair when Minns retired, and that he never got a Fellowship at Trinity.

Do you understand why Trinity would have not given him a Fellowship?

Oh well I think it does make sense. It is an example of publish or perish.

He had published a lot.

But these were compilations from Abbé Breuil, that was what he was good at. He did the same with Goodwin's material. That was not original research. Trinity never made him a Fellow. His father was a real scholar. Of course, when Burkitt didn't get the Chair, he devoted his energies to being a County Councillor and became Chairman of the County Education Committee.

Were you one of the people seated in the back of Grahame Clark's car when they discussed trying to get rid of Burkitt?

Yes, I was! In 1936. It was Phillips' car. Grahame Clark didn't have a car in those days. It was when we were driving out to the Fens, a couple of students in the back seat with long ears listening to this discussion of the plot to remove Burkitt because Clark regarded him as NOT in the forefront, not on the cutting edge of Archaeological research. He was right, and Grahame was on the cutting edge.

Burkitt started to teach in 1915 at Cambridge.

And, Grahame was only in his second year of lecturing when I sat at his feet. How would they get rid of Burkitt? The machinations of University politics! I don't remember. Glyn Daniel was only a Ph.D student then, so couldn't have been involved.

Who were the other students in your class?

There was Charles McBurney. He didn't pass his exams. He was very American. He was always trying to get people to talk about the Mesoamerican civilisations and I can remember one session with de Navarro in his rooms in Trinity. Charles trying to get him to talk. De Navarro was talking about the amber route in Bronze Age Europe and Charles McBurney tried to switch him to ancient Peru. Toty knew how to deflect that. There was Terence Powell, Betty Raven, the daughter of the Canon Charles Raven, the Master of Christ's, and Rainbird Clarke. Clarke, he was the best of us, and his father had been Head of Museum in Norwich. He became the Curator there as well, but went first to the Museum with Sir George Grey in Taunton. He was very useful to me because when we were revising for the Tripos, he had rooms in John's and we used to go out and sit on the grass by the river and revise together and spot the questions. We both got Firsts and he knew more than I did. In fact, Burkitt subsequently said that Rainbird knew more than I did but that I had the better brain. Then there was Terence Powell who became Professor at Liverpool; the first Professor of Prehistoric Archaeology at Liverpool. Betty Raven married. Her father was a leading ornithologist and a theologian and also was disapproved of by the establishment in Cambridge and in the Church. He was a proclaimed passivist and supported conscientious objectors. This was regarded as unpatriotic, coming up to the War. Desmond was the year after, along with Bernard Fagg who went to Nigeria. His daughter is still alive, Angela. She was working in Nigeria part of the time I was there but she married a soil scientist and spent the last 30 years bringing up a family. Bernard's widow, Catherine, and Angela, I am trying to think of her married name. Bernard left a lot of unfinished business and unpublished notes about the Nok stuff which is now being raped. All the sites are being illegally excavated and the artefacts are being sold off. It is being sold to wealthy collectors in Europe.

Catherine Fagg would have his notes?

Yes, she probably will. She is a very quiet person, a retiring person but she knows a very great deal about Bernard's work.

Well, we have gotten you up to Cambridge and almost through your degree. What was Cambridge was like? Was it quiet and rural?

Could we stop here. I am getting a bit tired.

END OF TAPE ONE

TAPE TWO recorded on 8 August 2000 at Professor Shaw's home in Great Shelford, England, by Pamela Jane Smith   pjs1011@ cam.ac.uk

Thurstan Shaw started to talk immediately about a man named Dr Willick who had been an amateur Prehistorian.

He used to live in Kent in the Canterbury area and it was at the time before you had large-scale mechanical extraction from gravel pits; still a lot of individual digging and people digging by hand, and he used to have people with a retaining fee at the site just outside of Canterbury; also at Swanscombe. These workman, who he kept in his pay, they could recognise hand axes. From time to time, he would get a parcel from Swanscombe or this other site. I was absolutely thrilled when he would get a parcel and when he spread them out on a table and showed me these Acheulean hand axes. I met him, Dr Willick, through the Devon Archaeological Exploration Society. He was very kind to me because he would give me one of these hand axes from his parcel and this was an absolute thrill! Then we went up onto Holden Hill between Exeter and Torquay and there was a Neolithic site there. We used to dig around there together. I was very critical of his digging methods. Piggott came to hear of this site and was very interested. So, he came down to Exeter one day and I remember him driving me and

Dr Willick. Piggott had his girl with him. She was absolutely, I remember her, she was absolutely stunning; all furs and jewels and that sort of thing. He had an absolutely smashing sports car. He drove us in this sports car up to the site in 1934. It was likely Keiller's car. Keiller was a great man for cars of course. That was another of Keiller's addictions; Archaeology and women were his other addictions as well as fast cars.

It was so funny that Piggott was so open about having affairs. I was surprised. It made me feel that during the late 1920s, after the war, for some people, things had really changed.

Yes, that was so in the 1920s after the war. I was not in that bit of society at all, being a Parson's son, and I had no affairs before I was married and can't rival Piggott at all.

He expressed freedom; vitality and exploration.

I was too young to experience that way at all. In 1924 I was only ten years old. When I was an undergraduate from 1933 to '36, there were very few of my contemporaries who had affairs or went with girls, and those who did, they were known as womanizers. They stood out. We went to dances and kissed them and so on, but didn't sleep with them. That was our misfortune, perhaps.

Maybe not, you were so much in love with your wife.

She came along at the later part of my time at Cambridge and we explored all that together. This discussion all arose out of my mishearing your word 'rural' for 'moral'. Was Cambridge more rural? Yes, it was. Yes, Girton was still quite a bicycle ride. I had a girlfriend out there with whom I would go and have a very decorous tea, and another one in Newnham, actually.

Did they have teas in the afternoons?

Oh yes, at Girton and Newnham and you could ask an undergraduate.

What were those tea dances that people talk about at the Dorothy Café?

The Dorothy Café was an ordinary tea-room, a Café restaurant. It was very popular with undergraduates and my brother was in a group who went almost everyday and had mid-morning coffee in the Dorothy. I never fell into that habit. I think that I was too conscientious about going to lectures, which for my first two years was a mistake, because they were a waste of time. That was when I was doing Classics. I had a very good scholar called Hackforth. He was my College Tutor in Sydney. I never once saw him smile, ever. He was humourless but a good scholar, but not a good teacher; quite boring and uninspiring. He was what you would call today my Director of Studies. Then he would suggest, at the beginning of each term, he would look through the lecture list and suggest the lectures you should go, all of which, with only two exceptions, were a complete waste of time. The exceptions were a Fellow of Trinity Hall called Angus, who I was persuaded to go along to his lectures by a fellow student from another College whom I had met through the Student Christian Movement, to which I belonged. This man, Angus, was not only an interesting lecturer but he invited one to his rooms, and there was always very good conversation there. He was a great reader and he read 365 books a year; a book a day. A lot of them he reviewed. It was he who recommended to me Geoffrey Görer's book, Africa Dances. Görer gave me this because I was already interested in Africa. Görer was a well-known writer of other books. Angus, who recommended that book, was one worthwhile Classics lecturer and the other one was Sheppard, the Provost of King's, who was not a good teacher but was a scholar of Homer. He was not merely a scholar but a fantastic enthusiast. He loved his Homer; he loved every word, every line, and knew it all. He used to lecture from an enormous lecture desk, like a pulpit, and he would take the whole lecture on one line of Homer. You would go to the next lecture and wonder if he would get onto the next line. He was so in love with it and conveyed this. He got so carried away with it that he used this enormous lecture desk as a climbing frame. As he lectured, he would climb up it and you always wondered where he was going to get to. It was an incredible performance and I remember him

declaiming from Homer; "Su ZU". He was such an enthusiast; he was a compensation for the dull lecturers.

Who recommended Archaeology?

Myself. I discovered Archaeology at the age of 15 or 16 while at school. My History teacher recommended that I read Breasted's *Ancient Times*. That was really what opened my eyes to it. I realised a bit about Archaeology because my father, as an Anglican Parson, was interested in Archaeology and the light it could throw upon the Old Testament. He had a copy of Woolley's Ur of the Chaldees. That was my first touch with Archaeology. Then I went on to Part Two. Having done Part One of Classics, people who stayed with Classics, the Part Two was either Classical History or Classical Philosophy or Classical Archaeology. Well, I can remember when my father and mother came for May week at the end of my second year, I had to decide. My father was interested as well. I knew that I wanted to read Archaeology & Anthropology, but I didn't want to say this outright to him. He said "Well, we will go to the Union and look at the Handbook and look at the various options." We went through them, pointing at the different options and pointing at them and, "No, not that, not that, what about Classical Archaeology?" I didn't think a great deal of Classical Archaeology. Having been immersed for three or four years in Prehistoric Archaeology, that seemed far more exciting. Classical in comparison seemed too easy. You had the assistance of a written language, inscriptions and what Classical Archaeologists seemed to do in their practical work was just moving sand away from stone buildings; that seemed so easy in comparison to trying to disentangle the section of a Prehistoric site. I can remember going through this exercise with my father in the Union. My mind was already made up. Anyway, we went through the motions of looking at all the various options and then didn't have any difficulty persuading my father that what I really wanted to do was Archaeology & Anthropology. That is what I did. The interesting thing is that, having made up my mind, I went to see Burkitt. I talked to him. I already planned to do some excavating during the Long Vac but thought it wise to prepare myself. So, I went to see Burkitt and asked him what I should read; how I should spend my Long Vac. I was fairly OK with French. So, he said. "Oh, well, learn German so that you can read the German literature." During that Long Vac, whenever I was going on trains or whatever, I had Hugo's German Course, trying to teach myself German. If I had been really serious about it, I would have done better to spend Long Vac in Germany but for me, in those days, the son of an impoverished country parson, travel on the continent was only for the rich and I wasn't in that class.

Was Burkitt interested in German Archaeology?

After all, the Prehistory that was taught at Cambridge at that time was largely Continental. The Continental Archaeological authors were very much a source. I could do French all right. So, he thought that it would be a good idea to make German literature accessible to me.

What was your impression of Burkitt?

Very genial, very kind and helpful man. When I was still at school, I used to read all sorts of Archaeology books. I would ask the Library in village to get them for me. It was one of the wonderful legacies that Carnegie gave to this country; the free public libraries. In my little village, there was one person who ran this in her private house. Anything that I wanted, I could get for the cost of postage, only a few pence. I could ask for it and they would get it for me from a neighbouring library; all these big expensive Archaeological books, which I certainly couldn't afford myself. It was so exciting as these books came. I can remember one of them was Keiller and Crawford's Wessex from the Air.

What about Burkitt's books; Prehistory *and* The Old Stone Age? *Were they used as textbooks?*

I think so. I don't remember him telling us to read it. One book would lead on to another.

What about the Proceedings of the Prehistoric Society *or Piggott?*

Piggott hadn't started publishing yet when I was in school. Yes, I did read the *PSEA* and I joined in the Prehistoric Society as soon as it was formed from the *PSEA* in 1935.

Tell me more about the classes and what it was like.

There were general courses in Archaeology and a general course in Anthropology. Which ever you came to specialise in, after the first few weeks, there was Driberg, who was Anthropology. There was a very good lecturer on Physical Anthropology, which I found absolutely fascinating. He even took the trouble to make beautiful little colour diagrams. There was Chadwick. We used to have to go to Papermills on Newmarket Road. I never got on with his lectures; and Toty de Navarro in Neville's Court, Trinity. He was exciting and an enthusiast, talking about his beloved Bronze Age Amber route but, of course, the most exciting of all was Grahame Clark. Burkitt was a good lecturer and teacher and we would bicycle out to Merton House in Grantchester at four o'clock on Monday afternoons and Peggy Burkitt would give us a wonderful tea. Then we would adjourn to Miles' study and sit around while he sat on a fender in front of a roaring fire, smoking a cigarette in a cigarette-holder made out of a piece of rubber tubing. He had an excellent library which he gave one the run of. When I started reading up and was pretty sure I was going to go to Africa, I started reading up stuff, everything I could find about Archaeology in Africa which, of course, there wasn't a great deal except he had quite a lot of French on Northern Africa. Louis Leakey was a Research Fellow. His book, Stone Age Africa, that came out just in time for me to choose it as one of my Tripos prizes for my First. I read Sollas, Obermaier. Both those I got from the Carnegie village Library.

Did you have lectures of Geology?

Not really. There was a certain amount of Quaternary Geology. Yes, and somebody who did sometimes lecture on Quaternary Geology, and I can remember going out with him on a practical expedition to look at a road cutting that had just been made near Barton Mills, beyond Newmarket. I remember his rubbing his hand over the gravel exposed in the cutting and saying "You can see that this is glacial." It was T.T. Paterson. He was only the Curator of the Museum for a short time. He took us out to his site at Barnham. He was sort of one of these absentee Archaeological directors. He had workman digging deep wells into these gravel deposits and would bring up all the stones and make them into piles and in these piles sometimes was a hand axe. When he was doing the Tripos, Bernard Fagg went out and helped T.T. Paterson. The publication of it was in both names.

Did you ever hear about Reid Moir or knew of and read about Eoliths?

Reid Moir I certainly knew of, and read some of his stuff, and at one point I went to Darmsden and looked around for Eoliths. The controversy whether Eoliths were natural or artefacts was still very much on and without being able to access the Geology, I wanted Eoliths to be human artefacts because they felt so nice and looked so nice. Clark was against them. Burkitt was sitting on the fence.

What was so exciting about Grahame Clark?

Clark was exciting because for one thing, the books I had read earlier had spoken about the hiatus between the Palaeolithic and Neolithic. The Mesolithic hadn't yet been invented, and Clark was involved in inventing it and all the stuff he told us about from Scandinavia. This was very new research, right at the edge. You felt you were in on discoveries being made, just as it was so exciting being in on discoveries about the English Neolithic, such as Windmill Hill and Hembury Fort.

Why do you suppose there was that explosion of interest in the Neolithic in that era?

There was the Curwens' work in Whitehawk in Sussex. I don't know. I think it was that it, the sort of final bursting into flower of the change from thinking of the Palaeolithic and Neolithic simply in terms of artefacts from the time in the French terminology, the Neolithic was simply defined by the

artefacts. This was a change over to where living sites like Windmill Hill were being excavated. It was the beginning of this shift from thinking in terms of artefacts to how those people lived. I think that's why there was this explosion. Other books which impressed me were Baldwin Brown's book, not Macalister's book, and Montelius once I got to Cambridge.

I was going to ask you about the atmosphere at Cambridge, the rowing?

It became important for me because at the age of nine, I had had measles and they said that had left me with a weak heart. I had stopped growing for a year, so I had an inch less in height and was less strong than I would have been for my age. I had to accept this all during my teenage years, but it wasn't easy to feel different and less strong. I was allowed to play rugger but in my last term, I got a concussion. They said therefore that I ought not go on playing rugger. When I went up to Sidney, I decided to play hockey because I had been told that I should never row. So when Freshers were asked to row, I said "No, I am sorry, I can't." I took up hockey. This was difficult because I was left-handed. It was not very satisfying. In the second term, when the Boat Club people came around and said "We're desperate for one or two more people to row. We want somebody particularly to fill a vacancy in the third boat, and after all you should be able to row, your brother was last year's Boat Captain." So at that time instead of saying "No" I said "I'll think about it." Thinking about it consisted of ringing up my parents and saying that I want to row. This was the last thing that they wanted to hear, but they were very wise and said "OK, go along and see the doctor and if he says you can row, you can start to row." I did that. It was a Dr Billington, and he said "Well, there is no reason I see that you shouldn't row. Start off and come see me in a week." Which I did, and after a week he said "Well, your heart has improved." I carried on. In that term, I rowed badly at number three in the third boat. I used to dig with my oar and had some difficulty in getting it out of the water. We did all right in the Lent bumping races, and they were very kind to me and said that I had been the salvation of the third boat and promoted me to the second boat. In the summer term for Mays, I was made to change sides from the bow to the stroke side and made to row in number six. I spent a lot of time tubbing and in using a fixed tub in front of a mirror. They put me at number six which is a heavyweight position. Imagine my astonishment when at the end of the May races, the Boat Captain came to me and said "Could you come to Henley?" I said "The Second Boat isn't coming to Henley, is it?" He said, "No, but Jack O'Swan who rowed number four in First Boat, he's ill and so I am inviting you to come and row in number four." It went on from there. Rowing at Henley is the cream of rowing. We rowed in the May's Plate. We got beaten in the first round but still I learnt a great deal and had very good coaching there and it was enormous fun. All that was quite important for me in my own personal development, having had to accept myself as a weakling during my school days, who had a weak heart, I now felt "I am a man at last!" That was the end of my first year; in less than six months, I went from starting rowing to rowing at Henley. Then, of course, the next year, the beginning of my second year, the Boat Captain at the time . . .

END OF side 1

Side 2

. . . he seemed to think that I had a good sense of rhythm. So, he tried me out as stroke for the First Boat. He couldn't himself because he was in a Trial Eight for the University. With the Head of the River Race in November, we did quite well with me stroking. That's very exciting, because I suppose more than any other oarsman position, you are directing and controlling what happens; more than any other place, apart from the cox who is not pulling oar. Particularly when it comes to bumping races, it's very exciting when to spurt, when to put the stroke up and when not to. Especially when you're being chased by another boat, it is the bow of that boat you are looking at because you are facing backwards. That boat is coming up and coming up, trying to get near enough to bump you. You can see it, watch it carefully and spot when they are making a spurt because, if you are going to keep away, you have to make your spurt with a sufficient gap in time for it to respond to their spurt. If you leave it until they make their spurt, it may not be soon enough. It is all very exciting.

Do you think that sort of activity trained you to be an Archaeologist?

No, but it is a character thing which comes into both.

It builds character and discipline; more clear about themselves in some way. It seems to have an important social function.

That was the other thing; the friendship and conviviality among the Boat Club members; this is so very much a team thing. This was certainly important to me. I kept a number of these friendships. I had a great friend in Sidney who lived across the staircase from me who went out to West Africa on same boat. But, you must remember that the War severed relationships and I sometimes go into the antechapel in Sidney now and see the list of names of my contemporaries killed in the War. Once I had gone to West Africa, I didn't come back to this country for six years, and sometimes it was difficult to pick up the threads, but the people I am still in touch with now are the survivors and were not from the Boat Club. In the immediate postwar years, I did go to the weddings of a couple of my Boat Club contemporaries and I saw one three or four year ago, Dickie Wheeler, who was the cox from the Varsity Boat as well as the Sidney Boat. He sat face to face to me. He was always forever infuriatingly singing 'Jingle Bells'! Another cox who was a terrible drinker; he used to have several whiskeys with his lunch and when he was sitting a few inches from my face, I had these whiskey fumes blowing over me when I was trying to row in the afternoon, six days a week, an hour-and-a-half daily. After my first year, I would spend another hour-and-a-half coaching the Second or Third Boat. I was spending about six hours a day on the river. It was terribly, terribly difficult to quit; one of the first big difficult decisions I had to make that taught me that life faces you with these sorts of decisions. Miles Burkitt came to me sometime during the Michaelmas Term in my third year, when I started to read Archaeology and Anthropology, and said "If you didn't spend so much time on the river, you might get a First". That was really difficult because I was Boat Captain then, and we weren't doing very well, and having difficulty in recruiting new members. To resign was a bit like leaving a sinking ship. This was terrible. I took two bits of advice; one my father's, who was very keen on rowing, but also keen that his son should do well. He was very understanding. The other person I went to was the Tutor of the College. It was a small College and in those days there was only one Tutor, B.D.D. Smith, who was very devoted to the College. He had been a Divinity Lecturer. He was an ordained parson. Although I didn't know it clearly at the time, he was in a difficult position because he had lost his faith. But he was a very, very good Tutor. He knew every undergraduate and their circumstances. He was very approachable. I went and talked to him. He said "Well, look, if you resign, you will not be letting the College down. The College will go on and the Boat Club will go on whether you remain Boat Captain or not. Whereas what sort of degree you get will affect you in your career the rest of your life." He put it so clearly. I was always grateful to him for that. Whereas there was a Research Fellow who had been a member of the Club. He did a tremendous amount of coaching and was very highly regarded in the Boat Club. So we saw a lot of him and he coached us a lot and he gave his time. When I resigned as Captain, he didn't say much but I knew he was fed up. When I finally got my degree the following summer, he was standing in the Porter's Lodge in Sidney, and I happen to walk in. He said "Oh, hello, Thurstan, I 'm glad you can do something properly." That was very painful at the time. My life at Cambridge had two concerns; being a hard-drinking and hard-swearing member of the Boat Club on the one hand and on the other, I was a member of the Student Christian Movement, which brought me into contact with people outside the College. I called myself a convinced Christian, and I got this idea floating around in the back of my head that I would be interested in being a Missionary in Africa. The University Boat Captain of the year or so before, called Charlie Sergal, a wonderful oar, he did go and be a Missionary in Africa. By one of these extraordinary coincidences, he became a Medical Missionary; when we moved to Shelford in 1948, he had retired to this country and he was my Doctor in Shelford. Going back to myself, when I was an undergraduate, I was aware of these two rather opposite bits of myself. I could see myself leading a double life. Members of the Boat Club, none were members of the Christian Movement. It wasn't very popular. There weren't large numbers. At the time there were two students organisations with Christian

allegiances. One was the SCM, which you might call the broad Liberal wing and then there was CICU, the Cambridge Intercollegiate Christian Union, of which Charlie Sergal was a leading member. They were the extreme, evangelical wing. After all, at the time, I suppose the percentage of students who called themselves Christians wouldn't be more than 15 or 20%. A lot of them were public-school boys who for 5 or 6 years had had to go to compulsory chapel every day and turned against that when they got their freedom. They would say "No, we have enough." Because I was a Day Boy, I had not been subjected to that but merely to my father and parents' influences, which were much gentler and less rigid.

How did you become interested in Africa?

My interest in Africa came from my father's interest in the Church Missionary Society. He was a strong upholder of the Church Missionary Society, and every summer we used to have a Church Missionary week and used to have African Pastors who would come and stay in the house. I suppose that was the first time that I had met and talked to Black men. So that was the source of the interest. I had this ambition to go to Africa, and David Livingstone had been my boyhood hero. Then, as things went on and a decision had to be made, although for a short time I was Lay Reader helping my father in his church, I thought that I might able to teach better than preach. It sort shifted sideways like that. It so happened that an uncle of mine, my mother's youngest brother, who was many years younger than she was, had a great friend called Dennis Herbert when he was at Oxford, who was the son of the Speaker of the House of Commons. He had gone to Achimota College in the Gold Coast, which was the nearest thing there was then to a University in sub-Saharan Africa. It was designed to build up into a University which, in fact, it did eventually. It wasn't missionary-run. It was government-funded but it was ecumenical, Christian-based. This seemed to me the kind of place I would like to work in. So when he was home on leave I spoke to him, and also managed to meet the Principal of this College when he was over in this country. During my second year, I asked him what subject should I read for my Part II. He said, "Doesn't matter, except History. We don't want any more Historians. Just get a good degree." That was a man called Alex Fraser who was the first Principal of Achimota, succeeded by Canon Grace. I approached Grace as well, in London sometime. He was an ex-CMS Missionary and had friends in Church Missionary Society. I had already made contact with the Church Missionary Society and been to their summer camps. I then became a body that was fought over by Achimota and the CMS. Canon Grace offered me a job and then the CMS people got a hold of him and said "Oh, but we had hoped that young Shaw would come to us. You should release him and let him come to us." I then got a very funny letter from Canon Grace more or less withdrawing the job offer, saying "Go to the CMS." My father was very upset about this and thought that it was bad faith. So I was given the job back at Achimota College. They sent me to London University Institute of Education to take the postgraduate Education Diploma, plus the Colonial Education course. I did two courses in London in one year, in 1936–37. By that time, I was engaged. My wife cleverly organised a job in London. At some point, Canon Grace wrote to me and said "I want you to take charge of the Anthropology Museum and I want you to go to the Museums Association in Newcastle." I remember saying to my fiancée at the time I had regarded it as my Christian vocation to go to Achimota, and then when I was put in charge of the Museum which included Archaeology, I remember saying "God has given me back my Archaeology." Achimota was the best of both worlds. It was an ecumenical foundation. It was teaching, not preaching, and this suited me well. When I was able to officially do Archaeology as well, this was wonderful!

You had three interests then; you had your rowing, your faith and your Archaeology.

And I also had a lovely girl!

How did you meet her?

I met her over a blackberry bush. I had an Aunt who lived in the village of St Tudy in Cornwall. Once when I was staying there, my fiancée was the daughter of the local Squire, she had been out driving with my Aunt and had had an awful motor smash. My fiancée had gone face first through the wind shield and was very badly damaged and disfigured. Well, it was a year or two after that happened that this same Aunt invited her to come out blackberrying. That is when I first met her, picking blackberries. No, no, wait a minute. That was before she had her accident, because at the time she had a gold brace going right across her top teeth. I can remember thinking "What a pretty girl; a pity she disfigured by that brace across her teeth!" I told her this years later. Then about a year after that, she had this awful motor smash which knocked all her teeth out.

Break to feed Lucy [the dog].

The motor accident and our getting engaged and so on — there was a court case to get insurance money out of the other car to pay for all the hospital fees and plastic surgery. She had to appear in court and the Barrister, who was trying to get as much money as he could, said "Well, look at her!" Then she had an awful scar down one cheek and a cut lip. "Someone who was a beautiful girl and now she is disfigured like this. She'll never get a first-class husband." When we got engaged, this was said to me. And it was alleged that I was providing her with a husband to preserve the family honour, because it was my Aunt who had caused the accident.

You were her first-class husband! Did Miles Burkitt ever tell you not to become an Archaeologist?

He never told me not to become an Archaeologist, but at the end of my Part II, he did say to me at a goodbye tea, "Do you hope to make a living out of Archaeology?" And I said "I'd very much like to have a career in Archaeology." He said "Well, don't consider it unless you have a private income of a thousand [pounds] a year." That was £1000 a year in 1936. At the time and for many years after that, I didn't have a private income of a penny a year. My College had offered me a BA Scholarship to go on and do postgraduate work but my father said that he couldn't afford it. The maximum the College could provide was £80 a year and being an Undergraduate cost £300 a year. So I was only able to get a Ph.D after the War, when they had brought in for the benefit of the people been hindered by the War, they brought in these new regulations that those who had done original research and published it could apply to be considered for a Ph.D on the basis of their published work instead of their dissertation. You had to have a viva as well. Bernard Fagg and John Fage, the Historian of Africa from Birmingham University, were my Examiners. They were very nice because they started off; we met in Bernard's house in Oxford and instead of leaving me in doubt, they said "Well, we might as tell you from the start that we are going to recommend you for a Ph.D, but we might as well go through the ritual." By that time I had already published the equivalent of three dissertations.

I wonder about when you first went to Africa?

Well, I can still see my feet very clearly on the 15th of September 1937, jumping out of a surf boat going through the water and setting my feet for the first time on the shingle of the beach, the first time I set foot on African soil. I can still see that quite clearly! I was met there by a young African member of staff from Achimota, with whom I became very friendly. Well, I can remember that particular moment, but the other early impressions of Africa have become so blended with 40-odd years mixed with other African experiences and impressions. I was very raw, although very keen and eager. I can remember that I was asked out to dinner by one of the senior members of staff that first day. Of course, in those days you had to have a tropical kit. It wasn't quite as bad as it had been earlier. We didn't have to have a Cholera belt, which was a belt which was supposed to save you from Cholera. And there was a thing called a spine pad to wear to stop getting sunstroke. It was just a long strip of heavy felt to wear inside your trousers to stop getting sunstroke. There was a firm called Long & Alder in London that one had to go to and get fixed up. They had certain special boxes like first aid boxes for various conditions and there was one I remember for dysentery and one for extreme constipation which was called the Livingstone Rouser. Of course all the newer tropical drugs which have come on the scene in recent years hadn't yet appeared. We all took quinine. You had to take it a fortnight before coming into Malaria areas. Then during the war all the supplies — the Dutch had captured the world market. It was all grown in Indonesia, and when the Japanese came

into the war and that area was lost, we couldn't get any quinine. That was when they started experimenting with other drugs, some of which turned one completely yellow. They had recently discovered an injection against Yellow Fever, which was endemic in Western Africa. While I was still in London, I was told to go along to the Wellcome School of Tropical Hygiene. So I dutifully went along at the prescribed time and was showed into a large room with an operating table in the middle and two white-coated figures standing here waiting for me. I marched up to them and started unrolling my shirt and they said "Oh no, please drop your trousers and lie on the table." I thought they were going to cut out my appendix or something. Anyway, I did as told. Then one of these characters lifted up from a nearby table something that looked like a garden syringe; a huge great glass cylinder and proceeded to fill it with liquid which looked like iodine; that sort of colour. He proceeded to come and jab it into my abdomen and press the plunger. As it went in, it felt like liquid iodine. He pressed until he couldn't get any more in. It had came up in a swelling the size of an orange. Then he walked slowly, but slowly, around to the other side of the table and proceeded to do the same thing on the other side. I had these two swellings on my tummy. Then he said "Right, come back in an hour's time for next lot." So, I dressed and at that moment I wondered if it was worth going to West Africa if it means all this. I went across to Euston Station and had a miserable cup of tea there and wondered if I should go back for the next lot or not. I hadn't quite got the guts not to. So I went back and these two characters were still there by this operating table. I went up to the operating table and started undoing my trouser belt. He said "Oh no, no, not this time. Just roll up your sleeve." It was just a tiny little injection in the arm and I felt like knocking him down. That was what was involved in a Yellow Fever injection in those days.

Did it work?

Well, I never got Yellow Fever. It didn't always work. One colleague was ill who had had this procedure, and they took various blood tests and it was something else, and they said "Did you know that you had had Yellow Fever?" and he said "No!"

END OF TAPE TWO

Professor emeritus Peter Shinnie

14 July 2000, SAfA, Peterhouse, recorded with Tony Bonner of Threshelfords, 21 Coggeshall Road, Earls Colne, Colchester CO6 2JP. tony.bonner@virgin.net. Interview conducted by Pamela Jane Smith pjs1011@cam.ac.uk.

Professor Shinnie, could you say something about your early love of archaeology, Egyptology and your education at Oxford University?

Yes, I went up to Oxford in Michaelmas term in 1934 with the intention of reading Egyptology, which had caught my imagination since I was a boy of 12 or 13. My interest then was almost entirely in the history and language and culture of ancient Egypt, but I had also begun to get an interest in field archaeology and had done some work in the south of England with the distinguished British archaeologist, Mortimer Wheeler; and I, along with many young men of my generation, in fact a whole generation of British archaeologists, was trained in field work at Mortimer Wheeler's site at Maiden Castle. But in spite of doing field work there on a British Iron Age site, my main interest was still in ancient Egypt, and that is what I went to Oxford to do. I spent my time at Oxford doing various things, partly academic, partly learning to fly with the University Air Squadron and partly playing a role in extreme left-wing student politics. As a result of that, I didn't do academically quite as well as I should have done, but ended up with a degree just before the beginning to the War.

I'm sorry, would you say something about the politics?

Let me tell you quite bluntly, I was a Communist in those days and at one time I was a full-time organiser of the Oxford University Branch of the Communist Party of Great Britain, and I have no shame in that at all. Many of us in those days saw Communism as the way to a better world, and we may have been naïve but we weren't really stupid. Many of us have gone on to have reasonable careers in one field or another and I have no regrets at all, except that it harmed me academically slightly because I put too much time into political work which perhaps would have been better spent reading Egyptian hieroglyphs, but anyway that is it. That was my choice and in the end, it has worked out quite well.

And then you graduated in 1938?

I graduated in 1938, yes, just the year before the War started, and went to work in the Ashmolean Museum as a temporary Assistant Keeper, a job that was previously occupied many, many years before by Lawrence of Arabia and also by the famous excavator of Ur, Ur of Chaldaea, Leonard Woolley. So I did that for a short time, and then the War came and because I had been a member of the University Air Squadron and a reserve Air Force Officer, I was called up. The next few years were spent being rather busy in the Royal Air Force and doing many very interesting things.

Did you work for Photographic Intelligence?

Yes, part of the time I did. I wonder how you know? I did, and that was in a way the most interesting part because it took me to North Africa, to Italy and to Greece, where I was dealing with general air intelligence, but with particular reference to interpretation of air photographs.

What exactly were you interpreting?

We were interpreting all sorts of things, enemy aircraft on their airfields, bomb damage done by our air force, a whole series of items of information which the Allied Forces required, movements of enemy troops, a whole range of things that were susceptible to being understood by photos.

Did your experience in Photographic Intelligence have any effect on your use of photographs later in archaeology?

Yes, but in a sense rather the other way around, because archaeologists had already started using air photographs to interpret archaeological features, and when the war came it was thought that archaeologists were perhaps the most suitable people to be taken into this study of photographs for intelligence purposes, and of course it did lead to a great increase in the use of air photography after the war for archaeological purposes.

Did you know O.G.S. Crawford?

I knew O.G.S. Crawford very well because slightly later in time, when I was in the Sudan, he came out or I got him out there as a visitor on two occasions, travelled with him in the Sudan and learnt very much from him.

Did you know him when you were at Oxford?

No, I didn't know. As a young undergraduate I didn't really aspire to know these great men of archaeology. When I had became a professional archaeologist myself, not so many years later, things were rather different.

I wonder if you could tell me something about the Wheeler dig. What Foreman did you work with?

Originally I was taught by Wheeler's first wife, Tessa, who taught me how to read an archaeological section when I was absolutely new and knew nothing, perhaps within my first few days, and then I also worked with Bill Wedlake, who was Wheeler's professional Foreman, a good Somerset countryman who knew the soil very, very well and had quickly acquired a very good, although uneducated, understanding of archaeology of stratification, the nature of soil and so on; and we, all of us youngsters then, learned a lot from him.

I wonder about Tessa Wheeler? I didn't know you knew her, and I think that is very important because she died so suddenly.

She died after the first season at Maiden Castle.

How important was she to that dig?

Oh, she was very important indeed, and I think that Wheeler himself had some difficult running it subsequently. She was very competent, both administratively and archaeologically. And he was a rather flamboyant character. She was the good solid one who kept things running.

I wondered about the Institute of Archaeology, because at that point they would have been considering setting up an Institute.

Yes, they were. I didn't really know anything about that. My nose was well in Oxford. I knew that there plans for an Institute of Archaeology in London. I wasn't especially interested in it because I was still set on what you might call straight-line Egyptology.

Can you say something then about after your experiences in the War? How did you get reinvolved in archaeology?

Yes, certainly. I had always intended to continue with archaeology if I could do it after the War. I had rather hoped I might go back to the job I had in the Ashmolean Museum in Oxford, but I knew I had no entitlement because it was a temporary job and, in fact, I didn't. And, my fellow student, Richard Atkinson, was the one appointed to the vacancy. He was a much more suitable appointment than I would have been because he knew a lot about British archaeology which I didn't. But I did go back to work again for a short time there in a temporary capacity, and looking for a post which would enable me to use my Egyptological training either in an academic sense in Britain or elsewhere, and because of my work done with Wheeler at Maiden Castle, I was more and more interested in field work. So I was hoping that I would somehow be able to do field work in Egypt. What then happened, by great good fortune, was the Sudan government, with antiquities in many ways similar or allied to those of Egypt, a study in which Egyptology was relevant, decided they wished to appoint an Assistant to the then Commissioner of Archaeology, Tony Arkell, and I was fortunate enough to get the job; and off I went, knowing nothing about the Sudan at all, in the summer of 1946. My only previous experience of work in the Near East had been a short season with Leonard Woolley at the site of Atshana in southeastern Turkey, just across the Turkish border.

I had been there in the early summer of 1946 for a full field season and therefore had learned something about the rather strange way in which he carried on his excavations.

Will you say something about that strange way?

I'd been trained in a very orderly and disciplined way of excavating by the Wheelers, both Tessa and Mortimer, and thought I knew it all, which of course I didn't, but also we had had a number of excavations around Oxford done by the University Archaeological Society, which were also done to the best standards of excavation, as then understood. Of course, people have much improved on that since, but we weren't bad. We were careful, conscientious, dug neat trenches, made careful drawings and excavated sites by their stratigraphy. I went to work with Leonard Woolley on this big ancient Middle Eastern site of Tel el Atshana, 'the mound of the thirsty woman' is its meaning, and was rather horrified by the wholesale way in which he excavated with about 100 workmen, spread all over the mound and under very little close direction. So I didn't think very much of the excavation techniques. I loved being in the Near East. I began to learn some Arabic and thoroughly enjoyed myself, but didn't take a very high opinion of the state of Near Eastern archaeology.

Thank you.

Well, he was a great man, with a tremendous imagination, did some marvellous work, but it wasn't the kind of standard of orderly discipline excavation that I had been taught.

Were you thinking in that era yet about pollen analysis or soil analysis?

No, I doubt if we knew anything about it at that stage. I certainly didn't, and I don't know if Woolley did. I suspect that all the new scientific techniques had developed since that time.

May we go back to the Sudan?

Yes; shortly after, I was appointed to the Sudan, went out there in late 1946, stayed in the Sudan, ultimately taking over from Arkell as the Commissioner for Archaeology in 1948, I think, and stayed on there until I was removed in the process of Sudanisation, just before the Sudan came to independence. So, I had some very happy and I hope profitable years there, did a lot of field work, organised the Sudan Antiquities Service, started its journal, then annual, KUSH, and arranged other publication series and started writing myself and publishing myself, although originally in a rather modest way. Then, I had to go because they decided they wanted the British Officials out, naturally enough, and to appoint Sudanese. But, bizarrely enough, my post was not filled by a Sudanese, because there is an interesting little note in the constitutional arrangement for Sudan Independence, which having said that all posts, the holding of which by the British might affect the future choice of the Sudanese and therefore the British should go and be replaced by Sudanese, but in such cases as there was no trained Sudanese to take over, then the new Sudan government might appoint a 'neutral' expatriate. And a 'neutral' expatriate meant somebody who was neither British nor Egyptian, since those two countries had governed the Sudan as an Anglo-Egyptian Condominium from 1899 to 1953 prior to achievement of independence. I was replaced by a rather distinguished French scholar, Jean Vercoutter, who made an extremely good job and carried on where I left off. I was, however, very disappointed in going back. I was unemployed for a time and spent a year in England looking around for jobs, found that my Sudan experience was not considered to be of much importance. Interestingly, given how much activity is going on in the Sudan today, at that time, 1955 and '56, nobody was interested in the Sudan. My experience there, if anything, was considered rather detrimental, and I was getting pretty anxious until Wheeler, who had always done his best to help me, arranged to have a post created in Uganda. Now, I am cutting very much short, of course, my Sudan activities. We could have a whole book on that, but that is just skimming over things. So I went off to Uganda to be the first and last, I think, Director of Antiquities in Uganda, because I needed a job very badly. I had a wife and two small children. There didn't seem to be anything going in

strict academic Egyptology at that time. My training had been not only in Egyptology but now considerably in the field, because I had been doing my own excavations now for several years, excavating and publishing the results. So off I went to Uganda and I didn't like it very much. The Antiquities were totally different, something I was not especially competent to deal with. I wasn't used to being right into Africa. Now I think that Africa is great, but I didn't feel strongly about it at that time and I wasn't very happy; but I knew I did my best to set up an organisation to look after the antiquities of Uganda, such as there were. Subsequently later workers, of course, have found out much more and the archaeology of Uganda under the auspices of some rather distinguished later archaeologists have been found to be of very considerable interest.

Who were some of the people who came after you?

Well, John Sutton who became Director of the British Institute in Nairobi has worked in Uganda. Merrick Posnansky who subsequently went to UCLA, came also to Uganda after I left, and a number of people have worked there and there has been a considerable amount of very interesting archaeology in Uganda subsequently, but I was not adjusted to it. I, my mind, was full of the deserts of the Sudan, the Nile Valley, Arabic culture, Egyptian antiquities and things of that sort, and Uganda didn't suit me.

How did Mortimer Wheeler help you get that job?

He put pressure onto the Colonial Office, as I fancy it was then called, to create a post.

He actually intervened and wrote them letters?

He must have done. I don't know the inner workings, but I know it was all part of a plot, perhaps we should call it that, by Wheeler to develop archaeology in East Africa to do the same for what was then called Tanganyika and for Uganda, and ultimately to get the British Institute in Nairobi (as it is now) founded, and his idea was if I could sit it out in Uganda for awhile, I would become the first Director of that Institute and I thought that that would be quite an interesting job because I slightly had my eye on the things on the Kenyan coast which, of course, I couldn't deal with from a government job in Uganda. Anyway, that didn't come about because I didn't stay in Uganda long enough. I was sitting having breakfast one morning in my house in Kampala, reading the London Times, in its great heyday as the great British newspaper, and I saw an advertisement for a Professor of Archaeology in the University of Ghana and I thought "Well, I know nothing about Ghana. It can't be more miserable than Uganda. Let's give it a try." So I applied, and I got it. So I packed up in Uganda after a year there with one smallest excavation which I proposed for Bigo where my friend and subsequent successor in Uganda, Merrick Posnansky, also excavated and I went off to be interviewed for the job in Ghana, to my surprise was appointed and went there to be Professor of Archaeology in the, rather new then, University College at that time, not yet a full University, of Ghana which had established a Department of Archaeology, the first University in Black Africa to have a Department of Archaeology. My predecessor in this Department, who founded it, was the very distinguished Cambridge Professor A.W. Lawrence, who had been Professor of Classical Archaeology in Cambridge but perhaps is better known for being the brother of the famous T.E. Lawrence. So I followed him there. I liked Ghana immediately. I wasn't sure about its archaeology. It took me some time to get really used to it, but I managed in a sense by good luck to get back to do some work in the Sudan. My first activities when I got to Ghana were to go to the nearest areas which looked like to Sudan — remember I had a fixation on camel riding, deserts, all that sort of myth that goes with Sudanic Africa. So I did two very interesting tours from my post in Ghana, and the fact that I could do them and be financed shows how liberal that University was, because there was no suggestion that I should spend my time entirely on the archaeology of Ghana. I did two very interesting trips. One of them was up to Borno in the northeastern Nigeria, in areas that were very much like the Sudan, where in a survey I investigated, rather superficially I would say, but I did investigate a number of monuments of the beginnings of the Kanuri civilisation in Borno and enjoyed that very, very much; went around Lake Chad, went boating in their marvelous papyrus boats, which they had on Lake Chad, and returned back to Ghana. The other trip was up into southern Mauritania, to the other well known Medieval site of Kumbi Saleh, often thought of as the capital of the ancient kingdom of Ghana; the modern Republic of Ghana having taken its name from a Mediaeval kingdom which didn't cover the same territory, but was at least in West Africa. So when the Gold Coast became independent, they decided to change the name and take their name from this Mediaeval state. So I went up to look at that, thinking that an excavation there in a country that looked very much like the Sudan, which was full of Arabs, people riding camels, would be attractive to Ghanaians because it was investigating what they rather mythically thought of as their ancestors, and which probably the Ghana government would support. So I was planning to do, there had been some small excavations in Kumbi Saleh, I was planning to do more there. While these plans were being developed, there was the archaeological crisis caused by the decision to build the new dam, the high dam at Aswan, and this immediately meant that there was the quest for all people with a knowledge of the archaeology of the Sudan, and a good many who hadn't, to participate in the salvage operation. So I thought, here is my opportunity to get back into the Sudan and do some archaeology in a country that really interests me, so let's see what we can do. I went to the Ghana government and I said, "Ghana is the only country in Africa equipped to participate. All sorts of European countries are going to be there in the Nile Valley, both in the part of Egypt that will be flooded and in the part of the Sudan, and nowhere else, except Ghana, because by your good fortune I happen to be here, is able to mount an expedition there." So the Ghana Government agreed. They funded a three-season excavation and off I went back to the Sudan, much to my delight, and had a very pleasant excavation there in which my friend here, Tony Bonner, joined me, and we worked at the site of Debeira West, right up in the northern part of the Sudan, which now of course is under many metres of water of the lake formed by the new high dam. So perhaps Tony would like to come at this point.

Tony Bonner:
My background is very undistinguished in comparison. I'm the end of four generations of farmers and seed growers in Essex, and quite by good chance I was at a party one day, and had always been interested in photography and archaeology and history and museums, and quite by good chance and with a gin and tonic in my hand, somebody said that "A friend of mine is taking a party to the Sudan and they are short of a photographer." And so I said, "I'll do that!" and the following day I was contacted and he said, "Are you serious?" and I said, "Yes, I'd love the chance." So, I wrote to Peter and I got a letter back from him asking about my experience, as it was pretty well nil in archaeological photography, but he accepted me. He must have been over a barrel, and he sent me a ticket to Cairo. I picked up a girl named Vanessa Wills, who was going to do the architecture, at the premises of the University of either Chicago or California near Luxor, and then went up the Nile by river boat and joined Peter at Wadi Halfa. We spent a number of months up there, and later on Peter was going to Meroë and I joined him there. Oh, you haven't mentioned that yet, have you?

Peter Shinnie:
Haven't gotten there yet.

Tony Bonner:
After that it was quite simple. My career went on. I went twice as a photographer to Kenya near Lake Borungo with Drs Ian Hodder and Françoise Hivernel. I went three times to Egypt with the Egypt Exploration Society, working at Quasr Ibrim with Prof Bill Adams and John Alexander, usually for about two months each season. Soon after I got married; my wife accepted this and seemed to think that married people did this sort of thing, went away for two-and-a-half months. After that it was quite easy to do it and I am here today.

Could both of you say something about the conditions you faced in the Sudan, the weather, the climate, the local people, how they reacted to your excavations? There must have been hardships?

Peter Shinnie:
No, I don't think there were any hardships. Sudan is a great country. I'm very much opposed to what is going on in the Sudan now politically, so I won't go there, but I love the country, very hot, bloody hot let us say, but

one can survive it all right, in the northern Sudan, very nice, dry climate, really no serious problems. When I was there, the people were delightful. I learned to speak Arabic quite well fairly quickly, as youngish people usually can do with languages, and I saw no disadvantages at all, except having to send my children back to England to school. I think that is what I would say on that angle, but let me just go on a bit after Tony came and joined me, an excellent photographer, we did our seasons there, finished it. I went back to Ghana, to my post there, and having sort of laid a few little seeds in the Sudan, as I will show in a moment, I was then invited to go to as a Visiting Professor to the University of Birmingham, where they had just set up a Centre for West African Studies, and I went there to be a West Africanist, because I was coming out of Ghana. Because I still had my eyes and mind still on the Sudan, I was writing and had written what for a time, until it was superseded by a later one, what was the standard book on the Meroitic civilisation of the Sudan, and had always thought that I would love to go back and dig at the main site of Meroë which had been the Royal residence and therefore presumably capital of this kingdom in the later centuries BC and first few centuries AD. While I was at Birmingham suddenly out of the blue came an invitation "Would I like to come to Khartoum to be the Professor of Archaeology there?"

Who was writing you?

The University; who was behind it I really don't know. I have no idea, but mind you I had been doing a little plotting there and dropping the idea that I would be interested if they wished or were planning to set up a Department of Archaeology in their University.

And who was setting up the Department of Archaeology at Birmingham?

It was the Centre of West Africa Studies at Birmingham and the first Director was a former colleague of mine in Ghana, John Fage, who had been Professor of History at the University of Ghana and then went back to England to the School of Oriental & African Studies and then became the first Director of the Birmingham Centre of West African Studies, and of course he had known me, and so he was responsible for inviting me for the six-months' stay. I got this invitation to Khartoum and I immediately accepted it and went back to Ghana and wound up and in 1967, I think, went back to Khartoum to start my life in the Sudan all over again, and then decided, oh I am sorry, I had already decided to start on the excavation of Meroë. Meroë was a big undertaking, big town site occupied from at least 800 BC to about 350 AD. Something like that. About a thousand years or more of occupation over a big area on the east bank of Nile, about 200-odd kilometres north of Khartoum, and so when I was invited back to the Sudan, I thought two things. One, it would be lovely to be back in the Sudan, and secondly how much easier it would be to excavate Meroë from a base in Khartoum rather than a base in West Africa, and surely the Sudanese would like this, and I was right on all these points. So back I went to the Sudan, had four years as Professor of Archaeology there and carried on excavating at Meroë at this time, and Tony came out for one season there and I can't remember which one.

Tony Bonner:
We were digging an industrial site at the time.

Peter Shinnie:
That was perhaps after I had gone to Canada. Yes, it was. I haven't quite got there yet. I had these few years in the University of Khartoum which were difficult because the University was short of money. I couldn't get very good premises for the Department. But generally speaking things went along all right, and we had this very exciting field work going where we had Sudanese students coming to learn and so on.

Was the student population primarily Sudanese?

Totally Sudanese. My students were all Sudanese. I had some Sudanese colleagues. So I did my time there and then I could see that politically it beginning to get rather difficult and the Sudanese were again getting fed up with foreigners doing all these things for them, particularly there seemed to be an over-supply of British, and it would be probably wise to look for a post somewhere else where I could still carry on the same work. And, at that time there was a big brain-drain from Britain across the Atlantic and, although I wasn't in Britain, I got caught up in this and Calgary University was looking for a Head of Department of Archaeology and I was again sitting reading at the Times over breakfast, I saw this advertisement, Head of Department of Archaeology, University of Calgary and I thought "Oh, Canada won't be bad. I think I would prefer that to the US." Also several America Universities were sort of hinting that there might be a position for me, but I thought that Canada might be nicer and at that time I was offered a six-month visit to USA to the State University of New York in Buffalo. So I accepted that and while I was there, I was called for an interview at Calgary. Now, that was a blessing, because I couldn't have got there from Khartoum, but of course from Buffalo it was comparatively easy. So I went up to Calgary, and rather to my surprise I was offered the job. We finished, by that time I had been having considerable marital problems. I had met my present wife and so you see there were problems and my first wife then, she had enough, and I think she was quite right. She was a very nice woman too. She packed up and went off, so with my present wife Ama, we went back to the Sudan and packed up and went to Calgary, where I have been ever since, and from where I have been able to carry on and have now finished the excavation to reasonable satisfaction at Mcroĕ, with of course more support and more possibility of having students to work with and to be able to get better funding. So, in every way the move to Calgary has been advantage.

May I ask, your wife is Ghanaian?

Yes, my wife is from Ghana. I met her in Ghana and because of that, even though I went back to the Sudan, part of my heart was left in Ghana and since I have finished at Meroë, since I decided I disapproved of the politics of the Sudan, my attention has turned to Ghana and for the last ten or more years I have been doing field work in Ghana. We have done two major projects in Ghana since about 1980, one in northern Ghana and one actually in my wife's area, Asante.

Is she Asante?

Yes, she is Asante. So there we are. That is a very brief run-down. I have now been retired since 1980, but still fortunately been able to be active and have continued excavation, did my final year in the Sudan in 1984 at Meroë and since then have been working in Ghana.

I wondered who it was who was at the University of Calgary. Was MacNeish there?

Richard MacNeish was the first Head of Department and had retired, and that is why they were advertising for another Head.

Who was there?

Dave Kelley, Jane Kelley, Richard Forbis who died a year ago who was really with MacNeish, the founder of the Department. Those were the main figures there at that time.

May I ask you about Khartoum? Were you the only Brit?

By no means. There were quite a lot of British, both professors and lecturers in the University of Khartoum at that time. When I say at that time, that means 1966 to 1970. Remember I had two periods in the Sudan. One was 1946 to 1955 and the second one was this one, 1966 to 1970.

How had things changed between those two periods?

They hadn't changed very much. Of course, the Sudan was independent. It was running itself. It had a different flag. It had a different coinage. Some things were nicer. Some things were worse. I mean this is always so and the worst aspects of Colonial society had gone. That was nice.

What were some of the worst aspects?

There weren't really any bad aspects. The British, of course, were not brutal

Colonial rulers but foreigners are always — nobody wants their country run by foreigners, however efficiently. They were efficient. Most of the British officials had a deep affection for the country and I think did the best that they could. Unlike British officials in many Colonial countries, they spent their whole career in the one country. They learnt the language properly. They got — really did identify with the Sudanese but the social side of British Colonial Society was rather laughable and stiff and strange to me with my left-wing background. I didn't care for that much. I adjusted to it. You can't fight against, kick against all the pricks. So we did this funny business of dressing-up dinner parties in a sort of bogus evening dress with black trousers and a white shirt and a black cummerbund and wearing a black tie only if ladies were present at the dinner party and silly little things like that. You didn't wear a tie at all if it were just men together, you'd wear your open-neck shirt, black trousers and your cummerbund. But if ladies were present, then you should wear a tie.

You should be more presentable?

You should be slightly more formal, yes. And the dinner parties were sort of funny. We would spend — a typical Sudan British dinner party, you would sit around on the grass. There are very nice gardens in Khartoum. The British officials, particularly the senior ones, had very nice houses, very nice gardens, plenty of servants to run them. Even my little house, and I wasn't all that senior, we had a cook, two houseboys, a nanny to look after the baby and a part-time gardener, which was quite a staff. So you could give quite a — and the cooks were very good and the servants were extremely good and you could give quite nice dinner parties but they always ran to the same pattern. Sat outside on the lawn, had drank very long whiskeys and soda in outsize glasses, perhaps two rounds, then the gentlemen would be sent off into the bushes to relieve themselves and the ladies I suppose would be taken indoors or somewhere and then we would go in to dinner and this was always the same. Started with a plate of rather good soup either made of peanuts, known as 'ful Sudani' in Arabic, or lentils, and you were served a glass of Sherry and of course the first dinner I went to, I started to sip my Sherry. Then I realised from observation, that everyone was pouring their Sherry into the soup. So the correct thing to do was to pour your glass of Sherry into your soup. It improved the soup a great deal. Then it was roast lamb and, oh, very occasionally there was a fish dish first and then roast lamb and then caramel custard as the sweet, and white South African wine, and that was the standard dinner almost every occasion that you went out to dine. Then after dinner you would go and sit out in the garden again and drink something, probably whiskey again, until the hostess decided that it was time you went and there was a nice social signal the hostess would call her senior servant and say to him "gib el moya", "bring the water", and he would come then with glasses of water for every guest and that was a signal to drink your water and go. Rather nice way of getting rid of your guests, I thought. So this was the standard British social party in those days.

That was in the 1940s?

Yes, by the time I went back, of course, to the University, the British official class, the administrators, were all gone and the only British were the academics in the University and commercial people.

And you said that at one point the Sudanese made it clear, or you were getting the idea, that you should leave?

Yes, we were getting — there was a bit of pressure but in the 1967 Israel–Arab War was one of the things that did it because it was felt that Britain and other countries too, of course, had supported the Israelis. So that didn't make us madly popular. There was this feeling, Sudan was moving a bit left under General Nimeiry. So, yes, we sensed that it was about time to be moving on. So when I got this offer to Canada, I thought it would be wise to go. I didn't have to but I was on a five-year contract. I had done four years. I wasn't at all sure that they would renew the contract or not. I thought "let's not test it. Let's take the chance to go while I can" and so —

You had quite a few Sudanese students. Were they interested in archaeology for their own heritage or what were their motives?

Mostly not, but there were some. There was a small group who were very keen and two whom I took on with me to Calgary to be graduate students there and one of them is Ali Osman who was chairing a session here yesterday. He was a student of mine at Calgary and then came on to Cambridge to do his Ph.D. But he did an MA with me in Calgary. I took the two best students to Calgary and we've had other Sudanese students. We've had five other Sudanese students in Calgary since,

So you've kept the contact?

We have kept the contact. It is sort of broken now because our funding has got more difficult and we can't pay for them anymore. That is not just Sudanese but African students. We have had Ghanaian students too.

So you kept the contact with the University of Ghana?

I've kept the contact with the University of Ghana. I've kept very close contact with Ghana since I married a Ghanaian wife and we spend, usually we spend half the year in Ghana. We built a house in Kumasi which is her town and we are on the way there now.

So Ghana did not become violent?

Tape ends. side 2

The British fled out of Ghana. I wasn't there at Independence. I didn't arrive in Ghana until just about a year after independence. So any of the tensions really had gone and what I realised about Ghana was that there were no tensions between Blacks and Whites. I think that is an old, old tradition from the days of the European traders, perhaps right back into the 17th century when there were close relations all the way along Ghana coast between the British, Danish, French, Dutch, and Portuguese merchants who intermarried frequently. There is a whole class of people who were their descendants in southern Ghana now, and there never seems to have been very much tension, and there isn't now, and I never found it. When I first went to Ghana, of course, it was a year after independence. The country was very euphoric, it has become a bit less so after its economic problems have hit it, but it hasn't affected relationships with foreigners of whatever skin colour, and so I have always felt very comfortable there. Mind you, it was only at times that I felt uncomfortable in the Sudan. Most of the time I found the Sudan — I always loved the country as such, and I found it quite socially agreeable too. Particularly after the big change from Colonialism. And, when I was back there the second time, I think it was pretty comfortable until we began to get political tension. Never found that in Ghana, even at the height of Nkrumahism. It was never really turned against any of us who were the foreign staff of the universities. Obviously Ghana was hoping to appoint its own people, and by now it almost exclusively has. There are very few foreign teachers left in the Ghana universities, but that is the time, and I suppose that the very considerable advantages, the economic advantages the foreign members of university staff had, have been quite rightly I think whittled away. There was never any tension. I have always been extremely comfortable in Ghana.

Are you primarily responsible for building up the Department at Calgary?

I don't think that I should say that. I think there were a lot of others. I did a number of things. I introduced the African side to the Department, did my best to build that up by bringing in students and by having field projects in Africa. That has been continued by my successor when I retired, Nic David, who has continued also to have students, both Canadian students and African students, and to take them out and give then experience in the field. He has worked largely in Cameroun, some extent Nigeria. So we have maintained this African link. The rest of the Department is heavily into New World archaeology, with a very strong Mexican and Latin American emphasis. The main emphasis is certainly there, and perhaps rightly. If that's what a Canadian university wants, then that is what it should have, but we have kept an African element going in the Department. I think I helped to build it a bit, but other people also played their part in that. I don't think that I have any special role except to emphasize the Africa side.

I wonder we don't have that much time.

Brief interruption in tape.

We were just briefly interrupted. Professor Shinnie will now discuss his experiences in the Sudan.

I was just going to say that during the course of the original excavation as part of the Aswan Dam salvage campaign, which was when Tony Bonner first came into my life and helped so much with his excellent photography, I also had John Alexander, who was a friend from before that time and ever since, came out for one season and worked with us there. And I think Tony has a little anecdote to tell about his association with John Alexander when they were both leaving after working on the site with me.

Tony Bonner:
Well, we were both waiting for the boat to take us to Aswan and we hadn't had a hair cut for a couple of months, and so we had a long while to wait because we had to wait for the train to come in from Khartoum, and that came in in the afternoon, if it didn't come in in the morning; and if didn't, it came in the next day. So we thought we would have a hair cut and so we went and saw 'Kitchener'. 'Kitchener' was the Barber there and as a small boy, he had held the pot while his father shaved Kitchener. The man who had cut my hair had also taken part in the shaving of Kitchener, which is a direct link as well to Kitchener! It is seems rather funny when you think of it now. Kitchener is an historical figure. Here was someone who has known Kitchener and known me. We caught the boat. It came in late in the afternoon, and we left late in the afternoon and we picked up James Myles and James Myles came from Ghana and Peter said "Will you pick up James Myles at the station?" and said "How will I know him?" and "Oh" he said "He's Black." I said "But everybody's Black here." So he said "No, he is Black." And of course — from West Africa — to the Nubian people.

So, you recognised him?

Oh, he recognised me. I was White.

Peter Shinnie:
Let me add a note to that to explain the role of James Myles. When I got funded by the Ghana government to take this expedition to the Sudan, they made one stipulation. They said, if this is to be a Ghanaian Expedition, then it must have a Ghanaian in it. That was perfectly reasonable. So we had to see who we could persuade to come with us. Our very first season, we had a Ghanaian historian, Adu Boahen, who has since become rather distinguished as he ran, unsuccessfully alas, for President at the last Presidential election but one in Ghana. He came the first season. The second season, this gentleman James Myles, who was then working in the Ghana Museum, came also and joined us, and as you have just heard from Tony, they met at the station and travelled on together. James Myles has subsequently continued to work in his own country on archaeology and on museology; and in the third season, we had James Anquandah, who was my first Ghanaian graduate student, and he came to work with us that one season and subsequently went on to succeed me, not immediately, but to follow after me as Head of Department of Archaeology at the University of Ghana, and has just recently retired.

Who came after you?

Who came immediately after me in Ghana was Merrick Posnansky, who had followed me to Uganda and then followed me to Ghana, and so he was there and he was a great success. He went on to UCLA and was followed by John Sutton, who subsequently became the Director of the British Institute in Nairobi and is now retired.

Once again a brief interruption in the tape.

Let me say that I am in the process of writing my Memories and a good deal of this and perhaps in greater detail is there. In writing them I have got as far as 1970 and I am hoping to spend the next few months sitting in my house in Kumasi with my laptop on my desk finishing it, doing the last 30 years, which is quite a big chunk of one's life.

I'd like to go back and say a little bit about Ghana when I first went there, because it has changed a great deal. It was a year after independence. I went to this University which had been founded mostly with Ghanaian money but partly with British, and certainly under British auspices, and absolutely on the model of Cambridge. The first Principal of the University whose name was Balme (Master of Jesus) was from Cambridge and he set it up on a sort of copy of the College system, with Halls of residence which were virtually independent Colleges, as at Cambridge. So each new arrival to academic positions was allocated to one of these Halls of residence. I was allocated to the one called Commonwealth Hall, and very nice it was, and in those days, all the students wore gowns. Each Hall had a different gown. Commonwealth Hall had, I think it was red or pink, something between the two. Legon Hall, the original one, had a blue gown. Another Hall had a blue with green facings, and so on. And we lived a sort of very dignified, slightly down-market copy of Cambridge life, with dinner in Hall with a High Table, all wearing our gowns in this quite hot, humid weather with students saying the Latin grace. So it was very much like an Oxford or Cambridge style university. I thought it was rather fun. Many people said "What nonsense, to run an African university like this." I didn't see anything wrong in it because I thought it gave a certain dignity to the place, and perhaps provided a decent academic atmosphere. Ghanaians, who have quite naturally and properly taken over, have rejected this and simplified and done away with the rather fancy stuff, and of course, why shouldn't they. It is absolutely their choice. I say I saw no harm in it. It was a bit of fun, but also a bit of nonsense, and wearing a gown to teach in wasn't very comfortable in that climate. They have certainly done away with that. It is not as it was, and the University then had plenty of money. I built up my Department there without any difficulties. We got more transport. We got money for books. We got money to set up a lab, to put in air-conditioning for a drawing office and things like that, which subsequently would have been quite impossible as the country ran into economic difficulties, but the country was prosperous then and everything was humming along in the dawn of independence. Everybody was highly optimistic. Much of that optimism has, alas, has disappeared, but it was fun then, even if it was nonsense, and we had very nice colleagues. The majority were British. There were Ghanaian colleagues. Many of them very able, but it was British and Ghanaian, and then gradually under the influence of the Nkrumah government with its professed socialist ideas, I was not opposed to this at all, it began to bring in a few people from Eastern Europe. We got some very nice Polish economists, who were only too pleased to get away and to get money that was interchangeable with Sterling, and most didn't go back. I thought that wasn't quite cricket. Anyway, we all had a great deal of fun there in those days, and I think we did a reasonable academic job, produced our first Ghanaian graduate and took the University to the point — when I arrived it was the so-called University College of Ghana, did not give its own degrees, it gave London University External Degrees. After a few years, it developed and became a fully independent University, giving its own degrees, and that was a natural progression and perfectly correct, and I saw this happen and I was totally in support of this move. So, I think it was well-founded. It was fun. It's gone on — if it had not been for the severe economic crisis the country had, it would be a rather distinguished University now. It struggled on. It has done very well, given the difficulties. The difficulties have been formidable.

What are some of the difficulties?

Shortage of money. It is as easy as that. No money, no equipment; it is difficult for the archaeologists to have money to get out and do field work or even to buy books for the Department Library.

Do you stay in touch?

Yes, I do stay in touch. In fact, you see Dr Kodzo Gavua who talked this afternoon; was a student of ours at Calgary, took his Ph.D with us. He was not directly my student. He was Nic David's student. We had, earlier, Ghanaian students.

What do you see as the future archaeologically there?

Difficult. Difficult to know. There are some good, promising Ghanaian archaeologists coming on. Some were trained initially by me. Others have been trained there, Merrick's students. I think it is going to go on, until there is more money, at a slightly low level. The standard of teaching is fine. It is ability to get field experience that is lacking, because the lack of money. As I say the teaching is fine, but my goodness they suffer from lack of things, books for one. So they are doing their very best; perfectly able, good people teaching there. There are considerable difficulties and the difficulties have been going on now for about twenty or more years and not getting any less.

What caused the difficulties there?

I am not an economist. I won't care to — originally it was over expenditure by Nkrumah government, but this is a very amateur view, of course, I don't think the country has recovered from that.

In comparison what is happening in the Sudan?

The Sudan is terrible now. I don't wish to go to the Sudan now. I think the War with the south is a disaster, both for the north and the south, and I very much dislike the Islamic fundamentalist government and I will not go there now.

Well, I want to thank you. That is a very exciting, good life.

I've enjoyed the things I done. I'm sorry that I didn't continue straight on in the Sudan and spend my whole working life there. That is what I would have liked to do. Fate decreed otherwise. I am not complaining at all. I have been very happy in Ghana, and we live quite a lot in Ghana. But had I had my choice, over 30 years ago, I would have stayed in Sudan, certainly because I was accustomed to it, I could speak the language well. I was absolutely comfortable there.

And that was the archaeology you wanted to do.

It was the kind of archaeology I wanted to do. I have adjusted and adapted myself, of course, and am very interested in what I am doing in Ghana now. I don't wish to downplay it at all, but my first love in archaeology is certainly the Sudan.

Professor Paul J.J. Sinclair

12 July 2000, recorded at the Museum of Archaeology & Anthropology at Cambridge University, SAfA Conference, by Pamela Jane Smith   pjs1011@cam.ac.uk

Professor Paul Sinclair of Uppsala University will now discuss aspects of his career.

Yes, I first came into contact with archaeology in 1968 in Cape Town. We'd taken over the University and the Archaeology Department was one of the few Departments in the University to continue their lecture course in the Administration Building. We had the South African police and the Army outside and there were about 400 students and teachers inside and we were creating a non-racist intellectual space in a very tight situation in the late '60s in South Africa. Following on that, most of us were excluded from our families or disowned formally with papers to the South African Police. And we felt that archaeology was interesting, and my own interests were in history and I was doing a B.Sc in Zoology and Statistics; and I thought that the archaeology had a good blend of the natural sciences and humanities and I wanted to follow it through. We saw the importance of teaching African history, and the archaeology came in as a component of that at that stage, and at Guguletu, outside Cape Town, I was working with Albert Luthuli's secretary on night-school courses for cadres of the ANC and the opposition, and we were doing adult education courses for the following 18 months; and my interest in archaeology grew and I really felt that it was a good combination of the arts and sciences. And then I was up in Namibia and Zimbabwe as well, working as a geologist, and I decided to go to Cambridge and there weren't any scholarships, in fact my grades weren't good enough, I suppose, but there weren't any scholarships for Whites from Southern Africa. So I borrowed some money at 17.5% interest and hitch-hiked to Cambridge, hitch-hiked to Nairobi and then took a student flight to Copenhagen and England, and I started in University in Cambridge in 1971. Previously Ray Inskeep and John Parkington had been very good to me, and I had participated as much as I could in the field work in South Africa, helping John in particular with his surveys of foraging community sites in the Western Cape. It was a very good basis for the interests I was later to pick up; and Ray was good on the peopling of South Africa and the whole stone-tool-using community framework in Southern Africa, which was very much owing to his inputs. Anyway, in Cambridge I met Grahame Clark whom I admired enormously just for his breadth of scholarship and his global vision. I think it was quite incredible, and his environmental orientation to archaeology, and I was lucky enough to have Charles McBurney and Eric Higgs as my teachers, and Grahame Clark used to give lectures; and David Clarke also was one of my supervisors. It was quite tough, actually. I ran out of money at the end of the two-year period and they passed the hat around the Department and got me back from a hotel in Belgium where I had been washing dishes to stay alive. They were very kind to me, especially Eric Higgs, and I got out of that and got through the exams and went down to South Africa, and it wasn't easy to get a job there. I had a chequered political background and I suppose it wasn't that easy to get on with in those days anyway, and I worked as a stoker on the tug boats in the docks in Cape Town for nine months and met a lot of the labourers who were migrated to and from the Transkei and working on the South African railways; and other Cambridge graduates seemed to take the tarmac road in a way and got good jobs. I was lucky, and I was offered a job for three months in Johannesburg by Mike Taylor, who was doing his research for his MA. So I went up and taught for the first year and at that stage, Frelimo was coming into power in Mozambique, and I went across and made contact with the colleagues in the Lourenço Marques University, later Universidad Eduardo Mondlane, and they told that there was a job coming up in Rhodesia and I should go and take it and they would get me out when they could; and I had a job offer in Mozambique and that is what I did. I went up and I was Curator of Archaeology at Great Zimbabwe, and in the war zone, and I managed to do some work in the rural areas because other archaeologists were, more senior to me, were interested in the central zone of Great Zimbabwe, and I was doing Higgsian archaeology in the rural areas, surrounding 25 kilometres, and there was quite a lot of guerilla contact and activity from the Rhodesia Army. So it was a bit uneasy doing fieldwork, but very good support from the local people, and it was there that I did my first excavations on my

own; and I was really surprised that I was asked to give a lecture in the Gokomore Secondary School near the Great Zimbabwe ruins, and 450 kids came to the lecture the same night when Papillon, the movie of the Devils Island and the Frenchman who escaped from it, was on, but they came to the archaeology instead of the film and I realised that there was a lot of interest in archaeology. And I started working more and more with school kids and we were doing our excavations and there was no money, and there were sanctions and there was no fuel, and I had a ten Rhodesia dollar excavation budget per year with support from builders, and so on; we managed to get a beautiful excavation done of an Iron furnace in the floor of a school chemistry laboratory. So the school kids saw it happening and this was very, very important for me because it wasn't just a thing of extracting information and processing it and publishing it somewhere foreign. It was information needed for ordinary people, for their own identities, and I was very lucky. I was offered a job by the Frelimo government in Mozambique and I went through and worked for them for the following five years. And essentially we were doing adult education work. Soweto militants had come in from Johannesburg. Hominid evolution was very important. The whole thing with the problems of human evolution and the place of human beings and mankind in nature, very important for people who hadn't had access to educational facilities, as the Blacks didn't have access in South Africa, very low level of primary education. High stress factors, and people really appreciated, anyway, the broader perspectives that were coming from the archaeology. We had problems too with censorship from the East Germans. We were using African examples instead of Steinheim man and Neanderthals and Cro-Magnon. So they didn't much go for the Australopithecines but ultimately we learned a lot; and what really happened was that up in Manyikeni, the Zimbabwe tradition settlement in south central Mozambique, 700 kilometres north of Maputo, there had been an excavation on-going, the British Institute supported Peter Garlake and Graeme Barker to do the work and the Mozambiqueans wanted to take a rather different approach to the extractive archaeology and publication outside. They wanted to work with people in the local community, and that is what we did. We had people coming in in groups of 25 per year, working on the sites. In the first part of the day we would talk to them about the history of Mozambique, pre-colonial, pre-Portuguese, and then they would work with us on the excavations in the afternoon; and this turned quite a sharp academic approach to archaeology to a more contributive one in terms of local consciousness-building and it is very, very important in Mozambique. In the war we had, at one stage, we had Rhodesian soldiers 22 kilometres from Mozambique and the South Africans were coming down the railway line and the Russian missile cruiser in the harbour, and it was kind of tense; and this dehumanising process from the South Africa regime and the Rhodesians was very, very intense indeed and the archaeology ordinary, straightforward, quite modern, but nothing too earth-shattering modern. Sort of Flannery approach to archaeology, really had a good role in demystifying the past and countering this dehumanising approach from Rhodesia. At that stage the censoring of archaeological displays in the Museums was on-going. You weren't allowed to put figures, especially Black figures, populating any reconstruction of the Zimbabwe, and you weren't even allowed to use carbon dates in the official exhibitions. So we tried very hard to give a balanced view. And for Lourenço Marques, which was then in a Marxist Leninist phase, actually should be congratulated for not putting any pressure on us, for not giving any particular slant to our interpretation of the past. And we built up a Department of Archaeology and we had 250 letters from ordinary school teachers and ordinary citizens in Mozambique, pleased with the line that we were taking and putting forward, through the media and newspapers and radio, the importance of archaeology for ordinary people. And that again made me stop and think a little bit. So I had this combination of a Cambridge background, where my academic teachers tried their best to put some sort of academic rigour into my approach, and then a rather different on-the-ground experience, both politically and socially, in southern Africa; and then I moved to Sweden in 1981 to do my Ph.D. It was the Thatcher time, and I was treated as a foreigner in Britain, and I had been away for longer than three years, so I had to pay foreigner's fees and I didn't have enough money from the salary I had been getting in Mozambique. And then the Swedish Government offered me a scholarship in Uppsala, and I moved there. There it was a very interesting situation. There was a really a good Department of Cultural Anthropology, quite idealist and symbolic anthropology orientated, rather different from the approach, the materialist approach, I had been used to in Mozambique. So I found this a very good development intellectually for me. It gave me a more rounded appreciation of Africa and I studied there for four years; and then I moved over to the Archaeology Department in Uppsala. I was invited by the Swedish government to set together a regional initiative for capacity building in African archaeology, and this was an issue that we discussed in 1979 with money from the Rockefeller Foundation in Nairobi, where we had actually, colleagues from different countries, had come together and put forward their ideas of what African archaeology should be. Kenyans, Sudanese, Tanzanians, Malawians, Mozambiqueans. It was fantastic, and they came forward with a series of issues that they felt were important, educational orientation, balanced approach to different periods of the past, because a lot of money had been going into the early Stone Age and we wanted some on the more recent periods. The British Institute boycotted the meeting, but they came around later on. So it wasn't, the problems with them weren't insurmountable, and anyway the Swedes then asked me to set together a group of colleagues and they wanted to link up bilateral programmes in Mozambique and Somalia. And when I started to contact with the Swedes I was accused of being a 'sell out' and I should deal only with Russia and China, at that stage, the late 1970s, but mercifully everybody followed track and the Swedes were supporting a lot of science in Mozambique and we had meetings in Stockholm with Heads of Antiquities and Museums and University personnel from eight countries in East Africa. First thing that happened, that a Tanzanian representative stood up and said "You never even asked what we wanted to do before, not once. Normally we have highly professional teams coming in with their own programmes and we have to battle to get educational facilities for colleagues from Africa." And the Swedish attitude is very different and they said "Well, what do you want? How can we help? How should we set it up?" And people in the National Science Foundation, I think it was Yellen, had been fighting to get money from the States to help and to have an African counterpart for the American research programmes. He told me that it was really difficult. So listening to the Swedes, I realised how important this opportunity was for colleagues in Africa. Anyway, to cut a long story short, we decided to focus on urbanism in Africa. We had Madagascar, Comores, Somalia, Kenya, Tanzania, Mozambique and Zimbabwe involved, and we decided to focus on the chronology, the geographical context, the morphological structure of towns and then how these developments should be interpreted from an ethnohistorical and ethnoanthropology point of view. So we set it up. We had the Madagascans saying, "We don't have any pre-colonial towns but we want to be part of this project." They didn't even know that they had pre-colonial towns. So there were a lot of problems, in fact, in all of this. I was accused of coming in the way of British interests in Eastern Africa, because we were supporting Tanzania or Zanzibar to excavate a site which the British Institute thought should be excavated by someone else. The French were keen that all contacts with Madagascar should be channelled through Paris, at least some of the French. Others, Claude Chanudet, Claude Allibert, Pierre Verin, magnificent scholars, open, supportive and absolutely fundamental to the success of the whole thing. We ended up with 19 Ph.D projects running concurrently, 19 field projects supported by the Swedish government and then implemented, each one implemented by African colleagues who could draw on technical support from the Swedish Antiquities Service or anywhere else in the world that they so chose. My problem was that I had 15 of them registered with us in Uppsala. So the day after I finished my Ph.D, I was supervisor for more than 12 Ph.D candidates. That was impossible to handle alone, and I really have to thank my colleagues, Henry Wright, Pierre Verin, colleagues from England as well. David Phillipson and others who were supporting this initiative throughout the years. I think that it has been indicative. Anyway, the perception was, and this is an interesting one, was that there wasn't really any urbanism in East Africa, not any African-based urbanism. So we had the Ras Hafun in the 1st BC and then the 1st and 2nd century AD documents and then commonly called the Black Hole afterwards in East Africa until the 9th and 10th century; and the Arabs and Islamic people coming in set up urban trading settlements. That crudely was the standard, orthodox view. Some colleagues, like David Phillipson and others, had found early farming community pottery, Robert Soper. There was some doubt then to the gap between the classical sources and the later expression of urbanism. So what we did, and not always very smoothly and I am sure that we could have done it better, but, anyway, these 19 projects, to cut a long story short, filled in that gap rather beautifully. The Tanzania results are fantastic. We

found Roman pottery, identified in the British Museum after first being identified in Uppsala, and checked in the British Museum, published in Antiquity, and the 5th century AD Roman pottery in Zanzibar, wonderful dates. We've got glass beads in the 2nd century BC to 2 AD from Dr Felix Chami in the Fufiji Delta now. We have a whole set of developments on East African coast which were just unknown. And Northern Madagascar, Princess Chantal Radimilahy, from the northern, from the Highland area, central Madagascar, she went down to the north. She excavated and she drilled 300 cores in a mosquito swamp, around the outside of a stone building, and she started to find archaeological deposits. She ended up, after 600 cores and 150 cubic metres of excavation and resistivity work as well, with the first pre-colonial urban settlement in Madagascar, two kilometres long and long ??one?? kilometre across, with a wall. And previously the French had just seen this as a stone trading fort from the Arabs; and in 1993 Pierre Verin with his black suit and Legion of Honour, stood up in front of 200 archaeologists and said, "There comes a time in the life of an archaeologist when he has to admit that he is wrong; and I was wrong when I went to do my work on this site and I found only the stone building, and I just focused on that, and Chantal Radimilahy has shown me that I am wrong. I am proud." Isn't that nice! He is such a big man. So, these labels 'Colonial', and this and that, you have to be very careful when using them against real people. Same thing with Neville Chittick, much maligned, and I really admire him; and at the same time that Neville was working, he was working underground for Amnesty in the Kenyan prisons and getting information out on the mistreatment of prisoners. So you can't just put labels on people and say this, people are conditioned by the time, just as we all are. Anywa,y now in Sweden what has happened is that in fact that we built up a little Sub-Department of African Archaeology at Uppsala, and now that the colleagues are trained and are running the projects and so on, we don't have a neo-colonial intention of maintaining long-distance control of production of archaeological knowledge in different parts of the world. So our management, we have just handed over a 9-million Swedish crown project, just a bit more than one million US dollars, to the colleagues, and they are running that now and we are extending from East and Southern Africa to West Africa. We have also been dealing with environmental change, and this is very, very important, because the success of the urban origins programme on the development of urbanism was in a cultural context; and now what is actually rather interesting is that some of these environmental issues, the forcing mechanisms, the beginning of the Little Ice Age, the land use cover changes and so on. We are now getting a better handle on them. Now, coming up to 2000, we have both the results of the different Ph.D programmes in Eastern and Southern Africa, and have a follow-through on the environmental side as well. That really has given us a bit of a more sound basis. Now it is possible, we hope, to extend this work to Nigeria and Malawi and elsewhere in Africa, and not only to have Swedes coming down to help in Africa, but basically colleagues from Eastern and Southern Africa working in West Africa. We would like to emphasise this south/south contact and what was interesting, in fact, was in the mid Nineties, Clinton's policy formulators in the United States asked me to come over, and heritage management, and they wanted to use this model in the Caribbean. So, we actually got a group of ten Caribbean countries together and this is the funding, after Newt Gingrich and so on has not been that easy for the US Department of Agriculture and Forest Service and the group is still there. So, in the background, we are rather thinking of the possibilities of doing something global and we think that the work that has been going on now in Africa, with the Eastern and Southern Africa colleagues working in West Africa supported by colleagues from external, colleagues from Sweden and elsewhere, we would like to link these programmes to Sri Lanka, and we have already done that. I have three Ph.D students working in southern Sri Lanka and there is another one at Stockholm University, these are Sri Lankans, working in the Highlands, doing environmental reconstructions. So we have a riverine system and we are linking together the different projects there with the colleagues in Africa; and further we have links in Nicaragua and Bolivia, and we would like to do things in South America. I have one student in Mexico and he is excellent, and would like them to, through the Swedish bilateral programmes of development assistance, to insure that the archaeology component is viable and that it provides a suitable framework for poverty alleviation for security programmes and so on in the countries concerned. Sustainable development, and I see the potential of archaeology for this, and we've been working also on the global change, the human dimensions of global change programme. People like Professor Fekri Hassan and others from Egypt, really very important, I think, breadth of knowledge and vigour and cultural acuteness. So, we have been working, we've been trying to work through — the international geosphere, biosphere programme, the human dimensions of global change programme as well, and I see there is some real potential of having colleagues in the Americas, all of them, linking in with colleagues in Southeast Asia and South Asia with Africa and Europe. And I have been in Laos, and we have links with the Laotian government, and would like to do something similar in Laos and then have the Sri Lanka component linking in with that. The idea is not just north/south relations but to stimulate south/south relations. We are looking at tropical urbanism, because I believe that urbanism is really important. It is an issue which is fundamental in social change facing us now. These big global change issues, and I think that this line of thinking, south/ south connections, models of trajectories of development using modern technology but deriving well-founded indigenous models of urban development and complexity formation, this is what we need. Until now we have been importing high latitude models into the tropics. I'd like to see that there is potential for building up some real insights. So from the Swedish side, we are investing in GIS computer systems, computer systems.We have good technology in our country. It is easy to apply it to archaeological problems, and then we form partnerships with colleagues in different institutions, in different countries in a Tropical area and it is an on-going fight. It is not easy at all, but ultimately one gets a feeling that it is worthwhile; and the fundamental issues as far as I can see are essentially the archaeologies of environmental change, human contributions to that, and responses to it. You got population dynamics. You have food security and you have urbanism. Those are the big issues. Of course there are other social issues, archaeological heritage management and the plundering of that, and so on. That is of course a big one, but in terms of the actual subject matter of the archaeology, another issue that is coming which is rather important in integrating, is the growth of capitalism, the modern capitalist world system, and of course there are many ways of doing that. But I would like to contribute to the thinking about these interrelationships between these major issues in global change and what archaeology can do to contribute to them. So that is essentially it. So we are still involved, and still fighting battles, in a sense, but I think the situation now is that the relevance of archaeology, that these issues are incredibly important in different countries. You know, vegetation, erosion in soils, food security long-term is really, really, fundamentally important, and archaeology has a role to play in all of this. And what I like about archaeology is that you don't have to keep to the temples, tombs and palace syndrome. You can focus on the lives of ordinary people in the past and interest ordinary people in the present about these issues, and that is not a waste of time. Thank you.

May I ask you some questions? We have about another five minutes.

OK.

Would you say a bit more about Neville Chittick, because he is deceased and no-one else offered anything about him?

Certainly. I met Neville in the late 1970s. I went up to Nairobi. I had found some pottery on a beach, which I am talking about at this conference, and I had read Neville's books on Kilwa and these were the only books I could use to compare the ceramic illustrations with what I was finding and find hits. The illustrations were beautiful and I could identify pottery and I wanted to meet the author, and so I went up and showed them, I showed Neville the pottery and he was extremely excited. I won't tell you what he said, but he was extremely excited and wanted to know where it had come from; and this was the beginning of the expansion of the Swahili trading system to South Africa and he was really helpful and we talked for hours, and his work has been extremely important in terms of his contributions in Kilwa, his contributions in other areas; and his interpretations, if they sound old-fashioned today, they are probably no more old-fashioned than my own interpretation of what's going on will be judged in 20 years' time. Everybody is coloured by the context in which they live. Neville had a very active and a good focus on the cultural remains, excellent on the imported pottery and architecture and the ceramics and essentially

those are the topics of a pioneer historical archaeologist and prehistoric archaeologist. That's what you start with, and he started. If he's wrong, we have the benefit of him showing us what he has done, and we can judge if he is wrong and do something better, but quite frankly I haven't seen too many volumes coming out that are better than the Kilwa in terms of presentation of basic material, and actually a beautiful presentation of it. If you can fault Neville, it is basically that he was very culturally oriented, and some of the osteological and ethnobotanical remains were outside his primary set of interests, but other people have filled in those later on. So I have a great respect for Neville Chittick.

We should have mentioned that he was the Director of British Institute in East Africa. Was he one of the founders?

I don't know. I suppose he might well have been. He was certainly very senor in the British establishment. He used to be called the Proconsul of East African Archaeology.

Was he, you said he had a social conscience?

Yes, he did and this, you know, Neville was quite flamboyant. He used to wear pink suits and take lots of bottles of wine on his excavations and made sure that he lived in a good way and he was a cheerful chap. This was the outside everybody saw, and round the back he was going, taking genuine risks, and finding out about conditions of prisoners in the Kenyan jail system. He was an active lawyer and defender. I've very great respect for him. He genuinely went out of his way to consider and act upon his considerations of basic human rights violations. At the same time, I don't suppose he was terribly keen when we had our regional meeting and wanted to set up other priorities than the British Institute for East African Archaeology had at that stage, in 1979. Things are not black and white, there are all sorts of nuances here. When I think of Neville Chittick, I just think of a very clever colleague and somebody to be respected and admired.

I wanted to ask you a bit, could you explain in greater detail one example of how your work is involved with poverty and how you knit an archaeological point of view with the present? One specific, more detailed example?

OK. For instance, in southeastern Madagascar we have Jean Aimi Rakotoarisoa, Head of the Museum in the University in Antananarivo. He has done his thesis in the last decade and following on from his thesis work on archaeological settlements, and as part of the human responses programme, we have had teams down there looking at the time series datasets, the settlements plotted on maps in time, and we could look at the development of the settlement system in southeastern Madagascar and my wife, Amelie Berger, has been doing ethnological studies in a one-kilometre grid over that whole area, looking at food production; and we can relate her information on animal and plant remains and present-day usage of animal and plants to the location of previous archaeological settlements. So this gives us a nice handle and very nice time depth to land use in this area today, which is fundamental if you are going to sort out long-term production systems. There has been an interesting development in this in that, you know, the fads change in the funding agencies globally. Rainforests are out and dry forests are in at the moment, and 50 kilometres away from where we are working, it is dry forest. It is spinney forest, and this is one of the 200 hot spots in the World Wildlife Fund assessment of global resources. The spinney forests are very threatened and very rare and they are in Southern Madagascar right next to this research area. We find that the spinney forests are pollinated by Lemurs. So, the zoologists are interested, the forest people are interested and where do these forests occur? They occur in sacred areas, areas which are grave fields, and so on, of the previous settlements. In other words, areas which were guarded from exploitation. So, the biodiversity people, the cultural people, the zoologists and the biologists are all linking together now in a new sort of project, focused on these spinney forests, and they need the archaeologists to give them the time framework of the use and regeneration rates of these forested areas. So that if we know that there was a cemetery, and that this area was cleared in 1600 and it takes at least 400 years or whatever in a forest to grow with trees of a particular thickness that you see today, and we, of course we have the time series data from the southeast and it is tying in rather nicely, and this is aimed at providing sustainable forestry resources for the populations living in these areas today. That is a very specific example. We have a few others. One in Sri Lanka is excellent as well. There's others coming. East Africa, Mozambique and so on. I am quite excited by this because I think there is a genuinely interesting contribution for archaeology to make. It is this business of not just being focused on the temples, tombs and palaces. You have a wide landscape approach, cognitive landscapes as well as physical ones and you don't have a differentiation between human and nature. You have, you know, landscapes are artefacts and they have been created via human activities and humans have been influenced by external forcing mechanisms. So we have a multi-scale dynamic perspective on the archaeology. And we are finding the same approach can be used in Laos or Nicaragua and this is what is kind of exciting. There are possibilities of really linking projects globally and I think that the funding agencies should look carefully at this, because there is a real need for the human dimension of the global change environmental issues. If you read Gore's book, Earth in the Balance, there is a whole chapter devoted to archaeology. It is not by mistake, and whether or not you agree with the politics that Al Gore, but the point is that the archaeology and the historical perspective and the human dimension is important in modern views of social environmental interactions. So this multi-disciplinary line is what we are building now in Sweden, linking up archaeology and the other disciplines. We have six Professors in Uppsala who have agreed to cooperate.

It is very exciting that it is applicable, highly applicable to a local community.

So in some way you have to link the global and the local and sometimes you manage and other times you don't. But there is a multi-scale of framework. For instance in Uppsala we have the Atlas of Africa Archaeology and information on all the archaeological sites on the continent. There is just no funding to do things with it, but there is a wonderful resource to really work with, and then you have continental and go right down onto the local level as well, and so you can integrate it. I just found out, kind of exciting, that the Smithsonian has similar information on the Amazon region. So why can't we compare? That is the situation that we are in now. These linkages are really exciting. They get you engaged. They make you want to get up in the morning and get down to work.

It is very exciting to hear you talk about, you have suffered a certain amount politically.

But I think that I was a sort of 'rough diamond' too so I can't just blame others for that, for what I have suffered. But yes, in a way I think that is a little bit true.

This isn't making you embittered.

No! The British actually went all the way to the Swedish Prime Minister to try to get rid of me because I was coming in the way of their interests in Zanzibar. That got me down a bit, actually, because as a Brit myself I get a bit depressed when my senior colleagues get down to that sort of game, but you know really everyone concerned is now very positively —

Why were they —?

We were supporting an African colleague to do the excavations in Zanzibar.

And that was —

That was basically seen as coming in the way of the other priorities, but we weathered those storms and I was lucky, I was working for the King. So they had to ask before they got rid of me. But the —

Was it so unusual to have an indigenous worker?

No, it wasn't unusual. I suppose the site was interesting, and I think the British Institute felt that it was important that they maintained control of that place. But you know, any of these things are part and parcel of archaeology. I think what I really like is that now that the colleagues in

East and Southern Africa have had genuine support, the xenophobia, the fear of the foreigner, has completely dissipated, and we have very good relationships. I think that is what I would like to emphasise in this context. You know you have bumpy rides and you have challenge to old structures if you do something new, that's par for the course, but really genuinely it is, what is so nice is, that colleagues that misjudged people earlier on actually acknowledge the contributions they are making now and when the Ph.Ds come up and get put forward and they are publicly defended, everybody has a chance to say what they think, and it is really nice to see that people's attitudes change and they change with good reason when the results are substantial. And fair enough. So I think that is the attitude, and I think that we must really focus, not on some of the problems of the past but really on to what can we contribute together in the future. I feel resources for archaeology globally are under threat, and we have to justify ourselves constantly. So let's do it together.

And if anybody listening to this tape would like to contact you?

I am Professor of African Archaeology in Uppsala University. That should be enough. Anything more? I think that it is very important that we work together on things, and we shouldn't be thinking in terms of nationalities, the Americans and the British, the Swedes, whatever, we really must be thinking globally and how we can link together resources, because we just don't have enough. We need to share.

Do others agree?

I think so. I get a really strong feeling of support from that. There was a whole set of circumstances around the South African apartheid issues that came up in the eighties. That was a main dividing line in African archaeology.

You are talking about the World Archaeological Congress in 1986?

Yes, and before the WAC that there was a lot of meetings in Botswana and Nigeria, before the Southampton scene. So it wasn't just Southampton that took that issue up. Colleagues in Africa has felt very deeply about that issue before the South Africa thing.

Yes, and they agreed?

Some agreed and some disagreed.

Did you think that was a positive move?

It was a move that we were all involved in, and we had no alternatives in the positions that we took at the time. It was very, very important indeed not to deny the fundamental human rights of people, and I think it is very difficult to support colleagues who did deny those or chose not to consider them. I can take Neville Chittick up as an example of somebody who actually maintained an interest in fundamental human rights all the way through his career. So I don't think that, I don't think it is so different, in a way, you know. The situation is important. I gave the Second Bassey Andah Memorial Lecture at Ibadan in Nigeria, in January this year, and all those issues came up again. The pressure on the educational system for Black South Africans is really terrifying, and it was very important indeed to combat that dehumanising process from the regimes in South Africa and in Rhodesia, as far as one could. There can be no compromise in certain circumstances.

How are the archaeologists in Nigeria?

Well, the situation in Nigeria is very run down and they have come out of a dictatorship period but I am amazed at the sense of cohesion in the Department. We are looking forward to strengthening that and helping colleagues get back out and do fieldwork. So that I think is rather positive. One has to be pretty tough-minded and make sure that checks and balances are in place, because it is a very difficult situation. I am just amased at how incredibly coherent the colleagues have managed to maintain themselves and how the teaching and structure and how encouraging the young students

A "Splendid Idiosyncracy": Prehistory at Cambridge, 1915–1950

are in Ibadan. I think there is something, that if Wenner-Gren wanted to do something good in Africa, they would give some funding in that direction. I really feel that. We need major institutions in Africa capable of granting PhDs. We mustn't just have it at European and American institutions, and Ibadan certainly has a role in that. So does Kenya. So does Dar-es-Salaam. I can name other institutions as well. But ultimately, what we need now in African archaeology is a strengthening of the teaching building capacity in Africa. I don't like these ideas of centralising things in particular institutions in Europe. We must form partnerships and and get stuck in, and really try to consolidate skills in Africa for African needs. This whole environmental development that we have had, what really struck me was what our environmental issues in Europe, i.e. issues which are almost non-social and cultural, they are environmental, in a category of their own; in Africa, when we had our meeting in Tanzania this year, I realised that those environmental issues had been made cultural issues by our colleagues, and that is not possible in institutions outside Africa. You need the local experience, you need the rapport and the linguistic skills, the cultural skills that colleagues like George Abungu and others really show. "Take them up and formulate them in simple words that ordinary people can understand". That is a poem by a Frelimo poet in the times when there was a strong humanist element in the Frelimo ideology. It changed, as things do change But there is this possibility, and this real need of trying to do something in terms of heritage management on the continent, and you can't do that at a distance. You have to have a hands-on approach, and it has got to be the people who have grown up in those areas, I think, that really take the lead. I see the role of the foreigners and outsiders in African archaeology as enormous. I really don't see that as problem, but it is, when it is only the foreigners and the colleagues from Africa are disengaged, or don't have the facilities to participate on an equal footing, that is when it just is sad and I don't think that either side benefits.

Side 2 of tape

What is interested now is, it is not just the Swedes that have taken this attitude to supportive archaeology and capacity building. There have been good American programmes and increasingly now the Norwegians, and there is a real potential now on the European level to get the European Union to further enlarge their heritage management approach. There is already one section in the fifth frame about this, and we would like to see more. What is exciting, I find, is that there can be a genuine north/south contributory movement of support, and archaeology is one component of a sort of Heritage Management initiative. I think it is the way it's going to go. But, it's going to happen in Africa. The Swiss have the same attitude as well. They also have been doing excellent work in different ways. And, I think it is easier now than it was in the seventies to talk about these programmes. Ultimately it will be the World Bank and the really big organisations. It is not just all positive, because there is also interesting internal critique of some of the UNESCO programmes. UNESCO developing from the League of Nations after the First World War and the destruction and putting together, if you want, Europe has a very building focus view of heritage, and now we find the changes that are coming, challenges from young Zimbabweans and others to a focus not just on buildings, more on landscapes and cultural, religious, spiritual landscapes as well as physical, architectural remains. It is kind of interesting now. There are some new developments coming and it is not always easy to predict which way things are going to go. So I really find that the ideas coming from the young students, that is what makes life stimulating.

End of tape

Professor emeritus Frank Willett CBE MA FRSE

13 July 2000, recorded at the SAfA Conference, Peterhouse, Cambridge, by Pamela Jane Smith   pjs1011@cam.ac.uk

Prof. Willett, you have a long history in Nigerian archaeology, is that true?

It depends on how long you consider long to be. I was at a conference once when a student came up to me and said what a long time I must have spent in Africa, which was in effect about 7 years, and I was standing next to Raymond Mauny and I turned to him and said, "How long were you in Africa, Raymond?" And he said, "Twenty-five years." So it depends on what you mean by a long time.

To go at it from the very beginning since you said you wanted to: my background is very much working class, north of England. My father was trained, was apprenticed as a spinner, went off to serve in the First World War and came back to find that his apprentice had been given his frames so, having no other qualifications, he was just a labourer. I was lucky enough to win a scholarship to go to the local secondary school, rather earlier than Merrick Posnansky went to the Church Institute in the same town (Bolton). Strange we should both turn out to Africanist archaeologists. From there, I was fortunate enough to get admitted to Oxford and did my undergraduate work in English Philology, Anglo-Saxon, Middle English and Old French. I was planning to work — went on after that to do the Diploma in Anthropology, the only qualification in archaeology apart from Classical Archaeology that you could get at Oxford in those days. It was sheer laziness that I didn't come to Cambridge, and I didn't really like the idea of coming to Cambridge to get another first degree. I thought I would rather have a postgraduate diploma. I think that was a mistake, but it worked in the end. John Sutton and I are the only two African archaeologists who ever trained in Oxford.

From there I had planned to concentrate on Anglo-Saxon Archaeology, but my first job effectively was at the Manchester University Museum. I was the Keeper of Ethnology and General Archaeology, and we didn't have a single Anglo-Saxon antiquity. It was rather difficult to specialise in the Anglo-Saxons. I also found that most of the people working in British Archaeology at that time were not awfully pleasant people. There was a lot of competition, because there weren't many posts. So I switched my interests. I did continue to do local archaeology — rescue digs. I concentrated my research interests on Pacific Ocean collections, particularly the Maori. I just was beginning to turn to that, indeed I had applied for a job in New Zealand, when the Museums Association reported that the Nigerian Museums Service wanted to have the help of a British museum official to prepare the National Museum in Lagos for opening. I asked for further information, but it happened that our lecturer in Egyptology had arranged an expedition to Egypt. This was 1956. That was the year of the Suez Crisis, when the British sent the Air Force rather as we used to send gunboats to settle their 'hash'. So with the serious diplomatic incident, there was no way the expedition could go ahead. I wrote to the Museums Association that I had had no answer to my letter, and they wrote back telling me that I had been selected. I think I was the only person expressing interest. I hadn't applied, most certainly. I had been given four months' leave to go to Egypt, so I said if I gave up a month of my leave (I had six weeks leave a year), would the University give me another month's leave? I was allowed to go for six months, 1956–57.

It was intended that I should go and help with the National Museum, but the number two in the Department was Bernard Fagg and I went to his brother, William Fagg at the BM, told him what had happened and could he give me any advice. He said, "You should go and talk to Bernard." I talked to Bernard, and he said, "If you are a field archaeologist, we really need field archaeologists much more than museum people. That museum has been all but ready for years. We desperately need archaeologists in the field." He suggested that I had a choice of digging in Benin with the Benin Historical Research Scheme, a city of which I had heard, or on behalf of the Yoruba Historical Research Scheme to go to work at Old Oyo, which turned out to be 20 miles from any road. He advised me that Old Oyo would be more interesting and something quite new, because Benin was already fairly well known.

I went and worked there initially, and then returned when we were driven out by lack of water, made my base in Ife, and there he asked me if I would put one of the stone sculptures back into the Ore Grove. When

I did this, I discovered that I had to partly bury the cement plinth that we had made for it to stand on, and this disturbed some more sculptures in the ground. I had to conduct a small excavation to remove them. That trip took six months, and then I came back, and the following spring, I got a phone call from Lagos, from Bernard, saying that important bronze-castings had turned up in Ife and could I get leave to go and investigate the site. This was Ita Yemoo. I went to investigate that site for two months. I didn't think that I could ask for more time. At the end of the first season, he had tried to press me to give up my job in Manchester, and the second time, he repeated it, and said that they really did need someone urgently. I arrived home, and my wife was expecting our third child, and I don't think she has ever forgiven me for trying to get out of her an agreement that we should go to Nigeria while she was on the brink of producing the baby. Incidentally, going home from that trip, I had picked up dengue. I was taken off the aircraft in Kano and put in hospital, and I said, "Look, I've got to get home, my wife is pregnant and the baby is due any minute now." And they said "You'll regret it if you go." And I said "I'll regret it even more if I don't go". I got home in time, and I did indeed have another attack of it in a couple of weeks, but that was nothing compared to the attack I would have sustained if I hadn't got home in time for the birth.

We did decide to go back to Nigeria. By the time we went the baby was six months old and this time the Salk Vaccine had been produced. We all had it. We were required to by the Colonial Office, but the baby couldn't have it because they weren't giving it to anybody under two. We arrived in Nigeria and got settled in and got to the local hospital and said the baby needs various vaccinations, and they didn't have them in stock and said we would have to wait for them, and they subsequently lowered the age for vaccination against polio to six months, so we asked for that as well, and they notified us that both sets of inoculations had come through. We could hear children with whooping cough around us. They gave us a choice: do you want the polio shots first or the whooping cough, and we said that we would have the whooping cough. This was a mistake, because she contracted polio at the age of 14 months, before she had had the opportunity to have the inoculation. She is still handicapped in walking. She walks with crutches or sticks, but she is very happily married and just over a year ago, she produced a baby, much to our surprise. We are delighted that she's reached this fulfillment and she's obviously very happy as well. It was a pretty horrible experience for a first visit to Africa for my wife and the rest of the children. The other problem was that there was no school that they could go to, so my wife had to teach them. When she was home a year or two later, a local journalist heard about what had been going on, interviewed her and produced a headline report in the local paper, "Maths before Breakfast". Our son had complained, "We do our maths before breakfast."

Then the following tour, the child with polio stayed in hospital in Britain, my wife stayed with her and I had to go back to Nigeria to continue working. Then my wife came out for three weeks to join me and we spent a little time on the beach in Lagos — I took a bit of local leave. I discovered that the tires on my car, the two tires at the front, were rather bald, and went off to get new tires, and fortunately the Agricultural Officer in Ife had been pressuring us to leave the children behind when we went shopping in Ibadan because it was hot and sticky for them, so on this occasion we did; and it was very fortunate that we did, because on the way back, it was just the beginning of the rainy season and as we approached a bend in the road, I remarked to my wife, it had just started raining, how strange, that there was this dead sharp line across the road, and black and shiny behind as if it were fresh water, but it wasn't fresh rain water, it was oil. A gang had been oiling the roads quite deliberately with old engine oil to cause accidents, and I was the first victim they collected. My car spun around, ended up in the direction I had come from, and the wings (fenders in the US, I think) got crushed. I got out to ease them off and my wife had to get into the back seat to keep dry, because the tools were underneath the front seat of the car — it was a Peugeot 403. I eased the wings off the wheels and pulled the car well off the road. A lorry coming in the other direction spun around and also ended facing back towards Ife, where he had come from. A bus came around the corner. The driver had been smoking pot, as he told the police, saw the lorry facing him, thought it was moving toward him fast — actually it was stationary — drove deliberately into the back of my car in order to save himself. He knocked me over with the impact and ran over my leg, my right leg — fortunately my other knee was up in the air, so I had a rather bad fracture of the leg. A bit of the middle of my shin is still buried already in Nigeria.

We had really rather a bad start those first two years. I served a further five years that was from the first two years, I was on contract with the Nigerian government from '58 to '63. Of course when I came back from Nigeria, no-one wanted to employ me. I had a year as a schoolmaster daily paid, substitute teacher in American terms. Then I was lucky enough to get a Research Fellowship at Oxford for two years, which allowed me to write my book about Ife, which came out in 1967. One of the things I had done while I was in Nigeria was to take Gwendolyn Carter, who was Professor of Political Science at Smith College, Mass., around the Ife Museum, and that was 1959 when William Fagg was out for six months, and we were writing a paper together on ancient Ife that we hadn't published. We were working on it then. We were bashing off ideas against each other, and she enjoyed this as an academic, and knew enough about the background to be entertained, and it stuck in her memory. She was appointed to be Director of the Program of African Studies at Northwestern, and decided that it needed to be expanded on the Arts side, and wrote to me and asked if I would be interested to visit. So I went to visit in my second year at Nuffield, and they offered me a full Professorship. I stayed there, thinking that it would be temporary. It turned out to be ten years. And I was putting in for jobs back in Britain, but nobody was interested. After I had been there ten years, 1976, I got the Directorship of the Hunterian Museum and Art Gallery at the University of Glasgow. I retired from that in 1990. I now have Emeritus status and am an Honorary Senior Research Fellow there, which means I get my xeroxing done and a certain amount of photographic printing, and so on.

It is good that you spoke about the difficulties of being in Nigeria because many people told me from the 1930s that it was considered a 'grave' for Europeans.

They used to say "The Bight of Benin, the Bight of Benin, where were few come out though many go in." That was before they had antimalarial treatments or preventive drugs, but the roads were extremely dangerous, extremely dangerous.

And the gang, was there a certain amount of lawlessness?

There was a great deal of lawlessness. Wole Soyinka wrote a play called the 'The Road' a year or two later. He said he hadn't heard about the particular gang that I fell victim to, but somebody else at the University of Ife fell victim to them as well shortly after. The play is about a gang that removes the road signs at bends and narrow bridges so vehicles would shoot off the road, and then they stripped the bodies of their clothing and the vehicle of its parts. I didn't mention in my accident, there was somebody who had stopped to look at me to see what I was doing, and got hit by the bus and was killed. I think that is why they didn't strip my car down once we had to leave it.

How did that affect your archaeology?

That particular incident meant that I lost nearly a year's work. At the time it happened — again this is a strange story — I was working on a site on what is now a Catholic Mission and we had come to what I was convinced was going to be a grave, an area covered with offering pots, some with cowrie shells and others that had presumably had palm wine or meat. I knew I was going to Ibadan, so I left my foreman in charge and said "Be very careful, I'm sure you're going to come across a skeleton." They did, and they broke it through its right leg in the middle of the shin, within a few inches of where my own leg was broken the same day. Eventually a group of my labourers came to see me in hospital in Ibadan, and I could see who had made the fatal blow that had broken the bones. He was most embarrassed about it and felt totally guilty about it.

Was there a belief that they had caused the accident?

They were convinced that they had caused the accident. Oh yes. Not from the fact that they had disturbed the burial, but from the fact that they had broken the leg, which was what caused my break.

Could you say something about your experiences working with the indigenous people?

A lot of my time was spent doing rescue digs. This site had turned up with the bronzes at Ita Yemoo, and this first season there I had recovered a site with a number of sculptures in. There were four heads from figures, so there must have been four figures at least, but eventually we discovered that there were seven left feet. There must have been seven figures originally, but the site had been disturbed when they were digging for building. That site we decided to acquire. It was quite a big area. It took literally years to complete the negotiations and arrange to do the excavations. I lost a lot of time in simply administrative work, rather than the job I had gone out to do. In the meantime, I was doing quite a lot of rescue digs. People would turn things up so we would go and investigate and do a small excavation. Siemens undertook to lay telephone cables buried throughout the town. So along all the main roads they were digging continuous trenches. We had to keep an eye on these, and they cut through a number of potsherd pavements for which Ife is famous, and so we cleared a lot of these out and had to do a number of rescues; and on several occasions they came across burials and my labourers at that stage were very concerned about disturbing human bones and were much more concerned about their health, not any spiritual effect but their physical health, so I always had a bottle of Dettol antiseptic/disinfectant in the tool box so they could swab their hands before and after having anything to do with the skeleton; and eventually it ran out and nobody asked for it any more, and they got used to handling skeletons. Only last week I heard that in fact it was possible for diseases to continue in buried bones long after the excavation, and quite a lot of archaeologists have now been reported to have mysterious illnesses which seem to be attributable to the skeletons they have excavated.

So, it wasn't a spiritual, a cultural thing with disturbing . . .

No, it was a medical problem essentially.

Did the labourers feel it was OK what you were doing or did they consider archaeology a foreign activity?

They didn't regard it as particularly foreign. They were Northerners, they were not local people, which may have been a help. They were nearly all Muslims from the north. Some were pagans from the north. They weren't directly related to the people, so there was no sense that these were their ancestors that they were interfering with, so there was no problem that way. The Hausa speakers had a reputation of being harder-working than the local Yoruba people, but in fact it is not that they were harder-working, but as employees they worked harder. The Yoruba worked very hard on their farms and I'm not sure that I could generalise about the Yoruba, there are so many of them. But in Ife, certainly I was later able to recruit one or two Ife people who had a bit of education to do more responsible jobs, and they were very satisfactory.

Was there eventually the incorporation of the local people into the University system, and then did they start to study archaeology themselves?

Yes, the University of Ife was founded about the time of independence in 1960. It was achieved by taking over what had been the Niger College, which had three different campuses. One was in Ibadan. It became the basis for the University of Ife. It was there for many years, until after I left Nigeria. One of the rescue jobs I had to do was to go over the whole site of the University of Ife, which has the largest campus in the world. It covers 30 square miles, and what hope has an archaeologist of covering adequately 30 square miles of a site more or less single-handed? The contractor laid out clearings through the bush and we simply put down small sample cuttings. One of the things that Bernard Fagg introduced was well-diggers from the North, who were habituated to digging wells down to a depth of 30 feet, and he used them for exploratory work in Ife and recommended that I should do the same. For sampling a site, it was a very good technique. One or two of them were extremely careful. They could spot the smallest of beads as they went down. In many cases that wasn't all that important. One was trying to get an idea of how extensive the potsherd pavements were, for example. But they could be very helpful.

What were your goals?

The first thing about Ife was that it was totally undated. The art was known. It's naturalistic, portrait-like indeed, and Frobenius had thought that there had been a colony from the western end of the Mediterranean who had settled there and lost touch with home — somewhere in the 2nd millennium BC — a long, long time ago. They had lost contact and gradually run down into modern Yoruba civilisation. There was no real dating. Kenneth Murray first of all, and then William Fagg, had pointed out that the proportions of the figures suggested that this was African work, and not by an imported artist or an immigrant artist or a European who had been captured — slave-trade-in-reverse kind of thing — and of course he wasn't Egyptian either. The ideas were being bandied about with no reference to chronology, because there wasn't a real chronology for Ife. So the first site, we didn't get anything that would help us date things beyond the fact that the bronze figures showed what William Fagg called African proportion. The second season I was able to dig on that site, we were able to get radiocarbon samples. They produced 12th-century dates, and this gave us a nice firm basis for showing that this was before the first European contacts with the coast in the late 15th century.

It just occurred to me that some people may not know Bernard Fagg.

Bernard Fagg was the younger brother of the two. William became Keeper of Ethnography at the BM. They were both Cambridge-trained, and Bernard qualified as an archaeologist but became an administrator in the Colonial Civil Service; and in 1943, Kenneth Murray, who was an art teacher, was appointed to start a Survey of Antiquities and in 1947, he was allowed to have an assistant who was an archaeologist. Bernard was on the spot in Nigeria and suitably qualified, and so he was appointed. He went out just before the War as a Colonial Officer, and then he served in East Africa with the West African Frontier Force, and when he came back after the War it was as Resettlement Officer on the Plateau, so he was resettling the troops when they came back and got to know the tin-miners up there. He liked the Plateau. It is a very pleasant — the pleasantest part of Nigeria certainly. When he became Director after Kenneth Murray left, he moved the Headquarters from Lagos up to Jos and expanded the Jos Museum. But he built the Jos Museum and his field work was devoted very largely to the Nok terracottas which we can now date between the middle of the 1st millennium BC and the middle of the 1st millennium AD with both radiocarbon and thermoluminescence dates, and that is securely dated now, and that was his main contribution to the archaeology of Nigeria.

When you discuss the difficulties of being in Nigeria in terms of your health, I am struck by the courage of even staying within an environment which can be dangerous.

It wasn't easy. The worst thing was the tiny little sand flies, which are so small you could hardly see them, like a speck of dust, and the place was infested with them in the dawn and dusk. This is a terrible thing when bringing up children, because even though they are under a mosquito net, they could penetrate the net and then the children would scratch themselves and get the most awful blisters which could go septic, so that was really very unpleasant, not fatal but nasty for all of us. I had a rash when I came home from Nigeria once, and went to my local doctor and he said, well, he didn't know what it was but he could give me something to cure the itch. I said, well I'm used to itching all the time in Nigeria. That wasn't bothering me at all. I'm sorry to emphasize that.

Actually it is good, because everyone will say that to me but they won't put it on tape.
May I back up a little and could you say something about your education at Oxford?

My Professor was Christopher Hawkes, but I learnt my archaeology, as opposed to prehistory, from Richard Atkinson, who at that time was Assistant Keeper at the Ashmolean Museum, and he put a lot of effort into cooperation with the University Archaeological Society, the student society, taking us out to dig, always rescue digs all over Oxfordshire and the adjacent counties. I spent a lot of my time as an undergraduate digging with the Society. I remember one week, I was out every single day in the week with the Society. But, he was the one who really gave me my training. Also, even in the evenings, he gave a weekly course of lectures for those of us who wanted to go, entirely voluntary, not part of his job at all, and of course eventually he became Professor at Cardiff. He worked on Stonehenge. That was his most famous investigation.

Did you ever work with Wheeler?

No, I didn't work with Wheeler. My first encounter with Wheeler was on the programme 'Animal, Vegetable, Mineral', where the panel was supposed to identify things, and I provided a series of pieces from the Manchester Museum Collections. There was a rehearsal of the first few objects before it — it was a live programme — without it being transmitted, and he was extremely good. One piece I put up was from the Pacific. It was a deep bracelet made of beads, but it was copied from an ancient form in shell, so I put both of them there — put the beads as the one they were asked about, and after we took that off we said, and this is what it was based on. People were saying it was South African, South African, and it came to Wheeler's turn just before we went live and he said, "I think it's from the Pacific", and put it down. He had that wonderful instinct for where things came from. He was really brilliant, but unfortunately a lot of the other things they got wrong, including some things that they might have known better, and it was the first time they had ever been defeated, apparently. Wheeler got a bit moody, and I couldn't see the programme and I was behind, handing up the stuff. He turned his back on the camera and didn't seem very interested in the programme, and my wife was at home watching it. We shared a taxi from the studios going back to the centre of London, and I said had he been told that it had been recorded and the same samples were going to be sent out to America, where Fro Rainey at the University Museum ran a similar programme (on which it was based) at the University of Philadelphia? The same examples were going to be put up to an American panel. And he didn't know this, and he was even more upset and the next time I saw him, he more or less cut me dead. But he got over that. He came out to Nigeria to do a lecture tour for the British Council, and so I had to take him around Ife and over to Benin where Graham Connah was working at the time, and Graham was really quite seriously ill, so I had to take him around Benin as well. It worked very well indeed, and after that he was very helpful. He became Secretary of the British Academy and was very helpful in getting me money for continuing to write up my material. I am grateful to him. He was very supportive.

You know a great deal about what is happening to the art in Nigeria — the looting.

Those of us who were involved in Nigeria — I think I was effectively the third to spend any length of time there, and then Graham Connah of course working in Benin, and later John Picton and Keith Nicklin — we had all been involved in setting up museums in Nigeria. We tried to introduce internationally acceptable professional standards. We set up catalogues and cataloguing systems. What is happening now is that material is disappearing from the museums. There are thefts organised. Whole museums have been totally looted. The University of Ife Institute of African Studies Museum, the Institute of African Studies Museum at the Univ of Ibadan, pieces from the Archaeology Department at Ibadan, an important piece from the Univ of Ife Archaeology Department; there have been thefts from the Jos Museum, Lagos Museum — all the reserve Benin material was stolen. That almost certainly was done by someone inside, but the police said there wasn't enough evidence to convict him. There have been thefts from the Benin Museum which were perpetrated by a Curator. The Owo Museum has been totally looted. The night watchman was shot in the course of that. I think he was killed. The Abeokuta Museum has been robbed. And the Esie Museum has been robbed. It is a dreadful state, and in many places it seems that there is involvement of the staff.

When the oil price fell, there wasn't enough money to pay for staff to do fieldwork, so curatorial staff were told to re-catalogue the collections, but they weren't adequately instructed on what to do; and so in the case of the Ife Museum, they started a new numbering system that had no real relevance to the Museum. They were giving dates of acquisition before the Museum existed. All the bronze heads from Ife found in 1938 and 39 were dated 1939. The Museum was founded in 1953. This became a sort of nonsense. They totally ignored the numbers which had already been assigned to the pieces, but what is worst of all, they threw away all the records. So there is no way you can check one against the other. They miscopied information or omitted to copy information from the old records, and the records they had produced which were on A4 cards were hopelessly incomplete. A great deal of the material was never catalogued. Now that there have been all these thefts, I wonder if this was perhaps deliberate, that people were planning to steal things. I got a letter from Nigeria — I had written to draw attention to a piece that had turned up in a private collection in Europe and sent the information about it and photographs, and they said "We have no record of this piece. We are very grateful that you do." So what I am currently working on is trying to put all my records of what should be in the Ife Museum — which isn't complete — I haven't recorded minor things, but the major things certainly I have — I am putting all this onto CD-rom. I've been working on it ever since I left Ife and my Ife book was a preliminary try-out of the material, but this is a try to publish everything comprehensively and now runs to about a third-of-a-million words and 1800 plates. This is much too much to get published as a book, as I was originally intending, so I am trying to produce it on a CD-rom and I hope to get it out by the end of this year. It is the last little bits of putting your book to bed or putting your CD to bed that take all the time.

Interruption

Reverting to the thefts from museums. There are now a great many museums in Nigeria, and I welcome this greatly, because what they were planning to do was to use the museums as a way of promoting a sense of national identity. There are at least 600 different linguistic groups in Nigeria which means, of course, ethnic identity. It is not a natural country. It was an artificial one caused by the rush of the Colonial powers to grab as much as they could, so there is a great need to promote this sense of unity and it has been done by setting up a museum in every state and by putting something from Ife in every museum, from Benin in every museum, so that when they hear about these achievements, read about these achievements in the press, they can all feel that this is something that they have in their local museum and take a local pride in it. I welcome this. Indeed, I did an article some years ago for the WAC when it was held in Southampton, comparing the attitudes in museums, 'Two Reactions to Colonialism' I called it, in Scotland and Nigeria. In Scotland, we always had a sense of our own identity so we can have museums about our locality, promoting our local trade and what we do here locally, as opposed to Nigeria, where they were trying to use it to promote a sense of national unity.

One of the problems about the looting that is going on now is that we have had, for a good many years now, military governments that have been dominated by Muslim Hausa from the north. In the Colonial days, the missionaries used to discourage the worship of the traditional cults. This is paganism. It is all bad. The Muslim attitudes are much the same, so that successive governments have not been so interested in protecting these ancient sites and the monuments and the collections; and I am informed that one of the generals is responsible for, indeed owned, a site which had a lot of terracottas contemporary to those from Nok, and that he was exploiting it like a field of potatoes. I have heard rumours that senior officers from the Department of Antiquities are involved with it, and that is very distressing.

That can be explained by the historical development of Nigeria as an artificially bounded political entity?

Well, I don't think that the destruction of archaeological material can be explained in those terms at all. I think that it is simply a failure to recognise the importance of their heritage. Whether it is your personal heritage or not. In America you have great problems in preserving sites because the farmers say, that is nothing to do with us. We had a great fight in Illinois trying to get sites protected there. It is a problem everywhere. I think in Britain, we've got the problem largely won. People recognise the importance of these things, even though they are so remote that you cannot relate personally, but we still have the British Army using burial mounds on the Salisbury Plain as targets. Who are we to criticise what goes on in Nigeria? When the staff themselves are involved in the thefts — and I wonder if I would behave any better if I were badly paid in a country with enormous inflation and no certainty that your salary was going to arrive at the end of the month. It is a very unhappy situation to be in, and I do hesitate to pass judgement. But I do think that those at the top are adequately paid and don't need to exploit the collections in this way.

We have not talked much about my archaeology, have we? One of my problems having spent my time doing archaeology in Nigeria, the people of Ife were major artists and it is so much easier to write about the art than to write a full scale archaeological report. I built up a completely spurious reputation as an art historian, which is convenient when I am at conferences like this, because they all tend to regard me as an art historian so they half write me off, whereas if I go to a conference of art historians, they regard me as an archaeologist. So, protective colouration in both camps.

I did a little work in Benin. It was a rescue dig and I handed all my information about that to Graham Connah, who wrote a rather condensed version of it in his Archaeology of Benin. The other site I worked in was Ilesha, about 20 miles from Ife, which turned out to be a relatively late site with, I've called them fired-clay sculptures rather than terracottas. But again the art dimension is what leads to finding sites in Nigeria. Either you are going to go off because there are traditions about the site and you explore it, or you are going to have your attention drawn to it because people find things that they recognise as being artefacts. A lot of Stone Age sites have been destroyed because people don't recognise that they are artefacts that they are dealing with. Whereas where I was, people were seeing terracotta sculpture in the ground, recognising it as sculpture and reporting it to the Museum. I would pay them a small sum of money for their discoveries, with the permission of the Ooni of Ife, who claimed legally that everything found in the ground belonged to him. I could always invoke this when necessary, but we gave a small fee as a gesture of thanks, which had no relationship to the value of the object. The international trade has now got reported so widely, and the figures that the Benin objects in particular fetch at auction, that there is no way you keep this quiet — it gets spread across the headlines in Nigerian papers.

Where are the markets?

For antiquities? There used to be a market in Oyo for wood carvings run by the leather workers. Initially they had quite good material but in the later years whilst I was there in the 1960s, there was more and more material that was inferior, was made for the tourist trade and had been blackened deliberately to make it look older. You had to be awfully careful. But now in Benin, they are making deliberately copies of old well-known pieces and deliberately patinating them and passing them off as ancient. That has happened in the last ten or fifteen years. They were making copies before that, but they were selling them as contemporary work; but now with the big prices that you can get for pieces, they are trying to make fakes deliberately and this I find very disquieting. The trouble is they are getting so good at it, it is very difficult to detect some of them.

This entire industry had arisen from a few small discoveries — in the 1940s?

Yes, the major discoveries made at Ife and Igbo Ukwu were made just before that, 1938–39.

Was that Fagg?

No, he was an Administrator Officer then. They were found casually and the Ooni of Ife sent to have the stuff brought in and the local District Officer called Field in Igbo Ukwu was asked to collect this stuff together when he heard about it and save it against the possibility of having a national collection. As I said, it wasn't until 1943 that Kenneth Murray was asked formally to go and survey what he could and made a very comprehensive record, but he never published. I tried very hard to get him to publish things and he said "No, if I publish these things, it will just become a sale catalogue for anybody who wants to find these things and buy them." And it turned out to be only too true.

What do you advise as a solution?

Frankly, I don't think there is a solution. It is a very popular answer in America but it is growing as well here in Britain that if you can discourage collectors from collecting, the bottom will fall out of the market. On the other hand, a collector complained to me a some years ago that the price

of Nok terracottas in New York was only 1/10th of what it had been the previous year because so many had flooded the market. Either you flood the market or you try to stop anything getting out. I don't think you can stop things getting out. Bernard Fagg, I thought, was quite sensible the way he administered it. Kenneth Murray tried to make it almost impossible to get anything out of the country and Bernard was much more relaxed about it and said if it is important we should keep it, if it is of less than national importance, we should let it go. This more liberal attitude I think discouraged people from the need to smuggle things out, but that didn't continue, and it became again rather restrictive; and then, of course, you got junior members of staff going around asking for a payment to issue a certificate and coming to your home and offering you a service: "I will give you a certificate, if you will pay me a sum." One person who was involved in that was dismissed from the Service, but how many others were involved in that, I don't know. Stuff that was submitted for application for export permits, I had this happen to me personally, I bought an Ife tray when I was back in Nigeria visiting, not a good one, and I consulted John Picton who was in Ife at the time and he said "Oh, it is not worthy of a place in the national collections, it really is quite inferior. I am sure you can take it out." So I had a box made and sent it down to Lagos, and said that I'd like to take this piece out, but if the then Director (who was Kenneth Murray, who had returned from his retirement when Bernard Fagg left) thought it was worthy of a place in the national collections, I would present it. I never heard a word about it either saying yes, it was accepted, or I could have it. So, the next time I was back in Nigeria, couple of years later, I was in Lagos, I asked to see it. It couldn't be found. It had been sold out of the back door of the Museum and Kenneth Murray presumably never even saw the letter. It has been going on quite a long time.

And again, your recommendations?

I have none. I have none. I feel desperate about it but I don't think we're ever going to stop collectors collecting. I don't have that bug myself. I collected on behalf of museums, and I did acquire a few things myself whilst in Nigeria that were commonplace pieces because I could foresee the possibility that I could be teaching about it so I acquired things for teaching purposes but not for any other . . .

End of side 1

You were speaking about the Dan mask.

I was telling you about the Dan mask. I bought this because I was teaching about the Dan masks at the time and I still have it, in fact. My collection, such as it is, I have promised to the Hunterian Museum because I think it should go into a museum. Everything I published should be and will be. No, I have very little sympathy for collectors. I have colleagues like William Fagg and people who have worked with him who sort of cultivate collectors, because after all Bill Fagg, when he retired, got involved with Christie's and used to go around encouraging collectors to buy through Christie's and finding out what they had in their collection, and drawing their attention to things that might be coming up, and also having some eye on what might be coming to them to sell again from collectors, and that has never interested me at all. I find it rather painful to be taken around people's collections, for the most part. I mean, it is nice to meet people who have a real eye for things and a real serious interest in it, but for so many people it is just acquisition, simply acquisition. I find that very distasteful.

So much of the illicit trade, does it end up with proper private collectors?

Most of it involves, ends up in private collections. I know of one piece recently, a very beautiful Ife terracotta head that an America Museum was very anxious to acquire, but they had adopted an ethical policy so they couldn't, but they still wanted to. They wrote to the Nigerian Government and said, if they were to acquire it, would the Nigerian Government claim it back? And, they got a firm answer saying "No, they would not attempt to claim it back", so they went ahead and bought it. If it goes into a private collection, it just keeps on re-circulating and they would never end up in a museum as long as these ethical policies are imposed. Is that desirable for the sake of museums? Personally, I think that it would be better if they could go into museums and be kept in museums safely. I have put a lot of effort into trying to get things returned to Nigeria. In one case — I was not directly involved — a bronze head from Benin, of the early period, a unique one which had the cat's whiskers scarification, but it was an almost life-size head of the early period — this was stolen from the Jos Museum and it ended up in the hands of a dealer in Zurich, who put it through a local auction house who specialised in objets de vertu, watches and jewellery, not the place where you would expect a Benin head to come up for sale; because in Swiss law if you buy something in good faith, it is yours, even if it is stolen. The owner can not get it back. Of course the question is, how do you prove good faith? It tends to be assumed that any transaction was in good faith. What the dealer was doing was, he put it up in an unlikely place so he could buy it back at a minimum price, and that would give entire title to the head. But as it happened, a husband and wife who were collectors spotted it in the catalogue, went around and looked at it and then went home and looked at their books, and discovered that Philip Dark had published this as being in the Jos Museum. So they got on to the local museum in Zurich and also to the Nigerian Embassy in Bern, and got on to the Museums and Monuments Commission in Lagos. Eventually, it took a lot of pressure, eventually they sent someone quite junior out to look at it and he tried to say that it was not the same piece. Again, it took a lot of pressure to make him take it on the plane back to Lagos. One might have thought that that was the end of the story. No, the dealer was sent from Lagos a terracotta head from the Ife University Museum to sell, so that he could make his profit on that, since he had failed to make his profit on the Benin head. That piece is now in a private collection in Switzerland. So if one gets things back to Nigeria, one wonders how long they will stay there. I have been instrumental in getting some pieces back. The French police returned three Ife pieces some years ago. I have no evidence that they have reappeared on the market. How long they will stay in Nigeria . . . the situation is so bad that I'm frankly very worried about it.

The difficulty is, the local population doesn't benefit publicly from it.

No, the finder will get a fairly modest sum. Each person who handled it along the line puts his mark-up on it and it grows exponentially, so that the farmer who finds a terracotta head will maybe get the equivalent of five or ten pounds for it, perhaps 25 if he is lucky, but that is the order of magnitude for a piece which eventually ends up fetching scores of thousands of pounds. It's the nearer end of the sale which makes the big profits. It's not the local people who do. If they did, it would be much more equitable and more understandable in a way. Although it would be disproportionate in a country that is so poor as Nigeria. It shouldn't be. It is sheer corruption at the top that has made Nigeria so poor. I was told that every general got an entire shipping tanker of oil given to him every year by the oil companies as a personal gift. I mentioned this to a Nigerian friend of mine and he said "Every year! It's more like every month!" The scale of corruption is unbelievable. I can remember there was a big row when I was living in Nigeria about a contract that had been let, and the British company had paid a bribe and there was a great uproar about it. British companies don't behave that way. But they do now, and Shell Oil has even been buying weapons for a special military police force that was used to shoot up the Ogoni people in the Delta. So I have been boycotting Shell Oil for several years ever since I read Ken Saro-Wiwa's book.* Shell have been recently convicted about two or three weeks ago — were convicted in the Nigerian courts of destroying the environment of the Ogoni people and were fined 43 million pounds, maybe it was dollars. It was a strange figure, anyway. They are appealing it. When there is an oil spill they simply set fire to it and it bakes the ground until it is like pumice. There is no way they can cultivate it. And the oil runs off into the streams. It kills off the fishes. These are agricultural people who also fish, living in the Delta and it is killing off the food supply and so they protested and they got shot for it. Ken Saro-Wiwa — I was shocked to discover they had four attempts to hang him. Not only was he innocent, but they wouldn't accept when he failed to die the first time that this maybe was somebody up there intervening and suggesting that it was an unjust death. They had four goes before they finally killed him, which is unbelievable and unforgivable. But that is what happens in military regimes.

And corrupt international companies.

Yes who work hand and hand with them.

Have you seen the recent Shell campaign about how clean they are?

No I haven't.

What is the name of the book that you just mentioned?

By Ken Saro-Wiwa? I can't remember what it is called — genocide comes into the title. It was published in Nigeria. It was about five years ago now. Ken Saro-Wiwa. He was a writer, a poet, and he tried to promote a sense of cultural identity among the Ogoni peoples in the Delta, so he set up this organisation which was purely a cultural organisation, not a political organisation. It was to bring back masquerades and encourage masquerades to be continued, and these other things that were characteristic of the Ogoni people as opposed to anybody else, so that they had a sense of pride in their own traditions; and of course you can see why a military government, trying to force a sense of unity into the whole of Nigeria, might see this as objectionable, but I am convinced that it was done entirely innocently to promote a sense of pride in their past and this was misconstrued by the military who sent in this special force of armed police whose guns had been bought by Shell Oil.

This is all because you were a working-class child who was interested in a life —

I suppose I should trace it back to my primary school, because I learnt about the ancient Egyptians in primary school and was told that our local museum had a very good Egyptian collection. The reason was, it was a cotton-spinning town. My mother was a weaver. My father, as I said, had been a spinner. The local museum curator had been an expert on textiles and he had written up the textiles for Flinders Petrie during his excavations in Egypt. So as his reward he was given some of Flinders Petrie's material, not just the textiles, a very good general collection about daily life in ancient Egypt, not much which was spectacular, although there were two or three mummies in their cases. It was really a very good collection. Our teachers had said "If you can, whenever you have a half day holiday, get your mum to take you." Children were not allowed unaccompanied of course. My mother was very sympathetic and she took the care to make sure that I got to see the Museum because it was in my interests at school and that got me hooked. I thought I'd love to be an archaeologist from a very early age, but when I came up to Oxford and said I was interested "Unless you have a private income, there is no hope. There are no jobs in the field at all", and it was true at the time. Fortunately I just hit it when the archaeological field was expanding, just after the War. It gave me the opportunity. If it hadn't been for the War, I probably wouldn't have got to Oxford anyway. I wouldn't have been able to afford the cost of education, but because I served in the Air Force, I was entitled to have my fees paid by the government. Well, I got my fees paid by my local authority, but the maintenance grant came from the Further Education and Training Scheme.

Was it Christopher Hawkes who said that you had to have a private income?

Oh it wasn't Christopher Hawkes personally. He wasn't at Oxford when I arrived. I think he came afterwards. No, it just was generally said among the archaeologists, museum archaeologists and so on. I joined the Archaeological Society, as I said, so I could get some experience of it, because I was interested, and I didn't initially think of taking it up professionally but it became — I could see that it might be possible because there were expansions in archaeological posts in museums and in the Royal Commission of Ancient and Historical Monuments and such organisations. They were expanding. So I decided that I would gamble on getting a qualification. You asked about my postgraduate education. I was much better trained as a social anthropologist than as an archaeologist. I mean I was taught by Evans-Pritchard, Meyer Fortes, Max Gluckman. Meyer went off to be a Professor at Cambridge just after I left. Max Gluckman when I left also started at Manchester when I did. My other teacher was Godfrey Lienhardt. I can swap genealogies with any Social Anthropologist.

Could you say briefly what your impressions were of Evans-Pritchard and Meyer Fortes?

I found them very warm human beings and very caring teachers. I remember Evans-Pritchard used to have a little party when we all finished the examinations — a garden party — and I remember his wife saying to me, "You know, EP would never fail a student. He would be so upset." It was so heartening when you were convinced that you had made an awful mess of your papers! I'm not sure if it was he who introduced a special qualification so that if you took the Diploma, and didn't do well enough, you got a Certificate. That was introduced particularly for foreign students who were sent over from Colonial countries to get a qualification. He wouldn't send them back without a qualification.

Did he talk about his experiences in Africa?

Oh yes, about how he was taken as one of them, so they would pinch his tobacco when he was working among the Nuer. He couldn't get used to this. He found it very hard at first. Nothing belonged to him. Everything was communal. It was very irritating. I can quite see that too. Also at Oxford at that time, just back from doing their field work, were the Bohannons, Paul Bohannon and Laura, Dusty as she was always known, worked among the Tiv who were a very difficult group indeed. They were never "pacified" by the British Colonial authorities. I remember reading in the paper, when I was in Nigeria, that a policeman had stopped a Tiv crossing a market place with a sack over his shoulder because he had something bloody inside. The blood was oozing from it, and so he stopped him and opened the bag, and there were five human heads inside. Eventually they accepted the Nigeria Police. The local police couldn't do anything but the Nigeria — the Federal — Police, they did accept them as an authority because they felt that they were less corrupt than the local police were likely to be, but they had a dreadful reputation. I remember that Jim told me of a case that the District Officer had to try. The man was accused of murder. Apparently what happened was that he was walking down the street and this other man was walking on the same side of the street, and he just killed him. The District Officer was falling over backwards — "Well did he provoke you? Did he threaten you?" "No, he was just on the same side of the street as I was." This was a good reason for killing the man? The District Officer was doing his best not to have to convict him, but there was no way he could avoid it. They were very peculiar people. I had a couple of Tiv work with me as labourers and one of them spoke Tiv and English, and the other spoke Hausa and Tiv but not English, so we had a chain of communication when I wanted to speak to them. They worked very well, and they were good workers.

The stories about Evans-Pritchard — I didn't realise you knew him.

Oh, yes, I was very fond of Evans-Pritchard. Whenever I was back in Britain from Nigeria, I would always try to look him up and we would end up having a pint of beer together, usually in the Lamb and Flag, that was his favourite pub at the time. He was always most welcoming, and Meyer Fortes too. I didn't see much of Meyer after he went to Cambridge, but he had a visiting appointment in Chicago when I was at Northwestern, so we got together again then.

Did he speak about his experiences in the field?

Not that I recall off hand. There must have been, but I don't remember at the moment. I can remember one of Max Gluckman's stories. I think it is published. We were talking about witchcraft which, of course, Evans-Pritchard's real thing was to show how witchcraft works because you can't question it. Once you accept it, it explains everything. It is an enclosed system. Max's illustration of this was a nursing sister in South Africa whose father had died of pneumonia, and she was going on about him having been bewitched and the doctor said, "Look, you know very well, it was a pneumococcus that got into his lung and produced the illness and this is why he died. He died of pneumonia." "Oh yes", she said, "he died of pneumonia, but it was the witches who made it happen to him." It's one of those systems that you simply can't get behind it and any kind of questioning of the system reinforces the system, which was one of the great topics of discussion when I was student. Things have moved on since then.

Gluckman was in the Livingstone for awhile.

Yes, he was. I remember a remark he made about museums that the problem with exhibiting in museums, if you have something that is unusual, that is rare, you tend to put that on exhibition, which gives a totally distorted view. The example he gave was the fishing net, perhaps in the Rhodes-Livingstone, which came from a people who didn't normally fish. You got the impression that they were fishermen, when in fact they were agriculturalists. This is a serious risk. Museums do tend to put on unusual pieces.

I have often wondered about the influences of the anthropologists upon the archaeologists since so many worked with Gluckman — Fortes was in Ghana.

I think that there is a stronger influence in America than there is in Britain, because archaeology is taught in Anthropology Departments. Personally, I welcome that. I think the separation from social anthropology from the rest and their abrogation to themselves of the name of anthropology, they don't claim to be social anthropologists, they claim to be anthropologists and I resent that quite strongly. When I studied it, it was a unitary discipline, covering physical anthropology and even linguistics as it still does in America and I think that is right and proper. I don't like this increasing subdivision of subjects at all. I think it is much to be regretted. Of course, even archaeology is splitting up in all sorts of different groups and different movements and lots of different journals. It is happening with all disciplines, and it is becoming more and more difficult to keep abreast with the literature, because there is so much specialist literature.

In 1959, Thurstan Shaw was invited to investigate the site at Igbo Ukwu. It had been discovered in 1938–39 and there hadn't been any archaeologists in the country at the time and it was waiting to be investigated. He had been up at Cambridge with Bernard Fagg and William and subsequently worked in Ghana, and had been in charge of the museum at Achimota College. So he was invited to come out and investigate the site and I went over to visit him whilst he was digging and subsequently when he came back to work on the material; I was supposed to fly up to Jos and spend a week with him getting him settled in and discussing with him how he was going to do some of the work. Unfortunately, I was the only passenger to be picked up from the airport in Ibadan and the pilot said "I'm not putting down to pick up one passenger." So he just overflew the airport, and there were only two flights a week, so that made a real hole in the time I had to spend with Thurstan, because I couldn't stay longer afterwards, but I had few days with him getting him set with his work and discussing with him how he would describe these very complicated, extremely complex castings. We had a great discussion, which he can tell you about, about how they made the Igbo Ukwu vase. It was really quite hilarious how we tried to unravel how that had been done, and it is quite an astonishing piece of work. Now I find that in Benin, they are making copies of it on a regular basis. They have learnt a few things.

One of the things that Thurstan is concerned about: I have not yet published all my excavation reports. He has. He is up to date on all of his. My problem has been that when I came from Nigeria nobody wanted to employ me, and the only job I could get was as Professor of Art History, and I then had to turn myself into an art historian in which I think I have had some success, but I am now trying to get the Art of Ife completed on this CDRom so that I can now get back to writing up my archaeological reports. I have several of them partially written, but I have never been able to get them completely finished. I found I was rather schizophrenic when I was teaching at Northwestern because, although I had a research assistant, I used my research assistant to work on the archaeology for the most part. That kept things going along, but not far enough to have anything that was really substantial enough to publish. This is my next priority. I only hope that I live long enough to get it all done.

You were trained as an Anthropologist. You worked as an Archaeologist and Art Historian —

I was trained as an Anthropologist because that was the only qualification available, but it did include such training in archaeology as you could get in Oxford. When I came back here as a Visiting Fellow at Clare Hall, Cambridge in 1970–71, generously funded by the National Endowment for the Humanities in America, I was asked to give a public lecture at which Grahame Clark presided and he introduced me as one of the few people who had done archaeology at the other place and made a reputation. I was able to shout out quite loudly "Yes, I have come to make up for my misspent youth." I meant it entirely sincerely, but it went down very well with the audience. I think it was a great mistake not to come to Cambridge. They were teaching archaeology much better here than they were at Oxford.

But then you would have missed out on Meyer Fortes and Evans-Pritchard.

Yes, I would. That was the compensation, but I must say I am not a theorist at all. I don't care much for theorising. I am an empiricist. This is really why I gave up Social Anthropology. I got as far as registering to do a B.Litt in Soc. Anth. on the kinship systems of the Anglo-Saxons and it got more — as I went down without completing it — it got more and more remote from what I was doing, and Evans-Pritchard kept pressing me to complete it. He said "Someone else will write it up if you don't." And I said, "Well, if they do, maybe I will get the chance to review it." In fact, it has been written up in the British Journal of Sociology and I have read it, but I was not asked to review it as it was an article in a journal, not a book, so one doesn't review them.

      That was sparked off because of Radcliffe-Brown, who had said that the Anglo-Saxon kinship system was a classification based on the parts — the joints — of the body and I couldn't find out any support of this at all, and it was quoted by Evans-Pritchard and Meyer Fortes but they both quoted it in lectures; and I went to them and said "Look, what evidence do you have for this?" "It was, well, Radcliffe-Brown told us, you see". So I had to wait years and years before Radcliffe-Brown's book on kinship systems came out and I discovered that he was saying this applied to Anglo-Saxons* when in fact it was continental Germans of the 13th century, this source, not relevant at all to the Anglo-Saxons. The only word in Anglo-Saxon that is a part of the body is the knee, cneow, and they speak of kinship within the cneow but it doesn't really mean knee at all, because if you go back to Indo-European, in Latin it is genus for family, genu for knee. They are both very similar words because they both come from the same root. I believe it comes from the habit where the father acknowledges paternity by placing the baby on his knee, so this becomes an acknowledgement of kinship and it is also the word for knee. The two words have fallen together. They have the same form in Anglo-Saxon. But that is all it is. It is just a word for kin. It had nothing to do with the joints of the body and there is certainly no other joint involved in Anglo-Saxon. It took me a long time to discover this, and by the time I got it sorted out I was so much into other things that I never got around to publishing that. That would distract me from writing up my archaeology. If I live that much longer after I got all my excavation reports written up, then maybe I should put a note in somewhere about that. Otherwise, it is unpublished except for on this tape at the Wenner-Gren Archive.

Thank you.

End of tape.

References

The referencing style is derived from Antiquity *under Christopher Chippindale's editorial guidance.*

Abir-Am, P.G. & D. Outram (ed.). 1987. *Uneasy Careers and Intimate Lives: Women in Science 1789–1979.* New Brunswick (NJ): Rutgers University Press.

Aitken, M.J., C.B. Stringer & P.A. Mellars (ed.). 1992. *The Origin of Modern Humans and the Impact of Chronometric Dating.* Princeton (NJ): Princeton University Press.

Akazawa, T., K. Aoki & O. Bar-Yosef (ed.). 1998. *Neandertals and Modern Humans in Western Asia.* New York (NY): Plenum Press.

Annan, N.G. 1955. The Intellectual Aristocracy, in J.H. Plumb (ed.), *Studies in Social History: A Tribute to G.M. Trevelyan*: 241–87 London: Longmans, Green.

Arensburg, B. & A. Belfer-Cohen. 1998. Sapiens and Neandertals: Rethinking the Levantine Middle Palaeolithic Hominids, in Akazawa *et al.* (ed.): 311–22.

Armstrong, A.L. 1937. Review: *The Mesolithic Settlement of Northern Europe* by J.G.D. Clark, *Man* 37: 68–9.

Atkinson, R.J.C. 1983. Archaeology, in S.B. Chrimes (ed.), *University College, Cardiff, A Centenary History, 1883–1983*: 219–22. Cardiff: University College.

Bahn, P.G. & A.C. Renfrew. 1999. Garrod and Glozel: the End of a Fiasco, in Davies & Charles (ed.): 76–83.

Bar-Yosef, O. 1992. The Role of Western Asia in Modern Human Origins, in Aiken *et al.* (ed.): 132–47.

Bar-Yosef, O. 1998a. The Chronology of the Middle Palaeolithic of the Levant, in Akazawa *et al.* (ed.): 39–56.

Bar-Yosef, O. 1998b. The Natufian Culture in the Levant, Threshold to the Origins of Agriculture, *Evolutionary Anthropology* 6(5): 159–77.

Bar-Yosef, O. & J. Callander. 1997. A Forgotten Archaeologist: the Life of Francis Turville-Petre, *Palestine Exploration Quarterly* 129: 2–18.

Bar-Yosef, O. & J. Callander 1999. The Woman from Tabun: Garrod's Doubts in Historical Perspective, *Journal of Human Evolution* 37: 879–85.

Bar-Yosef, O. & J. Callander. In press. Dorothy Annie Elizabeth Garrod, in G.M. Cohen & M.S. Joukowsky (ed.), *Women in Archaeology: the First Generation, the Pioneers.*

Bar-Yosef, O. & D. Pilbeam (ed.). 2000. *The Geography of Neandertals and Modern Humans in Europe and the Greater Mediterranean.* Cambridge (MA): Peabody Museum of Archaeology & Ethnology. Peabody Museum Bulletin 8.

Beard, M. 1999. Classics in 19th and 20th Century Cambridge: Curriculum, Culture and Community, in C. Stray (ed.), *Classics in the 19th &20th Century: Curriculum, Culture and Community*: 95–134.

Cambridge: Cambridge Philological Society. Cambridge Philological Society Supplementary Vol. 24.

Bégouën, N.H., Count. 1929. The Magic Origin of Prehistoric Art, *Antiquity* 3: 5–19.

Belfer-Cohen, A., L.A. Schepartz & B. Arensburg. 1991. New Biological Data for the Natufian Populations in Israel, in O. Bar-Yosef & F.R. Valla (ed.), *The Natufian Culture in the Levant*: 411–24. Ann Arbor (MI): International Monographs in Prehistory. Archaeological Series 1.

Bertsch, K. 1931. Paläobotanische Monographie des Federseerieds, *Bibliotheca Botanica* 103: 1–127.

Bethune-Baker, J.F. 1936. Francis Crawford Burkitt, 1864–1935, *Proceedings of the British Academy* 22: 445–84.

Birley, E. 1958. *Archaeology in the North of England: An Inaugural Lecture of the Professor of Roman-British History and Archaeology.* Durham: Wilson & Sons.

Booth, D.C. 1979. Poisonous Place. Armistice Day Siege, in A. Phillips (ed.), *A Newnham Anthology*: 119–26. Cambridge: Newnham College.

Brennan, M.L. 1973. Robert Alexander Stewart Macalister 1871–1950, *Journal of the Royal Society of the Antiquaries of Ireland* 103: 167–76.

Breuil, H.P.E. 1906. L'évolution de l'Art Pariétal des Cavernes de l'âge du Renne, in *Congrès International d'Anthropologie et d'Archéologie Préhistoriques, Compte Rendu de la Treizième Session*: 367–86. Monaco: Imprimerie de Monaco.

Breuil, H.P.E. 1921. Preface II, in Burkitt 1921a: x–xii.

Breuil, H.P.E. 1926. Preface, in Garrod (1926): 5–8.

Brodrick, A.H. 1963. *The Abbé Breuil, Prehistorian. A Biography.* London: Hutchinson.

Brooks, F.T. & T.F. Chipp. 1931. *Fifth International Botanical Congress, Cambridge, 16–23 August 1930. Report of Proceedings.* Cambridge: Cambridge University Press.

Buckley, F. 1921. *A Microlithic Industry, Marsden, Yorkshire.* London: Spottiswoode, Ballantyne.

Buckley, F. 1924. *A Microlithic Industry of the Pennine Chain. Related to the Tardenois of Belgium.* London: Spottiswoode, Ballantyne.

Burkitt, F.C. 1929. Petra and Palmyra, *Proceedings of the Antiquarian Society* 29: 67–71.

Burkitt, F.C. 1931. Notes, *Proceedings of the Antiquarian Society* 31: 72–3.

Burkitt, M.C. 1920a. Pleistocene Deposits in England and the Continental Chronology, *Proceedings of the Prehistoric Society of East Anglia* 3(II): 311–14.

Burkitt, M.C. 1920b. A Visit to Crete. *Proceedings of the Prehistoric Society of East Anglia* 3(3): 580–86.

Burkitt, M.C. 1921a. *Prehistory: A study of early cultures in Europe and the Mediterranean Basin with a short preface by L'Abbé H. Breuil.* Cambridge: Cambridge University Press.

Burkitt, M.C. 1921b. A New Find in Palaeolithic Cave Art, *Man* 21(108): 183–5.

Burkitt, M.C. 1922a. Émile Cartailhac, *Man* 22(27): 42–3.

Burkitt, M.C. 1922b. Notes on the Chronology of the Ice Age, *Man* 22(104): 179–82.

Burkitt, M.C. 1923. *Our Forerunners: A Study of Palaeolithic Man's Civilisations in Western Europe and the Mediterranean Basin.* New York (NY): Henry Holt & Co.

Burkitt, M.C. 1924a. Further Notes Useful for the Study of the Chronology of Palaeolithic Cultures in Relation to the Various Glacial Deposits, *Man* 24(2): 2–3.

Burkitt, M.C. 1924b. Some Notes on the Prehistory of the Eastern Part of Central Europe, *Proceedings of the Prehistoric Society of East Anglia* 4: 179–81.

Burkitt, M.C. 1924c. A Newly-Discovered Transition Culture in North Spain, *Proceedings of the Prehistoric Society of East Anglia* 4: 42–5.

Burkitt, M.C. 1926a. *Our Early Ancestors: An Introductory Study of Mesolithic, Neolithic, and Copper Age Cultures in Europe and Adjacent Regions.* Cambridge: Cambridge University Press.

Burkitt, M.C. 1926b. The Transition Between Palaeolithic and Neolithic Times, i.e., The Mesolithic Period, *Proceedings of the Prehistoric Society of East Anglia* 5: 16–33.

Burkitt, M.C. 1926c. Archaeological Notes, *Man* 26: 220–21.

Burkitt, M.C. 1928. *South Africa's Past in Stone and Paint.* Cambridge: Cambridge University Press.

Burkitt, M.C. 1930a. Christ and Pre-history, *The Modern Churchman* 19: 265–72.

Burkitt, M.C. 1930b. Correlations of the Archaeological and Geological Records, *Nature* 126: 509–10.

Burkitt, M.C. 1932a. Investigation of the Fens, *The Antiquaries Journal* 12: 453.

Burkitt, M.C. 1932b. Man and External Nature, *The Modern Churchman* 21: 255–68.

Burkitt, M.C. 1933. *The Old Stone Age: A Study of Palaeolithic Times.* Cambridge: Cambridge University Press.

Burkitt, M.C. 1934. Some Reflections on Man and Nature in the Light of Past and Recent Prehistoric Research, *Scientia* (December): 347–57.

Burkitt, M.C. 1949a. Place of Archaeology in National Education: A Survey and a Plea, *Nature* 164: 392–3.

Burkitt, M.C. 1949b. Archaeology in Schools, *Education* 10: 413–14.

Burkitt, M.C. & V.G. Childe. 1932. Chronological Table of Prehistory, *Antiquity* 6: 185–205.

Bushnell, G.H.S. 1961. Louis Colville Gray Clarke 1881–1960: Obituary, *Proceedings of the Cambridge Antiquarian Society* 55: 3–5.

Butler, E.M. 1959. *Paper Boats.* London: Collins.

Callander, J. & P.J. Smith. 1998. *Handbook for Exhibition in Honour of D.A.E. Garrod.* Cambridge: CUMAA.

Callander, J. & P.J. Smith. In press. Pioneers in Palestine: the Women Excavators of el-Wad Cave, in R. Whitehouse (ed.), *Women in Archaeology and Antiquity.* London: University College London.

Caton-Thompson, G. 1969. Dorothy Annie Elizabeth Garrod 1892–1968, *Proceedings of the British Academy* 55: 338–61.

Caton-Thompson, G. 1983. *Mixed Memoirs.* Gateshead: The Paradigm Press.

Chadarevian, S. de. 2002. *Designs for Life: Molecular Biology after World War II.* Cambridge: Cambridge University Press.

Childe, V.G. 1925. *The Dawn of European Civilization.* London: Kegan Paul.

Childe, V.G. 1929. *The Danube in Prehistory.* Oxford: Oxford University Press.

Childe, V.G. 1931a. The Forest Cultures of Northern Europe, A Study in Evolution and Diffusion, *The Journal of the Royal Anthropological Institute of Great Britain and Ireland* 41: 325–48.

Childe, V.G. 1931b. Review: *Weltgeschichte der Steinzeit* by O. Menghin, *The Antiquaries Journal* 11: 296–300.

Childe, V.G. 1933. Review: *The Mesolithic Age in Britain* by J.G.D. Clark, *The Antiquaries Journal* 13: 180–82.

Childe, V.G. 1935. Changing Methods and Aims in Prehistory, *Proceedings of the Prehistoric Society* 1: 1–15.

Childe, V.G. 1942. *What Happened in History.* Harmondsworth: Penguin.

Childe, V.G. 1952. Review: *Prehistoric Europe: The Economic Basis* by J.G.D. Clark, *Antiquaries Journal* 32: 209–11.

Clark, J.D. 1942. Further Excavations (1939) at Mumbwa Caves, Northern Rhodesia, *Transactions of the Royal Society of South Africa* 29: 1–239.

Clark, J.D. 1950. *The Stone Age Cultures of Northern Rhodesia with Particular Reference to the Cultural and Climatic Succession in the Upper Zambia Valley and its Tributaries.* Claremont, Cape: South African Archaeological Society.

Clark, J.D. 1989. J. Desmond Clark, in Daniel & Chippindale (ed.): 137–52.

Clark, J.D. 1994. Digging On: A Personal Record and Appraisal of Archaeological Research in Africa and Elsewhere. *Annual Review of Anthropology.* 23: 1–23.

Clark, J.G.D. 1927. Some Hollow-Scrapers from Seaford, *Sussex Archaeological Collections* 68: 273–6.

Clark, J.G.D. 1928. Discoidal Polished Flint Knives: Their Typology and Distribution, *Proceedings of the Prehistoric Society of East Anglia* 6: 40–54.

Clark, J.G.D. 1931. Review: *Weltgeschichte der Steinzeit* by O. Menghin, *Antiquity* 5: 518–21.

Clark, J.G.D. 1932. *The Mesolithic Age in Britain.* Cambridge: Cambridge University Press.

Clark, J.G.D. 1933a. With Reports by W. Jackson, H. & M.E. Godwin, W.A. Macfadyen, and A.S. Kennard. Report on an Early Bronze Age Site in the South-Eastern Fens, *Antiquaries Journal* 13: 266–96.

Clark, J.G.D. 1933b. Review: *The Personality of Britain* by Cyril Fox, *Antiquity* 7: 232–4.

Clark, J.G.D. 1933c. The Classification of a Microlithic Culture: The Tardenoisian of Horsham, *The Archaeological Journal* 90: 52–77.

Clark, J.G.D. 1934. Derivative Forms of the Petit Tranchet, *The Archaeological Journal* 91(Pt.1): 32–58.

Clark, J.G.D. 1935. Fenland Research Committee. *Proceedings of the Cambridge Antiquarian Society* 35: xxix–xxx.

Clark, J.G.D. 1936a. *The Mesolithic Settlement of Northern Europe: A Study of Food-Gathering Peoples of Northern Europe During the Early Post-Glacial Period.* Cambridge: Cambridge University Press.

Clark, J.G.D. 1936b. With Reports by W. Jackson, H. and M.E. Godwin, and M.H. Clifford. Report on a Late Bronze Age site in Mildenhall Fen, West Suffolk, *Antiquaries Journal* 16: 29–50

Clark, J.G.D. 1936c. Current Prehistory, *Proceedings of the Prehistoric Society* 2(2): 239–43, 245–53.

Clark, J.G.D. 1936d. The Timber Monument at Arminghall and its Affinities, *Proceedings of the Prehistoric Society* 2(Pt.1): 1–51.

Clark, J.G.D. 1937a. Review *The Stone Age of Mount Carmel: Excavations at the Wady el-Mughara* 1, by D.A.E. Garrod and D.M.A. Bate, *Proceedings of the Prehistoric Society* 3(2): 486–8.

Clark, J.G.D. 1937b. Current Prehistory, *Proceedings of the Prehistoric Society* 3(1): 166–85.

Clark, J.G.D. 1937c. Current Prehistory, *Proceedings of the Prehistoric Society* 3(2): 467–81.

Clark, J.G.D. 1939a. *Archaeology and Society.* London: Methuen & Co.

Clark, J.G.D. 1939b. Professor D.A.E. Garrod, *Proceedings of the Prehistoric Society* 5(Pt.2): 280.

Clark, J.G.D. 1947. *Archaeology and Society.* 2nd ed. London: Methuen & Co.

Clark, J.G.D. 1949. A Preliminary Report on Excavations at Star Carr, Seamer, Scarborough, Yorkshire, *Proceedings of the Prehistoric Society* 15: 52–69.

Clark, J.G.D. 1954. *Excavations at Star Carr; an Early Mesolithic Site at Seamer near Scarborough, Yorkshire.* Cambridge: Cambridge University Press.

Clark, J.G.D. 1956. The History of Man, *The Cambridge Review* May 26, 1956: 613–14.

Clark, J.G.D. 1959. Perspectives in Prehistory: Presidential Address, *Proceedings of the Prehistoric Society* 1–14.

Clark, J.G.D. 1972. *Star Carr: A Case Study in Bioarchaeology.* Reading (MA): Addison-Wesley Modular Publications. McCaleb Module 10.

Clark, J.G.D. 1974. Prehistoric Europe: The Economic Basis, in G.R. Willey (ed.), *Archaeological Researches in Retrospect*: 33–57. Cambridge (MA): Winthrop Publishers Inc.

Clark, J.G.D. 1985. The Prehistoric Society: From East Anglia to the World, *Proceedings of the Prehistoric Society* 51: 1–13.

Clark, J.G.D. 1989a. *Prehistory at Cambridge and Beyond.* Cambridge: Cambridge University Press.

Clark, J.G.D. 1989b. Early Days in the Development of Postgraduate Research in Prehistoric Archaeology at Cambridge, *Archaeological Review From Cambridge* Occasional Paper 1: 6–12.

Clark, J.G.D. 1993. Foreword, in Spriggs *et al.* (ed.): i–ii.

Clark, J.G.D. 1999. Dorothy Garrod, in T. Murray (ed.), *Encyclopedia of Archaeology. The Great Archaeologists*: 401–12. Oxford & Santa Barbara (CA): ABC-CLIO.

Clark, J.G.D. & H. Godwin. 1940. A Late Bronze Age Find Near Stuntney, Isle of Ely, *Antiquaries Journal* 20: 52-7

Clark, J.G.D., H. & M.E. Godwin & M.H. Clifford. 1935. Report on Recent Excavations at Peacock's Farm, Shippea, Cambridgeshire. With Reports by W. Jackson, A.S. Kennard, and S. Piggott, *Antiquaries Journal* 15: 284–319.

Clark, J.G.D. & S. Piggott. 1933. The Age of the British Flint Mines, *Antiquity* 7: 166–83.

Clarke, L.C.G. 1925. The University Museum of Archaeology and Ethnology, Cambridge, *The Antiquaries Journal* 5: 415–20.

Close, C.F. 1928. Review: *A Report on the Galilee Skull* by Sir Arthur Keith, *Antiquity* 1: 373–4.

Coleman, W. 1985. The Cognitive Basis of the Discipline: Claude Bernard on Physiology, *ISIS* 76: 49–70.

Conway, R.S. 1926. Ridgeway, Sir William (1853–1926), *Dictionary of National Biography 1922–30.* London: Oxford University Press.

Cornford, F.M. 1908. *Microcosmographia Academica: being a guide for the young academic politician.* Cambridge: Bowes & Bowes.

Crawford, O.G.S. 1926. Review: *The Dawn of European Civilization* by V.G. Childe, *The Antiquaries Journal* 6: 89–90.

Crawford, O.G.S. & A. Keiller. 1928. *Wessex from the Air* Oxford: Oxford University Press.

Cuénot, C. 1965. *Teilhard de Chardin: A Biographical Study.* London: Burns & Oates.

Curwen, E.C. 1931. Excavations in the Trundle, *Sussex Archaeological Collections* 72: 100–149.

Curwen, E.C. 1934. Excavations in Whitehawk Neolithic Camp, Brighton 1932–1933, *The Antiquaries Journal* 14: 99–133.

Curwen, E.C. 1941. Review: *Prehistoric England* by J.G.D. Clark, *Antiquity* 15: 202–3.

Daniel, G. 1950. Prehistoric Archaeology in the Universities of Great Britain, *The Archaeological News Letter* 2(9): 137–9.

Daniel, G. 1986. *Some Small Harvest: The Memoirs of Glyn Daniel.* London: Thames & Hudson.

Daniel, G. & C. Chippindale (ed.). 1989. *The Pastmasters: Eleven Modern Pioneers of Archaeology.* London: Thames & Hudson.

Davies, W. & R. Charles (ed.). 1999. *Dorothy Garrod and the Progress of the Palaeolithic Studies in the Prehistoric Archaeology of the Near East and Europe.* Oxford: Oxbow.

Duckworth, W.L.H. 1912. *Prehistoric Man.* Cambridge: Cambridge University Press.

Dudley, B.L.H. 1928. Human Remains, pp. 57–85 in D.A.E. Garrod, L.H.D. Buxton, G. Eliot Smith & D.M.A.Bate, Excavation of a Mousterian Rock-Shelter at Devil's Tower, Gibraltar, *Journal of the Royal Anthropological Institute* 58: 33–113.

Ebin, V. & D.A. Swallow. 1984. *"The Proper Study of Mankind": Great Anthropological Collections in Cambridge.* Cambridge: CUMAA.

Ely, T. 1890. *Manual of Archaeology.* London: H.Grevel.

English, R. 1939. The Disney Professor Elect of Archaeology, *Cambridge Review* 60: (1478): 382.

Epstein, C.F. 1991. Constraints on Excellence: Structural and Cultural Barriers to the Recognition and Demonstration of Achievement, H. Zuckerman, J.R. Cole & J.T. Bruer (ed.), in *The Outer Circle: Women in the Scientific Community,* 239–58. New York (NY): W.W. Norton & Co.

Evans, J.D. 1987. The First Half-Century — and After, *Bulletin of the Institute of Archaeology* 24: 1–25.

Field, H. 1955. *The Track of Man: the Adventures of an Anthropologist.* London: Peter Davies.

Flannery, K.V. 1982. The Golden Marshalltown: A Parable for the Archaeology of the 1980s, *American Anthropologist* 84: 265–78.

Fortes, M. 1953. *Social Anthropology at Cambridge Since 1900.* Cambridge: Cambridge University Press.

Fowler, G.E. 1932. Old River-Beds in the Fenlands, *Geographical Journal* 79: 210–12.

Fowler, G.E. 1933. With Reports by W.A. Macfadyen and A.S. Kennard. Fenland Waterways, Past and Present. South Level District. Part I, *Proceedings of the Cambridge Antiquarian Society* 33: 108–28.

Fowler, G.E. 1934. Fenland Waterways, Past and Present. South Level District. Part II, *Proceedings of the Cambridge Antiquarian Society* 34: 17–33.

Fox, A. 2000. *Aileen— A Pioneering Archaeologist.* Herefordshire: Gracewing.

Fox, C. 1923. *The Archaeology of the Cambridge Region: A Topographical Study of the Bronze, Early Iron, Roman and Anglo-Saxon Ages, with an Introductory Note on the Neolithic Age.* Cambridge: Cambridge University Press.

Fox, C. 1932. *The Personality of Britain: Its Influence on Inhabitant and Invader in Prehistoric and Early Historic Times.* Cardiff: The National Museum of Wales.

Garrod, D.A.E. 1926. *The Upper Palaeolithic Age in Britain.* Oxford: Clarendon Press.

Garrod, D.A.E. 1928a. Nova et Vetera: a Plea for a New Method in Palaeolithic Archaeology. Presidential Address, *Proceedings of the Prehistoric Society of East Anglia* 5: 260–67.

Garrod, D.A.E. 1928b. Excavation of a Palaeolithic Cave in Western Judaea, *Quarterly Statement of the Palestine Exploration Fund* 60: 182–5.

Garrod, D.A.E. 1929. Excavations in the Mugharet El-Wad, near Athlit. April–June 1929. *Quarterly Statement of the Palestine Exploration Fund* 61: 220–22.

Garrod, D.A.E. 1930. The Palaeolithic of Southern Kurdistan: Excavations in the Caves of Zarzi and Hazar Merd, *Bulletin of the American School of Prehistoric Research* 6: 8–43.

Garrod, D.A.E. 1932a. A New Mesolithic Industry: The Natufian of Palestine, *Journal of the Royal Anthropological Institute* 62: 257–69.

Garrod, D.A.E. 1932b. Excavations in the Wady el-Mughara 1931, *Quarterly Statement of the Palestine Exploration Fund* 64: 46–51.

Garrod, D.A.E. 1934. Excavations at the Wady al-Mughara, 1932–3, *Quarterly Statement of the Palestine Exploration Fund* 66: 85–9.

Garrod, D.A.E. 1938. The Upper Palaeolithic in the Light of Recent Discovery, *Proceedings of the Prehistoric Society* 4: 1–26.

Garrod, D.A.E. 1942. Excavations at the Cave of Shukbah, Palestine, 1928, with an Appendix on the Fossil Mammals of Shukbah by D.M.A. Bate, *Proceedings of the Prehistoric Society,* 8: 1–20

Garrod, D.A.E. 1957. The Natufian Culture: The Life and Economy of a Mesolithic People in the Near East, *Proceedings of the British Academy* 43: 211–27.

Garrod, D.A.E. 1962. The Middle Palaeolithic of the Near East and the Problem of Mount Carmel Man, The Huxley Memorial Lecture, 1962, *Journal of the Royal Anthropological Institute* 92: 232–59.

Garrod, D.A.E. 1968. Recollections of Glozel, *Antiquity* 42: 172–7.

Garrod, D.A.E. & D.M.A. Bate. 1937. *The Stone Age of Mount Carmel. Volume 1.* Oxford: Clarendon Press.

Garrod, D.A.E., L.H.D. Buxton, G. Eliot Smith & D.M.A.Bate. 1928. Excavation of a Mousterian Rock-Shelter at Devil's Tower, Gibraltar, *Journal of the Royal Anthropological Institute* 58: 33–113.

Gathercole, P. 1971. 'Patterns in Prehistory': An examination of the Later Thinking of V. Gordon Childe, *World Archaeology* 3: 225–32.

Gathercole, P. 1974. Childe, Empiricism and Marxism. Ms. (this is not in my thesis).

Gathercole, P. 1975. Gordon Childe and the Prehistory of Europe. Ms.

Gathercole, P. 1976. Childe the "Outsider", *RAIN* 17: 5–6.

Gathercole, P. 1977. Cambridge and the Torres Straits, 1888–1920, *Cambridge Anthropology* 3(3): 22–31.

Gathercole, P. 1982. Gordon Childe: Man or Myth? *Antiquity* 56: 195–8.

Gathercole, P. 1984. A Consideration of Ideology, in M. Spriggs (ed.), *Marxist Perspectives in Archaeology:*

149–54 . Cambridge: Cambridge University Press.

Gathercole, P. 1989. Childe's Early Marxism, in V. Pinsky & A. Wylie (ed.), *Critical Traditions in Contemporary Archaeology* : 80–87. Cambridge: Cambridge University Press.

Gathercole, P. 1993. Cambridge: History, Archaeology and Politics, in Spriggs *et al.* (ed.): 1–5.

Gathercole, P. 1994. Childe in History, *Institute of Archaeology Bulletin* 31: 25–52.

Geertz, C. 1973. *The Interpretation of Cultures; Selected Essays.* New York (NY): Basic Books.

Geison, G.L. 1978. *Michael Foster and the Cambridge School of Physiology: The Scientific Enterprise in Late Victorian Society.* Princeton (NJ): Princeton University Press.

Geison, G.L. 1981. Scientific Change, Emerging Specialties and Research Schools, *History of Science* 19: 20–40.

Geison, G.L. 1993. Research Schools and New Directions in the Historiography of Science. Research Schools: Historical Reappraisals, *Osiris* 8: 227–38.

Godwin, H. 1934a. Pollen Analysis. An Outline of the Problems and Potentialities of the Method. Part. I. Technique and Interpretation, *New Phytologist* 33: 278–305.

Godwin, H. 1934b. Pollen Analysis. An Outline of the Problems and Potentialities of the Method. Part II. General Applications of Pollen Analysis, *New Phytologist* 33: 325–58.

Godwin, H. 1938. The Origin of Roddons, *Geographical Journal* 91: 241–50.

Godwin, H. 1978. *Fenland: Its Ancient Past and Uncertain Future.* Cambridge: Polity Press.

Godwin, H. 1985. *Cambridge and Clare.* Cambridge: Cambridge University Press.

Godwin, H., M.E. Godwin, J.G.D. Clark & M.H. Clifford. 1934. A Bronze Age Spear-head Found in the Methwold Fen, Norfolk, *Proceedings of the Prehistoric Society of East Anglia* 7: 395–8.

Goldberg, P. & O. Bar-Yosef. 1998. Site Formation Processes in Kebara and Hayonim Caves and Their Significance in Levantine Prehistoric Caves, in Akazawa *et al.* (ed.): 107–25.

Goodwin, A.J.H. & C. van Riet Lowe. 1929. The Stone Age Cultures of South Africa. *Annals of the South African Museum* 27: 1–289. Cape Town: Trustees of the South African Museum.

Gould, P. 1997. Women and the Culture of University Physics in late Nineteenth-Century Cambridge, *British Journal for the History of Science* 30: 127–49.

Gould, P. 1998. Making Space for Women Science Students in Early Twentieth Century Cambridge, in *The Transformation of an Elite*: 120–29

Graham, P.A. 1978. Expansion and Exclusion: A History of Women in American Higher Education, *Signs* 3(4): 759–73.

Green, S. 1981. *Prehistorian: A Biography of V. Gordon Childe.* Bradford-on-Avon: Moonraker Press.

Guba Egon, G. & Y.S. Lincoln. 1981. *Effective Evaluation: Improving the Usefulness of Evaluation Results Through Responsive and Naturalistic Approaches.* San Francisco (CA): Jossey-Bass Publishers.

Haddon, A.C. 1928. Obituary, Baron Anatole von Hügel, *Man* 28: 169–71.

Hagen, J.B. 1993. Clementsian Ecologists: The Internal Dynamics of a Research School. Research Schools: Historical Reappraisals, *Osiris* 8: 178–95.

Hall, D. & J. Coles. 1994. *Fenland Survey: An Essay in Landscape and Persistence.* London: English Heritage. Archaeological Report I.

Halliday, D.L. 1979. Years of Renaissance, in Phillips (ed.): 136–43.

Hardwig, J. 1991. The Role of Trust in Knowledge, *The Journal of Philosophy* 88(12): 693–708.

Harris, D.R. 1977. Socio-economic Archaeology and the Cambridge Connection, *World Archaeology* 9(1): 113–19.

Hawkes, C.F.C. 1989. Christopher Hawkes, in Daniel & Chippindale (ed.): 46–60.

Heurtley, W.A. 1931. Review: *The Danube in Prehistory* by V.G. Childe, *Antiquity* 5: 124–5.

Heyck, T.W. 1982. *The Transformation of Intellectual Life in Victorian England.* London & Canberra: Croom Helm.

Historical Register of the University of Cambridge: Supplement 1921–30. Cambridge: Cambridge University Press.

Historical Register of the University of Cambridge: Supplement 1931–1940. Cambridge: Cambridge University Press.

Howarth, J. 1998. Gender at Cambridge and Oxford, 1900–1950, in *The Transformation of an Elite*: 99–119.

Hublin, J.-J. 2000. Modern-Nonmodern Hominid Interactions: A Mediterranean Perspective, in Bar-Yosef & Pilbeam (ed.): 157–82.

Hutton, M. and G.H.S. Bushnell. 1962. Obituary Notices: L.C.G. Clarke, LL.D and FSA 1881–1960, *Proceedings of the Cambridge Antiquarian Society* 55: 1–5.

Illustrated London News. New relics of man 20,000 years old: the Gibraltar skull, 28 August 1926: 379.

Johnson, G. 1994. *University politics: F.M. Cornford's Cambridge and his advice to the young academic politician.* Cambridge: Cambridge University Press.

Johnson, R. & G. Dawson. 1998. Popular memory: theory, politics, method, in Perks & Thomson (ed.): 75–86.

Jordanova, L. 1993. Gender and the Historiography of Science, *British Journal for the History of Science* 26: 469–83.

Kaufman, D.R. 1978. Associational Ties in Academe: Some Male and Female Differences, *Sex Roles* 4: 9–21.

Keith, A. 1925. Galilee Skull: New Light on Early Man, *The Times*, 14 August 1925: 37. (CUL Microfilm Room.)

Keith, A. 1927. *Report on the Galilee Skull.* London: British School of Archaeology in Jerusalem.

Keith, A. 1929. Palestine as a home of Ancient Man, *The Illustrated London News,* 2 February 1929: 178–9.

Keith-Walters, S. 1979. She Shimmies Like the Deuce, in Phillips (ed.): 162–4.

Kingsford, H.S. 1934. Notes, *The Antiquaries Journal* 14: 53.

Kluckhohn, C. 1936. Some Reflections on the Method and Theory of the Kulturkreislehre, *American Anthropologist* 38(2): 137–96.

Koslowski, J 1999. The Evolution of the Balkan Aurignacian, in Davies & Charles (ed.): 97–117. Oxford: Oxbow.

Kuhn, T.S . 1963. *The Structure of Scientific Revolutions.* 2nd impr. Chicago (IL): Chicago University Press.

Lang, E.M. 1929. *British Women in the 20th Century.* London: T.W. Laurie.

Langham, I. 1981. *The Building of British Social Anthropology: W.H.R. Rivers and his Cambridge Disciples in the Development of Kinship Studies, 1898–1931.* Dordrecht: D. Reidel.

Leach, E.R. 1984. Glimpses of the Unmentionable in the History of British Social Anthropology. *Annual Review of Anthropology* 13: 1-23.

Leaf, C.S. 1938. Further Excavation in Bronze Age Barrows at Chippenham, Cambridgeshire, *Proceedings of the Cambridge Antiquarian Society* 39: 29–68.

Leakey, L.S.B. 1931. *The Stone Age Cultures of Kenya Colony.* Cambridge: Cambridge University Press.

Leakey, L.S.B. 1934. *Adam's Ancestors: an Up-to-Date Outline of what is Known about the Origins of Man.* London: Methuen.

Leakey, L.S.B. 1936. *Stone Age Africa: An Outline of Prehistory in Africa.* Oxford: Oxford University Press.

Leask, H.G. 1950. Obituary: R.A.S. Macalister, *Journal of the Royal Society of the Antiquaries of Ireland* 80: 269–70.

Leedham-Green, E. 1996. *A Concise History of the University of Cambridge.* Cambridge: Cambridge University Press.

Lethbridge, T.C. 1931. A Skeleton of the Early Bronze Age Found in the Fens. With Reports by G.E. Fowler and R.U. Sayce, *Proceedings of the Prehistoric Society of East Anglia* 6: 360–64.

Livingstone, D.N. 1996. High Tea at the Cyclotron: Science as a Social Practice, *Books & Culture* January/ February: 22–3.

Macalister, R.A.S. 1921. *A Text-Book of European Archaeology: Palaeolithic Period.* Cambridge: Cambridge University Press.

MacCurdy, G.G. 1937. Foreword, in Garrod & Bate (1937): v.

MacLeod, R. & R. Moseley. 1979. Fathers and Daughters: Reflections on Women, Science and Victorian Cambridge, *History of Education* 8: 321–33.

Marett, R.R. 1912. Further Observations on Prehistoric Man in Jersey, *Archaeologia* 63: 203–30.

Marett, R.R. 1916. The Site, Fauna and Industry of La Cotte de St Brelade, Jersey, *Archaeologia* 67: 75–118.

McBurney, C. 1976. A Tribute to Grahame Clark, in Sieveking *et al.* (ed.): xi–xiv.

McNairn, B. 1980. *The Method and Theory of V. Gordon Childe.* Edinburgh: Edinburgh University Press.

McWilliams-Tullberg, R. 1975. *Women at Cambridge: A Men's University — Though of a Mixed Type.* London: Gollancz.

Menghin, O. 1933. Review: *The Mesolithic Age in Britain,* by J.G.D. Clark, *Antiquity* 7: 242–3.

Merchant, C. 1982. Isis' Consciousness Raised, *ISIS* 73: 398–409.

Morrell, J.B. 1972. The Chemist Breeders: The Research Schools of Liebig and Thomas Thomson, *Ambix* 19: 1–49.

Morrell, J.B. 1993. W.H. Perkin, Jr., at Manchester and Oxford: from Irwell to Isis. Research Schools: Historical Reappraisals, *Osiris* 8: 104–26.

Mulvaney, J.D. 1980. Obituary, Charles McBurney, *Australian Archaeology* 10: 105–6.

Mulvaney, J. 1990. Review: *Prehistory at Cambridge and Beyond* by Grahame Clark, *The Cambridge Review: a Journal of University Life and Thought* 3 (2310): 115–19.

Mulvaney, J.D. 1996. Obituary, Grahame Clark (1907–1995), *Australian Archaeology* 42: 54–5.

Munro, R. 1921 *Autobiographical Sketch.* Glasgow: Maclehose, Jackson & Co.

Murray, L.J. 1999. *A Zest for Life.* Swindon: Morven Books.

Murray, T. (ed.). 1999. *Encyclopedia of Archaeology. The Great Archaeologists.* Oxford & Santa Barbara (CA): ABC-CLIO.

Needham, J. 1962. Frederick Gowland Hopkins *Perspectives in Biology and Medicine* 6(1): 1–46.

Needham, J. 1976. Interview, *The Caian* (November): 34–49.

Nunoo, R. 1993. Thurstan Shaw and West African Archaeology: The Case of Ghana, in *Imprints of West Africa's Past (Les Emprints du Passe d'Afrique de l'Ouest)*: 25–31. Ibadan: Wisdom Publishers.

Obermaier, H. 1924. *Fossil Man in Spain.* New Haven (CT): Yale University Press.

Ophir, A. & S. Shapin. 1991. The Place of Knowledge: A Methodological Survey, *Science in Context* 4: 3–21.

Oram, A. 1989. 'Embittered, Sexless or Homosexual': Attacks on Spinster Teachers 1918–39, in A. Angerman, G. Binnema, A. Keunen, V. Poels & J. Zirkzee (ed.), *Current Issues in Women's History*: 183–201. London: Routledge.

Palmer, S. 1977. *Mesolithic Cultures of Britain*. Poole: The Dolphin Press.

Partridge, F. 1981. *Memories*. London: Victor Gollancz.

Peace, W.J. 1988. Vere Gordon Childe and American Anthropology, *Journal of Anthropological Research* 44: 417–33.

Peake, H.J.E. 1921. Review: *Prehistory: a Study of Early Cultures in Europe and the Mediterranean Basin* by M.C. Burkitt, *Man* (112): 189–90.

Peake, H.J.E. 1924. Review: *The Archaeology of the Cambridge Region. A Topographical Study of the Bronze, Early Iron, Roman and Anglo-Saxon Ages, with an Introductory Note on the Neolithic Age* by Cyril Fox, *Man* 24(82): 111–2.

Peake, H.J.E. & O.G.S. Crawford. 1922. A Flint Factory at Thatcham, Berks., *Proceedings of the Prehistoric Society of East Anglia* 3: 499–514.

Percival, S.T. 1934. Neolithic and Early Bronze Age Settlement at Broom Hill. With Stuart Piggott, *The Antiquaries Journal* 14: 246–53.

Perkin, H. 1989. *The Rise of Professional Society: England since 1880*. London & New York (NY): Routledge.

Perks, R. & A. Thomson (ed.). 1998. *The Oral History Reader*. London: Routledge.

Phillips, A. (ed.). 1979. *A Newnham Anthology*. Cambridge: Newnham College

Phillips, C.W. 1932. The Roman Ferry Across The Wash, *Antiquity* 6: 342–8.

Phillips, C.W. 1951. The Fenland Research Committee, its Past Achievements and Future Prospects, in W.F. Grimes (ed.), *Aspects of Archaeology in Britain and Beyond: Essays Presented to O.G.S. Crawford*: 258–72. London: H.W. Edwards.

Phillips, C.W. 1987. *My Life in Archaeology*. Gloucester: Alan Sutton.

Phillips, C.W. 1989. Charles Phillips, in Daniel & Chippindale (ed.): 34–45.

Pickles, J.D. 1988. The Haddon Library, Cambridge, *Library History* 8(1): 1–9.

Piggott, S. 1935. Report by Stuart Piggott, in Clark *et al.* (1935): 302–3.

Piggott, S. 1936. The Pottery from the Submerged Surface, pp. 186–201 in Warren *et al.*, Archaeology of the Submerged Land-Surface of the Essex Coast, *Proceedings of the Prehistoric Society* 2: 178–210.

Piggott, S. 1963. Archaeology and Prehistory, Presidential Address, *Proceedings of the Prehistoric Society* 29:1–16.

Piggott, S. 1989. Stuart Piggott, in Daniel & Chippindale (ed.): 20–33.

Pollard, J.G. 1978. The Cambridge Antiquarian Society, *Proceedings of the Cambridge Antiquarian Society* 68: 105–16.

Porter, R. 1982. The Natural Sciences Tripos and the 'Cambridge School of Geology', 1850–1914, *History of Universities* 2: 193–216.

Porter, R. & G.S. Rousseau. 1998. *Gout: the Patrician Malady*. New Haven (CT): Yale University Press.

Price, T.D. 1981. Transitions in Time, *Quarterly Review of Archaeology* 2(4): 2–8.

Price, T.D. 1983. The European Mesolithic, *American Antiquity* 48(4): 761–78.

Quiggin, A.H. 1912. *Primeval Man. The Stone Age in Western Europe*. London: MacDonald & Evans.

Quiggin, A.H. 1942. *Haddon the Head-hunter: a Short Sketch of the Life of A.C. Haddon*. Cambridge: Cambridge University Press.

Quinton, A. 1987. Review: *Some Small Harvest: the Memoirs of Glyn Daniel* by Glyn Daniel, *Antiquity* 61: 139–40.

Read, C.H. 1906. Anthropology at the Universities, *MAN* 38: 56–9.

Read, C.H. 1922. Review: *Prehistory: a Study of Early Cultures in Europe and the Mediterranean Basin* by M.C. Burkitt, *The Antiquaries Journal* 2: 75–6.

Reinach, S. 1903. L'art et la magie. A propos des peintures et des gravures de l'Age du Renne, *L'Anthropologie* 14: 257–66.

Renfrew, A.C. 1986. Review: *Symbols of Excellence: Precious Materials as Expressions of Status* by J.G.D. Clark, *Antiquity* 60: 238–9.

Renfrew, A.C. & P. Bahn. 2000. *Archaeology: Theories, Methods and Practice*. London: Thames & Hudson.

Reporter. Cambridge: Cambridge University Press.

Richmond, M.L. 1997. "A Lab of One' Own": The Balfour Biological Laboratory for Women at Cambridge University, 1884–1914, *ISIS* 88: 422–55.

Roberts, A.J. 1999. The Path not Taken: Dorothy Garrod, Devon and the British Palaeolithic, in Davies & Charles (ed.): 19–34.

Rosenberg, C. 1979. Toward an Ecology of Knowledge: On Discipline, Context, and History, in A. Oleson & J. Voss (ed.), *The Organization of Knowledge in Modern America 1860–1920*: 440–55. Baltimore (MD) & London: Johns Hopkins University Press.

Rouse, S. 1999. Haddon, Missionaries and "Men of Affairs", *Cambridge Anthropology* 21(1): 9–27.

Samuel, R. 1998. Perils of the transcript, in Perks & Thomson (ed.): 389–92.

Sayce, R.U. 1933. *Primitive Arts and Crafts: an Introduction to the Study of Material Culture*. Cambridge: Cambridge University Press.

Schuster, A. 1921. Obituary: John William Strutt, Baron Rayleigh, *Proceedings of the Royal Society Series A* 98: I–L (1–50).

Sciama, L. 1984. Ambivalence and Dedication: Academic Wives in Cambridge University 1870–1970, in H. Callan & S. Ardener (ed.), *The Incorporated Wife*: 50–66. London: Croom Helm.

Scott-Fox, C. 2002. *Cyril Fox, Archaeologist Extraordinary*. Oxford: Oxbow.

Secord, J.A. 1986. The Geological Survey of Great Britain as a Research School. 1839–1855, *History of Science* 24: 223–75.

Servos, J.W. 1993. Research Schools and their Histories. Research Schools: Historical Reappraisals, *Osiris* 8: 3–15.

Shapin, S. 1992. Discipline and Bounding: The History and Sociology of Science as Seen Through the Externalism-Internalism Debate, *History of Science* 30: 333–69.

Shapin, S. 1994. *A Social History of Truth: Civility and Science in Seventeenth-Century England.* Chicago (IL): University of Chicago Press.

Shapin, S. 1998. Placing the View from Nowhere: Historical and Sociological Problems in the Location of Science, *Transactions of the Institute of British Geography* 23: 5–12.

Shaw, C.T. 1943. *Archaeology in the Gold Coast. African Studies* (Johannesburg) 2(3): 139–47.

Shaw, C.T. 1944. Report on Excavations Carried out in the Cave Known as Bosumpra at Abetifi, Kwahu, Gold Coast Colony, *Proceedings of the Prehistoric Society* 10: 1–67.

Shaw, C.T. 1946. The Anthropology Museum at Achimota College, Accra, Gold Coast, *Museums Journal* 45(2): 189–90.

Shaw, C.T. 1990. A Personal Memoir, in Peter Robertshaw (ed.), *A History of African Archaeology*: 205–20. London: James Curry.

Sherbakova, I. 1998. The Gulag in Memory, in Perks & Thomson (ed.): 235–45.

Shore, A.F. (ed.). 1985. *The School of Archaeology and Oriental Studies, University of Liverpool: its History and Collections.* Liverpool: School of Archaeology, Classics and Oriental Studies, University of Liverpool.

Shostak, M. 1998. 'What the Wind Won't Take Away': the Genesis of Nisa — the Life and Works of a !Kung Woman, in Perks & Thomson (ed.): 402–13 .

Sieveking, G. 1976. Progress in Economic and Social Archaeology, in Sieveking *et al.* (ed.): xvi–xxvi.

Sieveking, G. de G., I.N. Longworth & K.E. Wilson (ed.). 1976. *Problems in Economic and Social Archaeology. A Tribute to Grahame Clark.* London: Duckworth.

Skinner, Q. 1969. Meaning and Understanding in the History of Ideas, *History and Theory* 8: 3–53.

Smith, P.J. 1997. Grahame Clark's New Archaeology, *Antiquity* 71: 11–30.

Smith, P.J. 1997–8. "A Passionate Connoisseur of Flints": an Intellectual Biography of the Young Grahame Clark based on his Pre-war Publications, *Archaeologia Polonia*: 35–6: 385–408.

Smith, P.J. 1998. From "small, dark and alive" to "cripplingly shy": Dorothy Garrod as the First Woman Professor at Cambridge, in *The Transformation of an Elite*: 199–225.

Smith, P. J. 2000a. Dorothy Garrod as the first woman Professor at Cambridge University, *Antiquity* 74: 131–6.

Smith, P. J. 2000b. The coup: how did the Prehistoric Society of East Anglia become the Prehistoric Society?, *Proceedings of the Prehistoric Society* 65: 465–70.

Smith, P.J., J. Callander, P.G. Bahn & G. Pinçon. 1997. Dorothy Garrod in words and pictures, *Antiquity* 71: 265–70.

Soffer, R.N. 1982. Why do Disciplines Fail? The Strange Case of British Sociology, *The English Historical Review* 97(385): 767–802.

Soffer, R.N. 1994. *Discipline and Power: the University, History, and the Making of an English Elite, 1870–1930.* Stanford: Stanford University Press.

Solecki, R.S. 1972. *Shanidar: the Humanity of Neanderthal Man.* London: Allen Lane The Penguin Press.

Sollas, W.J. 1924. *Ancient Hunters and their Modern Representatives.* 3rd ed. London: Macmillan.

Sonnert, G. & G.J. Holton. 1995. *Gender Differences in Science Careers: the Project Access Study.* New Brunswick (NJ): Rutgers University Press.

Souter, A., R.H. Connolly, B.H. Streeter, E.C. Ratcliff & G.G. Coulton. 1935. Francis Burkitt, *The Journal of Theological Studies* 36: 225–54.

Spriggs, M., D.E. Yen, W. Ambrose, R. Jones, A. Thorne & A. Andrews (ed.) 1993. *A Community of Culture, the People and Prehistory of the Pacific.* Canberra: Australian National University. Occasional Papers in Prehistory 21.

Stephen, B.N. 1927. *Emily Davies and Girton College.* London: Constable.

Stephenson, A.M.G. 1984 .*The Rise and Decline of English Modernism: the Hulsean Lectures 1979–80.* London: SPCK.

Stocking, G.W. 1984. Radcliffe-Brown and British Anthropology, *History of Anthropology Newsletter* 2: 131–91.

Stocking, G.W. 1996. *After Tylor: British Social Anthropology 1888–1951.* London: Athlone Press.

Stoddart, S. & C. Malone. 2002. Editorial, *Antiquity* 76: 915–24.

Stray, C. 1998. *Classics Transformed. Schools, Universities and Society in England 1830–1960.* Oxford: Clarendon Press.

Stray, C. 1999. The First Century of the Classical Tripos (1822–1922): High Culture and the Politics of Curriculum, in C. Stray (ed.), *Classics in the 19th & 20th Century: Curriculum, Culture and Community*: 1–14. Cambridge: Cambridge Philological Society. Supplementary Vol. 24.

Sutherland, G. 1994. Emily Davies, the Sidgwicks and the Education of Women in Cambridge, in Richard Mason (ed.), *Cambridge Minds*: 34–47. Cambridge: Cambridge University Press.

Sutherland, G. 1998. " . . . nasty forward minxes": Cambridge and the Higher Education of Women, in *The Transformation of an Elite*: 85–98.

Swinnerton, H.H. 1931. The Post-Glacial Deposits of the Linconshire Coast, *Quarterly Journal of the Geological Society* 87: 360–75.

Tallgren, A.M. 1937. The Method of Prehistoric Archaeology, *Antiquity* 7: 152–61.

Tansley, A.G. 1935. The Use and Abuse of Vegetational

Concepts and Terms, *Ecology* 16: 284–307.

Tchernov, E. 1998. The Faunal Sequence of the Southwest Asian Middle Palaeolithic in Relation to Hominid Dispersal Events, in Akazawa *et al.* (ed.): 77–90.

The Times. Obituary: Francis Crawford Burkitt, 13 May 1935.

The Transformation of an Elite? Women and Higher Education since 1900. 1998. An Academic Conference to Mark the Fiftieth Anniversary of Women's Full Membership in the University. Transcripts of the Day's Proceedings. Cambridge: University of Cambridge.

Thersites. 1913–15. Cambridge: Newnham College.

Thompson, P. 1998. The Voice of the Past: Oral History, in Perks & Thomson (ed.): 21–8.

Thompson, M.W. 1990. *The Cambridge Antiquarian Society 1840–1990.* Cambridge: Cambridge Antiquarian Society.

Tillyard, E.M.W. 1958. *The Muse Unchanged: An Intimate Account of the Revolution in English Studies at Cambridge.* London: Bowes & Bowes.

Trigger, B.G. 1980. *Gordon Childe, Revolutions in Archaeology.* London: Thames & Hudson.

Trigger, B.G. 1982. If Childe Were Alive Today, *Bulletin of the Institute of Archaeology, University of London* 19: 1–20.

Trigger, B.G. 1984. Childe and Soviet Archaeology, *Australian Archaeology* 18: 1–16.

Trigger, B.G. 1986. The Role of Technology in V. Gordon Childe's Archaeology, *Norwegian Archaeological Review* 19: 1–14.

Trigger, B.G. 1989. *A History of Archaeological Thought.* Cambridge: Cambridge University Press.

Trigger, B.G. 1994. Childe's Relevance to the 1990s, in D.R. Harris (ed.), *The Archaeology of V. Gordon Childe*: 9–34. London: University College London.

Tringham, R. 1983. V. Gordon Childe 25 Years After: His Relevance for the Archaeology of the Eighties, *Journal of Field Archaeology* 10: 85–100.

Urry, J. 1985. W.E. Armstrong and Social Anthropology at Cambridge, 1922–26, *Man* 20(3): 412–33.

Van Giffen, A.E. 1938. Continental Bell - or Disc - Barrows in Holland, *Proceedings of the Prehistoric Society* 4(Pt.2): 258–71.

Ward Perkins, J.B. 1936. Proceedings of the Prehistoric Society for 1936, *The Archaeological Journal* 93: 295–7.

Warren, H.S. 1922. Man and the Ice Age, *Man* 22(105): 182–3.

Warren, H.S., J.G.D. Clark, H. & M.E. Godwin & W.A. Macfadyen. 1934. An Early Mesolithic Site at Broxbourne Sealed Under Boreal Peat, *Journal of the Royal Anthropological Institute of Great Britain and Ireland* 64: 101–28.

Warren, H.S., S. Piggott, J.G.D. Clark, M.C. Burkitt, H. Godwin & M.E. Godwin. 1936. Archaeology of the Submerged Land-Surface of the Essex Coast, *Proceedings of the Prehistoric Society* 2: 178–210.

Webster, D.B. 1991. *Hawkeseye: the early life of Christopher Hawkes.* Far Thrupp: Alan Sutton.

Weinstein-Evron, M. 1998. *Early Natufian el-Wad Revisited.* Liège: Etudes et Recherches Archéologiques de l'Université de Liège.

Westerman, W. 1998. Central American Refugee Testimonies, in Perks & Thomson (ed.): 224–34.

Wheeler, R.E.M. 1955. *Still Digging: Interleaves from an Antiquary's Notebook.* London: Michael Joseph.

White, G.M. 1934a. Prehistoric Remains from Selsey Bill, *The Antiquaries Journal* 14: 40–52.

White, G.M. 1934b. An Acheulean Hand-Axe from Chichester, *Proceedings of the Prehistoric Society of East Anglia* 7: 420–21.

White, G.M. 1935. A New Roman Inscription from Chichester. *The Antiquaries Journal* 15: 461–4.

White, G.M. 1936. The Chichester Amphitheatre: Preliminary Excavations, *The Antiquaries Journal* 16: 149–57.

Widnall, S.E. 1988. AAAS Presidential Lecture: Voices from the Pipeline, *Science* 241: 1740–45.

Willey, B. 1968. *Cambridge and Other Memories 1920–1953.* London: Chatto & Windus/New York (NY): W.W. Norton.

Willey, G.R. 1990. *New World Archaeology and Culture History: Collected Essays and Articles by G.R. Willey.* Albuquerque (NM): University of New Mexico Press.

Willey, G.R. 1991. Review: *Prehistory at Cambridge and Beyond* by J.G.D. Clark, *Journal of Field Archaeology* 18: 222–4.

Williamson, R.P.R. 1930. Excavations in Whitehawk Neolithic Camp, near Brighton, *Sussex Archaeological Collections* 61: 57–96.

Wordie, J.M. 1934. Comments, p. 38 in G. Fowler, The Extinct Waterways of the Fens, *Geographical Journal* 83: 30–39.

Wright, D. 2000. Gender and Professionalization of History in English Canada before 1960, *The Canadian Historical Review* 81: 29–66.

Wylie, M.A. 1989. Matters of Fact and Matters of Interest, in S. Shennan (ed.), *Archaeological Approaches to Cultural Identity*: 94–109. London: Unwin Hyman.

Wylie, M.A. 1992. The Interplay of Evidential Constraints and Political Interests: Recent Archaeological Research on Gender, *American Antiquity* 57: 15–35.

Wymer, J. 1999. *The Lower Palaeolithic Occupation of Britain.* Vol. 1. Salisbury: Wessex Archaeology/ English Heritage.

Zeuner, F.E. 1946. *Dating the Past: An Introduction to Geochronology.* London: Methuen.

Zollikofer, C.P.E., M.S. Ponce de Léon, R.D. Martin & P. Stucki. 1995. Neanderthal Computer Skulls, *Nature* 375: 283–5.

Manuscript Sources: Archived and Un-archived

Antiquarian Committee Minutes, CUMAA Box 19 mm/2/5.

Antiquarian Committee Minute Book May 1914–November 1924, in possession of CUMAA.

Board of Anthropological Studies Minutes, July 1908–May 1915: CUMAA Box 19 mm1/3/2.

Board of Anthropological Studies Minutes, 1915–26: CUA Min.V.92.

Beard, M. [2002]. Draft "Sir William Ridgeway", in possession of Mary Beard.

Browning M.E. 1989. *Theories, Facts, and Artifacts: R.G. Collingwood and the Baconian Revolution in Romano-British Studies.* Unpublished Ph.D thesis in History, University of Chicago, Chicago (IL).

Burkitt, M.C. Papers: CUL Add. 7959, Boxes 1–5.

Burkitt Family Archives, in possession of the Burkitt Family, held at the Burkitt home, Merton House, in Grantchester, Cambridge.

Burkitt Photographs, in possession of the Burkitt Family.

Callander, J. 2002. *"A Beautiful Mousterian Industry": Dorothy Garrod's Discoveries in Layer D of Shukbah Cave in Palestine Reconsidered.* Unpublished MA Thesis, Institute of Archaeology, University College London.

CAS Minutes of Ordinary Meetings: Volume 3: 1908–27, in possession of the Haddon Library.

CAS Minutes of Council Meetings: Volume 5: 1910–23, in possession of the Haddon Library.

Clark, J.G.D. Papers, CUL Add. 9409.

Clarke, L. 1934. Draft of Museum Report, CUMAA Box 120 mm2/2/3.

Class notes and examination papers donated by former students: Peter Gathercole; Robin Kenward, née Place; and Jane Waley, née McFie, in possession of P.J. Smith.

Council of the Senate Minutes 1938–1942, CUA Min.I. 26 & 27.

Correspondence relevant to this study in possession of P. J. Smith. Some are listed by their maiden names only: Abraham, R.G., Adams, L., Alexander, J., Anderson, C.W., Anderton, E.A., Armit, M.E., Ashbee, P. (6 letters), Bahn, P. (3 letters), Baker, A. (10 letters), Baldwin, M.W., Baldwin, P., Bank, J.M., Barke, J.W., Barnes, J. (4 letters), Barr, W., Bart, W., Beauchamp, F., Bennett, Mrs, Beresford, M., Bertram, G.C.L., Blake, A.I., Blue, G. (5 letters), Bonner, T., Bookless, R.G., Box, M.G., Braidwood, G., Bray, W., Britton-Strong, R., Bromwich, R., Brockway, E.F. (3 letters), Brown, H.R., Burkitt, C. (5 letters), Burkitt, M. (2 letters), Caesaranni, G., Callander, J. (30 letters), Callister, E.A.M., Champion, T., Chippindale, C. (20 letters), Charles, R., Chakrawarfe, P., Chardin, D., Chitty Kitson Clark, M. (15 letters), Christenson, A., Clark, J.D. (8 letters), Clark, E., Clark, J.G.D.

(8 letters), Clark, J., Clark, M. (3 letters), Coles, J., Conway, P.R., Conn, M., Connell, G., Coorlawala, M., Copeland, L., Cormack, J., Cox, J., Cranstone, I.M., Cra'ster, M., Cremona, P., Crew, E., Crook, U.M., Crookes, M., Daniel, R. (4 letters), Davials, J.A., Dent, J., Donnison, L.J., Duckett, D.G., Duke, A. (5 letters), Elston, J. (6 letters), Embree, L. (2 letters), Erskine, R., Evans, J. (5 letters), Fagan, B., Feachem, R. (4 letters), Fell, C. (7 letters), Finnegan, G., Fisher, J.M., Fitch, D., Forbis, F., Fotheringham, A., Fox, A. (4 letters), Fremantle, K.D.H., French, E., French, C., Furness, A.E., Gadd, J., Gamble, M., Gathercole, P. (12 letters), Gibbard, J., Givens, D. (10 letters), Gill, D. (6 letters), Glynn, J., Glemser, M., Golding, M.S., Golson, J. (5 letters), Goody, J., Gosset, M.B., Greene, K. (3 letters), Greison, P., Hallam, S. (6 letters), Hammond, N., Harper, K., Haughey, F., Hartley, B., Hawkes, S. (2 letters), Henderson, I.B., Hetzel, P. (4 letters), Hodgess Roger, F., Hogarth, J., Horne,(Macalister), E.M.S. (4 letters), Howe, B. (8 letters), Hoxter, S.C, Hughes, J., Hurst, J. (8 letters), Innes, J., Inskeep, A., Inskeep, R. (4 letters), Lech, J., Jeffreys, Lady, Jelinek, A. J. (2 letters), Johnson, E., Jones, T., Kehoe, A., Kenward, J.R.D., Kenward, M.R. (Place). (14 letters), Lane, V., LaFontaine, J.S., Lawes, C., Lawry, R.E., Leaf (Sharland) Freydis, M. (4 letters), LeSage, A., Lethbridge, M. (10 letters), Lillico, J.W. (2 letters), Livingstone, D., Lyons, Miss., McBurney, A., Macfarlane, A., McFie, (Waley) J.M. (4 letters), MacGregor, D.B., McKearney, P., McPherson, S., Maeg, D., Mason, F. (4 letters), Mason, J., Mayer, A., Mead, T., Miller, E., Millett, P.C., Mulvaney, D.J. (8 letters), Morris, J., Munn, M., Murdock, B., Munro-Harrap, M., Nanavutty, P. (Jungalwalla), Neild, M.B., Noble, W., Nutter, M.C., Oakey, L.J.; Orey, J., Orr, R., Osmund, A., Parker, E., Parry, J. (3 letters), Pedoe, N.M., Perry, E. W., Peter, A., Phillip, J.G., Phillips, J., Phillips, P. (4 letters), Pickard,O.G.., Pickles, J. (8 letters), Piggott, S. (3 letters), Platel, M., Plunkett, S., Pollard, J.G., Posnansky, M. (6 letters), Powala, S.M., Priest, S.C., Proudfoot, E., Pulvertaft-Green, L., Rawlence, J.M., Reynolds, J., Richards, C., Richardson, H.H. (6 letters), Robert, N., Roberts, J. (6 letters), Robertson, E.G. (2 letters), Roe, D., Ronan, A., Roskins, B., Rossiter, M., Rouse, S. (8 letters), Rowley-Conwy, P., Salazar, P., Salt, G., Saumarez Smith, B., Sears, H., Sewell, A.M.N., Shell, C., Sieveking, A., Sieveking, G., Smith, R.T., Speak, C., Spence, G.M (Tennant)., Stone, T., Summers, I.M.R., Sutherland, G., Thompson, M.W.(4 letters), Thomas, A.P., Thomson, A., Tomkinson, S., Townsend, J.P., Tremantes, K., Trigger, B. (4 letters), Underwood, M., Vaughan-Jones, Walker, J.M., Wallace, C., West, R., Wheatley, D., White, M., Whitaker, I. (4 letters), Wilkinson, M.E. (2 letters), Wilson, S., Winker, P.A., and Woodward, F.J.

CUMAA Letters and reports from Box 23 mm1/1/1; Box 19 mm1/3/2; and Box 19.

CUMAA Letter Boxes dated by year.

Cunning, J. Cambridge University Museum of Archaeology and Anthropology History, CUMAA Box 259 mm1/1/14.

Daniel, G. Letters, CUMAA Box 111 wo7/1/1.

Denston, C.B. no date, unpublished autobiography in possession of Charles Bernard Denston.

Elections to Professorships 1883–1944, CUA O.XIV.54.

Elections to Professorships 1944–1960, CUA O.XIV.54A.

Faculty Appointment Committee notes, CUMAA Box 206 mm1/2/23.

Faculty of Archaeology and Anthropology Board Minutes 1927–1943, CUA Min.V.92a.

Faculty of Archaeology and Anthropology Board Minutes 1944–1947,CUA Min.V.94.

Faculty of Archaeology and Anthropology Board Minutes 1947–1952, CUA Min.V.95.

Faculty of Archaeology and Anthropology Board Minutes 1952–1954, CUA Min.V.96.

Faculty and Appointments Committee Minutes 1926–1962, CUA Min.V.93.

Fenland Foraminifera: Fenland Research Committee File [1960], Dead Curator's Cabinet, Sedgwick Museum of Geology.

Fenland Research Committee File, Dead Curator's Cabinet, Sedgwick Museum of Geology.

Fenland Research Committee Minute Book, 1932–1948, CUL Add. MS 9426.

Fonds Suzanne Cassou de Saint-Mathurin de la Bibliothèque du Musée des Antiquités Nationales de Saint Germain-en-Laye: includes both Garrod's and Saint-Mathurin's papers. Saint-Mathurin's material is stored in separate boxes from the Garrod papers but contain some Garrod material. This material is not accessioned.

Fonds Germaine Henri-Martin de la Bibliothèque du Musée des Antiquités Nationales de Saint Germain-en-Laye: Henri-Martin's papers are stored at the MAN along with Garrod's and Saint Mathurin's papers. Henri-Martin's papers contain correspondence from and photographs of Garrod.

Fortes Papers, CUL Add. 8405.

Foundation Deed of the Disney Professorship of Archaeology, CUA O.XIV.4.

Fowler, G.E. 1933. A Report to the Fen Research Company. Unpublished Paper: Lethbridge Papers, CUL Add. 9258.

Garrod letters in possession of R. & D. Kenward.

Garrod Reports of Field Director, Wady El Mugharah Expedition, Autumn Season, 1932, to the Directors and Trustees of the American School of Prehistoric Research, in possession of J. Callander.

Garrod Papers, Fonds Suzanne Cassou de Saint-Mathurin de la Bibliothèque du Musée des Antiquités Nationales de Saint Germain-en-Laye.

Garrod Papers, CUMAA mm1/6/15.

Garrod 1934. et-Tabun Diary, Fonds Suzanne Cassou de Saint-Mathurin de la Bibliothèque du Musée des Antiquités Nationales de Saint Germain-en-Laye.

Godwin Papers, Clare College Archives, ACC 1992.

Godwin, H. On the Development of Quaternary Research in the University, Clare College Archives, ACC 1992.

Godwin, H. History of the Fenland. Paper Given at the British Association Evening Meeting, Cambridge, August 19, 1938, Clare College Archives, ACC 1992/2.

Gould, P. 1998. *Femininity and Physical Science in Britain 1870–1914.* Unpublished Cambridge Ph.D Thesis in History and Philosophy of Science, CUL Manuscripts 22659.

Haddon Papers, CUL.

Haddon, A.C. 1923. *A Brief History of the Study of Anthropology at Cambridge,* CUMAA Box 23 mm1/1/1.

Hawkes, J. 1990. Transcript of interview with Hawkes, in possession of J. Callander.

Hurst, J.G. 1986. The Work of the Medieval Village Research Group 1952–86. Manuscript in possession of the Hurst family.

Interviews noted on paper but not as yet officially transcribed: John Alexander; Paul Ashbee; John Barnes; Mrs Geoffrey Bushnell; Mr Miles and Mrs Caroline Burkitt; Desmond Clark; Grahame Clark; Mary Kitson Clark; Mary Summer Conn; Mary Cra'ster; Mrs Glyn Daniel; Hilda Davidson; Charles Bernard Denston; Alison Duke; John and Evelyn Evans; Brian Fagan; Clare Fell; Lisa French, née Wace; Peter Gathercole; Jack Golson; Sylvia Hallam; Lady Hamilton; Sonia Chadwick Hawkes; E.M.S. Horne, née Macalister; Bruce Howe; Margaret Joan Howe, née Mence; John Hurst; Bertha Jeffreys; Robin Place Kenward; Marie Lawrence; Mina Lethbridge; Joan Lillico; Miss Lyons; Fred Mason; Anne McBurney; John Mulvaney; Leslie J. Oakey; Joan Oates; John Osborn; John Pickles; Stuart Piggott; John Plumb; Merrick Posnansky; L. Pulvertaft-Green; Joyce Reynolds; Hilary Richardson; Antonia Rose, née Sewell; Sister St Paul Evans; Mrs Kenneth St Joseph; George Salt; Freydis Sharland née Leaf; Thurstan Shaw; Gale and Ann Sieveking; Chris Stray; I.M.A. Summers; Mary Thatcher; M.W. Thompson; Jane McFie Waley; Barbara Wallis; Richard West; Ian Whitaker; and Ursula Whitaker.

Lethbridge, T.C. [1965]. "The Ivory Tower", unpublished autobiography in possession of P.J. Smith.

Lethbridge Papers, CUL Add. 9258.

Macfadyen Dead File. [1960]. Sedgwick Museum of Geology, University of Cambridge.

Mount Carmel Photograph Album 1932–24, in possession of E. Dyott's daughter, Mrs Caroline Burkitt.

Newnham College Council Minutes 1939–1946, Newnham College Archives.

Newnham College Roll *Letter* 1928–1952, Newnham College Archives.

Notes from interviews with Rosemary Summers.

Opitz, D. 1999. *The Country House as Laboratory: Science and the Aristocracy in Late-Victorian and Edwardian Britain*. Unpublished History Ph.D thesis, University of Minnesota.

Paterson, T.T. 1938. Appeal for funds, CUMAA Box 111 mm2/2/9.

Phillips, C.W. [1975–1980]. Unpublished memoirs in possession of the Phillips family.

Photographs of Faculty staff and students donated by Mina Lethbridge, in possession of P.J. Smith.

Photographs of Garrod donated by Madeleine Lovedy Smith, in possession of J. Callander.

Photographs of Shaw donated by Thurstan Shaw, in possession of P.J. Smith.

Piggott, S. 1994. Transcript of Interview with Julia Roberts, in possession of Julia Roberts.

Plunkett, S.J. 1996. *Prehistory at Ipswich — an Idea and its Consequences*, manuscript in possession of S.J. Plunkett.

Prehistoric Society of East Anglia Minute Books 1908–35. Held in the Library of the Society of Antiquaries of London.

Ridgeway Manuscript. The Relationship of Archaeology to Classical Studies, Classical Library, University of Cambridge OL Box C.9.

Rouse, S. 1997. *Ethnology, Ethnobiography, and institution: A.C. Haddon and Anthropology at Cambridge*. Unpublished Ph.D thesis in Archaeology and Anthropology, University of Cambridge, CUL Manuscripts 20900.

Schlanger, N. 2002. The Burkitt Affair Revisited: Colonial Implications and Identity Politics in Early South African Prehistoric Research, manuscript in possession of Schlanger.

Shaw, C.T. [1975–95]. *Skeleton in my Suitcase*. Unpublished autobiography, in possession of Thurstan Shaw.

Smith, J. 1968. Letter to Barbara White at Newnham College, Fonds Suzanne Cassou de Saint-Mathurin de la Bibliothèque du Musée des Antiquités Nationales de Saint Germain-en-Laye, Box 72: Inventory 33433.

Smith, P.J. 1993. *Sir Grahame Clark: A Passionate Connoisseur of Flints: An Intellectual Biography of his Early Years*. Unpublished MA thesis, University of Victoria.

Smith, P.J. 1994. *The Fenland Research Committee and the Formation of Prehistory as a discipline at Cambridge University*. Unpublished MPhil thesis, University of Cambridge.

Status of Women in the University. [1946–48], CUA Registry File R2930.

Stone, T. 1998. *Sex, Lies and Audiotape: Constructing an Oral History of the Woman's Auxiliary Air Force*, manuscript in possession of T. Stone.

Stone, T. 1999. *The Integration of Women into a Military Service: the Women's Auxiliary Air Force in the Second World War*. Unpublished Cambridge PhD thesis in History: CUL Manuscripts 22579, 22580.

The Tea Phytologist was a "private botanical journal edited by members of the Cambridge University Botany School Tea Club."Copy in possession of Richard West. Other copies are in the Clare College Archives, Cambridge, ACC 1989/17.

Waechter, J.d'A. 1949. *The Mesolithic Age in the Middle East*. Unpublished Ph.D thesis in Archaeology, CUL Manuscripts, 1496.

West, R. [2003]. *A History of Quaternary Research in Britain*, manuscript in Richard West's possession.